# VARIETIES OF SEXUAL EXPERIENCE
## An Anthropological Perspective
## on Human Sexuality

Suzanne G. Frayser

HRAF Press
New Haven, Connecticut
1985

ABOUT THE AUTHOR:

Suzanne Frayser (Ph.D. in social anthropology, Cornell University) is an independent, social science consultant in the Denver metropolitan area. For six years, she worked with George P. Murdock as a cross-cultural researcher at the Cross-Cultural Cumulative Coding Center (at the University of Pittsburgh); topics investigated were community organization and theories of illness. She received a professional associate award from the Culture Learning Institute at the East-West Center to participate in a six month international, multidisciplinary cross-cultural project. She has been a member of the Society for Cross-Cultural Research since its inception. She has conducted cross-cultural research since 1968 and has both taught and researched the subject of human sexuality since 1970. She has taught anthropology, sociology, and psychology at SUNY-Potsdam, George Washington University, Colorado College, and the University of Denver (The New College). She is currently writing a reference book (with Thomas Whitby) on resources in human sexuality (to be published by Libraries Unlimited, Inc.)

Cover design by Marylou Finch.

INTERNATIONAL STANDARD BOOK NUMBER: 0-87536-342-3
LIBRARY OF CONGRESS NUMBER: 85-60217
© 1985
HUMAN RELATIONS AREA FILES, INC.
NEW HAVEN, CONNECTICUT
PRINTED IN THE UNITED STATES OF AMERICA

# ACKNOWLEDGEMENTS

The process of writing my first book was an initiation rite. After analyzing the work of others and developing my own ideas and research, I emerged with a new product. Like other rites of passage, an initiation rite melds the past with the present and provides background for the future. My rite served to remind me of the debts that I owe to those who instructed me to the point of transition, nurtured me during the marginal period of analysis and writing, and celebrated the result of my painful perserverence as a new point in my life. Consequently, I think back to the teachers who have had an important influence on my intellectual growth: Nathan Altschuler, who encouraged me to pursue the study of anthropology; Victor Turner, Robin M. Williams, Jr., and Bernd Lambert, who taught me the importance of the human element in social science research as well as the rewards of being specific in supporting theoretical points; George P. Murdock and John M. Roberts, who convinced a "particularist" of the value of cross-cultural research. From my students I have learned the importance of connecting theoretical points with issues relevant to our everyday lives.

I value the support that I have received from colleagues and friends throughout the marginal period. Raoul Naroll suggested that I write this book. Joel Gunn helped me with the statistical and computer analysis of the data. Joe Popper read most of the text and offered editorial advice. Marianne Stoller read the last chapter and offered suggestions to improve it. Thomas Whitby not only prepared the index but also provided valuable advice on the text and compilation of the bibliography. Elizabeth Swift contributed her meticulous editing skills to smooth out problems with the prose and bibliographic citations. Edith and George Lauer, Lynda Rush and Bob Wong, my parents, and especially Gary Kaake gave me the emotional support that bolstered my confidence that the book would really be finished one day.

TO MOM AND DAD

# CONTENTS

# FIGURES AND TABLES

# Chapter One
# Introduction:
# Theoretical and Methodological
# Problems of Getting It Together

Sex. Reproduction. Each word evokes dozens of images, thoughts, and feelings. We may remember the tenderness of a first love, the passionate embraces of a lover, the beauty of a wedding ceremony, or the wonder of a child's birth. We may equate "sex" with sin or link it to a traumatic experience, such as rape. "Reproduction" may trigger feelings of anguish associated with the pain of a difficult delivery or moral outrage about abortion laws. We are rarely neutral about these subjects. They capture our fantasies, occupy our thoughts, and elicit intense emotional responses. They infuse our behavior with meaning at its most intimate level.

The American media recognize the power of our emotions about sex and reproduction. "Sex" sells. American advertisers promote many of their products by associating them with attractive men and women in various states of dress or undress. Men and women spend millions of dollars a year to enhance their sex appeal. In the make-believe world of ads, powerful men attract beautiful women and vice versa; material goods help them to attain their desires.

Varieties of sexual experience are as diverse as the people who participate in them. Elements of danger and fear, exultation and ecstasy, good and evil can converge within the sexual arena; they comprise a small sample of the meanings with which humans endow their sexual experiences.

A few cross-cultural examples may indicate the flavor of this variety. Intercourse is often a focus for personal and cultural interpretation. The African Thonga (3) think that the pace of nature responds to the pace of their sex lives (Junod 1927:*1*, 188), "Hot" people (especially married couples) who engage in too much intercourse are dangerous, because

1

they can upset the fragile balance of nature with their activities and bring harm to those in a weakened state, e.g., the sick or the elderly. Bellacoola (132) men of British Columbia can use their sexual habits to their own advantage if they so choose (McIlwraith 1948:*1*, 110). Abstinence from intercourse can bring them power, because it strengthens their link to the supernatural. Consequently, if a man wants to increase his chances of being a successful hunter or gambler, he refrains from intercourse for four days. The people of Uttar Pradesh (63) in India believe that sex should occur for procreation, not for pleasure (Luschinsky 1963: 332), and the New Guinea Manus (96) regard it as "something bad, inherently shameful" (Mead 1930: 125). The meaning of sexual relations may expand to include other aspects of social life. "Eating" and everything connected with it are symbolic of sexual relations among the Kimam (93) (Serpenti 1965: 74), but the Palauans (111) interpret sex in monetary terms: "Love between men and women is on a money basis, and the man has to pay for every embrace" (Krämer 1929: 229).

Basic attitudes toward men and women are often linked to their sexual and reproductive roles. In one Egyptian (43) village, men regard a woman as an "envelope for conception" (Ammar 1954: 94), while the Gheg Albanians (48) refer to her as a "sack" to carry seeds, only to be discarded later (Coon 1950: 23; Hasluck 1954: 25). Tanala (81) proverbs express a different view of women and men. "Women are like the gourd vine; they bear children everywhere; men are like the sacrifice posts in the rice fields; some are long and others, short" (Linton 1933: 315). Sexual prowess is so important to men among the Banen (15) that they refer to an impotent man as dead (Dugast 1959: 159).

Even products of male and female bodies are subject to cultural interpretation. The Kimam (93) hold sperm in such high regard that they place it on bamboo poles at the entrance to the village to fight an epidemic. In contrast, menstrual blood and childbirth are often regarded as dangerous, polluting, and contagious. The Hill Maria Gond (60) sequester menstruating women in special huts on the outskirts of the settlement (Grigson 1938). The Micmac (126) put menstruation and birth in the same category as death; they are all forms of contagion (Wallis and Wallis 1955: 108).

When we move closer to home and consider some widely-held American beliefs about sex and reproduction, we find that some of our views may be just as strange to outsiders as those of other cultures are to us. Most people currently believe that a woman is emotionally and physically handicapped before her menstrual period (Offir 1982: 318). Masturbation reigns as a major taboo. Masters and Johnson found that not one of their male respondents believed that he could masturbate "excessively" without bringing on mental problems (Offir 1982: 190). Fear of the dangers of masturbation has a long history. Victorian men were so concerned about not wasting their seminal fluids that someone developed a spiked ring, which was worn around the base of the penis, to warn its unsuspecting owner that he was about to have an erection in his sleep. A female masturbator could try to cure her habit by having her clitoris removed or by placing a hot iron on her clitoris or thigh (Offir 1982: 17). Abortion, contraception, and sex education in the schools are issues that continue to arouse controversy and stir strong emotions. The fact that the Supreme Court ruled that obscenity applies only to sexually-oriented materials reveals our ambivalence about sexuality, despite reports of a sexual revolution.

We could generate many more examples of differences in cultural views about sex and reproduction, almost ad infinitum. The illustrations presented in the preceding paragraphs give us some idea of the variety that exists. Numerous surveys, case studies, and political issues related to human sexuality in American society combine with descriptions of sex and reproduction in other cultural contexts to establish the vast range of human sexual experience.

## Basic Questions about Variety

The existence of such variety raises several important questions. What is the nature of the variety we see and experience? Are there any consistencies that transcend the diversity and help us to better understand it? How can we explain the constants and the variants that we have delineated? These questions focus on three main problems: (1) how to elucidate the type and extent of variation in human sexuality by systematic description; (2) how to establish whether aspects of human sexuality are consistently related to each other and form patterns; and (3) how to explain the patterns that are identified.

The purpose of this book is to understand varieties of sexual experience by presenting and demonstrating a model that deals with the three basic problems I have defined. In this chapter, I will present the explanatory model that I have developed by describing the process I used to generate it. Each step of the description corresponds to one of the major problem areas I have singled out for study. The rest of the book is a demonstration of the usefulness of the model.

*The Problem of Elucidating the Type and Extent of Variation:*
*Systematic Description*

Descriptions of sexual behavior contain much more than meets the eye. They are filled with ideas about the role of sexuality in the society and the life of the writer. Nevertheless, we may assume that they are straightforward accounts of the facts.

The first error in our assumption overlooks the heart of the descriptive process — selection. Descriptions include only selected aspects of what we observe, because it is not possible to describe everything we see. Consequently, the way we think about the world affects the information that we decide to observe and to include in our descriptions. For example, Hrdy explains the lack of information on infanticide among primates as a result of selective observation and description: ". . . we discount the unimaginable and fail to see what we do not expect" (Hrdy 1981: 89). A corollary to this explanation is the realization that the concepts used in descriptions bring together selected aspects of the world. The meaning of "marriage," for example, varies according to the authors who write about it. A dictionary may define it as "wedlock," a "wedding," or a "close union." Murdock, an anthropologist, presents a different version in his classic work, *Social Structure*: to him, marriage is a "complex of customs centering upon the relationship between a sexually associating pair of adults within the family" (Murdock 1965: 1). Although concepts are efficient ways of packaging information, they link ideas together on the basis of implicit assumptions.

The second error in our belief that descriptions of sexual behavior are factual accounts is that we may think of "facts" as representing unalterable truth or reality. However, facts are subject to change. We label something a "fact" when it is supported by specific types of evidence. The basis for labeling something a fact can change, however, as our standards for evidence change with the prevailing scientific theory. One of the characters in an early Frankenstein film succinctly makes the point: "The superstition of today is (or can be) the scientific fact of tomorrow."

Therefore, an essential first step in systematically describing the types and extent of varieties of sexual experience is to identify the concepts that may prove useful in organizing the descriptive material. Furthermore, it is important to clarify the assumptions that lie behind these concepts and to use them consistently. Since the descriptive information on human sexuality derives from a variety of sources, its presentation according to common conceptual categories aids in comparison.

The main concepts in this book derive from an analysis of the meaning of the phrase "varieties of human sexual experience." The analysis focuses on dealing with a basic question: What is human about human sexuality?

One way of dealing with this question is to look at sexuality in a cross-species perspective. How are humans similar to or different from other animals in their sexual behavior? The process of placing human sexuality within the context of the animal kingdom helps to identify the major features that humans share with other animals and with other humans. In other words, it helps to define the forest within which the trees of human variety are contained.

A cross-species perspective channels questions about human sexuality into a broader arena, where it is possible to think of wider issues and alternative orientations. For example, Ember and Ember (1979) tried to deal with the classic anthropological problem of explaining why marriage occurs in nearly all human societies. However, they found that the universality of marriage posed significant problems for testing hypotheses and deciding between different explanations for why it is adaptive. Any other human universal—e.g., the division of labor by sex—could be invoked to explain the existence of marriage. Therefore, Ember and Ember used a cross-species perspective to present a new way of looking at the problem. They argued that looking at data from other species helps to clarify why marriage is adaptive. Since some species have bonding and others do not, there is sufficient variation to test hypotheses about why bonding is present in some species and not in others. The reasons for bonding in other species provide new clues for understanding why marriage developed in human societies.

Chapter Two, "Our Human Heritage," defines some of the major components of human sexuality by presenting them in cross-species perspective. First, it describes those aspects of human sexuality that humans share with other sexually reproducing organisms, mammals, and primates. Then, it goes on to demonstrate how these shared traits developed into a distinctively human pattern.

Organizing material about the variety of human sexual experience from a cross-species perspective is like being given a "hidden figures" puzzle. The task is to find faces and objects hidden within a larger picture. Once we perceive the figures, it is hard to look at the picture in the same way again. We see the whole scene *and* the figures within it. It enriches our appreciation of what we are seeing and allows us to broaden our view of what we have seen.

This perspective draws attention to the fact (and I use the term advisedly) that human beings are animals and are subject to many of the same constraints that apply to other animals. An initial cross-species overview helps to narrow down just what is human about human sexuality. It channels our attention to the past in search of the reasons why we developed the anatomy and physiology that we now use in our sex lives and in reproduction. It guides us into considering the limitations and potential that all humans share in organizing behavior associated with their sexuality. It leads to the realization that it is important to define the biological capacities with which humans must deal in their sexual functioning.

Humans distinguish themselves as animals that engage in or are capable of engaging in a large amount of nonreproductive as well as reproductive sexuality. The simple statement that "sex is not reproduction" has far-reaching consequences for understanding the place of human sexuality relative to that of other animals. Therefore, it is possible to distinguish between two major facets of sexual reproduction in humans: a sexual facet and a reproductive one.

In order to highlight the distinctiveness of these facets in human beings, I have formulated two concepts to refer to the processes associated with them: the sexual cycle and the reproductive cycle. I base these concepts on the fact that all humans share stages of biological development that provide them with the potential for intercourse and a capacity for the procreation and nurturance of children. These stages of biological development occur in sequences that each generation repeats. Therefore, I refer to them as "cycles." The stages of physical development that are relevant to the potential for and performance of sexual intercourse I refer to as the "sexual cycle"; the ones that constitute preparation for the procreation and nurturance of children I call the "reproductive cycle." Although there can be considerable overlap between phases of the sexual and reproductive cycles, they do not necessarily coincide. This lack of coincidence defines part of what is human about human sexuality. Therefore, my distinction between them is not merely an analytic device, but a description of a trait which all humans share.

The conceptualization of human sexuality into sexual and reproductive cycles provides the basic framework for organizing the description of other important human aspects of human sexuality — those based on shared learning experiences. Reliance on learning distinguishes human experience from that of other animals. Humans use learning to structure and pattern their sexual behavior more than any other species (Ford and Beach 1972: 259). This fact brings us to the second major way of dealing with the question of what is human about human sexual experience; a cross-cultural perspective, which focuses on describing the learning that people share about sexuality.

Learning defines a large portion of what constitutes a human experience, particularly a human sexual experience. It throws light on the richness of the variety we seek to explain. Bronowski's television series and book, *The Ascent of Man* (1973), were a celebration of the degree to which humans have used learning to shape their environment. As he says, "I use the word ascent with a precise meaning. Man is distinguished from other animals by his imaginative gifts. He makes plans, inventions, new discoveries, by putting different talents together; and his discoveries become more subtle and penetrating, as he learns to combine his talents in more complex and intimate ways" (Bronowski 1973: 20).

Psychological, social, and cultural features of our lives are all variations on a theme of learning. Each type of learning contributes an important ingredient to the blend of thoughts, feelings, behaviors, and physical features that makes up the human experience. Sociologists, anthropologists, psychologists, and philosophers, among others, have spend a considerable amount of time and ink trying to define each of these types of learning. I cannot claim to have found the best or final definitions of these terms — the social, the psychological, or the cultural. However, I will present some working definitions, which will allow us to distinguish one from the other and clarify what I mean when I refer to the psychological, social, or cultural aspects of sexuality.

A convenient way to sum up the similarities among these features is to consider the degree to which behavior and/or thoughts are shared, how long they persist, and the degree to which they are patterned (Wallace 1970). If behavior and thoughts are patterned and persist over time in an individual, we usually call them a part of the person's personality; they are psychological traits. If behavior or thoughts are shared by a number of people, are patterned, and persist over time, we usually refer to them as cultural or social traits. I distinguish between social and cultural traits on the basis of the type of pattern I am considering. If the pattern consists of interactions between individuals, I refer to it as a social trait. If the pattern consists of shared symbols or ideas of and for behavior, I refer to it as a cultural trait.

These distinctions are not an exercise in intellectual nit-picking. They represent complex dimensions of human experience. To complicate matters even more, they are all linked to the kind of bodies we have and to the type of environment we inhabit. Consequently, we are constantly dealing with all of these types of systems: biological, social, cultural, and psychological. We may not think of our behavior and ideas in these terms, because we take much of this terminology for granted. In fact, we become so used to the patterns of ideas and behavior that we grew up with that they seem "natural." This assumption is due to two developments. First, each of the patterns consists of parts that are connected to each other and persist, as a whole, over time. In other words, patterns have stability and are slow to change precisely because they are made up of so many parts. Second, many of these patterns overlap, so that we do not have to learn each one individually. Much of what we learn about our bodies, our selves, our group, and our environment occurs simultaneously. While the overlap in the kinds of information we learn is an efficient way to store knowledge, it makes it more difficult to separate the influence that each of these systems has on us.

These distinctions are useful in systematically describing the learned aspects of human sexuality, because they provide clear criteria to use in selecting and classifying information. For example, it is much easier to appreciate the complexity of a football game if the viewer is aware of the role that each of the team members plays. Of course it is possible to glean a broad idea of the organization of the game simply by noticing that the players strive to attain a goal, but such an approach provides little knowledge of how the players get there. Similarly, understanding the role that the psychological, social, cultural, and biological dimensions of sexuality play in human sexual experience is one way to order the cross-cultural variety of experience that we find. It is a preliminary step to explaining *why* the variety exists in the forms in which we see it.

After sifting information through these categories, I realized that there was a significant lack of valid cross-cultural information on psychological traits for a large number of societies. I also found that there were gaps in information on some of the social and cultural dimensions that I wanted to investigate. Overall, valid information on sexuality is hard to find, because of the biases of the writers, the difficulty of observing private sexual activities directly, the unwillingness of people to talk about it to an outsider, etc. Consequently, I have excluded several topics of interest because of insufficient information, e.g., homosexual relations, specific means of contraception, and types of incestuous relations. Although some of the information is sketchy, I decided to do the best I could with what was available. I concentrated on topics described in a relatively full, reliable way and eliminated those subjects about which there was little or no information. After surveying the range of descriptions available to me, I decided to focus on dimensions of human sexuality that people *share* with other members of their groups, i.e., the biological, social, and cultural aspects. Shared behavior and thoughts are often easier to observe and record than those that pertain only to specific individuals. The broad distinctions of biological, social, cultural, and psychological categories helped to narrow the scope of this study to the aspects of human sexuality that are shared. They also indicated the gaps in our present research.

I present descriptive materials on the biological, social, and cultural aspects of human sexuality in Chapters Three and Four. The sexual and reproductive cycles are core concepts around which the information is structured.

## The Problems of Pattern and Explanation: A Model

Concepts and descriptions are useful within a given context. Descriptions alone may be interesting, but they do not explain consistencies and patterns in information. In order to fully understand varieties of sexual experience, it is necessary to cope with two other problems, which I identified as: (1) how to establish whether aspects of human sexuality are consistently related to each other and form patterns, and (2) how to explain the patterns that are identified. Preliminary concepts for organizing descriptive materials on human sexuality become part of an anthropological model to facilitate research on and an explanation for patterns of human sexuality.

I propose to analyze the shared aspects of human sexuality as a system of components in their own right. I offer a model that connects biological, social, and cultural aspects of human sexuality in an integrated way. It is based on intersecting facets of three systems relevant to the sexual and reproductive cycles: (1) the portion of the biological system that relates to sexual and reproductive anatomy and physiology; (2) the portion of the social system that includes patterns of interaction pertinent to different phases of the sexual and reproductive cycles, e.g., ceremonies at birth, puberty, and marriage, and social actions that punish people for engaging in prohibited sexual activities; and (3) the portion of the cultural system that includes the shared beliefs and rules about sexuality that are transmitted from one generation to another to serves as guidelines for individual behavior, e.g., beliefs about whether it is right or wrong to perform abortions, the significance of menstruation, what is masculine and what is feminine, and the rules that govern premarital sex, divorce, and age at marriage. Figure 1.1 depicts how these facets feed into the system of human sexuality.

The key to this model is integrating the different shared aspects of sexuality, while maintaining a balance among the contributions made by each. My approach is to follow a definite sequence of steps in presenting and analyzing information. Each step relates to an important question. The first question is how to show the relevance of each of the three shared dimensions to the major concepts—the sexual and repro-

Figure 1.1 *Integrated Model of Human Sexuality*

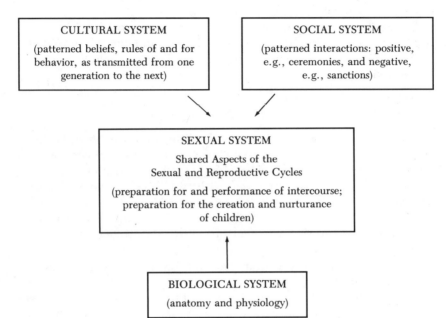

ductive cycles. Since human sexual and reproductive anatomy and physiology are more widely shared than specific social and cultural traits, I have established what I call the "biological baseline" to introduce the sequences of each cycle described in Chapters Three and Four. This baseline is the series of organic structures and processes in the life cycle that relates to sex and reproduction, e.g., prenatal gender differentiation, puberty, and the climacteric. As the term implies, the biological baseline becomes the initial line of continuity that defines the cycles.

A thorough description of biological structures and processes is essential to an understanding of the more variable shared aspects of the sexual and reproductive cycles. It allows us to begin our journey at the same starting point, carrying with us a fundamental knowledge of the biological features to which social and cultural attributes refer. Since social and cultural anthropology have veered away from such graphic descriptions in the past, a detailed introductory description of these facets may serve to balance past oversights. Generally speaking, we are not used to having full descriptions of anatomical and physiological processes presented in conjunction with social and cultural traits.

Therefore, such descriptions may seem too detailed, too lengthy, or irrelevant. Nevertheless, it would be difficult to generate hypotheses about links among the social, cultural, and biological components of human sexuality if the biological elements were left out or glossed over.

After establishing the biological baseline for each of the cycles, I describe social and cultural information relevant to each phase. This organization of information suggests some initial ways that each may relate to the other. For example, how does the significance that different groups attach to he physical changes that occur at puberty relate to the ceremonies held to celebrate the event? The general format of putting shared aspects of human sexuality in one framework conveys a message that it is appropriate to consider them together. It promotes balance, rather than preferential treatment for one to the exclusion of the other.

Once the components are described as phases of the sexual and reproductive cycles, another question arises: What consistencies and patterns are there within and between the cycles? Presenting the descriptions of the sexual and reproductive cycles as a series of phases makes it easier to suggest possible links between the phases in each cycle. For example, do societies that have strong incest taboos also have strong taboos against other forms of nonmarital sexuality, e.g., premarital and extramarital sexuality? Why do they or why do they not have such taboos? How does the involvement of relatives in a marriage ceremony relate to the extent of the celebration given on that occasion or to the difficulty of obtaining a divorce? Questions of the relationship of one phase to the next lead to larger questions and possible explanations. I have not assumed that there are close connections between the social and cultural aspects of the sexual and reproductive cycles. The degree to which groups choose to define sexual behavior in reproductive terms is a major way in which societies vary; it is a matter for research, not part of a foregone conclusion.

Chapters Three and Four describe phases of the sexual and reproductive cycles in an integrated fashion. Chapter Five establishes some patterns and suggests an explanation for them.

### Pursuit of an Integrated Model

This model represents an attempt to encourage interdisciplinary comparative research. An integrated orientation is particularly important in the study of human sexuality and would seem to be a straightforward and logical perspective. However, there are several barriers that face investigators who attempt to pursue this approach.

One barrier to an integrated approach is the scientists' traditional avoidance of interdisciplinary research. A major problem scientists have faced when they have considered participation in such research is whether and how to cross over into another, possibly unknown area of expertise. It may seem more comfortable to work in individual niches of specialization than to reach out into territory which we have not yet explored. While there are wellgrounded reasons for specializing (e.g., we have enough trouble keeping up with the information explosion in the one area of our own field, much less in another field), they are not legitimate grounds for refusing to look or to cooperate with others in a new direction.

Scientists may also have avoided an integrated approach on the basis that taking such an approach is not acceptable within the bounds of their own disciplines. We could call this the "paradigm problem.' In *The Structure of Scientific Revolutions* (1962) Kuhn introduced the concept of "paradigm" to describe the ideas in the scientific community that define acceptable ways of conducting research and developing theories. In a sense, working within one's own discipline is like living in a small, rural community, where people know each other well and live according to similar, though unspoken, assumptions and rules about life. Scientific communities also operate according to unspoken assumptions. Paradigms shift very slowly and do not easily accommodate new approaches. Consequently, a scientist may not baldly reject an interdisciplinary approach but rather subtly dismiss it as irrelevant or superficial.

A third and much more serious barrier to an integrated approach to understanding human sexuality is the fragmentation of research on the subject. The problem with many previous works is not so much what they discuss as what they do not discuss within the same covers. Our knowledge about sexuality is so widely separated into different specialties and books that may not be able to see how one area relates to the other.

The reasons for this fragmentation are complex. One possible explanation is that it results from resistance to interdisciplinary perspectives. Another possibility is that it stems from our own cultural taboos about the study of sex. While we usually reserve the term "taboo" for beliefs and practices of people in other cultures, I think we should consider how it applies to some of our own ideas and behavior; are they any less taboo because we do not call them that? At the very least, Americans are ambivalent in their attitudes about sex. This general cultural ambivalence about sex has hampered the scientific study of sexuality. Researchers are scientists, but they are also members of American culture and are subject to many of the beliefs of the general public. Personal discomfort with discussions of sexuality in a public context extends into the professional arena. Many scientists hesitate to place their professional reputations on the line by studying sexuality as a legitimate area of research in its own right. Rather, they skirt the issue and deal with the subject indirectly.

One indirect way of approaching sexuality is to study it by condemning it. The foundations for this avoidance were laid at the turn of the century; the social evolutionists were particularly adept at this approach, and their tradition has persisted ever since. They developed their theories by trying to reconcile Darwin's views on the origin of species with the strict morality and religious tenets of the late nineteenth century.

Darwin's view that natural selection, not special creation by God, was responsible for the origin of species not only uprooted established religious teaching; it also knocked humans from their unique pedestal as separate, superior creatures. Darwin's theory meant that humans developed from other animal forms and that they were subject to some of the same biological processes as other animals were.

Social philosophers came to the rescue of the thoughtful scientists who were pondering the implications of Darwin's works. The social evolutionists were so drawn to Darwin's ideas that they transferred many of them to the social realm. They hypothesized that social groups developed from simple to more complex forms as a result of more successful modes of adaptation. This was a social version of natural selection, whereby the fittest survive and the less fit die off. Therefore, societies could be ranked in stages, based on their relative success. Primitive groups became curious examples of earlier, less successful, and inferior forms of social organization. The gap between "primitive" and "civilized" societies grew. Primitive societies were biologically less fit than civilized ones. The implication was that primitives were just one step removed from beasts. Therefore, the social evolutionists insulated themselves from a basic acceptance of their relationship to other animals by putting themselves in a category apart from them. Primitives buffered civilized Europeans from the shock of being on par with other animals.

Not only was the association with animals objectionable, so, too, was the thought that the "immoral" customs of primitives were an inherent part of the human species. The study of the sexuality of primitives became an important way of proving the distance between civilized and primitive peoples. Therefore, it was acceptable to present ideas about sexual customs within the context of disapproving of them. Stability of the monogamous family and sexual restraint were central to nineteenth-century European morality. These concepts became the cornerstone of nineteenth-century definitions of "civilization." In contrast, the sexual customs of "primitives" were immoral, i.e., more sexually permissive and supportive of polygyny. The social evolutionists conveniently lumped together the societies that deviated from their own moral code as "primitive" and inferior. It was no wonder such societies were "immoral." After all, the rationalization went on, they are closer to promiscuous animals.

Unfortunately, some of these stereotypes about "primitives" and some of the nineteenth-century approaches to the study of sexuality linger on. It still seems to make us uncomfortable to deal with societies or groups that conform to different moral canons than we do or to face some of the ways in which we are similar to other animals.

Although sexual reproduction is a necessary feature of our existence, many scholars seem to have difficulty in dealing with the link between the social and cultural aspects of sex and reproduction and their biological components. These scholars may deal with this difficulty in at least two different ways. One is to transform sexual behavior into more abstract concepts or to embed it in other contexts. Gebhard, of the Institute for Sex Research, draws attention to this problem in a recent review of an interdisciplinary collection of research on human sexuality. He says the following:

> Most of the book is concerned with male-female differentiation in terms of physiology and roles, but there is amazingly little on sexual behavior in a fundamental physical sense. It is as though many social and behavioral scientists said, "I don't want to deal with gross simplistic behavior such as coitus, masturbation, or homosexuality; I want to deal with more scholarly and respectable topics such as roles, relationships, and meanings." To do so is to put the cart before the horse [Gebhard 1981: 205].

Sociological works on sexuality discuss a great deal about sex roles but bypass the relevance of intercourse. Social and cultural anthropologists have usually concentrated on general descriptions of social organization; the analysis of a particular institutional context, e.g., marriage; or the pursuit of a new theoretical scheme, e.g., interpretation of symbols. They transform sexuality into social or cultural organization. Consequently, the social and cultural aspects of sexuality are enmeshed in such diverse contexts that their relationship to each other is difficult to perceive. As Fisher put it in a recent survey of how anthropologists have dealt with "eros": "Although anthropologists have always been interested in sexuality, they have not always been interested in studying it"

(Fisher 1980: 170). Even early, well-known anthropologists, such as Malinowski, the "father of fieldwork," were very careful to defend themselves in advance for studying sexual behavior. Despite using such provocative titles as *The Sexual Life of Savages* (1929) and *Sex and Repression in Savage Society* (1965), Malinowski was quick to point out that the material in these books was only for the consideration of serious scholars. In fact, he talks more about marriage and the family than he does about titillating sexual practices. Like many anthropologists after him, Malinowski subsumed sexuality under kinship and emphasized how sexual and reproductive needs are channeled into social institutions.

A second way in which writers try to handle the link between the biological and the social/cultural components of sexuality is by concentrating on physiology and anatomy to the neglect of the social, cultural, and psychological factors that are integral to human sexuality. Handbooks on sexual technique, discussions of sex within the context of reproduction and childbirth, and medical explications of physiology are just a few examples of this orientation.

I have no quarrel with the specializations that people have chosen to pursue. However, I do wonder why we do not find more books that describe in detail the connection between the physiological components of sexuality and their social, cultural, and psychological dimensions. By and large, previous research has either investigated elements of sexuality without considering the whole domain of human sexuality, avoided the topic by subsuming it under more "acceptable" topics, or sidestepped it altogether. I think it is time that we changed our emphasis. The model I have presented is a step in that direction. Sociobiologists, physical anthropologists, and health professionals are also moving along that path.

As an anthropologist, I am particularly interested in the integration of the social, cultural, biological, and psychological dimensions of human life. Defined as the "holistic study of human beings," anthropology encompasses biological, social, cultural, and psychological changes and variations in humans from the past (including prehistory) to the present. Its comparative and interdisciplinary flavor is a fitting orientation for viewing human sexuality as a system of diverse components.

The cross-cultural method is the main anthropological tool I have used to aid me in drawing conclusions about the scope and patterns of social and cultural aspects of the sexual and reproductive cycles. Most of my data derive from a systematic study of sixty-two societies drawn from Murdock and White's Standard Cross-Cultural Sample (1969). I have added the results of several other cross-cultural studies, which are based on the same sample or on similar ones. Interested readers can refer to Appendix A for an extended description of the method.

This study draws on the principles of the anthropological tradition and tries to be true to the idealistic conceptualization of the discipline as a field that studies the diversity of humankind through time and across cultural boundaries. The remainder of the book demonstrates the fruits of this tradition as it applies to human sexuality.

# Chapter Two
# Our Human Heritage

We begin to unravel the complexity of human sexual diversity by asking what is human about human sexuality. Our focus shifts from our own personal experiences, from American society, and even from contemporary cultures and societies. We broaden our perspective until we can see twentieth-century human beings as one species in the animal kingdom. In order to answer the question of what is human about human sexuality we need an understanding of the ways in which our sexual and reproductive characteristics are similar to and different from those of other animals. Why have we humans developed the sexual anatomy and physiology that we currently have? Another part of the answer involves an appreciation of the biological heritage that has shaped the contours of our current sexual experience. How have the components of human sexuality changed from the past to the present? Tracing our sexual and reproductive characteristics as a species through time provides a broad, biological framework within which we can try to answer more specific questions about the nature of human sexual experience. This journey is our human heritage.

### Principles of Evolutionary Theory

Evolutionary theory offers a particularly appropriate scheme for helping us to define and explain a broad biological framework for human sexuality. First, its principles apply to all living things and therefore aid us in establishing a cross-species perspective. Second, it attempts to explain how and why species have changed from the past to the present. Consequently, its principles can help us to understand how and why human sexual and reproductive anatomy and physiology have developed in their present form. Why do certain traits persist, while others change or disappear?

*Darwin, Natural Selection, and Sexual Selection*

The term "evolution" refers to a gradual process of change. When applied to the creation of life on earth, evolution means that all living things diverged from a common ancestor in the distant past. As they occupied different ecological niches (land, water, and air) they gradually changed in form from simple to complex; their differences became more apparent the more they diverged from their common ancestor. Despite differences in appearance, there is continuity in nature because of a common heritage; all living things are ultimately related to each other, however small the link may be.

The idea of evolution was not new when the twenty-three-year-old naturalist, Charles Darwin, set sail on the H.M.S. Beagle for a five-year world cruise. Darwin's voyage around the world eventually turned the static, ordered world of Victorian England upside down. His zeal in classifying plants and animals led him to an interpretation of life's diversity, which challenged the prevailing Christian view of special creation. Special creation meant that God separately and uniquely created each organism on earth at one specific time. Darwin's view contrasted with creationism. He developed an evolutionary perspective that assumed slow, gradual change over long periods of time. In a few logical steps he formulated a theory that accounted for how organisms change through a process of natural selection. In other words, he specified a mechanism by which evolution operates.

Darwin made three basic observations: (1) All living things differ, and their differences are passed on to their offspring; (2) all organic things tend to increase at a high rate; and (3) the numbers in a species tend to remain fairly constant. He then drew two major inferences from these observations: (1) There must be a struggle for survival, and (2) in this struggle, the fittest survive. "Survival of the fittest" means that an organism has characteristics that help it to persist in its environment and make it more successful than others in producing offspring, who, in turn, are more successful than others in becoming adults. Competition occurs in the sense that individuals with traits that give them an advantage in a particular environment are more likely to produce more offspring in the next generation. Survival of the fittest does not refer to an actual tooth-and-claw battle, in which the biggest, strongest, or fastest organism survives. Natural selection refers to the process by which successful organisms in a particular environment survive and leave progeny, while less successful organisms recede in numbers or gradually die out altogether. The traits that are advantageous to survival and reproduction are more likely to be represented in the next generation. Species gradually change as more advantageous traits are represented in each succeeding generation. This process of gradual change in the makeup of each species is what we mean by evolution.

The concept of natural selection as a mechanism of evolution centers on three key elements: (1) variety in the population, (2) adaptation to the environment, and (3) fitness. First, of all the grist for the evolutionary mill is the variety that is already present within a species. Some traits are more advantageous than others in aiding an individual to survive in an environment. These traits will be passed on to the next generation. Second, evolutionary success occurs only in relation to a particular environment. A trait that aids an organism to survive in one environment may not help it in another. For instance, humans' characteristic lack of much body hair is an advantage for cooling off in a hot climate but a disadvantage in the snow of the Arctic. When an organism can shift in response to a change in environment, it adapts (Nelson and Jurmain 1982: 39). This sort of individual behavioral flexibility in the face of change is not necessarily passed on to offspring. Another, more specific meaning of adaptation is the way in which widely shared, species-wide characteristics enable an organism to "fit" with its environment (Konner 1982: 20). These characteristics can be passed on to later generations and are more likely to be an integral part of the evolutionary process. Those organisms with traits that allow them to adapt to a new or changed environment are more likely to be successful than those that do not have these traits. Environmental change is an ever-present challenge to an organism. In this sense, the environment is the "natural" part of natural selection, which selects for traits that are advantageous within its context. Finally, we can measure "fitness" in terms of reproductive success. The fittest organisms are those who produce viable offspring, who, in turn, are successful in reproducing themselves. Therefore, those traits that contribute to a reproductive advantage will be strongly selected for. Reproduction is central to the success of the individual and ultimately his species.

However, natural selection does not seem to explain sex differences, e.g., size, muscle mass, and physical adornment. Since natural selection depends upon the success of both sexes in relation to a given environment, it could not account for the differences between them. This conclusion led Darwin to hypothesize that a different type of selection was operating in this case — sexual selection. Sexual selection refers to the success of one sex relative to members of the same sex in producing offspring. It usually operates in two ways: (1) individuals of the same sex (usually males) compete with each other for opportunities to mate; and (2) individuals of the same sex (usually females) choose to mate with specific partners. In natural selection, the environment determines which traits or species are more likely to survive. In sexual selection, individual behavior (achieving an opportunity to mate or choosing a mating partner) shapes the types of characteristics that each sex is likely to have. For example, if larger males are usually more successful in competing with smaller males for opportunities to mate, large size may become more characteristic of males in general. Similarly, if females systematically prefer to mate with males who have more musculature, then more muscle mass may characterize males in succeeding generations.

Both natural and sexual selection focus on reproduction. The measure of fitness in natural selection is reproductive success. The payoff for sexual selection is an opportunity to reproduce or a specific choice of a mate. We might view sexual selection as a specific type of natural selection. After all, other animals make up part of the environment to which each individual adapts. If a trait confers an advantage on him or her in acquiring a mating partner, it contributes to his or her reproductive success.

Many contemporary biologists do not retain the distinction between natural and sexual selection (Daly and Wilson 1978: 71). Darwin thought the difference was a useful one, because sexual and natural selection could possibly oppose one another. For example, large size might make a male more attractive to a female but more conspicuous to a predator. I think the distinction is useful, because it draws our attention to the impact that individual choices and actions can make for individuals and for the species as a whole. Sociobiology, a branch of biology that applies the concept of natural selection to behavior, bases many of its hypotheses on the assumption that the purpose of some social behavior is to maximize individual reproductive success. What reproductive consequences does individual behavior have? Another useful consequence of having a concept of sexual selection is that it generates questions about what the differences are between the sexes and why they persist; furthermore, it suggests some answers to these questions.

*Mendel, Genetics, and a Synthetic Theory of Evolution*

A major problem in Darwin's formulation of evolution by natural selection was the fact that in spite of his conviction that natural selection operates on the variety within a species, he had difficulty in specifying how the variety developed in the first place. What was the source of the variety? He could not answer that question. Furthermore, he realized that traits were inherited from one generation to the next, but he could not clarify how parents transmitted traits to their offspring. The development of genetics has since filled in many of these blanks.

It is ironic that Gregor Mendel was laying the foundation for modern genetics in the garden of an Austrian monastery while Darwin's *Origin of Species* (1859) was shaking the creationist foundations of Europe. Until Mendel's hybridization experiments with garden peas, no one fully understood how traits were inherited from one generation to the next. By cross-breeding plants from different parental stocks, Mendel demonstrated that there are regularities of principles that govern heredity.

The specific factors responsible for inherited characteristics are now called genes (chemically they are DNA, or deoxyribonucleic acid). Each individual has two genes for a particular trait. During the production of sex cells (gametes), the pair of genes from each parent separate, so that a new sex cell has only one gene of each kind. Therefore, a parent contributes only one of each pair of genes to an offspring. (This is called the principle of segregation.) When pairs of genes separate, they do so independently of one another and distribute randomly in the gamete. The genes are unaffected by their association with others in the individual. They do not blend or merge; they retain their distinctiveness and emerge from a union as separate as when they entered it. (This is called the principle of independent assortment.) Consequently, genes from parents can enter into many combinations with each other to produce a variety of traits. The offspring expresses a constant trait when each parent contributes the same kind of gene. A hybrid results when parents contribute different kinds of genes. The principles of segregation and independent assortment fill the gaps in Darwin's concept of natural selection; they clarify the source of variation and explain how traits are passed down from parents to offspring.

The principles of genetics and natural selection were not combined into a consistent theory of evolution until the mid-1930s. The "modern synthesis" of Darwinian and Mendelian principles recognizes that changes in genetic material passed on from parent to offspring constitute the variety upon which natural selection operates. Each individual contains the genetic potential to produce a unique offspring, who may have traits that are even more advantageous in the environment. If so, the offspring will be successful in reproducing and passing on its genes; in the process, new sources of variety are added. Natural selection works on physical and behavioral characteristics already expressed in the organism (phenotype). The genetic endowment (genotype) of successful organisms is likely to be passed on to the next generation. The interaction between the phenotype and environment is the crucial factor in influencing which genes will be passed on and expressed in the phenotype. The development of sexual reproduction is the foundation on which much of this variety is based. Mendel contributed an understanding of the sources of variety and how variety is inherited. Darwin contributed an understanding of how natural selection works with this variety.

## Sexual Reproduction

Sexual reproduction is one of the most general reproductive characteristics that humans share with other animals. In fact, there are very few animals that do not reproduce in this manner. What features typify sexually reproducing animals? Why was sexual reproduction selected for? What consequences does a sexual mode of reproduction have for anatomy and for behavior?

### Typical Features of Sexually Reproducing Animals

All living things begin with one cell and reproduce in some manner. Simpler organisms usually reproduce asexually. Asexual reproduction means that the organism duplicates the genetic endowment of the parent. For example, a cell may divide and create a replica of itself by fission or splitting. The essence of this process is replication of the parent; no new genes are added to the offspring.

Sexual reproduction is more likely to take place as the complexity of the cell increases (Michelmore 1964: 97). This mode of reproduction requires the production and fusion of two specialized sex cells (gametes) — the ovum and the sperm. Ova and spermatazoa are specialized cells in that they contain only half the number of chromosomes that a normal body cell has; their only function is to create progeny and to pass on some of the genetic material of the parents to their offspring. The unique chromosomal composition of the sex cells is the key to an individual's particular genetic endowment. Chromosomes are a set of paired, rodlike structures in the cell nucleus that carry genes responsible for an organism's heredity. The gametes of the parents join together to form a zygote (fertilized egg), which contains the full complement of chromosomes. Since half of the chromosomes come from the mother and half, from the father, the genetic composition of the offspring is new. Part of each of the parents lives on in their offspring; the past links with the present and future. Equally important is the fact that the two parents introduce variety into the population.

The perpetuation of sexually reproducing animals depends upon the mating of individuals who carry reproductively incomplete cells, "sex cells." It is from this fact that the most fundamental definition of sex derives. The male is the organism that contains the sperm cells, and the female is the organism that contains the ova (eggs). Intrinsic to this definition of sex is the implication that males need to link with females in order to reproduce. Therefore, sexual behavior is necessary for reproduction to occur. As Bronowski says: "Two is the magical number" (Bronowski 1973: 388).

## Selective Pressures for Sexual Reproduction

Since sexual reproduction is so much more widespread than the asexual mode, it must have advantages. These advantages contribute to the prevalence of sexual reproduction.

Reproduction entails physiological strain, because the parent organism loses some of its cellular material in the process. This is particularly true for asexually reproducing organisms, whose whole bodies are involved in the act of reproduction (Michelmore 1964: 103). Sexually reproducing organisms limit the production of gametes to special organs in the body, the gonads (ovaries in females and testes in males). Therefore, specialized production of reproductive materials poses less strain on sexually reproducing animals.

Sexual reproduction also maximizes the use of successful types of reproductive cells. It is advantageous for the fertilized egg to begin to divide with an adequate mass of cell material (cytoplasm). It is also an advantage to produce a large number of sex cells, the most vigorous of which can fuse with another gamete. The problem is that the advantages potentially oppose each other; the former selects for size and the latter, for numbers. Since an organism invests a limited amount of material in producing gametes, an emphasis on size means minimizing numbers and vice versa. The development of males and females was a way out of the dilemma (Daly and Wilson 1978: 48–51). One organism, the male, produces large numbers of small gametes, spermatazoa, while the other organism, the female, produces relatively few, large gametes (ova). The small sperm merge with the large ovum to produce offspring. The egg provides the cytoplasm which the sperm lacks. Some authors define the sexes in terms of gamete size and the initial investment that each organism makes (Daly and Wilson 1978: 51). Females have large gametes, which substantially contribute to the early development and growth of the offspring. Males have small gametes, which supply few parental resources to the offspring. There is also a physiological difference between the gametes; the egg does not move on its own, while the sperm is always motile and able to maintain sustained movement. Although there is a wide variety of sizes and shapes of eggs and sperm, all sexually reproducing organisms retain these fundamental differences between the sexes.

However, differentiation into males and females produces some potential problems. Since separate organisms carry ova and spermatazoa, how will they get together to create a zygote? Courtship is one of the major ways that sexually reproducing animals secure mates and synchronize their activities so that they can produce offspring (Daly and Wilson 1978: 40). Courtship is often "elaborate, conspicuous, and stereotyped" (Barash 1977: 144). Consistent patterns of courtship seem to be typical of individual species and contrast with those of other species. Barash suggests that a large genetic component may underlie courtship, because so much of an organism's reproductive success depends on the choice of a mate (Barash 1977: 144).

The process of courtship may involve a great deal of time, energy, and risk. First, an organism has to attract another to it. Special scents, bright colors, and elaborate displays of behavior are just a few of the ways in which organisms attract each other. Second, an organism has to deal with aggression, either from competitors for the same mate or from the desired mate. Several males may be interested in mating with a particular female; their competition for her may result in injury to some of them. In addition, a female may not be initially receptive to a male; he may have to appease her and deflect her aggressive responses. Third, mates have to sufficiently coordinate their physiological and behavioral activities so that they can produce offspring.

How can mating proceed so that ova and spermatzoa can fuse? There is a great deal of variation in how fertilization occurs, and this has important implications for the nature of the link between males and females.

At one extreme are the animals that reproduce by external fertilization; fertilization occurs outside the bodies of the partners that have released their spermatazoa and ova. Fertilization occurs rather randomly, and the larva or embryo develops independently of the parents. Contact between parents is minimal, if it occurs at all. Mating requires little courtships or specialized reproductive structures.

At the other extreme are the humans and other complex animals (including most vertebrates) that reproduce by internal fertilization; fertilization occurs inside the female's reproductive tract. Courtship and greater contact between the male and female are essential for this mode of fertilization. The female needs to be cooperative to receive and retain the sperm. Some birds and fish have elaborate behavioral patterns, which help them to mate. They come in such close contact that they can easily transfer the sperm to the female. Specialized physical features may also facilitate the process of fertilization. Land animals have some special obstacles to overcome. Sperm only survive in a fluid solution of some kind. Consequently, terrestrial animals have developed specific anatomical and physiological features to deal with the problem. The penis, an outward extension of the male reproductive tract, carries sperm in a fluid medium directly into the female. The vagina, and inward channel into the female, is a protective pocket into which the penis fits and releases sperm. A variety of insects, reptiles, birds, and mammals have penises. The only animals in which penises have developed are those that fertilize internally (Michelmore 1964: 78).

A comparison of external with internal fertilization highlights the reproductive advantages of the internal alternative. Generally, a number of factors enhance the possibility of fertilization: (1) a large number of spermatazoa and ova released by the parents; (2) release of sperm and eggs at about the same time; and (3) deposition of eggs and sperm in a limited area. Animals that fertilize externally produce a large number of eggs, but this amount of production can strain the mother. Even though sperm and eggs may be released at about the same time in a limited area, they are at the mercy of environmental forces, such as bad weather (which may separate them) and other organisms (which may destroy them). Internal fertilization maximizes the proximity of ova and spermatazoa and therefore enhances the probability of conception. Gametes are less subject to environmental hazards, and therefore fewer eggs need to be produced (Michelmore 1964: 68). The precision of internal fertilization makes it particularly efficient.

Consequently, the nature of sexual interaction between males and females depends partly upon their mode of fertilization. Their contact may be confined to a brief mating period, or it may extend through an elaborate courtship ritual, mating, and a relatively continuous period of association thereafter. In this context, the relationship between males and females serves a vital function. It creates a situation within which reproduction becomes possible. We can view attraction, love, dating, and physical stimulation in this light. Such behavior is sexual, because each of the individuals engages in actions which could lead to the combination of one's genetic material with that of the opposite sex. Although contemporary definitions of sexual behavior have become more complex than the preceding one, the reproductive element is still there. Ultimately, sex is an intrinsic part of reproduction, although this does NOT mean that reproduction is the motivation for sexual activity.

Despite the potential problems that result from the specialization into male and female, one major advantage of sexual reproduction overrides its difficulties: variety. Sexual populations have the capacity to respond rather quickly to environmental change (Daly and Wilson 1978: 41). In *Sex and Evolution* (1975), Williams argues that sex is an adaptation to a special situation in the environment. When the young are faced with a new or different habitat, it is to their advantage to have a variety of traits that will help them adapt to living there. If the environment is stable and the organisms do not need to disperse, asexual reproduction is just as advantageous as sexual reproduction. If the parent adapts well to the environment, the offspring are likely to do the same assuming stable environmental conditions. Sexual reproduction allows greater flexibility and more options if the population needs to expand into new areas, or if the environment changes. As Darwin put it, variety is the raw material on which natural selection operates. Most species have evolved into sexually reproducing organisms. They carry with them some genetic insurance which allows their offspring to adapt to new conditions.

Given the large selective pressure that the environment exerts on reproduction, it follows that it is important to link habitat with sexual behavior and reproduction. Species-wide traits are part of the biological baseline that constrains the lengths to which social and cultural life can develop and effectively persist.

To Thurber's whimsical question: "Is sex necessary?" we can reply with a resounding "yes," because sexual reproduction introduces the variety that facilitates adaptation and increases the probability of our survival. As sexual beings, individuals link with one another to reproduce. Each of us has the potential to add to the rich variety of life, if only we make contact with other members of our species. Humans share this potential with each other and with other sexually reproducing animals. We all face the basic problem of how to ensure that males and females will mate in sufficient numbers to replace and perpetuate the population. How these arrangements proceed defines some of the other differences and similarities that humans share with other animals.

### The Mammalian Contribution

Since reproduction and survival of offspring are essential ingredients in evolutionary success, it is not surprising that as life forms have become more complex, characteristics that promote reproductive efficiency have developed and been perpetuated. The way in which members of a species ensure the perpetuation of their genes finds its "flesh and bones in the species' physiology" (Daly and Wilson 1978: 165). The reproductive advantages that mammals in particular have acquired constitute the next broad classification of biological similarities shared by humans and other animals.

Mammals probably began to develop about sixty-five million years ago. Warm-blooded vertebrates, whose skin is usually covered by hair, they have a decided advantage: a constant appropriate body temperature, which they can maintain regardless of external conditions. Homoiothermy (constant body temperature) gives them the continuous energy source that is necessary for an active life. Physiological and behavioral changes help to maintain body temperature. Sweat glands and fur or hair aid in raising or lowering body temperature. A change in dentition (heterodont, i.e., different kinds of teeth for different functions) allows them to take advantage of a variety of food sources. Mammals require more food intake to maintain their body temperature. Eating stimulates metabolic action, which generates heat. Given their homoiothermy, they can exploit a wide variety of environments during the day or night to support themselves.

These general anatomical and physiological changes related to homoiothermy are relevant to reproduction in that they enhance the overall survival chances of mammals and therefore increase their probability of reproductive success. However, other defining features of mammals are much more directly related to their reproductive success. Mammals have developed a number of traits that point to a general mammalian trend toward reproductive efficiency.

Males express this trend by their specialized reproductive structures. The testes of most species of mammals are outside rather than inside the body during the breeding season. The higher body temperature of mammals seems to impede the creation of sperm. Therefore, descent of the testes into the scrotum during the breeding season aids sperm production (Golanty 1975: 19). The scrotum — the sac that contains the testes — maintains the testes at a temperature lower than that of the rest of the body. The decrease in temperature is three to five degrees in humans and as much as seven degrees in other animals (Golanty 1975: 19). In many animals, the testes descend into the scrotum only during the breeding season and retract into the body at other times. Because humans do not confine breeding to one season, the testes descend into the scrotum before birth and stay there throughout the man's life.

All mammalian males have penises. The mammalian penis is distinctive, because it contains spongy tissue located between the arteries and veins. An alternative name for this tissue could be "erectile tissue," Since it is primarily responsible for the widening, lengthening, and hardening of the penis during erection. The flexibility of the penis allows it to remain small and protected when the mammal is not engaged in inter-course, yet it can become large, firm, and sufficiently long to enter the vagina and effectively copulate when the time is right. In some mammals, a penis bone (os penis) may help to retain the position or firmness of the penis during intromission. Despite some popular beliefs and jokes, it is not true that humans have penis bones.

Most mammalian changes involve an intensification of a trend already established with sexual reproduction: a major contribution by the female to the development and nurturance of the offspring. The mammalian emphasis is on maintaining the quality of prenatal and postnatal care of the infant that is needed to ensure its survival, rather than on producing a quantity of fertilized eggs. Mammals have more of an investment in the few offspring they do produce, in contrast to the animals that must rely on the probability that some of the large numbers of fertilized eggs they produce will eventually endure. The major contribution that females make to their offspring is directly connected to two primary defining features of mammals: viviparity and postnatal care (parenting).

Mammals are viviparous, i.e., the fertilized egg develops within the mother's body until an advanced stage of growth and is nourished there until she gives birth. However, viviparity entails several anatomical and physiological modifications, to make it possible for a fertilized egg to be transmitted to a place where it can be implanted and can then develop.

All female mammals regularly go through an ovarian cycle, which governs the production and release of ova and prepares them for receiving a fertilized egg. The endocrine system primarily controls the physiology of the ovarian cycle. Endocrine glands release chemical substances called hormones directly into the blood stream. The blood carries them through the body, and they stimulate responses from cells specifically attuned to them. For example, the follicle stimulating hormone (FSH) stimulates the development of ova.

When a female is not pregnant, the ovarian cycle consists of four phases, each of which is related to the effectiveness of viviparity. The first phase is the development of the egg in a follicle in the ovary. The second phase is the passage of the egg from the site of fertilization to a place where it can be implanted. The walls of the ducts through which the egg passes after its release from the follicle in the ovary facilitate this process. Lower mammals have oviducts, but higher mammals have developed fallopian tubes and uteri (wombs). The entire second phase involves the release of the egg from the ovary, its passage through the oviduct, and its arrival in the uterus, the third phase of the cycle is preparation for implantation. The tissues in the uterus form a special lining (the endometrium) to receive the fertilized egg. If fertilization occurs, the zygote receives nourishment for its growth from the mother's blood vessels in the endometrium; gestation follows implantation. If fertilization does not occur, the egg is shed in the uterus and the endometrium returns to its normal condition. This is the last phase of the cycle. It repeats itself when a new egg forms.

Since the egg is present in the oviduct for only a few days, copulation must take place during that interval for fertilization to occur. Most female mammals induce males to copulate with them during this time. The behavioral changes that females go through to attract the male are known as "estrus" or "heat." Since estrus usually coincides with the period of maximal fertility, the ovarian cycle of mammals is often called the "estrous cycle." Although humans share with other mammals the main physiological components of the ovarian cycle, they do not go through a pronounced behavioral period of "heat" to which most sexual activity is confined. Therefore, it is inappropriate to say that *all* mammals have an estrous cycle in quite the same terms.

Enclosure of the fertilized egg in the mother's uterus provides protection for future offspring during one of their most vulnerable phases of life — the period of embryonic life after conception. Development in the mother's body confers three important advantages for the fetus (Golanty 1975: 10). First, the mother is responsible for protecting herself and the fetus. Second, she provides nutrients for her growing offspring. Third, her body aids the fetus by providing a "relatively constant physical and biochemical internal environment" (Golanty 1975: 10).

The largest group of mammals, the placental mammals, illustrate the extent and importance of prenatal specialization. While monotremes (e.g., the platypus) and marsupials (e.g., the oppossum and the kangaroo) enjoyed a limited period of dominance in the past, they were soon outnumbered by the placental mammals. This fact seems to be connected with the nourishment and protection that the placenta provides for the fetus.

The placenta is a specialized organ, which develops within the uterus and is composed of tissues from both the fetus and the mother. It brings nutrients to the fetus from the mother, removes waste products from the fetus, and produces hormones, which help to maintain the pregnancy. Consequently, a unique relationship is set up between the developing offspring and its mother. The mother is the fetus' intermediary between itself and the external environment. Much of what affects the mother also affects fetal development. The life-sustaining substances that the mother passes on to her offspring foreshadow the nurturant role that the female is likely to play after the infant is born.

The reproductive efficiency of mammals is marked not only by specialized prenatal care inside the mother's womb but also by intense postnatal care. The mammae (breasts) provide a basis for continuing the protective and nurturant relationship of the mother with her infant. mammae are milk glands, which probably developed from the sweat glands and subcutaneous fat that originally helped to regulate body temperature. The number, location, and position of the mammae vary according to species. Their variations illustrate how closely the physical features of the mother correspond to the needs of the infant. The number of breasts characteristic of a species generally matches the number of offspring likely to be born at any one time (Goldstein 1976: 55). The location and position of the breasts relate to the ease with which the infant can reach specific parts of the mother's body (Goldstein 1976: 55). Human mothers generally hold their babies when they nurse. The position of the breasts on the chest allows the mother the flexibility to sit, stand, or lie down while she feeds her child. In addition, the amount of protein in maternal milk is specifically related to the rate of growth of the young: quicker growth requires more protein (Campbell 1967: 48).

Breastfeeding is often the infant's first attempt at social interaction. Both mother and infant must cooperate to accomplish feeding successfully. The infant's sucking sets in motion the process that ultimately results in milk production and the release of milk from the mother's breast. During feeding, the infant plays an active role in assuring its own survival. Its contact with the breast links it to its mother in a very intimate way and reinforces its attempt to establish a connection with another of its species by providing it with warm, nutritious milk.

The infant's protective network begins to expand after birth to include social as well as physical dependence. The infant has to interact with another individual in order to survive. It is not capable of surviving on its own. While the period of dependence on a caretaker varies among mammals, the basic necessity for cooperation and attachment to another animal does not vary. Bowlby suggests that attachment is not an option, but a mechanism under powerful selective pressure. Immature animals need to maintain close physical contact with mature members of their species in order to protect themselves against death by exposure or by predators (Bowlby 1969). Harlow also stresses the importance of the mother/infant attachment. The intimate interaction of breastfeeding provides a model for the formation of affectional relations in the future (Harlow 1973). The infant suckling at its mother's breast is an elegant image of the important role that social interaction will play in the survival of every mammal. Not only does the infant derive nutrients from its mother but it also acquires information about its environment, which prepares it to cope with potential dangers. It does not have to make the same mistakes its forebears did. The benefits of learning are added to those of attachment and food.

The female role in infant care far exceeds that of the male, even though he may participate in the process. There is no mammalian species in which the male assumes most or all of the burden of parental care (Daly and Wilson 1978: 144). However, it is important to note that most females do enlist the aid of males when they need it (Hrdy 1981). The infant has the opportunity to learn from both males and females in previous generations. Therefore, it can build up a complex repertoire of behavior without experiencing some of the drawbacks of learning by trial and error. This type of learning has developed only in animals that engage in parental care (birds and mammals).

Parental care enables the infant to explore its surroundings without immediate peril. The horizons of young mammals expand not only by imitative learning but also by a new determinant of behavior: "effectance motivation" (or, loosely, "play"). Young mammals can explore and investigate the environment without the goal of satisfying their primary biological needs of hunger, reproduction, or self-preservation (Campbell 1967: 49, 50; Nelson and Jurmain 1982: 230). They can then discover and learn how to interact effectively with their environment.

The increased input of information from effectance motivation is an important ingredient in the development of larger, more complicated, and more efficient brains. The caretaking responsibilities of parents require animals with brains large enough to deal with the environmental contingencies that could affect their young and to deal with their young while they are dependent. Parents are also an important source of information for the young on how to deal with the environment. Smarter parents are advantageous for the survival of their offspring. These combined sources of learning lay the groundwork for the greater role that experience and social life play in the lives of more complex animals.

## The Primate Contribution

The primate order is the mammalian group to which humans belong. Along with other mammals, primates began to develop the distinctive features of their order about sixty-five million years ago. Prosimians (premonkeys or early monkeys) were the earliest primate forms. They constitute one suborder of the primate order and include tarsiers, lorises, aye-ayes, indrises, and lemurs. Anthropoids, who make up the other suborder of primates, are more complex than prosimians and developed later; their families include the New World monkeys of South and Central America, the Old World monkeys of Africa and Asia, gibbons, apes (orangutans, gorillas, and chimpanzees) and humans. Of the approximately two hundred species of living primates, about 75 percent are monkeys. Despite a great deal of variation in size, structure, and behavior, primates share a general ability to adapt to a variety of environments. Part of the reason for their flexibility is their lack of structural specialization; there is no one anatomical feature that "exclusively and universally" applies to primates (Nelson and Jurmain 1982: 242). The basis for their generalized structure lies in their adaptation to life in the trees, particularly in their use of learning and social ties. Their mode of coping with their complex environment has far-reaching implications for the nature of reproduction and sexual behavior.

An arboreal existence requires the ability to move effectively in the trees. Two anatomical specializations derive from this necessity: modification of the limbs for climbing and jumping and increased reliance on vision to judge distances. Most primates climb by grasping with their hands, and some have prehensile feet. Among more advanced primates, e.g., chimpanzees and humans, the grip becomes more precise. They can oppose their thumbs to the rest of the digits on their hands and delicately feel the contours of objects. In addition, most primates have nails rather than claws at the ends of their digits. The sensitivity of tactile digits allows primates to derive more information about their environment; nails protect these sensitive pads, which allow them to feel smaller and more fragile objects. Whereas the sense of touch is confined to the nose in many animals, it shifts to the ends of the digits in primates. The snout takes up a proportionately smaller part of the skull, and the brain reflects the shift in sensory input; the region devoted to smell decreases.

The importance of touch extends into the realm of sexual behavior. Many mammals groom each other, but primates have developed it into a "fine art" (Jolly 1972 1972: 196). Social grooming is a unique primate trait (Napier 1973: 75). It may stem from the mother/infant bond, established when the mother reassures her infant with her attention via touch. Usually the mother licks and grooms her infant when it enters the world. Grooming also provides a basis for reinforcing social ties. Although the extent and uses of grooming vary according to the species, it often precedes copulation. Even New World monkeys that exhibit little or no grooming under ordinary circumstances may groom each other before copulation. A male Old World monkey may groom a female more assiduously when she is in heat. In many cases, touch may be more specifically sexual in nature. For example, male apes and monkeys may manually stimulate the females' genitalia before copulation (Ford and Beach 1972: 52, 53). Female apes and monkeys are less likely to stimulate the male genitalia (Ford and Beach 1972: 53, 54).

Primates also rely heavily on their eyes to gain information necessary for survival. Eyes have increased in size and now occupy a more central place in the face. Eye sockets have enlarged accordingly and claim a larger share of the skull. Bony sockets protect the eyes, and hairs guard against dust and moisture. Higher primates have both depth (binocular or stereoscopic) and color vision, which enable them to derive information at a distance about size, color, texture, movement, and distance.

Vision is also important, because it provides information about potential mates. Body posture may convey sexual cues. Often a female primate may solicit a male to mount her by "presenting" her rear end to him. Or, she may deliberately expose her genitals. Actual physiological changes may also provide a signal to the male that a female is fertile and possibly receptive to copulating. For example, some female monkeys and apes, e.g., baboons and chimpanzees, develop a "sex skin" when they are in estrus. The area of skin around the external genitalia becomes swollen and deepens in color. The male can respond to the prominent, brightly colored area as a visual cue of the female's sexual receptivity (Napier 1973: 63). The sex skin also provides the male with information about the females reproductive state; it is most swollen when she ovulates. If he copulates with her during maximal swelling, he is most likely to impregnate her. It is interesting to note that these swellings around ovulation occur most often in species that live in multimale groups (Clutton-Brock and Harvey 1976, in Hrdy 1981: 151). they may serve to increase competition between males for females in estrus. The female conserves her energy by having males approach her, rather than seeking them out. The swellings may help ensure that females have a range of choice of mates. Swellings may also serve to increase the female's freedom of movement between groups; a consort may accompany the female as she ranges beyond her usual community (Hrdy 1981: 152).

Variations in appearance may be sexually stimulating in and of themselves. And finally, recognition of characteristic colors, markings, and structures helps to ensure mating with members of the same species.

Like other mammals, primates focus their efforts on ensuring the survival of the few offspring they do produce. Mammals often have multiple births, but monkeys and apes are more like humans in that they rarely give birth to more than one infant at a time. Therefore, it is not surprising that they intensify the basic mammalian trends in reproductive efficiency—substantial prenatal and postnatal care of off-spring.

As animals become more complex, their gestation periods lengthen (Napier 1973: 66). Primates have longer gestation periods than do most mammals, and the duration of gestation among higher primates (e.g., chimpanzees thirty-four weeks; gibbons, thirty weeks) approaches the humans' thirty-eight weeks (Jolly 1972: 216, Napier 1973: 67). The uterine lining prepares more fully for the implantation of a fertilized egg. Some primates have a slight discharge of blood from the vagina during the ovarian cycle, because the build-up of the lining is so great that it cannot be readily absorbed into the body. In other words, some primates menstruate (mainly Old World monkeys and apes), although the amount of blood loss varies. New World monkeys do not bleed externally, but there is some evidence of increased internal blood flow. Humans lose appreciably more blood and tissue than other primates.

Their period of infant dependency after birth is also longer among primates than among most mammals. The infant is primarily dependent upon its mother for food and nurturance during the time that it is completing its growth. A close mother-infant tie is an intrinsic part of being a mammal. Primates intensify this bond and retain it as one of the most basic social units in their groups. The mother carries, feeds, grooms, protects, and imparts information to her infant. A significant consequence of the prolonged infant dependency period is that the infant has a longer time to learn about its complex habitat and the essentials of social interaction.

The learning that occurs during this period is important and plays a significant role in the young primate's survival. The Harlows' experiments with rhesus monkeys (Harlow 1973; Harlow and Harlow 1962; Harlow and Harlow 1966) suggest that an infant requires maternal care as well as contact with other monkeys in order to develop the ability to form bonds of affection with others of its species. If the infant is deprived of social contact with other monkeys, it will usually become antisocial, self-destructive, fearful, passive, and withdrawn. Some of these socially deprived monkeys may bite themselves to the point of bleeding. The pathetic consequences of deprivation are conveyed by the rocking movements of the solitary monkey, feebly attempting to provide some solace for itself in isolation from any other form of support. There seem to be few benefits derived from "independence" at such an early stage. If the lack of contact with other monkeys is extreme and prolonged, the infant may die.

The consequences of a monkey's deprivation in infancy reach to future generations. Deprived male monkeys rarely, if ever, mate. They may be physically abusive to females that approach them. The few female monkeys who do mate do not exhibit "maternal" behavior toward their offspring. Their behavior ranges from "indifference to outright abuse" (Harlow and Harlow 1962: 144). For example, one monkey repulsed an infant seeking the succor of her breast. The infants of "motherless mothers" play less, show more aggression, and lack interest in copulation (Harlow and Harlow 1962: 145). In sum, the quality of monkeys' early care and other aspects of their social lives can affect the success of their subsequent reproduction.

Most primates live and learn within a social context. This context is usually more extensive than the basic social unit of mammals, the mother-infant pair. Primate social groups span all age levels and include members of both sexes. Although most male and female mammals associate only during the breeding season, the composition of primate groups remains fairly consistent throughout the annual cycle. Males remain in the vicinity of females year-round and tolerate infants born within their group (Hrdy 1981: 35). Mammalian young generally do not remain with adults after puberty. However, the bond established between a primate mother and infant or between offspring of the same mother may persist past sexual maturity, especially among higher primates (Lovejoy 1981: 347). The longevity of primates gives them ample opportunity to learn during their lifetimes. It also means that elders are available as caretakers and models for effective behavior.

The nature of primate social life varies according to habitat. Groups of land-dwelling primates tend to be larger and more highly organized than those of tree-dwelling species. However, there are exceptions to these trends, and it is difficult to single out any one factor responsible for specific kinds of primate social organization.

Members of the social groups may contribute to the postnatal care of infants and thereby enhance their survival. There is a great deal of interest in a newborn in a primate group (Hrdy 1981: 97). Some monkeys and apes may even inspect an infant's genitals (Konner 1982: 114). Females may exhibit "aunt" behavior as they huddle around an infant and attempt to touch, groom, hold, or carry it (Nelson and Jurmain 1982: 281). In many species, females may share their infants by allowing others to take turns carrying them (Hrdy 1981: 96). The degree of willingness of mothers to share their infants varies considerably, but sharing may provide advantages for mothers, infants, and temporary caretakers (Hrdy 1981: 98). A mother can forage more easily without her infant clinging to her. An infant may also be cared for or adopted by another female if its mother dies or temporarily cannot nurture it. And, through sharing, other females, particularly those that have not borne young, can get some practice at mothering. However, sharing can have its drawbacks (Hrdy 1981: 98). The newborn are vulnerable to the incompetence of females that have not had offspring, and such other females may lose interest or abandon an infant altogether.

Males may also contribute to the care of infants. Male primates distinguish themselves by investing more in infants and juveniles in their own group than most mammals generally do (Hrdy 1981: 35, 72). They may directly care for the young by protecting, babysitting, and even feeding some infants (Hrdy 1981: 35). They may indirectly assist them by deferring to a mother and her infant for food or by defending the group as a whole and thus contributing to a safer environment for the young (Hrdy 1981: 35).

In some cases, primates may mate and stay together to raise their offspring ("monogamy"). They may copulate with others in their group, but they are usually somewhat restricted in the number of partners they seek. Hrdy thinks that under these circumstances the male has greater confidence in his paternity and is therefore willing to invest more in the offspring (Hrdy 1981: 35). The amount of time and energy he devotes to his offspring may approach that spent by the female. Less than 4 percent of mammals exhibit this pattern, but more than four times this proportion (18 percent) of primates live in breeding pairs that mutually care for offspring (Hrdy 1981: 36). Breeding pairs span the entire primate order and are not confined to the higher primates.

Ecology may play a large role in channeling the types of bonds that males and females form. Gibbons dwell in the confines of a small area of forest, which is only large enough to support a rather small group. Their existence is more arboreal than terrestrial. Their social organization is well suited to their environment. They live in small, familylike groups of a single male, a female, and their offspring. They maintain a balance between their resources and group size by compelling their offspring to leave when they are able to exist on their own. Both males and females protect the boundaries of their territory by keeping other males and females from intruding. Males have only one mate and make a substantial investment in the offspring. The similarity in male and female roles is reflected in their relative sizes. The adult female is approximately the same size (93 to 103 percent) as the male (Schultz 1969, in Symons 1979: 108).

Group organization may also affect the type of social and sexual interaction that takes place between males and females. Multimale groups are the most common type among both arboreal and terrestrial primates. For example, savanna baboons dwell in the open savanna and form troops of forty or more animals. They have a well-developed form of social organization, characterized by dominance hierarchies of males. The toughest, strongest, and most socially facile male becomes leader of the group. Other males rank below him in a definite order. The position of a male in the hierarchy may depend upon his age, strength, and social behavior and by the relationship of his mother with males in the hierarchy. Females may also have hierarchies.

Dominance usually means more access to desired resources, e.g., food and females. Therefore the place of a male in the hierarchy affects his sexual access to females. Dominant males are most likely to copulate with females in full estrus. Consequently, young males may be less likely than elder males to pass on their genes. In addition, they are less likely to produce offspring with their mothers, even if they do copulate with them.

For animals to assess an expanded social environment and adapt to a complex arboreal habitat (e.g., one with seasonal fluctuations, predators on the ground and in the trees, and activity primarily during the day, when they themselves are more visible) requires considerable skill. Animals with more complex brains have an advantage in dealing with these situations. The nervous system begins to play a more important role in the lives of primates, particularly higher ones. Primates are the most intelligent mammals (Lovejoy 1981: 347) and display the most striking reorganization of the brain of any of the mammals (Konner 1982: 66). The ratio of a primate's brain size to body size is greater than that of most other animals. The relative amount of brain tissue devoted to memory, association, and reflection has increased, resulting in a greater ability to process information about the environment. The brain plays a significant role in shaping the distinctive contours of primate sexual behavior.

As a consequence of these changes in the brain, the range of stimuli to which primates can sexually respond has expanded. Their heightened senses of touch and vision contribute to the variety of sexual stimulation. The clitoris, a small organ located at the front end of the small interior lips (labia minora) of the female's external genitals, is almost universal among female primates. It is exposed, often hangs down, and sometimes contains a small bone (Campbell 1967: 255). Like the penis, it can become erect and produce erotic sensations when stimulated by touch. Its only known function is sexual stimulation, and it may help raise sexual excitement to a level sufficient for the male to effectively enter the female with his penis (Campbell 1967: 259).

The way in which the brain processes clitoral stimulation may have important repercussions for the nature of a primate female's sexual experience. The clitoris provides the female primate with the potential for orgasm. Direct and prolonged stimulation of the clitoris occurs in all cases where orgasm seems to occur (Symons 1979: 83). However, it is uncertain whether female primates actually *experience* orgasm. Unfortunately, it is not possible to ask them about it and receive an understandable reply. Therefore, indirect indicators can only provide a partial answer.

Several primatologists report evidence that may indicate orgasm among nonhuman female primates. Some captive rhesus monkeys display a "clutching reaction" during copulation (Zumpe and Michael: 1968, in Symons 1979: 78). Baboons (Saayman 1970, in Symons 1979: 80) and chimpanzees (McGinnis, in Symons 1979: 81) may vocalize in characteristic ways after a number of thrusts by the male. Experiments by Burton demonstrate that a rhesus monkey may have a series of vaginal spasms when the clitoris is stimulated for five minutes or the vagina for ten (Burton 1971, in Symons 1979: 81).

There is a great deal of variation in the occurrence of apparent orgasms between species, between individuals within the same species, and even within the same female. Part of the problem in interpreting the primate evidence is that much of it is derived from captive animals. Captive animals do seem to provide convincing evidence of nonhuman primate orgasm in females (Symons 1979: 82). But to what extent can this finding be generalized to include primates in their natural surroundings? Prolonged stimulation of the clitoris is an important factor in producing an orgasmic response. Since most mammals mate rather quickly, they may not fulfill their potential for orgasm (Symons 1979: 88). Rhesus monkeys retain intromission for only three to five seconds in their natural habitat (Burton 1971, in Symons 1979: 81). However, higher primates may engage in more prolonged stimulation. Captive great apes often mutually stimulate each other's genitals. Galdikas observed wild orangutans that preceded copulation with the male orally stimulating the genitals of the female and then maintaining thrusting for three to seventeen minutes during copulation (Galdikas 1979, in Hrdy 1981: 137). Furthermore, lengthy stimulation need not come from just one of the partners. During a single estrus period, a female baboon may copulate as many as a hundred times (Hrdy 1981: 140). Hall and Devore (1965 in Hrdy 1981: 140) observed one female engage in intercourse twenty-three times in a ten-hour period, with three different males. Even when copulations occur in captive conditions, they may express what occurs in the wild. And even if they do not reflect "natural" conditions, they show the tremendous sensitivity of primate behavior to different environmental settings. At the very least, the reactions of primates indicate that they experience sexual excitement and seek it out under a variety of conditions.

Symons suggests that female orgasm is a by-product of the adaptive significance of orgasm for males, since orgasm aids ejaculation for fertilization (Symons 1979: 92). However, his conclusion dismisses the possibly important adaptive significance of the experience for females. Why would most female primates have developed a clitoris, the only known function of which is sexual stimulation? How does the brain process the intensity of increased arousal? Is it not possible that heightened sexual stimulation (culminating in orgasm) is just as adaptive for females as for males, but in a different way? The issue is broader than the question of whether orgasm occurs among nonhuman female primates; it centers on the nature of primate sexuality itself, particularly on the role that females play in relation to males.

A popular image of primate sexual behavior is that it is much like that of most mammals. According to this view, copulation occurs during a short breeding period and is confined to a few days around ovulation; sexual behavior rarely occurs at other times. Most lower primates (prosimians) conform to this basic mammalian pattern of strictly seasonal receptivity and breeding. However, higher primates exhibit more variability in the relationship between their ovarian cycles and their sexual behavior (Hrdy 1981: 145, 146). Not all primates are alike, and the complexity of primate sexuality may be more intricate than we suspect. Most researchers agree that nonhuman primates engage in nonreproductive (or extrareproductive) behavior, and that they do so under a variety of circumstances.

Symons provides some useful categories for summarizing the preceding evidence. First, primate breeding cycles vary according to species (Symons 1979: 100; Hrdy 1981: 146). Some, like prosimians, are strictly seasonal and cyclical. A few are nonseasonal and noncyclical and may occur at any time. Most primates fall into an intermediate category: breeding cycles may occur through much of the year, but mating may peak during certain seasons. Sexual behavior is often cyclical, but it can fluctuate according to the situation.

Some of this variation may be a response to environmental conditions. Ember and Ember (1983) present some cross-species evidence on the reasons why some species have breeding seasons while others copulate throughout the year. Where there is a great deal of seasonal fluctuation in the environment, animals are less likely to breed throughout the year. Breeding is timed in such a way that infants will be born during periods of optimal food supply. The relative length of the days according to the season may be an environmental trigger for the beginning of the breeding season (Rowell 1974: 113). However, when the dependency period of infants (the number of months during which the young typically get food from their parents) exceeds a season of optimal food supply, it is more advantageous to space births throughout the year. (An excess of six month's dependency is regarded as a long dependency period.) The Embers' data lend some strong support to their hypothesis about breeding seasons. They find that no species in their sample in regions above forty degrees latitude lacks a breeding season. Long dependency periods are most likely to occur in nontemperate areas of the world. It is only under those conditions that long dependency periods and nonseasonal breeding are likely to occur.

We can infer from the Embers' data that higher primates are likely candidates for developing nonseasonal mating systems, since their dependency periods may far exceed six months. They live primarily in tropical areas that are suitable for supporting the young all through the year.

Primates also show the sensitivity of their mating patterns to the environment by a change in sexual patterns during captivity. The breeding season that some primates experience in the wild may disappear under conditions of captivity, and copulation may occur throughout the year (Rowell 1974: 115). These changes may be due either to the absence of the seasonal cues that trigger breeding periods or to the consistency of the captive environment.

A second area of research that provides evidence of nonreproductive mating is the length of estrus. Ovarian cycles may range in length from eighteen to thirty-five days (Jolly 1972: 20) and may be repeated on an average of every twenty-eight days (Napier 1973: 62). Even though estrus begins around the midpoint of the cycle, it can last for seven to fourteen days. Therefore, it extends longer than is necessary for fertilization, and part of the behavior that occurs at the time is nonreproductive. Furthermore, females mate with many more males than are necessary for fertilization (Hrdy 1981: 147).

A third category of information about the occurrence of nonreproductive sexuality includes sexual behavior during pregnancy and after birth (Symons 1979: 100). Although estrus is usually absent during pregnancy, it may occur in some species. Similarly, all primates experience a period without estrus (anestrus) while they are lactating. Nevertheless, some females may go into estrus before their offspring are fully weaned. Therefore, sexual activity occurs at a time when fertilization is unlikely (during lactation) or impossible (during pregnancy). Conoway and Koford's observations of rhesus monkeys through an entire breeding season revealed quite a bit of variation (Conoway and Koford 1965, in Rowell

1974: 126). They found it difficult to tie sexual behavior to hormone fluctuations. Their analysis revealed that a large amount of cyclical sexual behavior (50 percent) occurred during pregnancy.

Symons sums up the evidence by concluding that primates engage in much more nonreproductive sexual activity than most mammals do (Symons 1979: 101). Hrdy concurs and suggests that nonreproductive sexuality indicates a trend in primate evolution "away from strictly seasonal and cyclical determination of receptivity" (Hrdy 1981: 145). Females appear to be just as interested in sexual behavior as males, even when it is not reproductive. The question, then, becomes "Why?" The answers may involve giving up some cherished views about the differences between human and nonhuman sexuality and those between males and females. Since "there is not a single species of primate for which adequate data on reproductive strategies exist" (Hrdy 1981: 136), much of what follows is speculative.

Symons suggests that a permanent social life may have permitted less precision in the link between copulation and ovulation without jeopardizing the possibility of conception (Symons 1979: 103). However, it would be a mistake to conclude that nonreproductive sexuality developed in order to maintain the group or bonding between males and females. Clearly, social life is advantageous for primates. However, Symons thinks that it is more productive to search for an explanation of nonreproductive sexual behavior, including heightened sexual stimulation, by examining the variety of ways in which the individual and/or progeny benefit from the behavior (Symons 1979: 103).

Symons identifies a number of factors which could hinder a female's reproductive success (Symons 1979: 92). These factors include anything that interferes with her ability to (1) make sure she reaps the greatest advantage from her sexual behavior; (2) conceive and effectively raise offspring; (3) choose a male who is the best available father for her children; (4) influence males to help her and her offspring; and (5) cut down on the possibility of violence or the loss of support from males, particularly her mate or her kinsmen. In sum, the circumstances that surround copulation, conception, and postnatal care are of vital concern to females.

Symons interprets female sexuality from this point of view. He finds it difficult to understand how heightened sexual activity (especially orgasm or nonreproductive sexuality) could contribute to a female's reproductive success (Symons 1979: 91). It could interfere with caring for offspring and obtaining food. Furthermore, a female might copulate so promiscuously that she would neglect to seek out the fittest mate for her offspring and would have difficulty in finding males to aid her in raising her offspring. He swiftly dismisses Sherfey's claim (in *The Nature and Evolution of Female Sexuality*) that a female's orgasmic potential is a deeply-rooted and adaptive part of her existence (Symons 1979: 94). Rather, he thinks it is most reasonable to conclude that orgasm and heightened sexual activity for females are possible because they are adaptive for males (Symons 1979: 93). Females do not have to compete for opportunities to copulate, but males do (Symons 1979: 153). Therefore, males are more likely to seek a variety of partners to enhance their reproductive success. The more females with whom they copulate, the more they increase their chances of fertilizing them and passing on their own genes.

Symons relegates female sexual activity to the category of a "service" or a "favor," which females "bestow" or withhold from males (Symons 1979: 253-285). Females are more likely to exercise choice in their selection of mates, because they have more to lose — the time and energy devoted to gestation, birth, and the care of infants. Unlike males, females are not likely to be aroused by the sight of the genitals of the opposite sex or to rely on cues of physical attractiveness (hair, facial features, age, etc.) in choosing mates. Symons sums up the "biological reality" of his perspective with W. H. Auden's comment on men and women: "Men are playboys, women realists" (Symons 1979: 92).

Although Symons stresses that the circumstances surrounding copulation, conception, and postnatal care are essential for a female's reproductive success, he does not give equal weight to these circumstances for males. He confines his emphasis to copulation and consequent conception. He promotes a stereotyped image of "Nurturant females" and "ardent males." However, nonreproductive sexual behavior among primates indicates that the significance of copulation goes beyond fertilization. Furthermore, postnatal care is of major importance to the survival of primate infants, particularly those of higher primates. A male primate does not necessarily ensure his reproductive success by flurries of sexual encounters. As Daly and Wilson put it: "The crucial question is not really 'Who mates with whom' but 'who fertilizes whom?'"(Daly and Wilson 1978: 83). I would add the question: "Who ensures the survival of offspring after they are born?" A male can enhance his own reproductive success if he contributes to the postnatal care of his offspring, even if the contribution is indirect.

Hrdy would probably agree with Symons' assumptions about the general factors that enhance a female's reproductive success. However, her interpretation of their relevance to female sexuality diverges rather sharply from his. Hrdy's recent book, *The Woman That Never Evolved* (1981) presents some intriguing information, which questions several widespread stereotypes about female primates. Far from being all-nurturant, primate females are intelligent, "highly competitive, socially involved and sexually assertive" (Hrdy 1981: 190). To characterize them as "naturally innocent from lust or power" is to paint a decidedly unrealistic picture.

Females express their sexual assertiveness and awareness of social networks by their participation in nonreproductive (and highly stimulating) sexual behavior. By so doing, they contribute to their reproductive success. Hrdy demonstrates her point by her interpretation of the way in which females solicit the sexual attentions of males in a multimale group.

Female primates in multimale groups copulate around the time of ovulation with more partners than are necessary for conception. It is possible that multiple matings may increase a female's probability of breeding with males that carry superior genes. Dominant males may compete with lower-ranking ones for access to her. If a female consorts with several males, she can assess their relative qualities as mates (Hrdy 1981: 15).

However, Hrdy suggests that the female may not be interested in attracting any single male but rather may want to mate with a number of males. Symons sees this as reproductively wasteful activity, but Hrdy views it as adaptive behavior. She relates it to the important role that males may play in the survival of the female's offspring. A primate female may try to attract and mate with a number of males, to enhance the quality of the care of her offspring. Male primates pay special attention to and care for offspring likely to be their own (Hrdy 1981: 76). Conversely, they may kill infants of unfamiliar females or be "brutally" intolerant to offspring of other males (Hrdy 1981: 76). By mating with a number of males, the female increases the uncertainty as to paternity and thereby induces more males to pay attention to and possibly care for her infant; each mate may regard the infant as his own. At the very least, he may not interfere with its survival. At the most, he may contribute to the well-being of an infant that is his own and thereby extend his overall reproductive success.

Hrdy considers the question of whether it is plausible to suppose that males would remember their past consorts; she draws on the work of two Canadian zoologists to reach her conclusion. Malloy and Brooks performed an experiment that showed that lemmings can remember exposure to the mothers of their offspring (Hrdy 1981: 154). Since rodents are not as intelligent as primates, Hrdy thinks it is reasonable to infer that primates also have this ability.

Both Symons and Hrdy view nonreproductive sexuality as a repro-

ductive strategy — a cost/benefit analysis of behavior in terms of ultimate reproductive goals. Another possibility is to interpret nonreproductive sexuality more directly as a product of the feedback between
some general primate trends — a greater capacity for sexual stimulation,
an expanded brain, and the complexity of social life.

Primates may engage in sexual behavior beyond that necessary for
reproduction, because it is enjoyable in its own right. Although copulation began as a means of facilitating fertilization, primates may have
generalized its significance as an intrinsically pleasurable activity. Their
expanded brains certainly have the capacity to process information in
this way. This conjecture seems more plausible in light of the fact that
primates, like many other mammals, touch and stimulate their own
genitals (Ford and Beach 1972: 163). At the very least, primates engage
in behavior to increase sexual excitement. Furthermore, they may associate their pleasure with specific individuals.

Since male and female primates typically reside together in permanent social groups, they recognize each other as group members, their
longevity (forty years for gorillas, thirty-five years for chimpanzees,
thirty years for orangutans) means that they have a long time to interact
and assess behavior (Campbell 1967: 247). As juveniles, they play together and may practice sexual interaction. Increased capacities for
association and memory can aid them in remembering their experiences
with other members. It is not too big a leap to conclude that their past
experiences may play a role in their willingness to engage in nonreproductive behavior.

Rowell suggests that we have underestimated the variety of ways in
which behavior may be determined among primates (Rowell 1974:
170). Few other mammals rely on affiliation with group members and
alliances between them as much as primates do (Hrdy 1981: 116).
Therefore, it is not surprising that primates express definite choices
about potential mates. Their preferences may override the dictates of
the ovarian cycle. A female may demonstrate a strong preference to
mate with a specific male, even in a species regarded as promiscuous
(Jolly 1972: 211). During estrus, the female may solicit the attention of
a specific male, who becomes her only consort for a short while (a few
hours to a few days) (Napier 1973: 64). In contrast, a female ape may be
very resistant to mating with certain males (Ford and Beach 1972: 206)
or she may alternate between single consorts and successive copulations
with different males. Tutin reports that a female chimpanzee may sequester herself with a single male, with whom she copulates five to ten
times a day (Hrdy 1981: 148). Or, she may accompany a small cluster of
males, with whom she copulates a total of thirty to fifty times a day.

Males may also show definite preferences for certain females. Van Lawick-Goodall observed that sometimes a chimpanzee male may force an unwilling female to travel with him until he tires of her, or she escapes (van Lawick-Goodall 1972: 194–199). She also noted an unusual relationship between two chimpanzees in which a high-ranking male became the faithful companion of an old female chimpanzee, especially while she was in estrus; the male accompanied her almost everywhere she went, and he slept in the nest next to hers (van Lawick-Goodall 1972: 97–99).

Other criteria beyond individual preferences seem to play a role in mate selection. Although some males may prefer to mate with females during their maximal swelling (if they have "sex skins"), others will copulate at any time. For some males, the difference between the most recent partner and a new one may be sufficient to arouse interest. Like other mammalian males, primate males may be rearoused by the presence of a new female (Symons 1979: 209), and they are able to differentiate precisely one female from the other. There is some evidence that the appearance of an unfamiliar male may also spark sexual activity in a female (Hrdy 1981: 146). However, it is also possible that she acts this way to prevent being attacked (Symons 1979: 103). Even the sight, sound, or smell of group members copulating may be enough to stimulate others to do the same (Rowell 1974: 177).

Rank may be another variable in the sexual equation. Conaway and Koford found that the highest-ranking male rhesus monkeys tend to consort with the highest-ranking females (Conaway and Koford 1965, in Rowell 1974: 126). Female orangutans may assertively seek out dominant, adult males as consorts (Hrdy 1981: 147). However, there is no consistent trend among species to suggest a causal link between rank and sexual interaction (Rowell 1974: 130). Rowell thinks that we may have given undue emphasis to "dominance" in mating patterns (Rowell 1974: 159, 160). Age may be as relevant a factor. For example, the "dominant male" may be a specific role that males adopt for a short time during mid-adulthood, rather than a position achieved solely through fierce competition (Rowell 1974: 172). If so, age and rank may go hand in hand to affect frequency of copulation.

Rowell thinks that kinship may emerge as one of the more important determinants of primate behavior (Rowell 1974: 171). The position of the young male's mother in the group may affect his relationship with other males and his access to potential mates. Kinship also provides some guidelines as to appropriate sexual partners. Sons rarely mate with their mothers.

The point is that primates make choices about their mating patterns.

They are not totally at the mercy of their endocrine systems. The behavioral interplay between primates and their environment is intricate. Learning and social interaction have more wide-ranging effects on all aspects of reproduction and sexual behavior. It is difficult to pigeonhole primates, because of their behavioral flexibility. Regardless of the hypotheses we accept about their sexual behavior, the evidence demonstrates that the line between nonhuman and human primate sexual behavior is a fine one. Human sexuality is part of the primate sexual continuum, not a separate category.

### The Human Family: Hominidae

Humans express the fruits of primate trends in behavioral flexibility and efficiency of sexual reproduction. In addition, humans have developed several anatomical and physiological characteristics that set them apart from other primates. These general changes indirectly relate to reproduction, because they enhance the survival of individuals and contribute to the perpetuation of the species. They have direct consequences for human sexuality in that they define the biological framework within which sex and reproduction occur. General changes are so intertwined with specifically sexual and reproductive ones that it is necessary to relate them to each other in order to derive a full understanding of what is distinctively human about human sexuality.

Humans belong to the family of primates called "hominidae"; this family includes contemporary humans and prehistoric fossil species related to them (*Homo* or "man," *Australopithecus*, and possibly *Ramapithecus*). How we piece together the series of events that led to and followed from changes in hominid evolution has a direct impact on how we interpret the sexual and reproductive roles of modern males and females. Therefore, it is necessary first to consider the development of hominid traits that preceded the appearance of true humans who belong to the genus *Homo*.

### The Significance of Bipedal Locomotion and Increased Brain Size

Two major physical characteristics that distinguish human beings from other animals are habitual bipedal locomotion with upright posture and a very large brain relative to body size. Controversy surrounds explanations of when, how, and why these characteristics developed.

It is not surprising that there are many different reconstructions of the events leading up to these changes. The scant fossil remains leave broad gaps for inventive interpretations. Furthermore, it is difficult to portray accurately the behavioral patterns of early hominids. Such portraits are inferred from the relationship between anatomical form and function, the material culture associated with the fossils, and studies that have been made of the social organization of contemporary primates, including humans. Finally, interpreters of this evidence are human beings who have a stake in the kind of picture they want to paint of their species; some bias is almost inevitable. Tanner likens the story of human evolution to the presentation of an origin myth (Tanner 1981: 1–7). There may be a tendency to reconstruct the past so that it legitimizes current values and social organization.

Nevertheless, prehistoric fossils, material culture, and current information about primate behavior constitute valuable clues for piecing together the novel components of the human heritage. Particular interpretations of the nature of human sexuality arise from broader hypotheses about general trends in human evolution.

Most researchers agree that the transition from the late Miocene (twelve to eight million years ago) to the early Pliocene (four million years ago) is a crucial one for understanding hominid evolution (Tanner 1981: 44). During that time interval, habitual bipedal locomotion with upright posture emerged. The problem is that at least four million years separate fossils of a likely hominid ancestor (*Ramapithecus*) from those of the earliest known and agreed upon hominid (*Australopithecus*). The key to the transition to hominids remains locked in undiscovered fossils between eight to four million years ago. The lack of fossils makes an answer to the basic question of when and why bipedal locomotion developed even more difficult to answer.

The initial clues with which anthropologists work are Ramapithecine teeth. Teeth are important, because they provide information about the type of food that may have been eaten and allow us to speculate about the kind of environment to which the animal was adapting. They also have the advantage of being hard and therefore more easily preserved than most human remains.

Ramapithecine fossils frequently occur in the mid to late Miocene, and they express some hominid traits — relatively small canines but large molars. On this basis, C. Jolly (1970) hypothesizes that Ramapithecines may have been seed-eaters. Large molars would allow them to crush and grind small, hard seeds, while reduced canines would allow some flexibility in their jaws; increased side-to-side movement could aid the molars in grinding the seeds. Pilbeam (1978) adds to this idea by concluding that Ramapithecine teeth have thicker enamel than that of most apes. If so, they probably relied on food sources in dry woodlands and open grasslands (Tanner 1981: 51). At the very least, Ramapithecines left the trees for the ground to seek out new food sources. At the most, they may have ventured into the open plains to eat small, hard grass seeds. Either way, they probably changed other behavior to adapt to their new habitat. How they changed may shed light on the path that led to habitual bipedal locomotion and increased brain size.

Most primates have the ability to walk bipedally for short distances and to stand upright. It is not unreasonable to suppose that Ramapithecines shared this ability. Therefore, they could use their hands for other purposes. What they used their hands for becomes an important factor in reconstructing other elements of our humanness.

*Male-oriented views of the transition.* Sherwood Washburn and Ruth Moore (1980) think that the use of tools, specifically weapons, was the stimulus that had a major role in producing a new mode of movement. Once on the ground, prehominids were more vulnerable to predators. Their small size (three to four feet tall) was not much protection, but weapons may have been. Initially they may have used their hands to throw sticks or rocks to scare off enemies. Later, they may have realized that rocks were useful as weapons. If so, they would have had an advantage, even in the face of bigger, faster, and stronger animals. Use of weapons could allow them to relinquish the protective cover of the forest and venture out into the savanna. More reliance on standing upright could help them rise above the tall grasses and scan the landscape for predators. More efficient use of weapons would require more freedom of the hands. Upright posture would permit that freedom. Bipedal locomotion by itself would provide few advantages; bipeds are slower and thus more vulnerable than quadrupeds. Therefore, the use of objects was probably the most important link in the process (Washburn and Moore 1980: 78); it conferred so great an advantage that it compensated for the "inefficient and costly" bipedalism that was required to free the forelimbs for tools (Washburn and Moore 1980: 123). As tool use and carrying the products of tool use became more important, selection favored more efficient bipedal walkers. One advantage fed into another. Their feedback led to *Australopithecus* ("southern ape"), a small biped with reduced canines who probably inhabited the African savanna three-and-one-half to four million years ago. Males had weapons. Females had infants. We begin to see the roots of the gender gap. They take hold more firmly as hypotheses develop about the kind of social organization that probably accompanied tool use and bipedalism.

Washburn and DeVore (1963, in Konner 1982: 39) suggest that baboon behavior is an appropriate model for understanding transitional and early hominids. Savanna baboons are Old World monkeys that have adapted to life on open stretches of land which make up the savanna. Since baboons have to deal with environmental conditions similar to those of early hominids, these authors think that we might infer some of the behavior of early hominids from the ways that baboons adapt.

The social organization of baboons stands out as one of the major ways to deal with the dangers that accompany life on the ground and in the open. In contrast to arboreal primates, baboons travel in relatively large groups. The troop contains an average of forty animals. Sheer numbers provide some safety. More striking is the way in which they organize their numbers. Dominance hierarchies of males are central to their survival and affect most aspects of their lives. Males express their dominance in a number of ways. Dominant males have access to safer social space. They accompany females, infants, and juveniles in the center of the group when they move from one place to another. Subdominant males defend the outer boundaries of the troop. Males express the importance of their protective function by their physical appearance. They are approximately twice as large as females and have large canine (or "eye") teeth, which they bare to ward off intruders or frighten subdominant males. Sometimes they make their hair stand on end to increase their apparent size. Females also have dominance hierarchies, but their ranks ebb and flow according to their reproductive states (pregnant, nursing, or in estrus). Higher-ranked females can speed the rise of their sons in male hierarchy by their relationships with dominant males. Dominant males also have priority of access to food and to ovulating females. Therefore, their genes are more likely to be passed on. Dominant males may occasionally band together to prevent younger, subdominant males from usurping their positions. Or, they may occasionally band together with other males to kill an animal.

Transitional hominids were probably just as well organized as baboons. Their social life and their tool use helped to effect the shift to more human characteristics. Because they used weapons, they did not have to rely on large size or menacing canines to protect themselves. Washburn and Moore regard relatively small canines as proof of increased reliance on tools, particularly weapons (Washburn and Moore 1980: 123). Therefore, the large differences in size between males and females decreased, as did the massive jaws and large canines. Weapons also allowed males to hunt for animals on a more regular basis. Like baboons, they probably joined together to kill their prey. Cooperative hunts may have developed from this practice, providing even more advantages over predators. Males' monopoly over weapons and hunting increased their dominance over females.

Males' use of weapons, hunting, and dominance became major stimuli for hypotheses about the origins of sexual differentiation. Robert Ardrey (*African Genesis* 1961) and Desmond Morris (*The Naked Ape* 1967) popularized DeVore and Washburn's early view of the transition to hominids. They gave males credit for blazing the path to distinctively hominid traits. Aggressive males forged ahead with their weapons and hunted cooperatively to create a new way of life. Through these activities, males became mentally and materially dominant over females. Meanwhile, females tended the young at the home base, gathered some vegetal food, and exerted little force over what was happening. They were passive clay to be molded into shape by the needs of males. In sum, savanna adaptation led to sexual differentiation along the following lines: males were aggressive, inventive, and dominant; females were passive, nurturant, and dependent.

Variations on this theme continue. Robin Fox (1980) explores the implications of this scenario in detail to explain the origins of a unique human rule: the incest taboo. In so doing, he offers an interpretation of how brain size in hominids increased to the extent that it did. Like others before him, Fox regards the beginning of the incest taboo as the mark of a shift into the truly human realm — a cultural domain where beliefs and rules govern behavior, especially sexual behavior. Since rule-governed behavior implies greater cortical control of actions, significant changes probably began with developments that led to increased brain size. The crucial stimulus was an environmental situation that required the ability to control impulses and weigh alternatives. Fox follows Chance (Chance and Mead 1953 and Chance 1962, in Fox 1980: 111) in positing that this ability to equilibrate (balance alternatives) lies at the core of our humanity. Changes in the breeding system made it necessary.

The social organization that gave rise to equilibration was a dominance hierarchy, much like that of baboons. Although humans are genetically closer to chimpanzees, they do not share the experience of the "timid chimp who stayed home and lost out" (Fox 1980: 87). Baboons and humans are closer in the savanna adaptation. Despite the differences in social organization and behavior between monkeys and apes, they share some common structural features. First, they are divided into three groups: (1) established males, (2) females with young, and (3) peripheral males. Second, males compete for breeding success. Dominance aids established males in winning the competition with young males for access to fertile females. The males best able to equilibrate would have an advantage over less cortically controlled males. Subdominant young males would refrain from aggression toward elders, and dominant males would cooperate with each other to retain their high position in the hierarchy. Although Fox concedes that females had their own equilibrating to do, "it is not so spectacular as the males" (Fox 1980: 114). The prehominid ancestor of the late Miocene/early Pliocene probably had a breeding system with similar elements (Fox 1980: 121). At this point, there seems to be very little difference between monkeys, apes, and prehominids.

One critical development that made humans different from other primates was their increased use of weapons and killing (Fox 1980: 138). The breeding system had to shift to deal with these factors. Weapons could equalize the differences among males and pose a considerable threat to elder males in competition with younger ones for access to females for breeding. The primate breeding system intensified to its limits; the stakes were much higher if males acted on their aggressive, competitive impulses. If they could exercise some restraint, they could balance some alternatives to enhance their overall success. By giving up short-term aggression (which could end in death), they could gain access to females in the long run. Larger brained males were more likely to equilibrate in this way and survive. Therefore, the breeding system sorted out the most cortically controlled males and caused the brain to evolve (Fox 1980: 145). A larger brain then provided the capacity to exert even more cortical control.

The shift from prehominid to hominid was subtle but far-reaching. Competition between males for a position in the dominance hierarchy led to the ascent of man. Dominant prehominid males had more access to females with whom they could breed. Dominant hominid males were more interested in gaining control over females to exchange for other females. The transition to hominids was a change from males "controlling 'own' females as objects of use to controlling 'own' females as objects of exchange" (Fox 1980: 139). Females participated in the process by seeking to mate with high-ranked males and by helping their sons to advance in rank (Fox 1980: 139).

The transition to full-scale hunting was the trigger for rapid expansion of the brain and the creation of rules, after the first hominids (Australopithecines) developed. Hunting affected social life in two ways. First, males needed to cooperate with each other in order to hunt. A display of aggression toward each other would be detrimental to cohesion for the food quest. It became advantageous to channel hostility into hunting and to restrain competition for mates. Second, a division of labor began. Males hunted, and females gathered. The nature of male/

female relationships shifted. Males needed females for more than sex, and females needed males for more than insemination and protection. They needed the products of each other's labor (Fox 1980: 143). Exchange of meat and vegetal products between males and females stimulated more equilibration. Females wanted meat for themselves and their offspring. Males realized that they might trade meat for the opportunity to control the sexuality of the females. The groundwork was laid for the development of rules governing mating.

Increased brain size, the economy (based on the exchange of the products of labor), cooperation of males in the hunt, and the traditional breeding system all meshed to generate a new, human, breeding system. Equilibration was carried one step further as brain size continued to increase from *Homo* (or *Australopithecus*) *habilis* to *Homo erectus*. Males were capable of classifying females as kin and non-kin. The control of dominant males over female kin would give them leverage in dealing with potentially dangerous young males. The elder males agreed to ally with the young ones if the young males would constrain their competition for mates. By keeping young males out of the breeding system, elder males would have more access to females. They would agree to allocate female kin to other males at a later time in exchange for their restraint. The payoffs for the young males were alliances and the assurance of having mates and similar positions of dominance later. The incest taboo assured the operation of the system. Fathers did not mate with their female kin; they saved them to allocate to young males. Sons could not mate with their female kin, because their fathers controlled sexual rights over them and would prevent such matings. The elders' political and economic control over female kin meant power over young males. Relinquishing sex with female kin was a small price to pay for such an advantage.

Once again, females became pawns in a male game of competition for dominance over them and younger males. Male strategies to control the breeding system and the products of female labor became the source of our humanity; their equilibration led to a dramatic increase in brain size and regulation of behavior by rules. Females were subsidiary to the process. As Fox puts it; ". . . I suspect that the equilibrational process is not so strong in females as in males, because the conflicts are not as great and hence the reaction less charged" (Fox 1980: 164).

*Female-oriented views of the transition.* Male-oriented views follow Darwin's bias in his presentation of sexual selection. They focus on the ways in which males compete with each other for access to females. they tend to minimize or neglect the role of female choice in selecting males. Other theorists try to correct this bias by considering the role that females played in effecting the transition to major hominid traits: bipedal locomotion and increased brain size.

Nancy Tanner thinks that many past and contemporary versions of human evolution are, at best, incomplete and, at worst, extremely biased toward a male perspective. Tanner accounts for Darwin's neglect of the female role in sexual selection in terms of acceptable Victorian sexual attitudes. Since women were characterized and treated as passive in this era, it was hard for Victorian males to assign a significant, active role in evolution to female choice. Contemporary books that emphasize the image of "man the hunter" play on sexual stereotypes. They pigeonhole males as aggressors, protectors, and providers and females as nurturant and passive recipients of male behavior. Evolutionary theory has almost become a rationalization for the continuation of the Western tradition, which has been characterized by social stratification, male dominance, and imperialism.

Tanner wants to add some missing pieces to the evolutionary picture — the roles of women and children — and to offer an orientation that stresses balance rather than bias. In her book *On Becoming Human* (1981), Tanner's aim is to present a "well-documented reconstruction of the human past that incorporates both sexes and the young as well as adults in a context determined by the ascertainable conditions of their own existence rather than a flashback of ours" (Tanner 1981: 28).

Like other theorists, Tanner attempts to fill in logically the crucial gaps in the information we have from eight to four million years ago, when bipedal locomotion developed. She relies on contemporary primate behavior to provide the clues for her reconstruction. She chooses chimpanzees rather than baboons as appropriate models for understanding the behavior of prehominids (Tanner 1981: 58). She makes this choice for four reasons. First, the genetic structure of humans is more like that of chimpanzees than that of baboons. Second, chimpanzees' anatomical features are not as specialized as those of other apes and therefore provide a useful idea of what generalized prehominids might have looked like. Furthermore, they are capable of bipedal locomotion and object manipulation. Third, chimpanzees inhabit environments similar to the ones to which Tanner supposes the early prehominids adapted: the forest, forest fringes, and savannas in Africa. The savanna areas where the first hominid fossils were found are a mosaic of habitats; they include open grasslands, clumps of trees, and riverine forests. The shift to hominids probably involved a transition from forest fringes to utilization of more open savanna. One of the early hominids' outstanding traits seems to have been their behavioral flexibility in taking advantage of a variety of habitats. Chimpanzees utilize a variety of food to sustain them: plants, insects and some animals obtained through predation (*not* through hunting). Therefore, they have some of the generalized behavioral patterns that prehominids may have had. To restrict the image of prehominids by positing only one form of terrestrial adaptation, e.g., dominance hierarchies, would be to deny them the complexity that they most likely had. Fourth, given the possible recency of the split between chimpanzees and hominids from a common ancestor (eight to four million years ago), chimpanzees may be particularly instructive in providing information about the behavioral potential of the more generalized ancestor of prehominids.

The behavior of chimpanzees may provide the most illuminating information available for piecing together the transition to Australoppithecines. It furnishes a foundation from which flexible human adaptation based on culture could have developed. Chimpanzees are intelligent, sociable animals that can effectively relate to one another via nonverbal communication and learn social tradition from their mothers and peers. They seem to have the capacity for variable, flexible behavior, which would have been present in prehominids that were adapting to a mosaic landscape.

Given these general capabilities, what process accounts for the transition from prehominids to hominids? Like Washburn, Moore, DeVore, and Fox, Tanner first considers the environment to which prehominids and early hominids adapted: forest fringes and open savanna offering a variety of foods, mostly available for exploitation during the day ("an omnivorous, diurnal niche") (Tanner 1981: 139). How prehominids exploited this new habitat was the key to hominid divergence.

In Tanner's view, a combination of gathering and tool use was responsible for the development of upright posture and habitual bipedal locomotion. Although considerable attention has been given to the use of weapons in hunting, evidence of cooperative hunting does not appear until much later in hominid development (a half a million years ago). The prehominid anatomy of the arms and shoulders would not have permitted very effective throwing, nor would the first stone tools (shaped like pebbles) have made much of an impact on predators. It is also unlikely that the lure of obtaining meat through hunting would have made much of a difference in the early stages. Both males and females probably killed and ate meat before the transition; chimpanzees and baboons do. They relied on predation, not hunting; they probably caught young or disabled animals with their hands.

However, a shift from foraging to gathering would have made a difference and provided a decided advantage for females and their offspring. Most primates rely on foraging to obtain their food; they find fruit or plants and consume them on the spot. Gathering means that the animal collects its food and carries it somewhere for consumption at a later time. Such an activity requires a knowledge of where food is and the foresight to collect it at the appropriate time. Since females are likely to experience high nutritional stress during pregnancy and lactation, they would benefit most from increased proportions of food obtained by gathering. The survival of offspring would also be enhanced, because mothers would most likely share food with their infants. The development of tools (objects used to modify the environment) might have occurred in conjunction with gathering. Simple implements, such as digging sticks or other organic materials used to obtain and open plant food, would increase the sources of nutrition. Gathering would allow females the option of ranging into a variety of settings to obtain food. They probably ventured into the savanna and then returned to the safety of the forest fringes or forest.

All of these factors converge to give a decided advantage to bipedal females. They could use their forelimbs to carry food; later they could use them to make tools to exploit their environment more effectively. As they became bipedal, they may have developed carrying devices to transport their infants. They also could have used their arms to carry and hold their infants. Upright posture offers some defense against the predators that are intimidated by the unfamiliar sight of a bipedal animal. It also aids the females in spotting predators more easily. In addition, females could use their arms to throw sticks to frighten off predators. They did not need a tight-knit dominance hierarchy of males to protect them. They were capable of providing for and protecting themselves and their young. The fact that gathering was a consistent rather than a sporadic activity would necessitate habitual rather than occasional bipedal locomotion.

Greater efficiency at gathering implies better communication skills and further development of cognitive capacities. It also means that the dependency period of infants is likely to increase; offspring have to learn how to use foresight to exploit their environment and to develop technical skills to make tools. The females that were more adept at communication and the infants that were more intelligent had an advantage. The intelligence of females would have a direct impact on the survival of their infants. They would be better able to provide for and transmit essential adaptational skills to their offspring. Although Australopithecines did not have brains much larger than those of chimpanzees, there is evidence that considerable reorganization had taken place; the temporal and parietal lobes responsible for memory and cognition had expanded (Halloway 1966). The innovation of gathering might account for this expansion.

Gathering meant a change in the relationship between males and females. Males had less reason to gather than females. They may have continued to forage for themselves, but the young males may instead have retained ties with their mothers and siblings. In other words, some kin selection may have occurred. Related animals may have contributed to the sustenance of each other. Just as important was sexual selection. With increasing cortical control over the food quest, females may have exerted more choice over the males with whom they mated. Given the gradual development of upright posture, a male would have fewer visual cues to determine a female's reproductive state; estrus swellings would be less prominent. Therefore, he would rely more on the behavioral cues of her interest. Estrus was not "lost." Physiological triggers for sexual activities and expressions of arousal became relatively less important as cortical control and choice ("equilibration") became more dominant. Communication became a more important element of sexual expression.

In line with their concern for their offspring, females were more likely to choose sociable males, who were not aggressive toward their offspring and who played with them and occasionally brought food to assist them. The females also were more likely to mate with males who associated with them regularly. Such choices would favor bipedal males who were better communicators than aggressors. Females' systematic choices of males of this type for mates would result in the reduction of anatomical features used in aggressive displays: large canines and large body size. More reliance on the products of gathering (seeds and nuts) might also select for smaller canines; grinding would be easier without them. Gathering and sharing food with kin would be advantageous for males and females. After bipedal locomotion became more firmly established, the stage was set for more extensive use of the cognitive capabilities of the brain.

The social organization of these prehominids was probably very fluid, unlike the rigid dominance hierarchies posited by "man the hunter" advocates. The mother/infant dyad was probably central to their social life; links between kin followed closely behind in importance. Sharing began in this unit and was found to be advantageous behavior. If a mother died, sibs might provide for the orphan. Since kin share genes, behavior that was helpful for the prehominids' kin would increase the possibility that their own genes were passed on.

This portrait of prehominids is not as dramatic as that of the "early hunter" story. The crux of the difference is the relative roles of tools and

behavior in effecting changes. Tanner relies on the cumulation of behavioral changes in obtaining food to explain the transition to hominids; tools supplemented the change. In contrast, prehominid hunters
became bipedal primarily because of their weapons. No weapons have
been found for the transitional period, however, although they do appear later. Perhaps reliance on the importance of technology in theory is
just as hazardous as too great a reliance on its magic in contemporary
society. Both theories deal with questions of how prehominids could
enhance their reproductive success. The weapons theorists give more
credit to males, while gatherer theorists give more to females. One need
not exclude the other. As Tanner (1981) pointed out, males, females,
and infants were all involved in the changes. It is unlikely that one
gender deserves all of the credit.

Recognizing the changes that affect *both* males and females is more
important than establishing a winner in a contest to determine which
gender contributed more to human evolution. Humans are still subject
to the basic constraint shared by all sexually reproducing animals: both
sexes have to participate in perpetuating the species. Survival requires
mutual effort, even though the tasks may not be the same. The relationships among anatomy, behavior, learning, material culture, and environment take precedence over any single factor.

Regardless of the theory we follow to explain the transition to hominids, both male- and female-oriented views conclude that two major
anatomical changes had occurred by the time the genus *Homo* appeared. Habitual bipedal locomotion with upright posture developed
early on and characterized the first hominids. A significantly expanded
brain developed later, between four and two million years ago. Humans
radiated into a variety of habitats by displaying an amazing amount of
behavioral flexibility and numerous survival techniques.

These general adaptive features provide the starting point for a more
specific discussion of their implications for the character of human
sexuality. Sexual interaction and the survival of offspring were central
to the prehominid/hominid transition. It is important to explore further
how these features changed in relation to the general hominid features
of habitual bipedal locomotion/upright posture and increased brain
size. These changes make up the distinctive human elements of the
pattern that defines the "human" in human sexuality.

### Distinctive Elements of Human Sexuality

Bipedal locomotion brought about changes in the physical structure
of early hominids. The pelvis became shorter and wider to facilitate the

new mode of locomotion and posture. For locomotion, humans depend upon extensor muscles, which extend the leg at the joint of the hip and move the leg backward. A horizontal extension of the pelvis aids the muscle power of the extensor muscles of the leg. The buttock muscles became more fully developed to aid in this process.

Changes in the pelvis also helped to accommodate an upright stance. Quadrupedal animals need a longer pelvic structure to support the muscles attached to them; the muscles hold in the internal organs between the forelimbs and hindlimbs. As hominids became upright, the pelvis became shorter to support internal organs placed vertically instead of horizontally in the body. The literal meaning of the word "pelvis," i.e., basin, is an appropriate image of the hominid structure.

Upright posture also caused the position of the sex organs to change; they shifted from a dorsal to a ventral position. The female's genitals were between her legs, below the trunk of the body; the male's genitals were more exposed and vulnerable in their new position at the lower, front portion of the torso. The loss of thick body hair increased the visibility of the features of the face, the sex organs, and the body contours.

These three general changes combined to produce specific alterations in sexuality. The nature of sexual interaction and of the reproductive process shifted into a more human configuration. First, the foci of sexual attraction changed for both men and women. Male primates respond to visual, olfactory, and behavioral cues to determine the sexual receptivity of females. Tanner has suggested that the position of the female's genitals made it difficult for the male to rely on his vision to determine whether the female was ovulating or not. The reddening and swelling of the genital area probably diminished, and a sex skin would have been more difficult to detect (Tanner 1981: 154). Habitual bipedal locomotion would also hamper the male's reliance on olfaction to determine the female's reproductive state; it would have been cumbersome to casually sniff the genital region. Consequently, males had to rely more heavily on females' behavior to determine how sexually receptive they were.

In contrast to the position of the female's genitals, that of the males' became more conspicuous with upright posture. The vulnerability of the male's genitals might account for a distinctive attribute of the human penis — its lack of a bone. Without a bone to facilitate intromission, males became more dependent on stimulation to produce and retain an erection. Furthermore, it was easier for a female to determine a male's state of excitement and sexual receptivity to her. The way that a female behaved toward a male became a more important factor in his ability to copulate and reproduce.

Therefore, physical changes that accompanied bipedal locomotion and upright posture placed a greater premium on interpersonal interaction between a male and a female to effect intercourse. There was greater potential for a more personalized relationship between the two. The basis for sexual attraction could range beyond the genitals to include other behavioral and physical features. The way that the female touched the male could be just as important as whether or not she was ovulating. The male might also respond to her overall physical appearance: her shape, the condition of her hair, her skin, and her stature. Human females generally have softer skin, more delicate facial features, smaller stature, and more prominent breasts than males. None of these features plays a necessary role in gestating or nurturing offspring. It is possible that males were more attracted to females with these features and chose to copulate with them more often.

The male's reliance on behavioral cues from the female to indicate that she is receptive means that females have a greater option to copulate at any time. Higher primates engage in some nonreproductive sexual behavior, and early hominids probably did so too. Hrdy suggests that females do so to enhance the survival of their offspring; males with whom they have copulated are less aggressive and may even be protective toward their infants. Early hominid females may have continued to copulate with several males for the same reason. Australopithecine remains indirectly indicate that they were probably not monogamous. They seem to show some pronounced differences in size between males and females. This type of sexual dimorphism rarely occurs in monogamous species. However, it is likely that females were using more discrimination in their choice of partners. Other higher primates show preferences for specific partners, and early hominids probably did the same.

Bipedal locomotion allowed males to be more sociable in another way; their arms were free to carry food to an attractive female. Prehominid males may have begun the practice by sharing food with their mothers and sibs; Tanner notes that this was consistent with the trend toward bipedal locomotion. Later on, hominids may have shared food with females with whom they wished to copulate. Access to females was not merely a function of intermale rivalry. Males were growing more dependent on how receptive females were to their advances. Males who brought food might have an advantage.

It is also possible that females preferred males who had certain physical characteristics. Since the penis and testes were more conspicuous, females may have preferred males with larger organs. Human males have the largest penises of any primate relative to the size of their bodies. Testes are sometimes referred to as the "family jewels;" they may have been regarded as an attractive adornment by females for millions of years.

Humans are notable for the wide variety of physical and behavioral features that they find sexually attractive in the opposite sex. A second consequence of upright posture and bipedal locomotion may have reinforced this trend toward more individualized sexual relations. The position for copulation changed from rear to frontal entry. The shift of the sex organs to a more ventral position as well as the trend toward more fully developed buttock muscles made rear entry unwieldy. Although other primates sometimes engage in face-to-face copulation, only humans do so on a regular basis.

Although the shift from rear entry to front entry intercourse may seem to be a minor adjustment, its implications for sexual intimacy are not trivial. Front entry clearly involves facing the person with whom one is having intercourse. Face-to-face intercourse creates a circumstance that fosters more interaction and intimacy between partners. At the very least, the partners can identify each other.

Face-to-face copulation while lying down expanded the range of stimulation possible for the partners. A human female has a much smaller clitoris than most other female primates have. Frontal intercourse may have contributed to that feature. Since the clitoris is extremely sensitive, vigorous stimulation of it while the male was thrusting might have been painful. During later stages of sexual stimulation, a small fold of skin (the clitoral hood) closes over the clitoris. Also, since humans do not have a sex skin, the clitoris would not have to be very prominent to receive stimulation. Masters and Johnson (1966) think that the clitoris is always stimulated during intercourse, either directly by manual or oral means or indirectly by the movement of skin around it. The main function of the clitoris in most mammals seems to be to raise sexual excitement to a level sufficient to accomplish intromission and to generate positive sensations during intercourse. A small clitoris facilitates that process in humans.

Scent may play an important role in sexual stimulation within the context of face-to-face, supine intercourse. More relaxed movement is possible between the partners, and they have easier access to different parts of the body. Given this proximity, scent can become a relevant sexual stimulus.

Apocrine glands are the major source of human odor (Doty 1981:

354). Their location coincides with the main areas where hair is retained on the head and trunk of the body: on part of the scalp, the
eyelids, the ear canals, the cheeks, around the nipples of the breasts, on
the chest, under the arms, around the navel, around the genitals, and
around the anus. As in other mammals, these glands secrete the odorous
component of sweat when humans are frightened or sexually stimulated. Although they serve to regulate body temperature in most other
animals, they do not do so in humans. Apocrine glands are highly
concentrated under the arms, where bacteria act upon them to produce
a person's characteristic body odor. The hair associated with them may
help to diffuse their odor in the air more readily. Such odors may have
become another basis for individual attraction and stimulation. It is
interesting to note that the position of these apocrine glands coincides
with areas that we label "erogenous zones." Perhaps subtle scents reinforce a tendency to pay particular attention to stimulating these areas.

Other sources of odor are relevant to sexual stimulation. The intensity
of vaginal odor shifts during different phases of the ovarian cycle; it is
weaker before and during ovulation and more intense after ovulation
(Doty 1981: 366). Sexual arousal itself can change the quantity of volatile organic secretions from the vagina (Preti et al. 1979, in Doty 1981:
366). This change may stimulate the male even more; it may even
trigger more testosterone production. Males are more likely than females to produce a discernable odor from their apocrine glands, especially from under their arms; their glands are larger than those of females (Doty 1981: 353). This odor gives females even more information
about the degree of their partners' sexual excitement and provides another criterion for sexual selection of mates.

Although scent is relevant to sexual stimulation, touch is probably the
most important sense. Freeing the forelimbs from locomotion meant
that the hands were left free for other activities. The sensitive pads on
the tips of the fingers and a fully opposable thumb combine to produce
a well-developed, delicate, precision grip. The hand can sensitively
hold and manipulate objects. It can also hold and caress different parts
of a sexual partner. This tactile stimulation can be especially important
in exciting a male so that he has an erection. Touching his nongenital
areas may be so intensely stimulating that it can result in orgasm. With
the loss of thick body hair, later in human evolution, the general naked-
ness of human bodies exposed more areas of the skin, which could be
stimulated by touch. The skin may well be our largest sex organ. By
stimulating the skin, humans are able to extend the pleasure that other
primates receive from more limited activities, like grooming.

All of these sources of stimulation provided the foundation for a much more sexually active primate. An increase in the variety and length of stimulation during foreplay may account for the ability of human females to experience orgasm more often than most primate females. Prolonged and intense clitoral stimulation certainly contributes to their potential. Both males and females have a wider range of criteria by which to choose a partner. Sexual relations could become more individualized, because both males and females were choosier. And, couples may have begun to engage in more nonreproductive intercourse.

Since prehominids and early hominids had a relatively small cranial capacity (400–550 cc), changes in pelvic structure probably posed few problems for birth (Leutenegger 1972, in Tanner 1981: 208). As brain size increased with the appearance of *Homo* (or *Australopithecus*) *habilis* (666 cc) and *Homo erectus* (873 cc), it posed a potential reproductive problem (Fox 1980: 124, 125). From then on, brain development and bipedal locomotion were inextricably connected in a feedback system; they affected the relationship between parents and their offspring and sparked further readjustments in the relationship between males and females.

When an infant is born, it must pass not only through the muscles of the vagina but also through the bones of the pelvis. The opening of the pelvis limits the size of the infant that can pass through it. Infants with larger brains could have difficulty in passing through the bony structure. How could humans retain both advantageous physical features— increased brain size and a pelvis suited for bipedal locomotion— without jeopardizing the survival of the mother or infant during birth?

One response was an increase in the pelvic size of the female. Females with larger pelvises have more room to accommodate the birth of an infant with a larger skull. While females generally have broader pelvises than males, an increase in the overall size of females facilitated this process. More sources of protein from gathering (nuts, seeds, and insects), predation, and hunting may have contributed to the general increase in the female's body size.

Another response to the limitation that the pelvis posed at birth was for females to deliver infants at an earlier stage of brain development. Napier and Napier (1967, in Jolly 1972: 217) note that primate pregnancies end when head size is suitable for a safe delivery. The infant's head would still be small enough to pass through the pelvis; further brain growth could occur after the infant was born. This seems to be the major way that humans escaped the dilemma of giving birth to large-brained babies. Like other higher primates, the length of human gestation is rather long. However, the developmental differences at birth are striking. Human newborns are much less advanced in motor control and percentage of growth at birth (Jolly 1972: 216). The brain has developed to only a quarter of the size it will eventually reach at maturity. In addition, the segments of the skull are not completely fused together at birth. The flexibility of the skull bones allows the head to pass through the pelvic ring and vagina more easily. Despite these aids, human births are still more difficult than those of other animals, because the human infant's head is large in relation to the mother's birth canal. Modern humans have a particularly difficult time giving birth; average cranial capacity for adults is 1300 cc.

Human births pose a number of problems (and potential disadvantages) for both mothers and infants. Delivering a big-headed baby temporarily damages the vaginal tissues. Occasionally the tissue between the vaginal opening and the anus (the perineum) may tear. The discomfort and possible infection of these wounds make intercourse unlikely until the injuries have healed.

Infants born at an earlier stage of development are vulnerable to harm from the external environment. The flexibility of the infant's skull during delivery can be hazardous to it after birth. Since the protective bones of the skull are not completely fused, the infant requires protection to ensure that the delicate tissues of the brain are not damaged. An underdeveloped nervous system gives the infant few immediate resources for dealing with its surroundings. In general the period of helplessness is longer and the period of dependence is more extended than in any other primate. Therefore, birth at an earlier stage of development is likely to be an advantage only if efficient prenatal development and/or lengthy postnatal care are available to ensure survival. Humans display both of these types of care for their offspring.

Changes in the human ovarian cycle have pushed mammalian prenatal reproductive efficiency to an extreme. The uterus prepares more fully for the fertilized egg, so that it can be swiftly implanted and begin its growth. The tissues and blood vessels of the endometrium build up to provide a rich environment for the zygote. As in other higher primates, the zygote develops by imbedding itself directly into the uterine lining, where it can begin to grow more quickly. After implantation of the egg, the placenta begins to develop sooner than in any other primate. Earlier placental development facilitates the flow of oxygen necessary for gestating a bigger-brained baby. All of these features serve to maximize the amount of prenatal development that can occur. Humans have the longest gestation period of any primate, and growth proceeds rapidly with the time constraints that head size poses for terminating gestation.

A discernible consequence of the elaborate preparation for implantation is menstruation. The difference between humans and other high primates is marked by the more pronounced amount of blood and tissue sloughed off from the uterus if fertilization does not occur. Although the endometrium of other higher primates also builds up to prepare for gestation, it does not do so to the degree present in humans. The body of other primates can absorb the tissues and blood or shed them by a slight discharge. Human females require several days to expel the endometrium. This event is so striking that we have labeled the ovarian cycle in humans the "menstrual cycle." The label can serve to separate us from other primates. However, the difference is a matter of degree, rather than kind.

The menstrual cycle may affect sexual behavior to some degree. If conception does not occur, the woman experiences an increase in the blood in the pelvic region. Vasocongestion also accompanies sexual excitement. It is possible that premenstrual vasocongestion stimulates a woman's interest in sexual activity, given its physiological similarity to a state of sexual excitement. If so, it may serve to lengthen a woman's interest in intercourse beyond ovulation, thus adding to an increase in nonreproductive intercourse. It is interesting to note that several researchers have found that sexual activity peaks around ovulation and menstruation; many women have difficulty reaching orgasm during the preovulatory portion of the menstrual cycle.

Physiological changes in the female also contribute to the postnatal care of the infant. Women have considerably more fatty deposits in their bodies than men; their breasts and hips have a particularly high concentration. The high proportion of body fat seems to contribute to the regularity of menstrual cycles; a certain amount is required to trigger ovulation. This may be related to the ability of a female to support an infant after birth. If food supplies are insufficient to maintain the woman alone, it is unlikely that they will be sufficient to nourish a mother and child. It would not be advantageous to conceive under these circumstances. Individual dietary habits could have the same effect. Contemporary females cease to menstruate when the proportion of body fat slips below a critical threshold.

Body fat is also important for lactation. Women use some of their fat reserves in each lactational episode. Given the long dependency period, infants may need to rely on their mothers' milk for a considerable length of time. Nutrition plays an important role in maintaining a mother's ability to nurse her baby. Breastfeeding enhances the mother/infant bond. Humans produce milk that is low in protein and fats. Therefore, an infant has to nurse more often to receive adequate nutrition; nursing may occur twelve to sixteen times a day in groups that practice extended lactation (Harrell 1981: 298). Suckling stimulates the production of more prolactin, the pituitary hormone responsible for generating and maintaining milk production; prolactin also induces cessation of ovulation and menstruation and thereby induces infertility (Harrell 1981: 797). If nutrition is poor, more prolactin is needed to produce milk, and amennorhea is even more likely. Thus, there is a significant interaction between the mother, the infant, and the environment. If nutrition is poor, the woman is not likely to resume ovulation soon and cannot conceive another child; part of the nutrition she has can be transferred to her infant. The infant plays a role in the process. If the baby does not suckle much, less prolactin is produced, ovulation may occur, and the probability is increased that the mother may get pregnant again; if so, she has fewer nutritional resources to provide for her infant. It is to the infant's advantage to suckle more often. If nutrition is good, the woman may ovulate sooner, regardless of her infant's pattern of suckling. However, behavioral factors, such as nursing on demand (rather than by a schedule) and not giving supplemental feedings, seem to influence physiology in the direction of longer anovulatory periods after birth (Harrell 1981: 802).

Therefore, as early hominid nutrition increased, the probability of bearing offspring in closer succession may have occurred. Lovejoy emphasizes the significance of closer spacing of births in his reconstruction of hominid evolution (Lovejoy 1981). He argues that other higher primates were already pushing "K-selection" to the extreme, i.e., they nurtured one infant at the expense of producing others. Humans were different, because they managed to space their births more closely and increase the number of offspring a woman raised in her reproductive life. This may have meant that a female was less able to provide for herself and her offspring; more dependent infants restricted her mobility. If she had an additional source of calories, which allowed her to remain in a more restricted range, she could manage to deal with more infants. Lovejoy thinks that this arrangement was responsible for the development of bipedal locomotion, but I think it probably occurred after bipedal locomotion and nearer to the time that brain size was substantially increasing. Before then, females were fairly skilled in gathering for themselves and did not have to deal with the long dependency periods that having larger-brained babies entailed. Furthermore, less sexual dimorphism in size (characteristic of monogamous species) occurred in conjunction with large brain size, not with the appearance of bipedal locomotion. Lovejoy is quite persuasive in his view that behavior was an important component of the development of hominid characteristics; our difference lies in when provisioning by males became significantly important. In any case, closer spacing of births increases the pressure to provide postnatal care for offspring. Hominids not only had to deal with a long dependency period; they may have had to cope with more than one dependent offspring at the same time.

Other features of anatomy may have aided them in caretaking. The number of female breasts could facilitate the process. Usually the number of breasts a female has relates to the number of offspring she bears. In this light, it may seem puzzling that humans have two breasts; they typically give birth to only one child at a time. It could be that women have two breasts because they occasionally have multiple births; the second breast is available for that contingency. Another possibility is that two breasts were advantageous in producing enough milk for infants whose dependency periods overlapped. The option of nursing more than one infant could override a possible disadvantage of the extremely long human dependency period, i.e., the danger of not being able to replace the population.

Both males and females had their arms free and could carry infants. So much attention has been paid to the significance of using hands for tools and weapons that the essential role that arms and hands played in caretaking is glossed over. Although a human infant can grasp, it cannot cling to its mother as other primates do. Therefore, the mother (or another caretaker) has to carry the infant in her arms or put it in a carrier designed for that purpose. One of the main causes of primate infant deaths is injury sustained after falling from their mothers' bodies (Lovejoy 1981: 344). Greater parental supervision and responsibility for the infant's mobility are reproductive advantages.

Although changes in anatomy aided caretaking, the bulk of postnatal care required changes in behavior. Humans have carried the mammalian theme of parenting to an extreme. They are unsurpassed in their efforts to provide postnatal care; the survival of their helpless infants requires it.

The length of infant dependency altered the relative reproductive advantages of copulation and postnatal care for both males and females. When infant dependence was fairly short, it was reproductively advantageous for a male to copulate with as many ovulating females as possible. He would maximize his chances of passing on his genes. This arrangement was also favorable for females, because male competition for inseminating them meant that they were likely to become pregnant by a competent male. Quality genes were the main contribution that males could make to their offspring. Females nursed infants and supplied postnatal care. As infant dependence became longer, copulation at ovulation was no longer a guarantee of a male's reproductive success. More important was the quality of care the infant received after birth.

Postnatal care became the primary determinant of reproductive success for both males and females.

Participation of males in postnatal care was clearly an advantage for females and infants. Early on, males participated sporadically by sharing food with their mothers and sibs as well as with females with whom they wished to copulate. However, when feeding requirements and the demands of child-care were not compatible, females could not rely on sporadic contributions of food to supplement their subsistence. Females with more assured sources of food had an advantage. Females with consistent sexual partners would fall into this category. Males who copulated with them were more likely to nurture their offspring and supplement their food. However, the hominid dependency period is longer than that of most primates. Therefore, the duration of a male's contribution could be lengthy. It would be advantageous for him to participate to such an extent only if he had some assurance that the female to whom he supplied food bore his children. He could then play a more direct role in ensuring the survival of his offspring by providing some subsistence to females nursing his offspring. Since males cannot nurse, contributing food to a lactating mother is the closest that they can come to direct nutritional support of their children.

However, this meant a change in the way that males and females related to each other. A male had to determine which children were his. Limiting his sexual activity to one or a few females would aid him in identifying the females that were possible mothers of his children. Limiting the female's sexual activity narrowed the possibilities even more. It was equally advantageous, however, for a female to limit the number of sexual partners she had if she could rely on one male to consistently provide food and aid her infant. The gamble paid off for both males and females. Long dependency periods channeled the male in the direction of more postnatal care. The conflict between subsistence needs and caretaking triggered a closer association between males and females in caretaking.

Ember and Ember suggest that this is the main reason for pair-bonding, i.e., the tendency for males or females to copulate with only one partner throughout a mating period (Ember and Ember 1979). The length of infant dependency is significantly associated with the duration of male/female ties, although the length of dependency does not in itself predict the existence of bonding (Ember and Ember 1979: 42). An important link became established between copulation and the care of offspring. An exclusive sexual arrangement was important insofar as it provided more confidence in paternity and validated a male's subsequent contribution to the care of his offspring. Moreover, the production of more offspring reinforced the soundness of contributing food to the female and thus benefited mother, father, and children.

Therefore, monogamy developed as a reproductive arrangement geared to the needs of males and females to assure that their offspring survived. Sexual exclusivity was a by-product of the process, not the reason for it. The amount of sexual activity between a male and female was less relevant than whether or not it was confined to a single partner. It is not surprising that monogamous species are usually involved in sexual activity less often than nonmonogamous ones.

Nevertheless, other developments have altered that pattern for humans. We do not fit into the mold of most monogamous species. Humans engage in more copulations per conception than any other primate; we qualify as the "sexiest primates." Several factors have contributed to that trend. Bipedal locomotion fostered more individuation in sexual relations. As brain size increased, cortical control over behavior did, too. Both males and females probably balanced alternatives (or "equilibrated," in Chance's terms) in their selection of mating partners. Hormones receded as the primary determinant of sexual activity. Sexual response was also tied into the brain. Males could have erections because of tactile *or* psychological stimulation. It became important that a male perceived a female as attractive, however he chose to define that attribute. It also became relevant just how attractive a male appeared to a female. In neither of these cases was physical appearance the sole criterion, although it probably entered in. Since postnatal care of infants was increasingly relevant to the reproductive success of both males and females, it is likely that physical characteristics related to reproductive viability may also have been relevant criteria for choosing a sexual partner. Both males and females probably considered how well their sexual partners would perform as parents.

For example, males may have chosen to mate with the more shapely females because of their reproductive attributes, *not* because big breasts or full hips were intrinsically attractive. The wide pelvis necessary to facilitate birth of the infant adds more contour to a woman's body. The fatty deposits that stimulate ovulation and maintain lactation accentuate a woman's shape. These "feminine" curves result from the realities of conceiving, delivering, and supporting a dependent infant. Males may have defined these females as attractive partly because their shape indicated the contribution they could make to their offspring.

Females may have relied less on physical appearance than on behavior as a criterion for choosing a mate; they may have observed the ability of males to obtain food and their willingness to share it with them and with their offspring. This consideration probably became very relevant when males hunted for large game. It was another instance of conflict between child-care and subsistence requirements. If females were not pregnant, animals might detect their scent when they were menstruating and avoid them. If they were pregnant, they would not be as mobile. If they had infants, they would not want to expose their offspring to the danger of an unpredictable animal. Therefore, they needed to be associated with males who would share with them the concentrated calories provided by meat. Males, in turn, had more to offer females in terms of contributions to their offspring. It is possible that the better hunters may have had more than one mate for whom they could adequately provide. If so, the potential for polygyny lay open for males. Females may have found certain males attractive because of their hunting prowess and their ability to supply food. They may also have found them attractive because of the pleasure they derived from intercourse. Or they may have liked the ways in which the males interacted with their infants.

The point is that an interest in nonreproductive sexuality and a choice of partners probably preceded monogamy. Cortical control over behavior meant that males and females could be more particular about the partners with whom they chose to share postnatal responsibility for their children. Copulation was not necessarily for reproduction, although it was tied to a male's decision to invest in the offspring of a specific female. At this point, we begin to see the disjunction of sex from reproduction. Intercourse did not necessarily result in conception, nor did joint postnatal care of infants mean that sexual interest was limited to this unit.

Nonreproductive intercourse could be retained within the monogamous context. By-products of human postnatal care may have enhanced this behavior. The long dependency period of the infant set the stage. Ember and Ember (1983) found that animals with long dependency periods (more than six months) usually lack a breeding season. Therefore, intercourse is likely to occur during each ovarian cycle if females are not pregnant. There already was a tendency to have intercourse at times other than at ovulation.

A longer period of lactation may also have stimulated intercourse during a nonreproductive period. Suckling not only stimulates prolactin production; it also triggers the release of oxytocin, a pituitary hormone that causes muscles around the milk-producing cells to contract and initiate milk ejection. Oxytocin also causes discernible uterine contractions (Meites and Kruyt 1973, in Harrell 1981: 799). Harrell notes that "an intriguing feature of the milk-ejection reflex is its apparent overlap with the pathways of sexual arousal and orgasm. Unlike the prolactin response, both milk ejection and orgasm are highly conditioned reflexes with a great deal of input from cortical centers" (Cowie and Tendal 1971, and Newton and Newton 1967, in Harrell 1981: 799). Some women may reach orgasm by nipple stimulation alone, and lactating mothers sometimes eject milk as the uterus contracts during a clitorally-induced orgasm (Harrell 1981: 799). It is not surprising that women may feel pleasurable sensations in their genitals while their babies suckle. These sensations may serve to enhance a mother's bond with her child. They may also maintain her interest in sexual activity. Suckling can be an erotic experience.

It is unlikely that a woman would engage in intercourse in the first few weeks after birth. The vaginal tissues are in the process of healing, and the vaginal lining is relatively thin and dry. During sexual arousal, the vagina is not as likely to fully lubricate or fill with blood; therefore, intercourse may be painful (Harrell 1981: 799). There is also an increased possibility of vaginal infections, because the vagina is more alkaline (higher in pH). And, the bloody discharge that continues for about four weeks after birth (the lochia) may be inconvenient and a cause of sexual restraint among some couples.

After this initial period, there is no physical reason why a woman cannot engage in vaginal intercourse (Katchadourian and Lunde 1975: 126). Nursing women are likely to be interested in sexual activity fairly soon; there is a positive relationship between nursing and sexual interest after birth (Katchadourian and Lunde 1975: 126). This may partially derive from the pleasurable stimulation of the breasts by the baby. Consequently, humans are more likely to engage in intercourse sooner after birth than other primates. Once again, physiological changes related to postnatal care influence behavioral patterns in a human direction.

Most primates experience a period of postpartum anestrus (lack of estrus), which coincides with the period of lactation and nursing. The females are not receptive to intercourse until their infants are no longer dependent on them. Therefore, they can concentrate their efforts on their offspring without the interference of additional pregnancies. However, human infants are dependent for a much longer period of time than other primates. Such a long period of sexual abstinence could be a serious drawback in replacing the population. If the infants who received so much parental care were not to survive, the parents would lose a substantial reproductive investment. Humans have overcome this possible disadvantage by copulating during the lactational period. Therefore, they are able to conceive soon after birth.

Breastfeeding primes females for sexual activity, and better nutrition increases the chances that ovulation will occur during lactation. If supplementary feedings start relatively early, the baby suckles less often; consequently, prolactin levels may decrease to such an extent that they do not inhibit ovulation. Therefore, lactation does not guarantee contraception. Nutritional levels and the degree to which a baby suckles are more likely to affect the possibility of conception after birth. Where nutrition is poor and the baby suckles often, conception is not likely to occur soon after birth. Where nutrition is good, chances for conception are raised. Because males participate in postnatal care by supplying food, parents are able to care for more than one infant at a time. This has given them a reproductive advantage over less prolific higher primates. Both males and females can benefit from intercourse during lactation. Unlike other primates, humans are able both to care for their infants and to be receptive to sexual activity.

Long dependency posed some potential problems in the relationship between the parents' and the infants' needs. The period of infancy lasts twice as long in humans as in apes (Jolly 1972: 216), and the length of the juvenile phase is much longer. Parent/child ties are an important source of affection and learning. However, too much attachment could impede the child's ability to be self-sufficient. It could also restrict the parents' availability to care for other offspring and for themselves. The onset of maturity occurs fairly late in humans (at from twelve to fourteen years). Greater dependence on parents could delay reproduction even longer. Attachment might also develop into sexual interest for parents; or parents might become sexually interested in their offspring, particularly after secondary sexual characteristics develop at puberty. Separation from parents is a particularly complicated process in humans, because dependency lasts so long. It is interesting to note that most primates actively encourage their young to separate from them when they reach the onset of sexual maturity. It is precisely at this point that offspring are ready to care for themselves, since the brain completes its growth at puberty.

Probably the most overarching factors in human evolution were the development of increased brain size and pronounced cortical control over behavior. As we have seen, they have influenced the direction of most aspects of human sexuality. Humans exceed all other primates in relying on learning to guide their behavior. Since the brain is only 25 percent of its adult size at birth, it is particularly susceptible to environmental influences. By the age of one year, it has reached 60 percent of its adult size; at two years, 70 percent; at four years, 80 percent; at eight or nine years, 95 percent; and, at puberty, 100 percent (White and Brown 1973: 128). Therefore, the period from birth to puberty is a crucial one for learning the skills to cope with adult life. Given the lengthy life span of humans, these early lessons have a significant impact on a large portion of humans' lives.

Humans explore and rehearse the roles they will play later in life. Like other primates, children learn how to interact in a social context. Play and other forms of interaction with peers contribute to the child's skills. Children can also model their behavior after the actions of adults, particularly their parents. They learn a great deal about sexual interaction from these sources. For example, primate mothers behave differently toward male and female infants (Jolly 1972: 245). Rhesus mothers may allow male offspring more independence and treat them more aggressively; in contrast, they may hold females closer to them and put more restraint on their mobility. Baboon males may display much more interest in male than in female infants. Humans accentuate these primate trends by interacting differently with male and female children.

Humans add a significant cultural dimension to the learning process. Culture means that learning is passed down from one generation to the next via symbols. Humans learn the rules that govern behavior and how to conform to them; they also attach meaning to their ideas. Although other primates may learn and may have some cultural traditions, humans have developed learning into a fine art. Given the increase in memory and forethought that accompanied increased brain size, humans have more of a sense of their past, present, and future.

The advent of rules has had a number of repercussions for sexual interaction. It affects access to potential mates. For example, the incest taboo discourages mating with kin and also affects the timing of sexual relations and even whether they can occur at all. For instance, menstrual taboos prohibit intercourse during menstruation, and premarital taboos channel sexual activity into a marital context.

The cultural context expands or restricts the meaning of sexuality and thereby endows the group with a great deal of power over an individual's actions. Increased cortical control over behavior means that humans have the ability to segregate sexual from reproductive activity. Not only can humans engage in nonreproductive sex but they can also *conceptualize* the distinction between sex and reproduction. The degree to which sexual activity overlaps with reproduction depends upon the rules that govern social interaction and upon the cultural constraints placed on behavior. The degree of disjunction between sex and reproduction is more pronounced in humans than in any other animals; culture can increase or bridge the gap.

Symbols add to the complexity of human behavior and provide a new dimensions of meaning for sexuality. Language is one of the most powerful sets of symbols that humans use. Language means more than verbal communication, because it alters the scope of human life. With the advent of language, a person's world could expand beyond the confines of material surroundings. Humans can endow their social and physical environments with a wide variety of meanings. Language is an important means of attracting and keeping a sexual partner. Ford and Beach emphasize the point: "[for] human beings speech is undoubtedly the most important single medium of sexual solicitation" (Ford and Beach 1972: 99).

Victor Turner interprets the power that symbols have over us in terms of two poles of meaning: a sensory pole and an ideological pole (Turner 1967: 28). The sensory pole refers to "natural and physiological phenomena and processes" and the ideological pole refers to "components of the moral and social orders" (Turner 1967: 28). These two poles combine to touch us at different levels of our lives. Their multiple meanings give them their power.

Sexuality is probably one of the most basic themes for symbolism, because so much of human anatomy and physiology relates to it. The special emotional sway that ideas about sex and reproduction have over us may derive from their use as raw materials for symbolic elaboration. Their power reminds us that we are still animals and that we are affected by the demands of our anatomy and physiology. We are also affected by our intellectual ability to expand or restrict our capabilities through our social and cultural life.

Our human world is linked to that of other animals, but it has altered appreciably. Its marks are its generality and its variability. The lesson of human evolution is one of feedback between anatomy, physiology, behavior, and environment. It would be a mistake to assume that the brain *alone* is responsible for most human traits. Any meaningful explanation of the social and cultural aspects of human sexuality must include their relation to anatomy, physiology, and environment.

# Chapter Three
# The Sexual Cycle

The sexual cycle includes the aspects of development that are relevant to preparation for and participation in intercourse. In essence, this cycle defines a framework within which we can examine how and when males and females will interact. How are males and females attracted to each other? What circumstances and ideas promote or delay their interaction with each other? What limits are placed on males and females when they do finally meet? Although much of our physical development provides guidelines for our interaction, still more of our interaction is structured by the rules of our social life and the ideas of our culture.

Human sexuality gradually develops over time. It is not a "natural" consequence of physical structure. John Money and Anke Ehrhardt emphasize the importance of looking at the development of sexual identity as a series of components (Money and Ehrhardt 1977). These components are the building blocks on which ideas of masculinity and femininity are based. Money and Ehrhardt prefer to use the term "gender identity," rather than "sexual identity," to define the end result of this process. Gender expands the definition of "sex" beyond its physical connotation. Its scope spans the social, cultural, and psychological aspects of sex. This point cannot be made strongly enough: the uniqueness of human sexuality lies in the interaction between biology and the social, cultural, and psychological worlds. Biology is *not* destiny; it is one of the many factors that shape human experience.

What are the components of the sexual cycle? What roles do social and cultural factors play in this cycle? I will modify Money and Ehrhardt's scheme of the development of gender identity as a basis for tracing the progression of the sexual cycle. Approaching the sexual cycle in this way allows us to be continually aware of a major aspect of human sexuality, i.e., the fact that sex is not a unitary phenomenon. It is not a physiological given. It is composed of physical, social, cultural, and psychological elements. The pervasive theme of the sexual cycle is the differentiation of males and females from each other.

### Prenatal Sexuality

The first phase of the sexual cycle consists of physical components, which include all of the physical changes from conception to birth that result in physical differences between males and females. When a child is born, the main physical difference that identifies the child as male or female is the appearance of the genitals. This seems to be a very straightforward means of defining sex. But even at this early stage of development, the physical components of sex are already complex.

Money and Ehrhardt divide the physical components of prenatal sexuality into three parts: chromosomal sex, fetal gonadal sex, and fetal hormonal sex (Money and Ehrhardt 1977). Each component makes an important contribution to sexual differentiation; it interacts with the one that follows it and affects the appearance and internal organs of the child. Together, these components channel the social and cultural responses to the newborn child.

### Chromosomal Sex

The fertilization of the egg and the pairing of chromosomes set the whole process of sexual differentiation in motion and start the sexual cycle. Fertilization is the union of two sex cells (gametes). The sex cell of the male is a sperm, and the sex cell of the female is an ovum. As I noted earlier, each of these cells is unique, because each contains only twenty-three chromosomes. All of the other cells of the body, the somatic cells, contain the full complement of forty-six chromosomes. When the sex cells join, their union fuses genetic information from the parents, which will influence the future development of the individual.

Each cell contains a spherical body called the nucleus. The chromosomes are colored, threadlike bodies within the nucleus. Within the chromosomes are genes, or units of inheritance (Bennett 1979: 36). Parents contribute part of their genetic heritage to their children; they transmit information about body build, hair color, eye color, nose shape, etc. Children become unique combinations of the variety of genes that their parents have passed on to them. Because children and their parents share some genes in common, we can see resemblances between parents and children in each successive generation. Comments like "He looks more like his mom than his dad" or "Fair skin runs in the family" are based on the fact that parents and children have genes in common.

Twenty-two of the twenty-three chromosomes that each parent contributes are responsible for the character of most of the physical features of the child. They are called autosomes. Only the twenty-third chromosome contributes to determining the sex of the child. It is called a sex chromosome. The twenty-third chromosome in the ovum is called the X chromosome. If the twenty-third chromosome in the sperm is similar in structure to the twenty-third chromosome of the female, it is also called the X chromosome. If it is different in structure, it is called the Y chromosome. The combination of an X from the female and and X from the male usually results in a female child. An X from the female combined with a Y from the male usually results in a male. From this description it seems that the male plays a larger role than the female in determining the sex of the child. Since only the twenty-third chromosome of the male varies at fertilization, it seems logical to assume that the presence of the Y chromosome is crucial.

If we limit the definition of sex to the chromosomal level, we can agree that the presence of the Y chromosome is important in determining the genetic sex of the person. However, even at this elementary level of pairing of the sex cells, it is difficult to say unequivocally whether the male or the female contributes more to the overall sex of the child. We can highlight the complexity of the influence of the X and Y chromosomes by considering what happens when the combination of the twenty-third chromosomes is abnormal. If the twenty-third chromosomes are absent, if there is a Y chromosome without an X, or two Y chromosomes without an X, the effects are lethal (Bennett 1979: 33). The effects are almost as severe when only a single X chromosome is present. Approximately 97 percent of these organisms die in the uterus (Bennett 1979: 33). The ones who survive have the physical characteristics of females. However, the ovaries are generally underdeveloped, and other sex organs are also immature. The physical changes associated with puberty do not occur, and the person is usually sterile (Money and Ehrhardt 1977: 32; Bennett 1979: 33). The chances for survival increase when either an abnormal number of X's or X's and Y's combine. The main effects of these types of abnormalities are (1) mental retardation, (2) variations from the usual pattern of development of the sex organs, or (3) sterility. For example, a combination of three or more X's results in a female body type, the possibility of mental retardation, irregularity of menstruation, and diminished fertility. An X with two Y's has a male body type, reduced production of sperm in the testes, some sterility, and slightly subnormal mentality (Bennett 1979: 34). Anyone with two X's and a Y is infertile and has a male body type, enlarged breasts, and small testes and penis. Generally, the androgen production and the sexual motivation of such a person are also low (Money and Ehrhardt 1977: 33).

In sum, if either an X or a Y is missing from the twenty-third pair of chromosomes, survival of the organism is rare. When one or more X's combines with one or more Y's, the body type of the person is usually that of a male. However, the sex organs are underdeveloped, and the person is likely to be sterile. Someone with more than two X's may survive but is generally mentally retarded. The presence of a Y is associated with the development of a male body type. Since a Y does not survive alone or in combination with another Y, it seems that the presence of the X chromosome is necessary for the production of viable offspring.

Even though XX = female and XY = male are fairly simple equations, the definition of sex at this early stage is difficult if an X or Y is added or subtracted. Since the X chromosome is associated with the development of a female body type and the Y with that of a male, more X's usually mean that the infant will be identified as a female, while more Y's lead to identification of the child as a male. However, we have only reached the first step in the definition of sex. The fetal gonadal and the fetal hormonal stages complicate the picture even more.

We might think of following the stages of physical sexual differentiation as going through a maze. The process begins at conception and continues until old age. The outcome of one stage has important consequences for development in the next stage. If we follow the wrong path, we may be blocked and have difficulty reaching our destination. When we reach a dead-end road, we can usually turn around, retrace our steps, and try another route. It may be difficult to change problems in prenatal sexual development, but fortunately, the physical phases of the sexual cycle usually progress smoothly and are not interrupted by obstacles in their development. The fact that so few deviations occur is a testimony to the amazing organization and efficiency of our physiological structures. It is easy to take them for granted, because we are so used to having our bodies function in a seemingly effortless way. They are like smooth-running machines. We do not question the ability of a car in top condition to take us where we want to go. We may only begin to appreciate the complexity of the components of a car when it breaks down. Then we realize that minor problems can prevent the whole car from functioning. In the process of sexual differentiation, a small change in the physical phases of development can snowball in its effects later on. This is especially true of the phases of sexual differentiation before birth. We shall see that the extreme care with which most societies treat pregnant women is well founded. The foundation for later sexual development is laid during this period.

## Fetal Gonadal Sex

Chromosomal sex is only the first link in the chain of sexual differentiation. The combination of male and female sex chromosomes stimulates changes in the fetal gonads. Gonads are sex glands, which secrete sex hormones. When the embryo is twenty-eight days old, the gonads have not developed into either male or female structures; they are neutral and undifferentiated. As the embryo continues to grow, the gonads begin to change. The way that they change depends upon the pattern of sex chromosomes. If the pattern is XY, then the undifferentiated gonads become testes (male sex glands) at about seven weeks. They later manufacture sperm in the adult male and secrete androgen, the "male" hormone.

In fetal development, testes secrete two substances: (1) androgen and (2) the Müllerian inhibitor, a substance that stops the growth of the fetal structures called Müllerian ducts. If the chromosomal pattern is XX, then the gonads become ovaries (female sex glands) at twelve weeks. They later produce eggs in the adult female and secrete estrogen and progesterone. However, at the fetal stage, ovaries do not secrete any hormones. Hormones are conspicuous by their absence. The testes and ovaries illustrate a further difference between male and female structures. Testes secrete androgen and a Müllerian inhibitor, but the ovaries secrete neither of these substances. The difference between the fetal gonads is important, because the presence or absence of fetal substances affects how the internal and external genitalia will develop.

Like the gonads, the physical structures that eventually develop into what we identify as male and female sex organs are neutral during the early part of fetal development. Until chromosomal and gonadal changes occur, they lie dormant. They begin to shift in form and grow in response to the presence or absence of hormones secreted from the gonads.

The gonads are in an "indifferent" state during the first four weeks of embryonic development. They are neither male nor female. The outer part of the gonad is the cortex, and the inner part is the medulla. If the chromosomal pattern is XY, the cortex disintegrates, and the medulla becomes a testis when the embryo is about seven weeks old. If the chromosomal pattern is XX, the medulla degenerates, and the cortex becomes an ovary when the fetus is about twelve weeks old. The defi-

nite appearance of ovaries or testes adds another ingredient to the definition of sex.

## Fetal Hormonal Sex

Both the ovaries and the testes influence the future development of
other fetal structures. Like the sculptor and his clay, the ovaries and
testes work with raw materials, which they shape into male and female
features. The materials with which they work are basically the same
structures. What changes is the development of their forms.

What are these raw materials? First, the structures that will become
the internal sex organs develop from one of two sets of ducts: the Müllerian ducts and the Wolffian ducts. Second, the structures that will
become the external structures develop from the genital tubercle, the
genital folds, and the genital swelling. At about five or six weeks into
embryonic development there is no difference in the physical materials
that will develop into the internal and external sexual structures. What
happens next depends upon secretions from the testes or a lack of them
in the ovaries.

The two substances that the testes secrete, the Müllerian inhibitor
and androgen, stimulate definite changes in the "raw materials"
(Money and Ehrhardt 1977: 42). The Müllerian inhibitor does exactly
what its name implies. It stops further growth of the Müllerian ducts.
They eventually disintegrate. The Wolffian ducts continue to grow and
become the internal sex organs of the male.

Androgen, the other substance secreted from the fetal testes, is responsible for stimulating the development of the external organs of the
male. It transforms the genital tubercle into the glans of the penis, the
genital folds into the shaft of the penis, and the genital swelling into the
scrotum, the sac that contains the testes. The transition of the neutral
fetal structures into male organs is now complete. The fetus has specialized sex organs, which can be identified as distinctively male.

As far as we know, the fetal ovaries do not secrete any substances that
stimulate changes in the "raw materials." Rather, it seems that the
absence of hormones is important for further differentiation of female
structures. Without the Müllerian inhibitor, the Müllerian ducts grow
and develop into the internal sex organs of the female: the fallopian
tubes, the uterus, and the upper three-quarters of the vagina. Like the
internal organs of the male, each of these structures is involved in reproduction in adulthood.

The external genitalia of the female fetus develop from the same fetal
structures as those of the male. However, no special hormone stimulates

their growth. In the absence of androgen, the genital tubercle develops into the clitoris, the genital folds develop into the labia minor (the small folds of skin that surround the vaginal opening), and the genital swelling becomes the labia majora (the large folds of skin that cover the labia minora). The process is gradual and needs no hormonal stimulation.

Complications can arise at the fetal hormonal stage that make it difficult later to identify the child as male or female. For example, chromosomal sex might not be consistent with the appearance of the genitals. If the chromosomally male fetus (XY) is insensitive to androgen production, or if the gonads produce an insufficient amount, the external genitalia will look like those of a female or will be incompletely developed (Money and Ehrhardt 1977: 46–49). It is therefore possible for a genetic male to be born with the external genitalia of a female. This could mean that the child is identified as a female at birth and is raised as a female. The "mistake" might not be discovered until puberty, when the child does not develop further female characteristics. At this point the effects of having raised the child as a female are probably too great to assign the child's sex as a male. In such a case, the physician may recommend that the child receive injections of female hormones, so that he will develop the external features of a female. Learning has taken too much of a hold on the child's sexual identity by then to allow him to function as a male.

Problems can also develop in the fetal hormonal stage of female growth (Money and Ehrhardt 1977: 49). If the pregnant woman has excessive androgen production, either from a tumor or from her adrenal glands, the fetus may form external genitalia that resemble those of a male. The clitoris may be enlarged and mistaken for a penis; the labia may look like a scrotum. The child could then be a genetic female, with the internal organs of a female but with the external organs of a male. The child would probably be identified as a male at birth and be raised a male. The problems resulting from this "mistake" would be particularly acute at puberty. The ovaries would secrete estrogen, which would lead to the development of such female features as breasts and rounded hips. The problem would become as apparent as the shapely figure that the child was beginning to exhibit. In this case, the child would probably undergo corrective surgery. The ovaries and other female organs would be removed. In addition, the child would probably be given androgens in order to develop the physical features of the male. By the time the child has reached puberty, the social forces that shape sexual identity are so deep that it would be difficult, if not impossible, to change such identity. In fact, Money suggests that sexual identity is well advanced by the age of eighteen months and that reassignment of sex in contradiction to this identity is ill advised (Money and Ehrhardt 1977:13).

In sum, the stages of the sexual cycle are already a complex network of components. If the child develops "normally," chromosomal sex will be consistent with fetal gonadal growth, fetal hormonal secretions, and the formation of internal and external genitalia. The XY chromosomal pattern will stimulate the growth of testes, which secrete androgens; these, in turn, promote the formation of internal and external genitalia. The XX pattern will lead to the presence of ovaries and the development of the internal and external sexual features of the female. As we have seen, problems can occur at one or more points in fetal development. The coordination and timing of the physical changes in the fetus are truly amazing. The "mistakes" about which I have written are rare, but their rarity does not make them any less important. They remind us that "sex" is a complicated combination of components, which mesh together and lead to the physical form of the child that is born. The difference in the genital structures of babies is the first visible basis upon which sex can be defined by other people. If the baby has a penis, he is defined as a male. If the infant has a vagina, she is defined as a female.

Up to this point, the components that define sex have been physical. It would seem as if biology *is* destiny — at least for a little while. The physical differences that develop between males and females during pregnancy are only partially expressed at birth. Many of them will lie dormant until puberty.

### Postnatal Genital Dimorphism

The most visible basis upon which a child can be classified as a male or a female is the structure of the external genitals. Humans have two forms, or manifestations, throughout their life cycles — a male and a female form. This is called sexual dimorphism. Every group responds to the differences in the same physical features, e.g., the genitals. The fascinating aspect of the human sexual cycle is the imprint that each person and group makes upon the biological baseline. For biology is only part of the story. After the child is born, social, cultural, and psychological forces can begin to weave their way into the fabric of the sexual cycle.

Money and Ehrhardt go so far as to say that "dimorphism of response on the basis of the shape of the external sexual organs is one of the most pervasive and universal aspects of human social interaction" (Money and Ehrhardt 1977: 12). Parents will behave differently toward infants, depending upon differences in the structure of their external genitalia.

In fact, parents may take their responses so much for granted that they hardly realize how much they are shaping the subsequent behavior of their children. Money and Ehrhardt present several examples to illustrate the subtle nature of this process.

The first example begins with the birth of identical, male twins. They were "normal" in every respect; there was no genital ambiguity or malformation. An unfortunate, dramatic accident in surgery changed the course of life for one of the twins (Money and Ehrhardt 1977: 118). When he was seven months old, he was taken into surgery to be circumcized. Circumcision is a routine operation, performed on many infant boys in American society. The operation involves removing the thin membrane that covers most of the tip of the penis. In the case in question, the circumcision was to be performed by electrocautery, i.e., removal of the tissue by burning it off with a powerful electric current. The current was too powerful. It burned the entire tissue of the penis. As a result, the tissue in the penis died, and it gradually fell off. The little tissue that remained lay flat against the wall of the abdomen.

After much anguish agonizing over what to do, the parents of the injured child decided that they would reassign his sex. When he was seventeen months old, the little boy was categorized as a girl. He underwent further surgery to continue the feminization of his genitals. The external appearance of the genitals was now that of a girl. The doctor would then wait until the child reached puberty to complete the physical change. At that time, the physician would administer estrogen, which would regulate further growth and development of female features. After body growth was complete, a surgeon would create a vaginal passage.

However, the effect of the accident on the little boy was much more than the loss of his penis and a change in his genital structure. The change in his genital structure meant that his parents behaved toward him in a way that was very different from their behavior toward his twin brother. John Money and his researchers closely followed the progress of the child's development. They could see the shift in the parents' behavior through the mother's eyes.

The first modification that the mother made in her behavior toward her child was to change the physical appearance of her reassigned boy to that of a girl. She let the child's hair grow, put ribbons in her hair, dressed her in frilly blouses coordinated with pink slacks, and gave her jewelry to wear. When she was tucked into bed at night, she wore gowns. Her mother stressed that she should pay attention to her physical appearance by making sure she was neat and clean. It was O.K. for her twin brother to be dirty. It made the mother feel good when "her little girl" seemed to naturally want to be "tidy," "daintier" than her brother—so feminine. The dirty/tidy distinction between brother and sister extended to more personal habits, e.g., how to urinate. The little girl's mother showed her how to urinate by sitting down rather than by standing up as little boys do. She tried to keep her from standing up and making an "awful mess" (Money and Ehrhardt 1971: 120).

As the twins grew older, their mother gave them information that could mold their ideas of what to expect from their lives later on. She was teaching each of them an appropriate sex role. Women menstruate, become pregnant, and give birth. They rehearse for womanhood by playing with dolls and learning how to do household tasks. Apparently she liked the idea that both of her children would go to college, but she did not view it as being as essential for her girl as for her boy.

The training sunk in. Before they were six years old, the little boy and the little "girl" had very different ideas about what they wanted from the future. The mother reported: "I found that my son, he chose very masculine things like fireman or policeman or something like that. He wanted to do what daddy does . . . [My daughter] said she wanted to be a doctor or a teacher. . . . She'll get married some day. She isn't too worried about that" (Money and Ehrhardt 1977: 122).

We do not yet know the end of this story, but we know enough of it to conclude that learning plays a vital role in shaping the direction that a little child will take in the future. As we have seen, the physical appearance of the infant's genitals makes an enormous difference in the scenario that is enacted after birth. Society begins to absorb the child into its network through child training by the parents. The stimulus for the process is the product of sexual differentiation in the fetus.

In another example related by Money and Ehrhardt, we can capture more of a glimpse of the father's response to his child's reassignment as a female. In this case, the child was born with ambiguous genitals. The penis was quite small (1 cm. long) and looked more like an enlarged clitorus. Although the scrotum was not completely joined together, it contained two testes. As in the previous example, the parents decided to reassign the sex of their child from a boy to a girl. A similar type of surgery followed. The external genitals were modified to resemble those of a female. The child could expect to develop other female body contours when she was given estrogen at puberty and in due time would have an operation to create a vaginal canal.

And again, the parents modified the child's appearance and play activities. She wore "female" clothing, let her hair grow long, and played with different toys than those of her brother. Both her father and her brother treated her in a gentle way. Since the parents had not stressed that their son treat his new sister in a more protective fashion, they assumed that he had picked up his behavior from watching his friends interact with their sisters. The father was conscious of a deliberate shift in his attitude and behavior toward his daughter. He said, "It's a great feeling of fun for me to have a little girl. I have completely different feelings toward this child as a girl than as a boy. . . . I treat my son quite differently — wrestling around, playing ball" (Money and Ehrhardt 1977: 124). Both parents were delighted when their somewhat "tomboyish" girl expressed "feminine" wishes at the age of three. For Christmas, she wanted a doll and glass slippers like Cinderella's.

In each of these families, a physical change in the appearance of the male child's genitals made a significant difference in the way that the parents treated him. They altered the child's wardrobe, hair style, and toys to conform to the "sex" of the genitals. More importantly, they changed the way that they interacted with him and encouraged him to mold his behavior according to their ideas of "masculine" and "feminine." They wanted the physical appearance of their child to be consistent with all they had learned that little boys and girls should be. Both families began to raise their children according to these ideas.

The parents in these families are like many parents in other parts of the world. The structure of an infant's genitals plays an extremely important role in channeling its future development. Why? To begin with, genitals are one of the few notable physical differences between infants that can be observed at birth. Most societies classify a baby as a male or a female soon after birth. They then assign social roles on the basis of this classification. More important than the physical structures are the social and cultural interpretations of the sex assigned to the child. Genital dimorphism provides the biological baseline for the roles of society and culture in sexual differentiation.

### Learning Sexual Differentiation

There is no society that does not maintain differences between the sexes. What varies is the extent to which the differences are elaborated.

Our evolutionary history has been a progressive elaboration of creative ways to survive. Learning is at the core of our existence as human beings. It has expanded our existence into the areas referred to as psychological, cultural, and social. Although the labels are different, there is a common thread of learning that pervades all of these realms. It is not surprising that the fruits of learning are consistently applied to assuring the perpetuation of human groups.

Sexual differentiation is important not only from the perspective of survival as a species but also for psychological stability. Money and Ehrhardt emphasize the importance of establishing gender identity at a very early age. Gender identity is the way a person feels about himself as a male or female. More specifically, it is the "sameness, unity, and persistence of one's individuality as male, female, or ambivalent, in greater or lesser degree, especially as it is experienced in self-awareness and behavior; gender identity is the private experience of gender role. . . ." (Money and Ehrhardt 1977: 4). The most crucial years for developing gender identity are from eighteen months to three or four years (Money and Ehrhardt 1977: 179). By puberty, gender identity is so firmly set in most human beings that it cannot be changed (Money and Ehrhardt 1977: 23). If gender is reassigned after three or four, psychological development of the child can be severely hampered. Freud and psychoanalysts following his tradition have stressed the significance of the psychosexual stages of childhood in promoting healthy personality development.

One way that children learn gender identity is by observation of the behavior of their same-sex parents and peers. In other words, there are role models for the child to follow. Money and Ehrhardt point out that another equally important but often forgotten aspect of learning gender identity and gender role is the contrast between the child and the opposite-sex parent and peers (Money and Ehrhardt 1977: 13). Each process complements the other. The boy can look at his father and see what he should do to be a male; he can look at his mother to see what he should *not* do to be a male. The importance of contrasts in gender roles and the specification of gender identity may be clues to the psychological importance of sexual differentiation in all societies.

Generally speaking, gender identity and gender role develop in conjunction with each other. Gender role is "everything that a person says and does, to indicate to others or to the self the degree that one is either male, or female, or ambivalent; it includes but is not restricted to sexual arousal and response; gender role is the public expression of gender identity" (Money and Ehrhardt 1977: 4). When genital structure, gender identity, and gender role do not coincide, the disjunction may pose difficulties for the individual, his group, or both. I have already discussed some of the rare cases of hermaphrodites who have ambiguous sexual structures.

Homosexuality and transsexuality are other examples in which physical appearance, gender identity, and gender role do not coincide. Narrowly defined, homosexuality refers to sexual behavior between members of the same physical sex and can apply to both males and females. However, in American society the term "homosexual" usually refers to a male, and "lesbian" refers to a female with a same-sex preference. In the case of a homosexual, his physical features, including his chromosomal and hormonal composition, would probably not distinguish him from the general population. Like other children, he was identified as male on the basis of the appearance of his genitals at birth. His gender identity may be in line with his physical features. He may perceive himself to be a male. However, the behavior he exhibits, which is part of his gender role, may not coincide with his perception of himself. He prefers companionship and sexual activity with members of his own physically-defined sex rather than with those of the opposite sex.

The gender roles we play are defined by the group of which we are a part and include rules about acceptable and unacceptable behavior. In American society, it is not generally an acceptable part of the male or female role to have sex with someone who has the same physically-defined sex. Consequently, homosexuals in our society may adopt a public gender role in line with their physical sex and express their preference for aspects of another gender role in private. If a homosexual expresses his preference publicly, he has "come out."

The confusion and animosity created by inconsistencies in physical appearance and gender role highlight the degree to which we expect people to conform to their gender roles. Until recently, the American Psychiatric Association classified homosexuality as a form of mental illness. The actress Anita Bryant created a storm of controversy by leading a campaign to try to fire homosexual teachers from the schools, because they were not living according to her interpretation of God's purposes.

Transsexuals are *not* homosexuals, but are another variation from the overlap between physical appearance, gender identity, and gender role. A transsexual is someone who was born with the physical features of one sex but who feels that he is a person of the opposite sex. In other words, the person's gender identity is not in line with his physical appearance. Sometimes he feels that he is trapped in the body of the opposite sex. Jan Morris is one of the most famous examples of this variation. She describes her experience in *Conundrum*. A conundrum is a riddle and provides an appropriate title for the book. Jan Morris was born a physically-defined male, and she was taught the male role. Yet very early in her life, she felt that she had the wrong body form: "I was three or perhaps four years old when I realized that I had been born into the wrong body, and should really be a girl. I remember the moment well, and it is the earliest memory of my life" (Morris 1975: 1). Yet it was difficult for her to define what was happening to her: "My conviction of mistaken sex was still no more than a blur, tucked away at the back of my mind, but if I was not unhappy, I was habitually puzzled. . . . I felt a yearning for I knew not what, as though there were a piece missing from my pattern. . . ." (Morris 1975: 5). Yet a major thought dominated her life, the "tragic and irrational ambition, instinctively formulated but deliberately pursued, to escape from maleness into womanhood" (Morris 1975: 8). She summed up her feelings about the relationship between her physical appearance and her gender identity: "To me gender is not physical at all. . . . It is soul . . . it is how one feels . . . it is more truly life and love than any combination of genitals, ovaries, and hormones. It is the essentialness of oneself, the psyche, the fragment of unity. Male and female are sex, masculine and feminine are gender, and though the conceptions obviously overlap, they are far from synonymous" (Morris 1975: 24,25). After serving in the English army, marrying, and having five children, James Morris had a sex-change operation and became Jan Morris, a person who felt that her physical appearance was now in line with her gender identity. She was forty-six years old when she had the operation. She could now adopt a gender role in line with her gender identity and physical appearance.

The agony of feeling so differently from what his physical appearance and gender role tell him he should feel may lead a transsexual to have a sex-change operation. He can reduce his anxiety by changing his physical form. As yet, we have no explanation for why this variation develops. It remains a dramatic illustration of the complexity of defining ourselves as male or female.

Transvestism is yet another variation on the theme of the relationship between physical appearance, gender identity, and gender role. A transvestite is someone who consistently derives pleasure from dressing in clothing appropriate for the opposite sex. The term is more often reserved for men who dress as women than for women who don male clothing. As in homosexuality, the person prefers to incorporate aspects of the opposite gender's role into his own. It is not generally considered appropriate for a man to wear female clothing unless he is acting in a play or film, is doing it for comic effect, or is going to a masquerade party.

Hermaphroditism, homosexuality, transsexuality, and transvestism all show that physical appearance, gender identity, and gender role need not coincide. The variations accentuate the precision with which society defines the components of gender role, shapes gender identity, and insists that they overlap with physical appearance.

Although I have been writing in terms of two sexes, some societies do not limit their gender classifications to two. Martin and Voorhies discuss a number of societies that have supernumerary sexes, i.e., more classifications of and roles for gender than the usual number of two (Martin and Voorhies 1975: 84–107). For example, hermaphrodites or "intersexual" people could constitute a third physical type and be recognized as socially acceptable. The Mohave peoples, who previously occupied parts of California, provided social positions for physically-defined females to adopt male roles and for physically-defined males to adopt female roles (Martin and Voorhies 1975: 96–99; from Devereux 1937). Among the Mohave, the transition to a gender role different from the one that physical attributes would suggest was in each case marked by a ceremony. The physical female/male gender and physical male/female gender person adopted new names and wore clothing appropriate to their new gender roles. The shift in gender roles was so complete that an individual in these categories could marry someone who had the same physical sexual characteristics but a different gender role.

The widespread acceptance of the berdache in aboriginal North America is another example that Martin and Voorhies cite as evidence for supernumerary sexes. A berdache dressed and behaved like a woman. He usually transformed his gender from male to female as the result of a vision (Martin and Voorhies 1975: 99,100). The rights and duties of the berdaches overlapped with but were not synonymous with those of women and religious functionaries. Therefore, they represented a separate, identifiable gender role.

While these variations are present in some societies, the dominant trend in most societies is to define two sexes on the basis of the physical appearance of the genitals at birth. Variations on the theme of sexual dimorphism are kept within some consistent boundaries. Variety is not infinite.

After birth, infants are subject to the social pressures and cultural beliefs of their group. The combination of a long period of dependency with rapid brain growth within the first few years of children's lives makes them particularly subject to the teachings of their caretakers. They acquire language skills very quickly and become adept at using symbols to communicate. Their lives expand in a network of meaning. Part of the meaning that they acquire is the meaning of their gender.

I noted earlier that children learn their gender identity not only by observing the behavior of their same-sex parent and peers but also by contrasting their behavior to that of their opposite-sex parent and peers. The role differences that they observe as they grow up lay the foundation for the development of their own gender identities and gender roles. At this point, they begin to observe how sex differences are elaborated by their own social groups.

In sum, bisexual differentiation is important for the survival of the

group, the psychological stability of the individual, and the maintenance of the social order. We can now begin to explore the social ramifications of sexual differentiation and why they are so difficult to change,
once they have been established. They do not have just one meaning.
Sexual differentiation becomes the basis for important social functions.
We can interpret the division of labor, child-training practices, and
incest taboos as major social mechanisms for showing the children the
importance of sexual differentiation. They can model their behavior
according to these practices and beliefs and develop a sense of gender
role and identity.

### Division of Labor

One of the first and most basic associations between gender and social
context is the sexual division of labor. Many tasks in the society are
assigned according to the gender of the persons who perform them.
Physical characteristics become the initial basis for the division of labor.
Since individuals have little control over the physical characteristics
with which they were born, the sexual division of labor is often described as an ascribed role. From the point of view of the members of
the group, assignment of tasks on the basis of gender simplifies their
task. They do not have to sift through a myriad of qualifications to
decide upon who can best fulfill a role. Rather, they ascribe the ability
to do a job to a person because he or she is classified as a male or a
female. Since the job is assigned on the basis of gender, it is a short step
to infer that it is "natural" for one gender to be adept at the job usually
assigned to it. The ability to do the job may seem innate, just like the
physical characteristics on which gender classification is based. Gender
becomes a convenient way to classify jobs as well as people.

What patterns of association between work and gender does the child
observe and learn in the process of growing up? Do children from
different parts of the world share similar experiences in terms of task
assignment, or do they grow up with diverse ideas about the nature of
male and female tasks? We can search for an answer to our questions in
a recent cross-cultural analysis of the sexual division of labor made by
Murdock and Provost (1973a). They classified the sex assignment of
fifty technological tasks in 185 of the world's societies. They found that
fourteen of the tasks are assigned to males, regardless of the world
region where the tasks are performed. Male activities are hunting
aquatic life and large land animals, trapping, fowling, lumbering,
woodworking, making musical instruments, boatbuilding, stonework-
ing, mining and quarrying, smelting ores, metalworking, bonesetting,

and working with bone, horn, and shell materials. Murdock and Provost classify nine other tasks as quasi-masculine activities, i.e., they are most commonly assigned to males, but they may also be assigned predominantly or exclusively to females. These nine tasks are soil preparation, land clearance, housebuilding, tending large animals, butchering, collecting wild honey, fishing, netmaking, and making rope and cordage.

When we look at the results of the analysis of tasks that are assigned to females, it is striking that there are no technological tasks that are assigned exclusively to females, as is the case with males. Furthermore, there are only nine tasks that were classified by Murdock and Provost as quasi-feminine activities, i.e., usually though not exclusively assigned to females. These tasks are fuel gathering, water fetching, gathering wild vegetal foods, preparation of vegetal foods, dairy production, cooking, preparation of drinks, spinning, and laundering.

The rest of the fifty tasks are male or female tasks in some parts of the world but not in others, and were classified as swing activities. Eighteen tasks fell in this classification. Swing activities are: crop planting, crop tending, harvesting, gathering small land fauna, gathering small aquatic fauna, care of small animals, milking, preservation of meat or fish, preparation of skins, manufacture of clothing, manufacture of leather products, loom weaving, matmaking, basketmaking, burden carrying, generation of fire, potterymaking, and bodily mutilation.

How can we explain the wide diversity of task assignments that Murdock and Provost found? The researchers offer some tentative explanatory factors to account for the variation. The two major factors that emerge are "masculine advantage" and "feminine advantage"; together they account for 93 percent of the variations in task assignment. "Masculine advantage" means that the task will be assigned to males if it has features that are definitely advantageous to males or disadvantageous to females in its performance. "Feminine advantage" means that the task will be assigned to females if it has features that give females a definite advantage in its performance. Murdock and Provost argue that males tend to have more physical strength than females and a greater capacity for mobilizing their energy in brief spurts. Females, on the other hand, are more attached to the home, because they get pregnant and have to care for their infants. Therefore, they would be at a disadvantage in performing tasks distant from the household.

Judith Brown specifies the elements of feminine advantage when she links them to child-care responsibilities (Brown 1970). Since women generally care for children, performance of other tasks depends upon their compatibility with child care. For a task to be assigned to a woman, it should not be dangerous or require the woman to be far away from home. Furthermore, a woman should be able to perform it in spite of interruptions. Therefore, feminine tasks would exclude pursuits that require intense concentration or periods of absence from the household.

Ernestine Friedl does not think that Brown's specification is adequate to explain the variety of tasks that women perform (Friedl 1975: 8). She notes that here are a large number of societies in which women consistently leave their households to gather, cultivate crops, or engage in trade. They leave their child-care responsibilities to older children or to elderly people, and they supplement their mother's milk with other foods. Furthermore, women may engage in dangerous tasks, such as attending to cauldrons of boiling food. Therefore, she thinks that the child-care responsibilities may be adjusted to the contribution that women make to subsistence, not vice versa, as Murdock and Provost (1973a) and Brown (1970) suggest.

White et al. (1975) attempt to understand patterns of the sexual division of labor in terms of the constraints placed on role behavior. They guide their discussion by logically tracing the implications of a few minimal assumptions. The first assumption is that the only innate difference between men and women is that women can nurse infants, whereas men cannot. This particular difference means that women are likely to have primary responsibility for the care of small children in preindustrial societies. Child care places constraints on the tasks that caretakers can perform if they are concerned about the welfare of the child. Therefore, their tasks are unlikely to be ones that require them to leave their children behind or consistently put their children in dangerous situations. It follows that women will not hunt, plow, herd large animals, or work with durable materials, using implements that are sharp or heavy.

Child care places constraints on the male role, also. If the group is concerned about the survival of its children and accommodates female subsistence tasks to the demands of child care, then the tasks that remain for males would be those that are *not* compatible with child care. They would probably be dangerous tasks, involve long absences from home or greater mobility, and utilize heavy or sharp materials. If this is the case, there is no need to assume that men perform these types of tasks because they are stronger or more energetic, as Murdock and Provost suggest.

White et al. make a second assumption, i.e., that a group will try to minimize its investment of time in training people to require the requisite knowledge and skills to perform their economic tasks. Therefore, tasks are likely to be continuous throughout the lifetimes of the individuals, and women who can no longer bear children will continue to perform the same tasks, such as child care, that they performed when they were reproductive.

The overall perspective provided by White et al. emphasizes the constraints that are placed on the assignment of roles if the social order is to function effectively. The underlying theme of their essay is that a social group operates in such a way that it maximizes its resources and minimizes the effort that it expends in developing them. The explanation of White et al. differs from the previous ones we have described, in that it tries to incorporate the patterns discovered by Murdock and Provost into a logical, theoretical framework. They try to get back to basics and follow their assumptions in a systematic way.

The explanations of the authors we have discussed have explicitly or implicitly pointed to the importance of understanding the constraints placed on the assignment of role behavior. They differ in the specific factors that they believe serve to constrain task assignment. Murdock and Provost point to physical strength and mobilization of energy as major factors in differentiating tasks. They agree with Judith Brown that child care restricts a woman to certain types of activities. Overall, their explanation points to physiological constraints on task assignment. Friedl, Brown, and White et al. share an emphasis on the constraints posed by the acceptance of social roles, e.g., caretaker of children. We can assume that such restrictions in task assignments would apply to any person who fulfilled the role of caretaker, regardless of that person's gender or genetic relationship to the child.

If we expand the discussion of the sexual division of labor to include nontechnological tasks that are exclusively male or female, perhaps we can gain more insight into the factors that make sexual differentiation so important in social life. At the core of the interpretations I have considered thus far is the important effect that child care has on the distribution of tasks. Barry et al. (1977) found that females are the primary caretakers of young children, regardless of their age or gender.

I was interested in following up on the issue of how child care responsibilities relate to subsistence requirements and task assignment. Using Murdock and Morrow's (1970) data on subsistence economy and Murdock and Provost's (1973a) data on the sexual division of labor, I constructed an index of the relative contributions of males and females to subsistence. I then related the index to the data offered by Barry and Paxson (1971) and Barry et al. (1977) on caretakers of children at different stages in the children's lives. I found that men rarely become caretakers of children, even when women are importantly involved in the economy. When men do participate in child care, they do so when the children are older. Generally men supplement rather than replace a woman's child-care responsibilities. More frequently, little girls or older women will be the alternate caretakers.

These findings are consistent with the expectations of White et al. that roles are efficiently assigned and continuously operative throughout the life of the individual and that child care is confined primarily to the female role. The findings also help to clarify the question that Friedl raises about the relationship between child care and task assignment. Child care, subsistence requirements, and technological tasks can be effectively managed by a *group* of women. If a woman engages in subsistence or technological tasks not compatible with child care, older women or female siblings can supplement her care. Problems arise if we assume that the caretaker has to be the mother. However, we do not need to make such an assumption.

Do these findings mean that it is natural for women to care for children? If the association between women and children is so consistent, perhaps there is an inborn characteristic that makes women more suitable as caretakers.

Sherry Ortner (1974) provides an alternative interpretation. She suggests that the constant association of women and children leads us to the conclusion that it is a "natural" link. The physiological association of women with children during pregnancy and lactation further strengthens the association of women with nature. Differences between men and women in terms of body type and procreative functions become the basis for viewing women as closer to nature than men. Because pregnancy and birth are exclusively female domains, a woman's body becomes closely identified with the perpetuation of the species. In most societies, lactation and the necessity of breastfeeding extend a woman's physiological functions to a social role — child care. The role of women as caretakers of children seems to deepen the identification of women with nature. Since infants are not yet socialized and require constant care and supervision, they, too, are likely to be regarded as closer to nature; they are more like animals than cultural beings (Ortner 1974: 78). We must be careful not to leap from physiological characteristics and social arrangements to assumptions that social roles are natural. "Natural" is a cultural category, which rests on beliefs assumed by the group that uses the term. We may take consistent aspects of our lives so much for granted that they seem a part of us. This has more to do with the major way that learning affects us. "Mothering" may seem natural for women, because we are so used to seeing women do it. However, a large component of mothering is learned.

The Harlows' experiments with rhesus monkeys may help to clarify some of the issues I have raised (Harlow and Harlow 1962; Harlow 1973). As I mentioned in the last chapter, the Harlows found that infant monkeys deprived of social contact with their mothers and peers not only were difficult to mate but also did not know how to respond to their own infants after they were born. Sometimes they would ignore or physically harm their helpless offspring when they sought attention. Monkeys who were raised in isolation but who had contact with their peers later in life were able to counter some of the problems that the completely isolated infants had. They were able to mate and to care for their infants. In other words, peer contact can compensate for a lack of mothering. Social interaction is an important aspect of adequate primate development. In the preparation of the female for mothering, learning seems to be more important than any specific physical characteristic. Since learning plays an even greater role in the lives of human infants, we might tentatively conclude that the ability of a woman to care for a child depends more on what she has learned than on the content of her genes.

Another social role linked to gender is the association of males with aggression, especially with war. Just as women are thought to be mothers naturally, men are thought to be suitable for war because they are "naturally" more aggressive than women. The cross-cultural evidence upholds the conclusion that warfare is primarily a male activity (Ember and Ember 1971; Rosenblatt and Cunningham n.d.). Although myths of Amazonian warrior women have captured segments of the popular imagination, there is no major society dominated by female warriors. It does not follow that the major role of males in warfare stems from physiological factors. Although there is some evidence that prenatal androgens may influence primate aggressiveness, current research also shows that aggression can be modified more than was thought possible in the past (Barfield 1976: 79). Environmental influences take their toll, and males are more aggressive in more severe habitats (Barfield 1976: 79). In addition, the degree of aggression expressed relates to child-training practices.

Margaret Mead's famous study, *Sex and Temperament* (1968), illustrates the impact that learning has on molding the expression of nurturant and hostile characteristics. Two of the three New Guinea groups that Mead discusses dramatically contrast to each other in the degree to which both males and females express aggression. Arapesh children grow up as "contented, passive, secure persons, while Mundugumor children develop as characteristically into violent, aggressive, insecure persons" (Mead 1968: 260). Arapesh men and women express nurturant behavior and are a very gentle people. The group punishes anyone who becomes involved in a violent interaction, whether it be a public argument or a hunting accident. Child rearing emphasizes the importance of minimizing violence by not provoking it. During the first few years of life, the child is "never far from someone's arms" (Mead 1968: 56) and is never left alone. Children are not subject to the pressures of growing up rapidly or becoming especially skilled or proficient at particular tasks. Children can become emotionally secure in their abilities and in the behavior they exhibit. People teach children to inhibit anger because it harms them, not because the control of emotion is desirable per se. Children may channel anger over rejection into temper tantrums, but caretakers do not give in by placating them. Parents verbally disapprove of fighting between their children, and children become very sensitive and responsive to an unfriendly comment. Overall, anger and aggression evoke fear and discomfort.

The violent and arrogant Mundugumor contrast to the gentle Arapesh men and women. The scattered residences of the Mundugumor are indicative of the social tension that prevails among them. Even brothers cannot live closely together. Hostility prevails between the females and between the males in the household. Mead puts it this way: "The Mundugumor man-child is born into a hostile world, a world in which most of the members of his own sex will be his enemies, in which his major equipment for success must be a capacity for violence, for seeing and avenging insult, for holding his own safety very lightly and the lives of others even more lightly. From his birth, the stage is set to produce in him this kind of behavior" (Mead 1968: 183). After birth, Mundugumor children are carried in harsh, stiff baskets, separated from the warmth of their mothers' bodies. Each baby's mother perfunctorily attends to the physical requirements of her child for food, warmth, and touch (Mead 1968: 188). Children have to learn to fend for themselves rather early and are hedged in by a number of prohibitions. They establish joking relationships with specific relatives. A joking relationship gives them the right to threaten, mock, and joke with people in this category. Insults, bullying, and hostility are the models of behavior that children see and according to which they shape their own behavior.

Mead effectively shows the influence of child rearing in shaping the expression of aggression in both males and females. She broadens the point about the effect of child rearing in her conclusion, when she sums up her findings as follows: "The material suggests that we may say that many, if not all, of the personality traits which we have called masculine or feminine are as lightly linked to sex as are the clothing, the manners, and the form of head-dress that a society at a given period assigns to either sex. When we consider the behaviour of the typical Arapesh man or woman as contrasted with the behaviour of the typical Mundugumor man or woman, the evidence is overwhelmingly in favour of the strength of social conditioning" (Mead 1968: 260).

"Dead Birds," a film about the Dugum Dani of New Guinea, graphically depicts the sway that social rules have over the expression of aggression. In the midst of battle, the fighting among the men suddenly stops. It has rained. The men retreat in haste, because they do not want the fine feathers they have worn to war to get drenched with water and be ruined. Wars, like other social activities, are conducted according to a specific set of rules, particularly in preindustrial societies, where combat consistently involves personal contact with the enemy.

If innate aggression does not lead to the assignment of war as a male role, what does? One possibility derives from the fact that females generally care for children. Like dangerous technological activities, fighting is a dangerous social activity. It is usually conducted at some distance from the household if possible. These are the qualities that are not compatible with child care. The caretakers of the children, the women, are free to tend to the needs of the future members of the social group. The people who do not care for the children, the males, are available to involve themselves in combat.

In conclusion, the pattern of technological tasks and social roles assigned to males and females suggests an even broader explanation for why males and females in different parts of the world engage in the activities they do. Women usually care for children and perform tasks near the household, and they rarely engage in dangerous activities. Men have occupations that take them some distance from the household; involve work with heavy, tough, or sharp materials; and are often characterized by an element of danger. We can view these patterns as socially effective ways to assure the replacement of the population. If women do not engage in dangerous activities, like making war or hunting large game animals, they are more likely to preserve their reproductive potential. Since a woman is pregnant for nine months and usually nurses her child for a significant period after that, participation in combat could endanger or terminate her ability to reproduce for her group. And since a human female has so few children relative to other animals, she, as well as the few children she has, are important to the perpetuation of the population. The loss of a woman would mean not only the loss of a member of the group but also the loss of her potential offspring. On the other hand, the reproductive consequences of the loss of a male in war are not as great as the loss of a female. One man can impregnate a number of women, but a woman can only bear one child at a time. The Huron (144), a native American group, concretely expressed their recognition of this fact. They participated in considerable warfare and might be expected to desire males to enhance their numerical strength in battle. However, they preferred the birth of girls, because they would eventually increase the population by bearing children of their own (Tooker 1964: 122). If a woman was killed in war, her group required that her death be compensated for by forty presents rather than the customary thirty given for a man (Kinietz 1940: 68).

Other aspects of the division of labor ensure the survival and psychological stability of the offspring. John Bowlby has presented some very convincing arguments about the survival value of consistent caretakers for children (Bowlby 1969). He hypothesizes that the proximity of mothers and their children served a very useful purpose when our ancestors lived primarily by hunting and gathering. Small children could be in continual danger from wild animals, dangerous insects, and reptiles; they needed the constant attention of their caretakers to ensure their physical survival. Therefore, the investment of women's time in their children became a valuable resource for the group, because the dividends it paid were the survival of additional group members. Women had to be able to interrupt their tasks to care for their children, and they were expected to participate only in those economic pursuits that would not put their children in danger.

The attachment of caretakers to their children is also important for the psychological well-being of the children. Bowlby shows that the nature of the attachment between children and their caretakers has significant implications for the future psychological growth of children. He does not say that the caretaker of a child has to be the child's mother; he only stresses the importance of a child having a consistent caretaker. Not only is consistency in the roles that women play important for the effective functioning of the social group; it also plays a vital role in the development of the child's personality. Children who are separated from their caretakers for a period of time may become fearful adults, who experience difficulty in social interaction.

### Child Training

Another way in which children learn sexual differentiation is by attending to the lessons of child training given them by their caretakers. We have seen that the social assignment of tasks and roles is related to but not determined by environmental factors. Subsistence requirements are also likely to affect the type of traits that caretakers emphasize in shaping children's behavior.

Why and how is subsistence related to child training? This is one of the main questions that prompted Barry, Child, and Bacon (1959) to undertake a cross-cultural study of the relationship between features of the economy and traits inculcated in childhood. They reasoned that different kinds of economic pursuits would be more successful if they were compatible with particular kinds of personality traits. For example, assertiveness and initiative are two personality traits that are highly compatible with the American emphasis on achievement. Boys are usually encouraged to be active and involve themselves in competitive team sports. They learn how to compete, win, and lose. On the other hand, girls learn to be more compliant and to involve themselves in individualistic and noncompetitive games, e.g., hopscotch and jumping rope. If women want to have careers as professionals in the corporate world, it is important that they develop the assertive, competitive skills that men have already acquired as they were growing up. As Betty Harragan points out in her book, *Games Mother Never Taught You* (Harragan 1977), women need to acquire an awareness of the rules of corporate gamesmanship and to develop personality characteristics and social skills that are compatible with the economic world they wish to enter.

The principle of compatibility between personality traits and economic pursuits is the same in other societies. It is helpful for both individuals and their group if personality characteristics mesh with the psychological requirements of the subsistence tasks that individuals will perform. Barry, Child, and Bacon (1959) found that societies that have a high accumulation of food resources, e.g., agriculturalists or pastoralists, train their children to be obedient and responsible. Conscientious, compliant, and conservative behavior aids the group in the preservation of its accumulated store of food. However, such conservatism would not be helpful in societies with a low accumulation of resources, e.g., hunters and fishers. Achievement, self-reliance, and independence would be more valuable traits, since they would increase the existing resources. For example, a workable new idea might lead to a more bountiful catch of fish or the pursuit of a richer source of game. The advantages of initiative would outweigh the mistakes made along the way. In sum, high-accumulation societies are likely to stress compliance, whereas low-accumulation societies are likely to emphasize assertiveness.

When there are differences in the ways in which boys and girls are socialized in the same societies, the researchers found that girls are more often pressured toward responsibility, obedience, and nurturance; whereas boys are more often encouraged to be independent, self-reliant, and achievement-oriented (Barry, Bacon, and Child 1957).

These observed differences in the socialization of boys and girls are consistent with the social assignment of tasks associated with the sexual division of labor, which was discussed in the last section. The repetitive, interruptible tasks performed by women, which are compatible with child care, are also consistent with traits of responsibility and obedience. The dangerous, nonhousehold tasks performed by men are compatible with initiative, achievement, self-reliance, and independence.

In sum, the physical environment constrains the types of personality traits that are likely to be taught to young children as they grow up. Some traits are more compatible with one type of subsistence economy than with another. Therefore, the group is likely to choose to teach its children those traits that are more likely to enhance their survival in the environment in which they live. The group molds its children to benefit from their environment by acquiring the social skills necessary for the survival of the population. Within these social and environmental constraints, the group can further differentiate between the sexes.

There is no wide variation in the treatment of males and females at different stages of their early childhood. In their study of infancy and early childhood, Barry and Paxson (1971) present data that show that the overall approach to boys and girls differs very little during infancy. The portrait that we can paint of infancy in the diverse societies of the world is one of nurturance. Of the 120 societies they rated on indulgence of infants, only 9 (8% of the total) are characterized as treating their children in a severe or neglectful manner. Of these 9 cases, only a single group is rated as being especially harsh or neglectful; the other 8 are characterized as severe or neglectful to a lesser degree. The dominant trend (111 of 120 cases, or 92%) is for caretakers to be affectionate and nurturant to their infants. This trend continues into early childhood (up to the ages of four or five) although to a lesser degree. By early childhood, 20% of the 136 societies surveyed exhibited harsh treatment of their children; however, only one of these societies fell into the category of extreme harshness. From infancy through early childhood, children are treated with gentle, affectionate concern by their caretakers.

As we saw earlier, subsistence tasks are assigned to women in such a way that they assure continuity in the attention that is paid to children. Barry and Paxson's data lend further support to this view. None of the 186 societies they surveyed arranged to have infants sleep in a room apart from their caretakers. One or both parents were available to their children should they awaken during the night. The mothers of the children always slept in the same room with their infants, either in the same bed (65%, or 82 of 126 societies) or in different ones (35%, or 44 of 126 societies). Only the sleeping place of the fathers varied. They were less likely to sleep in the same bed as their infants (19%, or 23 of 119 societies) but often slept in the same room (67%, or 80 of 119 societies).

These results are not surprising in light of the reproductive investment that humans have made in the survival of a few offspring. Rather than depending upon the vicissitudes of nature to ensure replacement of the population, humans have gambled on their ability to attend personally to their children. Proximity to caretakers, constant attention, and affection all play necessary roles in human development. During infancy, such considerations of survival of dependents take precedence over those of sexual differentiation.

By the time children are four or five, they can walk and use language with ease. Their brains have grown to a mature size. The group is assured that the children will be able to participate fully in the activities of the society. The children have passed the crucial, dependent stage of infancy and early childhood. They are now ready to receive more fully the imprint of society.

Socialization of the traits that apply differently to each gender begins slowly and proceeds at a more rapid pace in later childhood. Barry et al. (1976) document this process with the data they have presented in their article on traits inculcated in childhood. Their study is revealing, because they rate traits taught in early and late childhood according to gender. The earlier phase begins at four or five and can extend to eleven years or later. Childhood is short if it ends at seven years, medium if it ends at nine, and long if it extends to eleven years of age or later. Overall, they found that the differences in the traits taught to children are greater between the earlier and later stages of childhood than they are between males and females. In other words, socialization becomes more rapid with age, regardless of the child's gender. Nevertheless, there are some consistent differences in the kinds of traits for which parents train boys and girls. Boys are more often taught to be tough and mature, whereas girls are taught to be dutiful and submissive. The differences in these traits become even more pronounced as the children grow older. Once again, we see the compatibility between the characteristics inculcated in childhood and the social roles that males and females are expected to fill in adulthood.

Although the traits taught to males and females may vary from society to society, the agents and techniques of socialization are less likely to vary (Barry et al. 1977). Regardless of the age and gender of the child, the primary caretakers of children are female; the authority figures and disciplinarians tend to be male. The educators and companions of children are generally of the same gender as the children. This trend is particularly accentuated in later childhood. The children's network of social contacts expands to include nonparental figures of the same gender. The children can observe the consistency of same-gender behavior and contrast it with that of the opposite gender. The social requirements of gender-appropriate behavior become progressively more specific. A number of influences converge on boys and girls during their childhood. The children observe differences in the social roles and in the technological tasks of adult men and women. The children's caretakers educate them in the particular traits and rules that should guide their behavior.

Even though children cannot engage in reproductive sexual intercourse, child training includes very definite guidelines about appropriate partners for sexual relations. Ideas about gender-appropriate behavior can be learned in a variety of ways, both from individuals, as mentioned above, and from the group. Most groups establish rules about sexual behavior, which may either be articulated directly and publically or remain silently present.

## Incest Taboos

The incest taboo is a major social prohibition that influences the subsequent sexual behavior of the child. It also becomes a powerful basis for learning about sexual and gender-appropriate behavior. The incest taboo is a rule that prohibits sexual relations between kinsmen related to each other in specific ways. To our knowledge, there is no society that does not have a rule that prohibits sexual relations between a father and his daughter, a mother and her son, and a brother and his sister. Although sexual relations of a homosexual nature between brothers, sisters, a father and his son, or a mother and her daughter *could* occur, they are not explicitly defined as part of the focus of the taboo. Rather, the taboo applies to heterosexual relations within a limited kinship context. The apparent universality of this type of taboo, combined with the fact that it always applies to consanguineal or "blood" relatives in the nuclear family, make it a constant subject for study. In addition, it is probably the first rule that a child learns about sexual partners, and it is the only sexual restriction that is in effect for a person's entire lifetime. The last ingredient that adds spice to the incest taboo is our apparent fascination with the "forbidden" and with the "horror" that is associated with violation of this taboo.

Classical literature is steeped in the dramatic consequences of incest. The Greek playwright Sophocles portrayed the plight of his tragic character, Oedipus, in *Oedipus Rex*. Young Oedipus was separated from his mother and father. In the course of his life, he killed his father and married his mother. When he discovered the true identity of his father and mother, he was so remorseful and horrified by what he had done that he blinded himself.

Freud incorporated the classical theme of Oedipus' tragedy into his interpretation of psychosexual development. At the root of every healthy person's development is the resolution of what he calls the "Oedipus complex." He assumes that every male child feels hostile toward his father and desires to have sexual relations with his mother. Similarly, the female child would like to be with her father and dispense with her mother. When the Oedipal situation of the male applies to the female, Freud calls it the "Electra complex." The strong desires entailed by the progression of each complex are basic to every human being. However, the guilt that follows the expression of these desires outweighs any satisfaction gained from achieving them. Therefore, every human being must wrestle with the problem of how to transfer the desire for the parent of the opposite gender to a more appropriate sexual choice.

Why should avoidance of sexual intercourse with family members be so crucial for our development? Why should it be difficult for many of us to even think of having sexual relations with our parents or our siblings, much less of acting out such a fantasy? What is so important about excluding such thoughts and behavior from our minds?

Freud believed that the answer to these questions lay at the very core of our existence as human beings. He searched for the solution in the written pages of prehistory. By exploring the taboo's importance in a "simpler" society, he sought to discover its origin and to highlight its significance in his own time. From Freud's perspective, this was a logical procedure to follow, since he, like other great theorists of the late nineteenth and early twentieth centuries, thought that societies had evolved from the primitive to the more complex. In other words, he thought that it was possible to place societies on a linear scale and rank them in definite stages of development. Anthropologists were just beginning to describe the social and cultural organization of peoples who lived in all corners of the earth. Freud searched the pages of these reports to enlighten himself about the origin of the incest taboo. Spencer and Gillin's description of the Arunta (Spencer and Gillin 1899), a small group of aborigines in Australia, seemed to provide the key. Freud explained his discovery in the series of essays published in 1913, *Totem and Taboo* (Freud 1950).

Freud's explanation stems from his assumption that the Australian aborigines are the "most backward and miserable of savages" (Freud 1950: 1). Therefore, he would not expect that the "sexual life of these poor naked cannibals would be moral in our sense or that their sexual instincts would be subjected to any great degree of restriction" (Freud 1950: 2). In other words, Freud tries to explain what seems like a paradox to him. These primitive peoples have an incest taboo that extends far beyond relatives in the nuclear family; it incorporates an entire patrilineal kinship group of hundreds of people. Why? According to his reasoning, these "savages" should be close to animals in their sexual behavior, expressing their sexual urges whenever the opportunity arose. Yet they seemed unusually restrained and extreme in their restrictions on sexual behavior toward kinsmen. How could they be so primitive and yet so restrained? The two types of behavior were not supposed to be compatible, at least as far as early twentieth-century thought about nontechnologically sophisticated peoples was concerned.

Freud developed an ingenious and coherent explanation for the seemingly incongruous facts with which he was presented. He hypothesized that somewhere in the far-distant past, people like the Arunta gave sway to their promiscuous impulses. The sons in the group decided that they would fulfill their desires and have sex with their mothers. Therefore, they eliminated their arch rivals, their fathers, who had exclusive sexual access to their mothers, and consummated their fantasies. Unfortunately, acting upon their dreams produced an enormous amount of guilt about what they had done. Their fathers were dead, and they had violated their mothers. In compensation for what they had done and as a way of assuaging their guilt, they instituted the incest taboo. The taboo prohibited blood relatives in the immediate, nuclear family (brother/sister, father/daughter, mother/son) from having sex with each other. They hoped that such a rule would spare future generations the massive guilt that they had felt from committing such a heinous crime. To further bolster their confidence that their descendants would be protected from the horror they felt, they transformed their fathers into sacred figures, or totems, whom they would revere from that time forth. This gesture could help them atone for killing their fathers. Thus, totemism — regarded by some as the most primitive form of religion — and the incest taboo — one of the most common sexual taboos in the world — developed in response to our ancestors' guilt over committing incest.

Freud continues his reconstruction of our distant past. Our forebears felt such pervasive horror about their behavior that they extended the taboo to include all of the blood relatives tied to them as part of a kinship group. The extension of the taboo and the force with which "primitive" humans like the Arunta punished its violation was testimony to the weakness of their impulses. Freud reasoned that their emotions were so close to the surface and so likely to be expressed, because of their primitive natures, that a very strong prohibition of incest was necessary to circumvent a repetition of their destructive sexual behavior.

Freud's famous rendition of the origin of the incest taboo shows how ideas about sexual activities are embedded in the social thought of the period. The impetus for Freud's essays lay in his assumptions about foreign peoples and appropriate sexual behavior. For Freud, being "civilized" meant having control of sexual impulses and limiting their expression to a very few people. In contrast, his concept of "primitive" implied promiscuity and difficulty in restraining emotional outbursts.

The emotion of "horror" has continued to be associated with incest in many people's minds and has seemed to some to be a sufficient explanation of the taboo's existence. Although horror may not follow the commission of an incestuous act, some punishments for violation of the taboo are severe enough to justify a person'a fear of committing incest. The consequences of being found out could indeed by horrible in some groups. The Cayapa Indians (168) of Ecuador illustrate the extent to which a group may go in punishing those who violate the taboo. They regard incest as "heinous" and, in the old days, "anyone guilty of such a crime would be suspended over a table covered with candles and roasted to death" (Altshuler 1965: 156). Among the ancient Incas (171), the punishment for incest was uniform; death was the penalty that awaited any Incan who stepped across such an important social barrier. Some groups rely upon magical retaliation for incest. However, the offenders may be so overcome with shame and guilt that they do not wait for the supernatural to punish them. Honigman reports cases of native American Kaska (129) who express their remorse by leaping into fires or tearing off their penises (Honigman 1954: 91). Death, mutilation, sterility, and expulsion from the community are among the severe punishments for individuals who violate the incest taboo. (31%, or 9 of 29 societies).

However, punishment for incest is not always severe, despite the forebodings of Freud. Many societies (28%, or 8 of 29 societies) impose only a mild punishment, such as temporary disapproval and some ostracism by community members. Sometimes first cousins or closer kin among the Könkämä Lapps (52) marry, even though this is regarded as incestuous. The couple faces disapproval and possibly some ostracism (Pehrson 1957: 58). The Havasupai (150) of the Grand Canyon merely reprimand offenders verbally even though they strongly condemn incest. They rarely take public action against the offenders (Smithson 1959: 78).

Other societies only moderately punish the offenders (10 %, or 3 of 29 societies). Temporary body damage, e.g., whipping or ostracism for a limited period, may occur in these cases.

In general, the punishment that befalls offenders is either very mild or very severe. It is by no means uniform. Furthermore, punishment is not limited to the offenders, but may include someone else (17 %, or 5 of 29 societies) or the entire social group (14 %, or 4 of 29 societies). Quite often the offspring of the incestuous pair are thought to bear the brunt of their parents' transgression. Veniaminov (1840: 140) recounts the beliefs of the Aleutian Islanders (123). If children are born of incestuous unions, the Aleut believe that they will be monsters or at least will have a wart or blemish on their face. The most likely fate that awaited such children was death or at least a very grim future. The sea might "swallow" them and cast them on the shore. If they were lucky enough to remain alive, the Aleut believe that they would be marked as incestuous children by a walruslike tusk that would grow from the lower jaw or forehead of each of them (Veniaminov 1840: 141).

In other societies, the number of people affected by the actions of the incestuous couple extends beyond their offspring. If a brother and sister among the African Otoro become sexually involved, the Otoro (30) believe that leprosy will afflict their entire kinship group (Nadel 1947: 110). A Tanala (81) community in Madagascar believes that it may experience a series of calamities because of incest: crops will fail, the reproductive potential of the group will be destroyed, and the ancestors will be offended (Linton 1933: 264). The damage may be so pervasive that all of nature is thrown into chaos. The Toradja (87) of Celebes believe that if they do not kill a woman who is pregnant with an incestuous child, rain will continually fall, crops will fail, and the gods will strike the people with disease (Adriani and Kruijt 1912: 274).

Obviously, the social group believes that it has a big stake in discouraging its members from engaging in incest. The question arises again: Why? Why is this taboo taught to children so early in their lives? Why are the repercussions so severe or so extensive? Is Freud's suggestion of a primal crime sufficient to explain such sweeping adherence to the incest taboo?

Bronislow Malinowski, the "father of fieldwork" in anthropology, departed from Freud's philosophical and explanatory framework in grappling with some of these questions. He was one of the first anthropologists to offer an alternative to Freud's dramatic portrayal of the origin of the incest taboo. Malinowski's qualms about Freud's interpretation of the incest taboo stemmed from the assumptions Freud made about the nature of "primitive" social organization. Freud and Malinowski started from two different theoretical orientations. Malinowski preferred to view the social organization of the group he studied, the Trobriand Islanders, as a viable, contemporary expression of the people's needs. He refused to regard them as mere remnants of a primitive past. The Trobrianders represented a distinct group of people, whose customs should be appreciated on their own terms, as part of a functioning whole. In other words, each custom contributes something to maintaining the needs of the members of the social group. Malinowski tested Freud's theory through the lens of his own perspective. His interpretation meant a shift from the past to the present, from seeing customs as part of a grand, evolutionary scheme to viewing them as specific elements in a currently functioning constellation of customs.

*Sex and Repression in Savage Society* (1965) is Malinowski's most cogent statement on the subject of incest. He replies to some of Freud's formulations and presents his own theoretical stance. He brings us a step closer to understanding the importance of the incest taboo to social groups and gives us some insight into why there are variations in the extent and strength of the taboo in different parts of the world. He bases his conclusions on the ethnographic data that he collected in the Trobriand Islands. He begins by presenting Freud's argument and continues from there.

Freud claimed that the incest taboo is universal. It is derived from a psychological dilemma created by our earliest human ancestors. Since all humans descended from the same stock, they must deal with vestiges of a common problem, i.e., how to prevent the repetition of the guilt-producing crime of killing their fathers and having sex with their mothers. Malinowski carries through the implications of Freud's perspective. He reasons that if the taboo is universal, it should apply without exception to every society. Therefore, he should find evidence of the taboo among the Trobrianders. If he does not, he asserts that his single case could refute Freud's interpretation.

Throughout his exposition, Malinowski uses some of Freud's techniques of analysis. He accepts Freud's idea that dreams and myths may express unconscious wishes and conflicts; they should be in line with our innermost feelings. According to Freud's view, we would expect that the fantasies of all males would reveal hostility toward their fathers and attraction to their mothers. The necessity for restraint in acting out these desires underlies the incest taboo. However, when Malinowski examines the myths and dreams of the Trobrianders, he finds evidence of feelings that do not conform to Freud's formulation of the incest taboo. Sons express hostility toward their mothers' brothers, not toward their fathers. In addition, boys project desire for their sisters, not for their mothers. The incest taboo applies most strongly to brothers and sisters and to maternal uncles and nephews, not to mothers and sons and fathers and sons, as Freud would predict. Further, the taboo in the Trobriands extends to maternal relatives, not paternal ones.

Malinowski interprets this apparent deviation from Freud's expectations in terms of the possible conflicts inherent in Trobriand social organization. People pattern their lives according to a matrilineal kinship system; its rules govern aspects of the economy, politics, religion, and the family. All the descendants of females who share a common female ancestress belong to the matrilineage. Brothers and sisters are crucial links in the matrilineal organization, because they are the only consanguineal ("blood") relatives belonging to the group who are available to fill the male and female roles in the group. They would not assign responsibilities in the matrilineage to the spouses of matrilineal kin, because husbands and wives belong to different matrilineages. Descent group roles are confined to members of the matrilineage. David Schneider (1974) outlines part of the dilemma that matrilineal organization poses for the members of a family. The mothers, their children, and the mothers' brothers belong to the same matrilineage. The mothers' brothers fill the authority positions in the descent group. Therefore, the husband/wife bond is subject to a variety of socially imposed strains. In a sense, consanguineal kinship pulls them away from each other. The husband is the father of his children, but he does not belong to the same matrilineage. He does not have descent group authority over his own children. The wife is the mother of her children, belongs to the same matrilineage, and is subject to the descent group authority of her brother. If the father obtains too much power over his children, he could pose a threat to the operation of the kinship group; he is an outsider who might usurp the allegiance of the group's members, i.e., his children.

Phrased in one way, the problem for matrilineages is the distribution of authority. In his role as a husband, a man has domestic authority over his children and his wife. However, his authority can be superseded by the descent group authority of his wife's brother. Women and children should give priority to the dictates of their brothers/uncles. The role of mother's brother provides some consolation for the beleaguered husband; if he has sisters, he can exert descent group authority in his own matrilineage. Unfortunately, the requirements of matrilineal loyalty are not compatible with a peaceful domestic life. Husbands and wives live together, but their sisters and brothers usually live close by. Ties to spouses are qualified by allegiance to members of the husbands' and wives' own descent groups.

Where, then, can a man express his affection? One possibility is to direct it toward his sister and her children. However, full exploration of this path finds a major obstacle in its way: the incest taboo. In Trobriand society, the strongest incest prohibition applies to the relationship between a brother and sister. Furthermore, a boy seems to direct most of his hostility toward his maternal uncle. Freud's hypothesis of a universal incest taboo stresses a stringent sexual taboo between mother and son and hostility between father and son. What Malinowski finds in the Trobriands is not, therefore, in accord with Freud's hypothesis.

Malinowski revises Freud's explanation of the incest taboo by replacing the Oedipus complex with the "family complex." Social organization, not social evolution, becomes the crucial variable in explaining the strength and application of the incest taboo. The placement of authority, not a long-forgotten crime in a primal horde, triggers the necessity for restraint between related males and control over sexual relations between certain relatives. He reasons that authority itself may foster hostility toward the authority figure. Rules do not always conform to individual desires, and some conflict is inevitable. In addition, some emotional distance is necessary to maintain authority; it is difficult to enforce rules when there are close bonds of affection between the people concerned. Malinowski reasons that the Trobriand male would feel hostile toward his maternal uncle because that uncle has the most authority over him. Fathers and sons are not in the same situation, because a father's authority is limited to the domestic sphere. This frees fathers and sons to form more affectionate bonds with each other.

Distribution of authority could also explain the strong ban on sexual relations between brothers and sisters. If descent group authority is primary, and the maintenance of the group is essential for social continuity, sexual bonds between brothers and sisters could threaten the existence of the group. The intimacy involved might overpower the maintenance of proper authority. Extension of the taboo to the matrilineal group results from requirements for social cohesion, not from "horror" produced by an inability to control desires.

The principles of Malinowski's argument apply equally well to the patrilineal setting of the Arunta, which Freud described. Like matrilineages, patrilineages obtain group members by reproduction and recruit the children of their members according to specific criteria. Matrilineages include in the group only the descendants of female members, while patrilineages include only the descendants of male members. In patrilineages, fathers have both domestic and descent group authority over their children. Therefore, fathers do not have to divide their attention between their children and their nephews. Conflict is more likely to arise between a father and son in this situation, because the father has increased authority over his son. He does not have the matrilineal father's luxury of forming affectionate bonds with his son, unencumbered by the constraints of publicly significant authority. The mother/son bond is likely to produce more of a threat to the father's authority. If a mother and son become too intimate, then the mother, who is usually not a member of her husband's patrilineage, may threaten the descent group authority of her husband by manipulating her son. It is especially important for the continuity of the kinship group that mothers and sons keep some emotional distance from each other. Therefore, the incest taboo would strongly apply to the mother/son bond.

In sum, Malinowski concludes that the primary basis for the maintenance of society is the integrity of the family. Incest could disrupt the family in any social context. The focus and extension of the incest taboo depend upon the nature of kinship organization in the society and the placement of authority in the kinship unit. Given the importance of matrilineal kinship in Trobriand society, it is not surprising that sexual relations are also governed by its dictates. Restrictions on incestuous relations are patterned according to the rules that are most advantageous for the maintenance of Trobriand society.

The perspectives of Freud and Malinowski on incest illustrate how the society within which we live and the assumptions we make about other societies significantly affect the types of problems that we perceive and the solutions that we suggest for them. Freud was enmeshed in a society grappling with the philosophical dilemmas posed by Darwin's theory of biological evolution. Therefore, he considered it a problem that savages exhibited extraordinarily civilized behavior. His thoughts were channeled by his assumption that the Arunta were savages; his theory about incest taboos seemed to confirm his views. On the other hand, Malinowski assumed that the customs of a society function to fulfill the needs of the individual members of the group and thus sustain the group as a whole. This assumption led him to explore the relation of kinship organization to sexual restrictions. Malinowski broadened Freud's views to include different types of social organization.

The perspectives of Freud and Malinowski linger with us and continue to stimulate new insights. Robin Fox recently proposed his own interpretation of Freud's theory of the incest taboo in *The Red Lamp of Incest* (Fox 1980). He views his book as an "attempt to rewrite Freud's *Totem and Taboo* with half a century of hindsight" (Fox 1980: ix). He also addresses some of the issues about authority that were raised by

Malinowski. In so doing, he adds the benefits of recent research on human evolution, primate behavior, and learning theory.

Like his predecessors, Fox does not confine his discussion to the boundaries of one discipline, but draws "on any disciplines that help provide answers to the question in hand" (Fox 1980: ix). Incest becomes the focus for an intellectual journey that owes debts to Darwin, Freud, Marx and Engels, and Lévi-Strauss. Darwin contributed the theory of natural selection, the "major idea within which all else fits" (Fox 1980: x), as it is the basis of evolutionary change. Since the incest taboo is a human creation, principles of evolutionary change may provide some clues about why it emerged. Another of Darwin's theories, the theory of sexual selection, is even more relevant to the issues that Freud originally raised, e.g., the management of competition between males for sexual access to females. Sexual selection can account for differential distribution of genes and evolutionary change in terms of the preferences expressed by each gender for a mating partner. Freud adds the element of emotion. The sexual desires of young men led to aggressive behavior between sons and their fathers in our earliest social grouping, the primal horde. Incestuous relations with their mothers created such guilt in these men that they instituted the incest taboo. Marx and Engels provide another dimension to the story, i.e., the division of labor. Fox thinks that the establishment of a sexual division of labor provides a basis for understanding the transition from nature to culture. The combined ideas of Darwin, Freud, and Marx and Engels lead Fox to consider Lévi-Strauss, who concentrates upon the elements that define the shift from nature to culture. Lévi-Strauss stresses the importance of the human mind and its role in facilitating exchanges. The core of our humanity rests on these two major themes. Lévi-Strauss speculates that incest taboos are distinctively human traits that form the basis for exchange between groups (Lévi-Strauss 1969). If family members cannot mate, they must seek their partners elsewhere and thus establish links with other social units. Fox distills the focus of each of his "pantheon of savants" into four emphases: (1) Darwin and selection, (2) Marx and Engels and the division of labor, (3) Freud and emotion, and (4) Lévi-Strauss and the properties of the mind. These themes pervade what follows in *The Red Lamp of Incest*.

The "red lamp of incest" refers to a passage in a poem by Jacque Prevert (Fox 1980: 1), the story of a girl who commits suicide after her drunken father rapes and impregnates her. The red lamp flares up. The French word "lampion" means a small Chinese lantern that instantly lights up when someone throws the right switch. The term provides a fitting summary of Fox's goal—to illuminate the complex and intrigu-

ing questions of why we have incest taboos and why we are so fascinated with them. The beacon of light from the small, red lamp is an
appropriate image for the scope of Fox's discussion. Understanding incest taboos clarifies a broad range of evolutionary events.

Fox's perspective is relevant for our purposes, because he integrates
some of the main points I have discussed. He continually focuses on
incest taboos in the context of evolutionary trends, which incorporate
traits that all humans share. He describes the constant interaction between patterns of sexual behavior, brain development, and social organization. In the process, he offers some provocative suggestions about
the validity of Freud's theory of the incest taboo. In addition, he provides some cogent responses to the theme of this chapter, i.e., why and
how human groups establish guidelines for sexual differentiation of
males and females and channel appropriate behavior via social and
cultural rules.

As I mentioned earlier, Fox assumes that Darwin's theories of natural
and sexual selection provide the key to understanding why and how the
control of aggression and sexuality developed in the form of an incest
taboo. Avoidance of incestuous relations is *not* unique to humans, although some theorists prefer to believe that such avoidance distinguishes humans from other animals. Most sexually reproductive species
have mechanisms to avoid inbreeding, e.g., dispersal of the sexually
mature young. In terms of natural selection, outbreeding promotes variation in the gene pool; the possibility of variety enhances adaptability
to a range of environments. Incest probably does not occur in other
mammalian populations any more frequently than among human beings (Fox 1980: 13). This fact makes it difficult to argue that humans
are unique in their sexual restraint with close kin. Nevertheless, we can
make the case that humans are distinctive in their development of rules
about incest and in their mode of avoiding it. Sexual selection, brain
development, and learning enter the picture.

Fox argues that something like the primal horde to which Freud
refers must have existed in human prehistory and that it left its mark on
the nature of sexual regulation (Fox 1980: 61). He tries to support this
view by examining evidence from our close primate relatives, the monkeys and apes. Despite variations in the number of males and females in
a group, higher primates share a few features of social organization that
relate to sexual access of males to females. Primate groups are divided
into three segments: 91) females with their young, (2) established, elder
males, and (3) peripheral males. Generally, the established males try to
acquire dominance over the females and young males (Fox 1980: 106).
In other words, the elders try to maintain sexual access over females, so

that they can control the breeding situation. This entails retaining control over the behavior of young males, particularly in regard to mating. The development of strategies to retain control over breeding might have led to decreased brain growth. The successful males were more likely to equilibrate, i.e., balance alternatives. Fox hypothesizes that the more a species has to equilibrate, the more likely it is that selection pressures will favor a larger brain. Coping with the problem of sexual access to females and regulating competition between males may have entailed more brain growth and thus contributed to the foundation for the rest of our distinctively learned human characteristics. Fox is careful to point out that he is trying to establish a baseline for understanding human behavior, not trying to transfer nonhuman primate characteristics onto human social structure. Other developments, such as large-scale hunting and the manufacture of tools and weapons, also required equilibration. Our human ancestors were starting to balance alternatives in a variety of realms. Larger brain size enabled them to stretch their capabilities. They categorized kin as well as other aspects of their environment, and they developed rules based on these categories. The incest taboo and exogamous restrictions were products of this increased cortical control over emotions and of the production of rules. Successful breeding strategies were regularized and genetic variety was enhanced through fostering the exchange of mates between groups. Elder males could expect the compliance of young males with their authority in exchange for the assurance that they, too, would have mates. Organization of access to sexual partners for reproductive purposes meant that men needed women for more than sex and that women needed men for more than protection. They could both contribute to subsistence and exchange the products of their labor. The sexual division of labor arose — a truly human institution (Fox 1980: 143).

With more sophisticated hunting strategies and the sexual division of labor, the aim of male control shifted and covered a broader range of activities (Fox 1980: 152). Subsistence requirements led to the association of males and females in a domestic organization, where males provided protein to the mother/child units in exchange for the females' food-gathering activities and food preparation. Kinship organization linked individuals and provided the framework by which women were allocated to potential mates. All in all, the regulation of categories of activities became important. Elder males did not strive to monopolize intercourse with females, but rather attempted to maintain economic and political control over them. Women became important to men as reproducers, laborers, and links between groups (Fox 1980: 152); they were not merely sex objects. Elders used rules to constrain the choices that young men could make about mates. By controlling sexual access to females, men could maintain their power over young men. If young men depended upon their elders for mates, they would be less likely to thwart the authority of the senior generation (Fox 1980: 152).

Therefore, the process that produced the incest taboo was more complex than Freud imagined. The issue is not merely the control of sex but also the management of power relations between males and the manipulation of categories of relations between males and females. It is more to the point to regard exogamy as a unique human contribution (Fox 1980: 150), because it expresses the more general concern of males with controlling the allocation of mates. The evolutionary step of controlling incestuous impulses in the equilibrium process may have preceded our ability to develop exogamous restrictions. In sum, all primate breeding systems seem to achieve a balance between enough inbreeding to fix genetic traits and enough outbreeding to preserve genetic variability (Fox 1980: 139). Humans add rules and mechanisms for exchange (Fox 1980: 139). Fox stresses the continuity rather than the disjunction of humans from other animals. Incest taboos are a natural outgrowth of the evolutionary process, not unique human characteristics that developed in ways different from those of all other animals (Fox 1980: 182). Incest rules emerged as responses to selection pressures; their variety relates to the dynamics of social organization.

Fox explains rules against father/daughter, mother/son, and brother/sister incest in these terms. Elder males have authority over their wives, sisters, and children. Younger, related males are therefore precluded from access to their mothers and sisters. The father relinquishes sexual relations with his daughter in favor of the advantages that control over her gives him vis-à-vis other males.

Fox adds the provocative suggestion that Freud and an early twentieth-century social theorist, Westermarck, had complementary views about the necessity for a brother/sister incest taboo. He modifies the views of each and integrates them in a framework of learning theory. On the face of it, the two views seem to oppose one another. Freud argued that we have incest taboos because they restrain us from implementing sexual wishes that have destructive consequences. Westermarck (1925) said that brothers and sisters have an aversion to mating; they have no sexual interest in each other, because they grow up in close proximity to each other. Familiarity breeds nothing except a lack of desire. A study by Wolf (1966) seems to confirm Westermarck's point of view. Fox reconciles Freud's and Westermarck's views by specifying the conditions under which each is likely to occur. If siblings are in proximity, they could have a frustrating experience if they tried to have intercourse. Proximity entails physical contact between sibs, e.g., rough-and-tumble play. Although the children may feel sexually excited, they can rarely consummate their feelings in successful intercourse. They might feel angry, frustrated, and less likely to want to repeat the experience. Sexual aversion toward each other stems from such emotionally painful encounters. In this case, brother/sister incest prohibitions can be lax, because the aversion discourages the behavior. This conclusion is in line with Westermarck's hypothesis. In contrast, brothers and sisters who live together but are not given much opportunity to interact physically may be fascinated by the prospect of sexual contact with their sibs. Given propinquity and a sexually repressive tenor to their household, the sibs would not be able to find out how frustrating it could be to act on their desires; they would not have an opportunity to learn aversion. Therefore, stronger taboos may be necessary to quell the temptation to act on their desires. This conclusion is in line with Freud's hypothesis.

In sum, Freud's, Malinowski's, and Fox's views about incest are all significant, because they offer three major perspectives on the importance of the incest taboo. Freud sought to understand the origin of the taboo. He saw psychological forces giving rise to cultural beliefs about incest and plugged his interpretation into a scheme of social evolution. Malinowski was less interested in the origin of the taboo and more concerned with the role that the taboo plays in its social setting. He saw incest taboos as a way of preserving the social order by maintaining the integrity of the family. He also detailed the impact that current social organization has on the extension of the taboo. Fox adds another inter-disciplinary interpretation, linking the emergence of the taboo to the evolution of broad aspects of human behavior. Incest taboos are an outgrowth of major biological and social processes, e.g., the management of conflict between males, brain development, actions based on category formation, and exchange. He contributes substantial evidence from primatology and views incest taboos as part of an overall response to selection pressures.

Freud, Malinowski, and Fox gear their explanations to an understanding of what Yehudi Cohen terms the "core incest taboo," i.e., a prohibition on sexual relations between consanguineally related members of the nuclear family, i.e., father/daughter, mother/son, and brother/sister. All three touch upon extensions of the taboo beyond these members, i.e., the "extended taboo," but do not apportion a significant amount of their attention to it. Freud interprets the extension of the taboo among the Arunta as a product of the intense horror generated by the incestuous acts of young men against their fathers in the primal horde. Malinowski regards the extended taboo as a function of the type of kinship system in the society. Fox sees extended taboos as part of the controls that elder males exert over categories of kin, especially reproducing females.

One of the reasons that incest taboos are of major importance in our lives is the fact that they are our earliest experience with systematic social structuring of sexual partnerships. My discussion of them would be incomplete without a consideration of extended taboos. Every society extends the core taboo, and these extensions are the most variable aspects of the taboo. Because we call them "extensions," there may be a tendency to regard them as a product of the same processes that produced the core taboo. However, as Malinowski points out, all core taboos are not the same. The strength of the taboo may vary from one social context to another and may apply more stringently to certain pairs of relatives than to others. When we talk about incest taboos, we usually focus on their application to members of the nuclear family and sidestep the issue of extended taboos. Their variability makes them more difficult to explain than the seemingly consist core taboo. Perhaps one perspective is not sufficient to explain the complexity of behavior contained under the label "incest taboo." We need not only to distinguish between explanations for its origin and functions but also to try to understand the reasons for variations in its scope and intensity.

A popularly accepted justification for the incest taboo shows the kinds of explanatory problems that arise if the core and extended taboos are not distinguished. The inbreeding argument points to the destructive reproductive consequences of violating the incest taboo. The belief is that inbreeding is a genetically unsound practice, which may result in deformed or mentally unbalanced offspring. The theme of the belief is similar to many of those prevalent in other societies, i.e., that dire physical repercussions will follow from such unions. Offspring will bear the marks of their creators' sin.

The logic of the inbreeding argument is persuasive when we apply it to the core taboo. We know that inbreeding increases the possibility of recessive characteristics and that these are not often beneficial traits. Nevertheless, such inbreeding can also accentuate positive characteristics, which is one of the reasons that breeders of such animals as dogs, cats, and horses rely upon pedigrees to guide their mating for future generations of animals. We cannot assume that the genetic consequences of inbreeding will be uniformly detrimental. Nevertheless, it is difficult to dispute the fact that outbreeding is beneficial for the group as a whole, because it introduces more genetic variability into the population.

Even a modified view of the inbreeding argument, i.e., that incest taboos promote outbreeding, which has greater genetic benefits than liabilities, is less persuasive when applied to the extended taboo. In many societies, the extension applies only to matrilineal or patrilineal relatives. In American society, the taboo extends to first cousins, regardless of whether they are maternal or paternal cousins. In contrast, first cousins, e.g., mother's brother's daughter and father's sister's son, are preferred marriage partners in quite a few societies. Why is there such variability in the extension of the taboo if the genetic consequences of outbreeding are uniformly beneficial? The kinds of kinship categories to which the taboo applies seem more important than the absolute distance of blood relationship between potential partners. In addition, the inbreeding perspective frames its explanation for incest taboos in terms of reproductive consequences. Presenting the argument in this way is somewhat misleading, because it merges sexual and reproductive behavior. I have gone to considerable lengths to show the necessity for distinguishing these two aspects of our human sexuality. The incest taboo is a *sexual* taboo. A sexual relationship with a member of the prohibited kinship categories is incest, regardless of its reproductive consequences. It applies throughout the lifetime of the individuals, regardless of their age or reproductive capabilities. Although reproductive consequences of incest are relevant to the origin and function of the taboo, they do not provide a full or adequate explanation for the varieties of extension of the taboo.

In *The Transition from Childhood to Adolescence* (1964), Yehudi Cohen offers a cogent argument for extensions of the incest taboo. Like his predecessors, he tries to integrate the social, cultural, psychological, and biological aspects of incest taboos. He bases his interpretation on two aspects of social life: (1) the need for privacy, and (2) the nature of boundary-maintaining systems. The need for privacy is rooted in our biological makeup. When organisms are overcrowded, the activity of their glands shifts, especially that of the adrenals and the pituitary; such organisms may be less resistant to infection and have lower rates of reproduction. As social beings, it is important that humans reach out to others and establish bonds with them. However, people must distance themselves from others from time to time in order to function effectively. Most societies provide social techniques and cultural beliefs that are consistent with this need for privacy.

Because social groups vary, the means for attaining privacy will also vary. Nevertheless, the types of relationships to which such distancing techniques will apply are constant; they are the relationships that are a part of the networks in which people establish their social-emotional identity, i.e., the family and kinship groups. Cohen terms these networks "boundary-maintaining groups"; within these groups people are bound to each other by close ties, regardless of their feelings toward one another. Because their social ties with each other are so strong, they are the very ties most likely to threaten an individual's privacy. Sexual relations between members of a boundary-maintaining group would threaten the well-being of the individual and, ultimately, the existence of the group.

Cohen argues that the need for privacy, in association with the development of the individual's identity, account for the strength of the core taboo and for variations in the extended incest taboo. Incest taboos are a social means of enabling people to maintain a balance between approaching people and withdrawing from them (Cohen 1964: 169); they provide an individual with some freedom from extreme emotional and physical stimulation (Cohen 1964: 161). Since the child develops his sense of social and individual identity within the nuclear family and within more extended kinship units — e.g., patrilineages and matrilineages — sexual relations could overwhelm the fragile, developing ego of the child. Consequently, socializers must refrain from extreme intimacy with children. At the level of the core taboo, the specific reasons for insulation of the child vary. For example, father/daughter incest not only would be traumatic for the small child but also might create other problems for the family unit. It could hamper the effective identification of husband and wife with each other and undermine the maintenance of effective authority of a father over his daughter (Cohen 1964; 183). At the level of the extended taboo, Cohen expects that the incest taboo would extend to the kinship unit within which the child is socialized. Therefore, patrilineal groups would extend their taboos patrilineally; matrilineal groups, matrilineally; and bilateral groups, to both sides of the family. Cohen's cross-cultural data support this expectation, as do Murdock's in a separate study (Murdock 1965: 311). My data also confirm an extremely high association between the type of kinship organization and the extension of the taboo.

Kinship links form the contours that shape the extensions, but non-kinship extensions, such as those to a household or community, account for only one of the 41 cases (or 2.4%) for which I have information. This finding casts doubt upon the idea that physical proximity alone accounts for the application of the taboo. The most frequently employed extension (17 of 41 societies, or 41.5%) is distance of cousinage from the point of reference — i.e., ego — but this is balanced by emphasis on unilinearity (16 of 41 societies, or 39%). More specifically, I found that matrilateral extensions, i.e., those on the mother's side, occur most frequently (7 of 9 societies, or 78%) in matrilineal societies; patrilateral extensions, i.e., those on the father's side, in patrilineal societies (6 of 7 societies, or 86%); and nonlineal extensions, in societies that have bilateral, ambilineal, or double descent (19 or 25 societies, or 76%). Since descent is closely associated with residence patterns — i.e., the patterns that govern where a newly married couple resides after marriage — I would expect a significant association between postmarital residence and extension of the incest taboo. However, the association of residence and extension of the incest taboo is not as strong, nor is its significance as great, as with descent. It is more likely that the psychological anchorage of the individual in his kinship group exerts a greater influence over the application of social rules than the mere physical proximity of people to each other.

Cohen's argument is appealing, because it combines a number of important variables, e.g., the relation of individuals to their biosocial environment, the psychological requirements of the individual, and the realities of social life. In addition, the cross-cultural evidence that is available on social variation of the incest taboo substantiates his views. Cohen's view exemplifies the fruitfulness of looking at sexual restrictions from a variety of perspectives.

Nevertheless, a "need for privacy" is difficult to demonstrate. We do know that physical overcrowding produces stress. However, the effect of invading psychological boundaries is a more complicated issue. Yet the information we have on the subject is encouraging for Cohen's perspective. Psychologists working in the area of nonverbal communication have demonstrated that people space themselves at distances appropriate for certain types of interaction (Henley 1977: 33). In other words, the distance between people in social interaction is a clue to the degree of intimacy and the nature of the social relationship between them. These distances will vary according to the participants' age, social status, and cultural group. Improper distances can create psychological discomfort. The relationships to which the boundaries apply are learned, and they are first learned in the context of the family or kinship group. Therefore, it is not surprising that special rules apply to the maintenance of interpersonal distance in these units, as Cohen suggests. Such rules become a major part of the framework by which we judge other social situations.

Freud, Malinowski, Fox, and Cohen offer different but not antithetical views of incest taboos. Sorting out their perspectives becomes difficult unless we are clear about the questions we are asking and unless we clearly define the nature of the incest taboo. Like other aspects of the sexual cycle, the incest taboo becomes a focus for the intersection of the biological, social, cultural, and psychological dimensions of behavior.

Each of the theories I have examined taps the complexity of issues raised by the simple term, "incest taboo." All four theories share a cross-cultural, interdisciplinary approach to questions about the intensity and extent of the incest taboo.

A number of consistent themes emerge as being relevant to the development and maintenance of the incest taboo: human evolution, authority, affection, kinship groups, and the maintenance of social life. I would now like to draw upon these central elements and place them all within the same framework. I will also add a few other factors that shift the perspective back to the essential core of the taboo — sexual regulation.

One of the major similarities that humans have with other animals is sexual reproduction. Like other animals, humans have established mechanisms for introducing more genetic variability into the population and thus increasing their probability for survival. We can view avoidance of incest in this light. It is not uncommon for mammals to avoid mating with their parents or their sibs. Thus, incest taboos do not set humans apart from many other animals. Humans and other animals generally encourage outbreeding.

Mariam Slater (1959) points out how unlikely incest must have been in early human groups. She constructs a model of the probable age composition of small human bands early in evolutionary development. She assumes the existence of a sexual division of labor and a probable age at death of thirty-five. By estimating the impact of factors that affect fertility — e.g., age at menarche, length of nonreproductive periods, and duration of suckling — she concludes that "most sex and labor units would be outside the family" (Slater 1959: 1057); the units were simply too small to allow for matings between relatives. Given an appropriate age structure in the band, the lowest probability for the occurrence of incest is the mother/son relationship; father/daughter incest is slightly more likely, and brother/sister incest is most likely. "In the simplest of ecologies, most of the people most of the time mate out, not in order to survive but in order to mate at all" (Slater 1959: 1058). The relatively short life spans and periods of reproductive viability of early humans meant that they bred out of their natal units. The exigencies of the breeding system probably influenced the nature of future sexual regulation. The rules of incest seemingly originated when the ecological balance shifted, and there was a surplus of resources and people in categories appropriate for mating. The biological origins of the lack of incestuous unions are the importance of outbreeding for genetic variability and the practical problems of finding an appropriate mate within a small unit.

During the early period of human development, other characteristic modes of behavior emerged. As Fox points out, humans developed their capacity to equilibrate (balance alternatives) and relied more on their brains to aid them in coping with the challenges of their environment. Definite advantages stemmed from social life, e.g., more protein from cooperative hunting and more protection. The sexual division of labor enhanced the economic efficiency of the group and fostered a closer association between males and females in the group. Men and women had value beyond their reproductive potential. Learning played a larger role in the organization of human social life, and becoming a member of a social group played a larger role in the life of the individual. Therefore, we see three interrelated trends, all of which can affect the nature of sexual regulation: (1) the importance of social life, (2) learning, and (3) socialization. These trends mesh together in the capacity of humans to form rules. The distinctiveness of the incest taboo is not its avoidance of inbreeding, but its emergence as a *rule* for avoiding specific sexual partnerships. The question becomes why humans developed such a rule, not why we avoid inbreeding. It is the nature of the rule that varies. In order to understand the nature of incest restrictions, we have to examine the relationship between learning, cooperative social life, and reproductive viability.

The maintenance of a cooperative social life via learning entails the creation of mechanisms to ensure the continuity of beneficial patterns. Rules aid this process. Patterns of authority emerge as important elements in enforcing rules and resolving conflict. They pervade different layers of social life, from the domestic group to formalized political units. The important point for our purposes is to be aware of the relevance of rules to sexual regulation. Other terrestrial primates have dominance hierarchies to manage the potential conflict between males over sexual access to females. Human males utilize their authority to establish priority of sexual access over females. The control that males acquire over sexual rights to females becomes a basis for preserving adequate relations between different generations of males. Incest taboos offer one way for males to maintain control over something of value — sexual access to related females and assignment of their reproductive potential. The extension of the taboo would vary according to the social requirements of the group and maintenance of authority within it.

Social rules are learned from caretakers in the socialization process. The relationship of children with their caretakers taps another dimension of authority and shows why the taboo extends throughout the lifetime of individuals in the prohibited categories. As Harlow's studies of monkeys have shown, infants must establish an adequate relationship with their mothers and peers to perpetuate the group. Infant monkeys, isolated from their mothers and peers, have difficulty mating, if they do at all. If they do reproduce, females do not have sufficient skills to nurture infants. The nature of early social relationships has a major impact on future sexual and reproductive functioning. Socialization involves presenting children with models for roles they will play in the future. It functions to transmit a variety of information about sex life in a social group, e.g., rules. It establishes a basis for sexual differentiation, so essential for adequate sexual functioning. In addition, children learn to adjust their emotions according to their social appropriateness, but have the leeway to express themselves in an intimate environment. They also learn about the importance of maintaining authority to enforce the rules that society transmits through socializers. If socializers violate the rules they transmit, their behavior not only disturbs individuals but also disrupts the smooth functioning of the group. Expectations become confused, and boundaries, violated. Therefore, the group insulates individuals from sexual relations within the social unit in which they establish their social-emotional identity. The intensity of physical and emotional attachment to socializers would be harmful to the individuals' psychological and social functioning. A side effect of prohibiting sexual relations between members of Cohen's "boundary-maintaining unit" is the formation of sexual bonds outside of the unit. These bonds could foster links between groups and enhance social interaction.

Another dimension of the incest taboo is that it aids us all in dealing with a difficult human problem: How do we break away from those with whom we have shared such deep, affectional ties? It is a part of our humanity that we are dependent upon our caretakers for an extraordinarily long period of time. It is difficult to break away from these ties and establish our own lives. All humans share this dilemma. We see its roots in other primates. Harlow reports that the mothers of rhesus monkeys will encourage their young to break away from them if they have not initiated separation themselves. Bowlby emphasizes the psychological difficulty of separation, as well as the problems that result if separation occurs too early. Freud addressed the problem by assuming that our desires to attach ourselves to our opposite-sexed parent are deeply rooted in our prehistory. Despite the diversity of perspectives presented here, there is agreement that separation from caretakers is a difficult task. Still, separation is necessary—for the psychological integrity of the individual, for the perpetuation of the group, and for the well-being of the species as a whole. Perhaps this is the reason that incest fascinates us so. It is not just another sexual restriction. It is linked to the beginning of our social lives, to what we learn about appropriate sexual behavior toward others and about social distance in general. We learn that we are social beings who must form connections outside of our small, intimate groups. We learn that males and females have different roles and that authority entails distance. We also learn that it is difficult for socializers to satisfy some of our basic needs; we acquire the psychological and social techniques for doing that ourselves.

In sum, there is no one answer to the question of why human sexual relationships are subject to regulation by incest prohibitions. The complexity of the answer reflects the complex dimensions of human behavior to which the rule relates. The core taboo may have emerged as a response to the selection pressures that are associated with larger group size and the maintenance of cooperative relations among males. It would be one aspect of a general trend to organize social life by learning rules. In addition, it could encourage outbreeding, genetic variability, and links between social groups. The intensity of prohibition of relations within the core unit could derive from a number of factors. The management of male authority over younger males via controlling the sexuality of related females may account for the father/daughter, mother/son, and brother/sister taboos. Elder males could wield more power in the group by being able to manipulate the access of other males to their daughters and wives. The intensity of application of the taboo to each pair could derive from authority requirements in the kinship organization. The intensity of the taboo against brother/sister incest could also be affected by the proximity of brothers and sisters in their household and the opportunities available for their learning the difficulty of establishing a sexual relationship between them.

Overarching the core taboo and central to an explanation of the extended taboo are the requirements of the socialization process and the social and psychological necessity for individuals first to form and then to separate themselves from attachments with their caretakers. These factors become the basis for psychological differentiation of individuals from others; maintenance of distance between children and authority figures helps them to distinguish their own needs from those around them. Avoidance of sex within the boundary-maintaining unit ensures that they are influenced but not absorbed by what they learn. Therefore, the incest taboo extends to relatives in the group within which children establish their social-emotional identity. The emotional insulation that is fostered by the incest taboo helps children prepare for the changes that will inevitably follow when they reach puberty.

## Puberty and Adolescence

By the time that puberty arrives, a child has already observed many patterns of sexual differentiation and has developed a sense of his or her own sexual identity. However, the process is far from complete. Sex hormones begin to surge through the body again and produce other physical bases for sexual differentiation. Sex hormones have not played a significant role in the child's life since the fetal stage. Instead, they have stayed in the background, waiting to become central characters in the scenes of life that follow childhood. Money and Ehrhardt (1977) emphasize the significance of hormones when they refer to this stage as the "pubertal hormonal" period of sexual differentiation.

The definition of puberty has changed over time, as we have gained more knowledge about its components. Before 1960, the presence of pubic hair was a sufficient criterion for marking the beginning of puberty (Goldstein 1976: 80). Now puberty includes a wider spectrum of changes: maturation of the sex glands (the gonads), mature development of other genitalia, and the introduction of secondary sexual characteristics. All of these changes mean the beginning of sexual maturity and the potential for reproduction. They occur gradually and span a number of years. Technically, puberty ends when the person is capable of producing children (Goldstein 1976: 80).

The physical aspects of puberty may or may not coincide with the stage we call "adolescence." Adolescence is a culturally defined period in life between puberty and maturity or adulthood and does not necessarily occur in all societies. Some groups recognize childhood and adulthood but do not define a transition between them.

### The Biological Baseline

The physical changes that occur during puberty are the products of hormonal changes stimulated by two organs in the body: the brain and the pituitary gland. The hypothalamus is the portion of the brain most closely associated with the changes that occur in the hormonal system; it is located directly above the pituitary gland and is connected to it by a system of capillaries. These minute, thin-walled vessels transmit chemical messages from the hypothalamus to the pituitary. Although it is small in size, the pituitary gland's responsibilities are large. It releases six important hormones; these include growth hormones, which affect many organs and tissues; the follicle stimulating hormone (FSH) and the luteinizing hormone (LH), which affect the secretion of sex hormones from the gonads and the development of germ cells; and prolactin, which affects breast development and milk production (Bennett 1979: 441). With the exception of prolactin, the preceding hormones have a dramatic effect on the body during puberty. Although FSH, LH, and the growth hormones have unobtrusively circulated through the child's system, their production significantly shifts during puberty. The hypothalamus begins to stimulate the pituitary to release FSH, LH, and other growth hormones. Since the pituitary is an endocrine or ductless gland, the hormones that it releases are secreted directly into the body fluids to be carried to other parts of the body. Consequently, they have a direct impact on the body. At puberty, the links between the different hormones resemble a chain reaction; one hormone triggers the release of another, which in turn affects the production of others. This network of links is especially apparent at puberty.

Puberty generally begins earlier for females than for males; it usually occurs between the ages of nine and twelve, preceding first menstruation by a couple of years. The hypothalamus stimulates the pituitary to secrete FSH, which, in turn, stimulates the ovaries to produce estrogen. The bloodstream transports the estrogen to the breasts and stimulates the development of breast tissue. The breasts begin to swell in response to the increase in the ducts, tissues, and blood vessels; the areolae, the pigmented or colored areas around the nipples of the breasts, become elevated (Katchadourian and Lunde 1975: 93). Like other changes at puberty, increase in breast size is gradual. The nipples and areolae become enlarged during the first stage, between nine and eleven years (Bennett 1979: 448). Between twelve and thirteen years, the nipples increase in size, the areolae become elevated to the extent that they have a slightly rounded appearance in relation to the surrounding skin, and the coloring of the areolae becomes somewhat darker. During the last phase, the tissue beneath and around the areolae develops so that the areolae no longer rise above it; the nipples protrude from the rest of the breasts. The milk-producing aspect of the breasts does not fully mature or become functional until childbirth (Katchadourian and Lunde 1975: 93,95).

Other distinctively female characteristics also begin to develop during puberty in response to the secretion of estrogen and pituitary growth hormones. Estrogen stimulates an increase in the pelvic size of females, resulting in a wider bony frame for the hips. Fatty tissues grow not only in the breasts but also in the hips, buttocks, and thighs. The rounded contours that these fatty deposits create give women their "feminine shape"; the soft curves of the breasts and hips accentuate the relatively small waist. External genital organs also enlarge; the labia, or lips, which surround the vaginal opening and associated structures increase in size (Katchadourian and Lunde 1975: 95). Estrogen also spurs on the development of internal structures. The linings of the vagina and uterus are particularly sensitive to the amounts of estrogen in the woman's system; their thickness and alkalinity/acidity fluctuate in response to how much estrogen is present. The muscles of the uterus also increase in size. In addition, estrogen is responsible for the relatively short height of females; it prevents further growth of the long bones of the body so that no significant increase in height occurs in females after age seventeen (Katchadourian and Lunde 1975: 95).

Although estrogens are sometimes referred to as "female hormones" and androgens as "male hormones," such labels are somewhat misleading; they can suggest the absence of these hormones in the opposite sex. Both males and females secrete both estrogens and androgens; it is the proportions of each category of hormones that vary according to sex. The ovaries produce a small amount of androgen, and the adrenal cortex secretes a larger amount. The adrenal androgens are responsible for several changes in the female's body during puberty. Pubic hair and underarm, or axillary, hair develop in response to these adrenal androgens. Pubic hair appears when the girl is in the earliest stage of puberty, i.e., between ages eight and fourteen (Goldstein 1976: 80); it may precede breast development. After its initial appearance, the coarse, darkish hair grows primarily on the labia (twelve to thirteen years) and becomes thicker, darker, curlier, and more triangular in shape during the next year or so (thirteen to fourteen years). During the last stage, it may grow even thicker and spread to the thighs. Axillary hair develops later than pubic hair and continues to increase in amount until early adulthood (Bennett 1979: 448). The growth of axillary hair coincides with changes in the oil and sweat-producing glands in females. The adrenal androgens prompt increased production of oil and sweat by their respective glands under the skin. Secretions of sweat may mean that the odor of the body becomes noticeable, and oil may clog the pores to such an extent that acne develops (Goldstein 1976: 90). The sebaceous glands are associated with hair follicles; their oily secretions of sebum, lubricate the hair shaft. Because they produce sebum in larger quantities during puberty, the hair follicles can become irritated or blocked so that redness or blackheads develop. Clogged sebaceous glands may create pustules, or pimples, and blackheads, which appear primarily on the face but sometimes on the back and chest. Possibly because females have less androgen, they are less susceptible than males to acne.

Adrenal androgens may be associated with another important aspect of puberty: sexual motivation (the desire to engage in sexual activity).

There is ample evidence to show a link between androgens and sexual motivation. Money and Ehrhardt (1971: 22) hypothesize that pubertal hormones regulate the strength of sexual desire but not the stimulus to which it responds. They note that "falling in love" or having a love affair rarely occurs before puberty. Hormones seem to be related to the strength of sexual arousal to a particular object or image. Goldstein concludes that the "activation of sexual motivation requires the proper levels of hormones in combination with direct or symbolic erotic stimuli" (Goldstein 1976: 100). When women lose their adrenal glands, many of them experience a decrease in sexual motivation (Goldstein 1976: 99). However, they do not lose interest in sex when the ovaries, the source of estrogen, are removed or after menopause, when estrogen secretion significantly decreases. Some women experience increased sexual motivation when they are administered androgens (Katchadourian and Lunde 1975: 93). In addition, studies of the relation between intercourse and phases in the menstrual cycle show that women desire intercourse three to four days before their menstrual period more than during any other time (Kinsey 1953). Whether this is due to the high levels of androgen in the blood during this time (Goldstein 1976: 99), or to fluid retention, or to vasocongestion in the pelvis before menstruation is not clear. Overall, the results of these studies suggest that there may be a hormonal component that contributes to the strength of sexual desire. Such a conclusion does not discount the importance of learning in humans. We do know that removal of the sex organs may have little effect on sexual activity in adults (Katchadourian and Lunde 1975: 93), and that the strength of a person's desire does not determine the way or to whom the desire is expressed. Studies of the relation between hormone levels and sexual activity claim only that hormone levels should capture our attention as possible components, *not* determinants, in our overall sexual functioning. Since puberty introduces the possibility of reproduction to males and females, it would not be surprising if other bodily changes, including more physical differentiation and shifts in hormonal levels, enhanced the attraction of males and females to each other.

Menarche, or first menstruation, is probably the most striking illustration of the precision with which the hormones relate to each other and affect other organs of the body. Hormones stimulate finite changes in body structures by the age of seventeen or eighteen, but the hormonal stimulation that initiates menstruation continues to change the nature of some body organs throughout the woman's reproductive life. In addition, menstruation is marked by its cyclical nature. We infer from this that the hypothalamus in women is set up to trigger the release of FSH and LH from the pituitary at specific intervals. This contrasts with the apparently continuous flow of FSH and LH in males. Therefore, menstruation becomes a constant reminder of the physical differentiation of males and females and of the significance of puberty in this process.

The menstrual cycle demonstrates the intricate biological connection of sex and reproduction in the human female, for the menstrual flow is the product of preparation for efficient reproduction. Like other features of puberty, the impetus for menstruation comes from the hypothalamus; it stimulates the pituitary to release FSH and LH into the bloodstream. FSH and LH are primarily responsible for stimulating the maturation of the egg and for preparing the uterus for its implantation. During the first phase of menstruation, the follicles start to grow, but only one of the enlarged follicles develops to maturity. FSH stimulates a specific follicle to continue it development, but we do not know why only one develops (Goldstein 1976: 47). FSH also stimulates the secretion of more estrogen, which builds up the endometrium (lining) of the uterus. Estrogen production reaches its peak just before ovulation, i.e., when the mature egg is released from the ovary and begins its journey through the fallopian tube. The increase in estrogen has two effects on other hormones: (1) it decreases the amount of FSH released, and (2) it may trigger the release of LH. This process is called a feedback system, because the product of the system, e.g., estrogen, has an effect on its source, e.g., FSH. When FSH stimulates the production of estrogen, a high amount of estrogen results in a decrease of FSH and subsequently in a decrease in estrogen production. This is an example of negative feedback; the source of hormone production is decreased in its output by an increase in the hormone it produces. On the other hand, when the high estrogen level triggers the release of another hormone, LH, from the pituitary, which in turn begins ovulation, the process is an example of positive feedback. LH not only begins ovulation but also further affects the production of hormones from the ovary. After the egg is released from the ovary, cells of the follicle that contained it, the Graafian follicle, begin to change into the corpus luteum, or yellowish body. The corpus luteum begins to secrete progesterone and estrogens. During this phase, estrogen enhances the action of progesterone, which functions to maintain the endometrial environment and pregnancy, if it occurs. If pregnancy does not occur, an increase in progesterone inhibits LH production, and the corpus luteum gradually disintegrates. Its production of progesterone and estrogen decreases, and the uterine environment is not maintained. Endometrial tissue and blood from the arteries and capillaries connected to the uterine cavity are sloughed off and become the major part of the menses, or menstrual flow. The lack of estrogen triggers the release of FSH, and the cycle begins again.

The repetitive nature of the woman's menstrual cycle continues throughout her reproductive life. Unlike other physical changes at puberty, the first menstrual flow appears abruptly. In addition, the hormonal changes associated with its occurrence every month help to maintain the other physical transitions in appearance. Estrogen is particularly important in sustaining vaginal lubrication, skin tone, and the tissues that give the body its rounded contours. The recurrence of the menstrual flow each month is an indication of the cyclical pattern of hormonal release that is triggered by releasing mechanisms in the brain.

In contrast to the cyclical pattern of hormonal release in females, the hypothalamus signals the pituitary to release FSH and LH constantly in the male. Puberty begins when a boy is about ten or eleven, a couple of years later than the beginning of puberty in girls. There is no striking change in males, such as the appearance of the menstrual flow in females. Most of the changes are gradual. They result from the secretion of an androgen from the testes, testosterone. LH is the impetus for further changes. In males, LH is called ICSH, the interstitial cell stimulating hormone, because it stimulates the interstitial cells in the testes to produce androgen. The secretion of testosterone from the interstitial cells results in the gradual enlargement of the penis and the testes. Pubic hair also begins to appear at this time. As the testes enlarge, so, too, does their capacity for manufacturing more testosterone. Rapid growth of the testes and penis occur between ages twelve and fifteen. Greater production of testosterone triggers even more changes in the body. Pubic hair becomes more abundant and curly when the boy is twelve to fourteen years old. Axillary hair begins to appear between the ages of thirteen and sixteen (Katchadourian and Lunde 1975: 15; Bennett 1979: 447). Facial and body hair appear later, between the ages of fifteen and seventeen, and continue to develop, often until a man is in his early twenties. Katchadourian and Lunde (1975: 103) note that less than 50% of the young men in the United States have shaved by the time they are seventeen years old. The male hairline begins to recede slightly on each side of the head near the temple, whereas the female hairline partially circles the face in a more oval pattern. As also occurs in females, the sweat and oil-producing glands of the male begin to increase their secretions. Acne becomes a more acute problem for males than for females; males have greater amounts of androgen stimulating the production of oil in the skin. Boys may anticipate acne problems between the ages of fourteen and eighteen. Probably the most noticeable change in a boy during puberty is the deepening of his voice. Testosterone stimulates the growth of the larynx, or voice box, which is partially responsible for the deeper tones of the male voice (Katchadourian and Lunde 1975: 103); part of the deepness may be learned as part of the male role.

Testosterone also affects the overall stature and body contours of the male. While estrogen stems the growth of the long bones in the female's body, testosterone promotes their growth in the male. Consequently, males are usually taller than females; genetic factors may also contribute to differences in height. Unlike estrogen, which encourages the development of fatty tissues in the breast, hips, and thighs of girls, testosterone promotes muscle development in males. More muscle mass accounts for the greater strength and weight of males in comparison with females of the same height. The male pelvis remains relatively small; expansion is more likely to occur in the shoulders and rib cage. During the early stages of puberty, between the ages of twelve and fourteen, a boy may be subject to another hormone secreted from the testes, i.e., small amounts of estrogen. Estrogen may induce the development of fatty tissue in the boy's chest, so that he appears to have slightly rounded breasts. Breast enlargement occurs in approximately 80 percent of the boys going through puberty (Katchadourian and Lunde 1975: 103) and may be a source of embarrassment until the influence of estrogen wanes, when the boy is between fourteen and seventeen (Bennett 1979: 447). As I have noted before, males and females have different amounts of sex hormones, not exclusive monopolies on their secretion. However, the influence of adrenal androgens is more pervasive in women than that of estrogens is in males, in whom the effect seems to be rather transient.

Most of the internal changes that occur in the male during puberty are a consequence of the secretion of FSH and hormones produced by other glands, especially the thyroid (Katchadourian and Lunde 1975: 104). FSH is important, because it stimulates the maturation of sperm in the seminiferous tubules of the testes. The process is constant in the male; the continuous release of FSH in the male stimulates the maturation of sperm. Unlike that of the female, the male's potential for reproduction is not limited to one stage or time interval in his life. As far as we know, men do not experience anything like menopause or forty-eight-hour fertile periods. We do know that sperm production may be affected by external events in a man's life. Stress may result in a lowering of testosterone production. Extreme emotional disturbance — e.g., that experienced by soldiers in combat — may retard or eliminate testosterone production for a while. Heavy use of marijuana has been associated with decreased testosterone production. Even temperature changes and clothing styles may have an effect. Long, frequent, hot baths or a high fever may inhibit sperm production (Katchadourian and Lunde

1975: 105). Clothing styles can also affect sperm production by raising the temperature of the testes in the scrotum. Efficient sperm production occurs in the testes when the temperature is slightly below normal body temperature. The muscles of the scrotum, the sac that encloses the testes, relax and contract to maintain a constant temperature (Goldstein 1976: 9). When the temperature is warm, the muscles relax so that the testes extend from the warmth of the body. When the testes are cool, the scrotum pulls them closer to the body. Tight clothing or athletic supporters can draw the testes closer to the body for a long period of time and result in a decrease in sperm production. Furthermore, increases in temperature could affect the mutation rate of genes (Goldstein 1976: 8). Such findings show how our cultural creations, e.g., clothing, may affect our biological makeup and reproductive functions.

By the time a boy is between fourteen and sixteen, he usually produces mature sperm and is capable of fertilizing an egg. However, he may not ejaculate mature sperm during the early stages of puberty. Structures like the prostate begin to produce some of the fluids that make up the ejaculate; sperm are only a small portion of the fluid. Therefore, the first ejaculation does not necessarily mean the attainment of reproductive maturity. Montagu has coined the term "adolescent sterility" for the initial period of relative infertility that males and females experience while their reproductive systems are maturing (Montagu 1957).

The acyclical nature of male hormone production has generally been emphasized as an important contrast to the cyclical pattern of females. However, very little research has been done on the possibility that male hormone production may share some of the cyclical features of the female pattern. There is some evidence to show that hormone production in males may be more cyclical than was once thought. Some researchers have shown that testosterone levels may vary depending upon the time of day (Goldstein 1976: 30). Sperm production goes through six stages of development over a sixteen-day period in a particular area of the seminiferous tubules (Goldstein 1976: 30). We also know that LH is sensitive to the amount of testosterone in the system; the more testosterone, the more restrained the release of LH from the pituitary. As the testosterone levels fall, LH production increases. FSH may also fluctuate according to the amount of other substances in the system. One researcher has suggested that FSH responds to estrogen produced by the testes; as estrogen increases, FSH decreases (Goldstein 1976: 29). In contrast, Money (1980) suggests that the cyclical or acyclical pattern of hormonal release is permanently established during a crucial phase of prenatal development. Subsequent events are unlikely to shift the basic programming of the hypothalamus as male or female (Money 1980: 3). Males will be characteristically acyclical in their hormone production, while females will be cyclical.

Puberty ends somewhat later for males than for females; it lasts about five years and may extend into the male's twenties. Females usually begin puberty earlier than males and become reproductively and sexually mature sooner; a girl's puberty lasts about three years and is often complete by the time she is fifteen.

In sum, many of the physical changes that occur in boys and girls are the result of similar neurological and hormonal processes. The hypothalamus activates the pituitary gland to release FSH and LH. FSH and LH stimulate the gonads — ovaries in females, testes in males — to produce estrogen or androgen. Estrogen produces most of the physical changes in females — short stature, smooth skin, rounded body contours, vaginal lubrication, and enlargement of the labia, vagina, and uterus. Androgen, particularly testosterone, plays a large role in the physical changes that occur in males at puberty. Facial and body hair, muscle mass, voice, stature, and enlargement of the scrotum, testes, and penis are all responses to increased androgen production.

Males and females share some of the effects of androgen in their physical appearance; androgens are responsible for the growth of pubic and axillary hair and prompt increased secretions from the oil and sweat glands. It seems likely that sexual motivation is a response to the increased secretion of testosterone from the testes in males and androgen from the adrenal cortex in females. FSH and LH serve similar functions in males and females; they stimulate the maturation of the germ cells and aid in the completion of the individual's reproductive capability. At the end of puberty, reproduction is no longer a possibility. It is a reality. In fact, the end of puberty is usually defined as the attainment of reproductive maturity, with all of its attendant physical features.

It is difficult to disentangle the sexual and reproductive aspects of puberty, because they develop so closely together. There are few other times in the life cycle when the physical differences between males and females are so obvious. Changes in the body accentuate the contrast between the sexes. At birth, the difference in the appearance of the genitals is the main indication of gender. By the end of puberty, there are a host of subtle and striking expressions of sexual differentiation. Hormonal secretions intensify the strength of sexual urges. Males and females are not only capable of sexual intercourse; they are also capable of reproduction. At no other phase of the life cycle do we see more clearly how sexual differentiation complements the goal of reproduction. The contrasts between males and females can enhance and promote their attraction to each other. We share this trait with the rest of the animal kingdom; courtship behavior is based on a series of behavioral patterns that are triggered by stimuli from the opposite sex.

If we were not aware of the differences between the sexes before puberty, the physical changes of that period almost impose that awareness on us. It is difficult to ignore menstruation and breast development in females or facial hair, ejaculation, and differences in voice quality in males. Not only are the individuals themselves at an important juncture in their lives, but the society to which they belong is also at the crossroads of an important decision. How will it deal with the obvious sexuality and the potential reproductive powers of its youth? Will sex become synonymous with reproduction and be allowed only in specific contexts? Or, can sex be separated from reproduction and be permitted without reproductive consequences? Only humans have the option to decide upon the degree to which sex and reproduction will overlap. Social forces and cultural beliefs begin to play major roles in shaping the expression of sexual traits and reproductive potential. The raw materials for further social and cultural elaboration of differentiation are all there, in the form of biological changes. However, much more is at stake than accentuation of differences to establish gender. The social and cultural guidance of individuals from this time on could affect mating patterns, the pattern of genetic traits passed on from one generation to another, forms of sexual expression, and population size. For the sake of simplicity, I will consider the patterns that relate to sexual expression in the remainder of this chapter and discuss those that relate to the reproductive cycle in the next chapter.

### Sociocultural Dimensions of Puberty and Adolescence

Puberty involves a variety of physical changes over a period of years. How does the social group mark this time in a person's life? Does the group draw attention to it at all? If it does, which physical characteristics are emphasized? The biological changes provide ample possibilities for sociocultural elaboration. Do the changes mean the same thing in all societies? If not, what sorts of variations are there?

*Social attention and cultural interpretations of the onset of puberty.* A Goajiro (159) girl in North Columbia or Venezuela is not likely to forget the onset of puberty, especially if she is a member of the upper class. Upper-class people in that part of the world have more extended and elaborate versions of the same ceremonies that are conducted by people in the lower class. Despite differences in the scale of the ceremonies, the underlying theme remains the same for all of them: first menstruation is a signal to prepare a girl for womanhood. The period that she undergoes after first menstruation emphasizes the importance of the transition. I will focus on the upper-class ritual, since it is richer in its symbolic elements.

Constraint marks the life of a child approaching puberty. Treatment of the young girl's body symbolizes the restrictions to which she is subject. Many of her ordinary activities are curtailed. She is wrapped in a robe, and she must lie down in her house for five days. She should not move, scratch herself, spit, or eat. As if to emphasize the necessity for her to empty herself of her previous stage in life, she must drink an herbal mixture which makes her vomit. Her spatial seclusion and departure from her usual routine mark her withdrawal from childhood and her approach to womanhood. After her first phase of seclusion, her friends and consanguineal relatives join together in a feast and dancing. They express their feeling for the special nature of the occasion by dressing up, engaging in group activities—e.g., races—contributing food for the feast, and prolonging their participation over a period of days.

When the next phase of seclusion begins, the girl becomes even more separated from social life than she was in the first phase. She is lowered into a room separate from the main household, or she retreats to a room from which she can communicate to the household only through a small opening. Separation from men is a particularly important aspect of her segregation. Not only should she not be visited by men; she should not even see them. Needless to say, sexual relations are out of the question. Her seclusion lasts for a significant period of time. Poor people can manage social withdrawal of the woman for one month or less, while middle- to high-income people can extend her segregation from six months to a year.

Why does a young woman participate in such practices? In terms of Goajiro beliefs, the answer is permeated with some of the most significant aspects of a woman's life in Goajiro society. The point of the ritual is to ensure a successful marital life for the woman who takes part. The ceremonial elements are supposed to aid a girl in avoiding bad pregnancies, hard or abnormal deliveries, exhaustion from frequent childbearing, and ill children. In other words, the focus of the ritual is to prepare a girl for the Goajiro's version of womanhood, i.e., marriage and children.

An elaborate ceremony marks the conclusion of the ritual. Unlike the first feast, the young woman may participate in the festivities; she is now considered a marriageable young woman. Friends, family members, and important people from the surrounding region attend the celebration. The young woman's appearance expresses her new status. Her haircut, facial painting, and garment are now those of an adult woman. Her jewelry and ornaments supplement other physical indicators of adulthood by indicating her family rank. The lengthy ritual is now complete.

The social group has helped the girl to effect a transition from girlhood to womanhood. The girl has shown her commitment to the transition by observing the rules of her seclusion. The group has shown its recognition of her commitment and her new responsibilities by their affirmations of her new status; feasts, dances, and acceptance of her new appearance reinforce her new station in life.

Like the Goajiro, most societies regard first menstruation as an important event (39 of 42 societies, or 93%). However, the significance attributed to it varies considerably. Although some societies (9 of 42 societies, or 21%) interpret first menstruation solely in physical terms, i.e., as a cue that the girl is mature enough to engage in intercourse (6 of 42 societies, or 14%) or a sign that she can now reproduce (3 of 42 societies, or 7%), most do not. Such physical capabilities are usually combined with or overshadowed by social translations of the biological facts. Menstruation may mean that a woman is eligible for marriage (12 of 42 societies, or 28.6%) or that she is an adult (7 of 42 societies, or 16.7%). However, the significance of first menstruation need not be confined to one meaning. The power of the symbolic elements attached to it may derive from the layers of meaning that enfold it. Quite a few societies (11 of 42 societies, or 26%) attach multiple meanings to first menstruation. For example, the Goajiro believe that first menstruation signifies adulthood, eligibility to marry, and ability to reproduce. When the onset of menstruation has multiple meanings attached to it, eligibility to marry is always among them. Overall, eligibility to marry emerges as one of the most consistently important meanings attached to first menstruation (23 of 42 societies, or 55%).

The social definition of the onset of menstruation has implications for the type of attention given to the girl at this time. The severity of the ordeal that a girl undergoes is significantly associated with the meaning that is attached to initial menstruation. When adulthood and/or marriage are the primary emphases, the ordeal is likely to be moderate to severe; when sex and/or children are emphasized, it is unlikely that much of an ordeal will follow ($X^2 = 4.9$, 1 df, $p = <.05$, $N = 35$).

A sizable proportion of the world's societies (19 of 46 societies, or 41%) require a woman to undergo moderate to severe restrictions. Seclusion and rules that prohibit movement, touch, sight, sound, or physical alterations of the woman's body are frequent elements in such ordeals. For example, a young Hadza (9) girl of Tanzania submits to a painful clitoridectomy and removal of part of her labia (Woodburn 1964: 312). The Kaska (129) of British Columbia sequester the young girl for a few months; only women can visit her (Teit 1956: 121–129). She dresses in a robe and hood to hide her already blackened face. She is not allowed to comb her hair or scratch her head. She has to exclude fresh meat from her diet and sip water through a straw.

The significance of first menstruation, the ordeal that the girl undergoes, and the celebration that follows the girl's ordeal are linked together. When the group invests menstruation with the meaning of adulthood or marriageability, then a moderate to severe ordeal is likely to mark the transition. In addition, a moderate to elaborate celebration is likely to follow a relatively severe ordeal. The girl who has exhibited restraint and discipline during seclusion emerges into an arena of social celebration. Her transition to her new status and role is now complete. Friends, relatives, and community members may gather around her to acknowledge her difficult experience and to accept her as a new addition to her social context.

Although first menstruation is often the trigger for social elaboration of puberty, it is not the only physical change at puberty to which groups pay attention. The budding of a woman's breasts may become the focus for a shift in social attitudes toward her. After an Otoro (30) girl's breasts begin to fill out, she can go to the "girls' house" and receive lovers (Nadel 1947: 133). The Fon (18) call a girl a "woman-small" when her breasts begin to appear (Herskovits 1938: 1,277); while the Wolof (21) think that a girl should not marry or have intercourse before her breasts develop (Ames 1953: 53). Marriage transforms her into her adult status. Therefore, breast development becomes one step toward adulthood but does not signify adulthood. The Siuai (99) of the Solomon Islands think that a girl can have intercourse when her breasts fill out, but it is only when a girl actively does have intercourse that she becomes a young woman; first menstruation is incidental, and a woman reaches full adult status only after marriage (Oliver 1955: 141,143). These examples are sufficient to show that the definition of adulthood is quite variable for girls and not necessarily attached to any one physical aspect of puberty. Biology provides the baseline for social and cultural elaboration.

Schlegel and Barry's recent study of adolescent initiation ceremonies shows how variable the social recognition of adolescence can be (Schlegel and Barry 1979). They define an adolescent initiation ceremony as "some social recognition, in ceremonial form, of the transition from childhood into the next stage" (Schlegel and Barry 1979: 199). The ceremonies are absent more often than they are present. Since male initiations have been emphasized so much in the literature, Schlegel and Barry were surprised to find that initiations are held more frequently for girls than for boys; 21 of the 182 societies they studied held them only for girls, while 9 had them only for boys; 25 % held them for both girls and boys (Schlegel and Barry 1979: 201). One reason for this discrepancy may be that ceremonies for girls tend to include the immediate family or the local group, while those for boys tend to include a larger group, such as the total community. The elaborate scale of male initiations, as well as the preponderance of male ethnographers, may have led to more interest in male initiations.

Changes in physical functioning or appearance usually provide the impetus for the timing of the ceremony for both sexes. Ceremonies generally occur close to the time that boys first ejaculate and girls first menstruate (Schlegel and Barry 1979: 203). The initial signs of physical maturation, i.e., pubic hair, breast development, and masculine/feminine body contours, are the sparks for social attention to the developing child; most societies conduct ceremonies that parallel specific physical changes at puberty.

Although there are a number of similarities between male and female initiation ceremonies, there are also some striking differences. The Arunta of Australia provide a memorable contrast to the Goajiro's ceremony for girls. Although Freud referred to these Australian aborigines as "the most backward and miserable of savages" (Freud 1950: 1), the rich, symbolic matrix that marks the transition of Arunta males into manhood belies his characterization. It is misleading to mistake the quantity of material culture for the quality of a person's mental life.

While both boys and girls have initiation rites around the time of puberty, boys' rites last longer and are more elaborate. Service divides the series of ceremonies into four parts: (1) painting the boy and tossing him into the air, (2) circumcision, (3) subincision, and (4) fire ordeals and bloodletting (Service 1978: 29). The intensity of the individual ordeal, as well as the degree of social participation in the initiation, escalate with each phase of the ritual. The young, ten- to twelve-year-old boys may find some comfort in the Arunta practice of initiating a group of boys together, rather than individually. Many of the rites are quite painful and require discipline and courage. The boys know they are not alone in their pain and in their fears. A bond can develop between them in the face of their ordeal.

The first rite is relatively small and tame compared with those that follow. Until this time, the boys have associated primarily with other noninitiated children and the women. When they have passed through the initial rite, they can participate in some of the economic activities performed by adult men. Their status begins to change. To qualify for the change, the boys must submit to the actions of the men who initiate them. As the women dance in a circle around them, shouting and waving their arms, the men throw the boys in the air several times (Service 1978: 28). Prospective brothers-in-law paint the backs of their young, potential relatives. The men begin to modify the bodies of the boys by piercing their nasal septums; they can now lodge a nasal bone in the newly created opening.

Seclusion and secrecy mark the second phase of the initiation ceremony. The men snatch the boys from their ordinary setting and carry them to a secret place, which has been stocked with food and firewood. Their ritual singing and dancing transmit some of the tribal myths to the young boys. Once again, the boys submit to alterations in appearance. The men wrap their heads with fur strings and girdle their waists with bands of human hair. After this, they sequester the boys in an even more hidden spot, where the men reveal the tribe's sacred knowledge to them. Their instruction lasts almost a week and is followed by another painful rite: circumcision. While they recover from the removal of the foreskins of their penises, they must submit to further physical manipulation by their elders. The men intermittently bite the scalps of the boys until they bleed; they say that biting stimulates hair growth. The boys come out of seclusion after they have completely recovered from their wounds.

The third phase of initiation begins a few weeks after the second. The men return the boys to their last place of seclusion and transmit sacred knowledge to them again. The completion of this phase is marked by a physical modification in the boys' bodies: subincision; the men cut the underside of the penis to the urethra.

Physical modifications of the initiates' bodies continue into the last and most elaborate phase of the ceremony, the *"engwura."* The boys undergo bloodletting and fire ordeals as a final testimony to their stamina and value as adult men. They learn more details about the privileged reservoirs of secret information pertinent to the tribe and their group. At last they have become men and are accorded fully adult status by their group. The extensive dancing and feasting of the group express their evaluation of the importance of the occasion. Masses of people from miles around congregate to participate in the celebration. The festivities may continue for months.

Each boy's puberty provides an occasion for a peak in social activity. His initiation shows the gradual imprint of his group on him. He is physically and socially sequestered from the life he had led before. He withdraws from women's activities and begins to accept the tasks of men. He shares his transition with other boys and with the men who initiate him. He is filled with knowledge of the society he is about to enter as an adult. As if to symbolize the social importance of the transition, the group imposes its own physical transformation on the boy during puberty. His penis is altered by circumcision and subincision, according to social rules; these physical modifications remain permanent symbols of the boy's transformation to manhood. The group affirms his new status and their own solidarity by the communal ceremonies, which finalize the ritual.

The scale of participation in the Arunta boys' initiation ritual contrasts with that of the more subdued, individualistic initiation of the Goajiro girl. According to Schlegel and Barry, this is a common distinction between male and female initiations. Girls are usually initiated alone (87%, or 73 of 84 societies) within the context of their immediate families or the local group (Schlegel and Barry 1979: 201). Boys' initiations are more likely to include groups of young men and to draw the participation of groups of people beyond the local community (48%, or 29 of 61 societies) (Schlegel and Barry 1979: 201). Perhaps one reason that boys' ceremonies can be held in groups is that their initiations are less tied to the physical aspects of puberty than are those of the girls. Therefore, the group has more flexibility to decide when to plan its rituals. Schlegel and Barry find that 82% (68 of 83 societies) of the societies for which they have information initiate girls at the first signs of genital maturation or at genital maturation. On the other hand, only 39% (24 of 62 societies) of the societies use genital maturation as a cue for performing initiation ceremonies for boys; they may occur before genital maturation (21%), a year after maturation (27%), or later (13%) (Schlegel and Barry 1979: 202).

It is notable that boys' initiations are more likely to include pain and genital operations (40 of 63 societies, or 64%) than are those of girls (28 of 84 societies, or 33%) (Schlegel and Barry 1979: 202). Physical manifestations of masculinity at puberty are more subtle than those of femininity; no change in boys is as dramatic as the uncontrolled bleeding of girls at first menstruation. Does the group compensate for this difference by engraving the boy with its own assessment of his manhood? The focus of male initiation ceremonies is oriented more toward social than biological concerns. In other words, the male ceremonies seem to enhance the identification of men with areas of social concern, while those of women dramatize the classification of women with the physical, "natural" elements of life. I have discussed this theme as a major social belief about the foundation for assigning responsibility for child care. Since women bear children, the group reinforces the view that it is "natural" for women to care for their offspring. The evidence provided by Schlegel and Barry supports these inferences (Schlegel and Barry 1979: 203). They find that fertility and sexuality are the principal foci of female initiation ceremonies (62%, or 52 of 84 societies) while valor, wisdom, and, particularly, responsibility (65%, or 40 of 62 societies) dominate the emphases of male initiations. Both sexes share the importance of initiation as a status marker and as recognition of physical change or behavior change (males — 65%; females — 89%). Men's initiations are more likely to be interpreted in terms of spiritual changes or in terms of death and rebirth (29%, or 18 of 63 societies) than are those of girls (5%, or 4 of 84 societies). Once again we see that the group invests much of its creative, symbolic load onto the physical changes that signal the beginning of puberty.

However, the secrecy that characterizes the Arunta male initiation ceremony is not a common component of male or female initiations; only 5% of the male initiation ceremonies and 4% of the female rituals concentrate on learning skills and sharing secrets (Schlegel and Barry 1979: 202). More common is the importance of seclusion and observing taboos (males — 53%; females — 76%); males are more likely than females to have to deal with fear (males — 11%; females — 2%) and absorbing symbolic meanings (males — 32%; females — 18%) (Schlegel and Barry 1979: 202). Overall, the ceremonies seem to prepare men for participation in a wider social matrix than that of the women. The primary social consequences of female initiations are negligible, or else they merely revolve around their relationships to a small group of people, e.g., their families and their mates. In contrast, the main social consequences of male initiations are more likely to include the importance of same-sex bonding (males — 37%; females — 8%) and relationships to a larger group of people.

*Initiations as rites of passage.* Despite differences in participation and in emphasis on social responsibilities, several broad themes in the initiation rituals unite the experiences of men and women. If we shift initiation ceremonies into the framework of rites of passage, we can see more clearly the similarities between the male and female transitions.

"Rite of passage" is a more adequate term than "initiation ceremony" to describe the scope of what occurs; initiations into a new status/role is only one component of the transition. The ceremony is a public expression of a variety of rites that precede it, e.g., seclusion, taboos, ordeals, and instructions. Arnold van Gennep originally defined rites of passage as rites that accompany "every change of place, station, social position and age" (van Gennep 1960). He showed that they generally have three major phases: (1) separation, (2) margin (or "limen" which means "threshold" in Latin), and (3) aggregation. Each phase is one characteristic aspect of a shift from one social state to another. The scheme can apply to a variety of significant events in the life cycle, e.g., birth, marriage, and death. I will concentrate here on its relevance to initiation, the shift from childhood to adulthood.

During the first phase of a rite of passage, separation, the person begins to separate from a previous social state, e.g., childhood. Quite often the separation is spatial, as if to symbolize the distance from the person's former behavior and expectations. For example, the Goajiro segregated the girl in a small room; the Arunta removed the boys to a secluded, secret location. During this time, the initiates no longer engage in the tasks that they usually perform. Shifts in eating patterns and rules that prohibit the ordinary expression of sensations, such as seeing, hearing, and touching, reinforce the withdrawal of the initiates from their past behavior.

The second phase of a rite of passage is the marginal period. The individual has left a past social state but has not yet entered the new one. Initiates are in unknown territory during the marginal period, when their social attributes are ambiguous, and the sociocultural realm in which they must operate has little in common with either the past or the future state that they plan to enter. As Victor Turner puts it:

> . . . liminal [or marginal] entities are neither here nor there; they are betwixt and between the positions assigned and arrayed by law, custom, convention, and ceremonial. As such, their ambiguous and indeterminate attributes are expressed by a rich variety of symbols in the many societies that ritualize social and cultural transitions. Thus, liminality is frequently likened to death, to being in a womb, to invisibility, to darkness, to bisexuality, to the wilderness, and to an eclipse of the sun or moon [Turner 1969: 95].

The initiates pass through a marginal phase, and they share many of the characteristics that apply to the liminal entities that Turner describes. One of the most outstanding attributes of the marginal initiates is that they seem to have nothing. Their mode of dress expresses their lack of definition; they may be naked, wear only a token amount of clothing, or be covered with a robe or disguise. Other initiates are similarly dressed, so that there are no status distinctions between them. The Goajiro girl was wrapped in a robe, and the Arunta male wore only a strip of clothing and similar body paint. The uniformity in appearance parallels the similarity of liminal entities in experiencing the marginal period. They usually remain passive. The Goajiro girl was not allowed to move. The Arunta boys were carried into seclusion and had to obey the instructions of the elder men. Humility, passivity, and submission characterize the behavior of the initiates. They physically, socially, and psychologically strip themselves of their past lives and open themselves up to the new patterns that they will adopt. They allow themselves to be manipulated by their elders, and they accept the teachings, painful operations, and rules without question. The Goajiro girl did not move, scratch herself, eat meat, or have contact with men. Arunta males were tossed in the air, had their nasal septums pierced, were circumcised and subincised, and participated in bloodletting and fire rites. They even submitted to their elders biting on their heads until they bled. What is the point of these boys and girls enduring so much pain and seeming humiliation without complaint?

Turner says that the marginal period gives recognition to an "essential and generic human bond, without which there could be no society" (Turner 1969: 97). The uniformity and humility of the initiates free them from the usual distinctions of status and role that characterize the social group. All social groups have some sort of structure, i.e., patterns of thought and behavior that organize the interaction of people. The people in a marginal period step out of ordinary space and time for a while and can thus experience the common bonds that unite them with other human beings. Turner calls this temporary fellowship of equal individuals "communitas" (Turner 1969: 96). The spatial removal of initiates from their ordinary areas of living, their passive submission to painful procedures, and their uniform appearance emphasize their similarity in having no status. The experience of the marginal period is relatively fleeting, but profound in its social and psychological implications. Each initiate can glimpse into a world that does not exist, a world where individuals meld into a community of pure equality. Initiates are not called upon to participate actively or to contribute to their experiences. The have only to be receptive and suppliant and to acquiesce to pain. All of their other needs will be attended to by others. Turner thinks that the alternation between this ephemeral existence and the society into which the initiates are returned reveals two ways of life that are available to all of us. We can either be caught up into a structured, differentiated existence, or we can experience communitas, the human bonds that unite all of us. When we are in a state of communitas, we are all treated in an equal manner and can begin to truly empathize, or "feel with" others. A recognition of our common vulnerability can serve to strengthen us for life in the "real world" (Turner 1969: 96). We can be better prepared to act according to our limited roles and statuses, aware that other alternatives are possible. In a sense, the marginal period heightens our appreciation of the choices we make when we step into a society; it demonstrates that the group does organize our existence to a certain extent.

Turner's positive view of the marginal stage points out a fundamental contrast in our human existence. We are individuals, and yet we belong to a group. At times, we may alternate between what is best for us and what is best for our group. Rites of passage wrap up the strands of our divergent interests and mold them into an acceptable package. The events in the marginal period disentangle the threads of our individual and social lives for a temporary period. In the marginal phase, the individual becomes submerged and is close to being a totally social entity. In other words, little or nothing can be done to express a person's individuality. Structure is clearly present in this phase of the rite of passage, if only by implication. The initiates are humble and submissive to their elders. They are equal only among themselves. The social contrast between the two groups is stark. They learn the meaning of social differentiation between themselves and others in elementary terms; there are superiors and inferiors. Yet the marginal phase is an individual ordeal, even though an initiate shares it with others. Initiates not only submit to physical pain and deprivation with which they must cope on an individual level, but also tacitly agree to mask their personal coping styles to conform to the rigors of endurance that are suggested by social rules. Turner legitimately points to the formlessness of the marginal state from the point of view of the initiates. However, there is a structure and an adherence to the rules. The marginal period emphasizes social rather than individual concerns. Rites of passage take the individual's forbearance into account in their final phase.

Aggregation is the last phase of a rite of passage. The individual emerges from his or her seclusion into the main social arena. Group members await the introduction of the initiates to their new statuses and roles. The ordeal that the initiates endured receives recognition by the celebration that follows it. Feasting, dancing, and/or group participation mark the passage of initiates to their new state in life. The elaboration of the celebration is proportional to the severity of the ordeal, perhaps in order to impress the social importance of the event upon the individuals. If they have undergone a great amount of pain or deprivation, the final celebration may partially justify their toleration of the ways in which they were treated in the marginal period. The group compensates for the ordeal by providing approval and acceptance of initiates in new, responsible positions in society.

We can easily see that groups have quite an investment in a rite of passage. However, compliance of the individual is not as easy to understand. Why does a person submit to such treatment? I think that the answer lies in the compromise that every human being must make between personal desires and those of the group. We see elements of this interpolation throughout the ritual. The individuals lay themselves bare to the dictates of the group. The marginal period heightens their separation from ordinary social life. Aggregation presents individuals with an acceptable structure for the rest of their lives. They are likely to accept the structure because of the difficulty they have in tolerating ambiguity. As human beings, we find it hard to live in an unorganized way. Our evolutionary heritage has demonstrated the fruits of social organization. Structure enhances our survival and allows us to pursue our individual interests.

The last statement may seem to be paradoxical. How can organization aid individual flexibility? If there are aspects of our lives that we can take for granted, then we do not need to spend a great deal of our energy dwelling upon how to deal with them. Talcott Parsons states the point somewhat differently in his sociological work, *The Social System* (Parsons 1964). He maintains that we all need a stable set of expectations by which to organize our lives; the network of these expectations constitutes the social system. Beyond these expectations lies an unstructured area, which we are at liberty to mold ourselves. In other words, we can express our own personalities in the areas not already organized by our group. The freedom that such organization gives us resembles the process of learning to drive a car. At first we are awkward, thinking about the placement of the controls or the conditions of the road. As we become more used to these components, we drive with more ease and assurance. We no longer need to concentrate the bulk of our attention on the mechanics of driving. We are then free to talk to passengers in the car, respond to unexpected road conditions, and appreciate the scenery along the way. I think that rites of passage are similar in the freedom they give to individuals. Once individuals have accepted a new role and status, they have more leeway to express their own personalities. They have the tools for their future existence. They can mix them in a variety of ways that are characteristic of each of them as individuals.

My interpretation implies that there is a great deal of continuity between the social, cultural, and psychological aspects of our lives. I began with Parson's assumption that we all live according to shared expectations; I consider them cultural if they are primarily shared beliefs and define them as social if they are mainly behavioral in nature. Psychological traits or a personality are not necessarily shared with a group of individuals. Personality includes a set of personal and social expectations about an individual. Like cultural and social traits, psychological traits are usually consistent over time. Personality applies to one individual, whereas social and cultural traits apply to several individuals. The difference is quantitative rather than qualitative. Initiation ceremonies highlight this dimension. Expressions of personality can occur during the separation and aggregation phases of the ritual. However, they are held in suspension as the initiate passes through the marginal period. During this temporary period, the individual has no personality; this is the essence of the formlessness about which Turner speaks. The initiate has status, but it is uniformly inferior. The extreme emphasis on submission to social dictates and suppression of individual expression serves a dual purpose. It clearly focuses the initiate on the social component of life and frames the scope of individual variation. It gives the individual guidelines to psychologically and socially navigate in the world. It can also give the individual a sense of power.

Mary Douglas speculates that marginal periods are threatening to others, because the seeming lack of structure means that others do not know what to expect from liminal entities (Douglas 1966). Consequently, individuals structure these periods, or the social groups try to eliminate them as much as possible. When marginal periods do occur, they are held under extremely controlled conditions; to do otherwise would invite chaos and threaten the basis of social existence. Tight controls are precisely the conditions under which initiation ceremonies are conducted. Even though the initiates undergo a period free from usual social restraints, their lives are very closely controlled and supervised by others. The consequence is a paradoxical juxtaposition of freedom and extreme social pressure.

How can initiation result in greater possibilities for individual variation if constraints on behavior are so extreme? The marginal period exposes the individual to a state that is simultaneously structured and unstructured. The group structures it, in the sense that it establishes definite statuses and roles for the participants, i.e., inferior and superior. However, formlessness prevails within the inferior category. As individuals in the inferior category, initiates are required to behave according to the rules of their superiors. Otherwise, their thoughts are free to roam in limitless directions. They can also passively receive the sensations directed toward them. The activity that characterizes individual personality disappears; the individual has minimal impact or control over the marginal environment. Yet the withdrawal of initiates from their usual social setting gives them the potential power to see the possibilities they have for action when they leave the marginal state.

Without a definite structure, the individual can imagine a large range of variations in behavior for future action. In terms of psychodynamics, the person in a marginal state experiences something similar to an altered state of consciousness.

Price-Williams comments on some of the characteristics of altered states of consciousness in his book *Explorations in Cross-Cultural Psychology* (Price-Williams 1975). First, these "unusual" states of consciousness generally develop after a period of discipline, training, and initiation. Through such practices as meditation, intense concentration, and other forms of self-discipline, a person can transcend ordinary categories of thought. Individuals can begin to perceive their world transformed beyond the boundaries imposed by a specific culture and society. Second, altered states of consciousness often occur when the person is in a state of passivity. Some techniques of meditation stress that a passive attitude is one of the most crucial factors in eliciting relaxation (Benson 1976: 78). A person tries to empty the mind of any distractions that could hinder the attainment of a peaceful, relaxed state. One technique used to accomplish this is to concentrate upon an object, feeling, or word. Once again, we see the importance of discipline in attaining a release from structure. Such modes of thinking may be difficult for us to comprehend, because we are so used to perceiving our world according to fixed categories. The very term, "altered state of consciousness," suggests that there is a sense of unreality about such a state; it is not ordinary. What is normal has been transformed into an aberrant state. Castaneda expresses the frustration of trying to cross the bridge into another way of thinking about the world. He sought to know the world as his Mexican Yaqui mentor, Don Juan, saw it. He wanted to "see," a special way of sensing and perceiving the world. Time and time again he would say that he did not understand what Don Juan was trying to tell him. Don Juan would attempt to clarify the lack of understanding with his reply:

> Your problem is that you confuse the world with what people do. Again you're not unique at that. Every one of us does that. The things people do are the shields against the forces that surround us; what we do as people gives us comfort and makes us feel safe; what people do is rightfully very important, but only as a shield. We never learn that the things we do as people are only shields and we let them dominate and topple our lives [Castaneda 1971: 264]

One interpretation of Don Juan's statement is that the world is mysterious and not subject to order, except by people's behavior. To think that the world really is the way we have ordered it to be by our actions is folly; it prevents us from uncovering the complexity of what surrounds us. A life conducted according to social organization is limited by the boundaries of its rules of organization. We can know more about the world by going beyond those artificial limits. "Seeing" is a way of transcending boundaries; it is a perceptual shift, by means of which we open ourselves up to the untapped and uncategorized dimensions of our lives.

The fear associated with entering unknown regions of the mind and opening up ourselves to new experiences may account for the stringent rules that apply to new initiates. Entering a new realm of thinking may be fascinating and may induce feelings of power, but it may also be frightening. Some people are intolerant of ambiguity in their lives. The less structured or familiar a situation or set of categories, the more uncomfortable they feel. They may then rely on familiar categories to classify what they perceive. Gombrich's description of the first sketches of whales shows how this process applies to artists' representations of what they see. The strange-looking new animal was portrayed in familiar terms. The gigantic side flippers were sketched far above their actual position on the whale and represented as ears on the whale's head. This is only one example of many which Gombrich presents in *Art and Illusion* (1960), a book which illustrates how social categories influence visual perception and representational art.

The rules and structure imposed on the initiates by their elders during the marginal period may aid them in feeling more secure about the unfamiliarity of their isolation and passivity; they anchor the initiates to some sort of reality, even though they are drifting into unknown experiences. Consequently, the initiates can develop some temporary categories for interpreting their own behavior and that of others.

Another characteristic of the marginal period, which aids the individuals as well as the group, is the cognitive reorganization that occurs. During initiation rites, initiates may transform their cognition—i.e., how they process information—to a mode that seems to be appropriate for the smooth functioning of their social group. By so doing, they also prepare themselves more adequately for performing the requirements of their new status and role.

How does this cognitive reorganization occur? I think it is similar to what happens to a people during successful therapy. They separate themselves from the usual ways in which they have perceived and thought about their experiences; they may also separate themselves from their past behavior. By loosening themselves from the limitations of their previous patterns of thought and behavior, they open themselves to alternative ways of acting and viewing the world. Therapists guide clients into a new world by connecting the familiar with the unfamiliar. Techniques vary, according to the type of therapy. For example, present events may be connected with those of early childhood to provide a framework for explaining the form of present behavior; it becomes a clue to change. Forgotten aspects of clients' lives are brought to awareness and become the familiar material out of which they begin to make sense of their specific present problems. Therapists gradually guide clients into ways in which they can reorganize their lives; they may do this directly or allow the clients to discover the new patterns.

Although much therapy in our society is conducted on an individual basis, group therapy can also be an effective basis for cognitive reorganization. The development of support groups for such specific problems as alcoholism, physical abuse, and obesity is testimony to the effectiveness of change via a group. As in initiation ceremonies, the individuals try to effect a shift from one state to another, e.g., from drinking to nondrinking, violence to coping with problems, obesity to slimness. They derive support from those who have a similar problem and map out ways to confront their dilemma. The process is like that of initiation; they undergo separation from their usual ways of behaving, submit themselves to extreme discipline, and obey the dictates of those who have already experienced the process. Successful transit through the difficult period of discipline opens up a new world to the individuals. By attaining their goals, they have not only social approval but also a sense of well-being about themselves; they achieve more choice in their lives.

Bruce Kapferer documents a similar process of cognitive reorganization in ritualistic cures of demonic illness (Kapferer 1979: 110). He shows how the individual social self is negated and reconstructed in such a way that the patient is transformed from a state of illness to one of health. When afflicted by a demonic illness, a person is taken over by external force; the "self" dissolves. The negation of self is manifested by withdrawal from daily interaction, entrance into a trance, and participation in other dissociative acts (Kapferer 1979: 117). When the patient undergoes treatment, the rites represent the negation of the patient's self, but provide a basis for reconstructing it in a socially acceptable manner. The individual links up with the social group by participation in a ritual.

The curing ritual does not mean merely that the individual has passed from illness to health; it transforms the self to the individual. Therefore, curing rituals have much in common with other rites of passage, including initiation ceremonies. Although the occasions differ, cognitive reorganisation typifies much of the psychological impact of these diverse kinds of rites of passage. As Kapferer puts it:

Rites of passage do not simply mark the transition of participants from one status to another but actively transform one status into another. In many cases they are occasions for the presentation of socially defined and culturally accepted dimensions of Self . . . the ritual organization of symbolic action and content in performance reveals a process whereby the Self is constructed and reconstructed [Kapferer 1979: 130].

The psychological and social value of the marginal state partly derives from its contrast to the last phase of the rite of passage, the period of aggregation. The initiates enter the "real" world again and are subject to the social rules, cultural beliefs, and expectations of others. They enter a status, or position, in the social organization and behave as members of the group. They leave the rigidly controlled, passive state of marginality and enter a world in which they are expected to conform to the standards that others have for them. Marginality has prepared them for the psychological and social dimensions of their new role. They can attain a better balance between their individuality and the demands of their society. Their personalities emerge in their new forms; individuals have the flexibility to make choices for themselves, and they can appreciate their freedom to do so. The social constraints to which they are subject do not have the severity or force that the rigid controls of the marginal period had. The group expresses its confidence that individuals will abide by the rules of their new status by celebrating their completion of the marginal period. Aggregation constitutes the most elaborate social display in a rite of passage. It is a period of intense social interaction. Large numbers of people usually participate in the rich abundance of feasts, elaborate dancing, opulent clothing, and ingestion of alcohol or other drugs. The initiates have come home from their journey into communitas and the recesses of their own minds. They are transformed, and the celebration amply marks the transition. Their social acceptance may partially compensate for the ordeal they have endured.

*The symbolic load of initiation ceremonies.* Bruno Bettelheim (1968) probes more deeply into the psychological significance of the symbols that are characteristic of initiation rituals. He contrasts his view of initiation ceremonies with Freud's interpretation of them. Freud viewed the components of initiation ceremonies in the context of his theory of psychosexual development. According to Freud, initiation rites were one way to deal with the Oedipus complex. At the very least, a boy feels affection for his mother and competition with his father for her attention. The rivalry could pose a real threat to the father when the boy approaches puberty; he is capable of acting more effectively on his sexual desires and aggressive feelings. Freud reasoned that the custom of circumcision developed as an expression of the father's authority over his son and as a warning to the maturing boy not to act upon his sexuality with his mother. Freud thought that sons generally experience castration anxiety, because they fear the consequences of feeling hostility toward their fathers. The rite of circumcision in an initiation ceremony reinforces the boy's castration anxiety. As one of the elder males with authority over the young initiates, the father implies that he could castrate his son if he does not obey him. Consequently, circumcision becomes a daily reminder of the consequences of not following the social rules advocated by older males; it is a symbolic substitute for castration. In terms of the relationship between father and son, the most important rule that the son should follow is the incest taboo; the father retains his rights of sexual access to related females and maintains his authority over his related, younger males. Initiation rites become a way to maintain the force of the incest taboo.

Like Freud, Bettelheim sees initiation ceremonies in a larger psychological context. However, Bettelheim's context is quite different from the hostile, competitive milieu that Freud pictures. Bettelheim thinks that it is just as plausible to depict initiation ceremonies as a means of dealing with positive, creative forces in our lives. Fertility, children, and an emotional understanding of the opposite sex emerge as constant themes in boys' rites. Much of what occurs in the rites is an outgrowth of the child's awareness of the physical differences between males and females at puberty. As a girl's body develops, her growth sequence is punctuated by menstruation and breast development. However, male physical development emerges gradually and less dramatically. In addition, the reproductive significance of the male's development is not as clear as that of the female. Menstrual blood is connected with the creation of life; its cessation means that a woman is pregnant. The monthly flow of blood is a periodic reminder of the woman's creative power over life. Therefore, genital bleeding may come to signify creative potential.

Bettelheim suggests that male initiations serve to punctuate an inherently unpunctuated growth sequence in men. More importantly, they help males to cope with their envy of the reproductive capacity of a woman's body. Children gestate in a woman's body, not in a man's. Women give birth; men do not. Initiation can help males deal with these facts by stressing their own creative potential. Painful operations on the penis may be a way of symbolically acquiring some of the envied functions of the woman. Subincision aptly illustrates this point. When a boy is fully subincised, as an Arunta boy is, his penis is slit to the urethra, about one inch into the tissue. The opening resembles the vaginal opening, and the blood shed from the wound resembles the menstrual flow. Bettelheim thinks that the operation mimics the menstrual periods of women. It helps the male to feel that he, too, has some creative force in his genital bleeding. It also results in lessening an important, intimate difference between males and females. When men urinate, they usually stand up and direct the flow of urine away from themselves. When women urinate, they squat or sit. Subincision interferes with the flow of urine to such an extent that subincised men urinate in a squatting position as women do. Although subincision is relatively rare, it remains a dramatic illustration of the rich symbolic possibilities of initiation rites.

Bettelheim's interpretation may help to explain Schlegel and Barry's finding (1979) that painful rites occur more frequently in male than in female initiations. The physical modification may serve to mark socially the reproductive potential of the boy in a way that biology has neglected to do. The pain may imitate the pain that a woman feels when she gives birth to a child. The isolation of the marginal period in initiation rites resembles the seclusion of a woman at childbirth. Once again, Bettelheim's idea is that the rite attempts to duplicate aspects of the female role. Sometimes the identification with the female role takes the form of transvestism in initiation ceremonies; men put on women's clothes. It seems to Bettelheim that the rites express men's desire to have a more significant share in the creative process of producing children. Initiation ceremonies might be viewed as one form of fertility rite — for men.

The imitation of the female role in the male rites may also serve to delineate the distinction between males and females more clearly. "The efforts that . . . men and women make in most of the puberty rites . . . are aimed at an actual or symbolic understanding of the functions of the other sex and a psychological mastery of the emotions they arouse" (Bettelheim 1968: 147). For example, men may mimic menstruation by submitting themselves to painful operations that result in profuse bleeding from their genitals. By undergoing this rite, they may develop a more refined sense of the female experience of menstruation. Identification with the process not only allows them to sympathize with the female position; it also permits them to contrast more precisely their own lives as men with those of women. Therefore, it enhances cognitive and emotional understanding of the distinctive roles of males and females. In other words, it fosters an appreciation of sexual differentiation.

Bettelheim mentions another aspect of initiation ceremonies that is often overlooked. He explores the nature of the ceremony from the perspective of the initiators as well as from the initiates' viewpoint. How significant is their role in the rites? Freud responded to the question by interpreting the rites as a defense against incest. The father participates in the ritual to wield his authority over his maturing son and to remind him not to have sexual relations with his mother. Bettelheim sees the role of the initiators in more general terms. The ceremony helps elders deal with their ambivalence about the young. On the one hand, they may be pleased by the results of their child training and somewhat relieved that their children are not able to accept more social responsibility. On the other hand, they may envy the vitality of the youths' budding sexuality. The contrast between the old and the young reminds the older men that they are not as young as they used to be, either physically or socially. An underlying threat to their own sexual prowess and maintenance of power may account for the clearly superior position that they hold within the ceremony; it helps them to feel that they are still important. The ceremony allows them to adjust their feelings and roles to the emergence of a new group of men. It provides for an orderly social transition and emotional acceptance of the situation.

Bettelheim's hypotheses are provocative. They stimulate speculation about the symbolic load of the specific ritual elements in initiation ceremonies. They add depth to the comments I have made about the possible significance of the marginal period as a time for cognitive reorganization. It is not surprising that Schlegel and Barry find that learning skills and sharing secrets do not play a large role in initiations (males — 5%; females — 4%) (Schlegel and Barry 1979: 202). Knowledge is imparted through symbolic communication, not by teaching techniques. Transmission of tribal lore may provide a focus for other elements of the ceremony, but it is not the crux of the matter.

I think that the oscillation between contrasting emotional, cognitive, and social states gives initiation ceremonies much of their impact. Their power derives from the layers of meaning draped over the rites. Bettelheim suggests that initiation ceremonies are best seen as a type of fertility ceremony, wherein men cope with their sexual and reproductive roles. They express their desire to bear children themselves and acknowledge that they can contribute to the creative process in a different way. They come to terms with their role as impregnators rather than childbearers.

While Bettelheim poses his hypotheses as alternatives to Freud's, we do not have to accept an unidimensional interpretation. Symbolism allows for ambivalence, contrast, and synthesis of opposing elements. We can just as legitimately maintain aspects of both. Lévi-Strauss tries to demonstrate that the analysis of symbolic communication can proceed by the examination of pairs of binary oppositions, i.e., contrasts between two elements (Lévi-Strauss 1963). This approach gives us a basis for comparing symbolism in different societies, because it reflects a basic human thought process; our minds sift through information like a computer, sorting it out into successive pairs. The content may vary, but the basic pattern of operation is the same.

Lévi-Strauss' view of symbolism helps to clarify what seem to be competing elements in Bettelheim's and Freud's portrayals of initiation ceremonies. Freud stressed competition and possible death to others, but Bettelheim concentrates on positive, creative powers. I think that we can see both in the ceremonies. Their juxtaposition impresses the significance of each on the initiates. For example, the Arunta elders are in a position of clear superiority over the initiates; they subject them to painful ordeals, which highlight their submission. Here we can see the contrast between youth and age, inferior and superior, formlessness of the initiates and strict control of the elders, passivity and activity, the individual and social concerns, and emerging sexuality and waning sexuality. The painful ordeals ingrain the importance of the rites on the initiates. Since the rites entail such individual subjugation, they *must* be important. If the initiates believed that the rites were insignificant, they would probably feel psychological discomfort and unrelieved tension. There would be too great a disparity between the behavior they permit and the reasons they have for submitting to it.

The force of the initiates' beliefs derives from a process similar to one that Festinger, Riecken, and Schachter describe in *When Prophecy Fails* (1964). A group of people banded together around the belief that the world would be destroyed at a particular date and time. They created a great deal of social attention for themselves and proselytyzed to gain more followers. The book deals with the psychological readjustment of the believers when their prophecy fails. They experienced dissonance, i.e., tension produced by a disparity between beliefs and behavior. They coped with their disappointment by holding onto their beliefs more fervently; they rationalized the apparent failure of their convictions. Similarly, it is more comfortable for initiates to believe that the pain they experience during initiation rites has great rather than little significance. Pain becomes a socially effective mechanism for communication of important matters in life. It contrasts with the social acceptance and nurturance that follow it in the rites. It accents the shift from childhood to another, more socially responsible, state.

Other contrasts are implied in the symbolism that Bettelheim analyzes. Blood often plays a role in the rites. He links blood to the creative
power symbolized by the menstrual flow; its absence means pregnancy,
the creation of a new life. However, there are some disturbing aspects
about the presence of blood, which he does not discuss. Wounds, death,
and lack of control are a few of the associations we can make. Like
many other elements in the ritual, the meaning of blood is ambiguous.
Its significance may vary according to the context.

Ernestine Friedl (1975) views menstrual blood in a more negative
light than Bettelheim does. When a woman is not menstruating, she
cannot conceive. When she is menstruating, it means that she has not
conceived; it is the "antithesis of life" (Friedl 1975: 29). In this context,
blood may mean death. It retains its ambiguous quality, because it is
not like blood that flows from a wound; the uncontrolled bleeding at
menstruation is not the result of an injury and does not bring about the
woman's death. Menstrual blood provides a marked contrast to the type
of blood with which men are familiar, that associated with killing and
death. Friedl suggests that the different meanings attached to men's
blood and women's blood may account for the separation of men from
women during menstrual periods. Women's blood has an ambiguous
life and death quality; whereas men's blood is allied with death. The
separation of the types of blood restates the difference between the
sexes. Like other symbolic elements I have discussed, blood plays a role
in emphasizing sexual differentiation.

Blood is often shed during initiation rites. In addition, one of the
frequently used colors in the rituals is red. The full power of the ambiguity between men's and women's blood is brought into play. The categories of man and woman are not fully distinguished, but are allowed to
merge in the marginal period. As I have said earlier, initiates are able to
experience some lack of structure under the controlled conditions of the
marginal period. They can simultaneously experience the positive and
negative connotations of red blood.

Turner extends the significance of blood and the color red from the
context of initiations to a more universal plane (Turner 1967: 88). He
thinks that they are linked to a universal human organic experience
(Turner 1967: 89). They simultaneously express physical experiences
and social relationships. The red colors used in initiations may become
associated with a woman's blood, the mother/child bond, and group
formation. They could mean blood associated with injuries inflicted in
war, conflict, and other socially disruptive encounters. They might be
related to the animal blood associated with hunting, food preparation,
and other aspects of the male division of labor. They might mean the

blood that ties people together in terms of group formation. Regardless of the specific meaning of the color, Turner's point is that red can have more than one association at a number of levels. Multiple meanings are the symbolic elaboration of the biological baseline, blood. They help the individual to divide up reality into elements that are meaningfully connected with his life.

Turner suggests that the human organism and its experiences are the foundation of all classifications. A symbol captures the biological importance of an element in its sensory pole and the cognitive components in its ideational pole. Turner's interpretation of symbols is especially appropriate for understanding initiation ceremonies. The symbolic load of the experience reminds the growing child of the importance of personal, physical changes in the context of sexual differentiation. Money and Ehrhardt (1977) conclude that sex roles are less important to the formation of gender identity than the child's knowledge that sex differences are basically defined by the genitals and their reproductive capacity. Bettelheim stresses the role that initiation plays in helping the child to cope with issues of fertility and reproduction. We can conclude that initiation ceremonies involve larger issues than just the transition from childhood to adolescence or adulthood. They link up the strands of a child's future existence: by providing (1) a social interpretation of personal physical characteristics, (2) a rationale for the shifts in social relationships after childhood, and (3) a definition of reality in some basic terms, which relate to sexual differentiation, authority, and the forces of creativity and death.

*Variations in the occurrence of initiation ceremonies: a psychological view.* Symbolic interpretations of initiation ceremonies are very intriguing and point to their psychological and social power. However, they do not explain variations in the occurrence of initiation ceremonies. Such ceremonies do not occur in all societies, nor are they always conducted for men and women in the same societies. How can we account for the presence of initiation ceremonies in some societies but not in others?

John Whiting and his associates broach this more difficult task with their hypotheses about male initiation ceremonies (Whiting, Kluckhohn, and Anthony 1958). Like both Freud and Bettelheim, Whiting, Kluckhohn, and Anthony assume that initiation ceremonies relate to the psychological adjustment of individuals to sex roles. However, they limit their interest to the conditions that give rise to psychological problems of identity formation. They hypothesize that the impetus for initiation ceremonies comes with difficulties encountered in establishing ap-

propriate cross-sex relationships and sexual identity. Initiation
ceremonies clarify the roles that males play and reinforce their identity
as males.

The conditions that give rise to male initiation ceremonies revolve
around a tendency for the male child to identify too strongly with his
mother. Whiting, Kluckhohn, and Anthony test their hypothesis by
looking at the association between exclusive mother/son sleeping arrangements, patrilocality, and the presence of initiation ceremonies.
They reason that if a boy sleeps in the same dwelling with his mother
over a period of years, the living arrangement will foster a strong identification between the boy and his mother. Such an identification could
be particularly problematical in a society with patrilocal residence, i.e.,
where a married couple resides with or near the male relatives of the
husband. The residential association of males indicates that it is socially
important that men associate with each other. An identification with
women could pose problems on an individual as well as a group level. If
a male identifies with his mother and, by implication, with a feminine
orientation, it would be difficult for him to cement his masculine identity and function in a social setting that emphasizes the interaction of
males. Consequently, males go through initiation ceremonies to aid
them in separating from their mothers and forging a masculine orientation. The evidence that Whiting, Kluckhohn, and Anthony present
seems to support their hypothesis. Patrilocality, exclusive mother/child
sleeping arrangements, and initiation ceremonies are strongly associated with each other. Nevertheless, the strength of the association does
not mean that the assumptions on which it is based are valid. We can
only infer this.

*Variations in the occurrence of initiation ceremonies:   a social view.*
Frank Young (1965) issues a warning about accepting the validity of the
assumptions that underlie statistical associations. He thinks that a number of elaborate assumptions underlie Whiting, Kluckhohn, and Anthony's interpretation of initiation ceremonies. Their orientation is primarily psychogenic, i.e., they suggest that initiations arise in response
to underlying psychological processes. Their assumptions are necessary
to maintain their perspective. First, they assume that personality trends
begin in childhood and continue over the years before they have a
critical impact on the development of social institutions. Second, they
assume that the operation of psychological factors unfolds at an unconscious level; that the social outcome of psychological processes does not
occur as a result of rational, conscious deliberation between people.
Third, they assume that people are capable of complex mental proc-

esses, including subtle attention to conflict. Last, they assume that the unconscious dynamics of individuals can influence the character of social institutions, e.g., initiation rites (Young 1965: 36).

Young contends that a more sociogenically-oriented explanation can account for the same set of associations that Whiting, Kluckhohn, and Anthony present. He tries to persuade us that it makes more sense to adopt a sociogenic perspective, because we do not have to make so many assumptions about the operation of unconscious processes. In other words, it is simpler to give primary importance to the operation of social factors, rather than be weighed down by assumptions that are difficult to demonstrate, except by inference. Like Whiting, Kluckhohn, and Anthony, Young attempts to explain why initiation ceremonies occur in some societies but not in others. He links their presence to requirements for social solidarity.

Young defines "social solidarity" as cooperation of individuals in expressing a specific definition of a situation; there is a concensus that communicates a particular way to act (Young 1965: 63). Dramatization of classifications, such as age and sex, will occur in proportion to the requirements for solidarity in the society. In other words, initiation ceremonies can be viewed as a way for the group to maintain the integration of its various units (Young 1965: 24). The most important determinant of dramatization at puberty is the extent to which men's firm beliefs can articulate with each other into a coherent whole (Young 1965: 27). The more intense the focus is on adult solidarity, the more likely it is that highly dramatized initiation ceremonies will occur. The ceremony reinforces a boy's confidence in himself to perform the male role within his social setting (Young 1965: 31).

Young pits his sociogenic, solidarity explanation against the psychogenic, sex role conflict view of Whiting, Kluckhohn, and Anthony. He examines the presence of male sex role dramatization at puberty, i.e., initiation ceremonies, under a variety of conditions. Each set of conditions can be regarded as a test of the advantages of each type of explanation. The variables for which he tests are exclusive sleeping arrangements and patrilocal residence in relation to initiations; he looks at these both when male solidarity is present and when it is absent (Young 1965: 78). He predicts that the sociogenic explanation is more valid if initiation ceremonies occur more regularly when conditions of solidarity are present than when both patrilocal residence and exclusive mother/child sleeping arrangements are present. His data seem to confirm his view. He finds that in the crucial test, he can account for the presence of initiations, but Whiting, Kluckhohn, and Anthony cannot. There are three societies wherein male solidarity is present, but exclusive sleeping arrangements and patrilocality are both absent. In other words, the conditions that Whiting and his associates would say produce initiation ceremonies are not present. In two of these three societies, initiation ceremonies are conducted. In the reverse case, where male solidarity is absent and exclusive mother/child sleeping arrangements and patrilocality are present, dramatization is more likely to be absent. Young concludes that these bits of information are crucial tests which show the validity of his view.

However, as Young admits himself, the number of cases from which he draws his conclusion is small. He operates more on the basis of the logic of his conclusions than on their statistical significance. If we analyze statistically the data that Young uses to confirm his point of view, we derive a different picture of his crucial tests. If we compare the conditions of solidarity present without the variables used by Whiting, Kluckhohn, and Anthony, and solidarity absent with their variables present in relation to dramatization, we do see a trend in the direction that Young would predict. However, we have to be careful in drawing conclusions from such small samples. Fisher's exact test was devised to deal with such conditions. When we apply this test to the array of Young's data, we find that the variation Young presents could have occurred by chance (Fisher's exact test = .45). A statistical test of Young's crucial comparisons does not provide the strong confirmation of the view that Young favors.

This does not mean that Young's hypotheses should be discarded. He does present other data that show a strong correlation between male solidarity and status dramatization. It is possible that he might find stronger confirmation of his sociogenic view if he had more data. His basic hypothesis seems to hold, i.e., that the more important male solidarity is to the maintenance of the group, the more status dramatization there will be. All that Fisher's exact test shows is that Young cannot eliminate the psychogenic interpretation of the data.

Young's analysis has appeal not only because he attempts to provide a parsimonious explanation for male initiation ceremonies but also because he can offer a perspective on the presence or absence of female initiation ceremonies. He describes the more limited focus of female initiations. The domestic unit, rather than the community, is likely to be the primary, significant context to which the ceremonies relate. Community-based organizations for women or exlusively female activities are rare; a woman's sphere is domestic, whereas, a man's is public. Although the extent of the social context of men and women varies, the definition of solidarity does not. Solidarity refers to cooperation in maintaining a specific definition of a situation; in the case of women, the "situation" refers to the "institutionalized household" (Young 1965: 106). Young hypothesizes that female initiations facilitate learning of the female role; the greater the emphasis on the solidarity of the household, the more likely it is that initiation ceremonies will be elaborate. Young thinks that female initiations are less likely to reach the elaborate scale of male initiations, because the social context to which they apply is smaller. Schlegel and Barry's more recent study (1979) upholds this idea. This is an important observation. Otherwise, some might conclude that female ceremonies are less significant than male ceremonies because of their scale. On the contrary, the scope of the ceremonies is different because they apply to differing spheres of interaction.

Judith Brown (1963) explores the dimensions of female initiations along social lines similar to Young's. She probes beyond solidarity into some alternative reasons for why the domestic group conducts the ceremonies. One possibility is that residence is uxorilocal, i.e., the woman and her husband reside with or near her relatives after marriage. The purpose of the ceremony would thus be to impress upon the parents and other relatives, as well as on the girl, that the girl's status has changed. Otherwise, there might be little alteration in the way that household members interact with each other. The daughter might behave as a child or be expected to behave as a child for the rest of her life. The ceremony effects a transformation in expectations and attempts to change the psychological orientation of the girl and her relatives.

Another social reason that Brown suggests as an explanation for the occurrence of initiation ceremonies for girls is that they celebrate the contribution women make to subsistence. When women make a substantial contribution to subsistence, initiation rituals highlight their importance as females; the ceremonies provide social encouragement to perform the female role.

Schlegel and Barry (1980) suggest an even more extensive social view of initiation ceremonies than those suggested by the previous investigators. They attempt to explain variations in the presence of initiation ceremonies, their distribution by sex, and the features of which they are composed. They are not interested in the ceremonies as rites of passage, in the significance of their ritual symbolism, in their psychological impact on the initiates, or in the role that they play in expressing social organization and its conflicts. They concentrate on making inferences about "the generalized function and meaning of adolescent initiation ceremonies . . . the broader significance they have for societies at certain levels of development or with particular organizational patterns" (Schlegel and Barry 1980: 697). Therefore, their study focuses on relating initiation ceremonies to the complexity of social organization.

Their cross-cultural study of 186 societies reveals that the distribution of initiation ceremonies is not random. Food-collecting societies give prominence to female initiation ceremonies; first menstruation is usually the physiological event that triggers their occurrence. Since females are in short supply in small, foraging bands, the ceremonies highlight the women's productive and reproductive value as scarce resources (Schlegel and Barry 1980: 711). Middle-range societies are more likely to have initiation ceremonies for both sexes; they usually last longer and have more participants and initiates. These societies have incipient or extensive agriculture, but no compact or complex settlements; their jurisdiction does not extend more than two levels beyond the local community. Same-sex bonding seems to be more important in these groups than in foraging societies. Gender emerges as a major principle of social organization. Therefore, sexual differentiation is particularly important, and separation of the sexes is marked. Initiation ceremonies serve to formalize same-sex bonding (Schlegel and Barry 1980: 712). Complex societies are characterized by intensive agriculture, efficient food production, and a relatively elaborate social life; they are not likely to have initiation ceremonies for either sex. Gender recedes in importance as a significant category for social placement. Specialized economic and political interests are more likely to receive social attention. Life cycle transitions are relegated to specific contexts.

In sum, Schlegel and Barry conclude that there is an evolutionary trend in the occurrence of initiation ceremonies. They explain the differential distribution of the rituals in terms of the importance of gender as a principle of social placement. Initiation ceremonies are more likely to "incorporate young people into sexually defined categories" in simple and middle-range societies. They recede in importance in complex societies, as gender diminishes as a general principle for social organization.

Schlegel and Barry's extensive study supports the findings of some of the other studies I have reviewed. It confirms Brown's hypotheses that female initiation ceremonies are more likely to occur (1) in societies with uxorilocal residence, and (2) in societies where females make a high contribution to subsistence. Schlegel and Barry add that a high contribution of females to subsistence predicts the presence of initiation ceremonies for either sex. Their findings also give support to Whiting, Kluckhohn, and Anthony's hypothesis that male initiation ceremonies occur more often with patrilocal residence and exclusive mother/child sleeping arrangements. However, the findings shift the emphasis to a sociological one; initiation ceremonies could mark the extrusion of boys from the household and prepare them for peer-group activities. This socially-oriented explanation is consistent with Young's hypothesis about the role of initiations in fostering male solidarity.

It is clear that explaining the specific elements of initiation ceremonies, as well as their differential occurrence for males and females, is a complex task. Each perspective adds a piece to the puzzle and helps to clarify its dimensions. Schlegel and Barry contribute a broad evolutionary perspective, within which we can incorporate previous findings. Yehudi Cohen adds an interdisciplinary orientation, which taps other elements that Schlegel and Barry chose not to examine.

*Variations in the occurrence of initiation ceremonies: an interdisciplinary view.* The psychologically-oriented explanations for initiation ceremonies center on the resolution of psychological conflict related to sexual identity. The social explanations focus on the establishment of sex roles and the contribution that initiations make to the maintenance of the social order. Analyses of the ritual elements of initiations and views of them in the context of rites of passage provide further specification of these themes. Yehudi Cohen (1964) offers an elegant synthesis of three major perspectives associated with initiation ceremonies: biological, social, and psychological. He combines many of the questions raised by the studies I have considered thus far. Why do the ceremonies occur in some societies and not in others? What role do they play in the life of the individual, and what function do they serve for the society? Why do the ceremonies occur when they do?

Cohen asserts that puberty is a golden opportunity for society to make its mark on the individual. During the first phase of puberty, i.e., between the ages of eight and ten the body undergoes rapid biochemical and hormonal changes. The young boy may feel vulnerable as he begins to experience these physical adjustments. Usually he cannot observe a difference in himself from previous years. His external appearance has not changed much, but he is aware of a shift in his experiences and feelings. During the second state of puberty, he can observe the appearance of secondary sexual characteristics, such as hair growth, voice change, and muscular development. Cohen thinks that the social group can best mold the young boy in the first stage of puberty. During this period, he is confused about what is happening to him, and he needs some definition of his feelings. The social group can supply a socially advantageous interpretation and relieve the psychological tension that the boy experiences. After secondary sexual characteristics appear, the group can make less of an impact; the physical changes provide a ready-made explanation of the anxiety experienced in the first stage. It would seem that social intervention is so advantageous for the growing boy and the group that we would find it in most societies. However, this is not the case. Why? Why do some societies have initiation ceremonies for boys and others dispense with them during this time of psychological vulnerability? What are some alternative ways of dealing with the psychological and physical changes at puberty?

Cohen fuses the answers to these questions in his hypotheses about the role of social groups in the formation of the individual's identity. As I discussed in connection with incest taboos, Cohen thinks that the most important social group relevant to identity formation is the boundary-maintaining group. A boundary limits or demarcates a unit from other units. Boundaries provide a framework for individual action. Cohen likens a boundary system to a balloon; it frames the air it contains and delimits it from the surrounding air. In addition, it is subject to internal and external pressures; it can be very fragile. So, too, are individuals subject to pressures from within themselves, from their group, and from "outsiders."

Families and kinship groups are examples of boundary-maintaining systems, which provide emotional anchorage for children as they grow up. Emotional identification is "indissolubly related to a sense of responsibility" (Cohen 1964: 19). Responsibility can apply to a limited group of people, or it can extend to a wider network. Agents of socialization will reflect an appropriate amount of responsibility in their child-rearing techniques. Cohen divides responsibility into two types, social independence and social interdependence (Cohen 1964: 23). Training for social independence means that the child's sense of responsibility is limited to the nuclear family. Emphasis on social interdependence means that the child's sense of responsibility applies to the nuclear family as well as to a wider community of kinsmen, e.g., a descent group; the boundaries may stretch to a local group or beyond. Socializers will aid in fostering one of these types of responsibility. When children are being trained for social independence, their socializers will be compatible with that goal; their parents and nonmembers of their kinship group will train them. When they reach puberty, their children are likely to remain with their nuclear families. On the other hand, parents and kin group members will train the children for social interdependence. When children reach puberty, they extend their social network by separating from the strong ties of their nuclear families. They can emotionally withdraw from members of their nuclear families by avoiding them; brother/sister avoidance is the most common expression of this withdrawal. More commonly, boys shift their residence and no longer live in the same household as their parents; Cohen calls this "extrusion." The boys physically remove themselves from intense social interaction with their nuclear families.

The events in the first stage of puberty provide the setting for the activities in the second stage. Initiation ceremonies are most likely to occur in societies where children are trained for social interdependence. They separate the children even further from their nuclear families and foster more identification with the wider social group. Cohen finds that the presence of initiation ceremonies is significantly associated with socialization by parents and members of a child's descent group ($X^2$ = 26.44, p = < .001) as well as with the presence of unilineal descent groups ($X^2$ = 8.47, p = < .01) (Cohen 1964: 114). In other words, the wider the group to which the children are responsible, the more likely it is that they will participate in an initiation ceremony. Cohen notes that emotional identification with an extended social group is only part of an explanation for variations in the presence of initiation ceremonies. Nevertheless, he does account for their presence in a large number of societies.

Cohen's findings are compatible with more socially oriented explanations of the presence of initiation ceremonies. Young emphasized the dramatization of male solidarity; while Brown demonstrated the importance of initiations in defining a change to adult status when a woman continues to reside with her parents after marriage. Each perspective could be interpreted in terms of Cohen's idea that initiations serve to lessen the children's emotional identification with their nuclear families.

Cohen's ideas are elegant, because they combine many of the variables dealt with separately by other investigators. He tries to give us an integrated perspective about what goes on when societies elaborate puberty socially. He attempts to retain the complexity of the pubescent period by refusing to limit his explanation to social or psychological or biological variables. Clearly all three types of variables play their separate roles. He presents us with a theoretical framework that encompasses a range of activities that occur at puberty. He encourages us to look at the whole picture. He cautions us not to be misled into concentrating on initiation ceremonies as a major element of social concern with puberty. Social activities during the first stage of puberty are probably more influential in shaping a child's identity than the more spectacular ceremonies in the second stage.

In sum, biological changes occur in two stages, each with its own distinctive set of psychological and social problems. The children grope with the physical changes and confront the problem of emotional anchorage in their social group. The society deals with integrating the sexually developing children into its social network. The title of Cohen's book, *The Transition from Childhood to Adolescence,* indicates the scope of his concerns. He deals with social context as well as with general trends across societies. He also includes a discussion of incest within the same theoretical scheme that he applies to initiation ceremonies. His integrated approach is compelling, because it taps so many dimensions of the relation between physical development and social/cultural/psychological dynamics.

I, too, am inclined to link incest and initiation within the same explanatory framework. In addition to the aspects that Cohen analyzes, I think that incest taboos and initiations deal with sexual differentiation at different stages in the life cycle. Incest taboos define the range of people who cannot be considered as sexual partners. The introduction of such taboos early in life shows that the primary concern is not fear of defective offspring; children cannot be reproductive for many years. At their most basic level, incest taboos force children to differentiate themselves psychologically from their parents and to focus on other attachments. They foster awareness of the role that each parent plays in an individual child's life. By so doing, they encourage the process of healthy gender identity, as Money and Ehrhardt describe it. The contrast between the roles of mother and father helps children to see the distinction between boy and girl, man and woman.

Puberty intensifies the contrast between the sexes. The children separate further from their families and nestle into the social group within which they will function for most of their adult lives. If their responsibility is limited to the nuclear family, they are still able to maintain some emotional distance from the group; the incest taboo has developed that space. As the children's responsibilities to others become more extensive, so, too, does the group's investment in its children's acquisition of an appropriate sex role. Most societies perform initiation ceremonies to reinforce their social commitment to their children. As Cohen and other authors have pointed out, these ceremonies are likely to involve pain for boys. In addition to the psychological impact of pain, which I discussed earlier, there may be another reason for its imposition on boys. Cohen remarks that society can more easily mold children in the first stage of puberty. Children are vulnerable, because they experience new feelings which seem to have no basis; secondary sexual characteristics have not yet appeared. Most initiation ceremonies occur after secondary sexual characteristics have appeared. The task of the group becomes more difficult; it has to counter the appeal of explaining a change in role in physical terms. Men are more associated with the public expression of social concerns, while women tend to be embedded in the domestic sphere. Since men will take a greater share of the responsibility for the management of the group, the group makes an important investment in its men. It becomes crucial that men adhere to social rules. Therefore, male initiation ceremonies minimize the role of "natural" biological changes. They modify the male's body and link its alteration to social concerns and cultural interpretations. The social attention paid to the male intensifies the contrast between the public sphere of males and the domestic sphere of females. The difference in the nature of the biological changes in males and females at puberty aids the group in socially molding males. As Bettelheim reminds us, the changes in males are not punctuated by any cyclical events, like menstruation in women. The group is more flexible in adding its own accents to puberty in males. Meanwhile, women can be relegated to the sphere of nature and biology; they can be viewed as an extension of the "natural order" of things.

All of the views I have considered agree that initiations deal with sex roles and/or sexual identity. When a ceremony is conducted for a female, it emphasizes her social role either as a marriageable woman or as a major contributor to subsistence. Ceremonies are rarely conducted to celebrate fertility or sexuality alone. It is precisely in those societies where menstruation signifies a woman's eligibility to marry that she undergoes a painful ordeal. Otherwise, little attention is paid to the onset of menstruation. I conclude from this that the occurrence of initiation ceremonies for either boys or girls is significantly linked to the transformation of individuals into socially responsible persons, receptive to the rules that the group wishes to impose on them. Pain is considered necessary to impress upon the children the control that the group has over them. Otherwise, the contrasts between men and women can be more muted. It is sufficient to rely upon other mechanisms to maintain differentiation between the sexes.

The symbolic load of initiation as a rite of passage seems to reinforce the contrasts between men and women. Betelheim and Turner both draw attention to the psychological dynamics of initiation ceremonies. Male and female elements are consistently juxtaposed. For example, Turner shows that red, black, and white are constantly used as symbolic elements in initiation ceremonies (Turner 1966). I have already discussed the conflicting emotions that the color red can arouse. Similarly, white can relate to a variety of physical substances, e.g., mother's milk and semen. Black can relate to feces, rain clouds, and fertile earth (Turner 1966: 89). Each symbol evokes layers of meaning, many of which contrast with the others. Death and creativity and male and female emerge as major themes in the symbols. The symbols suspend contrasting elements and sensitize the mind to the nature of the conflicts with which the initiates must deal. Much of the power of the symbols derives from their capacity to arouse awareness of competing forces in our lives yet unify them in one symbol, e.g., colors; they are at once separate but unified. Bettelheim introduces another source of the power of symbols based on physiology. Women can bear children, but men cannot. Transvestism, incisions, and blood highlight the theme of the contrast between men and women. Once again, contrasting elements are juxtaposed, experienced, and then resolved in the final phase of the rite of passage.

*Spatial marking of adolescents: sleeping arrangements.* Initiation cere-monies are dramatic portrayals of the social and personal significance of the transition from childhood. However, other, more subtle adjust-ments in daily life also constitute a social recognition of the shift in a child's position in the group. A change in the child's sleeping arrange-ments is one of the most consistent forms of this type of recognition. Like the physical modifications at puberty, living arrangements can mark a change in the child's life cycle. They also serve to further differ-entiate males from females and parents from children.

Cohen links the extrusion of children from their households to the requirements of training them to be responsible to a wider group of kinsmen (Cohen 1964). Their spatial separation can help them to sepa-rate themselves emotionally from their nuclear families and to adjust to living within an expanded social network. I think that another dimen-sion of separate sleeping arrangements relates to their importance as an expression of or reinforcement for the explicit rules that govern sexual relationships. It is not accidental that puberty is often the point at which sleeping arrangements shift. Adolescents are no longer small chil-dren, unable to consummate their sexual desires in successful inter-course. The living arrangements may constitute a social recognition of pubescent children's maturing sexuality and reproductive capacities. They may serve to bolster the force of the incest taboo.

Izikowitz recognizes that the precise pattern of Lamet (72) sleeping arrangements is more than a matter of convenience and practicality; "it is an expression for the division of functions between the two sexes (Izikowitz 1951: 80). Marriageable girls occupy the far corner of the house, and unmarried adolescent males must sleep in the men's house, since it is "shameful" for the latter to stay at home with their parents (Izikowitz 1951: 60, 74). A husband, his wives, and their married chil-dren also have special sections of the house reserved for them. The couch of the head of the household is at the end of the house farthest from the entrance and opposite the unmarried girls' sleeping area. His senior wife sleeps in a berth next to him; the adjacent berth is the junior wife's. These areas are followed by berths for married children and their prepubescent offspring (Izikowitz 1951: 60). The significance of the *cong*, or men's house, is not restricted to its meaning as a masculine center where males congregate and adolescent boys sleep; it probably expresses the society's fear of the possibility of incest (Izikowitz 1951: 77).

The Nyakyusa in Tanzania are quite explicit in their recognition of the problems that sexually motivated young boys may produce for their families. It is necessary to segregate young boys from their natal households, in order to separate the sexual activities of boys from their parents and to avoid incest (Wilson 1963: 159). The Nyakyusa create age-villages, where young men between the ages of ten and eleven reside. These villages are on the fringes of the main settlement and become the nuclei for community development after the boys marry and start families of their own. Monica Wilson says that the Nyakyusa themselves link a proper sex life with residence in age-villages:

> When asked why small boys build apart from their parents they refer to the danger of a growing boy overhearing lewd talk between his parents, or seeing them unclothed; and they enlarge on the difficulties of father- and daughter-in-law avoidance where father and son live in the same village — an avoidance which is consciously related to the fear of incest between father- and daughter-in-law. We may add also the fear of young men seducing their fathers' junior wives, who are often girls of their own age [Wilson 1963: 159].

The sexual implications of sleeping arrangements are major elements in their living arrangements.

To what extent does the sexual segregation of adolescents in their sleeping arrangements prevail in most societies? Are the above examples aberrations from a more general trend? My data show that they are not unique. The majority of societies in my sample (70%, or 40 of 57 societies) spatially segregate adolescent males and females from one another. They do this by providing a separate section for adolescents of each sex within the parental household or by removing them to a separate, same-sex dwelling. Adolescents of both sexes sleep in the same room with their parents and siblings in close to one-third of my sample (30%, or 17 of 57 societies); a significant number of these societies are located in South America ($X^2 = 7.2$, 1df, p = <.01, N = 57).

A girl generally remains in the same dwelling as her mother or parents (88%, or 50 of 57 societies). It is uncommon for a girl to sleep in a structure apart from her parents (12%, or 7 of 57 societies); such separation occurs primarily in Africa but not in other world areas ($X^2$ = 21.6, 1df, p = <.001, N = 57). A girl is not usually sequestered in a separate section within the house, but she may be separated from her brothers and father by sleeping with her mother in her hut (6%, or 3 of 50 societies) or in a special section reserved for females (4%, or 2 of 50 societies). The most common pattern is for an adolescent girl to sleep in the same house as her parents, with no special provision for her to sleep in a section separate from theirs (61%, or 35 of 57 cases). This means that an adolescent girl is generally subject to potential surveillance by her parents or by her mother while she sleeps (70%, or 40 of 57 societies). This type of sleeping arrangement could allow the parents to protect their daughter from the untoward sexual advances of an enthusiastic young man or to restrain their daughter from expressing her desire to have intercourse. In addition, the mother's presence could restrain the father from making sexual advances toward his daughter. Therefore, the sleeping arrangements could shield the young woman from opportunities for premarital sex and from incest.

The character of male adolescent sleeping arrangements is very different for that of females. Rather than remaining in the same dwelling with his father or parents, a young male often sleeps in a men's house or some other dwelling separate from them (44%, or 25 or 57 societies). When he does sleep in the same house with his father or parents (56%, or 32 of 57 societies), he sometimes remains in the same section with his parents and sisters; almost as frequently, he sleeps in a separate section of his own or one that includes his father or other males of the household. Therefore, the most common sleeping arrangement for an adolescent male is for him to be separated from females by sleeping in a separate dwelling with his father or other males or in a separate section within the household. This means that he is not as likely as a girl to be observed by his father or parents while he sleeps (boys likely to be observed = 47%; girls = 70%). As I will show later, premarital sex is allowed more often for boys than for girls. Adolescent sleeping arrangements may facilitate the boys' sexual activities. Separation of adolescent boys may also serve to mitigate potential conflict between father and son for power or for sexual opportunities.

In sum, the overall tendency is to exclude young males and retain young females within the parental household. When male and female adolescents sleep in the same dwelling, the males sleep in a separate section more than twice as often as the females do. In addition, males are less subject to being watched by their father or parents than females are by their mother or parents. Two types of adolescent sleeping arrangements cluster significantly by area. Africa is one of the few areas where adolescent girls are excluded from the households of their parents and have their own dwellings. South America is the area where segregation of adolescents from their parents and siblings is least likely to occur.

Aside from the overall effect of separating adolescent males and females from the opposite sex while they sleep, these arrangements generally result in the segregation of brothers from their sisters (74%, or 42 of 57 societies) and mothers from their sons (61%, or 35 of 57 societies); a father is segregated from his adolescent daughter less frequently (44%, or 25 of 57 societies). The rarest pattern is for a husband and wife to sleep in the same dwelling with adolescent children of both sexes.

I have pointed out that initiation ceremonies in the second stage of puberty may provide a ritual expression of further sexual differentiation. Implicitly, that differentiation means a separation from family members as appropriate sexual partners. Cohen (1964) suggests that an effective social life requires some emotional distance between socializers and the young. Obviously, spatial separation may serve a variety of psychological and social purposes. The point I wish to make is that the sleeping arrangements of adolescents are particularly interesting, because they entail an organization of young males and females for whom intercourse is possible though not necessarily socially approved. They raise questions about whether the arrangements are conducive to conducting premarital affairs, preventing incest, or fostering the surveillance of adolescents by their parents. One way in which societies cope with the budding sexuality of their children is through their sleeping arrangements.

### Postpubertal Differentiation

The subtle processes of differentiation begun in childhood and emphasized at puberty pervade the adult lives of men and women. They surround many of the most basic activities in people's lives and are constant reminders of the contrast between men and women. Like adolescent sleeping arrangements, modifications in physical appearance as well as eating arrangements may mark the implicit boundaries that surround the social domains of males and females. The choices that a group makes in encouraging individuals to alter their appearances and in arranging them in physical space are symbolic statements about the nature of the group's impact on the individual.

Anthropologists and social psychologists have long recognized the significance of the organization of social space. Children learn many lessons by observation. They note differences in appearance and allocation between males and females. They can then associate these physical differences with behavioral ones. Children's observations of their parents' division of labor are particularly relevant to the formation of their gender identity; behavior of socializers in conformity with incest taboos is also significant. After puberty, children experience the physical and social fullness of sexual differentiation. It remains a constant, though perhaps assumed, contrast in their lives; it supports their adult gender identity and role. They may of course take sexual differentiation for granted, instead of considering the major impact it has on shaping their perceptions and behavior toward the people with whom they share their lives. After puberty, adolescents enter a world where sexual differentiation is well established and rules about intercourse are well defined. Their entry sets the stage for the complete expression of adolescent and adult sexuality.

### Physical Appearance

Differences in physical appearance are daily reminders of the contrast between males and females. Modifications of our bodies are not merely adaptations to organic needs and climatic conditions. The time and effort involved in selecting clothing, ornaments, and accessories testify to their individual and social significance. The care with which people apply makeup and body paint or submit to painful modifications of their bodies by scarification, tattooing, and genital mutilation is a clue to their importance. No society depends entirely upon intrinsic differences in physical development to differentiate the sexes. Each group places its social stamp on the person's appearance and invests it with cultural meaning. The human body becomes a canvas upon which society paints its own unique interpretation of the status and role of the individual.

The tailoring of clothing, the fabrics used, the colors, and the amount and quality of jewelry and makeup all provide subtle indicators of a person's social standing. John T. Malloy's book, *The Woman's Dress for Success Book* (1978), is a graphic illustration of the impact that clothing and accessories make on others. It shows how clothing may be varied to create a specific impression on a potential employer, colleague, or lover. The ways in which we care for our bodies, cloth them, and change the appearance they present may also reflect aspects of our personalities. We are the ones who select and coordinate aspects of our appearance. Appearance allows people to place others in categories, identify their positions in the social organization, and expect certain kinds of behavior from them. When someone's appearance deviates from the canons of acceptability, it may become symbolic of the conflicts inherent in society. In the 1960s in the U.S., for example, long hair on males was not merely a variation from acceptable grooming; it signified a liberal or nontraditional political orientation.

Mary Douglas suggests that "the body is a model which can stand for any bounded system. Its boundaries can represent any boundaries which are threatened or precarious" (Douglas 1966: 115). Because "no other social pressures are potentially so explosive as those which constrain sexual relations" (Douglas 1966: 157), the implications of physical differentiation of males and females may extend far beyond establishing a distinction between the sexes. Physical appearance may make statements about the person's marital status, age, receptivity to sexual encounters, etc.

Variations in modifying physical appearance can range from covering parts of the body with clothing or other parpaphernalia (footgear, headgear, belts, other accessories to the main garment) to severely altering the body itself by deformation or mutilation, e.g., cranial deformation, ear piercing, scarification, tattooing, and circumcision. The choice of style and color of clothing is one of the most important ways that men and women distinguish themselves from each other. It is the major way in which men alter their appearance (1 %, or 18 of 59 cases) and the second most significant way that women do (25 %, or 15 of 60 societies). Although styles may seem similar, there are subtle differences in tailoring, color, or the way the garment is worn that characterize it as male or female. For example, the Ganda (12) of Uganda attire themselves in garments that resemble a bark-cloth version of a Roman toga. The style is simple. How it is worn is the key to identifying this garment as male or female aparel. A man knots the cloth on his right shoulder and passes it under his left arm; a woman passes the cloth under both of her arms and cinches it with a girdle made from bark-cloth of a different color (Roscoe 1911: 442). It is considered improper for a man to expose any part of his body from his neck to his ankles. It is regarded as much more shocking for a man than for a woman to be naked (Roscoe 1911: 443).

The style of the garment may be less important than the portions of the body that it should cover. Comanche (147) men wear gee strings of braided cord to provide magical protection for their sex organs (Hoebel 1940: 77). When Siuai (99) girls reach childhood, they must cover their pubic regions with calico loincloths; during infancy they can be naked. However, we cannot be too quick to assume that a relatively uncovered body means that the person has no modesty. William Stephens (n.d.: 12) points out that people may be trained to refrain from looking at body parts that are exposed. The addition of a gee string may be enough to define the body as clothed, even though it may seem immodest to the untutored eye.

In his cross-cultural study of modesty, Stephens finds that people in most preindustrial, peasant societies are extremely modest. None of them allows exposure of the genitals, and most cover the breasts. He concludes that more extensive body coverings appear much later in human development, probably after the advent of cities, dense population and hierarchical political organization (Stephens n.d.: 14). His conclusions make sense when we think of clothing as a marker for social categories. More elaborate and extensive clothing styles would be an extension of the increased number of cultural components in life.

Jewelry overshadows the importance of clothing as the main means by which women differentiate themselves from men (30%, or 18 of 60 societies). Men rarely use jewelry for this purpose (5%, or 3 of 59 societies). Ganda (12) women wear as many ornaments as they can obtain; they adorn their bodies with colored necklaces made from seeds or beads and with bracelets and anklets made of iron, brass, and ivory (Roscoe 1911: 443). The Ganda (12) man's adornment is stark by comparison; he may simply wear a wire bracelet and a neck string (Murdock 1934: 520). Young Yukaghir (120) women of North Siberia sew brass buttons, tassels, and beads onto their garments and wear necklaces of curved brass. They take pride in their "tinkling metallic ornaments that serve to announce their approach to their sweethearts" (Jochelson 1926: 404).

Body deformation and mutilation are the third most important means of differentiation by women (15%, or 9 of 60 societies) and men (14%, or 8 of 59 societies). Tattooing and scarification are one form of body mutilation. Hill Maria Gond (60) women of Southwest India begin applying tattoos with needles and charcoal on the faces and foreheads of their eight- or nine-year-old daughters (Grigson 1938: 72). Marshallese (108) men heavily tattoo their bodies on the chests, shoulders, backs, arms, buttocks, and thighs as a confirmation of sexual identity (Krämer and Nevermann 1938: 91). The sexual connotation of tattooing on a Palauan (111) woman is particularly clear, for the tattooing covers not only the hands, arms, shoulders, feet, and legs up to the hips but also the mons veneris; unless the latter is marked, "no man would look at her" (Krämer 1929: 56). After the mons veneris is tattooed, the girl's family places a large piece of native money on it, with the hope that her sexual relations will be economically beneficial to them (Krämer 1929: 60). In addition to a few tattoos, Fijian (102) women have scars cut into their skin; they may also burn wartlike spots into their arms and backs (Williams 1884: 137). The ornamental scars of the Kafa (33) men distinguish them from the women (Bieber 1920–23: *1*,264). Cicatrization, i.e., deliberately cutting the skin to make scar tissue, of Otoro (30) males marks their entrance into manhood and their eligibility for sexual intercourse (Nadel 1947: 141,142).

Piercing the ears, cheeks, lips, or nose is another form of body mutilization. Tupinamba (177) men of Brazil pierce their lips and cheeks and then insert pieces of stone or wood in them; the women stretch their earlobes, sometimes down to their shoulders or breasts, by the insertion of large shell cylinders (Métraux 1948: 11). The holes that Marshallese (108) men used to make in their earlobes with sharks' teeth were so large that the lobes were ordinarily worn over the ears unless they were filled with ornaments, as on ceremonial occasions (Erdland 1914: 19).

Another form of body modification is deformation or removal of parts of the body. However, this does not seem to occur as much as tattooing, scarification, or piercing. Suku (16) women of the Southwest Congo attempt to lengthen their breasts by tying them down; they alter their incisors by cutting them into a "V" shape or by knocking them out altogether (Torday and Joyce 1906: 41). For the first six months of life, pressure is applied to the nose, cheekbone, and back of the head of a Marshallese (108) child, to make the child's appearance conform to socially acceptable standards (Krämer and Nevermann, 1938: 90).

Surprisingly, genital mutilation and deformation do not emerge as important modes of social differentiation of the sexes for either men (2%, or 1 of 59 societies) or women (no societies). This does not mean that practices such as circumcision or clitoridectormy (removal of part or all of the clitoris) are infrequent or unimportant. I have already discussed their symbolic role in the cognitive reorganization of males and females during puberty. They may be more relevant to personal than social identity, however. Since the genitals are usually covered, their modification would not be publicly observable. Therefore, they cannot be used as a basis for social classification in ordinary social interaction. Furthermore, where genital mutilation and deformation occur for men, they also occur for women and thus do not differentiate the sexes. The force of their meaning may be restricted to more intimate contexts, e.g., love relationships and mateships. They may enhance sex appeal, reinforce masculinity or femininity, and endow individuals with more confidence about themselves.

The last major modification of physical appearance that differentiates the sexes is the alteration of head, body, and facial hair. Changes in head hair, "hair-dos," are important for both men (15%, or 9 of 59 societies) and women (12%, or 7 of 60 societies). Yahgan (186) men wear their hair loose and groom it with blubber grease (Gusinde 1937: 421). Siuai (99) men are particularly diligent about their hair when sexual activities begin; variations in individual style include bleaching the hair and dying it a uniform black color (Oliver 1955: 23). Comanche (147) men pay particular attention to their head hair; they wrap their braids in beaver fur and ornament them with silver, beads, and feathers (Wallace and Hoebel 1952: 83, 144). Clearly women do not have a worldwide, exclusive claim on fashionable hair styles. Fijian (102) chieftains are so concerned about their hair's appearance that they have their own hairdressers (Williams 1884: 133).

The growth and accentuation of facial hair (13.6%, or 8 of 59 societies) and the removal of body hair (5.1%, or 3 of 59 societies) are outstanding modes of sexual differentiation for men. The alteration of all types of body hair emerges as a dominantly male (34%, or 20 of 59 societies) rather than female (13%, or 8 of 60 societies) style of sexual differentiation ($X^2 = 4.9$, 1df, $p = <.05$, N = 119). Yahgan (186) men and women both think that body hair is ugly; all Yahgan adults pluck out axillary and pubic hair, and men additionally depilate their beards. Comanche (147) men also pluck out their facial hair (Wallace and Hoebel 1952: 83).

Men may also style or ornament their facial hair to emphasize their masculinity. The Kurd (57) attribute great social significance to a man's moustache (Masters 1953: 156); if he has none, they think that he is "not quite a man." A Kafa's (33) beard may grow so long that he rolls it up for daily activities and extends its full length only during ceremonial occasions (Bieber 1920–23: *1*, 272).

The distinctively male practices of modifying their bodies and facial hair are further illustrations of the ways in which groups place their imprints on secondary sexual characteristics. Pulling out hair can be a painful procedure. Nevertheless, the "natural" distinctiveness of copious body and facial hair on males is obliterated in some cases. The dictates of the group replace biological characteristics in molding men's ideas about what is masculine.

In sum, men and women reinforce sexual distinctions in daily life by modifying their bodies or putting on clothing and ornaments. Clothes, jewelry, deformation, mutilation, and hair styles are the main ways that women do this; whereas clothes, hair styles, facial hair, deformation, and mutilation of the body are the usual ways by which men do so. The use of jewelry emerges as a primarily feminine mode of physical sexual differentiation. Modification of body hair is a more distinctively masculine mode of differentiating men from women.

*Eating Arrangements*

Sexual differentiation may also be expressed in daily activities by the spatial allocation of males and females during meals. Physical survival depends upon furnishing our bodies with food. However, eating patterns are not determined by the need for survival. Groups have a great deal of flexibility in deciding upon the way in which people should be placed together when they eat. Sharing meals is a very human characteristic. It may stem from the early evolution of humans as cooperative hunters with a distinctive division of labor: men hunted, and women gathered. Even though gathering could provide a stable source of nutrients, hunting was a more precarious endeavor. Food sharing could reduce competition between group members for scarce resources and thus enhance cooperation. The fact that food would be shared when it was available could promote a sense of psychological security. Food sharing could also aid in the survival of the group as a whole, not just a few fortunate hunters.

Regardless of its heritage, eating is a very social activity among humans. Eating binds each of us to our caretaker in our first human relationship. The pinnacle of major life cycle events may be expressed in elaborate feasting. Freud based one of his major stages of psychosexual development, the oral stage, on the gratifications that eating provides in infancy and childhood. If we assume, as Turner does (1967), that most symbols have a physiological component, eating is a ripe basis for symbolic interpretation.

Mary Douglas suggests that the body is symbolic of any bounded system (Douglas 1966: 115). Therefore, its apertures are particularly significant as points of access. Since eating and intercourse involve entering body openings, i.e., access to the bounded system, similar restrictions may be placed upon the two kinds of activities. For example, the Aweikoma (180) of Southeastern Brazil use the same term for eating and intercourse (Henry 1941: 35). Current American slang usage defines "eating" as cunnilingus or fellatio. An Otoro (30) man eats with the wife with whom he plans to have intercourse. The dinner that Tom and his lady friend consume in the film "Tom Jones" is a graphic illustration of the sexual implications of sharing a meal. Since consumption of food is a daily occurrence, eating arrangements can spatially reinforce sociocultural distinctions between the sexes and express restrictions placed on their relationships with each other.

Most societies qualify the places or times when men and women may share a meal (70%, or 33 of 47 societies), rather than allowing them to eat together at any time (30% or 14 of 47 societies). Most frequently, males and females eat in separate places (49%, or 23 of 47 societies). The separation between them may be so consistent that a special eating area is designated for each sex (11 of 47 societies, or 23%). Or, the separation may apply only to public occasions. Specific categories of individuals, e.g., husbands and wives, may eat together in private (25.5%, or 12 of 47 societies). When male guests are present in a Siamese (76) household (Sharp et al. 1954: 265), women eat separately from them and at a later time; otherwise the whole family eats together. Among the Ganda (12), a man may eat with his wife if he is alone or only has one wife; normally a woman eats in her own enclosure (Roscoe 1911: 95, 438). Even in a small Hadza (9) band, men and women may eat in separate areas; men eat by the fire, while women go elsewhere, apart from the men (Kohl-Larsen 1958: 99).

Another way in which the group exercises control over the eating patterns of men and women is to assign them specific places to eat when they are together (10.6%, or 5 of 47 societies). The Chinese (114) illustrate how seating arrangements can express social concerns. A new daughter-in-law sits at a lower place at the table until she has borne a child. Her position reflects not only her low status within her new household but also her husband's indifferent attitude toward her until she becomes a mother (Fei 1946: 46, 47). An Inca (171) wife generally sits back-to-back to her husband at the table, regardless of the length of time she has lived with him or the number of children she has borne (Cobo 1890–95: *1*, 172–173).

The last technique that groups use to differentiate the eating patterns of males and females is to stagger the times when they will eat (29.8%, or 5 of 47 societies). The main type of temporal separation is for the women to serve the men first and then eat later with the children. Miskito women (156), of Honduras and Nicaragua, serve their men prime, substantial shares of the food while they sit in their hammocks. The women and children consume the smaller, less desirable portions later (Conzemius 1932: 88). Even though the organization is not as precise, a similar pattern prevails among the Cayapa (168) of Highland Colombia. Although meals are prepared and eaten individually, women and children wait until the men have been served theirs before they begin to start to eat their own (Altschuler 1965: 59).

To summarize, eating arrangements can express social and cultural dimensions of sexual relationships. Men and women generally do not eat together unless some conditions are placed upon them. The most frequent arrangement is spatial segregation, while strict positioning at the table or temporal segregation constitute the less frequent types. There are no areas of the world where one eating arrangement dominates. There is a stronger tendency for African societies to segregate the sexes spatially than there is for most other societies ($X^2$ = 2.6, 1df, p = <.1, N = 47).

## Sexual Interaction

As we can see, the social constraints on interaction between males and females become progressively more pronounced and regularized as the individuals get older. Prenatal determinants of the physical features of sex become the foundation for the sociocultural elaboration of gender role when the child is born. Activities like the sexual division of labor impress upon children the behavioral importance of the distinction between male and female. Contrasts between the sexes and comparisons with the same-sex parent provide materials for the formation of a child's gender identity. The incest taboo introduces children to the idea of sexual restriction of partners. However, this restriction is not as relevant to their lives during childhood as the emotional separation from their parents and/or kinsmen that results from the incest taboo. They are dealing with a universal human problem. How do you separate yourself from those who have nourished you through your early years? How do you establish lasting emotional and social bonds with others? It is interesting to note that sexual maturity is usually the point at which many primates separate from their mothers. The human dilemma is more sharply accentuated, because our dependency period is so much longer than that of other primates. Therefore separation from the attachments that we formed in childhood is particularly painful.

The questions I have raised become crucial at the approach of puberty, for the children now have the sexual capacity to act upon their emotional needs. The potential for forming intense pair bonds via sex becomes a realistic possibility for them. Physical changes and their emotional concomitants highlight the sexual intensity of children at this stage. Sexual differentiation becomes pronounced physically and is emphasized socially. The group responds to a number of questions that it raises about the developing sexuality of its children. How can we maintain the incest taboo? How should we channel our children's sexuality in relation to appropriate partners, an acceptable time to begin sexual relations, etc.? How can we deal with the knowledge that if our children are sexually mature, we, too, are getting older and possibly changing in our sexual capacities? The ramifications of puberty are great, not only for the developing children but also for other members of the community.

Spatial segregation of adolescents and the application of more stringent rules to their behavior are two mechanisms that a group can use to handle the emotional changes that accompany the first stage of puberty. Another social response is to conduct initiation ceremonies in the second stage of puberty. These alternatives are sensitive to both social and individual concerns. Rules, spatial allocation, and ceremonies may help children to solidify and transform their gender identity; they may aid adults in their ability to accept their advancing age and the alteration in their own positions, which the introduction of children into adult roles implies.

By the time that children have gone through puberty, have reinforced their gender identity and are informed about the responsibilities of their sex role, they are on the threshold of a new expansion of their awareness of sexual differentiation. The differences can be pervasive. They look around their routine existence and observe sexual distinctions in their everyday activities. Arrangements for sleeping and eating, as well as body modifications, sort the sexes into specific categories. Children cannot avoid an awareness of the differences, even though they may take them for granted; by now they may seem "natural." The differences help them to maintain their gender identity. They also foster an appreciation of their biological incompleteness as sexually reproducing animals.

Social groups define physical sex in their own terms. They incorporate physiological details of appearance and behavior into socially meaningful idioms, "masculine" and "feminine." They also define the significance of intercourse — physical unity between males and females. The interpretation of intercourse in social, cultural, and psychological terms becomes the basis for its intriguing and elaborate complexity.

### The Nature of and the Occasions for Intercourse

The biological role of sexual differentiation is reproductive intercourse. Mammals other than humans generally have intercourse primarily during the periods when females are most fertile. With the loss of estrus, human females are potentially receptive to intercourse at any time. Since conception is possible during only a few days each month, a great deal of human coitus is nonreproductive. As I explained earlier, the disjunction between nonreproductive and reproductive intercourse is one of the distinctive features of human sexual relationships. Because of this difference, we can talk about intercourse both in a sexual context and in a reproductive context.

Our sexual relationships are subject to the rules and meanings that we learn as we grow up. Our social group has the power to channel our thoughts and feelings about sexual activity, as well as to regulate the occasions and partners with whom it is likely to occur. The social group has a basic investment in the sexual activity of its members, because sexual relations are potentially reproductive and can influence population size as well as group membership. As we shall see, the social ramifications of sexual activity extend far beyond these basic biological elements.

I found that there are few societies that actively encourage people to engage in intercourse at particular times. Most groups surround intercourse with numerous restrictions, which define activities that should *not* occur. Aside from its relevance to group survival, why should intercourse be surrounded with so many prohibitions? One clue may be the unrestrained passion with which couples may express themselves during intercourse. Masters and Johnson (1966) describe the physiological components of orgasm and claim that they are always the same. However, the sensations that people experience during orgasm are as varied as their individuality. For example, one woman describes her feelings in terms of two types of orgasm, clitoral and vaginal:

> I would say that clitoral orgasm is some shivery something that kind of runs out along the nerves . . . but with . . . vaginal orgasms, it's somehow something deeper . . . physical feeling. There's some kind of weight about it. One is along the nerves, the surface of the body, and the other has this, I don't know what . . . a kind of thing you get more submerged in feeling fully. And I recall that feeling as very overwhelming, washed over by something, that crying or sobbing was really the only place it could go to express itself. If it's a true vaginal orgasm, I can see here the quality of surrender is greater . . . [Schaefer 1973: 142].

Other women report sensations of "falling, opening up, mild labor pains, throbbing. Men may feel abandon when they know there is nothing they can do to stop ejaculation. Both men and women experience orgasm as intense pleasure" (Katchadourian and Lunde 1975: 59). Both describe their approach to a level of excitement where it becomes progressively difficult to maintain voluntary control (Katchadourian and Lunde 1975: 58). Other sensory perceptions may fade into the intensity of the moment; people may experience some numbness in their senses of vision, hearing, taste, and smell and may not be very sensitive to painful stimuli (Katchadourian and Lunde 1975: 60). Mental awareness and physical sensation blend in the uncontrolled moments of orgasm.

I think that the uncontrolled quality of orgasms may be related to social concern about intercourse. A lack of control implies a lack of responsiveness to rules. If the senses are partially numbed, how likely are people to respond to socially created guidelines for their behavior? When I discussed some of the characteristics of the marginal period of initiation ceremonies, I said that the formlessness of the initiates was bounded by the temporary nature of the marginal period and by the strict authority that the adult men had over the initiates. Similarly, symbols derive much of their power from their capacity to suspend contradictory forces, such as life and death; their position is not resolved in structure. During the physiological and emotional peak of intercourse, orgasm, people are in a formless state; they do not behave according to social and cultural requirements. Mary Douglas (1966) asserts that whenever something is not contained within a clear classificatory structure, it is apt to be categorized as "dirty," "abnormal," or deviant." Intense freedom from social constraints threatens the social order. The power of sexual relations suggests their potential to confound the rules that apply to relationships. It could upset our expectation of others and, with it, the main basis by which we form a social life. Consequently, the group invests sexual activity with very specific meanings, in an effort to tie the individual's uncontrolled moments into a socially controlled package.

Since our society regards intercourse as a private, personal encounter, it may be difficult for us to see how it can be tightly enmeshed in the social fabric. How can such a seemingly personal interaction be bound by social constraints? What are the cultural reinforcements that bolster the person's submission to these rules?

The meaning that a group attaches to sexual relations and teaches to its members influences the patterns of individual behavior. The Bellacoola (132), members of a North American tribe on the Lower Bella Coola River in Central British Columbia, illustrate how the cultural interpretation of sexual relations encourages men to be continent. The Bellacoola regard intercourse as a typically human activity (McIlwraith 1948: *1*, 111). Therefore, if a man practices ceremonial chastity, he dissociates himself from the human realm of behavior and draws himself nearer to the supernatural. Not only may a man acquire boundless strength by chastity alone but he may also be aided by continence in obtaining the good will of supernatural beings. Intercourse that occurs after a proper period of chastity increases a man's power tremendously. Chastity strengthens his supernatural attributes and increases the likelihood that he will have good fortune (McIlwraith 1948: *1*, 110). The practice applies to any activity in which a man wishes to enhance his luck. Continence is almost a necessity for hunters, since animals hide from men who have not observed the appropriate restrictions on intercourse. A man's ritual program of abstinence has important implications for his economic pursuits.

Following such a ritual program requires extreme restraint and discipline. The Bellacoola say that the best fortune awaits men who observe continence for a series of forty night intervals during a four-year period and have intercourse only on the proper nights (McIlwraith 1948: *1*, 113). However, the men do not usually practice the ritual in such a drastic form. Four nights of continence may be sufficient to gain success in some pursuits, e.g., hunting or playing cards. The primary emphasis here is the effect of abstinence on the individual. The group holds out the promise of supernatural power and social success if the man agrees to plan intercourse according to its guidelines. Nevertheless, the individual still retains his flexibility to reject the offer.

The restrictions that the African Thonga (3) follow contrast sharply with those of the Bellacoola. The timing and frequency of intercourse has significant repercussions for their social life, not merely for the individual who is continent. The implications of intercourse may intertwine with the pace and well-being of the total community (Junod 1927: *1*, 188). The Thonga say that sexual relations communicate their intensity to nature and accelerate the pace of life. Therefore, silence and continence help the community to maintain orderly relations with nature; protracted continence contributes to the welfare of the community. Married couples are referred to as "hot," because they engage in regular sexual relations. Since too much sexual activity could upset the balance of the community with nature, sexual restrictions apply particularly to married people. If people obey the rules of continence, they help to ensure that the sick will recover, that community crises will be resolved, and that economic activities will prove successful. Otherwise, sexual activities would tie up too much of nature's energy. Social life, nature, and sexual activity all mirror each other. The unrestrained passion of intercourse could be paralleled by social disorder and chaos in nature. The Thonga are explicit about their fears of lack of control. Their rules set limits on their anxiety and on their sexual encounters.

Both the Bellacoola and the Thonga abide by social rules that govern the pace and the occasions for intercourse. The pursuit of individual power motivates the Bellacola man to be continent when he desires to cultivate his good fortune. He has the choice of modifying his sex life according to his individual needs for economic and social success. The alternatives for the Thonga are not as wide as for the Bellacoola. The well-being of the entire community depends upon their maintaining a relatively calm balance in their sexual activities. The consequences of their "private" behavior could affect the welfare of everyone in their group; intercourse is fraught with social, not merely individual, implications.

Most restrictions on intercourse fluctuate between the two extremes illustrated by the Bellacoola and the Thonga. The restrictions usually parallel significant events in the individual's life cycle or major aspects of social life. A large proportion of the most important restrictions (54%, or 30 of 56 societies) are focused on events in the woman's reproductive cycle, especially birth. Postpartum sex taboos are almost universal prohibitions, applying to close to 94% of the world's societies. They usually do not last more than six months (53% of 146 societies), but they may apply for more than two years in a sizable number of groups (18% of 146 societies). Although humans do not have a period of anestrus after birth, they follow a pattern of abstinence similar to that of other animals. Another physiological event in a woman's life cycle that is surrounded by sexual taboos is menstruation. Contact with a menstruating woman or with the menstrual flow is thought to be dangerous; a man could spoil his luck at hunting, could get sick, or could even die. Many people link the ambivalent qualities of power and danger with the blood. As I discussed in relation to initiation ceremonies, menstrual blood may symbolize forces of creativity or death. Avoidance is one way to acknowledge its power and to deal with its danger. While other events in the life cycle may become a basis for sexual restriction, they are more likely to be a secondary (39% of 31 societies) rather than a primary focus (5% of 56 societies) for social attention.

In the public sphere of society, economic pursuits (20% of 56 societies) and religious occasions (16% of 56 societies) are the focus for the greatest proportion of restrictions. Military occasions are not likely to require abstinence (5% of 56 societies). Given the distinctively male character of such occasions, I was surprised that men did not reinforce their masculinity by sexually separating from women before they went into battle. Perhaps the de facto continence implied by absence from home during war eliminates the necessity for a taboo. Many societies tie restrictions on the timing and the occasions for intercourse to both individual and social events. A greater number of societies are likely to emphasize life cycle events alone (39% of 56 societies) than to limit intercourse according to social occasion alone (16% of 56 societies).

In sum, the occasions for regulation of intercourse almost always include episodes in the life cycle—particularly the woman's reproductive cycle—either alone (39% of 56 societies) or in combination with social events (45% of 56 societies). As was the case with initiation ceremonies, the group steps into people's lives and modifies their activities at a time that is intensely significant for them. At such a time, they may be more vulnerable and thus more receptive to social explanations and modifications of their behavior.

## Cross-Cultural Variation in the Sexual Response Cycle

Social rules and cultural beliefs not only affect the meaning, occasions, and frequency of intercourse; they can also modify the techniques we use and the responses we have when we have intercourse. It is important to understand the relationship between these rules and beliefs and the physiological aspects of the sexual response cycle.

*The biological baseline.* Masters and Johnson's description of the physiological components of sexual response gives us a a specific picture of the consistent physical characteristics of sexual functioning (Masters and Johnson 1966). On the basis of their empirical research, they attempt to define the biological baseline upon which groups press their social rules and cultural molds.

Both males and females can go through four phases of sexual response: (1) excitement, (2) plateau, (3) orgasm, and (4) resolution. Each phase is associated with definite physiological relations. In the first phase — excitement — effective and sustained stimulation lead to sexual excitement. The stimulation may be psychological — erotic thoughts and feelings — or physical — erotic touch, sight, smell, or behavior — or both. Males notice a number of physical changes during this phase. The penis becomes erect; the scrotum may thicken, flatten, and elevate; and the testes partially elevate and increase in size as stimulation continues. Women also experience some changes in their genitalia. The vagina becomes lubricated, its walls thicken, and the inner two-thirds expands. As stimulation continues, the clitoris swells and the cervix elevates. As in other phases of the cycle, both men and women may experience similar bodily reactions. For example, the nipples may become erect for both, although this happens more consistently in women than in men.

"Plateau" is an appropriate label for the next phase. This is the period when sustained erotic stimulation stabilizes the excitement at a high level. The sex organs of both the male and the female reflect the height of sustained excitement, providing intense expressions of the physiological reactions of the excitement phase. In males, the corona, or rim, of the penis increases in circumference and may take on a purplish hue. The testes elevate and rotate. Secretions from Cowper's glands, small structures beside the urethra in the penis, may produce a clear, sticky fluid on the tip of the penis during sexual arousal. In women, the outer third of the vagina becomes more congested with blood and develops into an "orgasmic platform." The inner two-thirds of the vagina expands more fully; this is called "tenting." The uterus and cervix elevate still further. The clitoris temporarily withdraws; Bartholin's glands, located near the vaginal opening, secrete mucous; and the labia minora, the small folds of skin that enclose the urethral and vaginal openings, change in color. As in the excitement phase, men and women share a number of general body responses. The surface of the skin begins to redden like a sudden rash. The reddish tinge begins in the center of the lower chest and spreads to the breasts, to the rest of the chest, and to the neck as excitement increases. This "sex-tension flush" is more common in women than men. The muscles and breathing of both men and women express their sexual excitement in characteristic ways. Breathing becomes excessively rapid and deep, and the heartbeat increases to 110–160 beats per minute, as if to keep pace with the accelerated breathing. Most of the muscles in the body become tense. The muscles of the hands and feet may become so tight that they have spasms called "carpopedal spasms."

The orgasmic phase, the third segment of the sexual response cycle, is the most intense of the four phases. Although the original meaning of the word "orgasm" is descriptive, it provides only a mild label for the intensity of response that characterizes it. Literally, orgasm means to swell or become excited. The contractions that mark orgasm express the height of sexual excitement. Most of the sex organs of the male participate in these contractions. Their spasms lead to the ejaculation of seminal fluid, the liquid that contains the sperm. The sphincter muscles, which surround the anus, also contract. As in the male, most of a woman's sex organs contract. The orgasmic response of a woman extends through her pelvic area; the uterus and vagina pulsate in rapid succession, while the cervix remains taut. The sphincter muscles and the urethra also contract. Breathing, heartbeat, and specific skeletal muscles all keep pace with the rest of the body. Both men and women continue to breathe vigorously; the rate of their already rapid heartbeats may increase slightly. Other muscles in the body may also contract.

The final stage of the sexual response cycle is the resolution phase. Both men and women may sweat. They continue to breathe heavily for a while, until their bodies gradually begin to relax. Heartbeat slows down. However, the sex organs of men and women are likely to respond differently in this phase. While their organs release much of the tension they have held during the previous phases, they do so at different rates. The penis loses its erection, and the clitoris returns to its unswollen state. The outer third of the vagina also returns to its normal position, and the coloring of the labia minora shifts to a less intense hue. The major difference between men and women during this phase is the rate at which the vessels of the pelvic area become less congested with blood. Men lose vasocongestion rapidly. Women lose vascongestion more slowly. Although men are likely to undergo a temporary period when they are resistant to sexual stimulation, i.e., a refractory period, women are capable of returning to the orgasmic phase rather quickly.

In sum, the physiological dynamics of the sexual response cycle relate to two general features that men and women share: (1) vasocongestion and (2) increased muscle tension. When a person becomes sexually stimulated, the blood flows into the arteries so rapidly that the veins cannot drain it all off. Consequently, the vessels and surrounding tissues are congested with an added amount of blood; this is what we mean by vasocongestion. The affected tissues become swollen, red, and warm. Increased blood in the spongy tissues of the penis makes it erect; likewise, the clitoris becomes swollen and more sensitive to stimulation. Other sex organs follow suit. Increased muscle tension complements vasocongestion to produce many of the sensations of sexual response. The impact of the muscles is most obvious during orgasm, when they contract rapidly in succession.

Masters and Johnson provide us with a precise description of the physiological components of the sexual response cycle. Our human heritage has endowed us with a general physical outline to guide our sexual activities. The impact of the rules and beliefs of our group is to create variations on the physiological theme. The ways in which males and females become attracted to each other, stimulate their partners during different phases of the sexual response cycle, or position themselves during intercourse reflect the influence of learning on our sex lives. They illustrate the intricate melding of knowledge, emotion, and physical response that constantly characterizes human behavior.

How consistently do people adhere to the dictates of their physiology when they have intercourse? How variable are the elaborations of sexual response that we learn? The rules and beliefs of our social group have a lot to do with the answers to these questions.

*Sociocultural aspects of invitation.* Few investigators have systematically collected information on sexual invitation, attraction, and intercourse in our own society, much less in others. Kinsey is a notable exception. More recently, the findings derived from the Hite reports, (1976, 1981) *Redbook*'s sex surveys, (Tavris and Sadd 1975), and the Institute for Sex Research show that the traditional, taboo-ridden nature of sex research is beginning to change. Even so, much of our information on these subjects has to be gleaned from innuendo, anecdotes, and polite avoidance of the subject. I was surprised to find that I could gather some of my most explicit information about sexual practices in other societies from the writings of pre-twentieth-century missionaries. Although they were quick to point out the sinfulness of the behavior they described, they were attentive to its fine details. Sometimes they would buffer their presentation of sexual materials by orienting it to a scholarly community; consequently, many shifted into Latin whenever they described these subjects.

Although *Patterns of Sexual Behavior* by Clellan S. Ford, an anthropolgist, and Frank A. Beach, a psychologist, is more than thirty years old, it remains a valuable source of information about cross-cultural and cross-species sexual practices. My discussion of sexual invitation, stimulation, and intercourse is drawn primarily from their materials.

Sexual interest begins before bodies ever come in contact. Potential partners need to interact and become attracted to each other before they can establish a sexual relationship. The elements of this phase cut across species and characterize what Money calls the "proceptive stage" of eroticism and sexuality (Money 1980: 73). This stage includes the solicitation, attraction, and courtship of partners (Money 1980: 75).

Physical appearance plays an important role in human sexual attraction, as it does in many other species. However, the traits that are considered attractive vary quite a bit from one society to another and from one individual to the next. In addition, standards of beauty apply more frequently to women than to men (Ford and Beach 1972: 86). Social and physical skill seem to have a more marked influence on defining a man's appeal to a woman than vice versa. At first, this distinction between the sexes seems puzzling. Why is the body of a man not evaluated as closely as a woman's? A possible reason for this is related to more general contrasts between the sexes. Ortner persuasively argues that groups tend to regard women as closer to nature than men (Ortner 1974). A woman's physiology and her reproductive role as a childbearer foster greater attention to her physical attributes. The contours of women's bodies are marked by fatty deposits in their breasts and hips. Men do not bear children, although they play a role in their creation. Social skill and achievement are more visible expressions of men's creativity. Greater attention to women's beauty could be an extension of an overall tendency for societies to categorize women in physical terms and men in social terms. Another possible explanation for differences in the social attention paid to the physical attributes of men and women has to do with the distribution of authority. Since men generally occupy positions of authority, they have more resources under their control to attract a sexual partner; they need not rely on their physical features alone. In contrast, women are not in positions of authority and rely on the limited resources they do have, e.g., physical appearance.

As I have emphasized earlier, groups go to a great deal of trouble to differentiate the sexes from each other. Sometimes the differences are more apparent in behavioral contexts, such as sleeping and eating arrangements, than they are in physical appearance. Nevertheless, the contrast between the sexes remains an important element in establishing gender identity and creating a basis for attraction. When we talk about standards of beauty or handsomeness, we are considering the values that a group or person attaches to the physical features. Therefore, less attention to standards of handsomeness for men does not mean that their physical appearance is unimportant. It means only that it is not explicitly singled out for cultural emphasis.

There are some features of women that men in most societies find attractive. Plump women are generally regarded as being more desirable than slim ones. A broad pelvis and wide hips are other female attributes with extensive appeal. There is considerably more variation in men's fascination with other physical qualities of women. Elongated labia majora (the large folds of skin that enclose the labia minora and urethral and vaginal openings) or the shape, size, and firmness of women's breasts are likely to be appealing in some societies (Ford and Beach 1972: 88). Beyond these few features that are singled out for attention in many societies, there is wide variation in what constitutes "good looks." The texture, color, and length of head hair; the shape of the nose, eyes, ears, or mouth: — each is regarded as a criterion of beauty in some societies.

It is easier to specify the traits that men and women *do not* find appealing in each other than to outline standards for beauty. A large number of societies consider a poor complexion and other disfigurations of the skin to be very offensive (Ford and Beach 1972: 89). Most people also think that filthiness is repulsive (Ford and Beach 1972: 89).

The senses of smell, sight, and touch play important roles in human sexual attraction. Most groups insist that people free their bodies from disgusting odors and regard cleanliness as sexually appealing. Some people use oils and perfumes to cover up body scents. As yet, the role of pheremones in human interaction is unclear (Money 1980: 74). There is some evidence to show that ovulating women release a pheremone-type of substance in their vaginas, but it is uncertain how much of a sexual stimulant this is to men (Money 1980: 74). There may be individual variations in receptivity to its influence, which could explain individual variations in the desirability of oral sex (Money 1980: 75).

Vision has a major place in our sex lives. The eyes themselves may be an indication of interest (Ford and Beach 1972: 152). Eyes are often decorated, and they have become significant as "windows of the soul." Exposure of the genitals is not likely to be a visual stimulus for sexual invitation in human societies, as it is for other mammals. When women wear clothing, the genitals are always concealed (Ford and Beach 1972: 95). Consequently, the specific physical features of the body, clothing, body gestures, and adornments are much more important as visual cues for attraction. Culture channels the eyes' perception and the mind's interpretation of the body.

The importance of touch as a symbol of intimacy is apparent in its role as a form of sexual invitation. As Alex Comfort puts it: "Skin is our chief extragenital sexual organ. . . . The smell and feel . . . of skin probably has more to do with sexual attraction than any other single feature, even though you may not be conscious of it" (Comfort 1972: 142). Cultures vary widely in their tolerance of touching. It is a major means of nonverbal communication and is patterned according to its symbolic significance (Henley 1977; Hall 1959). A mere touch between a man and a woman may be enough to encourage a relationship.

Finally, symbols constitute a major type of sexual invitation. Much of our communication with each other is verbal. Patterns of words and sounds influence our actions and elicit powerful emotions. Other animals make erotic overtures with their calls (Ford and Beach 1972: 96). Songs, music, poems, and the spells of love magic are powerful forms of human sexual solicitation.

*Sociocultural aspects of sexual stimulation.* Many of the elements of sexual attraction are elaborated during sexual stimulation. As with other aspects of human sexual functioning, sensations in the genitals and in the rest of the body are related to learning. They are particularly relevant during foreplay, the physical arousal that precedes intercourse.

Humans share with other animals some of the general features of foreplay. Males and females get close to each other and begin to mutually stimulate each other. The stimulation progressively focuses on the genitals, until the male mounts the female, and they engage in intercourse. However, the repertoire for stimulating a partner is limited in most of the animal kingdom. Their techniques and responses are confined to the use of their bodies.

The nature of the contact is different in humans; it is heavily overlaid with symbolic dimensions. Humans have the benefit of their minds in directing their stimulation and enhancing their responses. The combined effects of the mind and body immensely increase the versatility of human sexual stimulation. However, the mind can be a bittersweet addition to sexual response. While it expands our range of sensations, it can also limit them by constricting our knowledge and ability to respond. The symbolic association of sex with connotations of "dirty" can arrest sexual response and account for many sexual dysfunctions.

A certain amount of foreplay is necessary for effective intercourse. It helps to heighten the emotional excitement of the partners and to synchronize their actions so that they join. Sexual differentiation, specific markers of attractiveness, and courtship rituals pervade the animal kingdom and are equally relevant to human foreplay.

The duration of foreplay varies by species and by culture. The Lepcha proceed immediately to intercourse. Although the man may first fondle the woman's breasts (Ford and Beach 1972: 41). Other people, e.g., the Ponape and the Trobrianders in the insular Pacific, devote hours to foreplay, (Ford and Beach 1972: 41). Masters and Johnson (1966) describe the physical changes that occur in the excitement and plateau phases and emphasize the gradual progression of these transitions to orgasm. The excitement and plateau phases increase the woman's vaginal lubrication, so that she is more receptive to the penis. These two phases are also crucial in helping the man to achieve an erection. Many male animals have penis bones, which allow them to achieve intromission without much stimulation. Since human males do not have built-in skeletal structures to maintain their erections, they rely upon psychological or tactile stimulation to excite them. Vasocongestion of the penis produces an erection and allows intromission. Foreplay is more essential to the purely physical aspect of the male's sexual functioning than to the female's. This does not mean that foreplay is insignificant for females. The time involved may be a vital variable in determining whether a woman achieves orgasm. Gebhard's study of orgasm rate and duration of foreplay shows that close to 60 percent of the wives in his sample usually had orgasms if foreplay extended longer then twenty-one minutes (Gebhard 1966). Other investigators, e.g., Fisher (1973), found no significant association. Since some researchers have connected the contractions of the female's orgasm with aiding sperm to move toward the egg, effective stimulation may play an important, albeit indirect, role in conception.

Reciprocity in stimulation occurs in most animals. There is no infrahuman mammalian species in which sexual initiative rests solely with the male or the female (Ford and Beach 1972: 103). In the majority of human societies, initiative in sexual intercourse rests with the male rather than the female. Nevertheless, girls and women often counter the rules of their society and seek sexual relationships with men (Ford and Beach 1972: 101). The restriction of females in beginning sexual relationships is in line with the restraint they are supposed to show in premarital and extramarital relations.

Touch supersedes vision, smell, and hearing in human sexual stimulation; the latter play a larger role in the initial phases of attraction and invitation. The tender pads of the fingertips and the lips and tongue of the mouth are most frequently used to explore and stimulate a sexual partner. Caresses, hugs, and stroking are the most common ways in which people in other societies sexually stimulate each other by touch. Other animals rely on touch to stimulate their partners. Grooming—the removal of bugs, parasites, and other foreign matter in the hair—is a typical—social activity among primates. It often leads to sexual relations. Even the lower mammals that do not have limbs to grasp objects may rely on body contact and licking to establish intimacy. Humans often stroke their partners' hair and play with it as a preliminary to intercourse.

Touching the skin is a more complex process than it appears. The skin can detect five different sensations: pain, touch, pressure, warmth, and cold (Goldstein 1976: 128). The intensity of stimulation of receptors in the skin determines the type of sensation that the person will feel. Tickling, itching, and pain are variations of stimulation on the same receptors. Light stimulation produces the pleasurable sensation of a tickle, and moderate stimulation results in itching, mixture of pleasure and pain. Pain usually results from extreme stimulation of the skin. Since some parts of the body have a greater concentration of receptors than others, effective sexual arousal by touch may partially depend upon knowing how much stimulation to apply to different portions of the body (Goldstein 1976: 129). For example, the tip of the clitoris, like the glans or tip of the penis, is extremely sensitive to touch. Too much direct stimulation of these tender areas could be painful.

Other receptors are responsible for sensations of touch and pressure. Unlike pain receptors, they quickly adapt to continuous stimulation by becoming less responsive. Changing the patterns of touch and pressure is therefore more likely to enhance arousal of these receptors. For this reason, massage manuals emphasize awareness of the spots where it is more appropriate to apply pressure and to change the nature of the stimulation. Finally, changes in temperature can arouse another type of sensation in the skin.

Because people respond differently to tactile stimulation, it is difficult to establish definite "erogenous zones" that apply to everyone.

Erogenous literally means "producing love" and can apply to any part of the skin where stroking is sexually arousing. If we follow this definition closely, any part of the skin could qualify as an erogenous zone for a specific person. Cultures may parcel out certain areas for attention. For example, men in American society regard their thighs and lips as their primary nongenital erogenous zones, whereas women define their thighs and breasts as primary (Goldstein 1976: 130).

Stimulation by rubbing, handling, or stroking the genitals is a widespread form of sexual activity for humans and most other mammals. Male apes and monkeys often stimulate the females' genitals before intercourse; they may also lick them with their tongues (Ford and Beach 1972: 52). However, females are much less likely to stimulate the genitals of the male. Some of these general primate characteristics extend to humans. Mutual stimulation of the genitals commonly precedes intercourse. A young Dahomean girl of West Africa may try to enhance her sexual attractiveness by lengthening and thickening her labia, since a Dahomean man enjoys playing with his partner's labia before intercourse (Ford and Beach 1972: 51). The symbolic load of touch filters down to the interpretation of manual stimulation. Trobrianders believe that if a man can place his magically charmed finger into a woman's vagina, she will be irresistably drawn to him as a lover (Ford and Beach 1972: 50).

The frequency with which men and women orally stimulate the genitals is not clear. Ford and Beach do not report much oral stimulation (six societies where males use it and four where females do) by males or females. On the other hand, Athansiou, Shaver, and Tavris (1970) found that 35 to 40 percent of the 20,000 Americans who responded to their survey experienced oral-genital stimulation regularly; there was little difference between the sexes in giving or receiving this stimulation (Athanasiou, Shaver, and Tavris 1970; Goldstein 1976: 134). These two sets of results are not necessarily in conflict. Reports of sexual behavior are often unreliable. People are hesitant to reveal these details to an outsider. It is difficult to elicit the information from members of our own culture. How much more difficult it must be to give this information to a foreign scientist! The anthropologist is not often in a position to observe the behavior. Therefore, the lack of evidence of oral stimulation in other societies may be a reflection of the problem of data collection rather than a characterization of the actual practices in other societies.

Breast stimulation and kissing are confined to the human species (Goldstein 1976: 132; Ford and Beach 1972: 49). In most mammals, the breasts are well developed only during lactation, when the female is producing milk for her newly-born young. In humans, the female's breasts are conspicuous physical characteristics after puberty; their appearance does not depend upon the birth of a child. In most societies, the man stimulates the woman's breasts manually as an integral part of foreplay. Oral stimulation occurs less frequently. A few societies entirely dispense with stimulation of the breasts (Ford and Beach 1972: 47). Breast stimulation can be an intensely pleasurable experience and can help a woman in maintaining high levels of arousal. Masters and Johnson found that some of their subjects could attain orgasm through breast stimulation alone. Mouthing and sucking the nipples may trigger further physiological changes in the woman that add to her pleasure. Oral stimulation may prompt the release of a hormone, oxytocin, which induces the uterus to contract. Many women report that oral stimulation of their breasts is associated with contractions in the pelvis. Since sucking the nipples is common to both nursing and oral stimulation of the breasts as a part of sexual arousal, they may each lead to the release of oxytocin and its subsequent effect on the uterus (Goldstein 1976: 132).

Kissing is another primarily human form of stimulation. Although some male chimps may grab a female's lower lip and suck on it during intercourse, there are few examples of mouth-to-mouth stimulation in other animals. It is not common among subprimate mammals (Ford and Beach 1972: 49). Although it is a relatively common form of foreplay in human societies, there are some groups in which kissing is unknown or regarded as an amusing but strange custom. When the Thonga saw Europeans kissing, they laughed and remarked, "Look at them — they eat each other's saliva and dirt" (Ford and Beach 1972: 49). Despite its almost universal presence in American society, it occurs less often cross-culturally than manual and oral manipulation of the genitals.

Humans infrequently use anal and painful stimulation. Once again, our species contrasts with many others. Ford and Beach say that fighting and mating may be so closely associated that "it is not an exaggeration to state that physically aggressive behavior forms an integral part of the sex pattern for vertebrates of every major phyletic class, though it does not follow that this is true of every species" (Ford and Beach 1972: 56). During intercourse, many mammals bite their partners. Some humans find that pinching, scratching, and biting increase their sexual arousal. Although inflicting pain during intercourse is primarily the male's prerogative among most animals, it rarely takes this form in human societies. When it occurs, both males and females mutually inflict pain on each other (Ford and Beach 1972: 55). As sexual excitement increases, a person's sensitivity to pain may decrease. Therefore, experiencing pain in a sexual context may be different from the pain of other circumstances.

Masters and Johnson's clinical division of the sexual response cycle into four phases does not focus on the kinds of stimulation that lead to excitement, plateau, and orgasm. They assume adequate stimulation and confine their description to its physiological concomitants. We glean a clearer view of the definition of "adequate stimulation" from their second volume, *Human Sexual Inadequacy* (Masters and Johnson 1970). Although they are dealing with various forms of sexual dysfunction in American society, their format for therapy spells out the essential components of sexual arousal. Their approach provides a good summary of the points I have made about sexual stimulation.

As I have pointed out, the bodies of men and women are structured in such a way that some forms of stimulation are more likely than others to be effective. Freedom of the hands is a big bonus for human sexual arousal, and it is not surprising that tactile stimulation is the most prevalent form of arousal. Stimulation can become more intense as specific parts of the body become the focus of attention; kissing, breast stimulation, and genital manipulation are a few of the major emphases. Masters and Johnson put all of these forms of sexual arousal into human perspective by emphasizing that we must deal with sexual problems like other types of human behavior — on a relational level. Intercourse is primarily a social activity and is mediated by the influences of our culture, society, and individuality. Therefore, to aid clients in achieving satisfactory sexual interaction, therapists need to approach them as whole persons who participate in a variety of social relationships. Since the mind constantly channels sexual expression, therapists confront a sexual problem both from an emotional and from a physical perspective. They help a couple to develop a "sensate" focus. Each partner becomes more familiar with the other's body and preferences for stimulation; one asks the other to indicate what type of stimulation feels good. Each learns a variety of physical techniques and develops an awareness of the other's individuality. Each member tries to withdraw from social demands for performance by taking turns stimulating the other. In order to defuse stimulation from performance anxiety, the therapists recommend that the couple not engage in intercourse at first. The important point to understand is the relevance of feeling, giving, and individuality to sexual functioning. After both members of the couple sufficiently understand these components, they can engage in intercourse. By then each one can effect a balance between personal psychological and physical needs and those of the partner.

I do not mean to suggest that people in all societies achieve this equilibrium in their sexual functioning. The approach that Masters and Johnson take is enlightening, because it highlights the main features that compose human sexual response. They establish a biological baseline, the physiological components of the sexual response cycle, and proceed to show how social and psychological factors enhance or hinder its progression (Masters and Johnson 1970).

Goldstein synthesizes the findings of a number of studies (Kinsey et al. 1953; Ford and Beach 1972) into a succinct summary of the main methods of foreplay that are used in human groups. His summary provides a fitting conclusion to my discussion of the sociocultural aspects of sexual stimulation. He has arranged his methods of stimulation in order of decreasing frequency of use in human societies (Goldstein 1976: 131):

1. General body contacts, e.g., hugging, body caresses
2. Simple kissing
3. Tongue kissing
4. Manual manipulation of the female breasts
5. Manual manipulation of the female genitalia
6. Oral stimulation of the female breasts
7. Manual stimulation of the male genitalia
8. Oral stimulation of the male genitalia, i.e., fellatio
9. Oral stimulation of the female genitalia, i.e., cunnilingus
10. Oral stimulation of the anal area, i.e., anilingus
11. Painful stimulation

All of these techniques of stimulation emphasize the sense of touch. Vision, hearing, and smell add spice to the preceding techniques and show wide variability in their symbolic roles as sexual stimulants.

*Sociocultural aspects of the sexual response cycle: coital positions.* Humans show considerable variety in their techniques and responses to sexual stimulation. Their characteristic versatility extends to coital positions. The hundreds of positions that humans can use for intercourse contrast markedly with the rather sparse repertoire of other animals. Anatomy may be one of the reasons for the distinction. The vaginas of most female nonhuman primates are placed toward the rear of their bodies. Nonhuman primates generally use a single position, rear entry. The development of upright posture in humans facilitated frontal entry. The vaginal opening of the female is toward the front. In addition, muscles and fatty tissues are concentrated in the buttocks and make rear entry more difficult.

Humans in most societies adhere to these biological guidelines. Ford and Beach found that the preferred position in most groups is face-to-face, woman below, man above (Ford and Beach 1972: 24). Aside from the physical ease of maintaining this position, they thought that it was used more often because it enhances clitoral stimulation of the woman, thus making orgasm·more likely for her. However, Masters and Johnson have found that indirect stimulation of the clitoris may occur in any position in which the erect penis fully penetrates the vagina (Masters and Johnson 1966: 59). The thrusting of the penis moves the labia minora, which moves the skin covering the clitoris, the clitoral hood. An alternative explanation for Ford and Beach's finding is that the face-to-face position may aid reproduction. Masters and Johnson describe changes in the position and shape of the vagina and uterus relative to each other during intercourse. As excitement increases, the inner two-thirds of the vagina widens and deepens. This increases the space where semen can pool in the vagina. The outer third of the vagina constricts, forming the orgasmic platform. Its constriction helps to prevent the seminal fluid from leaking out. The uterus elevates to a position above the vagina. After orgasm, the vagina and uterus gradually return to their usual size and positions. The neck of the uterus, the cervix, soaks in any of the seminal fluid that is collected in a pool in the vaginal enclosure. Other positions are not as likely to maximize the pooling of the seminal fluid and the immersion of the cervix in it. The face-to-face, man above, woman below and lying down position would seem to increase the possibility of pregnancy more than other positions. Its reproductive advantages could partially account for the widespread use of the position in human societies.

Psychological and social factors may also contribute to the widespread preference for the face-to-face, man above, woman supine position in human groups. The person on top is in a psychologically more dominant position (Goldstein 1976: 151). Some men do not like the passivity that being below implies and some women do not like the activity that the top position allows (Katchadourian and Lunde 1975: 300). The position may also express social dominance. Woman-on-top positions seem to occur more frequently in societies where women have a greater opportunity to express their own needs (Goldstein 1976: 151). Man-on-top positions seem to prevail in societies where men have more social prerogatives than women (Beigel 1953).

Nevertheless, couples rarely restrict their positions to a single one, even though they may prefer one more than others. The variety of positions used depends upon such factors as psychological makeup, previous experience, information, the cultural context of sex, the statuses of the sexes, and the relative sizes of the partners. Reproduction requires only that the male and the female are attracted enough to each other to engage in intercourse, and that the man deposit his sperm in the woman when she is fertile. The position they use to accomplish this is not of major significance in this context. When we add the potential receptivity of women to intercourse throughout their menstrual cycles and the large amount of nonreproductive sexual activity, the strictures of reproduction need not affect sexual positions. Our biological makeup leaves a lot of room for us to achieve sexual variety as well as reproductive viability.

Comfort (1972) graphically describes and illustrates a sample of possible positions. The physical variations seem to be limited only by the agility of the couple's bodies. There are some common denominators: (1) direction of entry, from the rear or from the front, (2) posture, e.g., sitting, standing, lying supine, lying side-to-side, (3) position of the trunk of the body, e.g., bent backward, forwards, upright, (4) position of the bodies relative to each other, e.g., one on top of the other, side-to-side, crossed like an "X," upside down, (5) position of the limbs, e.g., restricted or stationary, and (6) movement, e.g., fast or slow. Add to these basic combinations the nuances of stimulation of various kinds (touch with the fingers, toes, nose, tongue, lips, or general body surfaces plus smell, sound, etc.). The possible variety of positions for humans is immense.

### Sociocultural Dimensions of Choosing a Sexual partner

The person with whom an individual decides to have a sexual relationship is as relevant to the group as the occasion for sexual encounters. Groups provide guidelines to channel a person's choice of a sexual partner. Social restrictions limit a potentially wide and diverse pool of sexual partners to a definable range of acceptable companions. The expression of the restrictions may be explicitly codified in laws, e.g., definitions of incest, fornication, adultery, and sodomy, as criminal offenses; or they may be forcefully communicated via informal social pressure. An American black woman describes the potent nature of social pressure against her relationship with a white man:

> I had been in Washington one day walking . . . with John, when a car full of young black men drove slowly toward us. Suddenly the men made sucking sounds and hand gestures and yelled out versions of "Hey, bitch, what you doing with that white boy?" and "Hey, bitch, you better leave him alone.". . . Farther down the street a teen-aged black boy bicycled past us, a disbelieving look on his face. "You ought to be ashamed of yourself," he finally said . . . [Other people] . . . force you to think about whether you should keep seeing each other . . . or whether to make life simpler again by

going back to a neatly segregated life, back to "your own kind" [McQueen 1981].

Although criteria such as skin color, status, and attractiveness play a role in the choice of sexual partners, the main bases for selection are kinship and marriage. They include constraints on incest, premarital relationships, age at marriage, spouse selection, number of spouses, post-marital opportunities for sex, and extramarital relationships. I will focus on purely sexual relationships in this chapter and reserve my consideration of reproductive relationships, which are primarily confined to marriage, in the next chapter on the reproductive cycle. Since I am going to discuss many types of partnerships, I want first to sketch how each type affects the overall availability of sexual partners and how one relates to the other.

*The overall view.* The incest taboo is one of the first rules that circumscribes the range of potential sexual partners. It prohibits sexual intercourse between consanguineal kin up to a specified range. It is distinctive as a type of sexual regulation, because it persists throughout the life cycle of the individuals to whom it applies and is not subject to change as they grow older or alter their marital status. Because the taboo can extend well beyond the nuclear family and include hundreds of kinsmen, it can effectively exclude a large number of individuals from sexual relations with each other for an interminable period.

Marital status emerges as another prominent criterion for regulating sexual partnerships. Even the terms we use to specify the restrictions refer to different points in the marital process: (1) premarital, or before marriage, (2) extramarital, or outside of marriage, and (3) postmarital, or after marriage. Social guidelies designate the appropriateness of exercising our human choice to engage in sexual partnerships outside of the bonds of a more centrally reproductive relationship. They define the degree to which purely sexual experiences can become a part of our lives. Unlike incest taboos, they do not precisely designate the statuses, e.g., kinship categories, to which they apply. They contrast to incest taboos in that none of the marital restrictions is as consistently and unequivocally negative as the taboos. They complement primarily kin-based incest taboos by restricting non-kin partners.

We can view both marital and incest prohibitions as reflections of human malleability in channeling the nature of sexual and reproductive relationships. We are introduced to incest taboos quite early in our childhood; their persistence is as indelible as the ties to which they extend. As our social life expands beyond our kin, so, too, do the sexual restrictions that apply to us. By framing the prohibitions in terms of reproductive relationships, they explicitly recognize the potential of the maturing young man or woman to reproduce. They speak to the question that all human societies must answer: To what extent will we allow our people to engage in nonreproductive relationships? Like incest taboos, nonmarital sexual restrictions may apply to a large segment of a person's life. We can follow adolescents through the rest of their sexual cycle in terms of the nonreproductive sexual restrictions that apply to them.

Premarital restrictions follow incest taboos as the major form of sexual restriction on partners to which children are subject. Premarital relationships are those that occur before one or both of the partners marries. They are particularly relevant to maturing adolescents whose physical changes during puberty have enhanced their sexual awareness. The children are physically capable of engaging in intercourse. Premarital rules, like initiation ceremonies, are one mechanism that a group has for defining how it will deal with the children's sexual and reproductive potential. On a broader scale, they are one component of the group's overall evaluation of the extent to which sexual relationships will coincide with reproductive ones. If the prohibitions on premarital sex are slight or nonexistent, the unmarried youths have a wide array of choices; they need not confine sex to one or a few of the parters they select. In some cases, the only limitation on the number and variety of companions seems to be sheer physical stamina. For example, the Aranda of Australia engage in intercourse as much as three to five times a night, pausing only to sleep for a while between each encounter (Ford and Beach 1972: 78).

Marital sexual relationships are likely to follow premarital ones. Marriage generally entails priority of sexual access to one's mate as well as the expectation of continuous availability. This expectation sets marital sex apart from premarital and extramarital sex, for the latter do not delimit specific partners for whom intercourse is allowed. Variety and individual preference usually characterize premarital and extramarital unions.

Another major distinction between marital and nonmarital sex is the desirability of reproduction within each context. Reproduction is usually expected from marital unions, whereas this is rarely the case for premarital and extramarital ones. Ford and Beach classify marriages as "mateships" and categorize premarital and extramarital relationships as "liaisons" (Ford and Beach 1972: 106). They define mateships as relatively permanent sexual unions based on economic cooperation, while liaisons are less stable partnerships in which the relationship is more exclusively sexual. Although the characteristics of stability and continuity are usually sufficient to distinguish between the two types, I have found that eligibility to reproduce is a clearer and more consistent principle, which singles out "marriage" from other types of sexual unions, regardless of their stability or endurance through time. Since marital relationships are the main sexual alliances within which reproduction is not only approved but encouraged, I will discuss them more fully in the chapter on the reproductive cycle.

Suffice it to say that marriage has a profound effect on the variety and extent of available sexual partners. Because marriages generally last longer than other sexual unions, they withdraw a significant portion of potentially available sexual partners from the field for a considerable period. The constriction is even greater with polygyny, i.e., the marriage of a man to more than one woman. One man has priority of access to multiple mates. Not only are the polygynously married women unavailable for sex with men other than their husbands but each of them must share and confine herself to sex with one man.

Age at marriage establishes a boundary that separates premarital from extramarital and marital relations. The intensity of sexual restriction that each nonmarital rule entails depends upon how long a person remains in each context. Some societies define prohibitions on sex for one nonmarital context and not for the other. Such discontinuity in rules would also affect the amount of time and the circumstances under which a person can have nonmarital sexual relations. If prohibitions or allowances are the same for premarital and extramarital contexts, age at marriage is not relevant to availability of partners for sexual access. For instance, if a woman marries relatively late, and if premarital relations are allowed, then her opportunities for sexual partnerships increase. If she marries early, but extramarital relations are allowed, she may look forward to gaining new opportunities for sexual encounters. In contrast, if prohibitions of sexual relations are strict for both premarital and extramarital relations, the age at which she marries will make little difference in terms of the number of partners available to her. Her choice is slight or nonexistent, regardless of when she marries.

A sizable disparity between the ages at which men and women customarily marry for the first time can also affect the availability of sexual partners. For instance, if females marry very early and males marry very late, there will be an excess of premarital males available for sexual activity in relation to the number of females in the same category. This unbalanced ratio of unmarried males to married females is especially characteristic of societies that practice full polygyny, regardless of the overall sex ratio, i.e., the relative number of males to females in the society.

Regulations or customs concerning divorce are similar to those governing age at marriage; they divide one type of sexual restriction from another. In this case, the transition is from an extramarital to a postmarital context, rather than from a premarital to an extramarital one. The death of a spouse effects the same transition but is not usually a matter of choice and is instead bounded by social rules. Difficulty in obtaining a divorce lessens the probability that men and women will be available for other sexual relationships after they marry, unless extramarital restrictions are lax.

The postmarital period includes divorced and widowed persons who are no longer bound by the strictures of marital sexual rules. The regulations that govern this period have been given little attention in the literature compared with other nonmarital rules, e.g., premarital. Due to lack of data, I have been able to include very little discussion about them. Difficulty of remarriage and the person's age determine the duration of the postmarital period. If remarriage is difficult, a person may belong to this pool of available sexual partners indefinitely. At this point, age may affect a person's desirability, and the options for relationships may decrease proportionately. Widowed and divorced women often provide young men with their first sexual experiences in societies where younger women are either married or prohibited from having premarital sex. On the other hand if remarriage quickly follows divorce, the postmarital period becomes too insignificant an interval for much social manipulation to occur. Another restriction on the availability of the formerly married as potential sexual or marital partners is created by customs requiring or encouraging them to marry kinsmen of the former spouse. This sort of restriction controls a widows's choices much more often than it does a divorcée's.

I want to emphasize that I am discussing the rules that affect the availability of sexual partners. The force of these rules is tempered by the degree to which they (1) apply to both sexes, (2) result in punishment when deviations from the desired modes occur, and (3) are obeyed by individuals. The absolute number of males and females in the pool is subject to other qualifications, such as the age structure of the population, the sex ratio, and migration patterns. My main aim is to show that rules that apply to the sexual cycle are linked not only to each other but also to elements of the reproductive cycle. Furthermore, the overall effect of variations in these rules can significantly widen or restrict the number of sexual partners that are available at any one time.

The regulation of sexual relationships can have a powerful impact on the structure of the population for years to come. For example, if sexual activity is confined to marriage and couples marry early, the population could reproduce itself at a rather fast pace. Later marriages, less emphasis on reproductive relationships, and fewer restrictions on nonmarital sexual relations could produce a smaller population, unlikely to replace itself very swiftly. Population size interacts with environmental resources to place further demands on the group. For instance, if population is too large, the group may have to explore alternate food sources and deal with problems of housing and sanitation, which had previously been taken care of through individual decisions. The decision-making process may have to become more elaborate in order to deal with increased population.

These vignettes are sufficient to show that restrictions on sexual relations have extensive consequences for the well-being of the group as a whole. Whether the society explicitly recognizes these repercussions or merely acquiesces to the rules, the effects remain. We need to seriously consider restrictions on sexual relationships in relation to each other and within their total sociocultural context, not as quaint or bizarre customs. The patterns of these relationships have social, cultural, biological, and psychological ramifications. Table 3.1 summarizes some of the most important factors I have discussed.

Table 3.1 *Sexual Restrictions that Affect the Pool of Available Sex Partners*

All of the following restrictions may be subject to differential application to men or women:

|  |  |
|---|---|
|  | Premarital (comprises total sexual encounters) |
|  | Age at Marriage (delimits time in premarital and extramarital periods) |
| Incest Taboo | Marital (number of mates, primarily reproductive) |
| (continues regardless | Extramarital (additional to an ongoing relationship) |
| of stage in | Ease of Divorce (delimits time in extramarital and |
| the life cycle) | post-marital periods) |
|  | Postmarital (affected by age) |
|  | Ease of Remarriage (determines duration of the postmarital period) |

*Premarital restrictions.* As children grow older, they find that their personal experiences of sexuality are very much bound up with the rhythm and organization of their group. After puberty, they have the knowledge and the physical capacity to act upon their sexual desires; they are on the threshold of physical and emotional intimacy with others. Whether they can enter sexual relationships at this time depends partly on their group's restrictions governing premarital sex. Incest taboos exclude a number of kinsmen as potential sexual partners. What opportunities do adolescents have for sexual encounters with people who are not banned by the incest taboo? How does a group deal with the possibility of premarital sex?

The Marquesans (105) on Nuku Hiva Island in Eastern Polynesia and the Egyptians (43) of the village of Silwa and its environs provide starkly contrasting experiences for adolescents. The two societies dramatically illustrate the amazing degree of divergence between groups in their beliefs and rules about the premarital period.

By the time that they reach puberty, most Marquesan boys and girls know about or have already participated in a wide range of sexual experiences. Homosexual encounters between boys and possibly between girls are not unusual during this period; they are condoned even after heterosexual relations are established (Suggs 1966: 25). Suggs estimates that aboriginal girls may have engaged in intercourse for the first time by the age of ten, while boys may have done so after circumcision, between the ages of seven and twelve (Suggs 1966: 99). Young men and women acquire the benefits of years of sexual experience from the older generation. A boy has intercourse for the first time with a married woman in her thirties or forties, while a girl has hers with an older man. As the development of secondary sexual characteristics progresses, so too does the frequency of nocturnal meetings with males in the girl's home. A girl's parents can modulate these encounters. They can arrange an inaccessible sleeping area for their daughter or force her to sleep with a particular young man if it is economically advantageous for their family to establish ties with him (Suggs 1966: 29). The expectation that girls will pursue relationships with men is so strong that their exploits are a source of pride to their mothers, especially if their daughters have a great number of lovers (Suggs 1966: 40). The image that best conveys a sense of Marquesan adolescence is that of a group of youths, fragrant with the scent of saffron and other herbs, who band together in the pursuit of the exciting pleasures that await them (Handy 1923: 39–41; La Barre 1934: 70–72).

The Marquesans' and the Egyptians' views of premarital sex are as divergent as the differences in their appearance. A Marquesan girl's skin is rubbed with coconut oil and scented with saffron. An Egyptian girl's skin is covered with a long, black garment, her face is hidden behind a veil; and the shape of her breasts is camouflaged by extra cloth which pads them.

The constraint of the Egyptians of Silwa represents an extreme reversal of the uninhibited flair of the Nuku Hivans. Chastity is a "moral and religious idea [that] implies the avoidance of any pleasurable influence from the opposite sex or talking about sex" (Ammar 1954: 185). This belief provides the rationale for removing the clitorises of young girls when they are seven or eight (Ammar 1954: 118). Since the clitoris is regarded as a primary focus of sexual stimulation and excitement, its removal is supposed to decrease the probability of premarital intercourse (Ammar 1954: 121) and quell a groom's suspicions that his bride is not a virgin (Ammar 1954: 118). Since it is not unusual for girls to marry at twelve or thirteen, the premarital period is extremely short. Even so, the fear that a woman will bring shame to her family by engaging in premarital sex is sufficient to justify the desire for male rather than female children. "Fire is preferable to shame" (Ammar 1954: 95).

The Marquesans and Egyptians represent polar extremes in their regulation of premarital sex. However, they express a general trend of their world areas. The Insular Pacific, where the Marquesans are located, leads the areas of the world in the extent to which its groups permit premarital sex (90% of 10 Insular Pacific societies). Africa and Eurasia follow closely in their tolerance of premarital sex (88% of 8 African societies; 82% of 11 Eurasian societies). The Egyptians are also in line with the character of their region. The Circum-Mediterranean diverges sharply from other world areas ($X^2 = 6$, 1 df, p = <.02, N = 61) in its emphasis on prohibiting sex during the premarital period (73% of 11 Circum-Mediterranean societies).

Most adolescents do not enter environments as saturated with sexual activity as that of the Marquesans; nor are they likely to experience contexts as devoid of sexual activity as in the Egyptian village of Silwa. Most societies (64% of 61 societies) allow one or both sexes to have premarital relationships. However, permission does not mean unrestricted license to form relationships. Usually social and cultural qualifications apply to the apparent freedom.

One major stipulation on premarital sex is that the rules may apply differently to males and females in the same society. In other words, there may be a "double standard." Under a double standard, premarital sex is allowed for males but not for females (18% of 61 societies). I found *no* groups where the bias is in favor of permitting premarital sex for females rather than for males. Double standards do not prevail in most societies (82% of 61 societies); both sexes are either subject to stringent rules or left free to engage in premarital sex.

The other main qualification to premarital rules occurs as frequently as differential application of the rules by gender (16% of 61 societies).

Premarital sex may be allowed as long as the unmarried girl does not become pregnant (36% of 28 societies in which premarital sex is allowed for both sexes). The proviso clearly reinforces the idea that premarital relationships should be sexual in nature, without reproductive consequences. Even where the nonreproductive qualification is not explicit, it is implied by individual and social responses to premarital pregnancies. Generally the girl destroys the child by abortion or infanticide; or, she may marry the child's father, thus shifting their relationship to a "proper" context for rearing a child. These behaviors point to a definition of marriage as the major reproductive context for sexual relationships.

However, the rules that provide guidelines for behavior give us only a partial glimpse of what actually goes on in a premarital context. We do not always do what we are told to do. Disobeying rules is as human as creating them. Therefore, we need to look at the actions that the group is willing to take to enforce the maintenance of their rules. These sanctions give us a more realistic idea of (1) how firmly invested the group is in upholding the rule, i.e., its social importance, and (2) how highly motivated a person is to violate the rule, i.e., its psychological significance. The implications of a premarital restriction are quite different when its violation is severely punished than when it is overlooked.

A substantial number of societies do not censure men or women for engaging in premarital sex (37% of 51 societies). However, the tolerance that characterizes premarital rules in most societies (64% of 51 societies) does not extend to the consequences of their violations. The majority of societies (63% of 51 societies) do express their disapproval by punishment of some kind. Just as women tend to be restricted by premarital restrictions a little more than men, they also bear the penalty for deviation from the rules slightly more often than men (women — 37% of 51 societies; men — 26% of 51 societies).

In most cases, retribution for the woman's actions is swift and harsh (79% of 19 societies where the woman is punished) rather than mild (21% of 19 societies). In cases where punishment is severe, death is the most common penalty (72% of 7 societies where punishment is severe). For example, the Kenuzi Nubians (39) strongly impress upon a girl the importance of her being a virgin when she marries. They remove the clitorises of three- and four-year-old girls and sew up their vaginal openings to hinder any premarital intercourse; only the woman's husband has the right to penetrate the opening (Herzog 1957: 101, 102). If the girl does not heed her group's demands, her nearest male relative must kill her (Herzog 1957: 94). The same punishment awaits a Kurd (57) maiden if she violates her group's premarital restrictions. She may try to escape death by leaving the chiefdom with her lover. However, if the woman's kinsmen catch the pair, they must slay both of the fugitives (Masters 1953: 186). Even a Kurd bride's inability to prove her virginity to her new husband will result in her return to her kinsmen and subsequent death at their hands (Masters 1953: 186).

Where punishment is severe, the woman's actions seem to be regarded as an offense to the men in her family or to her prospective husband. For example, the friends of a young Fijian (102) girl strangled her because of a premarital transgression. They then apologized to her fiance for her disloyalty to him (Williams 1884: 155). The fact that male relatives or friends slay the woman attest to their interest in the maintenance of her sexual integrity.

The Hidatsa (141) represent one of the few cases where a girl and boy encounter only mild retribution for their premarital activities. Although girls are told that they should not have intercourse with any of the eleven-and twelve-year-old boys who fraternize in groups, they do so. Unless this draws the boy away from his duties, he is not punished. The girl is merely scolded (Bowers 1965: 134).

Between these two extremes of severity and tolerance lie more moderate consequences for the the woman. From the woman's point of view, even they may seem devastating. Fear of what may follow a violation of rules looms over her. A Yahgan (186) woman checks any inclination she has to engage in premarital sex for fear that she might only have male children (Gusinde 1937: 749). Young Japanese (117) women in the fishing village of Takashima fear that their reputations will be ruined if they engage in premarital sex. Young men acquire their premarital experience with prostitutes rather than by having intercourse with virgins. The importance of an unblemished reputation is so great that there have been no cases of premarital pregnancy in the village in twenty years (Norbeck 1954: 162). Premarital relations irrevocably ruin a girl's reputation in Uttar Pradesh (63). Marriage becomes extremely difficult for a girl who breaks the rule (Luschinsky 1963: 254). Invalidation of marriage arrangements already in progress or the subsequent difficulty or inability of the woman to make a desirable marriage is a common type of retribution for her premarital activities. A Wolof (21) man has the right to demand an immediate divorce if his wife is not a virgin when he marries her (Gamble 1957: 68).

It would be misleading to assume that women always bear the brunt of the consequences for premarital sex. In some societies (26% of 51 societies), the man is the only one punished, or he is punished more severely than the woman. The Kafa (33) of southwestern Ethiopia highly esteem the virginity of their women. Castrated males guard nubile girls of the nobility. If the Kafa discover that a young girl has had premarital sex, they give her the benefit of the doubt and presume that it has been against her will. She does not escape unscathed by the loss of her virginity, for it may make it more difficult for her to marry, but the man who violated her may be punished by having his head or hands cut off. In addition, he must pay a fine of two cows to the girl's father and to the emperor (Bieber 1920–23: *1*, 267). A young Tiwi (90) man can also anticipate death if he has relations with a young woman who has not left her father's house to live with her husband (Hart and Pilling 1960: 127). Although a Thonga (3) boy can gain permission to have sex with an unmarried girl by giving her presents, he may do so only on the condition that she not become pregnant. If she does, he must kill a goat for the girl's parents and pay them a fine. In addition, the boy and girl must wander around the village naked for a few days and put a pre-scribed potion on the fence of the village to prevent a disease from infecting the inhabitants. Usually the boy must marry the girl (Junod 1927: *1*, 91)). A bias toward punishing the man is typical of Africa ($X^2$ = 4.0, 1 df, p = <.05, N = 51). In sum, the violation of premar-ital restrictions does not evoke a similar response in all societies. The punishment falls primarily upon the woman (37%) in a few more soci-eties than it does upon the man (26%). In many cases there is no punishment at all (37%). The nature of the punishment ranges from a mild scolding through the moderate consequences of finding it difficult to get married to the severe penalty of death. When punishment does occur, it is more likely to be severe than mild. The most severe retribu-tion is likely to occur in the Circum-Mediterranean. Males are more likely than females to bear the consequences in African societies.

*Age at marriage.* Age at marriage may extend or shorten the premari-tal period and affect the amount of time over which social guidelines apply. For example, a late age at marriage intensifies the permissive or restrictive character of the premarital period. An extremely early age at marriage results in the effective obliteration of the premarital period; nonmarital sexual unions would be primarily extramarital or postmari-tal. The Tiwi (90) of North Australia are a vivid example of the way that age at marriage channels and restricts sexual relationships.

Young Tiwi women never experience premarital relations, because they are betrothed at birth and reside with their husbands as soon as they are able to have intercourse. Early betrothal of women places young unmarried men in a difficult position. There are no unmarried young women with whom they can share premarital experiences. Their dilemma is compounded by the fact that even the most promising youth cannot reside with his bestowed wife until he is at least forty. The age gap between a woman and her first husband is at least twenty-five years. A young man is motivated to contract a marriage by bestowal, because it is the most prestigious form of marriage. However, a twenty-five-year wait to cohabit with his wife and consummate the union imposes strain on even the most virtuous youth. How can the man deal with the suppression of his physical sexuality, which prepares him for intercourse by the time he is twelve to fifteen years old? Does his group offer him any compensation besides the prestigious status of contracting a marriage by bestowal?

The alternatives available to the man are consequences of the relative ages of spouses when they involve themselves in a marriage by bestowal. Since women initially marry men so much older than they are, there is a sizable group of widows. Unfortunately, compulsory widow remarriage specifies a kinsman of the deceased husband, whom she *must* marry; it seizes the young widow from a potential pool of unmarried women with whom an unmarried man could share sex. In some cases, widows are available for young men to marry. Among the Tiwi (90), many bachelors exercise their option of marrying widows much older than they while they wait for their betrothed wives to mature (Hart and Pilling 1960: 29).

The older the man, the more likely he is to have a variety of sexual partners. Successful old men might have as many as twenty wives each. Men under forty can marry elderly widows. Men under thirty may have no wives at all. The possibilities for legitimate outlets for sexual expression for men under thirty seem bleak. Nevertheless, this does not mean that the young men have no alternatives. They can choose the risky option of having extramarital affairs with married women.

Once again, age at marriage channels the likelihood of particular types of relationships. The combination of no unmarried young women with a disproportionate number of single men results in frequent extramarital activity. Young wives find it difficult to be faithful to their old husbands (Hart and Pilling 1960: 37). Seduction by younger men becomes a much more attractive alternative. Consequently, elder males feel threatened by the presence of young men. Extramarital affairs with the elders' wives often precipitate conflicts between younger and older men. The older wives of the elder men may attain a great deal of power over their husbands if they successfully monitor the sexual activities of the younger wives for them.

Age at marriage among the Tiwi has pervasive consequences for the types of sexual encounters that men and women are likely to have in their lifetimes. Men marry late, because they want to enhance their prestige by acquiring bestowed wives. A man may also want more than one wife, but he is rarely in a position to acquire one until he is older. Prestige motivates the men to contract for wives as soon as female infants are born. However, the extreme age gap between husbands and wives severely restricts the type of premarital experiences men will have. It channels most of their early sexual encounters into less prestigious first marriages with older widows or into the conflict-ridden context of extramarital unions. Women have a better opportunity for engaging in a variety of sexual relationships. By menopause, women will have had a succession of extramarital relationships and more than two husbands each (Goodale 1959: 227).

Although the repercussions of age at marriage are generally not as dramatic as those among the Tiwi, they do affect the relative length of time that men and women are subject to the restrictions of the premarital and extramarital periods. In the majority of societies (74% of 42 societies), males marry when they are eighteen or older; females marry when they are seventeen or younger (69% of 45 societies). The most frequent ages at marriage for men fall in the eighteen to twenty-one category, while those for females cluster in the twelve to fifteen-year-old category. When we compare the ages at which men and women first marry, there is a consistent and strong pattern between them. When men first marry, they are always within the same age group or older than women (Gamma = .71, z = 4.04, p = < .01 two-tailed). The strongest trend is for men to be at least one age group older than women (44% of 39 societies) or even more than that (33% of 39 societies). This means that men are generally subject to premarital rules for a longer period than women, even within the same society. However, this does not entail sexual restriction, because premarital encounters are generally permitted to men. A later age at marriage implies an expansion of both time and freedom to engage in a variety of sexual relationships. In contrast, women experience a constriction of the premarital period, the time when women are usually freest to enter nonmarital sexual relationships.

*Extramarital restrictions.* Extramarital relationships are more complex than premarital ones. By definition, they involve a sexual relationship additional to and outside of an ongoing marital union. They can affect the husband/wife bond, children, and the investment of others, e.g., kinsmen, in the continuity of a marriage. The ramifications of extramarital unions are potentially quite extensive. They are not confined to the people in the illicit affair and are often a matter of social concern. The group's interest in preventing extramarital relationships is expressed by the restrictions and qualifications with which they surround them. Extramarital relations rank after incest as the most strictly prohibited type of sexual relationship. They are forbidden for one or both sexes in most societies (74% of 58 societies). Even where extramarital sexual relations are permitted for both sexes, they are circumscribed by numerous qualifications, which limit the occasions when they can occur (79% of 14 societies that permit extramarital relations). The eruption of too many illicit unions could threaten the organized functioning of the community. The group exercises as much control as it can in channeling the circumstances of these relationships if and when they occur.

Wife-lending illustrates how tightly extramarital relations can be structured. As part of the hospitality that they extend to visitors, Aleut men may give their guests permission to sleep with their wives. The husband controls sexual access to his wife. The "affair" is not likely to be a mutual, passionate attraction that leads to intercourse. Rather, it is a more measured extension of the social graces.

More frequently, kinship criteria limit the range of individuals between whom extramarital sex can take place. The Marshallese (108) of Jaluit Atoll allow a woman to have sexual access to her sister's husband (Erdland 1914: 115). A Comanche (147) man may have intercourse with his brother's wife (Wallace and Hoebel 1952: 138), but only with the express consent of the husband. If a woman voluntarily pursues her husband's brother or arranges to meet him secretly, her husband becomes incensed. The crucial difference is that the husband should make the decision about how to deal with his wife's sexual relationships, not the wife herself; her assent to extramarital relations defines the liaison as adulterous. Hidatsa (141) custom allows a man sexual access to his wife's sister only when his wife is in the advanced stages of pregnancy (Bowers 1965: 110). The woman's parents think it is preferable to offer him another daughter than to risk having him get involved with an unrelated woman.

Sometimes license for extramarital intercourse is permitted only during certain ceremonial periods. The Fijians (102) frequently engaged in extramarital intercourse after the men returned to the village with war captives (Thomson 1908: 96; Williams 1884: 43). Mardi Gras and some conventions in the United States seem to fit into a similar category. All of these situations are bounded by a definite period of time, after which the relationships are not tolerated. Once again, the group attempts to control the occasion during which sexual relations may occur. In this case, it also specifies the partners who can become involved.

Another way of limiting the opportunity for extramarital relations is to reduce the number of people who are allowed to become involved. A common method of doing this is to allow the husband but not the wife to have extramarital affairs (26% of 58 societies). I did not find one society that gave women the option of having affairs while denying this alternative to men. Once again, the double standard excludes women from participating in nonmarital sexual relations.

If groups go to such trouble to limit extramarital relations, why do they allow them at all? It would seem more efficient to dispense with the myriad qualifications that surround them. One rationale for maintaining extramarital relations is economic. Extramarital relationships among the Aweikoma (180) of St. Catarina, Brazil, can considerably benefit both the woman's husband and the band as a whole. An affair may motivate a man to join his paramour's band and thus increase the number of hunters in the group. "Even adultery plays a constructive role in . . . society for it keeps men within the band who might otherwise go elsewhere for satisfaction. . ." (Henry 1941: 56). Sometimes the economic advantages of extramarital sex come in the form of payments. The *bai*, or men's clubhouse, is the location for many of these transactions among the Palauans (111). Men and women conduct their affairs there with the full knowledge of their spouses. A man compensates a woman's husband or father if she restricts her sexual relationships in the *bai* to him (Krämer 1929: 369). Occasionally married women will enter the *bai* to earn more money (Krämer 1929: 370). The wives of club members have no alternative but to tolerate their husbands' affairs in the *bai* (Krämer 1929: 369). Despite the open toleration of liaisons, a woman must never go to the *bai* in the village where her family resides and where she grew up (Krämer 1929: 328).

Another reason for allowing extramarital affairs is political. Sometimes the residence of outside Palau women in the *bai* helps to soften tensions between villages. The wife-lending of the Aleut may help men to solidify their friendships with each other.

However, social tolerance of extramarital affairs may create a difficult emotional experience for the spouses. Social and individual needs may be at odds. Among the Hidatsa (141), a husband might endure the loss of his wife to another man rather than show anguish to his relatives; they would ridicule him for trying to take his wife back. The most honorable alternative for the husband is to feign disinterest and to publicly reject his wife. He might go as far as presenting his wife and her current lover with a grand display of gifts. He retains his honor but loses his wife (Bowers 1965: 248).

The overall tenor of the restrictions on extramarital relations conveys a picture of them as primarily forbidden, dangerous unions. Groups try to exert control by hedging them in on all sides with a variety of qualifications, if not outright prohibitions. They drive home the force of their discontent over such relationships by allowing particularly ruthless punishments of participants when they disobey the rules. Unlike the penalties for premarital sex, those for extramarital sex have a consistently cruel bent to them. Although one or both of the offending pair receive mild punishment in a few societies (15% of 54 societies), most societies (85% of 54 societies) inflict moderate to severe punishment. Even where the response is mild or moderate (52% of 54 societies), divorce or death are both alternatives that may occasionally be invoked. The Siuai (99) of the Solomon Islands and the Saramacca (165) of Surinam are among the few societies that inflict comparatively little punishment on the couple. A Siuai woman's husband may fine or incarcerate her lover if he finds out about their relationship (Oliver 1955: 147). In some cases, the couple receives only mild disapproval (Oliver 1955: 272). Numerous violations of the rules express how little regard people have for them.

The Saramacca are not quite as lenient toward the lover. The woman's partner must defenselessly submit to a public beating by her husband. In some regions he must also pay a fine (Herskovits and Herskovits 1934: 74). Although the woman's husband can beat her, he rarely does. He does not think that she is responsible for what has happened (Hurault 1961: 228). His belief in his wife's impunity endures even when she is pregnant by her lover. The Earth Mother, who bestows fertility, protects a pregnant adulterous woman from injury (Herskovits and Herskovits 1934: 74).

A range of specific, moderate punishments are often available to fit the spouse's current social situation. A Suku (6) woman's husband or group responds to adultery in a manner appropriate to their social status and the circumstances under which the offense occurs. In the past, adultery with the wife of a chief could precipitate a small war against the lover's village (Van de Ginste 1947: 45). Where no special status is involved, the man pays a fine to the woman's husband and a smaller payment to his wife's brother, if he is also married. However, it is a much graver offense to have intercourse with a wife who is especially protected by fetishes. Such an act endangers the health of the woman and her husband. Therefore, the man must pay more than the usual compensation for adultery; he must pay a fine to the fetish for offending its influence, to the husband and wife for the back pains that they incur, and to the woman's mother's brother (Van de Ginste 1947: 45–47).

Moderate punishments include a fine, a beating that does not result in permanent physical damage, and temporary public ostracism. People are not blind to the advantages and disadvantages of retribution for extramarital relations and may adjust their responses accordingly. In some cases a husband may reap substantial economic benefits from his wife's affairs, because of the penalty he can impose on the paramour. Some Miskito (156) men are reputed to retain their wives for the income that they receive in fines from their lovers. The main circumstance that provokes a husband to beat, choke, or drown his unfaithful wife is her unwillingness to name the man from whom he can expect a payment (Conzemius 1932: 103). Sometimes a group can go too far in punishing extramarital violations. The Nicobarese (78) had to change their usual penalty of death to a more moderate punishment. They put so many people to death for their transgressions that the population began to decrease significantly. Therefore, they substituted a fine and sometimes a flogging for the previous penalty of death (Whitehead 1924: 221).

The wounds of a beating or the financial deprivation of a fine seem lenient in comparison with other "appropriate" reactions to extramarital affairs. Divorce, mutilation, or death are frequent forms of severe punishments. A Comanche (147) woman is not naive about the potentially dangerous consequences of her relationship. In anticipation of possible punishment, she chooses a brave man as her lover, with the hope that her husband will fear him and possibly forego some chastisement of her. A man risks the loss of all of his property. If he is poor, he endures the degradation of a public flogging with a horsewhip. A worse fate awaits the woman. The husband not only whips his wife but also slashes the soles of her feet and usually cuts off her nose (Hoebel 1940: 58, 59). If his wife refuses to confess the name of her lover, her husband can subject her to further tortures until she replies. He can try to choke her or gradually lower her over a fire. His methods may bring about a confession if the woman does not die first (Hoebel 1940: 96). Fear of the ancestors' wrath upon her kinsmen and her husband's temper vented against her are enough to deter most Manus (96) women from adultery. They have seen the results of misbehavior. One husband was so angry that he branded his wife's vulva (Fortune 1935: 43).

Death is the preferred and most frequent punishment in a few societies (9% of 54 societies) and a likely alternative in many others (56% of 54 societies). If there is even the slightest suspicion of a wife's infidelity, a Kenuzi (39) husband can kill her (Herzog 1957: 94). The fear of death as a consequence of such suspicion probably explains the tenacity with which women cling to the practice of excision (the removal of the clitoris and labia minora). Excision is supposed to lessen a woman's sexual feelings and aid her in averting the temptation to have extramarital relations. Nevertheless, women think that abstinence for the months and perhaps years of their husband's absences at migratory labor requires a good deal of self-control (Callender and El Guindi 1971: 32). As an added precaution against extramarital sex, a woman closes her vaginal opening by sewing it together (Herzog 1957: 101). She might do this three to ten times in the course of her marriage. Although these measures may aid her in escaping death because of the suspicion of adultery, it is ironic that she risks death by the procedures she follows to prevent suspicion.

The social support for death as a punishment for violation of sexual standards is illustrated by Lebanese homicide statistics. A 1974 report showed that almost 8 percent of all homicide convictions were for the murder of women by their male relatives (Worden 1974). Fathers, brothers, and husbands killed their daughters, sisters, and wives because they engaged in premarital sex, extramarital sex, or prostitution. Because of the "extenuating circumstances" of the crimes, the judges were often lenient in passing sentences. It was a question of preserving "honor."

Not only is there consistency in the severity of punishment for extramarital sex; there is also near-uniformity as to the person who administers the penalty. The husband punishes his wife and/or her lover in the majority of societies (72% of 54 societies). A man's family or kinship group does not usurp his right to punish one or both of the pair. A member of his wife's family or kin group only rarely intervenes in this matter (5.6% of 54 societies). Even supernatural repercussions rarely apply to the couple (3.7% of 54 societies).

The consequences of extramarital sex are usually direct, severe, and confined to the parties involved. The immediacy and violence that often accompany punishment for extramarital sex seem almost to have a primal character. Social acceptance of extramarital relations does not mean that a spouse can accept the situation at an emotional, individual level. At the very least, the psychological foundation for the kind of punishment a man administers to his wife and/or to her paramour deserves more attention.

John Money suggests that love means the establishment of a pair-bond (Money 1980: 64). The experience of pair-bonding is similar to imprinting, in that the person projects a sort of ownership onto the partner. If both partners have similar experiences, then the attachment between them becomes very intense and durable (Money 1980: 65). However, if there is little feedback in the relationship, and it is one-sided, then it will become unstable and be likely to falter. The consequences of a one-sided relationship may erupt in arguments, hatred, and destructive violence (Money 1980: 66). If Money is correct about some of the biological mechanisms that underlie pair-bonding, then we may have a clue to the inordinate violence that characterizes the husband's punishment of his wife and/or lover.

Sometimes the community as a whole or its representative punishes one or both of the extramarital pair (14.8% of 54 societies). Caste leaders in Uttar Pradesh (63) feel compelled to punish a couple whose affair is well known or who are discovered *in flagrante delicto*. The status of the caste would suffer if it allowed such a blatant circumvention of its standards (Luschinsky 1963: 601). The captain of a Warrau (162) rancheria bears the responsibility for carrying out the couple's punishment. Only after he has struck them with his bare fists, suspended them between two stakes, and cut their hair will the spouses of the extramarital pair forgive them and allow them to return home (Turrado Moreno 1945: 257).

The most variable aspect of punishment for extramarital sex is the degree to which it falls upon the woman, the man, or both. A woman and her partner receive approximately similar punishment in most societies (40% of 48 societies). When both are punished, the man's punishment is usually (31% of 48 societies) more severe than the woman's (12.5% of 48 societies). Severe punishment of the man occurs particularly in Africa and the Insular Pacific ($X^2 = 11.4$, 1 df, p = < .001, N = 48). When the penalty is not shared, the woman is more likely to be chastised than the man (woman — 12.5% of 48 societies; man — 4.2% of 48 societies). However, in comparison with the number of societies that inflict punishment on the pair (83.4% of 48 societies), very few require one of them to suffer for both.

*The patterning of premarital and extramarital restrictions.* By the time that youths become familiar with extramarital restrictions, much of their social education about purely sexual relationships is complete. They will discover the nuances and exceptions to the rules as they progress through their own lives. Restrictions on premarital and extramarital sex are particularly relevant to the constriction or expansion of their sexual expression. These restrictions shape the degree to which the youths will be allowed to have nonmarital — i.e., nonreproductive — sexual relations with a variety of partners.

Premarital and extramarital restrictions provide guidelines for behavior in terms of approved and prohibited channels for sexual activity. However, the rules alone do not communicate the commitment of the group to allowing or preventing nonmarital sex. The actions taken in relation to the rules are more likely to express the investment the group has in maintaining the rule. There are at least three possible courses of action that a group can take. First, a group can reward people for observing its rules by celebrating their conformity or willingness to obey social guidelines. We saw this approach with initiation ceremonies. Second, a group can convey its involvement by punishing people when they do not adhere to its restrictions. Third, a group may express its indifference by not acting at all in relation to its rules; it neither exhorts nor dissuades people from obeying them. In sum, we have a clearer idea of a group's view toward nonmarital sex when we consider not only its expressed rules but also the actions it takes in relation to them. What consistency is there between the rules and the social actions connected with them?

It is rare for groups to encourage people to engage in premarital or extramarital relations. Groups generally censure nonmarital relationships when they do not conform to socially approved guidelines. The messages are much more likely to be consistent for premarital sex than for extramarital relations. When premarital rules are lenient, punishments are likely to be mild. When premarital restrictions are stringent, the punishments have a severe cast to them. Social actions are in line with the force of premarital restrictions. In contrast, punishments for extramarital relations are not in line with the rules against them. Even when extramarital relations are allowed, a person can be killed or severely mutilated for engaging in them. In fact, the punishments for extramarital relations are more severe than those for incest (moderate/severe punishments for incest — 72.7% of the societies; for extramarital relations — 85.2%). As I discussed earlier, individual responses to extramarital liaisons, e.g., the husband's, may explain the lack of congruence between the social rules and the actions taken to enforce them. After all, extramarital relationships are the only ones that add another relationship to an ongoing sexual and reproductive one. We need to consider the emotional commitment of the spouses as well as the social investment in a relationship when we examine the intensity of response to extramarital relationships.

Another apparent inconsistency in the social regulation of premarital and extramarital relationships is that different rules apply to different segments of the population. For example, men and women sometimes receive different kinds of punishment when they violate the same rule. In addition, groups may have very different guidelines for men and women to use in channeling their sexuality in the premarital and extramarital contexts.

I have shown that premarital intercourse is allowed for one or both sexes in more societies than it is not. Extramarital relationships are subject to greater restriction than premarital ones. In addition, a

Table 3.2 *Association of Premarital Sexual Restrictions with Extramarital Sexual Restrictions as They Apply to Females*

*Extramarital Restrictions*

| | | Allow, Limited Contexts, No Pregnancy | Weak Prohibition | Strong Prohibition | |
|---|---|---|---|---|---|
| | Allow, Limited Contexts, No Pregnancy | 10 | 6 | 8 | 24 |
| *Premarital Restrictions* | Weak Prohibition | 2 | 3 | 3 | 8 |
| | Strong Prohibition | 3 | 5 | 17 | 25 |
| | | 15 | 14 | 28 | 57 = N |

Gamma = .4955; z = 2.63; p = .01, two-tailed

greater number of societies permit men to engage in both premarital and extramarital sex than allow women to exercise the same privileges. There is more emphasis on the restriction of female sexual relationships in premarital as well as in extramarital contexts. The pattern of association between premarital and extramarital restrictions reveals their social significance and the force of the rules on individuals. How consistently are premarital and extramarital rules applied to males and females in the same social setting? Does the combined effect of premarital and extramarital rules mean that men's and women's sex lives have very different patterns?

Table 3.2 shows the application of premarital and extramarital restrictions to females; Table 3.3 shows their application to males.

These tables show that both men and women can expect some continuity in the severity of the rules that apply to them in the premarital and extramarital periods. In other words, when premarital restrictions are minimal, extramarital ones are also likely to be; when they are severe, extramarital ones will probably be too. Men experience a great deal of consistency in the rules they are expected to follow from the premarital to the extramarital period. Although women also share a significant portion of the experience of consistency in rules from one period in their lives to the next, the outlines for their sexual expression may begin to look very different from those of men. In the first place,

Table 3.3 *Association of Premarital Sexual Restrictions with Extramarital Sexual Restrictions as They Apply to Males*

*Extramarital Restrictions*

| | | Allow, Limited Contexts, No Pregnancy | Weak Prohibition | Strong Prohibition | |
|---|---|---|---|---|---|
| *Premarital Restrictions* | Allow, Limited Contexts, No Pregnancy | 26 | 9 | 1 | 36 |
| | Weak Prohibition | 3 | 3 | 2 | 8 |
| | Strong Prohibition | 1 | 2 | 10 | 13 |
| | | 30 | 14 | 13 | 57 = N |

Gamma = .8388; z = 4.92; p = .01, two-tailed

women may have to cope with curtailment of nonmarital sexual relationships after a previous period of premarital freedom. Men have to deal with this disjunction in rules much less often (women — 14% of 57 societies shift from premarital freedom to extramarital restriction; men — 2% of 57 societies). Secondly, women have to consistently restrict their nonmarital sex lives more often than men (women — 49% of 57 cases where prohibitions apply to premarital and extramarital contexts; men — 30% of 57 societies).

When we look at the contrast between the application of rules to men and women *in the same societies*, gender differences emerge even more dramatically. Table 3.4 shows the differential application of premarital and extramarital restrictions to males and females. When I developed the indicators for degree of restriction on males and females, I took into account the relative length of time that the prohibitions would be in effect. As I discussed earlier, age at marriage is an important marker of the extent to which individuals can express themselves in a nonmarital context. It can lengthen or shorten their time for experimentation.

Once again we see our general trends reflected in the application of rules to sexual relationships in which males and females are involved. There is a significant association between the degree of sexual restriction placed on men and women in the same society. This means that where a man's sexual activities are curtailed during the premarital and

Table 3.4 *Contingency Table of the Cross-Tabulation of the Degree of Premarital and Extramarital Restriction on Females with that for Males*

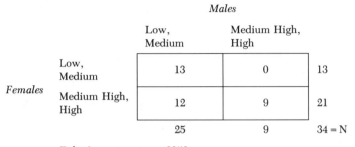

Males

|  | Low, Medium | Medium High, High |  |
|---|---|---|---|
| Females Low, Medium | 13 | 0 | 13 |
| Medium High, High | 12 | 9 | 21 |
|  | 25 | 9 | 34 = N |

Fisher's exact test p = .0056

extramarital periods, a woman's are also. However, a large number of exceptions to the general trend reveal one striking deviation from this consistency. If a man experiences a low to medium degree of constriction on his premarital and extramarital sexual encounters, a woman may not enjoy the same opportunities. Greater sexual opportunity is rarely allowed for females when the same option is unavailable for males. In other words, males do not experience the double standard.

We now have a partial answer to our original question: Do premarital and extramarital restrictions foster differences in males' and females' patterns of sexual expression? Yes, in a sizable number of societies. However, we have only a partial view of how male and female sexuality is channeled, because we have not yet discussed another major avenue for sexual expression — reproductive relationships. The significance of sexual expression in a reproductive context is likely to give us a better understanding of sex in a nonreproductive one. I shall discuss the relationship between sexual and reproductive relationships in a later chapter.

*Hormones and Sexual Response:*
*Adulthood through the Climacteric*

Learning plays a significant role in framing the biological changes that occur as individuals shift into adulthood. Social restrictions affect sexual response and the selection of sexual partners. The physical changes of puberty and the social attention given to them heralded a confirmation of the differences between the sexes. Consequently, later hormonal changes seem subdued in comparison to their dramatic expression during the first two decades of life. However, hormones continue to exert an important influence over the pace of sexual response throughout people's lives.

The basic hormonal paths that guide the sex lives of men and women segment into two types: cyclical and acyclical. The release of hormones from the hypothalamus of women is cyclical, while that of males is acyclical. These sex-linked characteristics are significant, because they trigger the release of other hormones in our systems, which, in turn, may influence the way that we feel about ourselves and affect our receptivity to sexual relations.

*The menstrual cycle: biological aspects.* Menstruation derives its name from the periodicity of the event. "Mensis" means month, and "menses" means months. "Menses" has come to refer to the flow of blood from the uterus, which occurs approximately every four weeks. The root of the word emphasizes the cyclical nature of the event.

Although the other two species with menstrual cycles (Old World monkeys and apes) retain peak sexual activity at ovulation, humans seem to be freer from the hormonal constraints that confine sexual activity to ovulatory periods. This does not mean, however, that hormones do not exert some influence on the periodicity of sexual relations. The emphasis on learning and cortical control over sexual activity in humans has been so great that we are tempted to reply without hesitation that human sexual receptivity and activity are different from those of other animals. Nevertheless, the question is open to empirical investigation. Do a woman's sexual desires fluctuate according to the pace of hormonal release so that she, too, experiences something like a period of heat?

Quite a few studies show that there is fluctuation in a woman's desire for and receptivity to intercourse according to specific points in the menstrual cycle. The earliest study of the relationship between sexual desire and hormone production (Benedeck and Rubenstein 1942) concluded that the emotional cycle parallels the hormonal cycle. The researchers found that women felt most loving and receptive to intercourse during ovulation; they were most likely to feel intensely sexual around menstruation. Udry and Morris (1968) found that intercourse and orgasm occurred most frequently around midcycle, although women also experienced sexual peaks before and after menstruation. Kinsey et al. (1953) found that most of their subjects felt most sexually aroused just before the beginning of menstruation. Weideger's study of menstruation (1977) shows that most women experience peaks in sexual desire just before, during, and after menstruation.

Although the empirical evidence is not conclusive about the association between sexual desire and hormonal release, it points to a couple of important conclusions. The first is that women (in samples drawn primarily from American and European cultures) are most sexually aroused around the time of menstruation. As I pointed out earlier, increased vasocongestion in the pelvic and genital areas before menstruation may heighten a woman's sensitivity to sexual stimulation. In addition, progesterone production is at its peak. Progesterone is chemically similar to androgens, which have been linked to increases in levels of sexual motivation. Therefore, there may also be an association between maximal progesterone secretion before menstruation and increased sexual desire. The second conclusion is that ovulation may also be associated with heightened sexual activity. Some studies do not differentiate between self-reports of arousal and activity based on those desires, e.g., initiating intercourse. In other words, they do not distinguish between sexual desire and sexual activity. The distinction is a significant one. Since we do not always act upon our desires, the reproductive repercussions of these sexual desires are unclear.

If we assume that human females experience two major peaks in sexual arousal during the menstrual cycle, i.e., one during ovulation and the other one during, before, or after menstruation, how can we account for the finding that most sexual activity and orgasms occur around ovulation rather than during menstruation (Udry and Morris 1968)? Given reports of heightened arousal during, before, and after menstruation and the physiological condition of vasocongestion, I would expect a greater frequency of intercourse around the period when a woman menstruates. Why does the intracultural and cross-cultural evidence point to more sexual activity during times other than that period?

Even though the physiological differences between estrus and menstrual cycles are slight, their consequences are not. The event from which the name of the cycle derives, the menses, holds the center of attention in many societies. Other activities may be adjusted to it. The cultural interpretation of the menstrual flow has more significant repercussions for the pace of sexual activity than the ebb and flow of hormones.

*The social significance of regular menstruation.* What, then, is the significance attributed to "regular" menstruation? I have already noted that many societies require that a woman undergo moderate to severe restrictions when menstruation first begins. However, there is no significant relationship between the type of ordeal that she undergoes at first menstruation and the restrictions that she incurs during subsequent cycles. This finding supports my view that its onset is used as an occasion to emphasize socially important concerns, e.g., the acceptance of adult responsibility and marriage. The attention given to the onset of menstruation does not establish procedures that will be followed in the periods that ensue. Therefore, we have to give separate consideration to the interpretation of regular menstruation and the types of behavior associated with it.

One of the major themes that surrounds the regular occurrence of menstruation is the danger linked to contact with or the sight of a menstruating woman. Most societies (70% of 30 societies) regard the menstrual flow or a menstruating woman as dangerous to others in the community. Fear of menstruation touches individuals and groups, in both past societies and contemporary ones. Orthodox Jews and some Christian sects follow the traditional proscriptions of Leviticus in the Old Testament. He forbade intercourse for seven days in order to deal with the abomination of the menstrual flow:

> And if a woman have an issue, and her issue in her flesh be blood, she shall be put apart seven days: and whosoever touches her shall be unclean until the even . . . And if any man lie with her at all, and her flowers be upon him, he shall be unclean seven days; and all the bed whereon he lieth shall be unclean . . . But if she be cleansed of her issue, then she shall number to herself seven days, and after that she shall be clean [Leviticus 15: 19, 24, 28].

Women were also cut off from religious practices. A Jewish woman could not shake hands with a rabbi or enter a synagogue. Early Christian women could not partake of communion (Weideger 1977: 99).

Other major religious traditions have some similar ideas. Islamic women are "a pollution" (Koran 1930: 77) during menstruation and are not allowed to enter a mosque or to pray (Weideger 1977: 197). Until recently, some Catholic theologians thought that it was sinful to seek or have intercourse during menstruation (Weideger 1977: 197). The early Roman historian, Pliny, distilled in his *Natural History* some of the aversion to the perceived destructiveness of menstrual fluid in the following description:

> . . . if this female power should issue when the moon or sun is in eclipse, it will cause irremediable harm; no less harm if there is no moon; at such seasons sexual intercourse brings disease and death upon the man; purple too is tarnished by the woman's touch. . . . it is certain that when their hives are touched by women in this state bees fly away, at their touch linen they are boiling turns black, the edge of razors is blunted . . . mares in foal if touched miscarry . . . [Pliny 1938–63: *8*, 55, 57].

Although death might not be the consequence of contact with menstrual blood or a menstruating woman, many societies believed that serious social or individual consequences might develop. Illness might be an automatic consequence of contact with a menstruating woman. Crops could wither, and luck in hunting could diminish. Defying the taboo could affect the health of the individual and/or the well-being of the group as a whole.

Fear associated with menstruation can be just as intense for women as for men. Psychotherapist Leah Schaefer (1973) presents some vignettes of how some of the women she interviewed felt about menstruation. Thirty-seven percent of the thirty women she talked with associated the onset of menstruation with physical injury. One woman said that a friend of hers told her, "You begin to bleed and if you don't put on a girdle, you'll bleed to death" (Schaefer 1973: 81).

Attitudes toward menstrual blood can translate into differences in receptivity to intercourse during menstruation. Some women were quite positive about sex at that time:

> About sex during my period — well, I don't mind if my husband doesn't mind. In fact, I rather like it . . . it's fine with me. Terrific, in some ways, because there are no worries about getting pregnant; also, I find that I feel strong sexual feelings in all phases of the menstrual period — that is, before, during, and after — although the strongest are before and during, and the least strong, right after [Schaefer 1973: 82].

In this case, the woman recognized the intensity of her sexual feelings around the time of her menstruation and was able to act on them. However, the majority of Schaefer's respondents (63% of 30) expressed neutral or negative feelings about sex during menstruation. Although I would categorize the following statement as negative, Schaefer uses it as an example of neutral feelings about menstruation:

> I don't know how I feel about it. I always thought that it wasn't good for a woman at that time because the flow comes from a sloughing off of the inner lining of the womb, and this always seemed like something rotting inside me. Also, you can get an infection at that time [Schaefer 1973: 83].

One woman thought that it was impossible to have intercourse while she was menstruating. Another expressed a definite aversion: "I'm not crazy about it at that time — it's a messy, dirty time of the month with blood and all that and I'd rather not" (Schaefer 1973: 83). The negative attitudes of the women themselves show how pervasive the influence of a cultural belief can be on the emotional lives of the people who are influenced by it. Women as well as men share the fear. Despite scattered beliefs about the danger of menstrual blood causing an infection in the male, there is no current medical evidence to justify a woman's abstinence from intercourse during menstruation (Katchadourian and Lunde 1975: 100).

The group may try to contain its anxiety about menstruation by specifying that the woman adhere to specific rules during this period. In many societies (55% of 38 societies), the restrictions are mild and involve only a slight modification of the woman's usual social or personal habits. Although a Garo (69) woman does not need to follow specific rules, she usually abstains from intercourse and wears dark clothes. She might also stay near the house for a couple of days to avoid any embarrassment she might feel in the presence of her neighbors (Burling 1963: 98). Otherwise, she goes about her daily activities as she normally would. Mild restrictions of this type tend to occur in Eurasia and the Insular Pacific ($X^2 = 3.4$, 1df, p = < .07, N = 38).

A substantial number of societies impose moderate (24% of 38 societies) to severe (31% of 38 societies) restrictions on a woman at this time. These types of menstrual restrictions occur significantly more in societies in North America (Fisher's exact test, p = .025, N = 38). For example, the Swedish Könkämä Lapps (52) require women to follow numerous, though moderate rules. Because the Lapps think that a menstruating women is especially vulnerable to supernatural dangers and is in an impure state, she must not touch sacred instruments or attend an important religious ritual; her mere presence could desecrate the area (Karsten 1955: 100). She modifies her appearance by removing her belt and cape. Her sleeping habits change somewhat, because she does not rest under the same covers with her husband. Her activities are slightly curtailed, because she cannot, among other things, milk a reindeer cow, step over a man's foot, or go to the shore (Karsten 1955: 101).

The Hill Maria Gond (60) of southeastern India and the Eastern Pomo (135) of central California indicate the extreme lengths to which groups go to evade the dangers they perceive are inherent in a menstruating woman. A Gond woman supposedly has special magical powers during menstruation. It would anger the clan god and the deceased to allow her freedom from seclusion. Therefore, menstruating women occupy a communal hut or a small hut apart from the other houses. The door faces away from the center of the village and is distinguished by the castor-oil plants and seeds placed upon it, which protect others from the women's magic (Grigson 1938: 104–106, 263). They cook their meals in special pots within the hut, or, lacking these, their food is placed by the door. Under no circumstances should a man come near the area. Women on the North American continent are subject to other, more severe constraints. Because an Eastern Pomo woman could harm herself and others at this time, both she and her husband follow special rules (Kroeber 1953: 254). Not only does she occupy a separate hut but she also follows other rules while she is there. She scratches her head only with a stick, for fear of losing her hair. She refrains from washing, because she does not want her face to become wrinkled. She eats no meat, because she believes it would sicken her. She weaves no baskets, because this activity could blind her. Her husband should not hunt, fish, dance, or gamble during the five to seven days that his wife is secluded (Kroeber 1953: 273). Although a husband does not usually have to adhere to special restrictions during his wife's menses, such restrictions are not rare (16% of 38 societies).

Young and Bacdayan (1965) revised William Stephens' scale of menstrual restrictions and tried to establish which restrictions are most likely to apply to a woman during this time. A woman has to occupy a menstrual hut (18% of the societies) and refrain from cooking (38%) least often. She has to submit to personal restrictions (62%) and refrain from intercourse (80%) most often. Between these rules lie others, which specify that the woman not touch male objects (49%). My data suggest that most personal restrictions entail distance from or avoidance of men. Young and Bacdayan, Stephens, and I agree overall that avoidance of men and abstinence are the most prominent features of menstrual taboos. Cultural beliefs about the danger of menstruation, in addition to the social restrictions imposed upon a menstruating woman, have the effect of concentrating sexual activity during specific periods within the menstrual cycle. Avoidance of intercourse during menstruation means that it is more likely to take place during a woman's fertile period. It also means that the social rules and cultural interpretations of menstruation may be at odds with the woman's sexual desires. Groups choose to restrict the sexual activity of women at a time when they are most likely to be aroused.

Weideger thinks that a woman's acceptance of the belief that it is wrong for her to have intercourse during menstruation has very negative effects on her well-being (Weideger 1977: 135). First, she faces increased sexual frustration, because she cannot satisfy her desires when they are most intense. Second, she may be angry, because she is not as convinced as her partner that intercourse is wrong during this time. One woman put it this way:

> I recognize why, for example, men might be disgusted by making love with me while I am menstruating — intellectually. Emotionally, I feel strongly, as a woman, that he should be able to accept my body, my being, at all times of the month. That I accept into my body his discharge of semen and that my

body is not "unclean" while I am menstruating. Also, I become quite easily sexually aroused at this time and do not feel that I should have to inhibit my activity [Weideger 1977: 136].

Third, the negative evaluation of menstrual blood and avoidance of a menstruating woman may promote low self-esteem in women. It would be interesting to find out the degree to which women in other societies are aware of similar feelings.

*Hormones, moods, and sexual activity: the premenstrual syndrome.* In addition to social rules and cultural beliefs that clearly discourage intercourse during menstruation, there are other aspects of the menstrual cycle that may affect the periodicity of sexual relations. The link between hormones, physical changes, moods, and behavior needs more detailed research. Previous studies in the area suggest an association between menstrual cycles and mood cycles. Robert L. Frank's paper, "The Hormonal Causes of Premenstrual Tension" (1931), was one of the earliest efforts directed at showing a relationship between hormones and premenstrual mood swings. He connected fatigability, irritability, lack of concentration, and attacks of pain to fluctuations in hormone levels. Katharina Dalton (1964) elevated the physical and emotional problems that appear before menstruation to the status of a syndrome. She admits:

The premenstrual syndrome is an ambiguous phrase. . . . This title covers a wide variety of cyclical symptoms, which regularly recur at the same phase of each menstrual cycle. The commonest time for recurrent symptoms is during the premenstrum or early menstruation, but occasionally symptoms occur at ovulation. The onset of the full menstrual flow usually brings dramatic and complete relief [Dalton 1964: 1].

The onset of symptoms may be gradual and may begin as much as a week or two before the menses. They generally develop somewhere between the twenty-third day premenstrum to the third day of the next cycle; the most frequent times for the onset of symptoms are the twenty-seventh and twenty-eighth days, i.e., a day or two before menstruation begins. The intensity of the symptoms may increase if the woman is in a stressful situation. Dalton brings together a wide range of psychological and physical expressions of the syndrome, many of which had not been previously linked to the menstrual cycle. She qualifies her work in two important ways. First, it is difficult to specify a consistent pattern of characteristics of the premenstrum that is applicable to the general population of women. Second, probably less than half of all women are affected by the premenstrual syndrome.

Psychological symptoms occur so frequently before menstruation that some researchers think that the premenstrual syndrome always includes premenstrual tension. Premenstrual tension has three elements: (1) irritability ("crabbiness"), (2) depression ("the world looks like a sour apple"), and (3) lethargy ("fall of energy") (Dalton 1964: 7). The woman may express her irritability by being agitated, on edge, impatient, spiteful, or bad-tempered. She may have the feeling that "it wasn't the true me who caused all this" (Dalton 1964: 7). Depression and lethargy also add to her tension. She may cry and have a pessimistic outlook on the world. A number of studies (MacKinnon and MacKinnon 1956; Dalton 1964) show a substantial increase of suicide attempts during the premenstrum and menstruation. However, Dalton cautions us not to conclude that the premenstrual syndrome causes these attempts. Irritability and depression accentuate psychological tendencies that are already present in the woman; she seems to have less tolerance for incidents that mildly upset her at other times. The point is that the psychological symptoms are not completely new experiences. Premenstrual tension may add to depressive tendencies to trigger more serious behavior, e.g., suicide. Lethargy may be related to the depression. In any case, women may sleep excessive amounts and feel mentally exhausted (Dalton 1964: 8).

Although the irritability, depression, and lethargy of premenstrual tension occur most often, other symptoms may also occur. We could interpret some of them as further elaborations of the basic elements of premenstrual tension. Sleep disturbances are common. The woman may still feel tired after a long period of rest. Or, she may suffer from nightmares and insomnia (Dalton 1964: 9). Other accompaniments may be excessive alcohol consumption, "distortion phenomena," "feelings of unreality," and some form of sexual disorder, e.g., an excessive desire for sex (Dalton 1964: 9). The last symptom is interesting in light of my discussion of the finding that increased sexual arousal occurs most frequently around or during menstruation.

Premenstrual tension is not purely psychological; it can affect most of the major systems of the body. The most frequent neurological symptom is a headache (Dalton 1964: 9). It may vary in its severity and in its location. Some women have intense headaches that last several days and make them ill to the point of vomiting. Others experience only mild discomfort. Fainting (syncope), dizziness (vertigo), a pricking or tingling sensation in the hands and feet without "objective cause" (paresthesia), and epilepsy (convulsive motions and loss of consciousness) may develop.

Gastro-intestinal symptoms may complement the neurological ones.

Nausea and vomiting often accompany headaches (Dalton 1964: 11). Lowered blood sugar (hypoglycemia) may relate to the irritability, agitation, weakness, and tension that are characteristic of premenstrual tension. The abdomen may be involved in a variety of ways. It may become bloated, or it may intermittently ache with pain (Dalton 1964: 11). The woman may become especially aware of constipation and hemorrhoids at this time of the month. her weight and digestive processes may be affected by her increased appetite for especially fattening foods. Some women become "addicted" to carbohydrates, such as bread or chocolate (Dalton 1964: 12).

The urinary system may become affected in a variety of ways. The woman may urinate less frequently than usual (oliguria) or be unable to exercise control over her urination (enuresis). The respiratory system is not exempt from the effects of the premenstrum. Asthma attacks, nasal problems — e.g., stopped-up nose, runny nose — and sinus headaches may relate to changes in the body tissues. A woman may even experience voice changes. The vocal chords may increase in size and result in a hoarse character to the voice (Dalton 1964: 11).

Joint and muscle pains are common, as are changes in the condition of the skin (Dalton 1964: 12); acne most commonly recurs during the premenstrum (Dalton 1964: 13). Breast changes, e.g., enlargement, pain, breast masses, and tenderness of nipples, are not unusual (Dalton 1964: 14). Less frequent but observed symptoms of the premenstrum include rapid beating of the heart (palpitations); vericose veins; a tendency to bruise more easily (due to capillary fragility); red, watery, and irritated eyes; styes, glaucoma, and ulceration of the mouth and genitals (Dalton 1964: 14).

We can view many of these individual symptoms as products of tension in the tissues, produced by an excessive accumulation of fluids and vasocongestion. In some women, the buildup of the endometrium is paralleled by a buildup of other tissues. The physical as well as the psychological symptoms could conceivably be traced to these processes. Nasal problems, hoarseness, constipation, headaches, abdominal pain, fainting, dizziness, muscle and joint pains, urinary problems, and changes in the skin all relate to fluid retention and/or pressure on the vessels. Dalton speculates that parts of premenstrual tension, e.g., irritability and nervousness, may be traced to lowered blood sugar. Rather than viewing these symptoms as a "female problem" specific to menstruation, Dalton places them in a more general context (Dalton 1964: 100). She notes that men as well as pregnant women periodically experience similar symptoms. She concludes that the premenstrual syndrome is a specific example of problems in electrolyte balance. Sodium and water retention, as well as potassium depletion, seem to have a major impact on physical and psychological functioning. They form the link that ties together depression, migraine headaches, and specific body disorders (Dalton 1964: 101).

Both Money and Marx point to research that shows that prostaglandins may contribute to menstrual cramps, pain, nausea, vomiting, and headaches (Money 1980: 41; Marx 1979). Prostaglandins are hormone-like substances, which occur in most body tissues; they are chemical compounds that aid in stimulating or relaxing smooth muscles, regulating cell behavior, and inhibiting or expanding hormonal action. There is a definite link between menstrual cramping and excessive prostaglandin released from the uterus (Marx 1979). Since men also secrete prostaglandins, the action of these substances could explain similarities in symptoms between men and women.

Obviously the symptoms and the causes of the premenstrual syndrome are diverse. The chemical processes of the body clearly play a role. They show the subtle connection between the body and behavior. It is conceivable that the discomfort produced by the physical and emotional correlates of the menstrual cycle affects the degree to which a woman wants to engage in sexual relations at that time. Cramps, sinus headaches, and muscle pains have little to offer as inducements to engage in intercourse. Dalton says that the physical symptoms may be so severe that they override the psychological impact of irritability, depression, and fatigue (Dalton 1964: 3). They might also override sexual arousal. Even without severe physical discomfort, premenstrual tension might not enhance a relationship. It could be part of the explanation for why intercourse does not occur as frequently around menstruation, despite women's reports of high levels of sexual desire or arousal at this time.

However, this view of the relationship between sexual relations and the menstrual cycle assumes that women significantly contribute to the initiation of sexual encounters. In these circumstances, a woman's desires would affect the periodicity of intercourse. Ford and Beach indicate that the majority of human groups believe that only men should initiate a sexual affair (Ford and Beach 1972: 101). Yet initiating and maintaining an affair are two separate issues. Initiation has to do with attraction, whereas maintenance relates more to the pattern of behavior that develops after a relationship has been established. Within the latter context, the woman may be able to take more initiative. In most mammalian species, both partners contribute to the arousal of the other (Ford and Beach 1972: 102); initiative does not rest exclusively with either the male or the female (Ford and Beach 1972: 103). Therefore, the female's desires may have an impact on periodicity of sexual relations. Unfortunately, there are too many unknowns to resolve the issue. We do not know the extent of the premenstrual syndrome across cultures. Is it a Western phenomenon, or is it more widespread? Could its symptoms reinforce the common taboo on intercourse during menstruation?

We do know that social context may shape the type of symptoms likely to occur during the premenstrual syndrome. The dominant symptoms may relate to the person's work. For example, women in a packing department, who had to stand and lift, experienced backaches, while those whose job required more concentration, e.g., assembling parts, had headaches before menstruation (Dalton 1964: 6). Some symptoms run in families (Dalton 1964: 4); the contributions of genetics and of the similarity of the learning environment are difficult to specify. Other symptoms may shift over the years, so that the syndrome is not consistent over time for one individual (Dalton 1964: 5). Additional psychological stress may increase the severity of the symptoms.

*The impact of social factors on the menstrual cycle.* McClintock's studies (1971) bolster the notion that social context can affect the functioning of the endocrine system. She found that female residents of a college dormitory showed definite patterns in the timing of their menstrual cycles. Roommates and/or closest friends tended to cycle together, even when each was not aware of when the other menstruated. McClintock is not sure whether the basis of the synchrony is pheromonal, linked to a level of awareness of the cycles, or related to some other process. Overall, the most important factor seems to be that the women spend time together. In a related study she showed that interaction with males may affect the length of the menstrual cycle. When women see males less than three times a week, e.g., within the context of an all-girl's school, they experienced significantly longer cycles than women who spent more time with males. One woman said that her menstrual periods were spaced six months apart until she began to spend more time with men. After that, her cycle shortened to four-and-a-half weeks. However, her cycle's length began to lengthen again when she dated less often (McClintock 1971: 245).

Psychological stress can also affect the timing of menstruation. Environmental changes, disturbances in sleep patterns, and fear of pregnancy are a few of the situations that may cause a woman to have a late period or skip one altogether (Goldstein 1976: 171). The close association of the hypothalamus with the release of gonadotropins — i.e., substances responsible for the release of hormones from the gonads — from the anterior, or front, lobe of the pituitary gland is probably a crucial link in the relationship between hormone levels and behavior. The connections of the hypothalamus to other parts of the brain may be responsible for the effect of individual life experiences on hormonal rhythms (Money 1980: 39).

Early childhood experiences may also play a role in determining the timing of the onset of menstruation. Whiting's cross-cultural study of fifty societies (1965) suggested that infant stress, e.g., pain, exposure, or separation of an infant girl from her mother, was associated with earlier onset of menarche (Goldstein 1976: 90). Vandenberg's experiments with rats (1972) show that females raised in isolation or with other females reach puberty later than those raised with a male and no females (Goldstein 1976: 90). In other words, the nature of social stimulation and interaction between the sexes in childhood may affect when menarche occurs.

Changes in diet can also have an impact on menstrual functioning. Although there is considerable speculation about what triggers the onset of menstruation, weight and body composition seem to play important roles. Weideger (1977: 90) thinks that critical body weight and composition must be reached before menstrual cycles will begin. Frisch and McArthur present findings to demonstrate that a "critical minimum weight appears to be necessary for the onset and maintenance of normal menstrual cycles in the human female" (Frisch and McArthur 1974: 951). The essential weight level is represented is represented by the amount of fat relative to overall body weight. A loss of 10 to 15 percent of body weight after the onset of menstruation results in the cessation of the menses (Frisch and McArthur 1974: 949). Subsequent weight gain can restore the woman's cycles. This may explain why women who have rapidly lost weight from new diets, e.g., fad diets or changes in the types of foods eaten — experience menstrual loss or irregularity. We see the effects of weight loss on reproductive functioning most stikingly in cases of starvation due to inadequate food resources or in cases of self-inflicted starvation, e.g., anorexia nervosa. Since a certain amount of fat is necessary for the body to manufacture hormones, significant reductions in fat can upset the hormonal balance. The body does not have adequate building materials to function "normally."

Although it is easier to measure and is more attractive as a variable, critical body weight may be less important in influencing the onset of menstruation than the overall nutritional state of the woman. Frisch and McArthur acknowledge that amenorrhea, i.e., absence of the menstrual flow, may follow rapid weight loss or chronic undernourishment;

undernutrition may also delay menarche (Frisch and McArthur 1974: 949).

Tanner (1962) has shown that menarche has occurred four months earlier in every decade since 1830. The median age of menarche in the U.S. is around twelve whereas it was sixteen one hundred years ago (Goldstein 1976: 88). Better nutrition has been one of the reasons why this has happened. Frisch and Revelle (1970) link better food supplies and improved health and nutritional standards to the earlier attainment of critical body weight and, thus, earlier menarche. Frisch maintains her previous emphasis on critical body weight, but gives improved nutrition more priority.

The most likely explanation for the timing of menstrual cycles is a combination of factors — genes, diet, climate, stress, and social interaction. There is wide variation in the age of onset of menstruation between and within groups. A Somali girl of Somaliland begins to menstruate when she is nine-and-a-half years old, whereas a Wogeo girl in Melanesia does not begin until she is sixteen. Genetic composition may influence the maturation of the hypothalamus (Goldstein 1976: 88). However, the evidence related to this is scant. One study showed that identical twins are more likely to experience the onset of menarche within a few months of each other than are nonidentical twins, whose ages of onset may vary by as much as a year (Goldstein 1976: 89). Genes may also control what type of body a woman has. If she has a genetic predisposition toward plumpness, and if critical body weight does trigger the onset of menstruation, then genetic constitution may play a larger role than nutrition in influencing when she begins to menstruate.

At the very least, we can conclude that social and psychological factors influence the pace of hormone production. It is very difficult to separate biological/social/cultural/psychological factors from each other, because they are closely interwoven. Therefore, it is a mistake to assert that a woman is a prisoner of her hormonal cycle. A more balanced view takes into account the fact that psychological and social situations affect hormone production and vice versa. All of these factors, in turn, will affect the pace of sexual response at different times in the cycle. The most important conclusion we can draw is that the factors affecting sexual response are multifaceted. To pit biology against sociocultural/psychological influences is to miss the point. Culture is part of our makeup as human beings; in essence, it means that we behave according to learned, patterned responses. It is an integral part of our lives, not a gilded overlay of traits that have superficial import. In addition, a balanced view of the relationship between hormones and sexual response requires additional material on their importance in male sexuality. Money (1980: 42) notes the exaggerated attention given to women's cycles and strongly suggests that the picture be balanced by studies of the behavioral endocrinology of both men and women.

*Age and sexual functioning:  the biological baseline of the climacteric.* Aging is the last major biological process that can significantly affect the pace of adult sex life. Gradual shifts in the hormone levels of both men and women occur with advancing age. Although men may experience emotional changes during middle age, there is no parallel to the marked physiological changes that occur during the year or two that women go through menopause. A woman experiences a shift from cyclical to acyclical hormonal release and a change in the relative type and quantity of hormones released. A man retains the acyclical nature of hormonal release and experiences a lower level of hormonal secretion. However, a man goes through a climacteric just as a woman does. The climacteric is a critical period, or "change of life," during which the production of sex steroids, i.e., compounds with estrogenic and androgenic properties (Masters and Johnson 1966: 344), decreases in both sexes. Menopause is only one part of a more extended period of changes associated with aging. I prefer to broaden my inquiry about the sexual cycle and age to include questions about both men and women. What changes in the sexual/reproductive organs do both men and women experience when they begin to age, i.e., approximately between the ages of forty and sixty? How do these changes affect the nature of the sexual interaction between men and women?

Masters and Johnson (1966) give us some preliminary data on the physiological changes that occur. The processes that began with puberty begin to slow down as the person ages. I will first consider the changes that occur in women and follow this discussion with alterations that occur in men.

A surge of estrogen production is responsible for the appearance of most of a woman's secondary sexual characteristics and changes in her reproductive organs. The release of estrogen throughout her menstrual cycle helps to maintain many of these changes. The pituitary continues to release FSH, the follicle stimulating hormone, but with middle age, the ovaries do not respond. The follicles stimulated by FSH during the proliferative phase of the menstrual cycle eventually decay (Weideger 1977: 29). Although some estrogen is manufactured by the follicles, it is not enough to trigger release of LH, the luteinizing hormone. In the absence of sufficient estrogen, the pituitary continues to release FSH; it does not secrete LH. Furthermore, the ova decay. When this happens, a woman has entered menopause, the cessation of the menses. There is no egg to be fertilized, and there is no buildup of the uterine lining to receive a fertilized egg. Since blood and tissue of the endometrium are the primary elements of the menstrual flow, the menses cease; the materials out of which the menstrual flow was composed are no longer available. Like the changes at the onset of menstruation, these transformations are gradual and generally last a couple of years. When a woman has had twelve consecutive cycles without menses, she has reached menopause; this usually occurs when she is about fifty years old (Weideger 1977: 29).

Like puberty, menopause involves physical and emotional changes. Interestingly, postmenopausal women exhibit fewer psychological symptoms of distress than adolescent girls (Neugarten and Kraines: 1965). Nevertheless, the American media stress the emotional trauma of menopause; they advertise products for menopause by showing women with nervous, lined faces, who seem to gaze into an empty future. Until 1976, five million women in the U.S. ingested estrogens to relieve the symptoms of menopause. By replacing some of the hormones lost after menopause, women felt that they could retain some of estrogen's beneficial effects during menstrual cycles, e.g., vaginal lubrication and firm skin. However, the FDA found that estrogen ingestion for more than one year may carry with it a number or risks. For example, a woman may have a higher chance of developing uterine cancer. They advised that a woman not take estrogens if she already has uterine or breast cancer, undiagnosed or abnormal vaginal bleeding, clotting in the legs or lungs, heart disease, angina, chest pains, or a stroke. Furthermore, they found that estrogens are not effective in treating simple nervousness, keeping the skin soft, or helping women "feel young" during menopause. They suggested stronger health warnings on the labels of sex hormones, so that women could balance the risks against the benefits. The advisability of estrogen replacement therapy (ERT) at menopause remains controversial.

The main symptoms that postmenopausal women experience are physical (Weideger 1977: 211). Levine and Doherty list the "classical symptoms": flushes of the head, face, neck, and chest; profuse sweating; sensations of cold in the hands and feet; dizziness or faintness; headaches; irritability; depression; insomnia; pruritas (intolerable itching and tingling) of the sexual organs; constipation; and an increase in weight (Levine and Doherty 1952, cited in Weideger 1977: 59). At this point, it is not clear whether the symptoms derive from a deficiency in estrogen, the rate at which estrogen levels drop, or a physical withdrawal of the body from addiction to certain levels of estrogen (Weideger 1977: 62–66). We do know that estrogen replacement therapy relieves some of the symptoms, e.g., hot flashes (Weideger 1977: 69). Although 80 to 90 percent of American women experience some of these symptoms, only 30 percent find them severe enough to disrupt their usual routine; only 30 percent seek medical treatment to deal with the symptoms (Weideger 1977: 59).

Yet the climacteric is broader than menopause. Other changes occur, which can have important implications for sexual functioning in later life. Masters and Johnson (1966) give us some preliminary data on the physiological alterations. The responsiveness of the external genitals varies as women age. The fatty deposits under the labia majora, or major lips, decrease or disappear; they appear thin. The labia minora, or minor lips, retain some of their responsiveness. Clitoral response remains unchanged well into seventy-year-old age groups.

Changes in the reproductive organs are more pronounced. The vagina shortens in length and width. Its thick, corrugated texture becomes paper-thin. The change in its well-stimulated color of reddish-purple to a light pink parallels the structural alterations. Without its thick walls, the vagina is less flexible and cannot expand as easily in response to sexual tension. The thickness of the vaginal walls previously buffered the bladder from the impact of the penis during intercourse. The thin, vaginal walls provide less protection for the bladder, and intercourse may irritate it. Some women experience pain when they urinate after intercourse. Other changes in the vaginal environment may also lead to discomfort. During the excitement stage, vaginal lubrication does not occur as rapidly, nor is it as profuse as when the woman was younger (ten to thirty seconds in youth; one to three minutes when the woman is over sixty). Although vasocongestion in the outer third of the vagina is somewhat reduced as a woman gets older, she continues to experience the orgasmic platform in response to effective stimulation in the plateau phase. When she reaches orgasm, the contractions may be reduced in length and frequency. After orgasm, the organs tend to return to their unstimulated state at a more rapid pace than before.

The deterioration of the uterus is more pronounced than that of the vagina. It shrinks so much that the cervix and uterus are approximately the same length five to ten years after menopause. Nevertheless, it continues to respond during orgasm. The intensity, duration, and recurrence of the contractions vary within and between individuals. Some women feel the contractions so intensely that they are painful, "almost like labor pains except that they occur more rapidly" (Masters and Johnson 1966: 238).

Other general body responses diminish in their intensity or become more taxing. The anal and urethral sphincter muscles do not respond as readily. Increased heartbeat and faster breathing may be more stressful than before. The breasts may not become as tender, but the nipples continue to become erect in response to effective stimulation.

Overall, Masters and Johnson conclude that the aging female is capable of "significant sexual capacity" and "effective sexual performance" (Masters and Johnson 1966: 238). The reduction in steroids reduces the duration and rapidity of her response. However, she is fully capable of orgasm, especially if she receives regular, effective stimulation.

The climacteric affects the sexual response cycles of males also. The changes a man experiences have elements similar to those that a woman experiences. His responses become slower and less intense than before. Even though he receives effective stimulation, the older a man is, the longer it takes him to have a full penile erection (young male — three to five seconds; older male — 15 seconds). However, he can maintain the erection longer without ejaculation. If he loses the erection and has not ejaculated, he may find it difficult if not impossible to return to a full erection. Full erection is not as likely to develop until just before orgasm. When he reaches orgasm, he may experience a shift in its intensity. The number and duration of contractions during ejaculation diminish. The force of his ejaculation also lessens (young men can expel seminal fluid from twelve to twenty four inches; men over fifty, six to twelve inches). Like a woman in the resolution stage, the man quickly returns to his unstimulated state after orgasm. The penis becomes flaccid again very quickly, and his refractory period (the period when he is not as susceptible to sexual stimulation) becomes increasingly longer.

The scrotum and testes also react less immediately and emphatically. The relaxed, sagging folds of scrotal tissue become even looser; they are not as elastic as before. The vasocongestion of the scrotum that young men experience may be reduced or eliminated. Overall, scrotal response to sexual stimulation is slow. The testes in the scrotum are neither as likely to increase in size nor to elevate as quickly or as much with effective stimulation.

The sensation of ejaculation is transformed by its reduced intensity. An older man may not feel the inevitability of ejaculation that a young man does when the penis begins to contract. The older man may not be able to identify any first-stage contractions or feel an increase in pressure in the penis. The two-stage process of ejaculation in youth fuses into a one-stage experience.

*Common elements in the sexual responses of aging males and females.* The sexual response cycles of both men and women diminish in intensity as they get older. Definite physiological changes occur, which contribute to alterations in the sex lives of men and women. We can view these as part of the overall process of aging. People generally experience a decrease in sensory perception; vision, taste, hearing, smell, and touch are all affected (Weiss 1960). The nerves generally become more "sluggish," requiring stronger stimuli to prompt them to carry messages. The brain may not discriminate as easily between different kinds of stimuli. Circulation of blood through the receptors may decrease. The capacity of different senses to pick up stimuli from the environment diminishes. The receptors in the skin may become distorted, as the composition of the skin gradually breaks down. Bones in the middle ear may become more rigid and can impair hearing. The operation of the lens of the eye wanes and may affect vision (Newman and Nichols 1960; Newman 1970; Goldstein 1976). In essence, the main bases for experiencing effective sexual stimulation, i.e., touch and vision, may dwindle.

The force of two major elements in the sexual response cycle ebbs. First, vasocongestion may decrease. We see this expressed in the woman's partially attained orgasmic platform, slight or lack of enlargement of the breasts and uterus, and the pink color of the labia minora — a pale reflection of their vibrant, deep-purplish youth. A man notices its effects in the difficulty he has in quickly attaining and maintaining a full erection. The degree of penile erection depends upon the amount of vasocongestion in the penis; with lessened vasocongestion, erection lessens. In addition, a second major element in the sexual response cycle, muscle tension, or myotonia, decreases with age. Although contractions continue to occur during orgasm, they are less intense; they are neither as frequent nor as long as before.

Men and women have more in common during the climacteric than has been acknowledged. Concentration on menopause has drawn us away from some basic similarities in the effects of the aging process on the sexual responses of both genders. One of my friends whimsically commented that the section on sexual response and aging should not be difficult to write, because "there is none" when you get old. A more serious point underlies the humor. Our culture has assumed that sex lies within the province of youth and possibly middle age. The sexual ability and interest of youth are supposed to wane gradually with advancing age. The assumption that aging involves progressive deterioration of sexuality is carried to such an extent in our culture that older men and women may be classified as "asexual."

Weideger captures the essence of some of our beliefs about aging and sexuality by naming her chapter on menopause "unveiled and invisible." Doris Lessing's description of her main character, Kate Brown, in

*The Summer Before the Dark*, impressed upon Weideger the acute anguish that recognizing this invisibility entails. The scene she cites is of Kate going for a walk after spending considerable time to make herself attractive. She notices a group of young men standing by a street lamp. She felt hesitant to walk past them, fearing a barrage of untoward comments. Instead,

> No one took any notice. She received indifferent glances, which turned off her at once, in search of stimulus. Again, she might have been invisible. Her whole surface, the shields of her blank, staring eyes, her body, even her trimly set feet, had been set to receive notice, like an adolescent girl who has spent three hours making up and who staked everything on what will happen when she presents herself to batteries of searchlight eyes. Kate felt light, floating, without ballast; her head was chaotic, her feelings numb with confusion, she was suppressing impulses so far from anything she had ever had, or could have imagined as hers, that she was shocked by them as if reading about them in a newspaper; she knew that if she were not careful she would march up to one of those groups of lolling men and lift her skirts or expose herself: There, look at that, I'm here, can't you see? Why don't you look at me? [Lessing 1973: 197–98; Weideger 1977: 224]

Men as well as women are subject to the constraints of assumptions about their sexuality and their age. Asexuality is one end of the spectrum. As one postmenopausal woman characterized the transition: "When you're older, people tell you that you 'look good' rather than saying you are 'good looking'." On the face of it, "looking good" would not seem to be a source of irritation. But it is the implication of the shift from "good-looking" to "looking good" that is troublesome. It suggests that the body has been preserved or retarded, in its assumed, rapid deterioration. The comment also implies that looking good "at your age" or "for your age" is so exceptional that it requires notice. Although the undertones of the comments cited may not be as extreme as I have described, they are suggestive. Age brings with it a change in physical appearance, a more negative evaluation of the body, and the assumption that sexual vigor disappears.

The other end of the spectrum of assumptions about aging and sex in our culture is that an older person's interest in sex is, at best, inappropriate and, at its worst, unnatural and disgusting. The jokes about "dirty old men" express the gist of these assumptions. Nevertheless, older men are not as burdened by cultural restrictions on their sexual functioning as older women are. In our culture, older men continue the pattern of marrying younger women. When they father children, this fact is often received with a mixture of admiration for their potency and mild amusement that they have continued to be sexually active. As the saying goes: "When there's snow on the roof, it doesn't mean that there isn't a fire in the furnace." Approval for relationships between older women and younger men is not given readily.

Cultural beliefs about sexuality in old age shift from one extreme, asexuality, to another, disgust at elderly people's possible interest in sex. Even where relationships receive some approval, an undercurrent of suspicion about the appropriateness of the pairing remains. The young woman must have been after the old man's money. Why else would she marry him? A young man who marries an older woman may be suspected of similar, economic motives. Cultural interpretations of such relationships focus on wealth and power as the main reasons for having them, rather than on sexual desire.

The difficulty that many children and grandchildren experience in trying to imagine their parents and grandparents as sexual beings reinforces the cultural notion that sexual functioning ceases after a certain age. Children know that their parents had to have intercourse a few times — to conceive them. Children are not likely to transpose the aura of excitement that may infuse their own sexuality to that of their parents, however. They may prefer to confine their images of their parents' sexuality to reproduction. Other factors may also contribute to this view. For example, denial of parental sexuality is an effective way to support the incest taboo.

Thus far, I have considered assumptions about aging and sexual response from the point of view of American culture. Cross-cultural evidence about physiological aspects of sexual functioning is generally difficult to obtain. Cross-cultural findings about sex and aging are even more elusive. Cultural beliefs about age and sex have hampered investigations of the topic. Freud's assertion that prepubertal children have sexual desires and responses shocked much of Europe and America in the first half of the twentieth century. We are now considering the other end of the sexual cycle, and the results seem just as difficult to accept. Therefore, it is not surprising that the evidence about sex and aging within our own culture, much less about other cultures, is scant.

Our own cultural blinders may not be the only reason for lack of research in the area. Another factor could be that life after menopause formerly did not extend very far. At the end of the nineteenth century, women went through menopause in their forties and died when they were abut forty-nine years old. The postmenopausal period in America has considerably lengthened since the turn of the century. A woman now goes through menopause when she is about fifty, but she can expect to live until the age of seventy-five (Weideger 1977: 209). The effect of aging on sexual functioning becomes a more pressing problem when life expectancy is so long. Less attention to sexuality in old age may be a product of general discomfort with confronting age in a dominantly youth-oriented culture. Like death, it is a subject that Americans veer away from. Nevertheless, the proportion of older Americans is increasing in relation to general population size. Avoidance of the issues will not make them go away. The recent public support for programs in gerontology over the last decade shows more recognition of the necessity to define the consequences of aging and to design effective social policies in relation to them.

Throughout my discussion of the physiological changes that may affect sexual functioning in later years, I was careful to qualify my description with "may." Information on sex and aging is scattered and incomplete. Even Masters and Johnson warn their readers that their information on "geriatric" sexual response is "presented to suggest clinical impression rather than to establish biologic fact" (Masters and Johnson 1966: 223). Nevertheless, we can piece together some of the information we have and reach some tentative conclusions about sexual response in the later years of the life cycle.

I think it is important to keep in mind that we are discussing one part of an overall sexual cycle, which extends throughout our lives. We are physiologically capable of sexual response from birth to death. How we choose to manifest our sexuality and how our culture and group channel its expression account for the high degree of variability that we find within and between societies and individuals. One possible reason that Gail Sheehy's book, *Passages*, became a best seller was that Sheehy acknowledges that change occurs throughout life; each decade of our lives presents new problems with which we have to cope (Sheehy 1976). Unfortunately, she ends her descriptions at the fifth decade of life.

If we view sex life after the midforties as one of a number of shifts in functioning in our lives, it becomes part of the continuity of our development. The available evidence on the physiological aspects of sexual response provides support for adopting this point of view. Masters and Johnson's description of the geriatric sexual response cycle indicates that functioning becomes slower and more attenuated, but *it does not cease.* They stress that hormone levels and their effects on sexual physiology do not necessitate the termination of sexual activity for older males and females:

> There seems to be no physiologic reason why the frequency of sexual expression found satisfactory for the younger woman should not be carried over into the postmenopausal years. . . . There is no reason why the milestone of the menopause should be expected to blunt the human female's sexual capac-

ity, performance, or drive. The healthy aging woman normally has sex drives that demand resolution. The depths of her sexual capacity and the effectiveness of her sexual performance, as well as her personal eroticism, are influenced indirectly by all of the psycho- and sociophysiologic problems of her aging process. In short, there is no time limit drawn by the advancing years to female sexuality [Masters and Johnson 1966: 247].

Briefly, if elevated levels of sexual activity are maintained from earlier years and neither acute nor chronic physical incapacity intervenes, aging males usually are able to continue some form of active sexual expression into the 70 and even 80 year age groups. Even if coital activity has been avoided for long periods of time, men in these age groups can be returned to effective sexual function if adequate stimulation is instituted and interested partners are available [Masters and Johnson 1966: 263].

The vigor of some of Masters and Johnson's older clients is notable. For example, three women, two between sixty-one and seventy, and the other, seventy-three years old, responded to sexual stimulation in a manner more typical of twenty-to-thirty-year-old women. Despite the changed vaginal environment, lubrication of their vaginas during the excitement phase was quick and full. Further, they had maintained active sex lives; they averaged one or two episodes of intercourse per week (Masters and Johnson 1966: 234).

The Hite report on female sexuality indicates that interest in sex does not diminish the sexual desires and activities of many women (Hite 1976). One woman commented,

I am sixty-six and sexual desire has not diminished. The enjoyment is as great as ever. I think it might diminish if you couldn't have sex. But enjoying it has nothing to do with age. . . . Age does not change sex much. Circumstances determine it. I have had much more sexual pleasure, both with my husband and other mates in recent years . . . [Hite 1976: 510].

Another woman eloquently expresses the place that an active sex life can have in the developmental process of life:

I think that sexual desire, attitudes, pleasure, etc. certainly change with age, but the change is qualitative rather than quantitative. It's a matter of growth and development, from a simplistic yes-or-no view of sex to much greater complexity, variety, subtlety, fluidity. I don't mean this so much in terms of increasing sophistication in "technique," though I suppose that's part of it. It's like the difference between a young shoot and a tree with many branches and a unique shape and structure and pattern of growth all its own. This is a natural growth process, but I believe that in our culture this process is often inhibited and retarded; we've all been told that all cats are gray in the dark, and many of us come rather to the recognition and appreciation of his own unique and intricate sexual personality. I find it much easier now to know and accept and act on what I want and feel, instead of worrying about what I should want and feel [Hite 1976: 510].

Masters and Johnson were perplexed by the sexual vigor of men and women in their sixties and seventies in view of the physiological drawbacks of their advancing age. They suggest that regularity of sexual expression may be an important clue to the maintenance of sexual capacity and effective sexual performance (Masters and Johnson 1966: 240). A study by Newman and Nichols (1960) lends support to this view. They investigated the attitudes and sexual activities of 250 people ranging in age from sixty to ninety-three. Although sexual activity generally declines with advancing years, there seems to be a pattern in how it affects different groups of people. They found that if the people had strong sexual desires in youth, activity became more moderate in old age. If sexual interest was weak in youth, sexual activity almost disappears in old age. In other words, if people enjoyed regular sex lives when they were younger, they are likely to continue similar sexual activities into old age. Newman and Nichols conclude that a couple in reasonably good health are capable of and often do engage in sex well into their sixties, seventies, and eighties. "Use it or lose it" communicates some of the conclusions of the studies. The lack of continuity in sexual expression seems to relate more to learned restraint than to physiological capacity. Although the organs themselves do not atrophy, desire for intercourse may. The climacteric may be a relief for people whose sex lives were repressed or were active only because of the requirements of marital "duty." Physical changes associated with aging can justify sexual withdrawal. But if people's interest was high in the first place, they may deal with the physical changes in the same ways in which they cope with other kinds of transitions.

Psychosocial factors feed back into the nature of sexual response in later years. Masters and Johnson outline some of the major elements that they think contribute to sexual difficulty in older men (Masters and Johnson 1966: 264–270). They include: (1) monotony or boredom with the partner, (2) concentration on economic and career goals, (3) mental or physical fatigue, (4) too much food or drink, (5) physical and mental problems of either partner, and (6) fear of failure in performance. In contrast, women may experience an increase in sexual interest. They are freed from the constraints of raising a family and the fear of pregnancy. The younger generation may not have to deal with freedom from this fear, since they may have practiced adequate contraception throughout their reproductive years. Many women become more interested in their husbands and go through a "second honeymoon" (Masters and Johnson

1966: 243). Release from social pressures may not be entirely responsible for a woman's renewed interest in sex. Although estrogen levels decrease markedly, androgen production does not diminish as much. If the hypothesis that androgen is related to sexual desire are true, the relatively higher amount of androgen in the woman's system may add to her sexual interest. Also, a man may find that his ability to maintain an erection for longer periods of time without ejaculation enhances his partner's pleasure.

However, continuity in sex life depends upon having a partner. Many aging women in American society do not have one. Even though a woman may be interested in continuing an active sex life, she may not be able to do so, because of having no one with whom she can share the experience. Her vigor may decline because of lack of opportunity, not lack of desire. Masters and Johnson introduce the sobering thought that the "trend of our population toward an aging society of women without men must be considered. Roughly 10 percent of women never marry. In addition, the gift of longevity has not been divided equally among the sexes. As a result, there is a steadily increasing legion of women who are spending their last years without marital partners" (Masters and Johnson 1966: 246).

Availability of partners in other societies depends upon a variety of factors. These include ideas about relationships between older women and younger men, the relative number of men to women in the older age categories, the number of years that women survive their husbands' deaths and vice versa, and the society's views about postmarital sex. As I described earlier, Tiwi women are able to begin their sex lives earlier and maintain them through a significant part of their life cycles. Because her first husband was about twenty-five years older than she, a woman became a widow at a relatively young age. A young man would marry her while he was waiting for the infant girl he betrothed to grow up. He gained sexual experience, and the widow gained a young sexual partner. When his young betrothed wife reached the age of marriage, the man gained a younger sexual partner. The older wives accumulated power by protecting the young wives from the sexual advances of young men. Both men and women reaped the advantages of a diverse sex life at different points in the life cycle. Women increased their power as they got older. Their husbands looked to them to help them protect their interests, sexual and otherwise.

Other aspects of the social setting can affect sexual functioning during the latter phases of the life cycle. A noteworthy element is the way in which the group regards aging in general and menopause in particular. I have tried to place menopause within the more general framework of the climacteric. Like menstruation, it is one expression of a broader process of aging. Nevertheless, many groups latch onto dramatic physiological events to make a social point. Menopause can be a significant transition in many women's lives, because of the cultural interpretation and the role change it may entail. Pauline Bart (1972) has conducted studies on menopause in both the U.S. and in other cultures. Her review of the status of women in 150 cultures showed that in all of them, the ideals and attributes of feminine behavior during the reproductive years *reversed* at menopause. Although the physiological shift in their functioning is gradual, the psychological transition to a new social phase of women's lives may be more challenging. The two cases that Weideger cites emphasize the positive aspects of the change. Like the elderly Tiwi woman, women may gain power. In addition, they may be freed from male domination and from numerous restrictions that applied to them during their reproductive years. Weideger uses Mead's account of the Balinese and Levy's account of the Chinese to drive home her point. In Bali, the reproductive period of a woman's life is regarded as impure and "ceremonially disqualifying." After menopause, a woman is regarded as being as pure as the virgins, and she is included in ceremonies. She does not have to adhere to the canons of delicate feminine speech; she can use obscene language as much as the men do (Weideger 1977: 216). Similarly, the postmenopausal Chinese woman is freed from many restraints, especially male domination. Her new role is so highly approved that attempts to relegate her to a subservient status would be censured. The older women in China has a "secure and coveted position."

Unfortunately, a release from the reproductive period may also bring heartache and rejection. If femininity is tied up with reproduction, then it may dissipate with the woman's reproductive ability. Weideger thinks that this is what American women have experienced. If menstruation means that a girl is a woman, menopause implies a retraction of that status. In addition, a woman may have an "empty nest" when she experiences the physiological changes of menopause. She loses not only the comfort and nurturance she gives and receives from her children but also an important goal and function in her life — raising children.

I think that it is curious that more emphasis has not been placed on the effect that the "empty nest" has on men. Although gender roles in American society gear a man to his work, he does participate in the family. A suppression of his nurturant qualities in the service of the masculine role does not mean that many of his emotions are not tied to his family. Is the emotional impact of the "empty nest" so minimal for men that we are justified in glossing it over, pretending that it is not relevant? Career changes or the end of a career may loom large in a man's life at this time. The changes in his job and in the composition of his family may influence his sex life.

Sex is not reproduction, even though some cultures try to equate the two. The crux of the issue seems to be how to deal with this elementary fact. When a woman ages, she loses her reproductive capacity at menopause. But, as Masters and Johnson have so emphatically shown, she does not lose her capacity to function sexually. She is capable of having an active sex life. Aging does not bring as dramatic a change in reproductive functioning for men. Sperm production continues, and a man is capable of fathering children until very late in life. Both men and women experience a diminution of their former patterns of sexual response. This is far different from experiencing an obliteration of sexual activity. However, cultural interpretations of aging and social rules about appropriate behavior may affect the sexual experiences of aging adults. At the very least, they may introduce fear and anxiety about sexual feelings and behavior after a certain age.

Throughout this chapter, I have emphasized sex in terms of a cycle. A cycle implies continuity and sequence, but it also allows for variation. Even so, variation is patterned in such a way that certain elements repeat themselves. In the last part of the sexual cycle — the later years associated with aging — we see some continuity with the patterns set up in childhood. The cyclical nature of a woman's reproductive system fully develops during her menstrual phase. With the advent of menopause, her hormonal secretions become acyclical. A woman has a smaller amount of estrogen relative to androgen. A decrease in a man's testosterone production as he ages means that the proportion of estrogen to androgen also shifts later in his life cycle. Even the gap between relative quantities of the "male" and "female" hormones changes when men and women age, as if to indicate the freedom from their past roles. They have to acknowledge this fact and act upon their awareness if their lives are to change significantly in conjunction with their physical forms. The groups to which these aging men and women belong have a lot to do with whether or not they will be able to experience positively the changed dimensions of their sexuality in their later years.

# Chapter Four
# The Reproductive Cycle

The reproductive cycle includes those stages of physical development that prepare males and females for and contribute to the procreation and nurturance of children. During childhood, the reproductive organs develop, and gender differentiation prepares children for forming sexual relationships. The way that a group channels sexuality at puberty affects whether sexual activity will be regarded as primarily reproductive or both sexual and reproductive, depending upon the context. After puberty, the link between sexual and reproductive relationships becomes a matter of cultural and psychological interpretation, not a biological imperative. Since sexual reproduction requires partners, puberty can become a crucial point, at which the nature of sexual partnerships is defined.

Reproductive unions are relationships in which the conception of children is not only allowed but encouraged. Sexual activity in reproductive relationships can and, in some cases, should have reproductive consequences. This chapter deals with questions that relate to reproductive relationships. The first part of the chapter defines the scope of human reproductive relationships and specifies some of their major components: the availability and selection of partners, entrance into reproductive unions, important rights associated with reproductive unions, and problems linked to terminating reproductive relationships. The second part of the chapter deals with social and cultural aspects of the reproductive cycle that relate to the desirability of having children, conception, pregnancy, and birth.

### Definition of a Reproductive
### Relationship: Marriage

Like sexual relationships, reproductive ones do not escape the careful scrutiny of a group. The group obviously has a big stake in influencing which partners will perpetuate the social unit, when they should begin

245

to reproduce, and how long they should continue to reproduce. The very existence of the social unit could depend upon its response to these issues.

In order to specify the ways in which groups organize reproductive relationships, we must first define them. I regard marital unions as the main reproductive relationships that occur in most societies. However, the problem of definition remains. If we are to investigate adequately the dimensions of reproductive relationships in a cross-cultural perspective, we need a definition of marriage that allows us to identify it in a variety of social and cultural contexts.

Much ink has been spilled in the pursuit of a satisfactory definition of marriage. One of the main obstacles to this goal is confusion between the essential ingredients and the chief functions of marriage. In other words, definitions of marriage include a potpourri of attributes that confound what marriage is with what it does; they mix its identity with its role. For example, economic responsibilities, coresidence, religious rituals, socialization of children, and permanence are attributes often included in definitions of marriage. However, I suggest that they are attachments to the marital relationship, not its defining qualities. Distinguishing between the identity and the functions of marriage may seem unnecessary. However, a failure to do so may bias research in terms of factors that are assumed but that ought to be investigated. For example, if we assume that marriages begin with religious rituals and involve coresidence of the marital partners, we are limiting the scope of the relationships we can investigate as marriages.

Kathleen Gough's attempt to define marriage among the Nayar of Kerala Province in India illustrates how difficult defining marriage can be (Gough 1968). She describes a group in which sisters and brothers live together, share economic functions, and socialize the sisters' children. A brief ceremony establishes a "marriage" between the sister and her "husband." After the ritual ceremony, neither the bride nor the groom has to have any further contact with the other (Gough 1968: 56). If both of them wanted to have sexual relations, they could. However, other men in the neighborhood group could also have sexual access to the bride, either as alternate "husbands" or as lovers. If the union endured for a while, a husband was expected to give his wife gifts at the year's three main festivals. If he did not give these gifts, it was a sign that the relationship had ended. However, the crux of the "marriage" related to the birth of children. It was essential that one or more men of the appropriate social group claim paternity when the "wife" became pregnant. If no man came forth to establish his probable fatherhood, the woman and her child would face ostracism by her entire village.

Her consanguineal ("blood") relatives would be so outraged that they would banish her from the lineage and caste groups as if she were dead; they would even perform funeral rites for her. Gough provides a definition of marriage that could include the relationships that the Nayar regard as marriages:

> Marriage is a relationship established between a woman and one or more other persons, which provides that a child born to the woman under circumstances not prohibited by the rules of the relationship, is accorded full birth-status rights common to normal members of his society or social stratum [Gough 1968: 68].

In other words, marriage establishes the legitimacy of children.

Gough's aim was to define marriage as simply as possible, in order to aid cross-cultural comparisons (Gough 1968: 51). I agree with Gough that it is essential to parsimoniously describe the criteria by which to identify marriage. Only then can we discover the range of functions that marriage does serve. If we include as many functions of marriage as possible in its definition, we limit the range of variation that we can explore and unnecessarily restrict its usefulness for comparative research. Therefore, the definition should be broad enough to facilitate the identification of a "marriage" in each society, but not so broad that it does not sufficiently differentiate marriage from other relationships.

I have found that Ward Goodenough's proposed definition of marriage contains some particularly fruitful criteria for the identification of a marital relationship in cross-cultural contexts:

> Marriage is a transaction and resulting contract in which a person (male or female, corporate or individual, in person or by party) establishes a continuing claim to the right of sexual access to a woman — this right having priority over rights of sexual access others currently have or may subsequently acquire in relation to her (except in a similar transaction) until the contract resulting from the transaction is terminated — and in which the woman involved is eligible to bear children (whether she is capable of bearing them is another matter) [Goodenough 1970: 12, 13].

His definition contains three characteristics that are especially relevant for identifying a marital relationship in any social context. The first is the jural or legal dimension of the marriage. Marriage involves a transaction in which people transfer rights to one another. In other words, marriage is guided by a set of rules. The second element specifies that a person or group has priority of sexual access to a woman. The third component is that marital relationships involve eligibility to reproduce. Goodenough unnecessarily restricts his definition of marriage to rights that a person acquires over a woman. He does not extend it to include the rights that a person acquires over a man. Such an orientation implies that a woman is more restricted than a man by marriage. Although the cross-cultural evidence may substantiate his implication, I do not think that it is necessary to include this assumption in a cross-culturally applicable definition of marriage.

Gough and Goodenough share some common ground in their search for an adequate definition of marriage for cross-cultural purposes. Gough stresses the importance of establishing rights for children born in the context of a particular type of relationship. Goodenough describes rules that establish priority of sexual access and eligibility to reproduce. Both of their definitions are concerned with orderly arrangements for reproduction and the connection between children and their parents.

My own definition of marriage derives from a review of the careful attempts to define it made by other social scientists, e.g., Gough and Goodenough, as well as from my analysis of ethnographic reports of marriage in a variety of societies. I have found that I can most consistently and usefully identify marriage in cross-cultural contexts by using the following definition: Marriage is a relationship within which a group socially approves and encourages sexual intercourse and the birth of children. Unlike Gough, I emphasize the nature of the relationship between the couple, instead of focusing on the possible consequences of the relationship, i.e., children. When we talk about marriage, we are considering the dimensions of a relationship, regardless of its consequences. In a marriage, people *can* be reproductive. In purely sexual relationships, they *should not* be reproductive. Unlike Goodenough, I choose to investigate rather than to assume and specify the jural rights related to this relationship. I agree that rules are an important aspect of marriage. However, I think that most of them are more properly allied with its functions in a particular group. Rules are part of the definition of marriage in the sense that marriage is an intrinsically human social relationship. Humans partially organize their lives in conformity with the rules they have created. I have incorporated this human trait in my definition, by specifying that the relationship is subject to social approval and encouragement of its activities. Since, reproductive relationships are influenced by social rules, I will discuss the nature of some of these rules in the next section.

### Spouse Selection

The selection of reproductive partners is subject to rules in human societies. The first part of the human reproductive process is the attempt to define a group of available partners and select a mate from among them. This may sound simple, but the reality is considerably more complicated. Social criteria and cultural categories can narrow the range of potential mates. The degree to which they restrict the number of partners a person has during a lifetime depends upon how a variety of choices are limited or expanded for the individual and the group. I will begin with the most general guidelines for spouse selection and become progressively more specific in my consideration of the rules and beliefs that apply to reproductive relationships.

## General Guidelines

*Implicit consequences of the incest taboo.* The first instruction that children receive about the selection of reproductive partners comes early in their lives, when they learn the scope of the incest taboo. Although the taboo is a sexual restriction, it has reproductive implications. The prohibition on intercourse between specified relatives effectively precludes a reproductive relationship in which intercourse and reproduction are encouraged. Therefore, one consequence of the taboo is the message that people should seek mates from outside the boundaries of their nuclear families and the kinship categories to which the taboo extends. Since the taboo remains in force throughout people's lifetimes, specified categories of kinsmen remain perpetually out of reach as socially approved reproductive partners.

*Explicit criteria for spouse selection: kinship.* When we review the main explicit criteria that people employ to aid them in selecting mates, kinship dominates as the primary criterion used (86% of 59 societies). Status (8.5% of 59 societies), age (2% of 59 societies), locality (3.4% of 59 societies), and tribal affiliation (0 of 59 societies) lag far behind as the most important explicitly used factor. Groups generally identify categories of kinsmen between whom marriage is or is not permitted. Bilateral (30.5% of 59 societies) and patrilineal or patrilateral considerations (27% of 59 societies) occur with approximately equal regularity. Matrilineal or matrilateral and nonlateral specifications (12% of 59 societies) occur less often.

The overwhelming priority of kinship as a guide for selecting a reproductive partner suggests that the presence or absence of a rule of descent would probably be strongly associated with the type of kinship distinctions used to select a partner. If this is so, I would expect that bilateral or non-kinship factors would prevail in societies with bilateral, ambilineal, or double descent systems; while matrilateral and patrilateral criteria would be associated with unilineal descent systems. My expectation was significantly confirmed ($X^2$ = 26.7, df, p = < .001, N = 59).

We can interpret this finding as part of a general human tendency to classify kin (Fox 1980: 181). We learn to act in terms of our classification scheme and to channel our reproductive relationships by selecting mates according to our created categories. Our mental structuring of the world guides a larger share of our behavior. Although using kinship criteria as bases for deciding whom to marry seems relatively straightforward, most anthropologists are well aware of the intricate and complex adjustments that their application entails (Lévi-Strauss 1969; Fortes 1969; Buchler and Selby 1968; Fox 1974).

*The impact of physical space: community marriage patterns.*  Kinship criteria parcel out the social space within which selection of reproductive partners can proceed. Physical space can also have an impact on partner selection, because it can provide a context for meeting and interacting with others. The fact that people associate with each other in a specific locale can encourage or dissuade them from establishing a relationship with those whom they meet there. In addition, rules that apply to the advisability of intracommunity (within the same community) or intercommunity (between different communities) marriages may also influence the chance that individuals will establish reproductive relationships with people in their own or in another community.

Although considerations of locality are relevant to spouse selection, they emerge as factors of secondary rather than primary importance (36% of 42 societies where they are of secondary importance). Nevertheless, there are patterns of intercommunity marriage that do reflect consistent behavioral preferences for choosing mates who reside in the same or another community (Murdock and Wilson 1972). Societies in which individuals marry members of their own community slightly outnumber (42% of 62 societies) those in which people marry people outside of their community (35.5% of 62 societies). In the remainder of the societies people do not express any clear preference for marriage in or out of the community (32% of 62 societies).

Kinship overshadows locale as a basis for structuring the potential pool of mates. Physical contact alone is not enough to stimulate relationships. The distinctive spice of human interaction includes the structured imprints of thoughts and emotionally charged beliefs about appropriate behavior. Categories become essential ingredients in the choices that channel our interactions and our decisions, particularly in the important domain of reproduction.

*Age at marriage.* I have pointed out that kinship is a broad principle that segments the social space within which a person selects a mate. Community organization and patterns of marriage within or outside of the community are other broad factors that affect mate selection; they reflect the organization of the selective process according to physical boundaries. Age at marriage structures another major aspect of mate selection — its timing. It shapes the rhythm of our reproductive lives by influencing when we first establish a reproductive relationship. The consequences of age at marriage are important (though implicitly applied) criteria for selecting a spouse.

Men are almost always within the same age group or at least one age category older than women when they first marry. Men usually marry when they are eighteen or older (74 % of 42 societies), but women are usually seventeen or younger (69 % of 45 societies). The most frequent ages at first marriage are between eighteen and twenty-one for males (36 % of 42 societies) and between twelve and fifteen for females (40 % of 45 societies).

One practical reason for the difference in age may relate to the attainment of reproductive maturity. The reproductive organs of males and females mature at different rates. Girls begin puberty between the ages of nine and twelve, whereas boys do not begin until they are ten or eleven. Not only does puberty usually start later for boys; it also lasts longer. Girls reach reproductive maturity earlier than boys. Therefore, marriages between adolescent girls and boys could result in reproductive problems. A later age at marriage for boys helps them to maximize their chances for reproductive success.

Differences in age at marriage may reflect individual assessments of the attractiveness of potential mates. Power and status are more likely to enhance a man's attractive qualities than physical appearance alone. A man may not attain the requisite status until he is beyond his first youth. Physical appearance is likely to play a larger role in a woman's appeal to men. In addition, if a man or the man's family select a woman for her reproductive potential, youth would be in her favor.

Another consequence of different ages at marriage for males and females relates to the number of partners a man can have. Different ages influence the proportion of males and females who are available within the preferred categories. It is impressive that there are *no* societies where females are older than males at first marriage. This reveals a general tendency for groups to ensure that the supply of females for marriage equals or exceeds the supply of males. This tendency at least introduces the possibility that a man can have more than one reproductive partner at the same time. In other words, a discrepancy in age at marriage could facilitate the development of polygyny. The cultural definition of appropriate ages at marriage has the effect of increasing the pool of marriageable females relative to the number of marriageable males in a given age group.

If the differential ages of males and females at marriage do affect the possibility of polygyny, I would expect that the number of societies with full polygyny would increase as the age differences between men and women increase at first marriage. I found that there is a tendency in the expected direction (Fisher's exact test, p = .07, N = 37). Monogamy and limited polygyny occur primarily in societies where the husband is the same age or one age category older than his wife. Full polygyny occurs more often when the husband is two or more age categories older than his wife. A more precise model for explaining polygyny would have to take into account the intervening circumstances of war, disease, and actual ages at marriage. The sex ratio, i.e., the number of males relative to the number of females, varies at different stages of the life cycle. Women generally live longer than men and are not engaged in as many dangerous activities. By the time women are older, there are considerably fewer men in the appropriate age categories whom they can marry. My main purpose here has been not to explain polygyny but to show how restrictions on age at marriage can shape the availability of marriage partners.

### Restrictions on the Number of Partners: Monogamy and Polygamy

Groups generally have specific rules that govern the number of spouses a person may have. The first set of rules applies to the option of having more than one spouse at the same time. I term this type of marriage a "synchronous marriage" (syn = same, chronos = time). Polygamy is the general label for plural marriage. Polygyny is a specialized term, used to refer to a man who has more than one wife; polyandry refers to a woman who has more than one husband. Monogamy is the mode of marriage in which a person has only one spouse at a time.

Polygyny is by far the most widely preferred mode of marriage (82% of 62 societies). Limited polygyny occurs somewhat more often (48% of 62 societies) than full polygyny (35.5% of 62 societies); the latter is particularly associated with Africa ($X^2$ = 7.7, 1 df, p = <.01, N = 62). The least preferred modes are monogamy (16% of 62 societies) and polyandry (2% of 62 societies). These statistics do not mean that polygynous unions occur more frequently than monogamous ones. Rather they mean that polygynous unions are preferred and occur with discernible regularity. The distinction between a polygynous and a monogamous society is based on the percentage of people who have plural spouses. In a polygynous society, obtaining plural spouses is a socially acceptable practice rather than a deviation from the rules.

Murdock specified some useful guidelines for identifying modes of marriage in a cross-cultural context (Murdock 1965: 28). He concerned himself with polygyny, since polyandry is so rare. He based his distinction on the percentage of married males in the community who have more than one spouse. He concluded that a cutoff point of 20 percent was sufficient to distinguish adequately between full and limited polygyny. Demographic features of the population would counter the possibility that most males could have more than one wife. Therefore, "limited polygyny" characterizes a group in which less than 20 percent of the married males in the society actually have more than one wife, even though polygyny is approved and preferred to monogamy. "Full polygyny" describes a group in which more than 20 percent of the married males have more than one spouse.

It is surprising that more effort has not been given to explaining why monogamy rather than polygyny occurs as a preferred mode of marriage. Interest in polygyny may reflect ethnographers' fascination with what they perceive to be freedom from the constraints posed by the monogamous customs of their own societies. The popular press uses "polygynous nature" as a synonym for relatively unencumbered sexual variety. The implication is that a man has the option of partaking of the sexual favors of a number of women who are consistently available to him. The broader message is that "by his nature" a man will want sexual diversity. As the King of Siam sings to Anna in the musical "The King and I," "A girl must be like a blossom, with honey for just one man. A man must live like honeybee and gather all he can. . . . [but] blossom must not ever fly from bee to bee to bee."

Some of these ideas may stem from comparing humans with other primates. Some primates form multi-male groups or, less frequently, "harems," in which one male is consistently associated with a number of females. However, even at this level, access to females is structured. More dominant males have priority of access to females in full estrus. Furthermore, sex is *not* the main feature that binds the group together. Banding together affords protection in a terrestrial environment and helps to effect a balance between group size and resources; this is particularly true where the male segments form a larger group with a number of females. However, as Fox (1980) points out, we have to be careful about analogies with other primates. Humans "must have been doing something different from desert baboons or there's no reason to suppose we should not have remained as they are" (Fox 1980: 119).

Polygyny is a form of marriage, a reproductive relationship structured by social rules. It is not a sexual relationship per se, nor is it legalized promiscuity, as our popular magazines would lead us to believe. Neither jealousy nor attention to rules disappears when people have more than one spouse. Household arrangements reflect some of the dimensions of the marital relationship. Generally a man does not reside in the same household with his wives unless they are sisters (Murdock and Wilson 1972). The more common arrangement is for each wife to have her own dwelling. The husband either has his own abode or shares the dwellings of his wives. He usually works out an arrangement for eating and sleeping with each of his wives on a specific schedule. He does not have the leeway to let his passions guide his choice of sleeping arrangements. Since the man generally relies on his wives for their domestic services, he could be in a very precarious position if he were to antagonize them. He has to pay attention not only to his relationship with each wife but also to the relationships among the wives. His situation may be particularly volatile if he has no dwelling of his own and rotates his residence with each of his wifes. Too much tension could result in his literally having no place to sleep.

The power that women can wield in a polygynous situation has been underplayed. The emphasis has usually been put on the dominance of the male over a number of women. This emphasis distorts the reality of polygyny just as much as too much emphasis on its importance as a sexual outlet. It is not that these elements of sex and power of men over women are not there. What is lacking is a perspective on how the components are organized as part of a reproductive relationship. Ernestine Friedl appropriately points out that in "whatever spheres of life men or women have legal or jural rights, their ability to enjoy full use of them always depends on some degree of cooperation, or at least of acquiescence, on the part of the other sex. Men and women are everywhere interdependent" (Friedl 1975: 97). She discusses three major tactics that women can use to gain some autonomy for themselves in the face of men who have authority over them. All three tactics can apply to the polygynous situation, in which the man has authority over his wives. First, a woman can add the weight of her support to her own kin or to those of her husband when men are in competition with each other. Second, she can aid in settling a dispute by helping to promote harmony between the men with whom she is in contact. Finally, she can resort to "subversive activities like sullenness, nagging, complaints, ridicule, gossip, and, in the extreme, witchcraft" (Friedl 1975: 97). Feigned incompetence at domestic chores could also be included in the last category. "Inadvertently" burning dinner, becoming ill when the husband desires sex, or making embarrassing mistakes when guests are present are all tactics a woman might use to annoy her husband, which illustrate the necessity for a man to retain his wives' cooperation. The man whose four wives conspire against him is not in an enviable position. Polygynous wives can exert power, even if it is not publically recognized or sanctioned.

It is true that polygynous marriages can affect the nature of sexual activity and rates of reproduction. However, counter to what our popular literature would lead us to believe, polygynous wives are *less* fertile than wives in monogamous unions (Daly and Wilson 1978: 289). One reason for this low fertility rate may be the reduction in coital frequency that a plural mateship entails for the female. A man generally organizes the time he apportions to each wife. Since his time and energy are limited, he has less time to spend with each wife than he would if the number of wives were less. Since there are very limited periods of time when a woman can conceive, a decrease in the frequency of intercourse can considerably reduce her chances of getting pregnant. Second, a lower reproductive rate may stem from the man's reason for contracting the polygynous marriage. If a man marries another wife because the first one is barren, lower reproduction would be a logical consequence of this situation. Third, long postpartum sex taboos are associated with polygyny. Therefore, the wife who has just given birth to a child will not be available to conceive again for a while. The man's other wives provide him with domestic services and sexual relations in the interim.

It seems, then, that polygyny does not provide a man with sensational sexual opportunities. Furthermore, it may not guarantee evidence of a man's reproductive prowess. What can it do? It can become an expression of a man's status. Perhaps more importantly, it parcels out reproductive partners in an organized way and facilitates the management of potential conflict between elder and younger males. Status, cooperation between males, and control over reproductive resources, i.e., women, become linked to each other in a polygynous marriage.

Permission to form a polygynous union does not mean that the path to attaining one is easy. Qualifications of age, status, and wealth often determine whether a man can obtain more than one spouse. A younger male may have to depend upon an elderly one to acquire the position and resources necessary to contract plural marriages. The elderly man's status and wealth help him to maintain authority over the young men. If a young man steps out of line, the elderly one may withhold valuable resources from him. Therefore, they work out a cooperative balance between their individual needs. The elderly male tries to retain his

position of authority, while the younger man tries to acquire the resources he needs to obtain a wife or wives.

The Massa (27) of Cameroon illustrate how complicated the balance
of resources, marriageable women, available men, and relations between the generations can be when a marriage is transacted. The circulation of cows, the enhancement of a man's prestige, and the acquisition
of a wife are all closely associated with one another and center on
marriage (de Garine 1964: 131-153). Cows are allowed to leave the
herd only as bride-price to procure spouses for males in the group; the
group that gives a daughter in marriage ought to receive cows for her. A
man's stock of cows can severely limit the choice of spouses available to
him. Since a father may put suitors in competition for his daughter to
increase the number of cows he receives, a man's ability to obtain the
woman he desires may depend upon the number of cows he is willing to
relinquish to her father. The cows the father receives provide the resources he needs to obtain even more wives for himself and to continue
the cycle of producing daughters, who will, in turn, give him further
opportunity to receive more cows when they marry. The number of
cows a man receives for his daughter is an important index not only of
her beauty but also of his renown. Thus, the chief of the canton has
numerous marriages and children, which assure him of the support of
affines, or in-laws and a constant flow of women and cows. A further
complication of the system is the allocation of the group's resources to
procure spouses for its members. Is a man going to distribute cows to his
sons and younger brothers to obtain wives, or will he keep them to
secure more wives for himself (de Garine 1964: 173)? The nature of the
interaction between the elder and younger men may have a lot to do
with the answer.

The only society in my sample that practiced polyandry was the
Marquesan Island (105) group. Polyandry occurred most often in the
families of chiefs (Suggs 1963: 111). The young men whom a chief's
wife attracted to her as additional spouses could be advantageous to the
husband and his retainers. Therefore, a chief might encourage his wife
to have more husbands. In addition, men could have more than one
wife. Secondary wives and their husbands could aid the chief or primary husband by working to maintain his household (Handy 1923: 47).
The primary husband's control over sexual access to his wife brought
him economic advantages. Once again, we see that the polygamous
situation is not a sexual free-for-all. control over sexual access and the
organization of marital relations are consistent features of plural marriages. In this case, the woman has more than one husband, but the
relationships between them are ordered in terms of the status of the

primary husband. The import of the marital relationship extends beyond sexual and reproductive bonds.

### Restrictions on the Number of Partners: Divorce, Widowhood, Remarriage, and Diachronic Marriage

Mode of marriage usually refers to the number of spouses that a person has *at any one time*. I labeled this class of unions "synchronic marriage." A neglected but equally important mode of marriage is defined in terms of the number of spouses that a person has *over time*. I term this category of unions "diachronic marriage" (dia = through, chronos = time). The rules associated with divorce and widowhood are important limitations on this type of marriage. The extent to which diachronic marriages are possible is shaped by the number and types of grounds for divorce that a man and woman may exercise, the ease of divorce for each, and the difficulty of remarriage. In addition, the rules that control the remarriage of people whose spouses have died can further affect the possibility that a person will have more than one spouse in a lifetime. Full flexibility in these areas gives an individual the option of experiencing a variety of reproductive relationships. Full limitation restricts the individual to synchronic marriages. What choices are open to the individual whose marriage ends, either by choice (e.g., a divorce) or by death? The alternatives are defined and assessed in terms of a variety of considerations related to the previous marriage.

*Divorce and remarriage.* Divorce terminates a current reproductive relationship, but it can be a preliminary step to the beginning of another. Because divorce is initiated by the decision of one or both of the spouses, ending a marriage in this way implies some individual control over the number of unions a man or woman might have. However, the control may be illusory.

One impediment that spouses may face in trying to divorce their partners is the necessity of conforming to a range of socially acceptable grounds for divorce. The narrower and more precise the range of these grounds, the more constricted people are in dissolving their relationships. Usually a group requires that individuals justify their behavior. They cannot merely decide that they do not like the arrangement and leave. Table 4.1 presents the primary grounds for divorce used by men and women to terminate their marriages.

Table 4.1 *Comparison of Primary Grounds for Divorce Used by Men and Women*

| Grounds | Men | Women |
|---|---|---|
| No Divorce (Regardless of Grounds) | 7.1% | 10.4% |
| Reproductive Problems | 28.6% | 6.3% |
| Illicit Sex | 16.1% | 10.4% |
| Physical Violence | 0 | 14.6% |
| Incompatibility | 21.4% | 22.9% |
| Desertion or Neglect | 5.4% | 2.1% |
| Incompatibility with Affines | 1.8% | 4.2% |
| Failure in Economic or Domestic Duties | 14.3% | 18.8% |
| Trivial Reason or No Reason | 5.4% | 10.4% |

N = 56          N = 48

Women most frequently divorce their husbands on the grounds of incompatibility, failure to meet economic responsibilities, and physical violence. For example, if a Thonga (3) husband is extremely selfish or keeps most of the meat to himself, his wife may divorce him because of it (Junod 1962: 1, 198). If a Palauan (111) wife dislikes her husband and has difficulty living with him, she can divorce him (Barnett 1949: 132). Failure in economic duties is primary among the Goajiro (159). If a man cannot pay his bride-price installment on time, his marriage may be dissolved (Bolinder: 1957: 95). Constant brutality by a Yahgan (186) husband may provoke his wife to divorce him (Gusinde 1937: 648).

Men also use one of the major grounds for divorce that women do — incompatibility. The similarity ends here. The two other most frequent grounds that men use are not among the main ones that women use: reproductive problems and illicit sex. Barrenness is the most common reason that a man uses to divorce his wife. Men in the Circum-Mediterranean area are particularly likely to justify a divorce on this basis ($X^2$ = 15.91, 1 df, p = <.001, N = 56). Conversely, a woman infrequently claims a divorce on the grounds of her husband's reproductive problems.

I was surprised to find that illicit sex, mainly extramarital sex, ranked third rather than first in importance as one of the primary grounds for a man divorcing his wife. Women use it almost as much as men. Its low incidence as grounds for divorce may be partially explained by the severity of punishment that can be imposed on a woman for engaging in illicit extramarital relations. It is possible that many of the marriages that would be terminated by divorce on the grounds of illicit sex never reach a stage of litigation; they cease with the death of the wife. As I discussed earlier, violent retaliation for extramarital liaisons seems to be mainly a male prerogative. Although I have read many descriptions of cases where the husband kills his wife for an extramarital affair, I have not found one that says it is a socially accepted alternative for the wife. In contrast, a man does not kill his wife for her inability to bear children. Why is there a difference between the responses to a violation of the sexual components of the marriage and the reproductive ones? Failure to have a child can threaten a major reason for marriage. Why does a man divorce rather than kill his wife for this transgression? I have already suggested some possibilities in the section on extramarital restrictions. Several alternative explanations specifically relate to the significance of extramarital relations to reproductive relationships. I think that the difference in the husband's responses to his wife's barrenness and to her extramarital relations relates to the degree of control that he perceives his wife has over her conception of children and the expression of her sexuality. In the case of an extramarital affair, the woman has direct control over what she is doing. The degree of control is not as clear in the case of barrenness. Control over the sexual activities of females is an important aspect of male dominance among many primates. A woman's conscious violation of her husband's apparent right over her sexual activities not only breaks a social rule but also attacks the man's basic sense of control. In addition, the woman risks pregnancy with another man. This assaults a man's investment of resources; he is likely to commit them to his own children but not to those of another man.

Given the importance of physical violence as grounds for a woman divorcing her husband, we can infer that men resort to violence as one way of maintaining control. If we add to this the leeway that men have in killing a wayward wife, the mechanism of physical control looms even larger in the marital relations of men and women. Perhaps further investigation in the field will reveal that the threat of physical punishment and death plays a more prominent role in the control of sexual and reproductive relationships than is commonly assumed.

*Ease of divorce.* Grounds for divorce are one part of an interconnected chain of restrictions that constrain a person's options of having more than one spouse in the course of a lifetime. Other constraints that may affect a person's decision to dissolve a marriage include the ease with which a divorce is likely to be granted and the amount of difficulty that can be expected in remarrying. Too many social obstacles to divorce may not only discourage a person from trying to obtain a divorce; they may eliminate the possibility altogether.

Divorce is usually difficult for one or both of the marital partners to obtain (62% of 45 societies). A smaller proportion of societies allow both husband and wife to secure a divorce (38% of 45 societies). A significant number of Insular Pacific societies ($X^2$ = 8.6, df = 1, p = <.005, N = 45) permit divorce rather easily. Nevertheless, the brunt of restrictions on divorce does not fall equally upon males and females. Like other rules applied to sexual and reproductive relationships, a woman bears an unequal burden of the constraint (women — 29% of 45 societies; men — 16% of 45 societies). Some biases against males and females obtaining divorces are significantly associated with specific world areas. Women are more likely to encounter difficulties in the Circum-Mediterranean area ($X^2$ = 4.08, 1 df, p = <.0, N = 45); men are more likely to face obstacles in African societies ($X^2$ = 7.49, 1 df, p = <.01, N = 45).

The Babylonians (45) and the Otoro (30) contrast sharply in the initiative they permit men and women to take in obtaining a divorce. A Babylonian wife cannot divorce or leave her husband at all unless she publicly justifies her refusal to have intercourse with him. The husband's options are easier than his wife's. Even though a woman has borne her husband a son and done nothing to offend him, he can still divorce her on a whim; he has only to utter a phrase to declare that he has terminated the relationship (Driver and Miles 1952–55: *1*, 289–299).

We see a reversal of the Babylonian situation among the Otoro. An Otoro man has a limited range of reasons that he may use to divorce his wife, i.e., leprosy, suspicion of witchcraft, and blatant and continual adultery. Even under these extreme conditions, he rarely tries to divorce her. In any case, he certainly would not attempt to divorce her if he could not receive a refund of the bride-price he gave for her. In contrast, a woman most frequently divorces her husband simply on the grounds that her feelings toward him have changed or that she has fallen in love with someone else (Nadel 1947: 125–127).

It is equally difficult for a man and woman to obtain a divorce in some societies (18% of 45 societies). The Bellacoola (132) and the Cayapa (168) go to great lengths to prevent a divorce. The respective families of a Bellacoola husband and wife will put pressure on them to stay together, even if one of them has run away with a paramour. Sometimes they resort to performing an "obscene" ceremony to shame the one who wants the divorce and thus discourage his or her intentions. The

Cayapa are even more forceful in their tactics of dissuasion. If Cayapa officials catch a person who tries to leave a spouse, they punish the culprit severely and try to effect a reconciliation between the couple. In addition, the person who wants to divorce a spouse has to face general public scorn for his or her desire. As a result, an unhappily married Cayapa spouse may prefer to leave the community rather than to receive both official and informal public chastisement (Barrett 1925: 329–32).

*Difficulty of remarriage.* Even if a divorce is granted, the divorced person may encounter difficulties in developing another reproductive relationship. Remarriage may be difficult, because no unmarried person is available or because the divorce stigmatizes a person. Most groups do not create these obstacles for divorced people. They generally allow the divorced person to remarry (78% of 37 societies), and they do not unduly constrain the individual in the process. When remarriage is difficult (22% of 37 societies), most societies make it more difficult for the woman than for the man (88% of the 8 societies where remarriage is difficult). For instance, public opinion would deter a Khalka Mongol (66) woman from remarrying if she were at fault in the divorce, particularly if she had children. If the husband were at fault in precipitating the divorce, he would not be hampered from remarrying (Vreeland 1954: 76).

If we look at the two main constraints on remarriage — ease of divorce and difficulty of remarriage — in relation to each other, we find that they allow men and women similar degrees of flexibility to form new reproductive relationships. In other words, if divorce is difficult to obtain, remarriage may be difficult. If divorce is easy, remarriage is likely to be also. The main deviation from this tendency is in the direction of permitting remarriage even though obtaining a divorce is difficult. This pattern prevails for men in more societies than for women.

*Pressures against divorce: considerations of children and property.* A group may impose subtle constraints on divorce through the type of guidelines it offers for determining child custody and allocation of property or other resources shared in the marriage. Although the procedures need not be punitive, they can deeply affect one or both partners. In a sense, they provide a way for the social group to punish one or both of the marital pair for failing to meet the cultural expectations and social obligations of marriage. At the very least, they can motivate a husband and wife to think seriously about the consequences of their actions. Although a woman might be anxious to leave her husband, she might not be as willing to lose her children or the economic security that the marriage provides. The object of the social guidelines at this point seems to be to mitigate the consequences to the group, despite the individual anguish they might entail.

The criteria for awarding custody of some or all of the children born in the marriage are quite variable. Most groups (44% of 41 societies) base the decision to grant custody on the circumstances that precipitated the divorce (17% of 41 societies) or on the wishes or ages of the children (27% of 41 societies).

A few examples may help to clarify the kind of circumstances upon which custody may depend. Among the Hadza (9) of Tanzania, coresidence is the main basis for legitimizing a marriage. If a man leaves his wife, not only does he have no further rights over her but he also has no grounds for securing custody of the children he has had with her (Kohl-Larsen 1958: 75). Among the Klamath (138) of south-central Oregon, custody of the children depends upon an evaluation of whose fault the divorce is. If the wife is at fault, the husband may choose to take custody of the children or demand the return of the bride-price he transferred at marriage (Spier 1930: 51). A Goajiro (159) husband may claim the children if his wife has committed adultery. However, if the wife's relatives can show that her husband mistreated her before she engaged in adultery, the husband has no such claim to the children (Gutierrez de Pineda 1948: 158).

The ages and preferences of the children may also be taken into account in custody arrangements. When a Bellacoola couple is divorced, the children may stay with either parent; the decision is left up to the parents and the children (Boas 1891: 419). Among the Wolof (21) of Gambia, the boys in the family remain with their mother after divorce until they are seven; the girls stay with her until they are fifteen or sixteen. Their father has custody of them after that (Gamble 1957: 60). The Kaska (129) allow infants to remain with their mothers, but older children go with their fathers. When the sons are grown, they may return to live with their fathers (Honigmann 1954: 134).

A sizable number of societies (42% of 41 societies) do specify that children should be only in the custody of the husband (22% of 41 societies) or of the wife (20% of 41 societies) after divorce. Not all groups feel that it is "natural" that the children stay with their mothers nor do all women think that it is "natural" for them to want to remain with their children. For example, most Banen (15) divorces are initiated by women rather than men. The men are happy if their wives are "fecund and hardworking" (Dugast 1959; 2, 222). Currently, women no longer feel great devotion to their husbands' families. They will abandon their children to follow other men, to return to their people, or to engage in "immorality, frivolity, or fantasy" (Dugast 1959: 2, 222). Therefore, the husband's prerogative to retain custody of his children may not impose a burden on his wife nor deter her from divorcing him. Miskito (156) children generally remain with their mother after a divorce that has been decided upon by mutual consent. The husband has the right to ask his wife or her family to return to him all of the presents that he made to them up to that time (Conzemius 1932: 150). Among the Otoro (30), the return of bride-price to the husband and the woman's custody of her children are interconnected. Regardless of the grounds for divorce, bride-price must be returned to the husband. After that, the woman is allowed to claim her children. Otherwise, the husband has the right to keep all of her legitimate or illegitimate children (Nadel 1947: 117).

Dissolving the marriage may also mean distributing the material products of the couple's labor. The circumstances that precipitated the divorce are also considered in deciding upon the appropriate allocation of property or attendant financial transactions. Individual circumstances of divorce govern these arrangements in the greatest number of societies (41% of 39 societies). For example, the Somali (36) are very specific about the return of dower and bridewealth according to the circumstances of the divorce. This is in keeping with the tone of the beginning of the marriage; they are very specific about the kinds of rights and relationships for which the exchanges at marriage are intended to pay (Lewis 1962: 36). If the husband has not paid the dower at the proper time, and the wife wants a quick divorce, she may renounce her right to it. The return of bridewealth depends upon the husband's reasons for divorcing his wife. If she deserts him or commits adultery, he will calculate the amount of bridewealth to be returned on the basis of: (1) the amount of dowry that was given for her (2) the number of sons she has borne, and (3) the amount of livestock that he has himself. A husband is entitled to partial return if he is physically incapable of maintaining his wife or if he refuses to do so. If the husband divorces his wife on any other grounds, he is not entitled to claim the return of any bridewealth.

Among the Garo (69), marriage is not initiated with extensive exchanges, and compensation after divorce is not subject to the detailed rules that characterize Somali divorces (Burling 1963: 259). The principle is straightforward: whoever initiates divorce pays compensation to the other spouse. The compensation is given for failure to maintain kin responsibilities and is divided among the relatives of the spouse who is divorced. Adultery or beating one's spouse are not adequate grounds for divorce. Only when a couple is incompatible is divorce justified. If both husband and wife equally desire the divorce, neither has to pay compensation to the other.

Economic obligations after divorce may depend upon the wishes of the couple. For example, the Micmac (126) show little concern with the distribution of property. Divorce occurs because of incompatibility. Mutual happiness rather than property is their main aim. They "retire without a fuss for they say one shouldn't marry only to be unhappy the remainder of one's days" (LeClercq 1910: 262).

In some societies, the economic resources are equitably divided between the spouses (21% of 39 societies). In others, one spouse or the kin of one spouse are more likely to incur greater financial consequences. The wife or her kin absorb an economic loss somewhat more often (23% of 39 societies) than the husband or his kin (15% of 39 societies). The fact that kin partially or totally contribute the economic resources for the marriage broadens social interest in maintaining the marriage. Kin may try to dissuade a relative from getting a divorce because of the investment they have made in the marriage. Their advice may constitute another subtle restriction on the choices that are available to the members of a troubled marriage. Nevertheless, the large contributions that the families of both the bride and groom make to a Siamese (76) couple at marriage do not deter the pair from divorce. The only stipulation that accompanies their families' gifts is that the couple return them if they separate or divorce (Sharp et al. 1954: 82).

The next question that arises is whether there is any consistency between the types of pressures a person is likely to encounter about children and property when a divorce is decided upon. In other words, if there is flexibility or harshness about granting custody of children, is there likely to be a similar tone in the allocation of property? My data confirm the idea that there is a significant association between the way that children and property are distributed to the divorcing spouses ($S_r = .4178$, p = <.006, N = 36). When each spouse receives custody of some of the children, there is usually (80%) either an equal division of the property or no economic transaction at the divorce. When custody of the children depends upon age, the husband is usually (80%) responsible for paying compensation to his wife or making a settlement according to the circumstances of the divorce. When one spouse regularly receives custody of all of the children, the woman or her kin must usually (82% of 11 societies) incur an economic loss or reimburse her husband according to the conditions that led to the divorce.

*Widow remarriage.* Death of one of the partners, rather than a conscious choice to dissolve the union, may terminate a marriage. This is a less controlled avenue to acquiring another spouse. The way in which a marriage ends affects the kinds of restrictions placed on remarriage. However, there is no consistency between the strength of restrictions placed on a woman subsequent to a divorce and after widowhood. Overall, the rules that surround a widow are often quite precise and are certainly more restrictive than the ones that govern the remarriage of divorcées.

Although a widow is free to marry anyone she chooses in many societies (37 % of 57 societies), she often chooses not to remarry at all (33 % of the 21 societies where she can remarry). Despite claims that she has a choice, there may be considerable social pressure against remarriage. DeVos (1965: 65) notes that a Japanese (117) woman might decide not to remarry, because remarriage would deprive her children of the right to inherit from the household of their deceased father. Furthermore, a subsequent husband would have no responsibility toward the children of another man. He could totally ignore them if he wanted to. Therefore, the woman usually remains in her late husband's house, dependent upon the support of his family. A woman is supposed to "remain faithful to her husband even after his death . . . [and] . . . to sacrifice herself for her children . . . [she] shouldn't be selfishly concerned with her own happiness" (DeVos 1965: 65).

The dedication that a wife is supposed to exhibit after her husband dies is sometimes carried to the extreme. There are a few societies where remarriage is prohibited (5 % of 57 societies), regardless of the circumstances of the marriage of the husband's death. For example, a young girl in Uttar Pradesh (63) may be deprived of ever having experienced married life. If she is a high caste girl who marries before puberty, she cannot remarry if her husband dies (Luschinsky 1963: 261). Even this sacrifice pales in intensity next to the alternative for a Fijian (102) widow. When a Fijian husband dies, it is the custom for his wife to be strangled and buried with him (Williams 1884: 118). The strangulation of a wife may sometimes be prompted by the jealousy of her dying husband, who wishes no other man to have her (Waterhouse 1866: 311). The Fijians say that the woman wants to die after her husband dies, apparently because she is so grief-stricken. Unfortunately, there is probably a more practical reason for a Fijian widow to prefer to die. "They know that life would thenceforth be to them prolonged insult, neglect, and want. Death offers an escape from suffering and wrong that await the woman who survives her husband" (Williams 1884: 169–171).

Most groups are not as extreme in their demands of widows. However, they often expect the woman to remain committed to the family or kin group of her husband. By far the most usual constraint (58% of 57 societies) on a widow is the requirement that she marry or at least give first priority to one of her husband's relatives when she contemplates remarriage. These kinship limitations on widow remarriage occur with almost equal frequency in the three main types of descent systems (patrilineal — 31%; matrilineal — 25%; bilateral — 34%).

In addition to strictures on whom she can marry, a widow is generally subject to restrictions on the amount of time that should elapse before she marries again. There is a "respectable" duration for mourning. In most societies (77% of 31 societies), this period does not extend beyond two years. However, the length of time can vary a good deal from one society to the next. The most frequent intervals for mourning are less than six months (29% of 31 societies) and between one and two years (32% of 31 societies). Intervals of six months to a year (16% of 31 societies), more than two years (13% of 31 societies), or for an indefinite period (10% of 31 societies) occur less often. Although a widow's choice is bound by precise rules, she does have the possibility of remarriage open to her in a large number of cases *if* she follows the prescribed route for obtaining another husband.

### Restrictions on Partners for Reproductive Relationships: A Summary

Marriage defines a relationship within which intercourse and the conception of children are not only encouraged but approved. In other words, it is a reproductive relationship, subject to social rules. Using this definition of marriage, I interpreted the rules that surround partner selection and availability as social mechanisms that aid the group in exerting some control over the nature of reproductive relationships. The marital process is like a path, which has many forks in its route. One fork may lead to more possibilities for an individual to have a number of partners; another may entail a progressive restriction of individual choice.

The consistent thread that runs through the rules governing the possibility of a person obtaining more than one reproductive partner, either by synchronic or diachronic marriages, is that they generally increase the options for a man and decrease or strictly control those open to a woman. Nevertheless, broad conclusions about single rules are less informative than an investigation of the pattern of rules that is followed in each society. Does a double standard regarding reproductive relationships occur in most societies?

In order to deal with this question, I constructed an index to assess the

Table 4.2 *Comparison of Males' Confinement of Reproductive Potential to One Union and/or Family with the Confinement of Females' Reproductive Potential to One Union and/or Family*

|  |  | Confinement of Male Reproductive Potential | | |
|---|---|---|---|---|
|  |  | High, Medium High | Low, Medium Low |  |
| Confinement of Female Reproductive Potential | High, Medium High | 13 | 6 | 19 |
|  | Low, Medium Low | 1 | 19 | 20 |
|  |  | 14 | 25 | N = 39 |

$X^2 = 14.39$; df = 1; p = < .001

degree to which reproduction is confined to one union or family. I combined a number of the restrictions that I had dealt with individually in my discussion of rules affecting spouse selection. I wanted to find out the overall impact of the pattern of rules associated with the marital process. I based my index of confinement of a woman's reproductive potential to one union or family on two main factors: difficulty of divorce and limitations on remarriage after divorce or widowhood. If divorce was allowed, and if a woman could marry anyone she chose after the termination of her marriage, I regarded it as low confinement of her reproductive potential. If the opposite held, I regarded it as high confinement of her reproductive potential. I based the index of confinement of a man's reproductive potential on the extent of polygyny, difficulty of divorce, and the likelihood that a man would inherit a widow from his kinsmen. If there were full polygyny, easy divorce for a man, and obligatory transference of a kinsman's widow to him, I regarded this as low confinement of his reproductive potential. If monogamy prevailed, divorce was difficult, and there was no widow remarriage, I regarded this as high confinement of his reproductive potential.

I then related the confinement of a woman's reproductive potential to that of a man's in the same societies. I found that there is a high degree of association between the degree of restriction on men's and women's reproductive potential in the same societies. Table 4.2 presents a summary of these findings.

The important point that emerges from these findings is that there is a general consistency in the extent to which a woman's and a man's reproductive potential is confined to one union or family. Although it is true that there are some cases in which woman's flexibility to have more than one reproductive partner is highly confined, whereas a man's is not, these double standards are in the minority (15% of 39 societies). In addition, the fact that a woman is not concurrently married to more than one man with whom she can bear children does not mean that her reproductive potential is necessarily restricted to one man. The main restriction on a woman in this regard is that she not have simultaneous reproductive relationships; she is allowed to have a series, or sequence, of relationships at different times. Therefore, although both men and women can have a variety of reproductive partners in their lifetimes, their means of accomplishing this end differ. Polygyny may be a dramatic illustration of variety in reproductive partnerships. However, we need to balance our focus on synchronic marriages with a consideration of the impact of diachronic relationships on the availability of variety in reproductive relationships.

### The Social Investment in Marriage

Thus far I have dealt with the main ways in which cultural beliefs and social rules can limit or expand the possibilities for forming reproductive relationships. The next phase of understanding the social and cultural dimensions of marriage is to consider the impact that the group has on: (1) individual consent about whom to marry, (2) the rights and functions attached to marriage, and (3) social involvement in the celebration of the marriage. These factors give us more specific clues about the special place that marriage has within particular social settings.

In the last section I pointed out the value of thinking of different aspects of spouse selection in relation to each other — as part of an overall framework for restricting reproductive relationships. It is profitable to think of the next three elements in a similar fashion. Each one is a facet of the way that the social group chooses to invest itself in marriage. The degree to which a marriage is primarily a bond between two individuals or, instead, part of a wider network of social relations depends upon the links between these elements.

### Restrictions on an Individual's Consent to Marry

In American society, we tend to think of marriage as an individual matter. We think we are free to choose, within some bounds of respectability, whom we will marry. Just as intercourse is regarded as a private matter between individuals, so, too, should marriage be a personal decision. Once again, it may be difficult for us to leap into another social context, where the relationships we consider to be matters of individual choice are the focus for social concern. Even more unsettling may be the fact that other people may intervene and influence an individual's decision of whom to marry. Our understanding of these groups depends partly upon our being able to think of other ways that marriages can begin and function.

Marriage is not usually a transaction confined to the bride and groom. It extends beyond them, to include members of their families or kin groups. In most societies, the families of the bride and groom (52% of 58 societies) or the kin groups of both (35% of 58 societies) play an important role in the initiation of marriage. Responsibility for proposing marriage falls much less often upon the family of the bride alone (10% of 58 societies).

When others play a major role in the choice of whom a person will marry, the marriages are sometimes referred to as "arranged marriages." An "arranged marriage" usually does not mean that the prospective couple has no say in the marriage transaction. A prospective spouse's opinion about a proposed marriage is usually taken into account for both men and women (men — 83% of 54 societies; women — 72% of 57 societies). However, an individual's consent is necessary in only half of these societies (men — 43% of 54 societies; women — 33% of 57 societies). In an approximately equal number of societies, a prospective spouse may be consulted, but an individual's consent is not necessary (men — 41% of 54 societies; women — 39% of 57 societies). Less frequently, a man (17% of 54 societies) or a woman (28% of 57 societies) is not consulted at all about the choice of a prospective spouse. Overall, a woman has slightly less flexibility than a man has in consenting to a marriage.

Some of these modes of consent are more characteristic of specific regions of the world than others. A man's consent to marry is usually necessary in South America and Eurasia ($X^2$ = 4.5, 1 df, p = <.05, N = 55), while a woman's is required in Africa and Eurasia ($X^2$ = 10.04, 1 df, p = <.005, N = 56). Women in the Circum-Mediterranean are very much confined in their choices. In most societies in this area (78% of 9 societies), a woman is not consulted at all about the choice of her prospective marriage partner ($X^2$ = 11.29, 1 df, p = <.001, N = 56).

However, summaries of statistics about consent to marriage for each gender do not tell us very much about what happens to men and women in the same societies. In order to find out how much flexibility about consent men and women have relative to each other in the same society,

I correlated male consent to marriage with female consent to marriage. I found that there is a consistent association between the modes of consent that apply to both males and females in the same societies (Gamma = .9778, z = 5.54, p = .01, two-tailed). When males do not have much to say about whom they will marry, females do not either. If the group allows more scope to individual choice, it usually applies to both males and females. If there is a double standard in flexibility about consent, it is less likely to work in the woman's favor than in the man's e.g., the man's consent is necessary, whereas the woman's is not required.

The pattern that emerges with regard to the sociocultural aspects of the initiation of marriage is not unlike the one I have described for the confinement of reproductive potential. Men and women are generally subject to the same degree of social involvement in their decisions to marry. The exceptions are societies where males are consulted more than females (13% of 54 societies); the opposite almost never occurs (2% of 54 societies). In most societies the couple must consider the wishes of their families or kin groups in their seleciton, rather than adhere solely to the dictates of their own wishes. Marriage *is* a family affair in most parts of the world.

*Framework of a Marital Relationship:*
*The Rights Transferred at Marriage and*
*the Factors that Finalize the Union*

After two people agree to marry, they increase their ties to each other by committing themselves to transfer specific rights. The group may participate in this phase of the marital process by means of the qualifications they attach to it. First, they may specify which rights the bride and groom should transfer to each other. Second, they can establish criteria to determine when the marriage is regarded as final. Finality of marriage means that the couple has completed all of the steps necessary to gain full social acceptance of the union. Since the social organization of different societies varies, it is not surprising that the rights transferred at marriage and the factors that finalize marriage vary across societies.

The West African group, the Fon of Dahomey (18) presents a prospective spouse with an intricate array of marriage choices. Imagine being faced with a range of thirteen different categories of marriage! Each one has distinct rights and obligations associated with it. Depending upon an individual's social status, concern for the future of children that might be born, and the type of relationship desired with a prospective spouse, a person can choose a variety of arrangements. A couple of examples show how variable the nature of marriage is in Dahomey (Herskovits 1938).

In one form of marriage, "money with woman," control of the children is vested in the father. The kin units of the bride and groom play a large role in the negotiations. When the girl's family is satisfied that the groom has fulfilled all of his financial obligations, the groom can request that his bride-to-be be sent to his house. He goes to the girl's residence to deliver his gifts of shells, goats, salt, and clothing and to display them to his fiancée's relatives. The value of his fiancée's virginity is reflected in the payments he makes. After his gifts have been accepted, the groom participates in a marriage ceremony. Subsequent to the cermony, the couple can leave for the groom's home.

The wedding night has significance for the couple's future, because the husband finds out whether or not his wife was a virgin when he married her. Previous sexual activity may lower her value in his eyes. If the mat on which the newlyweds slept shows that the bride was not a virgin, the girl's father forces her to name her previous lover. Her family has the right to beat her until she confesses a name. Admission of a previous affair is sufficient to warrant a variety of punishments to the offenders. The wife's family can beat her and fine her lover; the woman's new husband can reject her as his wife. If she was not a virgin, her husband can give fewer gifts for her and be less rigorous in his adherence to obligations performed for the girl's parents.

When the woman is given her married name, social participation in the event may vary according to her sexual experience previous to marriage. Usually the families and friends of both the bride and groom are present for the daylong festivities. The ceremonies are less elaborate if the girl was not a virgin. The emphasis on giving gifts to procure rights in a woman's fertility becomes tied to her sexual activity. Her value declines in this type of marriage if her sexual experience has been extensive. In fact, it may exclude her from such marriage altogether. This marriage arrangement shows that marriages are tied to very specific sets of rights and obligations, which are explicitly recognized from the outset.

Another type of marriage, "giving the goat to the buck," shows how flexible marriage arrangements can be. This type of marriage occurs frequently among upper-class families, in which the women may be independently wealthy. The woman's economic independence allows her to form her own household unit and to participate in economically lucrative enterprises after marriage. She may own a great deal of property and economic resources. Therefore, it is in her interest to have some control over the resources that will come to her children.

In this form of marriage, control of the children is vested in a woman. The main goal of the marriage is to enable the woman to retain control over her resources by making sure that her children will perpetuate the business of her household. For all practical purposes, she takes on the role of a man and marries a girl from another family. She becomes the "husband," and the girl she marries becomes her "wife." She establishes the union in much the same way as a man does in the "money with woman" arrangement. The obvious exception to a parallel with the previous example is the nature of sexual activity between the partners. How does the women have children if she marries another woman? She arranges to have a man live with or sleep with her "wife," so that they will have children. Her economic contribution to her "wife" defines her right to claim the wife's children as her own. The man who slept with her wife has no rights in the children. A woman with a lot of economic resources can marry more than one woman and arrange to have men come to the compound to produce children with her wives. None of the ethnographers mentioned how the "husband" satisfied her sexual needs or whether she also gave birth to children.

This type of marriage shows how broadly the definition of marriage can extend. Even in this case, marriage remains a context for reproduction, and intercourse is approved between the wife and a genitor. The economic functions of the marriage and the nature of the rights transferred at marriage allow for this unusual pattern of two people of the same gender establishing a reproductive relationship.

As both examples illustrate, marriage entails a variety of rights and obligations. Although the relationship can be identified by the couple's eligibility to reproduce, the rights that each partner transfers to the other at marriage vary not only in kind but also in the importance attached to them. In addition, societies have different rules and procedures to define the point at which the marriage transaction is considered complete. In the first example, a man may terminate the marriage if he finds that his wife is not a virgin. The constellation of rights and procedures for completing a marriage gives marriage its unique flavor in a specific society. It also provides a framework to embrace other rules connected with marriage. The transfer of rights that marriage entails is probably the clearest indication of the meaning that the social unit attaches to the union.

The rights that a man transfers to his wife at marriage vary less from one society to another than do those that a woman transfers to her husband. The most important right that a man gives to his wife in an overwhelming number of societies (89% of 37 societies) is the right to his economic labor. In a third of the societies in which the husband transfers his economic labor to his wife (33% of 33 societies) he also transfers to her his choice of postmarital residence. A woman rarely receives the prerogative of having priority of sexual access to her husband (8% of 37 societies) *and* the right to the children they have together.

The number and types of important rights that a woman transfers to her husband at marriage vary from one society to another. The privileges that a woman gives to her spouse are usually more numerous than those her husband gives to her. The most important right that a woman transfers in the largest number of societies is a claim to her economic labor (34% of 50 societies). She also explicitly transfers the right to her children (20% of 50 societies) and control over sexual access in a sizable number (18% of 50 societies). She transfers domestic services (16% of 50 societies) and choice of residence (12% of 50 societies) less often. African and Circum-Mediterranean societies are the context within which a woman is most likely to give her husband the right to their children and control over sexual access ($X^2$ = 6.6, 1 df, p = < .01, N = 50).

Additional events finalize the marriage. Until these events occur, rights exchanged at marriage may be in suspension. The birth of children (44% of 45 societies), bride-price (22% of 45* societies), or both (13% of 45 societies) are the most important criteria used to finalize marriage. While cohabitation (9% of 45 societies) or the marriage ceremony itself (11% of 45 societies) is the most important conclusion to the marriage transaction in some societies, neither holds the central place of children and/or bride-price (80% of 45 societies).

Like the rights transferred at marriage, the factors that finalize marriage tend to cluster in some areas of the world more than in others. Bride-price finalizes marriage most often in African and Circum-Mediterranean societies ($X^2$ = 6.15, 1 df, p = < .02, N = 45). The birth of children alone or in combination with a factor other than bride-price tends to be most important in societies in the Insular Pacific and South America ($X^2$ = 3.32, 1 df, p = < .10, N = 45).

I wondered whether there were any patterns of association between the types of rights that men and women transfer to each other at marriage and the factors that finalize the marriage. I found that bride-price is the only factor that is consistently associated with the rights that the man or the woman transfers. A man's transfer of the right to his economic labor is significantly related to his paying bride-price to finalize the union (Fisher's exact test, p = .002, N - 29). A woman is most likely to transfer rights over the children she bears, as well as control over sexual access, when bride-price is the factor that finalizes the marriage ($X^2$ = 3.69, 1 df, p = < .06, N = 38).

In sum, two consistent themes pervade the process of transferring rights and finalizing the union: (1) economic exchange and (2) reproduction. Their pervasiveness supports the view that marriage functions as a basis for exchange between groups, management of economic resources, and a context for reproduction. Their reproductive relationship allows the couple to set up a basic sexual division of labor, which becomes a major function attached to the marriage.

*The Marriage Celebration*

The most striking expression of the investment that a group has in a reproductive relationship is the marriage celebration. The ceremony may include a public summation of the rights transferred between the husband and his new wife. The people who contribute to the preparations for the celebration or participate in the event itself publicly express their interest in the marital union. They may bring food, gifts, and other material manifestations of their links to the couple. The number of people associated with the celebration may reflect the range of social interest in the continuation of the marriage. The ceremony itself may encapsulate many of the marital rights and standards that will be activated after the ceremony.

Even though other aspects of sociocultural involvement in marriage are restrictive, marriage celebrations are likely to be expansive, positive events. Their influence extends beyond the occasion of the marriage. Kinsmen can cement ties with each other. In-laws (affines) can establish rapport in a relaxed, supportive atmosphere. Feasting, dancing, music, elaborate dress, and special utensils used for the occasion all add to the festive air. People who are already married can remember and reaffirm the meaning of their own ties with each other. Unmarried boys and girls who share in the joy learn the importance of social approval in forming relationships. They can see vividly the wider significance of marriage. Marriage celebrations are the most positive means that a group has of offering its stamp of approval for the relationships that it wants to encourage. Thus, the degree of social elaboration present at the celebration may be a preview of the amount of social concern that will be associated with later phases of the marital relationship.

Some societies give little or no public attention to a couple's transition from an unmarried to a married state (28% of 57 societies). For example, the Tupinamba (177) have no public rites that accompany marriage. A man delivers his sister or daughter to the man to whom she is betrothed. This simple act completes the marriage, and nothing further occurs to mark it (Staden 1928: 147). The Havasupai (150) express slightly more concern. Marriage can begin in two ways. One way is for the families of the bride and groom to agree upon the marriage in advance. The transfer of a gift from the groom to the bride's parents and his subsequent residence with the bride in the parents' dwelling show that the marriage has taken place. The second method is for the man to make a series of nocturnal visits to his future bride at her house. He later presents a gift to the woman's parents and takes up residence in their home (Smithson 1959: 94). Both the Tupinamba and the Havasupai finalize marriage by living together.

This sort of minimal public attention given to the beginning of marriage contrasts with the moderate (26% of 57 societies) to elaborate (39% of 57 societies) celebrations held by most societies (65% of 57 societies). Relatively elaborate types of celebrations are likely to occur significantly more often in Africa, Eurasia, and the Circum-Mediterranean ($X^2$ = 5.76, 1 df, p = <.02, N = 57) than elsewhere. The Garo (69), who live in Assam, in northeastern India, show moderate public concern when a marriage begins. The celebration occurs after the potential bride's brothers successfully capture the husband. When the woman decides that she likes a particular young man, she tells her father and brother(s). Neither the young man nor his parents need to be consulted about her decision to marry him, unless the potential bride is an heiress. The woman's brothers then venture out to capture the unsuspecting groom-to-be, take him back to their sister's village, and participate in a celebration at her house. The girl, her family, interested friends, relatives, and neighbors all attend this joyous (at least for the bride) occasion (Burling 1963: 83–86). Marriage becomes final only after the groom establishes continual residence with the bride. Captured grooms are prone to run away repeatedly. Therefore, continuity of residence with the bride is a sign of a groom's acquiescence to his new situation in life.

The Somali (36), a pastoral group in Somalia on the horn of Africa, illustrate the complexity of individual and social concerns that may be expressed during the elaborate celebration that accompanies a marriage (Lewis 1962: Paulitschke 1888). Women of the bride's lineage sing hymns, and the couple becomes the focus of a series of rites. After these preliminaries, the bride and groom retire to a hut, where they are served meat and other food. The kin of the bride and groom attend the wedding and present gifts to the couple. The wife's kin prepare most of the food for the participants in the celebration. While the bride and groom remain in the wedding hut, the singing, dancing, feasting, and processions continue outside for seven days. The seclusion of the couple from the events around them succinctly shows that their wedding is an occasion for the expression of other important social matters, one of which centers on the exchanges that take place in the course of the celebration.

Three distinct transactions occur at a Somali marriage: (1) transfer of bridewealth, (2) payment of dowry, and (3) giving the dower. The groom gives bridewealth to his bride's father. The groom's father allocates some of his stock to his son, so that he can contract a marriage. Although the transfer of bridewealth has broader implications, its overt purpose is to compensate the bride's parents for the cost of raising her. In addition, it pays for specific rights that the woman will render to her husband and his lineage. It pays for the woman to cook for her husband, to manage the flocks, and to produce the children, especially sons, who will be necessary for the continuation of her husband's patrilineage (Lewis 1961: 21). No effective affinal relations can be established without the payment of bridewealth. The distribution of the payment shows its wide-ranging importance to the bride's kin group. The bride's father shares it with the *dia*-paying group, a mutual-aid group based upon patrilineal ties and contractual obligations.

The dowry is any gift given from the wife's kin to the husband. It usually includes the hut in which the newly married couple will live, camels for transport, a flock of sheep and goats, and other camels. There may be little difference in economic terms between the value of the dowry that the wife's kin gives and the bridewealth that the groom gives. The main purpose of the exchange of economic goods is not their simple monetary contribution to the maintenance of the couple. The amounts transferred are important in determining the strength of the social ties that are established between the bride's and groom's kin (Lewis 1965: 340–341). The formation of links between the two groups is in fact the predominant aim of the transactions. The members of each group do not consider that their contributions cancel each other out, even though the value of the goods exchanged is approximately equivalent (Lewis 1961: 7). The exchange itself becomes symbolic of the new association between the kin of the bride and groom. The meaning of the transaction derives from this added dimension. In more practical terms, the mutual exchanges ensure that a member of a deceased husband's lineage has priority in marrying his widow (Lewis 1965: 341). Ties between in-laws are important as a means of access to the pasture and water of people to whom they are not patrilineally related. The association between the groups is means to last a long time. Therefore, the beginning of their bond is important, because it establishes links between them and sets the tone for future interactions.

The dower, the personal gift that the groom gives to his bride, is a crucial transaction for the couple. It is the only exchange that establishes a personal relationship between the man and woman. Although bridewealth pays for the husband's rights to the children his wife bears, the activation of this right is not possible without the transfer of the dower from the groom to the bride. Only the dower entitles the groom to have sex with his bride and to reproduce with her. If the groom does not give his wife a dower, her children are regarded as bastards.

In sum, the Somali wedding integrates a number of social concerns connected with marriage. It marks the establishment of a reproductive relationship between a man and a woman and specifies the rights and obligations of each to the other. It also creates affinal ties between the wider groups to which the couple belongs and aligns their rights with each other.

Both the celebration of the marriage and the identity of the participants or contributors to it indicate sociocultural aspects of the union that extend beyond the couple. Although the amounts of individual and social interest that are expressed in the celebration differ, recognition of the marriage is never confined to the couple alone (0 societies in my sample). Nor is participation in the celebration usually restricted (20 % of 50 societies) to the friends of the couple (4 % of 50 societies), the family of the bride or groom alone (8 % of 50 societies), or solely to the kin group of either the bride or groom (8 % of 50 societies). By far, the most widespread trend (80 % of 50 societies) is the participation of a large group of people in the celebration. The most likely candidates for participation are the kin groups to which the bride and groom belong (38 % of 50 societies). The other probable celebrants are the families of both the bride and groom (18 % of 50 societies) or most of the members in the community to which one or both of the pair belong (24 % of 50 societies).

When we look at the components of the celebration and the social participation in it, we find that the two features parallel each other in their extent. As the elaboration of the celebration increases, so does the extensiveness of the group that participates in it ($S_r$ = .51, p = <.001, N = 50). This association supports the view that each component is one facet of a pattern of social actions that encourage marriage.

*Continuity of Social Interest: Postmarital Residence*

As the exchanges between affines imply, the transactions at a marriage are only a preview of the expectations that the couple and members of their groups will have of each other in the future. These expectations include the couple's choice of residence after marriage, i.e., postmarital residence. Where the couple decides to live becomes a significant spatial expression of the social factors involved in their marriage. Residence with or near relatives usually fosters interaction and communication with them. Direct access to relatives may affect the nature of the relationship between the married couple. For example, a woman may complain to her relatives about a violation of the rights she was supposed to have when she married. The support of her kinsmen may exert sufficient pressure on the husband to remedy an unsatisfactory situation for the wife.

Patrilocality — residence with or near the husband's father — dominates (60% of 62 societies) as the main type of postmarital residence pattern that couples adopt (Murdock and Wilson 1972). The clustering of males through avunculocal residence — residence with or near the husband's uncle — is rare (5% of 62 societies) in comparison. Groups in Africa and the Circum-Mediterranean are most likely to choose patrilocality ($X^2$ = 4.59, 1 df, p = <.05, N = 62). It is less likely (21% of 62 societies) that a couple will prefer matrilocality — residence with or near the wife's mother. Nevertheless, matrilocality occurs more often than neolocality — the establishment of a new residence, apart from the kin of the husband or wife — or ambilocality — a choice of residence with the wife's or husband's kin (15% of 62 societies).

The possible importance of residence patterns for understanding different aspects of social organization has long been recognized in anthropology (Lowie 1920; Fox 1974; Bohannan and Middleton 1968; Otterbein 1968; Ember and Ember 1971; Murdock and Wilson 1972; Divale 1975). However, I am less interested in the relationship of residence to general features of social life than I am in the impact that residence has for reproductive relationships. For example, the presence of clusters of related males or females may influence a number of events related to the reproductive cycle, e.g., attention paid to the birth of a child, preference for a particular gender of child, and selection of a spouse.

The association between unilocal residence with unilineal descent has been confirmed for some time. Both emphasize ties traced through one sex, rather than through the other. However, the reason for the association has not been clear. In the past, it seemed logical to conclude that residence patterns derived from the importance of males and females in the sexual division of labor. In other words, if males contributed more to subsistence, then it was likely that patrilocality would prevail. Recent studies, e.g., Ember and Ember (1971), show that this assumption does not hold.

Divale (1975) presents an alternative hypothesis to the residence/ contribution-to-subsistence view. He relates residence to the management of conflict between males and to obtaining access to females. Groups generally have to face two problems that require reconciliation: (1) How can men maintain sufficient cooperation with each other to protect the community? and (2) How can men be sure that they will have mates if they avoid open competition with each other? Divale sees residence patterns as one response to these problems. Matrilocality can be a temporary solution to the problem of conflict between males. Divale sees its development as an outgrowth of patrilocality.

The coresidence of related males in a patrilocal pattern is ripe for internal warfare, i.e., fighting between communities in the same culture. Rivalry over women may become a major disruptive influence in men's interactions with each other. Although they may participate in social mechanisms that may stem conflict — e.g., succession to power based on age or access to women governed by bride-price — men may barely maintain an uneasy peace with each other. However, if they cannot establish cooperation in their residence group, they are in a weakened position for teaming up under conditions of external warfare, i.e., fighting between communities not in the same culture. External warfare is most conducive to the development of matrilocality. Divale's research shows that this is most likely to occur when a group has recently migrated to an area. Men have to band together to maintain their social unit. They are in a better position to fend off an alien group if they cooperate with each other and jointly pursue a common goal.

The persuasiveness of Divale's argument derives from its parsimony and its compatibility with what we know about primates in general and their reproductive strategies in particular. The management of conflict between males and the maintenance of access to females are two basic problems with which other primates have to deal. Despite our human embellishments, we still have to attend to such basic survival tasks as protection. Reproduction, and maintenance of an adequate number of people in the group. Divale's argument points to a way to tie all of these themes together.

Although political and economic aspects of residence are important, their importance may have overshadowed other equally significant features, which relate to reproductive viability of the population. For example, residence patterns may create social support networks, which aid a woman after she has her first child. My data show that a couple often reside with or near a woman's relatives either permanently or temporarily when the woman has her first child (Wilson 1975). Raphael (1966) postulates that physical, emotional, and social support during the onset of lactation are necessary conditions for successful breastfeeding; they promote the survival of the infant. Her cross-cultural study showed that most groups provide social support for the woman when she begins to breastfeed her child; maternal kin are most likely to offer help. She concludes that the reassurance that others provide for her after the birth of her first child may be an important factor in aiding the woman to satisfactorily establish lactation. My data support this view (Wilson 1975).

The general point that derives from Divale's and Raphael's work is that the patterned clustering of males and females can affect conflict resolution, the establishment of support networks, and reproductive viability. Robin Fox's discussion of residence patterns (1974) also deals with some of these issues, e.g., patterns of reproduction. He describes the conditions under which residence patterns are likely to develop and then tries to show how descent groups might derive from residence patterns.

Fox begins his analysis by assuming four "facts of life": (1) women have children, (2) men impregnate women, (3) men usually exercise control, and (4) primary kin do not mate with each other (Fox 1974: 31). Local group formation precedes and is basic to the kin ties. Residence patterns take into account the practical difficulties of links between men/women/children and the problems of reproduction under different environmental circumstances. For example, an environment that requires hunting and gathering as the main mode of subsistence would encourage the formation of groups of related males. Hunting in a band has demonstrated its advantages over millions of years of human development. Cooperation between men could result in their having a better subsistence base plus the assurance of sharing resources and being able to rely on each other for protection. Different types of reproductive arrangements associated with subsistence requirements may lead to the formation of different kinds of groups. Fox then tries to show how kinship patterns derived from residence arrangements. He hypothesizes that people conceptualized their bonds with their children and their parents in terms of the ways they were clustered in local groups. He finds it difficult to imagine any alternative path that could explain the close association between residence and descent. He does not think it is plausible to argue that descent systems preceded residence patterns. To illustrate his belief, he follows the development of the Shoshone Indians from loosely defined matrilocal groups to matrilineages (Fox 1974: 33–91).

Matrilocality began when the Shoshone gradually moved into new territories, suitable for small-scale agriculture. The women tended the crops, and the men supplemented the food supply by hunting. They could not form large groups because of the military and ecological situation. Their settlement pattern reflected their response to their environment. They lived in relatively isolated houses, with the women clustered together; the men were intermittently and loosely attached to the households. As time went on, some of the households formed more compact settlements or lived in villages taken over from previous residents. Matrilocal households continued to be the main residential units. Concentration in villages meant that brothers could be near their sisters, and husbands could remain with their wives. Males and females could establish more continuous ties. Matrilineality probably grew out of a recognition of the residential ties and the previously established ties between parents, children, and siblings. Fox concludes that matrilineal groups most commonly develop from residential pattens that have been responsive to concerns of property and defense.

Fox's discussion centers on the effect of patterns of reproduction on group formation and residence patterns. Divale focuses on the conditions under which the residence patterns are likely to develop. Both agree that defense of the group plays a major role in the development of residence patterns. Fox's example of the Shoshone traces them through phases that Divale hypothesizes are ideal for the development of matrilocality, i.e., migration to a new territory and reliance on ties between males for defense. As population increases, the established groups would segment and create new settlements. The names assigned to kin would be a way of continuing their bonds and association with each other. The step from local group formation to principles of descent would be an easy one.

I agree with Fox that many anthropologists tend to take descent as given and ask about its implications rather than question its influence (Fox 1974: 95). There is no doubt that the principle of descent exerts a powerful sway over the structure of social relations. This is not the question. The question relates to the direction and force of influence between descent, principles of local group formation, and reproductive viability. I think that we need to look more closely at kinship as one type of response to reproductive arrangements. When kinship bonds become established as principles of social behavior, they may then begin to shape future reproductive arrangements. Recognizing feedback between kinship and reproductive arrangements seems to allow for more flexibility in the variables we examine than confining ourselves to a narrower view by focusing on kinship as a determinant of behavior. Kinship has its place, but it is only one of a number of important social concerns that relate to where a couple lives after they marry.

## Continuity of Social Interest:
## Eating and Sleeping Arrangements

Residence patterns influence the choice of relatives with whom a couple is most likely to interact, but other social arrangements channel a couple's access to each other. Daily activities provide good clues to the structure of the marital relationship after the honeymoon.

The majority of societies require males and females to eat separately in public (11 % — eat at different times; 23 % — designate separate areas; 26 % — eat separately in public, but not in private). Yet even these rules bend for husbands and wives. Close to half of the societies that specify separate eating areas for males and females allow husbands and wives the option of eating together in private quarters. I interpret these exceptions as a social recognition of the importance of communication and regular contact between married people. After all, meals occupy a constant, relatively significant amount of time in each day.

Sleep is another daily activity that consumes a large amount of time. It provides an opportunity for body contact, private interaction, and intercourse. Sleeping arrangements may express how close a unit the group expects the marital pair to be. The allocation of space for sleeping may be a constant reminder of the impact of social arrangements on individual preferences.

Half of the societies in my sample (50 % of 60 societies) provide specific sleeping areas for married couples. In some societies (29 % of 60), this means a single dwelling for the nuclear family; if there are separate rooms within the dwelling, the married couple sleeps together in the same room. In other societies (22 % of 60 societies), the husband and wife reside in a dwelling with more than one nuclear family. However, they sleep in their own room or in a partitioned area, thus keeping their unity intact. For example, the Yukaghir (120) hang a small sleeping tent over the area where a married couple will sleep. This partitions them from other occupants of the house (Jochelson 1926: 344, 345).

The remaining half of the societies (50 % of 60 societies) do not provide separate sleeping areas for married couples. Some make no special provision at all for where people will sleep (18 % of 60 societies). For example, a number of families may sleep together in the same area, with no partitions or other markers to assign them space. The Aweikoma (18) of Brazil do not divide their dwellings into rooms, nor do they delimit a special area for sleeping (Henry 1941: 10, 11). The most relevant consideration for their sleeping arrangements seems to be how close their feet are to the warmth of the fire. The ease with which they accept this flexible situation extends to their interaction with each other at night. A married man may shout across the area to converse with a young man on the opposite side.

Sleeping arrangements may de-emphasize the unity of the married pair by separating their sleeping areas within the dwelling or requiring each of them to sleep in a separate abode (32 % of 60 societies). One form of this arrangement is to cluster the women in one area of the house and the men in another (8 % of 60 societies). Not only does this play down the association of a husband with his wife; it also emphasizes groups composed of only one gender. For example, the homes in Uttar Pradesh (63) are divided into men's and women's sections. The women occupy the main building, while the men sleep in a room attached to the house, or sometimes rest in a separate building. If the extended family is particularly large, the men rarely visit the women's quarters except to take a drink of water, eat a meal, or sleep with their wives (Luschinsky 1963: 19). If a husband wants to have intercourse with his wife he is placed in the rather inconvenient position of visiting his wife very late at night and returning to his own quarters before dawn (Luschinsky 1963: 262).

Another way in which sleeping arrangements may de-emphasize the association of the married couple is designation of sleeping places for the husband and wife in separate dwellings (23 % of 60 societies). In some societies (7 % of 60 societies) the husband sleeps with his wife for a certain period, but rests elsewhere the remainder of the time. For example, each Thonga (3) wife has her own hut, but her husband has none (unless he is headman of the village). Therefore, he divides his time (and his sleep) among his spouses. In other societies (17 % of 60 societies), the couple sleeps together when one or both want to have intercourse. If a Banen (15) man is polygynously married, he resides in a separate hut. His wives sleep with him in a definite sequence, regardless of his desires at the time (Dugast 1959: 2, 271). Husband and wife usually have separate huts, even when the man has only one wife; she usually goes to his hut to sleep with him (Dugast 1959: 2, 154). The provision of separate quarters or dwellings that segregate husband and wife from each other occurs primarily in African societies ($X^2 = 10.49$, 1 df, p = < .005, N = 60).

*Summary: Social Involvement in Marriage*

From the initiation of marriage to its maintenance in the daily activities that follow the celebration of the union, we can see that the meaning of marriage is quite different from one group to another. Although marriage focuses on the relationship between a man and woman in a reproductive context, it does not necessarily mean that they will thenceforth walk through life as a "couple." Social concerns and cultural beliefs are woven into marriage, just as they are in sexual relationships. The group attempts to maintain some control over its own interests.

The theme that emerges from these sociocultural aspects of marriage is that group interest in the union is usually high. Extended families, kin groups, and the community preserve their own interests by structuring the circumstances within which the couple interacts. The interests of the group and those of the individual intersect at marriage. How much one overshadows the other after that depends upon the integration of the social and cultural factors I have discussed in the previous sections.

## Guidelines for a Reproductive Relationship: Conception, Pregnancy, and Birth

The social and cultural aspects of reproductive relationships extend beyond rules and constraints on the selection and interaction of the married pair. They include beliefs about the nature of conception, pregnancy, and birth. These are some of the dimensions of the reproductive context that surrounds the couple; they constitute the marrow that infuses the rules with their substance and meaning.

### Responsibility for Conception and Barrenness

*The biological baseline: a scientific view.* Our knowledge of the physiological basis of conception is rather recent. The first observation of spermatozoa occurred in 1677 and provided some information about the male role in mammalian conception. Observation of the ovum is even more recent, stemming from the work of Carl Ernst von Baer in 1827 (Money 1980: 1). Until then, we had to rely upon inferences about the mysterious process of conception.

The mystery that surrounds conception derives from the fact that every act of intercourse does not result in conception. This leads us to question how sexual activity relates to reproduction and why conception occurs when it does. The "scientific" answer is a wholly physiological one. Conception occurs when the mature sperm penetrates the mature ovum, fuses with it, and forms the zygote (the fertilized egg). The timing of conception is explained in terms of the occurrence of intercourse relative to a specific phase of the menstrual cycle. Theoretically, a woman ovulates (releases an egg from her ovary) once a month, approximately fourteen days *before* the beginning of her menstrual flow. The egg is available for fertilization for only a short time, within approximately forty-eight hours of ovulation. Furthermore, the sperm are viable for only a limited time, about forty-eight hours. Therefore, intercourse can lead to conception during a very limited period of time.

Even when the timing of intercourse coincides with the release of the egg, it may not lead to conception. A man usually ejaculates approximately 2.5–5 cc. of spermatic fluid, about a teaspoon. The fluid contains 150–600 million sperm (Katchadourian and Lunde 1975: 113). Even so, the odds of fertilizing the egg are quite low (Katchadourian and Lunde 1975: 112). The sperm have to survive a number of obstacles before they ever have a chance to meet the egg. First, vaginal secretions may hamper their journey. Sperm are very sensitive to the acidity of the vagina. Too much acidity can destroy them. They are more comfortable in a pH of 8.5 to 9.0; with that degree of acidity they can survive and swim more freely up to the cervix (the neck of the uterus) (Katchadourian and Lunde 1975: 114). A second factor that influences the sperm's probability of surviving the trip to the ovum is the position of the woman during intercourse. The sperm's chances are enhanced when the woman is lying down during intercourse and remains supine afterward. The sperm can pool more easily near the cervix. If the woman has intercourse while standing up or if she gets up soon after coitus, some of the sperm may be lost. The man may contribute to sperm loss if he continues to thrust into the vagina after he ejaculates, or if he does not penetrate the woman completely (Katchadourian and Lunde 1975: 114). Although we do not know whether female orgasm aids in propelling the sperm from the vagina into the uterus, we do know that it produces contractions in the uterus. Sperm usually move at a rate of one inch an hour, but they may move faster with uterine contractions (Katchadourian and Lunde 1975: 114). They may arrive to meet the ovum in the uterine tube within an hour or an hour and a half after intercourse. Such a quick pace cannot be explained by their usual rate of movement, but uterine contractions probably help. Cilia, hairlike structures in the uterine tubes, represent a third impediment for the sperm. The cilia aid the egg in moving down the uterine tube, but they become a current against which the sperm must swim in order to meet the ovum. Since ovulation occurs in only one ovary, only one uterine tube carries a ripe egg. The other is empty. Some of the sperm may complete the arduous journey to the uterine tube, only to find that it contains no egg.

By the time the sperm reach the uterine tube that contains the egg, only 2,000 of the original 150–600 million remain candidates for penetrating the egg (Katchadourian and Lunde 1975: 115). Only one sperm penetrates the egg. The twenty-three chromosomes in the sperm join with the twenty-three in the egg, thus contributing the forty-six requisite for conception of a new human being. Over the next four days, the zygote travels down the uterine tube into the uterus. After it arrives in the uterus, it takes a couple of days for the zygote to attach itself to the uterine lining. The zygote becomes completely implanted on the eleventh or twelfth day after conception. The uterine lining continues to build up to cushion and maintain the womb's environment. Therefore, the menstrual flow ceases, because the tissues and blood are being used by the uterus to help embryonic and fetal development.

*Other beliefs about conception.* Although the details differ, many societies give a physiological explanation for conception (62% of 26 societies). In fact, it is the first and most prevalent type of explanation for conception in many societies. Such an explanation is likely to emphasize the central role of body fluids in conception. The contribution that each parent's fluids make to the child's formation may vary from one interpretation to another, as does the role attributed to intercourse in conception.

In some societies, intercourse is not explicitly mentioned as necessary for conception, but its role is strongly implied. Sperm is repeatedly mentioned as one of the main elements out of which the child is formed. In Uttar Pradesh (63), the people believe that the bones and brain of the child come from the father's semen, while the blood comes from the mother; nine months of the mother's blood is stored before the child is born (Luschinsky 1963: 62). In contrast, the Gheg Albanians (48) believe that the soul and body of the child come from the father and that the child contains none of the mother's blood. A woman is merely a "sack" for carrying the child (Coon 1950: 23; Hasluck 1954: 25).

In other societies, the relationship between frequency of intercourse and conception is more clearly specified. The Siuai (99) of the Solomon Islands believe that a fetus is formed from the sexual fluids of a man and woman. The semen must coagulate with menstrual blood before a woman can conceive; therefore, a man must continue to have intercourse with a woman night after night to form a child (Oliver 1949: 4, 20). This sort of belief attributes fatherhood to the man who is a continuing sexual partner of the woman, rather than to someone with whom she may have had a casual liaison. The Tanala (81) share a similar idea. The parents form the child by contributing their blood. They regard semen as a form of blood. It mixes with the woman's menstrual blood at her next period and coagulates it. The child continues to develop when a new clot is formed each successive month (Linton 1933: 282). In all of the societies that believe that conception results from a mixture of body fluids, the male element is semen, while the female contribution may be blood, menstrual blood, or vaginal fluids. Most of these ideas about conception also explain the absence of the menstrual flow after conception.

However, there are a considerable number of societies (38% of 26 societies) that do not subscribe to a purely physiological view of conception. A second category of beliefs about conception consists of those that assert that intercourse is a necessary but not a sufficient condition for the conception of the child (27% of 26 societies). Other factors, especially supernatural ones, are thought to play an important role. This view contrasts with the first category of beliefs, where frequent sexual activity, usually under the couple's control, is thought to lead to conception. The Saramacca (165) believe that a woman may become pregnant by the river god. Nevertheless, continuous sexual activity is necessary to create the child's mind (Hurault 1961: 405). A Tiwi (90) man must dream of a child before he can conceive one in intercourse. After the prospective father dreams of his child, intercourse is likely to result in pregnancy. Tiwi women say that the child enters the woman's body through the vagina, goes to an egg in the placenta, and develops there (Goodale 1971: 143). The Manus (96) believe that the fetus is a fusion of semen and blood. However, this union will not occur without the blessing of the ancestors of the female descent line (Mead 1930a: 66; Fortune 1935: 82).

The last category of beliefs about conception is associated with societies in which ethnographers have claimed that the people have *no* idea of the relationship between intercourse and conception (12% of 26 societies). Bieber says that the Kafa (33) have no idea of how conception occurs (Bieber 1920–23: *1*, 268). Roth claims that the Warrau (162) think that intercourse may not always be necessary for conception; a woman may conceive a child by eating a plant or miscarry when pregnancy was caused by a water spirit (Roth 1915: 325; Kirchhoff 1948: 875). Nevertheless, I am particularly uneasy about the validity of this category because of the lack of supplementary information to corroborate the writers' statements. When the ethnographer's opinion is amplified, the description leads me to doubt the conclusion that "they have no idea of how conception occurs." Dugast's summation of Banen (15) views about conception aptly illustrates my point: "It is evident that everyone ignores how conception takes place. They know only that when a woman has relations with a man, she can have a child. The women explain that the blood becomes, at first, a ball; then it is like a lizard with small limbs. Then it takes the appearance of a child. That's all they know to describe" (Dugast 1959: 2, 365).

Each category of explanation for conception represents a different cultural dimension of the reproductive process. Another way in which we can glean some idea of how people think that conception occurs is to ask why conception does *not* occur. By looking at beliefs about conception and barrenness, we can form a more balanced view of the values placed on the relative roles of men and women in conception. We can also gauge the extent of the group's interest in the couple's reproduction. The more widely the group extends the responsibility for barrenness, the more social concern there is about their relationship. Shifting the responsibility for conception or barrenness to persons or factors beyond the reproductive pair dilutes the couple's own contribution to reproduction. It also means that they are likely to be influenced by rules that they believe will aid them in having children. For example, if conception requires the ancestors' blessing, as in Manus (96), people who want to have children believe that they must obey the rules of their deceased kinsmen. The motivation to have children becomes a basis for social control. Barrenness can be the punishment for breaking social rules. The individual becomes more and more wedded to the teachings of the group.

The most frequently used explanations for barrenness contrast with those given for conception; they do not rely on physiological reasons. They imply that a woman's infertility is due to the effect that the actions of others, whether human or supernatural, have on her (70% of 30 societies). One type of reason given for barrenness is that it is due to the malice that others have toward the woman (23% of 30 societies). If a Manus woman is old enough to have children but has had none, they think that someone has cursed her (Fortune 1935: 81). For example, a woman's children have the power to curse the children of their mother's brother with barrenness (Fortune 1935: 77). Gond (60) widows are often suspected of practicing black magic, which may result in making another woman barren (Grigson 1938: 358).

Other people may also hinder a woman's fertility if they break taboos (23% of 30 societies). For instance, an animal may eat a woman's afterbirth if no one buries it after a Klamath (138) woman delivers. This negligence can cause the new mother to become sterile (Spier 1930: 55). The consequences of breaking a rule are more extensive among the

Thonga (3). No children would be born in the community if someone other than an elder brother became master of the village (Junod 1927: *1*, 327). Even political activity can have reproductive implications. Ideas that stress the ways in which the behavior of others can bring about barrenness are especially prevalent in Africa (Fisher's exact test, p = .03, N = 30).

Actions of the supernatural compose the third and final way that external forces may affect a woman's fertility (23% of 30 societies). The attitude of deceased relatives toward a Yukaghir (120) woman can result in her sterility. They send their souls to facilitate conception only in relatives they like (Jochelson 1926: 105).

Cultural beliefs about barrenness reflect a great deal of social interest in conception. Individuals are given their glory as participants in conception. They are less likely to bear the burden of responsibility for barrenness. In my sample of societies, primary responsibility for a woman's barrenness is never attributed to her husband's reproductive failure or impotence (0 of 30 societies). However, a woman is not free from being blamed for barrenness. She may contribute to her own infertility if she has a reproductive dysfunction (20% of 30 societies) or is being punished for breaking a rule of some kind (10% of 30 societies). The disproportionate blame on women for barrenness is interesting in light of the prominent role that men are believed to play in conception. Men's reproductive powers glow in the light of fruition; they are not diminished by the darkness of barrenness.

A comparison of the types of explanations given for conception with those given to account for barrenness reveals very different perspectives about success or failure in the reproductive process. When beliefs about conception involve supernatural intervention, the cause of barrenness is also attributed to the supernatural or to people other than the woman herself. When the merging of male and female body fluids is primarily responsible for conception, barrenness is thought to be a result of the actions of others or of the supernatural toward the woman. Just as often, barrenness is thought to result from the physical condition or the behavior of the woman, but not of the man. Failure to reproduce becomes linked with failure in other areas of social life. It can pressure an individual into conformity with social guidelines. On an individual level, the shift in responsibility to others may mitigate some of the disappointment or guilt that may accompany barrenness.

*The importance of children to a marriage: alternatives to barrenness.*
Given the tendency to shift responsibility for barrenness away from a husband and wife, does it follow that neither of them experiences social

consequences for infertility? Alternatives open to a couple in the event of barrenness can indicate the amount of social censure that they must bear if they do not have children in their marriage, a context within which the group encourages them to have children.

The attribution of blame for barrenness to people other than the couple who experience infertility does not relieve the couple of all social consequences. If a woman is barren, her husband divorces her in an appreciable proportion of societies (29% of 51 societies). Her group may ostracize her in a smaller portion of societies (8% of 51 societies). Either of these alternatives is more likely in Circum-Mediterranean or South American groups ($X^2 = 4.53$, 1 df, p = < .05, N = 51) than in other regions of the world. The birth of children confers the appropriate status of motherhood upon an Egyptian (43) woman. Without children, she is in a very tenuous position. Her husband can divorce her and remarry a woman who is able to have children. The husband's justification for his actions is based on the idea that "the proper woman is the one who is an envelope for conception" (Ammar 1954: 94). The Ganda (12) despise a barren woman. Therefore, a Ganda woman hopes to become pregnant as soon as she marries. If a husband is especially fond of his wife, the couple uses charms or other remedies to aid them in conceiving. If these attempts prove to be unsuccessful, the husband may despair of ever having children with his wife and consider her sterile. As a result, the husband gradually withdraws his favorable attitude toward her, and she is relegated to the position of a drudge (Roscoe 1911: 46). If a Tanala (81) couple has no children, they are more likely to occupy a low status (Linton 1933: 311). Since children are greatly desired, the inability to have any is regarded as a calamity (Linton 1933: 292). The barren wife of a polygynously married man must endure more concrete consequences than depression because of having no children. Not only does she lose her rights of inheritance but also she has to face the possibility that her husband may send her away at any time (Linton 1933: 280).

In some societies (14% of 51 societies), a husband may decide to marry an additional wife rather than to divorce the one unable to bear children with him. Although a Thonga (3) woman is despised and can be divorced if she does not bear children, her parents may find a young woman to give to her husband as his second wife (Junod 1927: *1*, 190). Spier repots that a Havasupai (150) man would never divorce his wife if she were barren. It is preferable to marry an extra wife who can bear children (Spier 1928: 225).

Most of the preceding alternatives to barrenness entail punishment for the woman (divorce or ostracism) or a change in the nature of the marital relationship (a second wife). In many societies (49% of 51 societies), adoption or recourse to remedies to cure the woman of her condition are the most common solutions. Adoption is a particularly important alternative in the Insular Pacific ($X^2 = 18$, 1 df, $p = < .001$, $N = 51$). Adoption is the favored means of dealing with barrenness among the Marquesans (105). The practice is so common that there is an adopted child in practically every family on the islands (Suggs 1963: 73). It is clear that the importance of adoption in the Marquesas extends beyond its role as an alternative to barrenness. Couples who already have children adopt others. Suggs thinks that the main motivation that encourages adoption is economic (Suggs 1963: 25). If a family without any economic resources gives their child in adoption to a wealthy family, the adopted child might receive a portion of his new parents' land. Adoption may also facilitate economic cooperation between the families involved.

### Preference for Children

A couple's ideas about the importance of reproduction in their marriage include various cultural beliefs that influence their preference for children. Cultural beliefs may affect the intensity of a couple's desire to have a child of a specific gender or to have children at all. They may also specify the circumstances under which it is preferable to give birth to a child. We can gauge the type and strength of cultural influences by looking at expressed preferences for children as well as at rules that pertain to the practices of abortion, infanticide, and other means of birth control.

*Expressed preference for children.*  Do certain groups desire one gender of child to be born in preference to the other? How many children do people generally want? is the birth of a specific gender of child a more important indication of reproductive success than the number of children a couple has? What are the bases for their choices?

Only one report describes a society where people expressly desire very few or no children (2% of 46 societies). The Nambicuara (174) of the Western Mato Grosso area in South America consider children a burden, because the group has difficulty in obtaining enough food for everyone. In addition, women find it hard to transport more than one child who is nursing (Lévi-Strauss 1948b: 72).

A considerable number of societies (25% of 46 societies) prefer a large number of children, regardless of their gender. For example, the Lamet (72) of Laos desire as many children as they can have. A large number of children ensures them of a sufficient number of workers (Izikowitz 1951: 304). A Kimam (93) family can enhance its opportunities for strengthening its kin group, the *kwanda*, by having a large number of children. Other members of the group can adopt their children. The network of adoptive relationships reinforces the kinship ties between them (Serpenti 1965: 83–86; 143).

Most societies have a bias toward having children of a specific gender (72% of 46 societies). They definitely desire males more often (41% of 46 societies) than females (31% of 46 societies). The Circum-Mediterranean and Eurasia dominate other areas of the world in their preference for males ($X^2 = 8.2$, 1 df, $p = < .005$, $N = 47$). For example, one of the main purposes of marriage among the Gheg Albanians (48) is to have sons. Their adherence to this goal is so firm that they do not perform the marriage ceremony until the woman has borne a male child. The fact that a woman has given birth to several females is irrelevant; females are "worthless" children (Durham 1928: 193). The emphasis on the birth of a male is so great that it is accompanied by gunfire; there is only disappointment when a girl is born (Durham 1928: 191). The Fijians (102) justify their disdain for female children, as well as their practice of female infanticide, by pointing out a woman's uselessness in war. One man put it this way: "Why [should she] live? . . . Will she wield a club? Will she poise a spear?" (Williams 1884: 155).

Other societies prefer to have girls. Although the Huron (144) have considerable warfare, they want to have girls. Why? Women eventually increase the population by having children of their own (Tooker 1964: 122). The Huron show the value of women in absolute terms by the increased compensation they ask if a woman is killed in war (Kinietz 1940: 68). A Palauan (111) family may be disappointed when a boy is born, because a girl might become a prostitute and increase their economic well-being with her earnings (Krämer 1929: 231).

Some societies do not have a bias in favor of either sex (29% of 46 societies). The Thonga (3) are happy when a girl is born, because she will bring bridewealth to her family when she marries. They can take these economic goods and use them to acquire wives for the men in their own group. They also desire boys, because they strengthen membership in the clan and exalt the names of their fathers (Junod 1927: *1*, 45).

*Preference for children: contraception.* The group can express its involvement in a couple's fertility by the restrictions it places on contraception. It can publicly state its views about the desirability of a couple having children but imply quite different messages in the regulations that it imposes on birth control, i.e., techniques designed to prevent or control the birth of children. The regulations specify the desirable conditions for having a child. They do not necessarily promote a negative attitude about having children.

Contraception is one method a couple can use to control their fertility. Approximately half of the societies in my sample are reported to use some form of contraception (51 % of 41 societies). However, their methods do not necessarily conform to those current in American society.

Contraceptive techniques in our society are based primarily on physiological principles, aimed at preventing the union of the sperm and the egg. Foams, douches, and other spermicides are inserted in the vagina to kill the sperm before it can enter the uterus. Condoms, diaphragms, and cervical caps are physical barriers, which block the sperm from entering the uterus. A condom, or "rubber," is placed over the penis before intromission and contains the sperm after ejaculation. Diaphragms and cervical caps are used in conjunction with spermicidal creams to block the cervix. An interuterine device (I.U.D.) makes the uterine environment inhospitable for implantation of a fertilized egg. "The pill" inhibits the release of the egg, so that sperm have no ovum with which to join.

Some of the less reliable methods do not focus upon mechanical or chemical techniques, but upon knowledge about the likelihood of conception under specific conditions. The contraceptive efficacy of withdrawal or coitus interruptus relies upon the idea that removing the penis from the vagina before ejaculation will effectively prevent the release of any sperm into the vagina; therefore, no sperm are available to join with the ovum. Aside from the difficulty of controlling ejaculation, withdrawal has another obstacle to its effectiveness. Ejaculation is not always a reliable indicator of the transmission of sperm into the vagina. Small amounts of sperm may seep into the vagina before orgasm and ejaculation (Katchadourian and Lunde 1975: 164). The "rhythm method" is based on the idea that conception is possible during only a few days of the month. If a couple can avoid intercourse during these periods, they can be "safe" from conception. The sperm and egg cannot meet if sperm are not deposited in the vagina for the short time that the egg is in the uterine tube. The practice is risky. The major problem with this method is how to determine exactly when ovulation occurs. Without precise knowledge about ovulation, the method is based on some guesswork. Additional difficulties in gauging when ovulation occurs are that a woman may not ovulate at the same time each month, or she may ovulate more than once in a month, or she may fluctuate in the timing of ovulation because of climatic changes, stress, etc. Though rare, some women ovulate during menstruation.

More drastic measures are effective, although they may not be pleasant. Sterilization entails modification of the body in such a way that pregnancy is practically impossible. For example, the removal of the ovaries eliminates the production of ova; therefore, there are no ova with which the sperm can fuse. A vasectomy is a minor operation in which the man's vas deferens is cut, thus preventing the passage of sperm from the testes during ejaculation. Alternatives to sterilization include long periods of abstinence from intercourse; they eliminate the possibility of pregnancy because the male does not transfer his sperm to the female.

Information on contraception in other societies is not adequate enough for us to form any conclusion about peoples' attitudes toward contraception or about the extent of its use. However, I found some descriptions about whether contraception was used and, if so, what type was preferred. Contraceptive techniques that involve individual control over sexual activity, e.g., coitus interruptus and abstention, are used in some societies (15% of 41 societies). The effectiveness of these methods depends upon the cooperation of the man and the woman. More frequently (29% of 41 societies), the woman alone is responsible for providing contraceptive measures. The procedures that women employ to prevent conception are quite variable. For example, a Balinese (84) woman stands up after intercourse and assumes that she will expel the semen in her vagina (Covarrubias 1937: 123). Toradja (87) women think that they can prevent pregnancy either by warming their stomachs or by eating grains of rice that have dropped off alone from the plant on which they grew (Adriani and Kruijt 1912: 2, 335). An Eastern Pomo (135) woman visits a native doctor, who gives her the appropriate medicine (Kroeber 1953: 248). A Yahgan (186) woman thinks that throwing the placenta from her last birth to the dogs will prevent further pregnancies (Gusinde 1937: 706).

Some methods of birth control are implicit in the sexual practices of the group. They effectively prevent or at least space the number of children that a couple is likely to have. A long prohibition on intercourse after the birth of a child (a long postpartum sex taboo) is a sexual restriction that has reproductive implications. I consider a postpartum taboo to be long when it specifies that a woman should abstain from intercourse for more than a year after the birth of a child. Nag (1962) reinforces my view that a long postpartum taboo may significantly affect fertility. He found that "there is in general a negative association between the period of postpartum abstinence and fertility level. Societies with long periods of postpartum abstinence have generally low fertility" (Nag 1962: 79).

Birth is one of the most common occasions to which sexual restrictions apply. Postpartum taboos emerge as a potentially important, implicit means of birth control in a substantial number of societies (46% of 41 societies). Long postpartum taboos may supplement other methods of contraception (20% of 41 societies) or occur in their absence (27% of 41 societies). Some societies explicitly acknowledge that birth control may be one of the purposes of a long postpartum sex taboo. For example, the Klamath (138) disapprove of a couple if they have children less than two or three years apart. It is a disgrace for a woman to be pregnant while she is nourishing another child. Therefore, a Klamath couple abstains from intercourse for two or three years while the woman nurses her child (Pearsall 1950: 314).

Saucier (1972) conducted a comprehensive study of the correlates of the postpartum taboo. He was interested in discovering whether he could find a significant association between the taboo and other social factors. He concluded that one factor alone could not explain the taboo. Furthermore, he could not suggest what minimum combination of variables could predict its use and length. He remarks that a postpartum taboo is not a method of birth control, because the couple use it regardless of the number of children they have. However, my data suggest that the taboo's purpose *is* birth control. Its aim seems to be literally to control birth by spacing them, rather than to prevent the birth of children altogether.

Ethnographic accounts are more likely to report the presence of knowledge about contraception than to comment on its absence or the failure of individuals to practice it. Circum-Mediterranean groups are most likely to disavow knowledge of contraceptive techniques ($X^2 = 6.95$, 1 df, p = < .01, N = 41). However, we should not leap to the conclusion that an absence of contraception as we know it indicates an unwillingness to use it. It may mean that a group's theory of conception does not lead to a physiological basis for contraception. Because their beliefs direct them to conform to social rules to ensure conception and prevent barrenness, some groups may place more of their faith in their social behavior to prevent the birth of children. We could say that they have a method of birth control, but it is not based on mechanical, chemical, or physiological principles.

If my line of reasoning is correct, I would expect explicit means of contraception to be more likely to occur in societies that emphasize the merging of body fluids as the basis of conception. Theories of conception that emphasize the formation of a child by the merging of body fluids without the necessity for supernatural intervention imply more individual control over conception. On the other hand, I would think that societies that have no theory of conception or that believe that physical events are not sufficient to produce a child would adopt a different approach to contraception. They would either practice no contraception at all or effectively reduce births by having a long post-partum sex taboo. My data support this conclusion. I found that a society's theory of conception is significantly associated with the type of contraception the people practice, if any (Fisher's exact test, p = .02, N = 19). In the absence of a solely physiological belief about conception, groups do not practice contraception as we know it.

The data also suggest that the use of contraception does not necessarily mean that a man and woman do not want to have children. Rather, they may use contraceptive techniques to have some control over the circumstances under which they will have their children. Unfortunately, the information on contraception is so scant that it is possible only to suggest the nature of these circumstances on the basis of sporadic references in the sources. The most commonly mentioned reasons are to prevent the birth of a child outside of the marital context and to avoid the birth of a child while another is still an infant. I found no significant relationship between the presence of contraception and the desire for children, regardless of their number or gender.

*Abortion and infanticide.* A society may also imply the strength of its preference for a couple to have children by its social approval or disapproval of abortion and infanticide. Both abortion and infanticide can serve as means of controlling the birth of children under specific circumstances. The similarities end there, for each method of eliminating a conceived child has quite different justifications associated with its use. I will discuss some of these reasons after I present an overview of the occurrence and approval of abortion and infanticide.

Abortion and infanticide occur in most societies (79% of 47 societies perform abortions; 75% of 40 societies perform infanticide), but social approval of their practice varies. Most groups publicly disapprove of them. Infanticide is likely to be rejected as a legitimate practice in slightly more societies (68% of 22 societies) than abortion (60% of 30 societies). Acceptance and censure of abortion and infanticide are associated with specific areas of the world. Abortions are more likely to be acceptable in societies in South America (Fisher's exact text, p = .06, N = 47) and unacceptable in Africa (Fisher's exact text p = .06, N = 47). Disapproval of infanticide clusters in societies in the Circum-Mediterranean, Eurasia, and North America (Fisher's exact text, p = .05, N = 47).

Generally, groups are consistent in their approval or disapproval of both abortion and infanticide. Where abortion is allowed, infanticide is also likely to be permitted. When abortion is disapproved, so, too, is infanticide (Fisher's exact text, p = .06, N = 14). However, general approval or disapproval of both practices does not necessarily mean that abortion and infanticide are alternative solutions to the same kind of problems. On the contrary, they are different dimensions of the ways that societies qualify their desire for children. Variations in the reasons used to justify each practice reinforce this view.

Justifications for abortion most often relate to the conditions under which and with whom the child was conceived (35 % of 34 societies). In some cases, the prospective parents are not married to each other (24 % of 34 societies). In other cases, partners in the sexual relationship that led to conception do not qualify as potential parents, because they come from inappropriate kinship or status categories. The Toradja (87) aptly illustrate the importance of all of these concerns. When a girl becomes pregnant before she is married, she usually aborts the fetus (Adriani and Kruijt 1912: 2. 339). If she carries the fetus to term, she has to endure a lot of social ridicule. A Toradja woman is also likely to abort a fetus conceived in either an incestuous or an inappropriate status relationship, e.g., a liaison between a freeborn person and a slave (Adriani and Kruijt 1912: 2, 342). These justifications for abortion point out the stake that individuals have in maintaining appropriate distinctions between sexual and reproductive relationships. It is incumbent upon men and women to retain premarital and extramarital relationships as primarily sexual unions and to select reproductive partners who are socially appropriate. If they do not, they may face the consequences of their actions by aborting or killing the infants they have conceived in socially inappropriate contexts.

In some societies (18 % of 34 societies), a woman aborts her fetus because she does not want to have another child. However, the circumstances that lead her to this decision are quite diverse. An Abipon (183) woman may abort the fetus because she is afraid that the birth of the child will result in her losing her husband. An Abipon woman is subject to a three-year postpartum sex taboo. During the interim, her husband may tire of waiting to resume sexual relations with his wife and decide to marry another woman (Dobrizhoffer 1822: *1*, 97). A Fijian (102) woman may prefer to have an abortion, even though she strongly desires to give birth to a male child. If she delivers a son to her husband, she will have to endure the jealousy of her co-wives. She prefers to have an abortion and live amicably with her co-wives rather than receive the transient favors of her husband (Williams 1884: 153).

Women are less likely to justify abortions by claiming that they did them out of revenge or concern for the welfare of the unborn child (9 % of 34 societies). If the husband of a Kiman (93) woman fails to care for her properly, commits adultery too often, or drinks excessively, she may resort to taking a drug to induce abortion (Serpenti 1965: 145). However, this can be a dangerous expression of anger. If her husband discovers what she has done, he may kill her or, in less extreme cases, leave her. In contrast, a Micmac (126) woman of eastern Canada considers the ultimate well-being of her unborn child when she decides to have an abortion. If she is already nursing a child, she aborts the fetus because she thinks there would be insufficient nourishment for both of them (Denys 1908: 404). Tupinamba (177) women often abort children they have conceived with war captives in order to spare them from being eaten (Levy 1880: 43). They base their behavior on the logic of their theory of conception. The child is primarily the product of a man's semen. Therefore, a child conceived with a captive would, in effect, result in the creation of more enemies. The Tupinamba think it is necessary to kill and eat the child in order to destroy the potential enemy. However, selling the child into slavery is sometimes an alternative (Anchieta 1846: 259).

It is important to keep in mind the behavioral consequences of following the preceding theories about abortion. When a woman decides to abort a fetus on the basis of the justifications I have described, she undertakes a task that may put her own life in jeopardy. The impact of the group's guidelines for having children with the appropriate partner is so great that a woman may risk her life rather than deal with the social disapproval she would face in continuing the pregnancy.

In the absence of modern medical technology, trained personnel, sanitary conditions, and *social approval*, women resort to self-help procedures to effect an abortion. Devereux (1955) studied abortion in 400 nonindustrialized societies and categorized sixteen techniques that are used by women to abort a fetus. I will briefly discuss six of these, to convey an idea of the danger involved. These techniques are also of interest in that some of them are used by women in the United States when they cannot or do not choose to allow a physician to perform the abortion. Sarvis and Rodman (1974) discuss these medical aspects of abortion in more detail in *The Abortion Controversy*; the following discussion relies heavily on their work.

The first two techniques are attempts to kill the fetus by mechanical means or strenuous activity. Mechanical means include procedures designed to damage the fetus through the wall of the abdomen. For example, a woman may squeeze, massage, rub, pinch, or twist her belly. Or, someone may place a heavy weight on it. She may lie down and allow someone to jump up and down on her. Jolts and strenuous activity are another way that a woman may try to abort the fetus. She may lift heavy objects, take on very hard work, jump from a high place, or go horseback riding. All of these techniques can cause injury to the mother or to the fetus. They are rarely effective as abortive techniques. Their ineffectiveness demonstrates how well developed a woman's reproductive system is. Even when the fetus is subjected to such extreme procedures, its protective environment is often sufficient to keep it unharmed.

Three other techniques are attempts to kill the fetus by inserting objects or fluids into the uterus. Instrumentation is one such method. A woman inserts some sort of instrument into the uterus to kill and dislodge the fetus. The implements may include such objects as sticks, coat hangers, knitting needles, or curtain rods. The woman risks bursting her uterus and bladder with the object. She could die from infection or hemorrhage. Another technique designed to dislodge the fetus is the insertion and retention of extraneous objects in the cervix. The goal is to dilate the cervix so that the fetus can be cut out of the womb or expelled by contractions. For example, the Romans used to insert papyrus into the cervix to induce abortion (Devereux 1955). A variation on this theme is the insertion of a catheter into the uterus; this tubular instrument is left in place until the cervix begins to dilate. This procedure may induce contractions sufficient to expel the fetus. The problem with the technique is the risk of infection, hemorrhage, and perforation of the uterus. Yet another technique used to kill the fetus is the insertion of fluids or the injection of substances into the uterus. Boiling water, soap suds, alcohol, and lye are a few of the liquids that a woman may introduce into her body. Not only may they burn the tissues; they may also cause hemorrhaging, shock, and death. Some substances may be poisonous and cause death if the doses are too large.

A sixth technique used to induce abortion involves ingesting drugs or other preparations to harm the fetus. The variations are almost infinite. For example, a woman of the Loyalty Islands might boil sea water and drink it when she wants to abort. Other compounds include herbs, kerosene, castor oil, ergot compounds, strong purgatives, and irritants. Some of these, e.g., castor oil, are useless as abortifacients. Others, e.g., ergot compounds, are poisonous and can harm essential organs in the body. At the very least, they may irritate the tissues and harm the woman.

These brief descriptions of techniques employed to induce an abortion without proper medical facilities show how deeply a woman probably feels about having a child in socially inappropriate circumstances.

The justifications for these desperate measures center on the social definition of the proper context and partner for having a child. Social rules
and cultural pressures have such force that a woman may be unwilling
to have a child when she is not married or has had a purely sexual
relationship. Having an abortion rarely means that the woman does not
want to have children at all. In come cases, pregnancy prompts a couple
to marry. Instead of abortion, the couple prefer a change of circumstances, so that the context is no longer inappropriate for reproduction;
they marry and form a reproductive relationship.

There is some overlap in the reasons given to justify abortion and
those given for infanticide. However, they are more important as rationales for abortion than for infanticide. Revenge and considerations of
the unborn child's welfare play a small part in the justification of infanticide (3% of 38 societies). Although a woman might kill an infant if it
were conceived in an illicit sexual relationship, she is not likely to use
this circumstance as a reason for infanticide (16% of 38 societies). Infanticide may occur because a woman does not want to have a child,
but this reason is used less frequently for infanticide (11% of 38 societies) than for abortion 18% of 34 societies).

A substantial number of societies (42% of 38 societies) justify infanticide on the basis of the characteristics that the infant exhibits after
birth. Multiple births may become the occasion for infanticide. One of
all of the infants born in this manner may be killed (21% of 38 societies). The Nicobarese (78) believe that they improve the future chances
of the elder twin by killing the younger. "It is impossible for twins to
grow up together for many years" (Man 1932: 120). In some cases, the
gender of the infant, rather than the timing of the birth, is the decisive
factor in triggering infanticide. When twins of the opposite gender are
born, the Lamet (72) kill the girl rather than the boy (Izikowitz 1951:
104).

Even if the infant is not a twin, disappointment about its gender may
be sufficient justification to kill it (5% of 38 societies). When a group
uses gender as a basis for infanticide, it usually chooses to kill females
rather than males. For example, the Yangtze Chinese (114) of Kaihsienkung village use infanticide to help them balance population size
with scarcity of land. If there were not enough resources for an increased population, the birth of more children might entail a rise in
poverty and crime. They usually choose to kill female rather than male
infants, because a girl will leave the group when she marries to reproduce for her husband's descent line (Fei 1946: 31–34). Williams estimates that the rate of female infanticide among the Fijians (102) may
have reached between 50 and 60 percent of all female births in some

parts of Mbau Island (Williams 1884: 155). The Fijians condone the practice, because women are "useless in war or, as some say, because they give so much trouble" (Williams 1884: 155).

Even a physical deformity or an unusual physical or behavioral trait at birth is sufficient cause for infanticide in some societies (16% of 48 societies). The Kimam (93) destroy a deformed infant because it will not be able to participate sufficiently in the economy to support itself in adulthood (Serpenti 1965: 146). The Marshallese (108) are less generous in their reasoning. They kill a crippled infant because they regard it as "useless and burdensome" (Erdland 1914: 125).

In sum, the meanings attached to abortion and infanticide are quite different. Justifications for abortion center around the circumstances of the child's conception. Abortions are one solution to inappropriate mating, i.e., reproduction in a sexual context. Infanticide deals with a different set of problems, i.e., the characteristics of the infant itself. Although there are some societies where abortion and infanticide are performed for the same reasons, there is no consistent relationship between the reasons given for both types of behavior. Therefore, although abortion and infanticide may occur in the same society, their coexistence does not imply that one leads to the other or that they are interchangeable alternatives, undertaken for the same purpose.

*Preference for children: summary.*  Individuals and groups may express their preferences for children in a number of different ways, each of which taps an aspect of the social and cultural complexity of reproductive relationships. Individuals and groups most often express their preference for children in terms of the gender and the number of children they would like to have. Less obvious than stated preferences for children but just as relevant to evaluating a group's desire for children is the acceptability of birth control practices. We need to look at what people do before and after children are conceived, not just at what they *say* they do or would like to do.

A man or a woman may use contraception to space births or to prevent the birth of a child in a nonmarital, sexual context. Reasons for abortion imply that incestuous, premarital, or extramarital relationships should not be reproductive. Rationales for infanticide stress the importance of having one child at a time and of delivering a child who is free from deformity. All of these beliefs qualify the publicly expressed view of the desirability of having children. Most groups want women to give birth to children only under certain conditions. Cultural beliefs define the appropriate partners and contexts for the conception of children; the suitable intervals for spacing their births; and the characteristics of children that are most likely to be socially acceptable.

## Pregnancy

Rules and beliefs about pregnancy and birth center on the reproductive process itself. Aside from its significance to the individual and the group, pregnancy involves some major alterations in a woman's physical appearance and functioning. Conception triggers a series of hormonal and physiological changes that prepare her body for containing and nourishing the fetus. All human females who become pregnant go through these changes. The alterations constitute a biological baseline, which individuals and groups interpret in their own terms during the course of the pregnancy.

*The biological baseline.* After conception, the fertilized egg (zygote) wends its way through the uterine tube and nestles in the wall of the uterus. The zygote becomes firmly attached to the uterine wall by the ninth day after fertilization. After another day or two, it is completely embedded in the uterus. The lining of the uterus completes the process by growing over the implanted egg. The endometrium becomes a lush, nutrient source of survival for the fetus. It is retained rather than shed; thus, there is no menstrual flow.

Even before implantation, the zygote starts to develop. It begins as a single-celled structure, which contains genetic information from the sperm and egg. Then it undergoes a number of divisions, which increase the number of cells it contains. These cells eventually differentiate and make up the tissues and organs of the body.

Two aspects of cellular development are relevant to the future fate of the zygote. The first is the formation of the blastocyst, i.e., the series of cells that surround a fluid-filled cavity. The second is the development of the trophoblast, the series of cells that surround the blastocyst. The trophoblastic cells secrete enzymes that digest and liquefy the endometrial cells (Guyton 1966: 1153). The blastocyst absorbs some of the fluids and nutrients released by the action of the trophoblast. In addition, the trophoblastic cells form a series of cells that attach to the edges of the endometrium. The blastocyst, with the aid of its trophoblastic cells, eats its way into the uterine lining and becomes firmly entrenched. Further changes proceed from there.

The trophoblastic cells rapidly increase. They combine with cells from the endometrium to form the placenta. Therefore, both the zygote and the mother's body contribute tissues for the fetal life-support system. The placenta is the specialized organ that provides materials for the growth and maintenance of the developing child. Until the placenta fully develops, the action of the trophoblastic cells provides nourishment for the developing embryo by continuing to digest the cells of the endometrium, which in turn release nutrients. Although the placenta provides some nutrition for the embryo after the sixteenth day following fertilization, the trophoblastic cells help to support the embryo for the first eight to twelve weeks (Guyton 1966: 1154).

During the first few months of pregnancy, the placenta grows rapidly in comparison with the pace of fetal development. The circulatory system of the fetus links to that of the placenta via the umbilical (navel) cord, which is a major point of connection between the fetus and the mother. The umbilical vein transports oxygen and nutrients to the fetus. The two arteries of the umbilical cord remove waste products from the fetus to the mother's circulatory system, which then eliminates them.

The circulation system of the placenta may carry substances other than nutrients to the developing fetus. For example, it may transmit drugs taken by the mother, which may have harmful effects on the fetus. Women addicted to heroin can produce addiction in their children (Katchadourian and Lunde 1975: 127). The placenta can also transmit disease from the mother to the child. This is one reason for serious concern when a woman in the first month of pregnancy contracts German measles, or rubella. The virus introduces a 50 percent possibility that the child will be born with abnormalities, e.g., deafness, mental deficiency, or congenital heart disease (Katchadourian and Lunde 1975: 127).

The placenta is a life-support system for the fetus. The fetal body begins to develop during the second week after fertilization. The inner cell mass of the blastocyst differentiates into two layers of cells. A third layer of cells grows between the first two during the third week of development. Each of these groups of cells is a germ layer. All of the specialized cells of the human body derive from them. Their differentiation into the tissues and organs of the body occurs during the fourth to eighth week of fetal development. The major organ systems of the body become established at this time. It is remarkable how quickly the fetus develops. By the end of the eighth week of development, the external appearance of the fetus has distinctively human features, e.g., arms, legs, fingers, toes, and a head with eyes, ears, a nose, and a mouth.

As the fetus develops, it is contained within the amnion. The trophoblastic cells, which contributed to the development of the placenta, also help to form the membranous sac called the amnion. The amnion encloses the fetus and eventually separates the fetus from the uterine walls. Amniotic fluid fills the amnion and surrounds the fetus. The fetus is free to grow without the interference of contact with the mother's internal organs. The fluid also cushions the fetus from damaging movements made by the mother. Shortly before birth, the amnion ruptures and loses its fluid. The loss of amniotic fluid is often called "breaking the bag of water" (Golanty 1975: 128).

The course of the pregnancy involves the growth and development of the processes already begun in the first eight weeks. The fetus gets larger, and its body systems mature. It begins to become active between the fourth and fifth month. By that time, the mother can feel the movements of the fetus. She may also be able to seek the kicking of the fetus in her abdomen. Gestation lasts an average of 266 days, from conception to birth.

As the fetus matures the outward appearance of the mother begins to change. The woman's waistline expands and her abdomen begins to protrude during the second three months of her pregnancy (Katchadourian and Lunde 1975: 131).

During the third trimester, or three months, of the pregnancy, the mother becomes much more aware of the fetus she is carrying. The fetus is so active that its movements may interfere with the mother's sleep (Katchadourian and Lunde 1975: 135). The support systems for the fetus increase as it continues to develop. The expectant mother gains more weight. It may be difficult for her and for others to ignore her condition at this point. If a woman gains a lot of weight, she may move more awkwardly and tire more easily.

The support systems that maintain the pregnancy and protect the fetus are complex. Many of the changes in the woman's physiology are due to the actions of hormones, especially estrogen and progesterone. For about three months after conception, the corpus luteum secretes estrogen and progesterone. These hormones stimulate the further growth of the endometrium and aid it in storing more nutrients for the fetus. The development of the endometrium is essential to the growth of the placenta and fetal tissues.

By the twelfth week, the placenta is sufficiently well developed to function on its own. The corpus luteum's influence wanes. Not only does the placenta remove wastes and transmit oxygen and nutrients from the mother to the fetus but it also acts as an endocrine gland, to produce the hormones that maintain the pregnancy. Estrogen enlarges the uterus, breasts, and external genitalia of the woman; it may also affect the rate of cell proliferation in the early development of the embryo. Progesterone promotes cell development in the endometrium, which, in turn, provides nutrients for the fetus. It may also deter contractions of the uterus and prepare the breasts for lactation.

Most groups connect the absence of menstruation with the possibility of pregnancy. Nausea or morning sickness, frequent urination, and tender breasts can also be signals for pregnancy. Awareness of fetal movements and changes in the woman's abdominal size provide direct evidence of pregnancy if the subtle, earlier signs are not sufficient to do so.

Just as the prepubescent boy or girl may become anxious about what happens to him or her during puberty, so too may expectant parents be subject to a host of fears about the development of their offspring. They cannot observe the progress of the child's growth directly. They infer information about the child from the condition of the mother. Their psychological vulnerability may motivate them to accept social restrictions and beliefs about the fetus. Adherence to pregnancy restrictions allows the husband and wife to participate in fostering the well-being of their child.

*Pregnancy restrictions.* Most pregnant women are subject to restrictions of some sort. Usually the restrictions focus on the well-being of the mother and her infant. The extent to which their goal is to preserve the welfare of both is striking. Groups rarely (8% of 40 societies) justify pregnancy restrictions in terms of the welfare of others beyond the mother/child dyad. The scope of the social guidelines is limited. Most often (53% of 40 societies) the purpose of the restrictions is to ensure the good health of the baby and prevent pain or a difficult delivery for the mother. When they center on either the child or the mother, they are more likely to concentrate on the welfare of the child (33% of 40 societies), rather than that of the mother (8% of 40 societies).

The main adjustments that a woman must make during her pregnancy are modifications in her diet (38% of 45 societies) and changes in her responses to sensory stimuli (24% of 45 societies). Both of these types of constraints reflect a recognition of the intimate connection between the prospective parents and the developing child. Fear motivates the couple to abide by social rules during pregnancy. They are afraid that their experiences will be communicated to the unborn child and harm it in some way. Cultural beliefs in the effectiveness of conformity to rules can assuage their anxiety. Thus, both husband and wife avoid a variety of specific behaviors. For example, the Aztecs (153) believe that a pregnant woman who looks at the sky during an eclipse will have a child with a harelip. If the potential father sees a ghost, his child will be born with heart disease (Soustelle 1961: 189). If a Tiwi (90) woman spits into the flames of a fire, or if she cooks, she may cause her unborn child to twist in the womb (Goodale 1971: 144). If she eats new yams, she may kill the baby. A Thonga (3) woman thinks that she should not eat eggs when she is pregnant, because the child might be born bald (Junod 1962: *1*, 184). She should keep her belly bare, to prevent the birth of a baby with a membrane covering its head (Junod 1927: *1*, 191).

Although pregnancy may entail some changes in a woman's daily social life, it rarely limits the range of people with whom she is usually in contact (4% of 45 societies) or curtails her participation in group activities (2% of 45 societies). More often, pregnancy limits her mobility (9% of 45 societies) or forces adjustments in her usual household or economic duties (11% of 45 societies). The Ganda (12) recommend that a pregnant woman remain in her enclosure as much as possible. Confinement makes it easier for her to avoid the sights and sounds that might endanger her unborn child. If she does venture out of her dwelling to visit someone, boys of her husband's clan attempt to protect her. They beat the grass on the path to remove the evil effects that some male might have left as he walked there (Roscoe 1911: 49). During the last three months of his wife's pregnancy, a Siuai (99) husband may take over responsibility for some of the heavier tasks she usually performs. He helps her, because he hopes that he will contribute to ensuring a safe delivery and a healthy child (Oliver 1955: 170).

Groups often believe that the actions of a pregnant woman's husband also affect the development of the child (56% of 45 societies). Therefore, a husband may be subject to restrictions, which complement the ones that affect his wife. Pregnancy restrictions apply to both expectant parents among the Eastern Pomo (135) of central California. If either kills a rattlesnake, their child will be born with a harelip. In addition, the husband should not hunt, fish, or gamble during his wife's pregnancy. The woman should not eat hot foods, meat, or fish. If she eats fish, they think that the "fish would drink up the liquid in her and she would die" (Loeb 1926: 249).

Sexual taboos during part or all of the pregnancy mean an alteration in the husband's usual sexual access to his wife. Their purpose is in line with other pregnancy taboos, i.e., to prevent harm to the unborn child and its mother. For example, the Goajiro (159) believe that prospective parents should refrain from sex during pregnancy. Otherwise, the woman will have a prolonged delivery and give birth to a sickly child (Gutierrez de Pineda 1948: 8). The Tiwi (90) do not engage in intercourse during pregnancy because they fear that such activity will terminate it. They justify their belief in terms of their ideas about menstruation. They believe that intercourse causes the beginning of menstruation. Therefore, intercourse might result in the reappearance of the menstrual flow and, by implication, the disappearance of the child (Goodale 1959: 144).

Specific rationales for pregnancy restrictions center on a few major themes: (1) the ingestion of certain foods or liquids, (2) sensory input, (3) the extent of daily activities, and (4) intercourse. It is difficult to assess the full consequences of each type of concern. In a recent review of the relation between nutrition and pregnancy, Robson concludes that we know very little about the nutritional status of a mother during pregnancy (Robson 1975). Furthermore, we do not know the effect of inadequate nutrition on offspring and on the group as a whole. The evidence we have shows that inadequate nutrition adversely affects physical growth, development, and viability. Abortion, a premature birth, and a low birth weight are all possible consequences of an inadequate diet.

Curtailment of daily activities may reduce the energy output of the pregnant woman. Energy balance may affect fetal development, especially in adolescents. If the woman uses more energy than she consumes in her food, the imbalance may hamper fetal development (Robson 1975: 51). The weight gain that accompanies the progress of the pregnancy may fatigue the woman more than usual. Fewer daily responsibilities could provide some relief from her lethargy.

The advisability of sexual relations during pregnancy depends upon a number of factors. Generally there is no reason why a woman cannot continue her usual sexual activities during the first trimester of pregnancy (Katchadourian and Lunde 1975: 125). There is no foundation to the idea that intercourse may abort the fetus during these early months (Katchadourian and Lunde 1975: 126). The failure of jolts and strenuous physical activity to effect an abortion are further corroboration for this point. Nevertheless, fatigue, nausea, anxiety about being pregnant, and tenderness of the breasts may affect sexual receptivity. During the second trimester, vaginal lubrication usually increases, while breast tenderness decreases. The disappearance of the discomfort that some women feel early in pregnancy may renew their sexual interest (Katchadourian and Lunde 1975: 131). The most likely change in sexual relations in the second trimester is a shift in positions for intercourse. The increased size of the woman's abdomen may make the man-on-top position more difficult. Woman-on-top, side-by-side, and rear entry may be more comfortable (Katchadourian and Lunde 1975: 131). The advisability of intercourse during the last trimester is more controversial. One study shows a relationship between sexual activity and premature labor (Goodlin et al. 1971). The authors think that the strong uterine contractions that accompany orgasm may rupture fetal membranes or induce premature labor. Another study (Wagner and Solberg 1974) finds no association between sexual activity and premature births.

### Labor, Birth, and the Postpartum Period

In addition to their potential physical benefits to the child, pregnancy restrictions can be psychologically beneficial to the woman and her husband. They aid the prospective parents by providing ways for them to contribute to the safe delivery of a healthy child. In other words, they provide a framework for interpreting the physical changes associated with the pregnancy. These social rules derive their force from the parents' belief that their daily activities do have meaningful consequences for the well-being of their unborn child. Therefore, the active roles played by both wife and husband in the reproductive process can continue beyond conception. In addition, pregnancy restrictions imply that the woman has a special status. Her behavior departs somewhat from her usual routine. This adjustment can raise her own awareness of the new social role she will play after her child is born; it also attunes others in her social group to her role.

Just as marriage adds the statuses of husband and wife to those of man and woman, the birth of a couple's first child enlarges the scope of their statuses to those of father and mother. Dana Raphael coined the terms "patrescence" and "matrescence" to refer to the processes by which a man becomes a father and a woman becomes a mother (Raphael 1976). She emphasizes the point that becoming a parent requires learning; it does not develop "naturally" as a consequence of conception or gestation. Social rules and cultural beliefs parallel the physical changes that accompany pregnancy to prepare the woman and her husband for their new roles as parents.

Birth ends the pregnancy, but starts a series of adjustments that the couple and their group must make to the arrival of a new member of the society. The long dependency period of the infant requires the parents or other members of the group to provide adequate arrangements to care for its needs, e.g., eating, sleeping, and protection.

Until birth, the woman's body nourishes and protects the growing fetus. After birth, the new mother's body can still provide for some of the infant's needs, e.g., milk to nourish the newborn child (neonate). However, the bulk of the responsibility shifts to the social realm. The first part of this section describes the physiological components of the birth process, as well as some of the changes that occur after childbirth, e.g., lactation and weaning. The second part deals with the social and cultural dimensions of these major physical events.

*Birth and lactation: the biological baseline.* The organs and hormones that help to maintain pregnancy also play a role in preparing the woman's body for birth and the postpartum (post = after, partum = separation) period. Preparation for birth focuses on changes in the uterus and the breasts. During the last three to four weeks of the pregnancy, the fetus changes position or "lightens"; it drops down into the uterus, so that its head descends into the pelvic outlet near the cervix (the neck of the uterus, which opens into the vagina). Changes in the uterus accompany the fetal shift in position. The upper uterus contracts, and the cervix softens. Up until this point, the upper uterus had been expanding to accommodate fetal growth, while the cervix remained firm to sustain the weight of the fetus and the placenta in the uterus. These uterine changes suggest the types of developments that will follow. During the last few months of pregnancy, the woman may periodically experience some weak, slow uterine contractions (Guyton 1966: 1163). She may also have a small, barely discernible discharge of blood, a "bloody show"; this is made up of cervical mucous, which previously stopped up the cervical opening (Katchadourian and Lunde 1975: 138). The previously closed, protective environment of the womb gradually changes to facilitate the movement of the fetus through the vagina.

The most dramatic alterations occur in the woman's breasts (Raphael 1976: 63–65). Unlike other parts of the body, the breasts do not develop in proportion to the rate of general body growth. They reach their maximal development only during pregnancy and lactation; nursing maintains their condition. After nursing ceases, they resume their diminished size. Early in the pregnancy, the surge of estrogen stimulates the growth of the system of ducts in the breasts and increases the amounts of the fat and connective tissue that serve to pad and protect the intricate internal structure. The secretion of progesterone develops the lobules, alveoli (small sacs), and cells that line the alveoli and absorb raw materials for milk from the bloodstream. This proliferation of milk ducts, fat, and tissues in the breasts increases their size and weight by as much as 300 gm (approximately two-thirds of a pound) each (Golanty 1975; 171). The nipples and the aerolae (the pinkish areas of skin that circle the nipples) enlarge to as much as twice their usual size. The nipples can become very sensitive to touch and may stiffen. These alterations in breast structure may account for the tenderness and pain that women may feel in the early stages of pregnancy.

Toward the end of the pregnancy, the cells in the breast prepare for the production of milk by secreting colostrum, a fluid thicker than milk. The high levels of estrogen and progesterone inhibit the pituitary from releasing much prolactin, the hormone primarily responsible for milk production.

Labor usually begins when the fetus is able to function outside of the womb. However, it is not known why labor begins precisely when it does. Parturition, or labor, includes the entire process of uterine contractions and the cervical and vaginal stretching that effect the passage of the fetus from the mother's body (Guyton 1966: 1163). Most people can recognize the signals that indicate when labor has begun. Strong abdominal and uterine contractions mark the first stage of the birth process; the cervix progressively dilates. At first the contractions may occur at relatively long intervals, e.g., every thirty minutes, and may not be very intense. However, they increase in frequency and intensity until they occur every one to three minutes. Women in our society generally go to the hospital when the contractions are four to five minutes apart (Katchadourian and Lunde 1975: 138). The uterine contractions trigger abdominal contractions, which provide extra pressure to force the fetus from the uterus. The combined impact of these contractions exerts about twenty-five pounds of downward force (Guyton 1966: 1165). The initial pain of labor may derive from the compression of the uterine blood vessels (Guyton 1966: 1166). Since the contractions are so strong, they hamper the flow of blood into the placenta and are, therefore, rhythmic, rather than continuous. If it were otherwise, the life of the fetus could be in jeopardy (Guyton 1966: 1165). In 95 percent of all births, the head of the fetus is already positioned near the cervix. The head acts as a wedge to open the vagina after it has passed through the cervix. Presentation of the head first has two advantages. First, since the head is larger than the trunk of the fetus, the cervix can expand to its maximal size in the beginning. Second, the head is compact and has less difficulty in emerging (Golanty 1975: 161). The first stage of birth ends when the cervix has completely dilated to about ten centimeters.

The second stage of birth begins when the cervical dilation is sufficient to accommodate the passage of the fetus' head. Strong uterine and abdominal contractions help to push the fetus through the vagina. The pain that the woman may feel at this stage derives from the stretching of the muscles in the uterus, the dilation of the cervix, tears in the vagina, and expansion of the perineum — the area between the vaginal and anal openings. The flexible skull of the fetus adjusts to its surroundings, as does the rest of its body. The vaginal opening stretches to permit the passage of the fetus from the mother's body. In American society, physicians often cut the perineum to facilitate birth and prevent tearing; this is called an episiotomy. However, there is some debate about the necessity for this procedure if the tissues have had sufficient time to stretch (Newton 1975). It is important that the woman be conscious during this stage, so that she can actively bear down, or "push," and thus aid the delivery (Golanty 1975: 160).

The third stage of birth begins after the fetus has passed through the vaginal opening. The uterus begins to reduce in size. However, the placenta does not get smaller. Therefore, the placenta separates from the uterus. Contractions in the uterus diminish the flow of blood from the tissues surrounding the placenta. Uterine contractions expel the "afterbirth" (the dislodged placenta), blood from the placental site, and fetal membranes (Golanty 1975: 166).

The entire birth process rarely lasts more than a day and often requires a considerably shorter period of time. First births generally last longer than subsequent ones. The first stage may continue for eight to twenty-four hours, and the second may last as long as eight hours. The third usually requires less than an hour. However, there is a wide range of individual variation.

After birth, the woman's body continues to change. The absence of the placenta results in a sharp reduction of estrogen and progesterone. Since their secretion inhibited the release of much prolactin, their absence allows a larger secretion of prolactin from the pituitary. Therefore, the expulsion of the afterbirth triggers the release of prolactin, which, in turn, begins the process of manufacturing milk in the breasts. In the meantime, the breasts continue to secrete colostrum, a thick, yellowish liquid, which was already being produced before birth. Colostrum contains protein, enzymes, and antibodies, which provide nutrition and resistance against disease to the newborn. Its presence encourages the baby to suck the nipples and toughen them in preparation for nursing.

As the infant begins to nurse, it empties colostrum from its mother's breasts. Milk gradually replaces the colostrum. Once lactation begins, it continues for a few days, regardless of whether the woman is breastfeeding. However, further milk production depends upon the breasts being emptied. Otherwise, the process gradually slows down, less milk is produced, and lactation eventually stops (Raphael 1976: 70). The body reabsorbs the milk that is being produced.

Breastfeeding requires the cooperation of the infant and its mother and serves to establish one of the child's earliest social relationships. It forecasts the impact that social life will have on the individual's life from this time onward.

The baby's sucking stimulates the release of prolactin and the production of milk. It also helps to initiate the mechanism for releasing the milk, i.e., the ejection, or "let-down" reflex. Regardless of the amount of milk a woman has produced or how fervently the infant sucks at its mother's breast, it cannot draw milk from her if this reflex is inhibited. Because the crucial hormones for milk production and release are secreted from the pituitary gland in the brain, successful breastfeeding depends somewhat upon a relaxed, psychological state in the woman (Golanty 1975: 172; Guyton 1966: 1167). Social support is an important ingredient in fostering the relaxation so essential to facilitating lactation (Raphael 1976). When the baby sucks at its mother's nipple, the nerves in the nipple send messages to the pituitary to release oxytocin, the hormone responsible for stimulating the release of milk. Oxytocin circulates through the blood and into the breasts to initiate the release of milk. A woman can breastfeed for several years, but the amount of milk she produces may decrease after seven to nine months (Guyton 1966: 1168). At the height of milk production, a woman may manufacture as much as 1.6 quarts per day (Guyton 1966: 1167). The mother's milk provides a number of advantages for her infant. The infant experiences less diarrhea, better protection from disease, and a well-balanced diet (Golanty 1975: 172). A woman's milk contains 50 percent more lactose (sugar) and two to three times more protein than a cow's milk. Other advantages of breastfeeding derive from the skin contact, body movement, and response to their hunger that infants receive from their mothers while they suckle (Raphael 1976: 85).

Breastfeeding is also associated with a number of advantages for the mother. It has been associated with a reduced incidence of cancer, less hemmorrhage after delivery, and quicker afterbirth (Raphael 1966: 83–85). However, a woman who is used to sleeping for long, continuous periods of time may experience fatigue from trying to satisfy the cries of hunger from her baby.

Although lactation is one of the more dramatic aspects of the postpartum period, other significant developments may follow birth. One of these is the possibility of postpartum depression. The woman may feel "blue" rather than radiantly excited and happy about the new arrival. Raphael attributes these feelings to the psychological adjustment of the woman to becoming a mother (Raphael 1976). A study by Gordon, Gordon, and Gunther (1961) showed that the women who were most prone to postpartum depression had had no previous experience with babies, had the least help, and did not know their neighbors very well. In other words, the depression was associated with the women's psychological responses to the new social adjustments that they had to make.

The birth process may briefly alter a woman's sexual relationship with her husband. In American society, physicians suggest that a woman wait at least six weeks to resume intercourse. Their main concern is the possibility that the woman may contract an infection through the vagina (Katchadourian and Lunde 1975: 142). Physical discomfort and fatigue may be other factors that contribute to a woman's delay in resuming intercourse. However, current evidence shows that there is no reason why a woman cannot engage in intercourse after the tears and lacerations of birth heal and the flow of the lochia ends (Katchadourian and Lunde 1975: 142). In the meantime, sexual activity does not need to cease. Manual manipulation of the genitals, oral stimulation, and other erotic activities may provide adequate substitutes for a while (Katchadourin and Lunde 1975: 142).

The body gradually begins to assume its prepregnant state over the six weeks that follow birth. A few days after birth, the site of placental attachment autolyzes, or self-digests. This produces a vaginal discharge called the lochia. The discharge continues for about a week and a half. It is bloody at first and contains remnants of tissue; later the discharge may become a clear, yellowish fluid. After the cessation of the lochia, the endometrium resumes its prepregnant state. Other tissue damage begins to heal. The lacerations produced by the fetus passing through the vagina, as well as the tears or incision at the vaginal opening, also begin to return to their normal state. Subsequent to birth, a woman may lose a substantial amount of weight. The absence of the uterine contents alone may account for sixteen pounds of weight loss; the dissipation of water stored in the blood and tissues may account for another four pounds of weight.

Lactation itself may accelerate the speed with which the uterus returns to its prepregnant state. It may also affect when ovulation and the menstrual cycle resume. Lactation usually reduces the production of FSH (follicle stimulating hormone) and LH (luteinizing hormone) while the pituitary is preoccupied with the release of prolactin. Therefore, the menstrual cycle does not begin for a while; in a few months, when FSH and LH are secreted again, the menstrual cycle reactivates. There is wide variation in the time when ovulation resumes. Since ovulation precedes the menstrual flow, it is possible that the woman may ovulate while she is nursing and before the menstrual flow begins again. Although breastfeeding may retard ovulation after birth, it is unclear how effective a method of birth control it is. Some people contend that continuous breastfeeding is a natural form of birth control (Raphael 1976: 83); others regard this point of view as a distortion (Katchadourian and Lunde 1975: 142). In any case, the uterus, vagina, and general body changes that occur during pregnancy return to their prepregnant state after a couple of months. The breasts may be included in this process, depending upon whether the woman breastfeeds or not. If a woman is nursing, the breasts gradually return to their pre-pregnant state after weaning. Weaning begins when the child starts to ingest other foods. As the child relies less upon the nutrients in the milk and suckles less, the flow of milk concomitantly decreases. The tissues, ducts, and milk production in the breasts diminish proportionately.

*Sociocultural aspects of birth: where birth occurs.* After the woman notices the first signs of labor, she prepares to give birth according to the guidelines provided by her social group. Although some societies make no special provision for a place where the woman will deliver the baby (23% of 47 societies), most societies do so (77% of 47 societies). In the former cases, the woman may have the infant at the place where she happens to be at the time (2% of 47 societies); more commonly (21% of 47 societies), she has the baby in her usual dwelling; it has no partitions or similar provisions to segregate her from the rest of the household.

The specific arrangements made for childbirth are quite diverse. In some societies (23% of 47 societies), the woman remains in her usual dwelling, but is set apart from the rest of its occupants by a partitioned area or room. A Kurd (57) woman gives birth in one of the rooms of the dwelling that she shares with her husband's father, mother, brothers, and brothers' wives. She is attended by her female friends and relatives; no males are allowed in the area (Masters 1953: 253).

In other societies (13% of 47 societies), the woman goes to a place near her dwelling or to a place outside the area in which most social activity occurs. The Bellacoola (132) select the location for childbirth according to the season of the year. A woman leaves her house with a group of assistants as soon as her labor pains begin. In the summer, they go to a solitary place in the woods and erect a crude windbreak to shelter her. In the winter, they withdraw to a protected spot under the dwelling (McIlwraith 1948: *1*, 363). A Hadza (9) woman gives birth under a tree, about 150 feet away from the main settlement (Kohl-Larsen 1958: 145).

A good many societies provide a special structure in which the woman can have her baby (23% of 47 societies). Among the Nicobarese (78), birth houses are located outside of the village areas; wealthier people may choose to build their own. Husband and wife move there before the baby is due and remain for a period of from three to six months. The rationale for this procedure is that the woman is unclean when she gives birth; contact with her usual dwelling would make it impure too and necessitate its demolition (Man 1932: 66). Not only are there female attendants who help provide for her during this time; also her husband is responsible for taking care of her. Man says that there are always a number of couples inhabiting the birth huts at the same time, because of the long period during which they reside there (Man 1932: 118, 119).

In the remainder of the societies (17% of 47 societies), the woman leaves her usual residence and goes to live with a relative; the dwelling is usually the home of a consanguine (15% of 47 societies), rather than that of an affine (2% of 47 societies). A Palauan (111) woman prefers to be in the house of her mother, sister, or mother's sister when she delivers her infant; when she gives birth to the baby, one of her close female relatives is present to attend her (Barnett 1960: 23). The woman remains in confinement for a period of five to ten days; the midwife not only bathes her daily and rubs her with coconut oil and tumeric but also gives her a steam bath on the final day of her seclusion (Barnett 1960: 102).

The emphasis on a woman being with her maternal relatives when she gives birth may be more pervasive and important than statistics on spatial segregation indicate. When the societies in which a woman shifts from patrilocal residence to temporary residence with her relatives (8% of 52 societies) are combined with those in which she is already resident matrilocally, either permanently (21% of 52 societies) or temporarily (17% of 52 societies), the result is that a woman gives birth while she is living with her maternal relatives in close to half (46% of 52 societies) of the sample societies. The link between birth and residence is particularly striking in cases of matri-patrilocality, because the birth of the first child is the specific event after which the couple resides patrilocally. This fact points to the importance of understanding the significance of the parturient woman's proximity to her kin (Wilson 1975).

Even though a woman is usually segregated in a separate place during birth, she is generally not removed from surroundings that are familiar to her. My impression is that the woman usually delivers her baby in the presence of women friends or relatives; the husband may or may not be present too. Ford (1964) corroborates this impression. He found that women usually attend the birth of an infant; men and menstruating women are ordinarily excluded.

Contrary to popular opinion, childbirth is not necessarily an easy and painless process in other societies (Ford 1964: 62). It does appear to be the case that birth is aided by the position in which the woman delivers her baby and that women in other societies generally give birth in an upright or semiupright position, rather than lying down (Ford 1964: 59). In addition, the social support that a woman receives from female friends and kin may lessen her anxiety about birth and aid her in establishing successful breastfeeding (Raphael 1976; Wilson 1975).

*Sociocultural aspects of the postpartum period: lactation and weaning.* In many other societies, women do not take milk production for granted as an automatic consequence of birth. Raphael estimates that only 5 percent of all women are physically incapable of lactating to some extent; however, a woman may not be able to produce and release a supply of milk sufficient to ensure the survival of her infant (Raphael 1976: 67). Therefore, the concern that surrounds successful breastfeeding seems well placed, particularly where alternative sources of nutrition for the baby are not readily available. It is ironic that anxiety about not being able to breastfeed may increase a woman's difficulty in accomplishing her goal. The woman's psychological state is important, because the brain is central to milk production and release. Psychological stress can hamper the release of prolactin and oxytocin from the pituitary gland.

Some groups respond to possible anxiety about successful breastfeeding by establishing specific techniques to guarantee an adequate milk supply (Ford 1964: 81). For example, Thonga mothers take a medicine or drug to ensure the proper quality of their milk. Other techniques focus on improving the quantity of milk. These methods include massaging or mechanically "pumping" the breasts, cold baths, and drinking nutritious liquids (Ford 1964: 81).

Another way to deal with insufficient milk production is to provide an alternate milk supply. A woman may choose to use either a bottled formula or cow's milk. However, many groups do not have adequate facilities to sterilize bottles or to maintain the quality of the milk. An additional choice may be more suitable in societies where women breastfeed for several years. Another lactating woman, usually a female relative of the child's mother, can feed the child (Ford 1964: 82).

The time at which nursing begins varies in different societies. Some groups do not allow newborn babies to nurse immediately after birth. For the first seven days of its life outside of the womb, a Thonga baby receives substitute foods (Ford 1964: 77). Ford links this type of custom to the yellowish appearance of the colostrum that is produced for the first few days after birth; initiation of breastfeeding may begin after the colostrum disappears (Ford 1964: 77).

The times at which a woman feeds her baby are also variable. Most groups encourage a woman to nurse her baby whenever the infant is hungry, instead of imposing a fixed feeding schedule on the baby. The fact that an infant often sleeps with its mother increases the ease with which the mother can feed her baby at night. Breastfed babies often need less of their mothers' milk but more frequent feedings, because they assimilate human milk more "efficiently and rapidly" (Raphael 1976: 53). The interaction between mother and infant during non-scheduled breastfeeding can be very helpful for the baby. The infant can regulate the amount it drinks according to its hunger; there is less danger that it will be overfed (Raphael 1976: 54).

Finally, groups vary in the length of time that their women generally continue to breastfeed. An analysis of Barry and Paxson's data on weaning (1971) shows that the most common ages at which children cease to breastfeed are between twenty-four and thirty-six months (45% of 166 societies). In only 20% of the 166 societies do women wean their babies before they are two years old; in almost twice as many societies (35% of 166 societies), women extend breastfeeding beyond three years. Bororo women of South America may nurse their children as long as seven years, while the Spanish Basques may shorten the period to as little as three months (Barry and Paxson 1971). Ford's cross-cultural study of reproduction showed that "regardless of the availability and use of other suitable foods, weaning seems to be delayed as long as it is at all possible in the great majority" of the societies he surveyed (Ford 1964: 79).

*Sociocultural aspects of the postpartum period: restrictions.* In addition to the practices that surround breastfeeding, groups provide still other guidelines for the new parents to follow after their child is born. These postpartum restrictions structure the behavior of the husband and wife for a definite period and may aid them in adjusting psychologically to their new child.

Postpartum restrictions primarily emphasize the welfare of the child (35% of 37 societies) or that of the child and his mother (38% of 37 societies), rather than showing a dominant concern for the mother alone (8% of 37 societies). Postpartum restrictions emphasize spatial confinement as a mode of limitation, the necessity for a prohibition on sexual intercourse for a period after birth, and the extension of these restrictions to protect a wider range of people (19% of 37 societies).

Many of the reasons given for adherence to postpartum restrictions are reminiscent of the purposes of menstrual restrictions. A Micmac (126) woman is encouraged to eat alone for a month or two after she bears a child. When she does have a meal, she is not allowed to drink from the kettles or eat from the bark dishes, which she would ordinarily use; if she did so, she would spoil the men's success in hunting beaver and moose (LeClercq 1910: 229). A Warrau (162) woman is secluded after she gives birth, because the group believes that anyone who came into contact with her food, clothes, or blood would fall ill and die (Turrado Moreno 1945: 264). A woman who has recently given birth is explicitly considered impure for a month among the Khalka Mongols (66). She must remain at home for that period of time and abstain from sexual relations with her husband. A stranger should not enter her dwelling during that interval, because the contamination could spread to him (Ballis 1956: *1*, 338). The definition of a woman as impure after she has given birth occurs in a large number of societies (39% of 47 societies). Her delivery of the child not only marks her status as a new mother but also may signal the start of a transition period during which people fear her impurity.

Like pregnancy taboos, postpartum restrictions may apply to the husband as well as to the wife. Their extension to the husband occurs in approximately the same proportion of societies (59% of 47 societies) as extensions of pregnancy restrictions do. This holds true for all of the South American societies in my sample ($X^2 = 4.68$, 1 df, p = < .05, N = 47), but for none of the Circum-Mediterranean ones ($X^2 = 7.5$, 1 df, p = < .01, N = 47). New Yahgan (186) parents continue to observe some of the restrictions on food and behavior to which they adhered during the wife's pregnancy. The woman fears that she will cripple her child if she breaks a bird's bones, while her husband fears that the baby's skull will split if he breaks a sea urchin's shell. Consumption of the wrong foods can lead to deformity in the child and to the ill health of both the baby and its mother. In addition to obeying the foregoing restrictions for about three months, the couple avoids intercourse for at least six weeks and perhaps longer. Although the woman begins to work again fairly soon after the child is born, the new father resigns himself to a period of "dutiful inactivity" (Gusinde 1937: 710–712).

The prohibition of sexual relations is an important type of restriction on a man's relationship with his wife after she bears a child. It is absent in very few societies (7% of 41 societies) and is probably the most prevalent postpartum limitation that applies to both husband and wife. Although its occurrence is widespread (93% of 41 societies), its duration varies. Most societies limit the period of postpartum abstinence to less than a year (68% of 41 societies); a one-to-five month interval is the most frequent duration (34% of 41 societies). Nevertheless, a substantial portion of societies (32% of 41 societies) extend the taboo beyond one year; in these, it is not unusual to extend it more than two years (15% of 41 societies). Societies in Africa are significantly more likely than those in other regions to extend the taboo beyond six months ($X^2 = 8.2$, 1 df, p = < .005, N = 41); groups in the Circum-

Mediterranean and Eurasia usually confine the taboo to less than six months ($X^2 = 4.97$, 1 df, p = < .05, N = 41).

Just as the length of the postpartum sex taboo varies, so, too, does the length of time during which other restrictions apply. In most societies (41% of 50 societies), a woman resumes her usual economic and household duties within one week after she gives birth. In many cases (28% of 50 societies), she must wait between one and two weeks before she can perform her usual tasks; less frequently, such activities are postponed for from two to four weeks (12% of 50 societies) or for a period of between one and two months (12% of 50 societies). It is rare that she is restricted from resuming her tasks for more than two months (6% of 50 societies).

*Sociocultural aspects of the postpartum period: celebrations.* New parents show their awareness of the significance of the child's birth by their adherence to postpartum restrictions. However, there is no dominant trend in the way that a group publicly displays its attitude toward the arrival of a couple's first child. There is a slight tendency for minimal rather than more elaborate recognition to be given to this event (56% of 54 societies). Among the Cayapa (168), the couple and some of the closest friends of the family may gather for the naming of the child after the woman comes out of confinement; usually this practice occurs only among the Catholics in the group (Barrett 1925: 317, 318). The Eastern Pomo (135) express more enthusiasm. The new mother's relatives make her wampum and bring her the finest basket in the village Members of her husband's family bring her strings of beads to wear on her wrists (Loeb 1926: 251). The Lamet (72) perform a ceremony called the "tying of the wrists," which they also enact when the couple marries. In addition, they sacrifice a pig to the ancestral spirits (Izikowitz 1951: 103).

A considerable number of societies (44% of 54 societies) celebrates the birth of the first child by conducting moderate (15% of 54 societies) or elaborate (29% of 54 societies) festivities. The Fon (18) of Africa and the Bellacoola (132) of British Columbia moderately celebrate the birth of a child. Five days after a Fon child is born, the relatives of the couple bring gifts to the new mother. The entertainment consists of dancing, eating, and drinking (Herskovits 1938: *1*, 266). A social gathering also acknowledges the birth of a Bellacoola (132) child. One of the child's relatives invites the people of the baby's village to a naming ceremony, at which an ancestral name is given to the infant (McIlwraith 1948: *1*, 146).

The elaborate celebration at the birth of a Manus (96) child surpasses the moderate ones of the Fon and Bellacoola. The delivery of a child triggers an intricate set of social events, as well as a dramatic change in the young mother's life. A Manus woman usually bears her child in her husband's or her brother's house. If she is in her husband's house, he moves out of it, and the woman's brother and his wife come to stay with her. The latter take care of the woman by providing food and pleasant company for her. This is an enjoyable change for her. She begins to notice an improvement in her relationship with her brother's wife, as well as with her female relative who come to visit. a series of feasts follows the birth of her child. A small one in the household precedes the elaborate one that takes place the next day. A husband must provide sago and pots for his wife's kinsmen, to compensate them for the care that they have taken of his wife and newborn child. Otherwise he would not be permitted to see her or his child. The culmination of these events is a financial transaction between the woman's relatives and her husband. A change in her physical appearance accompanies the round of social activity. The long hair that the woman grew when she was pregnant is shaved off, and she wears the bridal costume that she donned when she first married (Mead 1930a: 61, 62). Her dress succinctly expresses her role in the celebration; she has given birth to a child, which becomes the occasion for elaborate exchanges between affines. The image of her position as a pawn in a game for social prestige is a graphic one. The young mother is so weighted down by her attire of shell money that she can hardly move.

The social interest in the birth of the child is shown not only by the elaboration of the birth celebration but also by the range of people who participate in it. Few societies (14% of 36 societies) limit recognition of birth to the couple alone. It is relatively rare for only the family or kin unit of the husband or wife to be present at the festivities (8% of 36 societies). More often the relatives and associates of both the husband and wife participate in the celebration (78% of 36 societies). The group may be made up of a combination of friends and neighbors (19% of 36 societies) or friends and relatives (22% of 36 societies), or of the kin groups to which each belongs (14% of 36 societies), or of members of the local community (22% of 36 societies). Just as in the case of marriage celebrations, the degree of elaboration that accompanies the celebration of a birth is significantly associated with the extent of social participation in it (Gamma = .91, p = < .01, N = 36).

The foregoing examples make it clear that the occasion of the birth of a first child is celebrated at different times and with variable degrees of elaboration. The timing of the celebration may be an important indicator of its significance. Does it mark the social identity of the child by bestowing a name upon him, or provide immediate support for a woman who has just undergone labor pains and delivery, or celebrate the end of a period of confinement and the resumption of the woman's usual activities? In most societies, the celebration occurs rather soon after delivery (49% of 45 societies). In a large proportion of societies, the celebration occurs when the baby is named or baptized (31% of 45 societies). The release of the mother and child from confinement or other occasions evoke celebrations in the least number of societies (20% of 45 societies).

The birth of the child becomes the basis for the beginning of social involvement in its sexual cycle. The group begins to impress its ideas of appropriate sexual differentiation on another new member of society. We have come full circle. The sexual and reproductive cycles start to develop in new generations.

# Chapter Five
# Patterns of Human Sexuality:
# Social and Cultural Aspects

The main idea that underlies the material presented in this book is that it is important and profitable to analyze the shared aspects of human sexuality as components of a system of behavior in its own right. The last two chapters were the first steps in demonstrating this point of view. They identified some of the main elements of which the system is composed, showed the extent of their variation in different social contexts, and suggested some preliminary associations of variables within the cycles. Each chapter focused on the components of one of the cycles, i.e., either sexual or reproductive behavior and beliefs.

Since use of the term "system" indicates that there are links between the elements contained within the framework, the next step is to demonstrate that there are, in fact, significant associations between the sexual and reproductive cycles that make up the system of human sexuality. The purpose of this chapter is twofold. First, it aims to show that many of the shared aspects of human sexuality described in the last two chapters form patterns. Second, it tries to demonstrate that it is fruitful to seek explanations for these patterns from a variety of perspectives.

## Sexual Restrictions and
## Reproductive Relationships

One way of approaching the association between elements in the cycles is to explore the consistency of the rules that apply to the sexual and reproductive cycles. A first step is to determine the degree to which rules within the sexual cycle are related to each other.

*Premarital and Extramarital Rules*

The chapter on the sexual cycle presented generalizations based on data bout the rules that govern premarital and extramarital coitus in other societies. First, there are more societies that do allow premarital coitus for one or both sexes than there are those that do not. Second, restrictions are more likely to apply to extramarital relationships than to premarital ones. Third, a greater number of societies permit men to engage in both premarital and extramarital coitus than allow women to do so. Overall, the rules emphasize greater restrictions on a female's option to engage in premarital and extramarital coitus than on a male's.

Another, equally significant, set of patterns emerged when I explored how premarital and extramarital rules apply to men and women within the same social context. There is a general consistency in the degree of restrictiveness that applies to both men and women when they shift from a premarital to an extramarital context. That means that when premarital restrictions are stringent, so, too, are extramarital ones, and vice versa. However, the pattern of consistency is much greater for men (gamma = .84) than for women (gamma = .50). The differences in consistency relate to the degrees of restrictiveness that apply to men and to women. When rules apply to men, they are likely to be lax about both premarital and extramarital coitus. In contrast, the rules in both of these areas are more likely to be strict when they apply to women.

The reason that the association between consistency of rules is not as strong in the case of women as it is for men is that there are a greater number of exceptions to the general trend. A woman's premarital period of freedom is more likely to be followed by relatively strict restriction of her extramarital activities. This sequence of rules suggests a "double standard" in some societies. To what extent does a double standard prevail in the societies in this study?

Once again, the exceptions to general patterns are revealing. When rules apply differently to males and to females, the difference lies uniformly in the direction of allowing greater sexual freedom for males to pursue premarital and extramarital liaisons, while denying similar opportunities to females. Not one society in my sample had rules that allowed women relative freedom to have nonmarital coitus and prohibited men from this same option. In other words, the double standard operates only in one direction. A woman is rarely permitted to engage in nonmarital coitus if men cannot exercise the same right.

*Implications of Sexual Regulation
for Reproductive Relationships*

A central question arises from these findings. How are we to interpret the degree of variation that we find in the strictness of the rules that apply to nonmarital relationships? Why are rules so severe in some societies and relatively lax in others? Further, when there is a double standard, why is there particular concern with restricting a woman's sexual relationships outside of marriage? These questions lead to a consideration of the implications of sexual restrictions for reproductive relationships, i.e., marriages.

What connection do we actually find between the rules that apply to sexual and to reproductive relationships? My data on sexual restrictiveness and the confinement of reproductive potential provide a partial answer to this question. "Sexual restrictiveness" refers to the degree to which a group restricts a person's option to form premarital or extramarital relationships. "Confinement of reproductive potential" means the degree to which a group confines a person's reproductive relationships to one marriage. I tested the association between these two variables for men and for women and found a striking divergence by gender in how consistently sexual rules are likely to carry over in their restrictiveness to reproductive relationships. There is no significant association between the two types of constraints for men (Fisher's exact test, $p = .32$, $N = 31$). In other words, when men are subject to sexual restrictions before or outside of marriage, they will not necessarily be similarly constrained in the flexibility they may have to form a variety of reproductive relationships. The exceptions are interesting. Almost half (48 % of 31 societies) of the societies in the test of association restricted sexual relationships but did not confine a man's reproductive potential to one or a few partners. In other words, where a variety of purely sexual partners for males are not acceptable, multiple marriages are.

In contrast to the men's pattern, the association between the regulation of the two types of relationships is strikingly consistent for women. When sexual rules are restrictive for women, their reproductive potential is also likely to be confined. When rules are more lax, women are likely to have the flexibility to form a variety of marital unions. Table 5.1 shows this highly significant association.

Table 5.1 *Association between the Index of Sexual Restrictiveness and the Index of Reproductive Potential for Females*

|  |  | Confinement of Reproductive Potential | |  |
|---|---|---|---|---|
|  |  | Low, Medium Low | Medium High, High |  |
| *Sexual Restrictiveness* | Low, Medium Low | 13 | 1 | 14 |
|  | Medium High, High | 7 | 16 | 23 |
|  |  | 20 | 17 | 37 = N |

$X^2 = 11.26$; 1 df; $p = < .001$

Of the few exceptions to the overall trend (8 of 37 societies, or 22%), the overwhelming majority (7 of 8 exceptions, or 87½%) restrict sexual relationships but do not confine reproductive ones. Like her male counterpart, a woman is most likely to experience inconsistency between rules that stress strict sexual restriction but allow more scope for forming reproductive unions. Even the exceptions suggest a connection between sexual and reproductive rules; they more frequently confine sexual relations of both men and women to a reproductive context.

These findings add to the intensity of our original questions. Why are there variations in the way that rules apply to men and women? Why is there particular concern with restriction of a woman's sexual relationships to marriage? The differences between the foci of the sexual and reproductive cycles becomes more relevant. If there are patterns of rules that govern options to form sexual and reproductive relationships, are there other social and cultural aspects of the sexual and reproductive cycles that are associated with them?

### The Degree of Coincidence between Sexual and Reproductive Relationships

When a group prohibits premarital and extramarital unions, it channels acceptable sexual relationships into marriage, a childbearing context. In other words this type of arrangement ensures that sexual relationships are reproductive relationships. By contrast, a group that allows its members to engage in premarital and extramarital relationships does not focus on confining sexual relationships to marriage, and sexual relationships are therefore less closely identified with reproductive ones. These hypothetical restrictive and permissive groups represent two versions of the ways in which sexual and reproductive relationships can relate to each other. They suggest that the next step in interpreting the nature of the rules that apply to sexual and reproductive relationships is to examine the consequences that follow both when sexual relationships coincide with reproductive ones and when they do not. Since there is variation in the applicability of the rules for each gender, we need to take into account the nature of the consequences for each gender.

Females are physically identified with their children during gestation, childbirth, and the postpartum period, particularly during lactation. Males do not have the same option for a close physical association with their offspring, because of the nature of their reproductive organs. Furthermore, the general association of children with women continues beyond birth and at least until early childhood. Men begin to interact more frequently with their children only after the children enter early childhood. The physical differences between men and women in their reproductive roles pose a problem for men that women do not have. Although the physical association of a woman with her child suggests a social link between them, a man lacks this preliminary identification. Therefore, sociocultural criteria are more likely to be used as a basis for linking a man with his children. If a man has a continuing relationship with a woman who confines her sexual relations exclusively to him, he can more easily identify any children she bears as his own. Therefore, a man indirectly affirms his physical link to his child by creating a close, social bond with the woman whose children he wishes to claim as his own. Cultural beliefs about his role in conception and the restriction of the woman's sexual relations to him further strengthen the basis for his connection with the child.

## The Importance of a Marriage Celebration

Marriage is a particularly important bond for a man to establish if he wants to be socially identified with the children of the woman or women he impregnates. Marriage becomes a social means of establishing the reproductive tie between a man and a woman. My definition of marriage is consistent with this idea; marriage is the main context within which the birth of children is acceptable and encouraged.

I am arguing that marriage and the restriction of a woman's sexual relationships to one man serve to socially identify children with their parents, particularly with their fathers. If this is so, I would expect a significant association between social interest in marriage and a woman's sexual relationships. The degree of celebration at marriage is an important indication of the amount of interest a social group has in the marital bond. Restrictions reflect social interest in the kinds of sexual relationships that women have. Table 5.2 presents the results of the association between sexual regulation of women and the extent of elaboration of the marriage celebration.

Table 5.2 *Association of the Elaboration of the Marriage Celebration with the Index of Sexual Restrictiveness for Women*

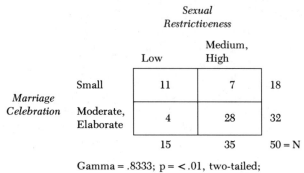

|  |  | Low | Medium, High |  |
|---|---|---|---|---|
| Marriage Celebration | Small | 11 | 7 | 18 |
|  | Moderate, Elaborate | 4 | 28 | 32 |
|  |  | 15 | 35 | 50 = N |

Gamma = .8333; p = < .01, two-tailed;
z = 3.25

The table shows that societies that restrict a woman's sexual relationships to a childbearing context, i.e., marriage, have elaborate marriage celebrations; those that do not have only small celebrations. This highly significant association indicates an important link between the sexual and reproductive cycles; rules that apply to a woman's sexual relationships are closely connected to the establishment of a reproductive relationship.

Confinement of a woman's reproductive potential to one man or family is also significantly associated with social involvement in marriage (Gamma = .67, z = 1.79, p = < .05, one-tailed, N = 38). However, it is not as strongly linked to the amount of celebration at marriage as is the sexual restrictiveness of women. It is more important as an additional factor, which escalates the importance of marriage for both the man and the woman. When a woman limits her reproductive potential to one man, she puts all of her eggs in one reproductive basket, thus intensifying the importance of the bond with her husband and strengthening his social identification with her children. Therefore, I would expect that the rules that restrict a woman's sexual relations to one man as well as confine her reproductive potential to him and his kin would be more strongly associated with the elaboration of the marriage celebration than either type of restriction alone. Table 5.3 presents a significant confirmation of my hypothesis.

Table 5.3 *Association of the Type of Marriage Celebration with Both Sexual Restrictiveness and the Confinement of Reproductive Potential of Women*

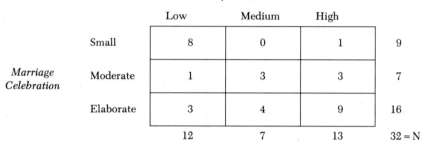

|  |  | Sexual Restrictiveness and Confinement of Reproductive Potential | | | |
|---|---|---|---|---|---|
|  |  | Low | Medium | High | |
| | Small | 8 | 0 | 1 | 9 |
| Marriage Celebration | Moderate | 1 | 3 | 3 | 7 |
| | Elaborate | 3 | 4 | 9 | 16 |
| | | 12 | 7 | 13 | 32 = N |

Gamma = .9487; z = 3.297; p = < .01, two-tailed

### The Importance of Bride-price

The way that a marriage transaction is finalized is another facet of a group's interest in the reproductive aspect of marriage. It is not surprising that there is a significant association (Gamma = .8571, z = 2.9578, p = < .01, two-tailed, N = 42) between the type of marriage celebration and the factors that confirm the establishment of a marriage in the eyes of the group. Both reflect the group's involvement in the marriage. The marriage celebration is almost always small or nonexistent when the birth of a child or cohabitation is the primary means for confirming the validity of the relationship (87% of 15 societies in which the marriage celebration is small). On the other hand, a moderate or elaborate celebration usually accompanies marriage when bride-price or ritual confirms the union (67% of 27 societies where the marriage celebrate is moderate/elaborate).

As social interest in marriage increases, confirmation of the union centers on factors that a group of people can share and control. The birth of a child or cohabitation of spouses may depend on fortuitous, individual circumstances, such as a couple's fecundity or compatibility. Ritual and the transference of bride-price are subject to social management. The group has the flexibility to encourage a reproductive union by participating in an elaborate marriage celebration and by investing its economic resources in the couple.

## The Importance to Marriage of Sexual Access and of the Birth of Children

Since marriage is a major context for childbearing and usually defines the relationship between spouses in reproductive terms, two elements are central to the marital bond: the right of sexual access to a spouse and the birth of a child. However, their vital contribution to the marriage may not be obvious in the celebration itself. Marriage celebrations are often solemn, yet festive, occasions, which stress the positive elements of the group's involvement in a new reproductive relationship. The centrality of sexual relations and fertility becomes more apparent in the negative repercussions that befall a couple if they do not conform to the group's expectations for their union. Grounds for divorce and alternatives to barrenness are some of the guidelines that a group can establish to protect its investment in reproductive unions. In other words, it is likely to counterbalance its positive social involvement in a union — e.g., participation in elaborate marriage celebrations and gift-giving — with negative social rules or actions, which express its discontent with the individual's contributions to the union.

*Grounds for divorce.* If there is an association between the positive and the negative aspects of a group's involvement in marriage, I would expect that there is a relationship between elaboration of the marriage celebration and the primary grounds that a man gives for divorcing his wife. Each may reflect a different side of the group's interest in restricting a woman's sexual relations to marriage and anticipating that a woman will have children. If this is so, I would expect that reproductive problems or a wife's extramarital affairs would more frequently be the main grounds that a husband would give for divorcing his wife when an elaborate celebration has accompanied the establishment of marriage. Table 5.4 presents the results of testing this hypothesis.

Table 5.4 *Association of the Type of Marriage Celebration with a Husband's Grounds for Divorcing His Wife*

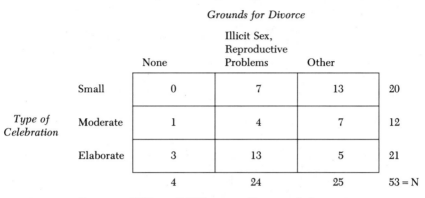

*Grounds for Divorce*

| | | None | Illicit Sex, Reproductive Problems | Other | |
|---|---|---|---|---|---|
| | Small | 0 | 7 | 13 | 20 |
| *Type of Celebration* | Moderate | 1 | 4 | 7 | 12 |
| | Elaborate | 3 | 13 | 5 | 21 |
| | | 4 | 24 | 25 | 53 = N |

Gamma = .5539; z = 2.7289; p = < .01, two-tailed

Table 5.4 confirms my expectation that there is a significant relation between the group's positive social actions, e.g, a marriage celebration, and its negative rules, e.g., grounds for divorce. Like the sociocultural aspects of the sexual cycle, aspects of the reproductive cycle are also linked together.

*Alternatives to barrenness.* Another way to indicate that sexual access to a woman and the birth of children are important ingredients in a marriage is to explore the relationships between the rules that restrict a woman's sexual relations to one union and the consequences for her barrenness. I showed earlier that one possible reason for restricting a woman's sexual relations to marriage is to establish paternity. What happens when a woman restricts her sexual relations to her husband, but does not have children? This situation focuses on the social and personal significance of having children in a marriage.

The couple faces social pressure, because they are not meeting the group's expectations that they have children. However, the personal impact of barrenness on the couple is more subtle. Earlier I showed that a man is rarely assigned responsibility for his wife's barrenness, even though he is believed to play a major role in conception. A woman's restriction of her sexual relations to her husband could cast doubt upon the idea that the couple's lack of children is unrelated to the man's reproductive powers. How does the man deal with this potential inconsistency? Both he and his group shift responsibility for barrenness away from himself and blame it on other factors.

One cultural mechanism for shifting responsibility from the man is to explain barrenness in terms of the wife's physical condition or to blame it on the harmful consequences that the actions of others have had on the woman's fertility. A more emphatic way to deflect responsibility for barrenness away from the husband is to infer that it is the woman's fault. The group can establish alternatives for the husband, which may have a punitive effect on the woman. Ostracism for the woman, divorce, and the husband's marriage to an additional wife to bear him children are some of the punitive consequences that can befall a barren woman. Therefore, I would expect that the societies that restrict a woman's sexual relations to marriage are likely to provide more alternatives that infer that responsibility for barrenness lies with the woman. Societies that do not socially identify a man with his wife's children by limiting her sexual relations to him would allow for less punitive alternatives to barrenness, e.g., adoption and remedies to correct the condition. I found that there is a significant association between the degree of sexual restrictions that apply to a woman and the degree to which alternatives to barrenness are punitive (Gamma = .5694, z = 2.8352, p = < .01, two-tailed, N = 48).

Earlier, I showed that confinement of a woman's reproductive potential to one man strengthens the social identification of her children with him. Therefore, I expect that punitive alternatives to barrenness are even more strongly associated with societies that restrict a woman's sexual relations and reproductive potential to one man. Table 5.5 confirms the greater significance of this association.

Table 5.5 *Association of Alternatives to Barrenness with Both Sexual Restrictiveness and Confinement of Reproductive Potential of Women*

|  |  | Sexual Restrictiveness and Confinement of Reproductive Potential | | | |
|  |  | Low | Medium | High | |
| | Ostracism, Divorce, Additional Wife | 0 | 3 | 9 | 12 |
| Alternatives to Barrenness | Adoption, Remedies | 9 | 4 | 3 | 16 |
| | | 9 | 7 | 12 | 28 = N |

Mann-Whitney U test z = 7.3; p = < .001, one-tailed

*Summary: Sexual Rules and*
*Reproductive Relationships*

We can summarize the pattern of associations that I have identified as a model, the elements of which define the extent to which a woman's sexual relationships overlap with her reproductive ones. At one extreme is complete coincidence between a woman's sexual and reproductive relationships. In terms of the variables investigated in this study, complete coincidence means that the woman confines intercourse to a single marital union. This restrictive extreme is associated with elaborate marriage celebrations, extensive social participation in marriage, the importance of bride-price in finalizing the marriage, barrenness and extramarital sex as a husband's grounds for divorcing his wife, and punitive alternatives to barrenness. At the other extreme, we find *no* overlap in sexual and reproductive relationships. In this case, a woman has the flexibility to engage in premarital and extramarital relationships; she can also have a succession of reproductive partners by easily remarrying after divorce or the death of her husband. This permissive extreme is associated with minimal social celebration at marriage, little social participation in the celebration of marriage, the importance of living together or the birth of children as confirmation of marriage, a husband divorcing his wife on grounds other than barrenness or extramarital sex, and a preference for adoption or remedies as alternatives to barrenness. Between these two extremes lie societies that have some overlap between sexual and reproductive relationships. Societies that conform to the intermediate position display the greatest variation in the rules and social actions that govern the sexual and reproductive relationships of their members. They may place restrictions on premarital or extramarital relationships, but not on both. They may have rules that constrain a woman in obtaining a divorce or remarrying after the death of her husband, but generally not both. Figure 5.1 illustrates the components of the model.

Figure 5.1 *Components of the Model of Coincidence of Sexual and Reproductive Relationships of Women*

|  | *Restrictive* | *Permissive* |
|---|---|---|
| *Indicators:* |  |  |
| Premarital Sex | Prohibited | Allowed |
| Extramarital Sex | Prohibited | Allowed |
| Ease of Obtaining a Divorce | Difficult | Easy |
| Ease of Remarriage after Widowhood | Difficult | Easy |
| *Associated Variables:* |  |  |
| Elaboration of Marriage Celebration | Elaborate | Minimal |
| Social Participation in Marriage Celebration | Extensive | Little, None |
| Factor(s) which Finalize Marriage | Bride-price, Ritual | Coresidence, Children |
| Husband's Grounds for Divorce | Barrenness, Illicit Sex | Not Barrenness or Illicit Sex |
| Alternatives to Barrenness | Divorce, Ostracism, Another Wife | Adoption Remedies |

## Two Examples of the Model of Coincidence of Women's Sexual and Reproductive Relationships

The model of associations that I have outlined does not demonstrate that a society that conforms to one extreme of the pattern is a carbon copy of the others that share similar characteristics. Rather, the model provides a preliminary framework for probing other social and cultural nuances that attach to its silhouette. The societies that conform to the model are diverse. I will describe two societies, which represent the model's permissive and restrictive extremes; each has its own way of expressing its central beliefs. The Kimam (93) inhabit Frederick Hendrick Island in southern New Guinea. They illustrate the permissive pattern. They are relatively flexible in allowing women to form sexual and reproductive relationships. The Kenuzi Nubians (39) starkly contrast with the Kimam in their emphasis on restricting the range of women's sexual and reproductive relationships. In both cases, I will tie my discussion specifically to the significance that each society places upon the birth of children. This orientation gives us a focus for interpreting the relevance of fertility to the degree of association between sexual and reproductive relationships.

The Kimam regard intercourse as "something given away or received" (Serpenti 1965: 165). Not only do they freely permit premarital relationships; they also expect a girl to take the initiative in encouraging premarital intercourse. Even after marriage, a man and woman have considerable sexual license. A husband may offer his wife to another man, so that he can engage in "ceremonial intercourse"; men may also exchange the right to sexual access over their wives for a few hours (Serpenti 1965: 183, 253).

An ideal marriage arrangement is one in which two men marry each other's sisters (Serpenti 1965: 124). This arrangement sets up a preliminary basis for later cooperation between them. The birth of children becomes important to a man for a number of reasons. He desires boys to work on his garden property, to inherit it, and to support him and his wife in their old age. He also wants to have girls, because they are essential for him to establish marriage exchanges for his sons (Serpenti 1965: 148).

Kimam men are very serious about their desire to have children. A man can divorce or kill his wife for aborting a child (Serpenti 1965: 145). Not only do men hope that their wives will have children; they also want their sisters to have them. A brother's partial support of his sister and her children has its compensation in the rights he has over her children. He has the right to adopt one of her children or to use one of her daughters as an exchange sister for his son. Marriage exchanges and adoptions establish a basis for a man to strengthen his ties with members of his local group.

Although adoption is an alternative to barrenness, its significance extends far beyond this role. Just as marriages may create alliances between groups, the exchange of children by adoption may foster social cooperation. The Kimam use adoption to reinforce ties with their kinsmen. They adopt children so frequently that they can readily offer "their children" in marriage exchanges; they do not rely upon the actual number of children a wife has borne. Adoptive parents are in debt to the couple who gave them a child. They not only invite the "natural" parents to every feast for the child; they also give them part of their harvest and allow them to use certain objects (Serpenti 1965: 197). The importance of marriage and adoptive exchanges to their social life is so great that a couple may adopt a child even before the wife has had any children or has proved to be barren.

Even though the Kimam give and adopt children with relative ease, they are not ignorant of the physical basis for conception. They acknowledge that a "man may produce life with his sperm" (Serpenti 1965: 164). However, the lack of emphasis placed upon the confinement of sexual relations to marriage means that they claim rights over a child on a basis other than a physiological bond. Conceiving or giving birth to a child is not sufficient reason to claim the right of parenthood; people acquire this right by taking care of the child. Caretaking overrides the physiological foundation for parenthood. Therefore, a woman who has not had children is not particularly set apart from other women. Adoption is widespread and is an expression of solidarity and good will between the couples who arrange it. No one would refuse to give away a child for adoption.

At the other end of the spectrum from the Kimam are the Kenuzi Nubians, a group located along the Nile River in Egypt. They are an example of the restrictive societies in the model. A woman confines her sexual relations and reproductive potential to one man. Regulation of a woman's sexual activity begins early, between the ages of three and four; her clitoris is removed (Herzog 1957: 101). In addition, the Kenuzi close a girl's vaginal opening, to ensure her virginity until marriage. After marriage, a woman confines her sexual relations to her husband, even though she may have only slight contact with him. Men engage in migratory labor and are often away from the village for long periods of time. Since a woman is alone a considerable amount of time, her husband may request that his wife's vagina be sewn up during his absence, to ensure her fidelity (Herzog 1957: 188). The sanctions of infidelity are even more extreme then the preventative measures taken to avoid it. A husband may kill his wife at the slightest suspicion of infidelity (Herzog 1957: 94). Therefore, it is not surprising that a woman regards a pregnancy as a catastrophe if it occurs while her husband is absent (Callender and El Guindi 1971: 32).

A woman also confines her reproductive potential to one man. She is reluctant to divorce her husband and fears his divorcing her (Herzog 1957: 94). It is essential that a woman remain married, because of her economic dependence upon her husband (Callender and El Guindi 1971: 45). Her fidelity to her husband may extend beyond his death. She should not remarry if her husband insists that she mourn him for the rest of her life (Callender and El Guindi 1971: 81).

Both men and women desire children, especially sons. However, their reasons for wanting them are not identical (Callender and El Guindi 1971: 21). The men desire sons to carry on the patrilineage to which they belong. The women want sons to ensure the continuation of their marriages, as well as their husbands' economic support.

Although a man may not want to divorce his wife for barrenness, he faces tremendous social pressure to remarry if his wife has not given birth to sons (Callender and El Guindi 1971: 21). Therefore, a couple's ability to produce children, particularly sons, is fraught with anxiety, especially for the woman. A woman expresses her anxiety by her belief in a set of dangers collectively termed *"mushahra,"* but vaguely glossed as "unknown peril" (Callender and El Guindi 1971: 13). This menace threatens a woman with sterility and a man with impotence throughout their reproductive years. In addition, the malicious influence of others can threaten a woman's reproductive ability. The effects of the evil eye or the attempts of barren women to steal the fertility of others are continual sources of danger. Ideas about pollution also express the fear that a woman associates with sex and reproduction; defilement centers on contact with blood, sexual fluids, and flesh, especially in the genital areas.

Infant mortality probably intensifies a woman's anxiety about having children; one-third to one-half of all the Kenuzi children born die young (Callender and El Guindi 1971: 23). Therefore, women take many precautions against barrenness. They try to avoid coming in contact with a suspected agent of *"mushahra,"* and they attempt to deflect the evil eye. They also pray to the saints for children (Callender and El Guindi 1971: 8). There is no abortion or contraception (Herzog 1957: 95).

The Kimam and the Kenuzi differ considerably in their reasons for wanting children. They also diverge in their interpretations of the significance of the birth of children to a couple. The Kimam do not appreciably restrict a woman's option to have a variety of sexual or reproductive partners. Caring for a child is of primary importance in establishing parenthood. Emphasis on social bonds allows for more flexibility in the kinds of ties that can link a couple, their children, and their close consanguineal relatives. Adoptive exchanges bind them together in a network of social cooperation.

The Kenuzi severely restrict a woman's sexual relations to marriage. A man's claim to paternity depends upon his marriage to the woman who bears his children. This may explain why it is difficult for a woman to remarry if she has young children. Her new husband does not have to accept them, because they are not *his* children (Herzog 1957: 96).

The Kenuzi desire descendants to perpetuate their kinship group. The Kimam desire children to set up links with their kinsmen and to have laborers. The Kimam system of exchange does not collapse if a man has a barren wife; in fact, sterility provides an occasion for setting up exchanges by adoption. Although there is an emphasis on parent/child links among both Kenuzi and Kimam, the focus on each component differs. A Kenuzi child derives his status from his father. A Kimam father reinforces his own position by giving his children in adoption to the people with whom he wishes to establish cooperative ties.


## The Relevance of Kinship

The Kenuzi and the Kimam illustrate the restrictive and permissive extremes of the model that relates the sexual and reproductive cycles. Although people in both groups desire children, they differ dramatically in their interpretation of parenthood. The restrictive Kenuzi place more emphasis on establishing a physiological basis for parenthood, particularly fatherhood. The more permissive Kimam broaden the definition of parenthood to mean the people who care for a child, not those who physically conceived or gave birth to the offspring. In technical terms, the Kenuzi give primary attention to the role of the genitor and genetrix, the man and woman who conceived the child — the biological parents. The Kimam prefer to stress the roles of pater and mater, the socially acknowledged roles of father and mother — the social parents. The Kenuzi equate the genitor with the pater and the genetrix with the mater; the Kimam do not assume that they will coincide.

Why is the nature of parenthood such an important focus of the relationship between the sexual and reproductive cycles? What is so crucial about being able to specify who the father and mother of a child are? Why do groups go to such lengths to reinforce these ties? These questions are basic to considerations of how sex relates to reproduction in human societies.

One of the main anthropological frameworks for dealing with the relationship between intercourse, reproduction, and parenthood has been kinship. Kinship translates into a variety of social institutions: marriage, the family, and kinship groups. Fox thinks that "kinship and marriage are about the basic facts of life" (Fox 1974: 27), i.e., birth, intercourse, and death. Intercourse provides the basis for a relationship between mates that establishes the groundwork for marriage and parenthood. Death leaves a gap in the social group, which the birth of a child can fill. Birth also sets up one of the most basic social bonds, the mother/child bond. The link between parenthood and birth becomes the foundation for providing an heir for a position in the social group — a means of replacing the members who have died or who can no longer function in an adequate way. Kinship deals with what humans do with the bonds that arise from mating, birth, and childrearing; it also includes the rationale behind the behavior, as well as its consequences. An "actual or putative genetic connexion, according to the local definition of 'genetic' or 'consanguineous,' is usually the basis of kinship relations" (Fox 1974: 34).

According to Fox, another human element of kinship is the classification of kin. There is no known human group that does not classify kin (Fox 1980: 18). Part of our human heritage is the ability to balance alternatives, make choices, classify, and generate rules about our behavior. These abilities stem from increased brain development and probably precede the beginning of kinship systems. The difference between humans and other animals lies in the human ability to make choices about the ties that arise from the basic processes of life.

Like other aspects of our lives, a number of alternatives are open to us in deciding whom we will include as our kin. In cognatic systems, people are related to each other through both male and female links. For example, in American society kin include people tied to us through our mothers and our fathers. Other societies limit the range of people whom they consider kin by paying attention to the gender of the persons through whom they establish their ties. Unilineal kinship systems, e.g., patrilineal and matrilineal systems, trace kinship links through either the male or the female line.

Groups use these major principles of reckoning kinship in a variety of ways. They may become the basis for forming local groups, deciding political succession, determining inheritance, and choosing marriage partners. They are the foundation of social life in many societies and guide people's interactions with each other. Therefore, it is not surprising that anthropologists have also interpreted many aspects of the sexual and reproductive cycles in terms of kinship organization. If kinship has such a profound influence on social life, it is also likely to shape the character of sexual and reproductive relationships. How?

Unilineal kinship systems would seem to be most directly concerned with the organization of sexual and reproductive relationships. Gender and reproduction are essential ingredients in the definition of unilineal kinship systems. Kinship is based on descent in a line from a common ancestor or ancestress. Reproduction creates more kinsmen, and the parent/child bond defines their relationship as kin. When societies form descent groups on the basis of unilineal kinship, reproduction becomes the major way in which they recruit members. Gender limits a person's inclusion in the kinship system as well as descent group membership.

There are two main types of unilineal systems — patrilineal and matrilineal. All of those people who can trace their descent from a common ancestor in the male line are patrilineal kin; those who can trace their descent from a common ancestress in the female line are matrilineal kin. The birth of descendants is important to both types of unilineal systems. However, patrilineal and matrilineal systems differ in the significance that each places on gender in continuing the line of descent. Patrilineal systems stress the importance of male links, while matrilineal systems focus on female links. Does the cultural emphasis on males and females in the kinship system affect the society's evaluation of the reproductive roles of males and females?

*Cultural Expressions of Parenthood*
*in Unilineal Systems*

Patrilineal systems have certain problems in evaluating a woman's reproductive role that matrilineal systems do not have. Luschinsky's study of the people of Uttar Pradesh (63) in India stimulated her to think about the dilemma that patrilineal systems face:

> . . . Motherhood cannot be ignored in a society which places great emphasis on the importance of the male. Mothers bring baby boys into the world and nurture them during the early years. Women can be viewed in two ways, as mothers upon whose cooperation the patriarchal system depends and as women who must be regarded as inferior if the system is to maintain its intrinsic character [Luschinsky 1969: 759].

In other words, patrilineal systems need to reconcile their cultural emphasis on males with the vital reproductive role that females play in giving birth to new members of the system.

One way of achieving this aim is to elevate the status of motherhood. Praise of motherhood is ultimately beneficial to the patrilineal system, because it may motivate a woman to desire children. The Egyptians (43) of Silwa village illustrate this alternative.

Hamed Ammar, a native of Silwa, acknowledges that the foundation of a patrilineal system is based on having children (Ammar 1954: 65). He emphasizes how much women want children by pointing out that they try to induce pregnancy in a variety of ways. He praises a woman's role as a mother by commenting that "a child is more valuable to her than her jewels" (Ammar 1954: 90). Her husband supports her reproductive role by giving her gifts and attention during her pregnancy (Ammar 1954: 87). She remains the center of attention for a period of time after she gives birth (Ammar 1954: 93). In addition, a woman gains status by having children, especially boys (Ammar 1954: 94).

Although the Egyptians clearly value and encourage motherhood, they do not similarly praise a woman's capacity to carry and deliver a child. Ammar reveals a low opinion of a woman's reproductive capacity when he writes that "even dogs, after all, have brought forth offspring"

(Ammar 1954: 100). Therefore, an emphasis on motherhood does not necessarily parallel a generally high evaluation of women. If a "proper woman is the one who is an envelope for conception" (Ammar 1954: 94), then the group culturally defines the importance of women primarily in terms of their reproductive role, which will benefit the patrilineal system. Culturally equating motherhood with womanhood acknowledges a woman's value to a patrilineal system while retaining an overall emphasis on males.

Another way in which patrilineal systems can deal with a woman's reproductive role is to downgrade it in conformity with a general view that women are inferior to men. Although this alternative may preserve an emphasis on males that is consistent with the patrilineal principle, it is a riskier means of encouraging reproduction. It could promote such hostile feelings in a woman that she might choose to abort her unborn child or kill her infant. However, it could be workable, if the controls over women were so strong that a woman would find it difficult to escape her reproductive role. The Fijians (102) provide an example of a society that has adopted this tenuous alternative.

The dominant role that Fijian men play in war provides an adequate justification for stressing the importance of males. War also provides a rationale for devaluing women. Because a woman cannot fight in battle, she is regarded as useless (Williams 1884: 155). Therefore, female infanticide occurs frequently. The devaluation of females may account for the treatment that a Fijian woman can expect to receive throughout her life. Wililiams says that "in youth, she is the victim of lust, and in old age, of brutality" (Williams 1884: 145). Even motherhood provides no respite from her degradation. One of the first lessons that a male child learns is to strike his mother. If he did not, it "begat fear lest the child should grow up to be a coward" (Williams 1884: 152).

These pervasive attitudes of male dominance have destructive reproductive consequences. Williams reports that it is common for women to hate their husbands (Williams 1884: 175). Women practice a rudimentary form of contraception in order to avoid pregnancy, and they frequently perform abortions because they do not desire children. Infanticide is also frequent. Male social pressure encourages the elimination of female babies, but women also kill their male infants, because they do not want them. In sum, the Fijians elevate the importance of manhood but lower that of womanhood, including motherhood. The consequences are that women hate their husbands and destroy the fruits of their reproduction. In the end, it seems to be a rather unsatisfactory way to produce males to continue the patrilineal system.

Unlike patrilineal systems, matrilineal ones do not have to reconcile an emphasis on males with a woman's reproductive role within the system. The matrilineal emphasis on descent through females gives more scope for a positive evaluation of motherhood and womanhood. For example, the Garo (69) say that a "woman is like earth that nourishes the seed" (Burling 1963: 99). They believe that her role in producing a child is so important that the father contributes no aspect of a baby's body, soul, or social affiliation (Burling 1963: 99). The Huron (144) regard women as more valuable than men because they produce children. They justify this evaluation by noting the contribution of women: "As they peopled the country, they were more valuable" (Tooker 1964: 52). The Saramacca (165) also express a high evaluation of women. "Women, it is said, are like hearthstones, men like axe handles. Once placed in a house, a set of clay hearthstones may never be moved; they endure. But an axe handle is made to travel, and once worn out from use, it is discarded on the spot; it leaves no traces" (Price 1971: 55). The Saramacca dominate their art motifs with sexual symbols, e.g., snakes and the vulva (Kahn 1931: 195). In addition, they participate in a fertility cult which personifies the earth as an earth mother, the giver of fertility (Herskovits and Herskovits 1934: 74).

In sum, the cultural emphasis on males or females that is implied by unilineal principles may influence the interpretation given to a woman's reproductive role. Patrilineal systems may attempt to reconcile her role with an emphasis on males. One way is to acknowledge a woman's importance as a mother and thus motivate her to bear children for the group. Another way is to consistently emphasize males and downgrade the importance of females, regardless of whether or not they bear children. The first alternative has more beneficial reproductive consequences to the group than the second one has. Matrilineal systems do not face the same dilemma that faces the patrilineal ones. Since people trace descent in the female line, they can extend the high evaluation of a woman's reproductive role beyond her value as a mother; they can esteem her as a woman.

### Sexual Restrictions, Reproductive Relationships, and Unilinearity

The dilemma that patrilineal systems face concerning the reproductive role of women does not end with an adjustment in their cultural interpretations of women. They have to deal with the practical problem of finding wives who will reproduce for their group, even though they are not members of it. Since they trace descent in the male line, the father/son tie becomes a central link in the kinship system. Therefore, establishing paternity takes on added significance. A father's investment of resources in his children, especially his sons, depends upon his knowledge that they are definitely his descendants. The perpetuation of the kinship system, as well as the rights gained by membership in descent groups, both center on confidence about who a child's parents are.

One way of dealing with this problem is to restrict the sexual relations and reproductive potential of the women. Such restrictions provide a basis for bolstering a man's confidence that the children his wife bears are his own. At a minimum, his wife is important to him as the mother of his children. Women nurture children both before and after birth, especially during breastfeeding. Therefore, a man who is interested in the survival of his descendants has a substantial interest in maintaining his relationship with his wife and in preserving the mother/child bond long enough for his child to exist independently of her. Restricting the wife's reproductive potential to himself or his patrilineal kin helps to ensure that the patrilineal system controls enough women to perpetuate itself. Difficult divorce and remarriage, as well as inheritance of widows by patrilineal kin, also help to preserve the bond between a woman, her husband, and her husband's patrilineal kin.

In contrast, systems that stress descent through females would be much less interested in affirming a child's paternity. Recognition of maternity is enough to maintain the link between mother and child that defines matrilineal kinship. Furthermore, a man's contribution to reproduction is relatively brief, compared to a woman's. As long as a woman becomes pregnant, she can assure the perpetuation of her line. As Schneider points out, "matrilineal descent groups do not require the statuses of father and husband. The statuses of mother and wife, on the other hand, are indispensable to patrilineal systems" (Schneider 1974: 14).

In sum, it seems clear that men in patrilineal systems would be more concerned than those in matrilineal systems with keeping their wives and establishing paternity. Therefore, I would expect that they would also be more concerned with restricting a woman's sexual and reproductive relationships as a way of establishing a firm link between a man and his descendants. Women in matrilineal systems would be less concerned with retaining their husbands for reproductive purposes, and men would be less concerned about paternity, because they owe kinship responsibilities to their sisters' children, not their own. Therefore, men would be less likely to confine the sexual relations or the reproductive potential of women.

My data confirm these hypotheses. Table 5.6 presents a summary of the findings.

Table 5.6 *Association of the Degree of Sexual Restrictiveness of Women and Confinement of Their Reproductive Potential with Type of Unilineal System*

| | | Type of Unilineal System | | |
| --- | --- | --- | --- | --- |
| | | Matrilineal | Patrilineal | |
| *Sexual Restrictiveness* | High, Medium | 1 | 11 | 12 |
| *and Confinement of* | | | | |
| *Reproductive Potential* | Low | 6 | 3 | 9 |
| | | 7 | 14 | 21 = N |

Fisher's exact test p = .0087

The table shows that patrilineal systems restrict a woman's sexual relations and confine her reproductive potential to one man significantly more often than do matrilineal systems. Matrilineal systems show the reverse of this trend: low confinement of a woman's sexual and reproductive relationships to one man.

## The Relevance of Residence

The influence of kinship systems on sociocultural aspects of the sexual and reproductive cycles seems convincing as long as we confine our attention to unilineal systems. Not only do matrilineality and patrilineality affect the cultural interpretation of womanhood and a woman's reproductive role but they also are significantly associated with different extremes of the model of coincidence of sexual and reproductive relationships.

However, unilinearity is only a partial answer to the question of why social confirmation of parenthood, particularly paternity, is more important in some societies than in others. Nonunilineal systems also rely upon the recognition of parent/child links to decide whom to classify as kin, but they may include descendants of both the mother and the father in each generation. If, as Fox suggests, kinship is concerned with the ties that revolve around mating, childbearing, and childrearing, then nonunilineal systems would also have an important stake in establishing parenthood. However, an ancestor's gender would not limit the descendants who are included as kin. If kinship generally shapes the nature of sexual and reproductive relationships, I would expect that nonunilineal systems would vary more in how they establish parenthood than either patrilineal or matrilineal systems. Emphasis on parenthood would shift according to the importance and function of kin ties in the society. Patrilineal systems are generally restrictive, while matrilineal systems are generally permissive. I would expect that non-unilineal systems would be, at most, moderately restrictive in the way that they deal with sexual and reproductive relationships. This is *not* the case, however.

Nonunilineal kinship systems seem to have more in common with patrilineal systems than with matrilineal or lineal systems alone. In fact, the contrast between patrilineal/nonunilineal systems and matrilineal ones in regard to sexual and reproductive restrictions is stronger and more significant than the one between patrilineal and matrilineal systems alone. Table 5.7 shows the association.

Table 5.7 *Association of Sexual and Reproductive Restrictions with Types of Kinship Systems*

*Type of Kinship System*

|  |  | Patrilineal, Nonunilineal | Matrilineal |  |
|---|---|---|---|---|
| *Sexual Restrictiveness and Confinement of Reproductive Potential* | High, Medium | 19 | 1 | 20 |
| | Low | 6 | 6 | 12 |
| | | 25 | 7 | 32 = N |

Fisher's exact test p = .0055

Why isn't there more variation in the ways in which nonunilineal systems restrict sexual and reproductive relationships? Nonunilineal systems restrict sexual and reproductive relationships (75% of 12 nonunilineal societies) almost as much as patrilineal ones (79% of 14 patrilineal societies). As I have suggested before, such restrictions effectively establish a basis for social recognition of paternity. Patrilineal and nonunilineal systems share a cultural emphasis on father/child ties. However, the reason for the emphasis is not as clear in the nonunilineal systems as it is in the patrilineal ones. Patrilineal societies systematically classify kin on the basis of descent links through males alone. Nonunilineal systems can include descendants of both males and females on both sides of the family. While links through males are relevant, they are not the only game in town. The question remains. Why do nonunilineal systems seem to stress paternity?

I have phrased the question in terms of kinship systems. Perhaps a rephrasing of the question would help. It is possible that the cart is before the horse. Although kinship principles may pervade many of the activities in our lives, other principles of behavior also wield considerable influence over us. Kinship systems provide a basis for group formation; much of the power of kinship is expressed in a group context. If we widen our discussion to include other principles of group formation, we can ask another question. Are there any other principles of group formation that would require emphasis on paternity and, thus, limitation on a woman's sexual and reproductive relationships? Principles of post-marital residence offer one possibility.

The parent/child tie is relevant in some types of residence pattern but not in others. When a man and his wife move near or with the husband's father after marriage, they reside patrilocally. When a bride and groom move near or with the wife's mother after marriage, they reside matrilocally. Neolocal residence means that the couple establishes a new place to live, independent of the location of either of their parents. Patrilocality results in a clustering of related males in a given locality, while matrilocality groups related females. Neolocality disperses related people. If we shift our focus from kinship systems to residence patterns, we find another reason that the parent/child bond is important; it regulates where a person will live after marriage. Paternity would be most important in patrilocal groups, because it is the only residence pattern whereby an individual's postmarital residence depends upon where the persons's father lives. In addition, patrilocal residence means that the raw materials for community organization consists of clusters of related males.

I have argued that establishing paternity is a significant aspect of the restrictions on sexual and reproductive relationships. Since patrilocal groups are formed on the basis of paternal links, I would expect that patrilocal groups would restrict sexual and reproductive relations, while nonpatrilocal groups would not. Table 5.8 shows the relationship between these variables.

Table 5.8 *Association between Residence and Restriction of a Woman's Sexual and Reproductive Relationships*

|  |  | Residence | | |
|---|---|---|---|---|
|  |  | Patrilocal | Other | |
| *Sexual Restriction and Confinement of Reproductive Potential* | Medium, High | 17 | 4 | 21 |
|  | Low | 4 | 8 | 12 |
|  |  | 21 | 12 | 33 = N |

Fisher's exact test p = .004

The table shows that patrilocality is significantly related to restrictions on a woman's sexual and reproductive relationships. In addition, it is more strongly related to these restrictions than is patrilineality alone. Therefore, residence may be a productive key to understanding why some societies are "permissive" and others are "restrictive."

Residence cross-cuts kinship systems to provide a broader basis for understanding variability in the restrictions that apply to sexual and reproductive relationships. Patrilineal systems are usually patrilocal (93% of 75 patrilineal societies), and matrilineal ones are usually matrilocal (69% of 26 societies) (Murdock and Wilson 1972). However, non-unilineal systems are not that closely allied with one type of residence pattern; they may be patrilocal, matrilocal, neolocal, or ambilocal (i.e., providing a choice of residence near the parents of either spouse). Focusing on residence allows us to consider similarities between groups whose modes of classifying kin are not the same. For example, patrilocality may be associated with patrilineal, nonunilineal, or even matrilineal kinship systems.

An emphasis on residence shifts us from the realm of cultural principles of kinship classification to the realities of social life. Patrilocal residence localizes male kin and channels the types of cooperation and conflict that are likely to result. This suggests that the nature of interaction *among* males may be another reason why strict rules apply to the sexual and reproductive relationships of men and women in these groups.

A number of problems can occur when related males are in close association with each other. Males generally have the authority (the legitimate right to control the actions of others) in groups. Disputes may arise if the group does not specify when and how males may have access to authority. Conflict also can erupt over the distribution of resources. Who can have which animals, movable property, or rights over land? A third area of potential conflict is access to women. How can a man stay on good terms with the men in his community, yet compete with them for women whom he wants to be his sexual partners and mates?

Otterbein and Otterbein (1965) picture life in patrilocal communities as being far from harmonious. Conflict filters through several levels of social organization. Men frequently feud with each other within the local community. Even though they belong to the same society, individual communities may go to war against each other. Men have to adjust their relationships not only with other men but also with women. How can they cut down on sources of potential conflict and maintain a somewhat cooperative, effective social life?

One way of reducing dissension is to establish rules that assure men that they will eventually have some of the things they want — authority, women, and resources. The price they pay for their security is obedience to the elder generation and a delay in attaining their personal goals. How do the elders motivate young men to obey their rules and delay gratification of their desires? Initiation ceremonies could serve this purpose. In the chapter on the sexual cycle, I went to great lengths to show the psychological impact that initiation ceremonies have on the initiates. These ceremonies interpret and channel the young men's budding sexuality in socially acceptable terms. They impress upon the initiates the authority that their elders wield over them, but they also stress their common bond as men. Although their theoretical perspectives differ, Young, Cohen, and Whiting all agree that male initiation ceremonies aid men in affirming their masculine identity and social solidarity.

If male initiation ceremonies aid in affirming solidarity between men, I would expect that they would occur more often in patrilocal societies. I combined Schlegel and Barry's (1979) data on the extent of participation in male initiation ceremonies with Murdock and Wilson's (1972) data on residence patterns to test his hypothesis. I found that there is a significant association between patrilocality and participation of the local community or a large group of people in initiation ceremonies for men. Table 5.9 presents the results.

Table 5.9 *Association of Residence and Extensive Social Participation in Male Initiation Ceremonies*

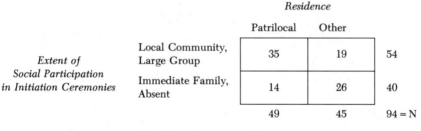

|  |  | Patrilocal | Other |  |
|---|---|---|---|---|
| *Extent of Social Participation in Initiation Ceremonies* | Local Community, Large Group | 35 | 19 | 54 |
|  | Immediate Family, Absent | 14 | 26 | 40 |
|  |  | 49 | 45 | 94 = N |

$X^2 = 8.5$; 1 df; sig. $= <.005$

Schlegel and Barry remark that male initiation ceremonies occur most often in societies within a middle range of social development. Gender is an important basis of social classification, and the basis for local power is fluid (Schlegel and Barry 1980: 709). Men create their own networks of followers by fathering children to be their subordinates.

Another way in which patrilocal groups can develop some coherence is to organize their groups around a principle of patrilineal descent. Localized males would have several bonds to unite them — kinship, residence, and gender. They could then use these ties to organize political, religious, or economic activities in the community. Rules of inheritance and principles for succession to political office could help to stifle competition between related males. The patrilineal principle emerges as one way of coping with conflict between males.

According to Divale (1975), many wars in patrilocal communities arise from disputes over women. Therefore, regulation of access to women plays an essential role in maintaining cooperation in the community. I have already shown that patrilocality is highly associated with sexual restriction and confinement of a woman's reproductive potential. In other words, the group generally prohibits a woman from having a variety of sexual and reproductive relationships. If a widow can remarry, the man she marries is often specified as having to be a patrilineal kinsman of the deceased. These rules can serve to cut down on hostility between men and can provide them with some security in the knowledge that they will have children, who will be subordinate to them in the future.

However, restrictions on sexual and reproductive relationships do not apply only to women. They are only half of the equation. If part of the problem in patrilocal communities is the relationship between men, then restrictions may also apply to their sexual and reproductive relationships. This idea is consistent with my findings that (1) the degree of sexual restrictiveness that applies to females is significantly associated with the degree that applies to males, and (2) there is a significant association between the confinement of men's and women's reproductive potential. Exceptions to both of these findings lay in the direction of giving males more flexibility to form sexual and reproductive relationships.

Patrilocal societies represent a specification of the general trends. Patrilocal societies are most likely to restrict a man's sexual relations as much as a woman's (67% of 9 societies where restriction is high for both) or to restrict a woman's sexual relations but allow a man to have a variety of them (83% of 12 societies where there is a double standard). The standards are stiffer in patrilocal societies concerning the variety of reproductive partners males and females are allowed to have. In patrilocal societies, both men and women are likely to confine their reproductive potential to one partner (85% of 13 societies where both males and females have high restriction on reproductive partners), although men may be less subject to these constraints than women (67% of 6 societies where women are subject to high confinement but men are not).

In patrilocal groups, the regulation of a male's reproductive relationships seems more important than the constriction of his sexual liaisons. Other details of life in patrilocal groups support this idea. Although most societies allow both the man and the woman some say in whom they will marry, patrilocal groups are more likely to deprive them of this choice. Tables 5.10 and 5.11 show the relationship between residence and consent to marry.

Table 5.10 *Association between Residence and a Woman's Consent to Marry*

*Degree of Consent*

|  |  | None | Consulted, Necessary |  |
|---|---|---|---|---|
|  | Patrilocal | 14 | 20 | 34 |
| Residence |  |  |  |  |
|  | Other | 2 | 21 | 23 |
|  |  | 16 | 41 | 57 = N |

$X^2 = 5.65$; 1 df; sig. = < .02

Table 5.11 *Association between Residence and a Man's Consent to Marry*

*Degree of Consent*

|  |  | None | Consulted, Necessary |  |
|---|---|---|---|---|
|  | Patrilocal | 9 | 21 | 30 |
| Residence |  |  |  |  |
|  | Other | 0 | 23 | 23 |
|  |  | 9 | 44 | 53 = N |

$X^2 = 6.32$; 1 df; sig. = < .02

By restricting the marital choices of the young, the elder generation can retain some control over the kinds of reproductive relationships that are likely to occur in the group. The influence of the group is even more dramatic in patrilineages, in which restrictions on consent to marry are greater than for patrilocal groups in general.

Polygyny is another way in which the elder generation of males can organize the reproductive relationships of men. The elders can foster the expectation that a man can have more than one mate when he is older and has acquired the proper resources. However, polygyny in patrilocal societies seems to create more conflict than it solves. There is no significant relationship between polygyny and patrilocality, but there is a strong link between patrilineal systems and polygyny ($X^2 = 7.63$, 1 df, sig. $= < .01$, N $= 62$). As I suggested earlier, the formation of patrilineal groups may be a way of developing solidarity among a group of related males. All patrilocal societies do not have the benefit of these additional ties. Therefore, the presence of polygyny is likely to vary among patrilocal groups. Where there are few other stabilizing ties, polygyny is a risky situation. It can create resentment and the kind of disputes that divide men who have more than one wife from those who do not. Restriction of a man's reproductive choices is a safer solution if the group is not well integrated.

Bride-price is another mechanism that elders can use to keep young men in line and to regulate access to mates. A young man depends upon his relatives to aid him in acquiring enough economic resources to have a wife. It would be difficult for him to amass enough resources on his own. Therefore, elders can limit a man's marriage options if he does not conform to the standards that the older generation lays down for him.

In sum, the presence of patrilocality is another reason why groups may stress paternity. It also draws attention to the problems that men face when they interact with each other and compete for positions of authority, and for resources and women. They can cope with their rivalry by adopting a number of strategies to reduce the intensity of competition. Most of these revolve around organizing males in such a way that they have access to what they want in a specific sequence. Elders retain their authority, resources, and women, and may then relinquish them to younger men at an appropriate time.

## The Relevance of Environment

An analysis of areal distributions provides another approach to understanding why there is so much variation in the rules that apply to the sexual and reproductive relationships of men and women. If restrictive or permissive societies cluster by region, there may well be environmental factors that contribute to the types of rules they have.

The Circum-Mediterranean area stands out as a particularly restric-

tive region. Among the strictures characteristic of the area are strong
prohibitions against premarital and extramarital sex, difficulty in obtaining a divorce, barrenness as the primary grounds a husband uses for
divorcing his wife, formidable obstacles to remarriage after divorce or
widowhood, and punitive alternatives to barrenness. The main rights
that a woman transfers to her husband at marriage are sexual access and
rights over her children. Circum-Mediterranean societies seldom seek a
prospective bride's consent in contracting marriage. They particularly
want women to have male children. Contraception is rarely used.

Jane Schneider introduces a persuasive interpretation of these facts.
She connects the Mediterranean emphasis on honor, shame, and virginity to conflict among groups over strategic resources. She hypothesizes
that the cultural unity of the Mediterranean area "derives from a particular set of ecological resources which have interacted to produce the
codes" of honor, shame, and virginity (Schneider 1971: 2).

Competition for similar resources by pastoralists and agriculturalists
in the same area creates conflicts within and between groups (Schneider
1971: 3). Therefore, political integration is difficult to maintain. The
lack of cohesion filters down to kinship organization. The family or
lineage is unstable and has no long-term, indivisible, economic interests. The codes of honor and shame provide a means of social control in
the absence of more explicit forms of political organization.

Family name can provide a focus of honor. Since the men of the
family share an interest in the women who are related to them in
determinate ways, "the sanctity of virgins plays a crucial role in holding
together the few corporate groups of males which occur in many traditional Mediterranean societies" (Schneider 1971: 18, 22). The sense of
shame that accompanies the violation of honor further reinforces the
group's feeling of unity. The regulation of a woman's sexual relationships and the confinement of her reproductive potential to one man or
family are interpreted as both the basis for and the expression of the
males' effectiveness as a group. The desire for male children stems from
the importance of males as a protective force for the group and its
resources (Schneider 1971: 10).

The cooperation of both males and females is essential to maintaining
the codes of honor and shame. Men identify their honor with the sexual
restraint of their women; violation of a woman is tantamount to challenging the integrity of the group. Men derive a sense of cultural unity
and social cohesion from the codes. What do women gain from this
arrangement? Why do they cooperate with men by rigidly confining the
scope of their sexual and reproductive relationships?

Schneider notes that the woman's sense of shame, the reciprocal of the man's sense of honor, is extremely intense in this area. It "defends or enhances patrimonies of families" and aids in defining the family as a corporate group (Schneider 1971: 21). A woman may feel quite proud of her ability to exhibit "shame." However, my data suggest that more practical considerations underlie a woman's compliance with such extreme restrictions on her behavior.

A woman faces harsh consequences if she does not conform to the canons of "shame." Circum-Mediterranean societies impose some of the most severe punishments for violation of premarital and extramarital restrictions. For example, they punish extramarital sex with divorce or death (70% of 10 Circum-Mediterranean societies). Two of the three remaining societies that punish a woman moderately for extramarital liaisons retain the option of divorcing or killing her for it. This means that it is rare that a woman cannot be divorced or killed for extramarital sex (10% of 10 societies) in the Circum-Mediterranean societies in my sample. The severity of the punishment is matched only by the swiftness with which it can be enacted. In most of these societies, the husband punishes his wife for extramarital affairs (79% of 9 societies). A woman seldom has time to deliberate with her husband about the harsh consequences of her actions.

A woman also faces extreme punishment if she does not fulfill expectations about her reproductive capabilities. These expectations specify not only that she should give birth to children but also that she should have sons (82% of 11 societies). If she does not live up to these requirements, her husband can divorce her for her "failure" (90% of 10 societies).

In sum, threats of divorce or death provide one set of reasons why a woman would be hesitant to cross the boundaries of "honor" or refuse to have children. However, it is somewhat puzzling that women would perceive divorce as such a catastrophe. It would seem that the termination of marriage could be an attractive alternative to the pressures of severe restrictions. Divorce may become a threat rather than an alluring route of escape, however, if it means that a woman loses economic support.

This suggests another reason why women adhere to the restrictions placed on their sexual and reproductive relationships. They do not want to forfeit the economic advantages that their husbands provide. This reasoning is even more plausible for the Circum-Mediterranean area when we consider a woman's role in subsistence. In Circum-Mediterranean societies, a woman's contribution to subsistence relative to a man's is lowest in comparison with all other world areas. Therefore, if a woman's husband divorces her, her consequent economic deprivation would be of major proportions. This economic loss could overshadow a woman's temptation to violate the regulations placed upon her sexual or reproductive relationships.

Most of the Circum-Mediterranean societies in my sample are patrilineal and patrilocal. However, corporate group organization is shallow and is ridden with rivalry and fragmentation. The social identification of a man with his father is one basis on which group cooperation can rest. The integrity of a woman's sexual and reproductive behavior can become another basis for solidarity. This suggests that the societies most likely to severely restrict sexual and reproductive relationships base their solidarity on the identification of a few men with each other, rather than with a large, corporate group organization. This also means that well-organized patrilineal systems are more likely to exhibit moderate rather than extreme restrictions over sexual and reproductive relationships.

## The Relevance of Reproductive Strategies

Kinship, residence, and environment all contribute to an understanding of the variations that I have found in patterns of sexual and reproductive relationships. Each taps larger domains of human life, which intersect with the system of human sexuality: the cultural (kinship), the social (residence), and the ecological (environment). If we broaden our perspective even more, we can consider how the cross-cultural patterns relate to reproductive strategies. By so doing, we come full circle and ask once again: What is "human" about human sexuality? With both cross-cultural and cross-species evidence available, we have more grounds on which to evaluate our speculations.

As I pointed out in the chapter on our human heritage, humans share a lot of characteristics with other species in the animal kingdom. It is not surprising that we also find an overlap with the reproductive strategies that male and female animals use. Daly and Wilson (1978) succinctly characterize the essence of these strategies as the "reluctant female" and the "ardent male." Although males and females both contribute to the conception of their offspring, their parental investments in them differ. Parental investment is "any investment by the parent in the individual offspring that increases the offspring's chance of surviving at the cost of the parent's ability to invest in other offspring" (Trivers 1972). The female reproductive strategy concentrates on the nurture of relatively few offspring. She invests her time and energy in assuring the survival of the offspring she already has. A male's investment is different. His reproductive strategy focuses on maximizing his reproductive potential by competing with other males for an opportunity to mate. Pregnancy, birth, lactation, and postnatal care all direct a woman's attention toward the intensive care of her offspring. A man's physical link with his progeny is neither as immediate nor as lasting as a woman's bond. He can gauge his reproductive success by the number of offspring he produces. A woman gauges hers by the number of offspring she nurtures to survival. A male is "ardent" because he potentially increases his reproductive success with each sexual encounter. A female is "reluctant" to engage ardently in sexual encounters without first selecting a mate who seems suitable to care for the offspring they might have. She risks wasting her reproductive resources and nurture on an unsuitable mate.

Therefore, reproductive strategies provide a more general answer to the question of why establishing paternity is important in human societies. Females can enhance their reproductive success by attracting males who will provide for the well-being of their children. However, males do not benefit from this arrangement unless they are sure that the children they invest in are their own. Men are particularly concerned, therefore, with assuring the paternity of their children. Infidelity could pose a major threat to a man's parental investment. It could arouse the suspicion that his mate's children are not his own and that he is supporting another man's child. Accordingly, a man tries to establish rules that confine a woman's sexual activities to the reproductive relationship he has with her; whereas a woman trades sexual variety for the assurance that her mate will care for her offspring.

Because of the close physical bond between a woman and her child, maternity is not difficult to establish. A man does not cast doubt upon his wife's maternal status when he engages in other sexual relationships. Consequently, sexual restrictions may apply less stringently to men than to women, because they are not needed to establish a woman's parenthood. Although my data show that social rules generally restrict the sexual relationships of men and women to a similar degree, there are quite a few exceptions, all of which lie in the direction of allowing men to engage in sexual relationships when women do not have the same privilege. This double standard fits with Daly and Wilson's view that males are likely to be more ardent in seeking sexual opportunities, in order to enhance their reproductive success.

However, despite strict rules against it, women also engage in extramarital affairs. Broude (1980) argues that a woman may aid her own reproductive success by doing so. She may marry early to maximize the number of children she can bear. And even though she selects a less-than-ideal mate in the process, she has some assurance that a male will invest in her offspring. She may then have affairs with men who are improvements over her husband and thereby enhance the genetic contribution that a male makes to her children — if she is not caught, or if she leaves her husband and marries the better-endowed man.

Daly and Wilson provide a large array of other examples, which show the consistency between the organization of human societies and reproductive strategies. They enthusiastically conclude that "there is an ultimate rationale underlying the cross-culturally consistent behavior and attitudes of men and women, and it is the same strategic rationale that applies to all reproducing organisms" (Daly and Wilson 1978: 310).

Symons takes up the banner of this interpretation, carries it throughout his book *The Evolution of Human Sexuality* (1979), and waves it at us with a vigorous flurry by emphasizing its application to psychological differences between males and females. He says that "enormous differences in minimum parental investment and in reproductive opportunities and constraints explain why *Homo sapiens*, a species with only moderate sex differences in structure, exhibits profound sex differences in psyche" (Symons 1979: 27). It is possible, therefore, that "uniformities of mind" may underlie the variety of human sexual behavior and custom.

Some of the behaviors that Symons highlights as expressions of "uniformities of mind" are compatible with the findings of this study: males involve themselves in polygamy more than females, respond in a jealous manner more often than females, and are likely to have the opportunity to have intercourse with a greater variety of partners. However, it is a big leap from documenting the occurrence of these behaviors to explaining them as "wired-in" sex differences in inclination, attitude, and desire. It is difficult to disentangle the multiple impacts of culture, society, physical environment, and physiology on psychological functioning in order to make even limited claims about the way the mind works. What we do know is that social, cultural, and psychological dimensions of behavior *all* involve learning, upon which humans rely more heavily for their adaptations than any other animals. Consequently, our reproductive strategies are likely to diverge from those of other animals in some rather important ways, despite some broad similarities.

The fact that humans have longer dependency periods than those of other animals means that an "ardent" male has to do more than inseminate a woman to ensure his reproductive success. He, too, has to become involved in the parenting process, at least to the extent of making sure that the woman he impregnates and her offspring can survive. Consequently, a claim to paternity becomes important. Paternity is fathering — a social behavior — not merely being a genitor — a physical contributor to conception. The social implications of parenthood weigh heavily upon both males and females in the human species. Therefore, it is a bit simplistic to see a wide range of human social behavior as the expression of an "ardent" male and "reluctant" female theme.

For example, Symons says that men "incline" to polygyny. However, polygyny is a socially approved reproductive arrangement, which does not by any means occur in all societies and does not serve primarily as a sexual orgy for a male; it is misleading to regard multiple reproductive unions as a formal expression of males' desire for sexual variety. As I pointed out in Chapter Four, women often have the option to engage in several marriages, though not at the same time. Synchronic, polygynous marriages are a male mode of engaging in a variety of reproductive relationships. To concentrate on polygyny is to ignore the culturally approved ways by which women engage in variety. We can interpret these arrangements as a way of affirming the links between father, mother, and child. Polygyny is most likely to occur in a patrilineal context, in which regulation of competition for mates is necessary to maintain the cooperation of men with each other. Even within some polygynous contexts, females can remarry or divorce. Plural marriages are more likely to be a result of social and cultural factors than the consequence of a psychological "inclination" of males (or females) to engage in them.

Nevertheless, many of Symons' generalizations seem to make sense and are in accord with the behavior we see around us. This is not surprising, since Symons used *The Hite Report* (Hite 1976) and *My Secret Life* (Anonymous 1966) as guides to the diversity of human sexuality. Both of these books derive from a Western tradition and reflect the dynamics of sexuality to be found within our own culture, rather than those of all humans. Symons' findings are persuasive, because they seem natural to us; we grew up with the male-oriented assumptions upon which he based his conclusions. Given different assumptions, we might not be so ready to jump on his bandwagon and proclaim that we have discovered that the basis for sex differences is localized in our brains.

It is easier and perhaps more comfortable to reinforce traditional patterns of male/female relationships by veering in the direction of saying that biology is destiny. By so doing, we deny ourselves the complexity of thought and action that our human heritage has given us.

However, to dismiss Symons' book as a simplistic interpretation of complex differences would be unfair to his efforts and would blind us to the benefits of his approach. He rouses us out of our complacency by challenging acceptance of a dominant social science paradigm, i.e., the view that we are almost totally a product of learning.

Jo Durden-Smith and Diane de Simone, authors of *Sex and the Brain* (1983), discuss how entrenched the "new orthodoxy" or viewing people as products of their environment really is. Applied to sex differences, it assumes that (1) the mind and body are separate; (2) psychological states are products of mind; and (3) gender is learned, not inborn, and can be changed (Durden-Smith and de Simone, 1983: 37). The conclusions of Symons and of many sociobiologists fly in the face of these assumptions and violate many of our long-held assumptions about ourselves and our capacity to control and change ourselves and our world.

I do not think that it is necessary to replace our belief in the importance of learning with equally hearty support for a reliance on biology. The nature/nurture debate seems to rear its head in all such decisions. Why is it necessary to polarize our interpretations? Part of the reason may stem from our tradition of separating conceptually the mind and body and giving priority to the mind as the spiritual side of ourselves. Darwin's revolutionary finding that humans are subject to the principles of selection, as are other animals, reconnected us with the physicality of our existence. It also spurred our creativity to discover other ways in which we are different. We latched onto the fact that our brains are larger relative to our body size and more fully developed than those of other animals. We used this information to explain social differences and to account for the apparent gap between "civilized" and "primitive" peoples. When we discovered the enormous role of learning in shaping our behavior, we threw over biologically-based explanations. We then became "human" in proportion to the degree to which our minds controlled our bodies and our behavior. Current research on the brain, as reviewed in *Sex and the Brain* (Durden-Smith and de Simone 1983), holds out the promise of putting the pieces of the mind and body back together again. Sociobiologists encourage us to do the same thing. By concentrating on the reproductive functions of many kinds of behavior, they snap us back into an arena where our actions are connected to our survival, where our behavior is linked to our biology. How it is linked remains a major unanswered question.

### A Holistic Perspective

Throughout this book I have emphasized the importance of a holistic perspective toward human sexuality — one that includes the biological, cultural, social, and psychological dimensions of our behavior. Each section of this chapter has attempted to demonstrate the valuable contributions that the shared facets of human behavior make to under-standing varieties of sexual experience. The biological, social, cultural, and psychological aspects of the sexual and reproductive cycles overlap. A feedback between learning and biology is at the center of that over-lap. Such a view links us with other animals, but it does not mean that we are ruled by biology. It acknowledges an important facet of our behavior, which is linked to other components of a system of human sexuality.

The advantage of looking at the sexual and reproductive cycles as part of a system of human sexuality is that it allows us the flexibility to look at relationships between a wide variety of components. The sexual and reproductive cycles are the cycles of life. They begin before birth in intrauterine development, and they have consequences beyond the life of one individual. Many of the major changes in our lives involve stages in the sexual and reproductive cycles. Sociocultural factors can channel sexual and reproductive behavior so that they completely overlap, mod-erately coincide, or seem to have no link to each other at all. The fact that human groups can have so many options, balance alternatives, construct classifications, establish rules, and act on the basis of their creations accounts for the variety of sociocultural aspects that make up the sexual and reproductive cycles.

# Chapter Six
# An Application of the Models: Unraveling Dilemmas of Sexuality in American Society

According to the media, American society has experienced a sexual revolution. In *Sexual Behavior in the 1970s* (1975), Morton Hunt tries to measure the extent to which the revolution has occurred and to describe the attitudes and behavior that characterize it. Assuming its existence as an established fact, one portion of *The Cosmo Report* Wolfe (1981) summarizes readers' reactions to the revolution. In their recent book, *American Couples* (1983), Blumstein and Schwartz provide convincing evidence that the "American family has changed more in the last thirty years than in the previous two hundred and fifty" (Blumstein and Schwartz 1983: 25). In *The End of Sex* (1984), Leonard proposes how we might deal with sexuality *after* the sexual revolution. And the April 9, 1984, issue of *Time* magazine ran a cover story entitled "Sex in the '80s: The Revolution Is Over" (Leo 1984).

For some, the sexual revolution is revolting. For others, it is an expression of human potential. The dizzying bombardment of our sensibilities by books on sex, magazines that capitalize on interest in sexuality, television programs and movies that portray lovers in the heat of passion, and advertisements that play on sexual themes lead us to believe that "anything goes," that we are free from the past strictures that bound us. However, announcements that America has at last found the Holy Grail of sexual freedom are premature. Americans are experiencing conflict and ambivalence about sexuality; they are not sighing with relief that they are "free."

How are we to understand what is meant by the "sexual revolution"? The holistic approach to sexuality that is advocated in this book is one way to put contemporary dilemmas of sexuality in American society into perspective. Doing this involves taking two steps. The first is to describe the traditional sexual values and behavior of American culture in terms of their shared cultural, social, and biological features. The second step is to trace the changes that have occurred over time to transform the shared dimensions of the traditional pattern into the forms we see now. The link between these two steps is the contextualization of sexual patterns at specific points in time. By analyzing how they acquire new meaning and shed previous elements over time, we can derive a clearer understanding of the interplay between the social, cultural, and biological aspects of sexuality and hypothesize how they might impact on the lives of individuals within contemporary society. American patterns of sexuality can then be compared with those of other cultures. If we look at American culture as one type of system relative to many others, we can assess more precisely how restrictive or how permissive it is. The specific (historical) and the general (cross-cultural) contexts overlap, like the separate lenses of binoculars, to develop a view of sexuality in America, which has both focus and depth.

### The Making of a Tradition: Sexual Values and Behavior in Nineteenth-Century America

The past seems to have a certain stability about it, because we feel it can no longer change; it has a consistency, which our current lives seem to lack. So we harken back to it in an effort to understand how we have developed and why. We can conveniently romanticize or debase it according to our interpretation of "the facts." Consequently, the "tradition" that preceded the twentieth century may seem particularly well established. Many of the values of the nineteenth century are like crystalline images, which conform to a particular mold. A mold can be comforting, especially in times of change. It provides a set of expectations upon which we can rely. However, the facets of the crystals glitter with more life than their form suggests. What was the mold of traditional sexuality as expressed in nineteenth-century America? How did it channel the behavior of the day and bias the direction of the future?

Nineteenth-century sexuality was set against a background of swift social change. By 1800, the new nation was adjusting to its political independence from Britain by stepping into the new waters of democracy, while departing from the solid shores of a well-defined class structure. Economic opportunities opened up for the adventurous and the hopeful; vast territories for settlement lay to the west, and industrialization was continuing to change the nature of work. While the potential for bettering one's lot presented a challenge, which promised great rewards, it probably engendered anxiety. Barker-Benfield (1978) argues that the freedom of choice that accompanied these opportunities carried with it "relentless pressure" for men to face competition and to have control over their lives. The realities of the economy wove their way into the ideology of the day and had an important impact upon gender identity and roles. Barker-Benfield describes the nineteenth-century view of sexuality as the "spermatic economy" and demonstrates how a man's body became a microcosm of some of the abilities required for competition in the larger society.

Men's activities required energy; men regarded their bodies as repositories of their vital powers. Since the mind derived its powers from the body, it was important to retain physical energy for the intellectual demands of success. Any excessive activity, including exercise, could undermine a man's vital resources. This was particularly true in the realm of sexuality. A man's "natural" sexual appetite and eruptibility constantly threatened his ability to exert self-control. Furthermore, ejaculation depleted him of some of his life's blood — sperm. Therefore, men thought that intercourse and masturbation were particularly dangerous activities, because they could be both excessive and draining. Masturbation could lead to insanity, paralysis, bed wetting, and sterility, to name a few of its consequences. Therefore, its prevention became the focus for the diligent efforts of parents in raising their children properly. They adopted a host of measures designed to avoid its dreadful effects. Mothers folded diapers wider than necessary and pinned them in a special way to prevent a baby boy from stimulating his genitals (Brecher 1984: 232). An older boy might be subject to preventative measures, such as a cold-water enema before sleeping, cauterization of the uretha, or a cord around the base of the penis (Rugoff 1971: 53). New technology supported these efforts; a metal ring with spikes on its inner side could be put around the penis to awaken the sleeper if he began to have an erection (Rugoff 1971: 53). The consequences of masturbation were thought to be so severe that mothers tolerated their sons' visits to prostitutes if intercourse would prevent them from "abusing" themselves (Brecher 1969: 232). But probably the worst repercussions of all were the guilt and fear that accompanied ejaculation by masturbation; a man was consciously giving in to his unruly nature, abdicating control over the energies of his body. Since sexual and mental activity were mutually exclusive, masturbation depleted the body of its resources and hampered the road to economic success.

A woman's role complemented that of a man's. While men actively pursued the material fruits of a competitive, public world, women lived in the private, domestic sphere. Within this context, a woman could admirably express the virtues that defined her as a "true woman": domesticity, submissiveness, piety, and purity (Welter 1978). The constancy of womanhood became an anchor for a society in the midst of change. To threaten its tenets was tantamount to threatening the social order. Home became a haven for men to enjoy after the pressures of their daily routines. Women were expected to provide as much comfort, cheer, and moral support to the members of their households as their self-sacrificing natures would permit.

Marriage was the proper context for expressing domesticity. A woman's natural desire to have and love children was an integral part of marriage and augmented her opportunities to express her virtues. Mrs. Gilman's *Recollections of a Southern Matron* (1938) aptly advised three major routes to domestic bliss: (1) repress a harsh answer; (2) confess a fault; and (3) refrain from self-defense by submitting to a man's opinion (Gilman, in Welter 1978: 319). Submission to men was a heavenly edict. By self-control and self-sacrifice a woman provided herself to be a spiritual guide for a man's volatile nature. Women cooperated with God and cultivated piety instead of undermining His purposes, as Eve had done. The temptress became a goddess on a pedestal, ever fervent in her attempts to purge the world of sin and unruliness. By guarding against excessive passions of any sort (anger, ambition, and love), she could aid her husband in controlling the loss of his much-needed energy.

Beliefs about a woman's sexuality closely paralleled the self-control that typified her domestic virtues. By her very nature, a woman lacked a sexual appetite. As Dr. William Acton put it in *The Functions and Disorders of the Reproductive Organs* (1857): "The majority of women (happily for them) are not very much troubled with sexual feelings of any kind. What men are habitually, women are only exceptionally" (Acton, in Degler 1978: 403). Given these differences between males and females, a woman had to expect assaults on her purity by men. Nevertheless, it was her duty to overcome these advances and exercise the self-control with which her innate lack of passion provided her. In this way, a woman could demonstrate some power and moral superiority over men. The converse was also true. It was unnatural and unfeminine to have sexual desires. Expression of sexual passion could lead to duplicitous behavior, madness, prostitution, and even death (Welter 1978: 315). The goddess could fall to a subhuman level, where she was not regarded as a true woman but as part of some lower order (Welter 1978: 315). Therefore, it was particularly heinous for a woman to masturbate, because this behavior showed her interest in sexual excitement. The dire consequences of being impure led to the implementation of some extreme measures to prevent masturbation. A woman might undergo surgical correction for her condition. In the 1860s, gynecologists began to remove the clitoris to treat masturbation and other "dangerously unappeasable irritations" of the clitoris (Barker-Benfield 1978: 388). The practice continued until 1904 and possibly until as late as 1925 (Barker-Benfield 1978: 388). A less extreme version of this treatment, circumcision, involved removal of the clitoral hood; according to some accounts, this practice may have persisted well into the 1930s (Barker-Benfield 1978: 388).

It is ironic that a woman's marriage meant the loss of a certain degree of her sexual innocence if she were to fulfill her natural inclination to have children. Nevertheless, she could manage to retain her purity if she engaged in intercourse without displaying passion. Consequently, both men and women connected marital intercourse with a lack of passion; women identified it closely with reproduction.

Despite her supposedly passionless nature, a woman's mind could be dominated by her reproductive organs. During the first part of the nineteenth century, the internal workings of a woman's organs were still as mysterious as they were to the Greeks over 1700 years before (Pearsall 1969: 283). The belief that the uterus resembled an animal, which moved itself to different parts of the body, continued to be accepted in some circles. Menstruation, a "curse" best not discussed between husband and wife or even reluctantly mentioned between a mother and her fourteen-year-old daughter, reinforced doctors' views that women were "natural invalids," suffering from internal wounds (Pearsall 1969: 206, 207). Menstrual blood was an indication of failure to conceive, since it would otherwise be used to form the fetus (Pearsall 1969: 208). It was not until 1879 that Dr. John Goodman hypothesized a link between the release of an ovum and menstruation in his article, "The Cyclical Theory of Menstruation," which was published in the American Journal of Obstetrics (Pearsall 1969: 209). It took almost twenty years before unequivocal evidence persuaded doctors to accept this view; Dr. E. Knauer found that removal of the ovaries resulted in cessation of the menses (Pearsall 1969: 213).

The ovaries were thought to have a central role in the control of a woman's personality (Scully 1980: 49). Like the Greeks of the fourth and fifth centuries B.C., nineteenth-century Americans believed that diseased ovaries could cause insanity. Therefore, doctors treated many nervous disorders and psychological problems by removing a woman's ovaries (Scully 1980: 49). By the late 1800s, gynecology had been established as a medical specialty, and the aggressive surgery advocated by its American practitioners supported a belief that the internal organs of women were not as mysterious as they had seemed to be in the early

1800s. The popularity of ovariectomy reached its height between 1880 and 1900, though some doctors continued to treat psychological disorders in this manner as late as 1946 (Scully 1980: 49). Much of a woman's identity was bound to her reproductive organs. Yet there was an inherent tension in believing that a woman was naturally able to exert more self-control than a man and in also perceiving her mind to be subject to domination by her sex organs (Barker-Benfield 1978: 383). A woman had the capacity to be both sexless and entirely sexual. By separating virtuous from "fallen" women, the ideology redefined sensual women as unfeminine semimales and retained the view of "true women" as lacking passion.

Religion and Victorian attitudes fed into the reinforced beliefs about the place of sex in the lives of men and women. The Judeo-Christian tradition established the belief that the main purpose of sexual activity was to procreate; therefore activities that did not lead to conception and the legitimate birth of children were wrong. Jews and Christians diverged in their acceptance of sex within marriage. Jews allowed more room for sexual expression by expecting everyone, including holy men, to marry rather than to remain celibate and also by encouraging husbands not only to procreate but also to satisfy their wives sexually.

The Catholic orientation derived from the teachings of the early Christian fathers, particularly St. Paul and St. Augustine. In the first century A.D., St. Paul expressed the idea that sexual desire was a weakness of the flesh — i.e., all that was temporal and transitory — and advocated celibacy as a path to Christ. Although marriage was a less attractive alternative, it could be a way for others to cope with their sexual desires. Four centuries later, St. Augustine, ever mindful of the story of Adam and Eve, articulated the view that sex was an inherently sinful activity. Though unpleasant, intercourse was necessary for procreation. However, any nonprocreational sex — e.g., masturbation, homosexuality, or bestiality — was sinful, whether in or out of marriage. The overall message was that sexual activity should lead to procreation.

Protestants had a different version of the role of sex. They broke away from the earlier Christian teachings by arguing that celibacy was not a necessary component of the religious life and that marriage was a noble context into which potentially sinful passions could be diverted. Procreation remained the main purpose of sexual activity, although pleasure might be a serendipitous side effect.

Despite our modern tendency to equate Puritanism with asceticism, the Puritans' brand of Protestantism was not the root of American squeamishness about sex. According to Edmund S. Morgan, an eminent scholar of Puritanism, the Puritans encouraged sexual expression within marriage as long as it did not interfere with their major goal of glorifying God (Morgan 1978). Marriage was a desirable state for all, and sex was an essential part of marriage. Puritans regarded sex outside of marriage more harshly. However, they recognized the frailty of human nature and began to lighten the punishments for adultery and fornication to fines and branding, rather than death and whipping, since so many people were violating the rules prohibiting nonmarital intercourse.

All of these religious traditions encouraged the confinement of sexual activity to a reproductive context, i.e., marriage. This dovetailed with the nineteenth-century belief that the main purpose of sex for a man was reproduction. Prohibition of nonmarital sex and "unnatural" activities, particularly masturbation, meant restriction of sexual activity to intercourse, a view compatible with the belief of the nineteenth-century man that he ought to conserve his energy and refrain from excess of any kind.

The attitudes that were current during Queen Victoria's reign (1837–1901) over Great Britain also provided major influences on the sexual values of nineteenth-century Americans. Although America declared its political independence from Britain in 1776, it did not isolate itself from British influence. Both immigrants and ideas crossed the seas. The century after 1820 had the "greatest Atlantic migration in human history" (Feagin 1978: 55). The themes that permeated these times were respectability, politeness, the development of good character, and the maintenance of spiritual and physical health. The strict guidelines for appropriate conduct accentuated the split between the body and the spirit (Leonard 1984: 140–141). The body was often a hindrance to the superior dictates of the mind, since it was basically a container for the more lofty directives of the spirit. Victorians distrusted bodily feelings and urges unless they were symptoms of illness or injury. It is interesting to note that the word "sex," a fairly recent addition to the English language (it first appeared in a 1382 translation of the Latin Bible to describe Noah's selection of pairs for the Ark), became more generally used during the Victorian era to describe a "separate, highly charged entity," which was independent of its context (Leonard 1984: 98–99). Therefore, sex became associated with the lurid longings of the body and was extracted from association with spirituality. After it was ripped from other aspects of life and abstracted as an independent force, many dimensions of "sex" were condemned. Public displays of affection and "unnatural acts," which did not lead to procreation — e.g., oragenitalism, masturbation, anal intercourse, and homosexuality — were severely censured.

Victorians went to great lengths to ensure that behavior fell in line with their moral guidelines. References to the body and "sex" were regarded as improper and were excluded from the language. A wide range of euphemisms for allusions to the body sprang up to replace unseemly words. Underwear became lingerie, pregnancy became "in a family way," and birth became "going into confinement"; even the leg and breast of a chicken became "dark meat" and "white meat" to avoid possible reference to body parts (Brecher 1984: 246). Covering up the legs of furniture with skirts and segregating books on bookshelves by gender were signs of polite consideration of others (Brecher 1984: 246).

Religion and Victorian attitudes therefore became elements of a distinctively American interpretation of sexuality. All of these values helped to reinforce the cornerstone of nineteenth-century American society: the married couple and the family. The mutual goal of a husband and wife while engaging in sexual relations was to establish a family, the ultimate symbol of their partnership. The family was bound together with love and affection and was accorded privacy from public scrutiny. These bonds were to last a lifetime.

Thus far I have described the cultural ideals for sexual behavior and some of the medical modifications of anatomy that followed from them. Social compliance with these beliefs was a different matter. The realities of life made strict adherence to ideals a difficult task for both men and women.

The separation of men in the public sphere and women in the domestic one limited the degree to which they could establish real communication with each other. Men rarely participated in the intimacies of a woman's family and kin, and women knew very little about a man's activities. Therefore, it was difficult for women to become real supports for their husbands, as the ideals of domesticity required, since they knew only scant details about the men's world; responsiveness and submissiveness provided a semblance of this support. Social restrictions on heterosexual interactions before marriage and lack of information during marriage may account for the formality and emotional distance that many men and women exhibited toward each other. Love and intimacy were expressed more by mutual concern for children than by sexual abandon. Morality meant capping passionate longings.

Some doctors and couples refused to go along with the restrictive ideas of the nineteenth century. In his article "What Ought to Be and What Was: Women's Sexuality in the Nineteenth Century" (1978), Degler argues that it is not clear how much of a consensus there actually was about female sexuality. A well-known Philadelphia physician, Dr. George Napheys, published a popular guide for women in 1869 entitled

*The Physical Life of Woman: Advice to the Maiden, Wife, and Mother.*
He described three types of women on the basis of their sexual appetites.
Women with no sexual feelings and those with very strong passions were
infrequent types; the vast majority of women had moderate sexual appetites, which Napheys validated as appropriate and dignified desires.
Other physicians hypothesized that women's illnesses might be due to a
*lack* of sexual expression (Degler 1978: 407).

Some couples were fairly public in their refusal to adhere to restrictive norms. The Oneida Community of John Humphrey Noyes was an
extreme example of this orientation. Noyes believed that the Bible encouraged all true believers in God to engage in communal love (including sexual intercourse) with each other (Talese 1980: 296). Since the
human body, including the sex organs, was designed by God, it was not
regarded as a source of shame. Although Noyes' views precluded his
ordination as a minister at the Yale Divinity School in the 1830s, they
appealed to a dedicated group of followers, who helped him build an
estate in New York in 1848 to house and support his utopian group, the
Perfectionists. The men and women not only lived and worked together
but also made love with each other regularly. Since no one was to have
an "exclusive" relationship with anyone else, a committee selected couples to have children, who then became the joint responsibility of the
community. The women did not regard the ideal of domesticity as their
primary purpose in life, and they worked along with men to fulfill
community objectives.

However, the majority of men and women in nineteenth-century
America found other ways of dealing with sexual restrictiveness. Each
gender developed different types of outlets for their passions.

Pornography was one major outlet that men used to cope with their
sexual feelings. Although pornographic materials had been produced in
the West since the seventeenth century for mass audiences and for monetary gain, their publication increased to record-breaking levels in the
last part of the nineteenth century (Offir 1982: 367–368). The influx of
pornography from Europe was so great that Congress passed a law in
1842 prohibiting the importation of obscene prints and paintings. Nevertheless, pornography continued to cross the national and state boundaries of the United States.

Then, as now, a precise definition of pornography was difficulty to
provide. Americans of the time took their cue from the Chief Justice of
England, who defined "obscene" materials as anything that could "de-
prave and corrupt those whose minds are open to such immoral influences and into whose hands a publication of this sort may fall" (Talese
1980: 56).

Pornographic materials included prose, verse, "dirty" jokes, illustrations, lithographs, and engravings (Pearsall 1969: 378). Despite differences in the medium of expression, these materials share a common theme: literal, repetitive documentation of a range of sexual activities, including fellatio, cunnilingus, anal intercourse, sado-masochism, masturbation, fornication, adultery, and homosexuality. Virgins were violated, women were passionate and sexually assertive, and venereal disease was humorous. Some writers were particularly fascinated by semen and would go into great detail about the copious amounts released during a sexual encounter (Pearsall 1969: 370). Penises were pictured as larger than life, and sex lives were described in terms almost larger than the imagination. An anonymous writer detailed his total sex life in one of the major pornographic productions of the period, *My Secret Life*; it totaled over 4,000 pages (Anonymous ["Walter"] 1966).

The themes of pornography could be a catalogue of the major sexual taboos of nineteenth-century America. In fact, the Austrian psychiatrist Krafft-Ebing's major work on sexual pathology, *Psychopathia Sexualis* (1886), became an important source of ideas for pornographic writings (Tannahill 1980: 382). Even the word "pornography" derives from a negatively evaluated activity, prostitution; it means "writing about a prostitute."

While some men were ardent consumers of pornography, others refused to condone its presence; they zealously sought to tighten their own actions and those of others to the restrictive ideals. Some formed religious communities and segmented themselves from the rest of society. Upstate New York became such a source of religious fervor that it was named the "burned-over district." Christian Science (1879) and Jehovah's Witnesses (1879) were both formed in the second half of the nineteenth century. Other people turned their zeal into secular pursuits. Anthony Comstock regarded himself as a "weeder in God's garden"; he believed that books and pictures depicting sexual acts would drive youth and adults to immorality by encouraging masturbation, fornication, and venereal disease (Talese 1980: 56). He was willing to violate other constitutional freedoms in order to combat the infringement of norms; the use of informants and spies and tampering with the mail were just a few of his suggestions (Talese 1980: 55). By 1873, Comstock mounted enough support to persuade the U.S. Congress to pass the "Comstock Laws," banning from the mail "every obscene, lewd, lascivious or filthy book, pamphlet, paper, writing, print or other publication of an independent character"; these materials included birth control information (Talese 1980: 57). Consequently, a person could be fined up to $5,000 and go to jail for as many as ten years for participating in the consumption of "sexual obscenity" (Talese 1980: 58).

Fantasizing about taboos and attempting to ensure adherence to moral standards by stamping out "deviant behavior" were two of the approaches that men used to deal with a strict code of morality. Many chose a more direct way of venting their sexual feelings. They broke cultural taboos and acted out some of their fantasies.

Given the dissociation of love and sex in marriage, a belief in male sexual eruptibility, and a knowledge that men were less able than women to adhere to canons of morality, it is no wonder that many men released much of their sexual energy with prostitutes. Since sex with prostitutes did not involve love, men may have rationalized that coitus with them was permissible, particularly if it was not accompanied by passion. Furthermore, a man might think that he was doing his wife a favor, because he was not imposing his unruly impulses on her delicate and pure nature. Intercourse once a month was deemed an appropriate frequency between spouses; they could engage in it once a week if circumstances were desperate, though never during pregnancy and menstruation (Tannahill 1980: 355). Consequently, prostitution flourished, despite the efforts of wives to prevent such wanderings with cheerful dispositions and comfortable homes. Social reformer Robert Dale Owen estimated that half of the adult male population of New York City in the 1830s visited prostitutes regularly (Tannahill 1980: 357). The Superintendent of Police in New York City said that there were at least 621 brothels in the city in 1866. Bishop Simpson of the Methodist Episcopal Church noted that there were probably as many prostitutes in New York city as there were Methodists (Tannahill 1980: 361). Young widows, unmarried mothers, and career women often resorted to prostitution because they needed the money (Tannahill 1980: 357–358); they joined the ranks of "fallen" women.

Although the disjunction between ideals and behavior may have resulted in some psychological discomfort, indiscriminate sex with prostitutes had an even more serious consequence; venereal disease increased at an alarming rate. Pearsall referred to it as the "Russian roulette of Victorian sexuality" (Pearsall 1969: 225). One expert estimated that more than half of the American male population may have had gonorrhea by 1914 (Tannahill 1980: 367). Although venereal disease was often a focus for jokes, its consequences were no laughing matter. Victims in the later stages of syphilis suffered paralysis, disfigurement, and death. At the time, there was no effective remedy for venereal disease. The cures were as harmful as the disease. Some thought raping a virgin was a cure for syphilis (Pearsall 1969: 226), while others used the favored remedy of ingesting mercury to remove their symptoms. Mercury not only gave them bad breath and turned their gums purple but also frequently led to death (Pearsall 1969: 226).

The sexual repression that contributed to a husband's visits to prostitutes and to the subsequent likelihood of his contracting venereal disease had some very real consequences for the relationship between a husband and wife. Intercourse became fraught with even more danger. Added to her fears of sexual excess was a wife's fear of the very real possibility of being infected with venereal disease from her husband. This possibility threatened to hamper or destroy one of the ideal expressions of their union — children. As many as 90 percent of sterile marriages may have been a result of gonorrhea (Pearsall 1969: 225).

Since the cultural definitions of male and female sexuality differed, men's and women's styles of reacting to cultural values also differed. Just as values establish a range of acceptable behavior, they also (sometimes only by implication) channel the direction of deviance from the "normal." Men were supposed to be in control of themselves, saving their energy for successful economic pursuits. Nevertheless, they had an acknowledged tendency to be sexually passionate and volatile. When men crossed the boundary of controlled decorum, they reverted to another part of their nature by fantasizing about sex with pornography or by acting out their desires with prostitutes. "Boys will be boys." However, these types of outlets were not as readily available for females. Women were defined as lacking sexual passion, nurturant (stemming from their interest in children), and constitutionally infirm (due to the "debility" of menstruation). They were supposed to be moral and domestic. When women deviated from cultural expectations, they could not revert to a culturally defined passionate nature, as men could. Therefore, dealing with feelings at variance with norms became more complicated for women. As Pearsall put it in his book on Victorian sexuality, *The Worm in the Bud*, working off repressions "was more difficult for women, often condemned to an endless round of social visits and needlework. Men, at least, could do something about it; too frequently, women who suffered from sexual repression were pinned like butterflies in transparent cases" (Pearsall 1969: 425). What did women do to deal with feelings at odds with what they were supposed to be? Like the men, they reverted to what was considered to be their "true" nature, i.e., the culturally defined traits of nurturance, infirmity, and lack of sexual passion.

Women channeled many of their emotions into nurturing their family members and into friendships with other women. The nursing role became one of women's most important functions as comforters in the home (Welter 1978: 321). Within this role, women were allowed to touch the body (within the bounds of their "delicacy") and to use medical terminology to "cultivate right views of the wonderful structure of the body" in the interests of consulting with the physician (Welter 1978: 321). Although presented for its humorous effect, a passage in *Godey's Lady's Book* probably struck a chord of truth: a man says that a husband's ailments sometimes provided joy for a woman, because she could have the pleasure of nursing him to recovery; in addition, a husband might suspect that his wife "almost wishes me dead — for the pleasure of being utterly inconsolable" (Welter 197: 321). Given the heavy cultural fetters on a woman's actions, it is not surprising that the activity and purposefulness of caring for the sick had an appeal.

Female friendships became another major outlet for a woman's emotions. Smith-Rosenberg (1978) asserts that the often emotionally intense and sometimes sensual ties between women were an essential aspect of American society between the late eighteenth and midnineteenth centuries, even though writing about them was rare. Basing her conclusions on a thorough analysis of correspondence and diaries of men and women from thirty-five middle-class families from the 1760s to the 1880s, she is able to provide a glimpse into the nature of these ties. Just as the family provided a sense of comfort and continuity for men in a rapidly changing world, it also became a course of emotional satisfaction for women. The bonds between consanguineal kin became the basis for an integrated network of ties, which radiated from them. The mother/daughter bond was characterized by sympathy and understanding, as the mother guided her daughter into the realm of domesticity (Smith-Rosenberg 1978: 342). Sisters expressed affection toward one another, as did unrelated adolescent girls. These positive emotions developed further after a young woman went to school, made friends of her own, and incorporated these ties with those of her kin. Mature women helped each other with domestic chores, comforted each other at important events in the life cycle (pregnancy, birth, menopause, and death), and frequently visited each other. A woman would often move in with a friend while her husband was traveling. Women nurtured other women during pregnancy and birth by secluding the pregnant woman for an extended period both before and after birth, thus exempting her from domestic chores and segregating from men the whole process of becoming a mother.

Through these networks, women were able to develop self-esteem and to feel the security of bonds that spanned distances to include kin who no longer lived nearby (Smith-Rosenberg 1978: 342). Given the restrictions on heterosexual interactions and the common biological realities that women faced, such bonds between them were accepted by both men and women. And since women were, by definition, "not much troubled by sexual feelings of any kind," there was no suspicion that these relationships might be homosexual. As Smith-Rosenberg puts it, "it was not these homosocial ties that there inhibited, but rather heterosexual leanings. While closeness, freedom of emotional expression and uninhibited physical contact characterized women's relationships with each other, the opposite was frequently true of male/female relationships" (Smith-Rosenberg 1978: 350). The segregation of the male and female spheres may also have channeled men's emotions in a similar direction. Pearsall notes that passionate friendships in the upper classes of English society were the "done thing" in public schools and that homosexual experiences were likely to occur, particularly by the time young men attended universities (Pearsall 1969: 452). However, these relationships may not have been defined as "homosexual" by the participants.

While friendships provided one kind of positive outlet for expressions of affection, a woman might also break through the repression of her sexual feelings in another way: through sickness. Hysteria was a common psychological malady among women of this era; some of its symptoms included "fits," paralysis, blindness, deafness, anorexia, bulimia, amnesia, trances, dream-states, fugues, and somnambulism (Hinsie and Campbell 1970: 366–368). All of these symptoms accentuated withdrawal from the realm of effective social life and thus made it difficult for a woman to perform the duties that were associated with domestic virtue. Since she was ill, she was not thought to be in control of her actions and therefore would be forgiven for the tasks she did not perform. While men vented their sexual fantasies in pornography, women repressed their sexual feelings even further and expressed them in what was considered to be an acceptable way by becoming sick. The conversion of a woman's sexual energy into symptoms of illness allowed her little pleasure. One payoff of a woman's illness may have been playing the sick role, in which she was herself nurtured instead of constantly being asked to be the nurturer. Afflicted women did not consciously set out to bring attention to themselves; the point was that hysteria was an unconscious process of repression, which erupted in physical symptoms. It is true that English pseudohysterics tried to feign the malady to their own purposes. Some women developed symptoms that required medical examination of the sex organs and thus provided momentary release from cultural standards, while retaining the woman's sense of being demure and ladylike (Pearsall 1969: 426–427).

Home nursing, friendships, and hysteria all provided avenues for dealing with sexual repression, but the emotional dilemma presented by the ideal of "motherhood" required a different coping style. The value of motherhood was central to the concept of the true woman; children demonstrated that a woman's sexual activities were reproductive, that a husband and wife had fulfilled their goal of establishing a family, and that a woman wanted to participate fully in the virtue of domesticity. Nevertheless, the reality of becoming a mother could be not only dangerous but also lethal.

Until the nineteenth century, female midwives had aided in the delivery of babies. In the early part of the century, obstetricians (or "men midwives," as they were called then) introduced the idea that childbirth was a medical problem, which required the expertise of trained surgeons to intervene in case of difficulties during birth. In other words, they departed from the commonly-held assumption that birth was a natural process. Gradual acceptance of this "modern" view meant that female midwives were eventually replaced by obstetricians, who used instruments to assist births. By 1910, only 50 percent of births were assisted by midwives (Scully 1980: 30), and by 1968, 99 percent of births were assisted by male physicians (Barker-Benfield 1978: 388). The United States is one of the few places in the world where male physicians rather than female midwives help to deliver babies (Scully 1980: 25). England went in the other direction by providing government sanction to the practice of nurse-midwifery (Barker-Benfield 1978: 388).

Despite claims of special expertise, better prenatal care, and an ability to reduce infant and maternal mortality, intervention in pregnancy and birth did not appreciably lower mortality. The inside of a woman's body was still regarded as a mystery in the first part of the century; therefore, there was very little aid for a woman who had complications during pregnancy. It was difficult for doctors to advance knowledge, given the taboos surrounding the body and heterosexual intervention. Some obstetricians regarded touching a woman's genitals as an "odious task" (Scully 1980: 25), and public opinion tended to favor the thought that it was indiscreet for a woman even to submit to an examination by a man. In an effort to preserve modesty, doctors covered themselves and their patients with sheets while conducting examinations, averted their eyes, or worked from behind their patients (Scully 1980: 26).

If a birth happened to be difficult, the new instruments in the hands of novices in a new specialty could be as much of a hindrance as an aid to the woman in labor. Hooks and cutting instruments were used to perform embryotomies; the fetus was removed piece by piece if it could not be delivered. The Chamberlens revealed their invention of the obstetrical forceps to the public in 1813. While the use of forceps may have aided some deliveries, in others it harmed the mother, child, or both. Infection, hemorrhage, a crushed fetal head, damage to internal organs, and intense pain were some of the effects of the sometime inept use of forceps. Prolonged labor or instruments could produce a particularly unpleasant internal injury, a tear between the vaginal wall and the bladder, which resulted in a constant, slow drain of urine into the vagina (Scully 1980: 30). The woman afflicted with this injury would not only be uncomfortable but also smell bad and often be socially isolated.

Another danger that new mothers faced was puerperal fever (childbed fever), which reached almost epidemic proportions throughout Europe and the United States in the nineteenth century (Scully 1980: 30–31). Its cause was not known early in the century, but doctors tried to deal with it by giving the woman opium and by applying leeches to her abdomen (Pearsall 1969: 199). The new practice of using "lying in" hospitals instead of giving birth at home exacerbated the problem, because it facilitated the spread of contagion. Physicians who had just worked with cadavers might deliver babies without washing their hands; antiseptics were not used during this period. Although some evidence from the 1840s suggested that unsanitary conditions contributed to the spread of the fever, it was not until 1885 that antiseptic techniques were generally used in U.S. hospitals (Scully 1980: 30).

Finally, infant mortality remained high. A new mother might have to endure the pain of losing her infant within the first year of its life. Acceptance of this part of life was probably one of the most heartrending challenges of a woman's virtue of submission to "fate" and social circumstances (Welter 1978: 320).

Some strides were being made toward easing the pain of childbirth, particularly in the last half of the century. In the 1840s, Dr. James Simpson encouraged the use of anesthetics to make childbearing as painless as possible. By the 1860s, the use of chloroform and ether had become a more acceptable part of birthing; Queen Victoria gave some legitimacy to the practice by using anesthetics during her own confinements.

Although eighteenth-century botanists knew that plants derived their characteristics from both parents, it was not until 1854 that the question of how conception occurred was firmly answered for humans; observation of the joining of the eggs and sperm of frogs lent more credence to the belief that both a man and a woman contributed to the formation of a child (Tannahill 1980: 345). This discovery boosted the evaluation of a woman's role in motherhood, since she was acknowledged to be one of the creators, not just a container that nourished the procreative result of sperm.

Nevertheless, the dangers of childbirth and the high infant mortality (it was estimated that as many as one in every four to six infants died before the age of one) probably engendered ambivalence about the process of motherhood. This ambivalence may have led some women to use birth control. Although abortions were legal for most of the century, they were dangerous (Epstein 1983: 120). Furthermore, the practice continued to meet with opposition. By the 1860s and 1870s, doctors began to campaign against abortions, on the basis that they were morally objectionable, could lead to disease, and represented the rejection of a woman's "natural" role (Epstein 1983: 121). Pessaries, condoms, and abstinence were among the contraceptive alternatives. Abstinence was a reliable means of birth control and was probably the easiest to justify. It helped a man to conserve his sperm and could therefore be interpreted as a woman's contribution to a man's need to control his energy. It also allowed a woman to conform to a major belief about a woman's sexuality, i.e., that she was not very much interested in sexual passion or by extension, in intercourse. By playing up this aspect of her womanhood she could avoid the fear, grief, and domestic responsibilities that were associated with the birth of children.

In summary, the cultural orientation of America toward sexuality was restrictive for most of the nineteenth century. Sexual relationships were expected to be procreative and to occur within marriage. As in the other restrictive societies that I have discussed, there was in the United States a consistent pattern of prohibiting premarital and extramarital sex; where deviations occurred, men were given more leeway in involving themselves in nonmarital relationships. Although women were not killed for engaging in sex outside of marriage, as in some of the most restrictive societies in the sample, social attitudes could be almost as deadly. A "fallen" woman might end up as a prostitute, whose punishment for momentary pleasure resulted in continual depravity and isolation from participation in a "respectable" world. Men and women lived in different spheres, and sex had a different range of meaning for each gender. For women, sex within marriage meant procreation. Barrenness meant that a woman could not fully participate in the domesticity that defined her as a true woman. Although a man might try to constrain his sexual activities within marriage to procreation, he might not always succeed. Furthermore, sex could be passionate for men, but not usually within marriage, and it was rarely accompanied by love. Love was on a more spiritual plane for both men and women.

Since sexual activity was meant to be procreational, the emphasis was on coitus; other sexual activities were forbidden, e.g., oragenitalism and masturbation. It was expected that children (who were prereproductive) and postmenopausal women (who were postreproductive) would not engage in sexual activity at all.

Physicians rather than clergy began to assume responsibility for defining the consequences of sexual behavior. Deviation from the moral code became as dangerous to a person's health as to the salvation of his soul.

As we have seen, ideology does not exist in a vacuum; it derives part of its strength from the degree to which people can abide by its values. The cultural constraints on behavior in the nineteenth century were difficult to "live up" to. Both men and women found ways to channel their ambivalence or discontent with the rigid standards. Nevertheless, the disjunction between ideals and behavior created a lot of individual stress. As Pearsall so aptly expressed it: "The pretense that widely varied sexual activities did not exist was so overpowering during the nineteenth century that many fell into mental confusion when persuading themselves that impulses they well knew they had did not exist" (Pearsall 1969: 239). This confusion became a wedge that opened the door to changes that took place at the end of the century.

### Changes that Transformed
### the Traditional Pattern

Most of the societies I discussed previously were presented as they were observed at one point in time. We are fortunate to have some detailed descriptions of the social and cultural activities that occurred in this country from the latter part of the nineteenth century up to the present time. They disabuse us of the idea that societies are static and give us some insight into change. Specifically, they provide us with a basis for understanding how and why a restrictive orientation can shift toward the more permissive end of the continuum, within the same society. This historical perspective ricochets to the cross-cultural information and renews our interest in both as avenues for interpreting our current situation.

Toward the end of the nineteenth century, social developments confronted established cultural precepts to challenge the existing ideology. Increased mobility gave people more room to move, both physically and emotionally. Darwin's *Origin of Species* (1859) defined the religious foundations of the day and knocked humans from their spiritual pedestal back into the animal kingdom. The principles of the scientific method were beginning to take hold as a basis for knowledge; more credence was given to the validity of observation than to belief in the unobservable, the spiritual. Even though the majority of people lived in rural settings (60 percent in 1900), the influences of the city and of industrialization impinged upon them. More goods became available, and mass-produced items began to replace the home-crafted ones. Even though their purchase eroded some of the necessity for domestic skills, it became acceptable to want and to buy them.

Although industrialization had been gradually redefining the roles of men and women in the family since the beginning of the century, the effects of the changes could be seen more clearly toward the end of the century. Working and middle-class women diverged in their adherence to a collective family ideal. Working-class families retained their emphasis on all family members providing assistance and support for each other, even when they were no longer members of the same household. Children were still an asset, because they could work in industry. The timing of marriage and parenthood was governed by the economic and social needs of the lower-class family (Hareven 1982: 455–456). Single women were likely to work. Motivated by a desire to help support other family members (e.g., a sick father, a widowed mother, a brother who wanted to go to college), young women worked long hours in factories (Cott 1972: 13). Although they received wages and had the potential to sever some of their dependence on men, their hearts remained tied to domesticity. Social pressures reinforced a working-class woman's inclination to regard her work as temporary until she could establish a home of her own. Higher status was accorded to a woman serving her family at home than to a woman who contributed by paid employment. Working conditions did little to encourage women to remain; eighteen-hour days and less pay than men received for the same work were hardly adequate incentives. Female factory workers demonstrated their strength and competence in dealing with machines and revealed an untapped potential for future development.

Descriptions of work in the city illustrated the pitiful straits in which an employed woman might find herself. In "'Charity Girls' and City Pleasures," Kathy Peiss (1983) chronicles the experiences of some working girls in New York City between 1880 and 1920. These young, white women were single wage earners who worked in the factories, shops, and department stores by day and participated in public amusements, such as dance halls, at night. The delights of dancing, dressing well, and eating and drinking out became a positive part of affirming heterosexual interaction (Peiss 1983: 77). However, they were counterbalanced by the widespread practice of sexual harassment at work. As Peiss puts it, the "sexual style that we have seen on the dance floor was often reproduced on the shop floor" (Peiss 1983: 79). Low wages and few financial reserves led some women to become "charity girls," who agreed to trade sexual favors for gifts and a good time; they did not conform to the ideal of delaying coitus for marriage.

Middle-class women followed a more individualistic path. Lower- and lower-middle-class women were more likely to work for longer periods than their upper-middle and upper-class counterparts, who cultivated the role of "lady" (Cott 1972: 13). Changes were taking place that should have facilitated the entrance of married women into the labor market. The birth rate was down at the end of the century (3.56 children per family in 1900, in contrast to 7 in 1800), labor-saving devices cut down on the time devoted to household chores, and transportation to new industrial and commercial facilities was now available (Hareven 1982: 455). However, the middle class had settled into a strict division of labor between men and women, instead of retaining the economic partnerships of working-class families. The middle-class ideology of maintaining separate spheres for men and women implied that domesticity and work outside the home were incompatible routes for women to take. As a result, most middle-class women (97 percent) preferred to stay at home after they married, although they dipped their skills into the world of employment while they were single (Hareven 1982: 455). In these families, children did not work until their late teens. A socially recognized period called adolescence was born.

In the interests of becoming good mothers and wives, many middle-class women went to institutions of higher learning in the late 1800s. However, college did not always fulfill its intended functions. The division of subject domains sought to reinforce the differences between men and women; men took science and mathematics, while women studied domestic and cultural arts. Nevertheless, an unexpected side effect of such education was the women's belief that they were meant for a special mission in life; that being a wife and mother was a restricted image of their aspirations (Sochen 1974: 187). Although more than half of the Vassar graduates from 1867 to 1900 married, some (beginning in the 1870s) organized settlement houses, women's clubs, and nursing schools. Many feminists emerged from their ranks.

Both working and middle-class families continued to rely on kin in effecting the transition from rural to urban life. In this respect, they retained some continuity with the past. Relatives could provide lodging, tips on job opportunities, and information about the new social context. However, industrialization meant that families relinquished some of their previous functions to social agencies. Schools helped to educate children. Hospitals and asylums took over some of the care of the sick. Employers took responsibility for training workers. The family was left with the tasks of economic support, childbearing, child rearing, and household maintenance (Hareven 1982: 451). By the end of the nineteenth century, the separation of the male and female spheres that was typical of middle-class life had become a model of the good life.

Given the increasing specialization of functions in the middle-class family, sentiment became more important as a bond between members. Nurturance and privacy were important themes of family life. "Love" became a major criterion for selecting a mate. Although the ephemeral quality of love as a feeling state was difficult to define, a mother might say to her child, "When love happens, you'll know." According to this nebulous description, a person could "fall in love" with practically anyone. The flexibility of the concept meshed well with the mobility of the life-style. Wherever a person lived, there was always the potential of finding someone with whom it was possible to fall in love. Emotions emerged as an important aspect of male/female relationships.

At the same time, technological developments were having important implications for reassessing the definition of sexuality. I have already discussed some of the consequences of an increasing reliance on medical instruments in birthing. The vulcanization of rubber by Goodyear and Hancock in 1843–1844 made it possible to produce a rubber sheath for the penis (Pearsall 1969: 215). The "rubber" was first introduced at the Philadelphia World Exposition in 1878 (Pearsall 1969: 215). Vulcanized rubber also allowed for the development of the diaphragm and of syringes to introduce contraceptive mixes into the vagina. Given the relatively low cost of mass production of vulcanized rubber, the new technology offered the possibility of low-cost contraception. This potential introduced a major dilemma for reconciling sexual behavior with moral precepts. Given the risks of pregnancy and birth, women were still ambivalent about having children and were probably inclined toward using some form of contraception. Some used abortions to control the number of births. Men were also well disposed toward using condoms to help prevent venereal disease. The needs of both men and women could be met by using condoms. This one device served two very different purposes; for men, it was a prophylactic against venereal disease, and for women, it was a contraceptive.

Cultural and social events made acceptance of some contraception timely in the nineteenth century. Malthus published his *An Essay on the Principles of Population* in 1798 and provided a reason for contraception beyond personal interests. He argued that the population was growing geometrically but that the world's resources were increasing arithmetically. Consequently, population would outstrip resources and would result in suffering for all. Limiting population could therefore be viewed as a way to serve the national interest, not just as a result of individual selfishness. In America, infant and maternal mortality remained rather high. Given the shift from the farm to the city, large numbers of children were not essential for economic purposes in middle-class families. In fact, they could prove a hindrance, because they meant more mouths to feed without the recompense of their economic contributions.

Despite an ideology that dictated that sex should be procreative, both men and women had reasons to violate its prescriptions. Contraception could bring benefits for the entire population. For a short while, men and women sought solutions to the contraception issue by behaving more vigorously in traditional ways. Men continued to transgress cultural boundaries by visiting prostitutes, as they had done in the past. They might use condoms in an effort to prevent venereal disease, not necessarily as a contraceptive measure. Women did not have this rationalization for using contraception. They faced a new problem; throwing out the baby with contraception might mean sacrificing the bath water of domesticity. In addition to the protests against abortions from physicians who stated that they violated a woman's natural role, there was pressure from husbands, who felt that contraception by women meant independence from the home. Such male attitudes engendered fear in women that they would endanger their marriages if they used birth control (Epstein 1983: 123). Since most middle-class women did not participate in the paid labor market, they were dependent on their husbands and on the institution of marriage to sustain them economically. Motherhood was a route to some autonomy. Therefore, they reasoned that separating intercourse from reproduction would destroy a major link they had with men. They feared that men would have less incentive to marry or, if they did wed, would be more likely to be unfaithful. Yet women had good reasons for agreeing to use contraception, particularly "rubbers"; they could avoid the risk of becoming pregnant before marriage and entering the degraded world of "fallen" women; they could lower their risk of contracting venereal disease; and, they could avoid the dangers of pregnancy and birth. Nevertheless, fears of losing their place in the domestic realm overshadowed public support for contraception. They used extant ideology to cope with the dilemma.

The "voluntary motherhood" movement attempted to preserve the traditional values of motherhood and purity, even though its effect was to control births. Its adherents extolled motherhood and emphasized its centrality to a woman's role. They asked for a woman's right to refuse to engage in coitus when she did not want to have more children. In so doing, they overturned a man's traditional right to his wife's body and introduced the idea of a woman's option to schedule intercourse. They reasoned that the option to *choose* motherhood raised its status. Consequently, they could retain their ideology and avoid pregnancy. This solution avoided the feared separation of sex and procreation. Sex could still occur for reproductive purposes, even though it would occur less often. Although many aspects of "true womanhood" remained intact with this stance, proponents of "voluntary motherhood" did break the silence about female sexual experience that existed before the 1870s and implied that women had sexual desires (Snitow, Stansell, and Thompson 1983: 21). Other changes had to occur, however, to make couples comfortable with contraception.

Social and cultural influences slowly but steadily made an impact on the way women viewed their sexuality and their relationships with men. "Love" was already being validated as an appropriate part of marriage. Havelock Ellis, an English cultural and political radical, reframed the link between sex and reproduction; he argued that the relationship between men and women (including husbands and wives) could be strengthened by dissociating sex from reproduction. Sex could be a bond rather than a hindrance to a relationship (Epstein 1983: 124). Some sex manuals encouraged the development of women's sexual feelings. Dr. George Napheys reached a receptive audience with his advice in *The Physical Life of Women: Advice to the Maiden, Wife, and Mother* (1869). He sold over 60,000 copies of his book in two years, even though his message was counter to public ideology. Since information derived from his medical practice indicated that most women have a moderate amount of passion, he thought that women ought to cultivate rather than suppress their sexuality (Degler 1978: 405).

European writers were also influential in promoting a link between intimacy and sexual fulfillment. Edward Carpenter's *Love's Coming of Age* (1911) advocated a fusion between love and passion, while Swedish authoress Ellen Key's *Love and Marriage* (1911) advocated a closer identification between "soulful sensuousness" and "sensuous soulfulness" (Trimberger 1983: 133).

Popular magazines and fiction began to promote the message that passion could be an expression of love. The March 1908 edition of the *Ladies Home Journal* included an article entitled "A Girl's Preparation for Marriage" (Time-Life Books 1969–70: *1*, 166). The writer, Alice Preston, extolled the virtues of love and linked them to the body:

. . . no gift, no happening of youth is comparable to this of the coming of Love; because when Love comes, it brings in its hands the keys to a Paradise which she could nowise else nor without Love's aid enter. . . . None of us can quite define what Love is; but this we know — that its crown and citadel is the human body. To keep healthy hours, to think sound thoughts, breathe pure air, to dress with loveliness, to strive to be a type of warm, chaste girlishness — these are all of them a preparation for Love's coming. [*This Fabulous Century* 1969: *1*, 166–167].

She retains the emphasis on marriage as a context for sex and describes procreation as the fruit of sexual love. Nevertheless, she makes a connection between love, the body, and passion. Romantic fiction described the passionate yearnings that a young woman might have for a man. Even though magazines vacillated between presenting stories of passion and providing restrictive guidelines about proper conduct with men, they agreed on the power of love (*This Fabulous Century* 1969: *1*, 166). Passion could enter the sphere of the respectable woman if it were connected to love. Love, in turn, could give some legitimacy to sexual feelings, although they would not necessarily be recognized as sexual.

Cultural ideology reframed traditional concepts. Although the labels of the major elements in the scenario of heterosexual relationships remained the same (love, sex, marriage, children), their meaning and link to each other were changing. Love not only was an affectionate bond between a man and woman but also could be a passionate one. Since love was a part of marriage, passion too could be part of marriage. The assumption that women were asexual was transformed into a "valorization of female sexuality" within a relationship that was marital or leading to marriage (Epstein 1983: 125). Passionate love could be an end in and of itself, even though it usually resulted in children. Children had to share the spotlight of significance in the family with love in a marriage between husband and wife.

One of the few surveys we have from this period indicates a shift in attitude about heterosexual love. The papers of Dr. Clelia Mosher, a physician at Stanford University, contained a small survey that she had conducted of women's sexual attitudes and behavior over a twenty-eight-year period (from 1892 to 1920) (Mosher 1980; Degler 1978: 413–421). Although the results were limited to 45 usable questionnaires and were biased in favor of middle-class and upper-class women, they are of interest because they provide direct information on the sexuality of some women who were born before 1890 (70% of the sample were born before 1870). Of these, 77% (35 of 45) reported a desire for sex independent of their husbands' interest. Although the majority (30 of 45) thought the main purpose of sex was reproduction, the high proportion of exceptions (33%) is striking. Answers to a question about the necessity for sex also reveal a mix of the traditional and the new: 20% (9 of 45) thought sex was necessary for men; 29% (13 of 45) thought it was necessary for both men and women; and 35% (15 of 43) thought it was necessary for males or females. A majority (24 of 45) thought that intercourse was pleasurable for both men and women; over 75% reported having orgasms.

Another source of information about the degree of attitude change at the turn of the century is a recent study by Consumers Union, *Love, Sex, and Aging* (Brecher 1984). The editors of *Consumer Reports* surveyed the attitudes of 4,246 men and women over 50 years old. The oldest respondents (77–93 years old) were born during Queen Victoria's reign, and many of the younger ones learned about life from parents who were raised during that era (Brecher 1984: 23). Of those 70 and over, 65% retain many of the Victorian sexual views (against sex without marriage or love), but 35% do not (Brecher 1984: 263). It is interesting to note that this percentage of "deviants" from the restrictive view parallels the findings of Mosher's study that the main purpose of sex need not be reproduction. The changes in attitude were not overwhelming, but nevertheless they were taking place.

Changes in attitude about the role of sex and love within marriage made acceptance of contraception a more acceptable option for both men and women. Quiet but widespread support for contraception increased over the later decades of the nineteenth century and the early part in the twentieth (Epstein 1983: 126). Margaret Sanger was primarily responsible for public endorsement of artificial contraception. She presented a variety of reasons for its necessity: reduction of maternal mortality by preventing pregnancy among women with various physical disorders; prevention of the social waste of abortion and infanticide; promotion of the welfare of children, who would be wanted rather than tolerated; eradication of poverty by restricting the number of children; protection of the upper classes from increases in the lower classes; and a contribution to stemming problems of worldwide overpopulation (Kennedy 1970: 109–113). Just as important as the social advantages of birth control was the individual enhancement of the quality of sexual relationships. As Sanger saw it, freeing the mind of sexual prejudices and taboos was probably the most important function of the birth control movement (Sanger 1922: 244). It would enhance the link between sex and love in a relationship, allow women to develop their sexuality, free the "feminine spirit," and deepen the emotional lives of both men and women (Kennedy 1970: 128, 133, 134). Abstinence and coitus interruptus were not desirable means of birth control, because inhibition of desire had damaging psychological effects.

Sanger thought that condoms and diaphragms were appropriate methods of contraception (Kennedy 1970: 130). Although the vulcanization of rubber had provided these safe, inexpensive means of preventing conception, public access to their use was limited. Before 1930, the Comstock laws prohibited importation, transportation, or mailing of contraceptive materials or information across state lines. Sanger opened the first birth control advice center in Brooklyn in 1916, but it was promptly closed down as a "public nuisance" (Peel and Potts 1969: 15). Her efforts with Emma Goldman to translate the birth control movement into a political issue, expressive of a class struggle, met with similar opposition. Only when she enlisted the aid of physicians in her efforts did she have more success. She persuaded Robert L. Dickinson, President of the American Gynecological Society, to lobby for more research on contraceptive techniques and to help establish the right of qualified medical personnel to legally provide contraceptive advice (Peel and Potts 1969: 15, 16). Nevertheless, most doctors continued to prescribe abstinence as the most effective technique, since they had little scientific data on the effectiveness of different methods. It was not until 1937 that the American Medical Association endorsed birth control (Kennedy 1970: 215).

The public was more flexible and increasingly relied on pessaries, suppositories, coitus interruptus, and condoms (Kennedy 1970: 184). Katherine Davis (1922) provided some statistical evidence for this trend. She interviewed 1,000 women, most of whom had graduated from college or were members of women's clubs, and found that close to 75% of them used contraception. Her investigation was the first published statistical study of contraceptive use in the United States. A 1929 study showed that negative attitudes toward contraception were in the minority; 89.7% of 1,200 unmarried women thought that contraception should be used in marriage (Epstein 1983: 125).

Acceptance of contraception expressed and reinforced changing attitudes about the roles of sex, love, marriage, and children. Other social changes fed into the shift in attitudes. Greater mobility of the upper and middle classes accentuated the increasing autonomy of the nuclear family.

The passage from the repressiveness of the first two-thirds of the nineteenth century to a new way of dealing with love, sex, marriage, and children was not an easy transition. The wrappings for the new package of norms were already cut. Popular books and magazines encouraged passionate love within marriage; sex/passionate love/marriage made up a new triangle. Men and women were using contraception, sex and procreation could be separated, and sex could be an expression of love and pleasure. Nevertheless, the new ideals entailed some problems of their own. Even though ideology changes, it may take a while before emotions and behavior fall in line.

Some adventurous people tried to implement the new ideals by casting aside the old restrictions and living in a very different way. During the first two decades of the twentieth century, Greenwich Village was the site of some of this experimentation. The problems that confronted couples trying to live according to the new ideology attest to the conflict that was inherent in the transition from repression.

Following the ideas of Carpenter (1911) and Key (1911), men and women publicly acknowledged their attempts to blend an active, sexual love with emotional intimacy, without the bond of marriage. Trimberger (1983) traced the course of three radical relationships, in which couples tried to mix the elements that their Victorian predecessors could not combine. The men wanted women who were their intellectual equals and were also sexually desirable (women you can "talk to and kiss"). The women wanted men with whom they could express their sexuality without the bonds of marriage and with whom they could share their most intimate thoughts and feelings. None of the relationships worked out, despite the good intentions of the participants. They cognitively desired a new type of relationship, but their emotions lagged behind.

It was difficult to link elements that had been so steadfastly dissociated for decades. First, they could not reconcile female autonomy with heterosexual love. Second, impotence was becoming a problem, because it was difficult for a man to respond sexually to a "valued love object." Freud pointed out the seriousness of this problem of male sexual response in a 1912 essay entitled "The Most Prevalent Form of Degradation in Erotic Life" (Trimberger 1983: 140).

Movies reflected the public's ambivalence about the transition to newer values. In *From Reverence to Rape* (1974), Molly Haskell interprets the virgin/vamp dichotomy in silent films as an expression of the difference between the old-fashioned and the new woman; country girls were pure and innocent, while city girls were portrayed as subject to corruption. The allure of women on the silent screen was a mixture of danger (unbridled sex) and innocence. Haskell sees the film images of this period as portraits of women who wanted the thrill of looking and acting free, without actually losing control. Even so, some directors — e.g., de Mille — provided ideas of how a wife could have sex appeal within her marriage.

The new cultural skeleton needed some flesh on it before it could function. Given the repression of the previous period, there were very few models for how to think and behave in a sexually expressive way. Two major figures helped to round out the ideology. Freud provided new concepts for thinking about sexuality, and van de Velde contributed some practical instructions for how to behave in a passionately loving way.

Freud tried to explain how sexuality and the mind relate to each other. By asserting that people's sexuality was not necessarily what they consciously thought it to be, he provided a new way to explore and open up repressed areas of sexuality. He expanded the concept of sexuality to include a variety of nonprocreative sexual behaviors. Brecher has succinctly summed up three major areas central to Freud's concept of sexuality (Brecher 1969: 174). First, sex life starts shortly after birth, not after puberty. Second, sexual activities are not confined to the genitals, but may include a wide range of nongenital behavior. Third, stimulation of erogenous zones produces pleasure, which aids procreation but does not necessarily coincide with that function; pleasure may occur independently of procreative purposes.

Freud thought that the body was infused with libido, a mass of sexual energy that seeks expression. The concept is similar to the nineteenth-century view of male energy that needed appropriate release, but it differs in that it applies to both males and females and is explicitly sexual in nature. The id, ego, and superego were new concepts, which provided a rational link between the restriction of the previous century and the permission in the twentieth for both men and women to be sexual. The superego represented parental (socially defined) "shoulds" while the id was a cache of unbridled impulses demanding gratification. Like the virgins and the vamps in silent films, the superego and the id portrayed a vacillation between authority and dangerous passion. The ego became the mediator between these two insistent forces and sought to balance them. The road to a healthy ego coincided with physical phases of development (oral, anal, genital, etc.) and the resolution of sexual conflicts at each stage. Former "perversions" — e.g., masturbation or homosexuality — became symptoms of emotional immaturity. Relabeling deviant behavior helped to remove the venom from the fangs of the moral censure that had previously been applied to it. The concepts of the unconscious and of repression gave people the option of realizing that everyone has sexual thoughts and feelings and that such thoughts and feelings are normal. Responsibility for dealing with sexual feelings lay ultimately with the individual. The ego was the bridge between ultrarestrictiveness and sexual gratification. Implicit in this idea was a shift from social surveillance of morality to individual responsibility for sexual decisions. Even so, sex retained its aura of danger, as it had in the past.

Despite the initial denunciation of many of Freud's ideas, particularly his idea that infants and children are sexual beings, discussion of his views represented a willingness to talk about sex. The taboo on silence about sexual matters was gradually eroding. Freud gave people a vocabulary for discussion. He also gave them a way to explain anxiety about sexual behavior; unconscious processes were at work and continually shaping their behavior. Like love, these forces could apply to anyone, even though an individual could not precisely define them or might not be consciously aware of them. They were psychological balm for people troubled by their inability to live up to the ideals of sexual love after many decades of repression.

While Freud provided a theory to explain why sexual problems arose, Theodoor Hendrick van de Velde, a Dutch gynecologist, hoped to circumvent difficulties by providing precise instructions for implementing the new cultural ideas. His *Ideal Marriage* (1926) provided a much-needed blueprint for guidance into an expanded world of sexual behavior. Part of its appeal was the sensitive way in which van de Velde opened the door to sexual responsiveness by using language that did not offend his readers. Another reason for the book's popularity (the American edition has sold more than half a million copies since 1945) was that it sought to describe how a married couple could achieve a fulfilling sexual relationship throughout their years together (Brecher 1969: 83). This approach meshed with the new view of marriage as one that included sexual love. Van de Velde was perceptive enough to realize that love and affection do not automatically lead to satisfactory sexual response. Therefore, he provided detailed techniques for translating emotional bonds into physical responses. He included such techniques as body kisses, stroking, cunnilingus, fellatio, manual clitoral stimulation, masturbation, assuming different positions, and after-play as ways to maintain excitement in a marriage. Within this framework, former "perversions" became acceptable behavior, as long as they enhanced the climax of love in coitus. By focusing on the link between emotion and physical expression and stressing the reciprocal give-and-take of a man and woman as a sexual unit, van de Velde "found a way . . . to make at least some of the joys of human sexuality aesthetically and ethically acceptable to a severely inhibited generation in many parts of the world" (Brecher 1969: 101).

The cultural pressures for change finally evolved into a middle-class solution to the dilemmas entailed by the new values: the "companionate marriage" (Trimberger 1983). Integrating love, sex, and intimacy was the core of this type of marriage. Although it was acceptable for a single woman to work, in order to develop maturity and to find a husband, she should become a full-time wife and mother after she married. Within her marriage, both she and her husband were to strive to fulfill each other sexually. However, the intimacy to which the Greenwich Village radicals aspired was more difficult, because the woman remained in the domestic sphere; she did not share her husband's world, even though he might confide his feelings to her (Trimberger 1983: 134).

The overlap between nineteenth-century social forms and the companionate marriage made the transition more palatable. Marriage and the family remained socially acceptable institutions. One more thread was added to tie spouses together: sexual love bound a husband and wife, just as children linked the spouses as mother and father. However, divorce became a more reasonable possibility if it could ultimately result in more fulfilling marital bonds. In fact, the divorce rate had shown a steady increase from the later nineteenth to the early part of the twentieth century (Smith 1978: 434).

Premarital and extramarital sex were also tolerated if they led to a more satisfactory marital relationship. Rationalization of nonmarital sexual relationships on the grounds of passionate love made previous outlets for passion less necessary, e.g., prostitutes and hysteria. Young men were less likely to have their first sexual experiences with prostitutes than with girlfriends, usually their fiancées (Epstein 1983: 125). A beneficial consequence was a substantial reduction in venereal disease. The widespread use of condoms during the first two decades of the twentieth century also contributed to the reduction (Tannahill 1980: 368). Increased acceptance and use of contraception by women lessened the possibility of unwanted pregnancies. In addition to being less objectionable morally, sexual relationships were less dangerous physically than they had been in the past. Both the cultural and the biological dimensions fed into each other to support different social behavior.

The "look" of women in the 'twenties was a manifestation of women's willingness to test the waters of liberation from repression. Since body image contributes to gender identity, transformations of body decoration are symbols of personal and cultural ideas about sexuality. Women *looked* liberated. Freed from the corsets that once bound their bodies and symbolized the tight constraint that culture exerted over their minds, they wore loose-fitting dresses, which revealed previously hidden parts of their bodies. Short dresses became fashionable for street wear and facilitated the national pastime of dancing (Brownmiller 1984: 146). Nevertheless, the newly exposed feminine leg brought constraints with it, much as new attitudes toward sex carried with them their own dilemmas. Garter belts and girdles held up the delicate silk stockings, which were vulnerable to snags and runs. Women began shaving hair from their legs and from under their arms to attain a chic, sexually appealing look. Rather than powdering their faces to accentuate a frail, almost infirm demeanor, they used vivid cosmetics; flappers dared to paint their faces with bright lipstick and rouge, cosmetics formerly associated with "fallen" women.

Movies accentuated these images. Some showed nudity and costumed their female stars in revealing clothing. Makeup for the eyes, mouth, face, and nails became glamorous and erotic accoutrements for the "new" woman. Mae West, Marlene Dietrich, and Jean Harlow were "sensualists without guilt," who could initiate sexual encounters without being portrayed as destructive or manipulative (Haskell 1974: 91). In contrast to the vamps (short for "vampires") of silent films, who drew their life force from men, the new stars were direct in asking for what they wanted and could desire sex without being evil or demented.

Like magazines and novels in the nineteenth century, movies were a means of communicating cultural aspirations and problems to a mass audience. They were the stage on which the play of elements of the new male/female scenario was acted out. The movies expressed the frustration of the public trying to rehearse satisfactorily their new parts as men and women, and they molded the public's views on how to behave. As American culture became more socially and ethnically diverse, mass media played a greater role in articulating cultural values that transcended geographical and social boundaries. In this light, the Production Code of 1933–1934 represented an important shift in attitudes toward sexuality. In response to pressure from the National League of Decency, moviemakers began to conform to a code that prohibited the use of "offensive" words and actions in films. Marriage was pictured as sacred, and displays of passion or the sex organs were discouraged. Adherence to the code was so strict that body stockings were put on Cheetah and other animals in the Tarzan and Jane movies to avoid shocking the audiences (Haskell 1974: 118)! "Wholesomeness" transmuted sex into romance, lust into love, and the body into the spirit. Just as twin beds were typical props in bedrooms, the difference between the male and female spheres widened once again. The jolt of the Great Depression may have knocked men and women back into more traditional, though unsatisfactory, roles. Or, perhaps people's discomfort with the newly emerging roles may have created too much anxiety to allow a publicly acknowledged transition. However problematic the old roles were, at least they were known. Gangster films, Westerns, war films, detective stories, and adventures expressed a male-dominated world of danger and thrills. Women's films concentrated on the limited options that women had to maintain in their middle-class state of mind. Sacrifice of a career, children, marriage, or a lover generally had a tragic ending, although some had bitter-sweet conclusions, which merged joy and pain (Haskell 1974: 163). A man's world was exciting and passionate, while a woman's involved sacrifice but a confirmation of her femininity. When women ventured into male realms, they were only provisional visitors; they eventually accepted marriage as the road to fulfillment. Work outside the home was fine until a woman became a wife and mother. Home and the family became the heart of a woman's existence.

As men and women sifted into their separate spheres, public discussion of sex and the family faded from view (Epstein 1983: 127). Several major social and cultural changes begun in the last century were firmly in place.

Technological developments clearly channeled changes in attitudes and behavior associated with reproduction and sex. All of them involved greater control over and specialization of certain aspects of the sexual and reproductive cycles.

The reproductive process became compartmentalized. As medical management and technological intervention in pregnancy and birth became more widely accepted, male doctors almost totally replaced nurse-midwives as the primary health providers for prenatal care of pregnant women and the delivery of babies. Births occurred more frequently in hospitals, away from home. Husbands were just as segregated from the process as they had been in the past. Wives were not as closely linked to social support during birth; they were cut off from their friends and relatives while they delivered. Instead, they were in the care of specialized medical personnel in a public facility. Birth became an individual rather than a family experience. Routine use of anesthesia and separation of mother and infant after birth sequestered women from several aspects of the birthing experience.

Additional technological developments separated women from a close physical connection with their babies. By the 1930s, bottle feeding enjoyed considerable popularity. Use of the rubber nipple, designed by Elijah Pratt in 1845, together with the ability to pasteurize milk, made bottle-feeding a safe alternative to breastfeeding by the turn of the century (Gerard 1970: 111). The practice was initially adopted by the well-to-do, who preferred to have their babies in hospitals and to defer to pediatricians in caring for their children. In 1900, most women breastfed their babies unless they were rich, ill, or irresponsible. By

1946, only 38 in 100 women were breastfeeding, and the proportion continued to decline into the 1950s (Gerard 1970: vii). The United States has the smallest proportion of women breastfeeding for its population of any country in the world. Although it loosened a close biological bond between mother and infant, bottle-feeding meant that a mother need not remain at home to feed her baby; alternate caretakers could feed infants. The potential opened for a way both to work outside the home and to have small children. Nevertheless, most women stayed at home.

Technological improvements and the routine use of antiseptics lowered infant and maternal mortality. The physical risks of becoming a mother were not as great as in the past, and a woman could look forward to the survival of the infants she had borne.

Having children became an option over which couples had voluntary control. Both men and women were using contraception. In the mid-1930s, more than 317 million condoms were being sold per year (Tannahill 1980: 411). By 1930, 55 birth control clinics were open in 23 cities in 12 states (Tannahill 1980: 416).

The separation of sex from reproduction had major implications for the nature of marriage and the family. Whereas marriage in the nineteenth century and early twentieth century was a rite of passage, marking both marriage and a transition to parenthood, contraception permitted a gap between marriage and procreation (Hareven 1982: 457). Decisions to marry did not have to be predicated on having children immediately. As voluntary factors became more important than involuntary ones in determining the timing of having children, marriage could be important in its own right. Marriage and having children became two separate phases in the modern family cycle. The addition of sexual love and intimacy as elements of marriage raised the standards for having a successful marriage.

A smaller number of children and a longer life span meant that a few more experiences were added to family life. Not only could husbands and wives have more years together but also they were likely to have distinct periods marked by having children and being without them after the child rearing was completed ("the empty nest"). Differential male/female mortality added another segment in a woman's life: being a widow without children at home. The timing of transitions within the family became more orderly and stable than it was in the past (Hareven 1982: 457). Age became a significant marker of the phases.

A major change in family values, which developed at the turn of the century, was set by the 1930s and 1940s. Emphasis on individual priorities and preferences superseded the collective view of the family that was prevalent among the middle class (Hareven 1982: 456). The family ceased to be a collective work unit, to which all members made economic contributions. The distinctions between the generations (children and adults, adolescents and adults, middle-aged and older adults) and between the male and female spheres were sharp. Consumption of economic goods and care of children and adolescents centered in the home. Housework lost its economic and productive value and contrasted with the highly differentiated and specialized work schedules to which men conformed. Communication between husband and wife suffered as their domains became more distinct. Work schedules made it difficult for a father to become an integral part of the domestic scene except during his leisure hours. Therefore, the mother/child unit was the most intense form of parent/child interaction. Emphasis on privacy within the family implied greater social isolation of women in their household compartments.

Further segregation of the domestic world of women and the public one of men was made impossible by World War II. Large numbers of women entered the labor market to support their families while their husbands were away at war. More education and training became available for women. The media supported women's transition from the home to "male" jobs. Films portrayed women as effective workers and shrewd business people. The superfemale and the superwomen entered the already wide array of movie images (Haskell 1974: 214). Superfemales were very feminine, but were too intelligent to be passively content with a life at home; they were ambitious, though they contained their rebellion within a comfortable, traditional framework. Superwomen were also very intelligent, but chose to adopt male characteristics because they needed to survive economically or because they wanted to attain the fruits of a man's world. Vivien Leigh and Bette Davis typified superfemales, while Joan Crawford and Katherine Hepburn played superwomen.

Clothing styles reflected these changes. In contrast to the flashy, short dresses of the flappers in the 1920s, women in the early 1940s looked almost mannish in their suits, pants, and tops with squared-off shoulders. Despite heavy media pressure to return home after the war, women were not so quick to relinquish their roles in the workplace; many became a permanent part of the workforce. Both husbands and wives who worked outside the home had the chance to develop new skills, opportunities, and friends.

Since the division of labor is one of the important sources of nonverbal modeling for children's development of gender identity, participation of both men and women in the workplace portended changes for the next generation, both in their view of themselves as males and females and in how they were likely to interact sexually.

Although the mass media generated considerable discussion and writing, as well as film portrayals, of sexuality, very little was actually known about what couples did in the privacy of their own homes. Alfred C. Kinsey, a mild-mannered biologist at Indiana University, changed all of that. His shocking but voraciously read reports on the sexual behavior of the human male (Kinsey, Pomeroy, and Martin 1948) and the human female (Kinsey et al. 1953), gave people a yardstick for determining the normalcy of their own behavior. More importantly, they placed the study of human sexuality on firm, scientific footing.

Ellis, Freud, and van de Velde did not use statistics to establish the validity of their generalizations. And even though some early sex surveys based on questionnaires and interviews were conducted in America, the samples were small and unsystematic, and the content was narrow in its focus. Kinsey's studies remain the most extensive and reliable sampling of American sexual behavior that has ever been made. As such, they give us a sophisticated body of data with which to examine the question of how coherent our cultural values and social practices were from 1900 to 1950. In addition, they remain a standard by which to gauge the type and amount of change that occurred from the time of Kinsey's reports to the "sexual revolution."

When Kinsey was asked to offer a course in sex education and marriage at Indiana University in 1937, he was chosen because his character and credentials seemed to be of impeccable quality for the task. He was forty-three years old, married, and settled into his profession, and he seemed to be the essence of conventionality and respectability. His parents were middle-class, devoutly religious Victorians, who had trained Kinsey according to the standards of the era (Brecher 1969: 110). He had been a biology professor at Indiana University since 1920 and had established himself as an authority on gall wasps. He had demonstrated his meticulous attention to detail by collecting over four million gall wasps as a basis for making generalizations about them. Who, including Kinsey, would have guessed that he would become a major figure in the study of sexual behavior?

A major clue to what unfolded was Kinsey's dedication to the principles of science and his insistence on following them, wherever they led. As he attempted to gather information for his new course, he was appalled by the lack of sound scientific information on human sexuality. He found that scientists had avoided the investigation of human sexuality to such an extent that it was one of the most poorly explored fields in biology, psychology, or sociology (Kinsey, Pomeroy, and Martin 1948:

21). Although the volume of written material was equal to that of other fields, it was "of such mixed quality that it is difficult to separate the kernel from the chaff, and still more difficult to maintain any perspective during its perusal" (Kinsey, Pomeroy, and Martin 1948: 21). Therefore, he decided to conduct a "fact-finding survey in which an attempt has been made to discover what people do sexually, what factors may account for their patterns of sexual behavior, how their sexual experiences have affected their lives, and what social significance there may be in each type of behavior" (Kinsey et al. 1953: 3).

Reacting to criticisms that the study of sexuality belonged to the province of moral philosophy, Kinsey remained steadfast in his adherence to science. He reiterated his faith in the truth value of science: "There is an honesty in science which demands that the best means be used for the determination of the truth . . . We do not believe that the happiness of individual men and the good of the total social organization is ever furthered by the perpetuation of ignorance. There is an honesty in science which leads to a certain acceptance of the reality" (Kinsey 1953: 9, 10). In conformity with these ideals, Kinsey deliberately veered away from making value judgments about his subjects or his findings. He wanted to discover the "facts" and avoid the emotionalism that had so clouded research in this area in the past.

Establishing "facts" meant having precise definitions, operational criteria for confirming the occurrence of behavior, and a systematic method. Therefore, he confined his investigation to those activities that could result in orgasm ("orgasmic outlets"). His subject matter included a broad spectrum of the taboo and private aspects of sexual behavior, including nocturnal dreams and emissions, childhood and adolescent practices, masturbation, premarital sex, marital sex, extramarital sex, homosexuality, and bestiality. He did not presume that these behaviors would not occur; rather, he assumed that everyone may have participated in every type of outlet, regardless of culture's labeling of them as normal or abnormal. He also assumed that sexual behavior might be affected by a number of social factors, e.g., socioeconomic background, marital history, sex education, age and decade of birth, and rural/urban residence; he tested for the influence of each social factor on orgasmic outlet.

The detailed sampling procedure and interviewing techniques that Kinsey discussed in Part One of *Sexual Behavior in the Human Male* (1948) show a breadth of knowledge about human behavior and the realities of conducting sex research, which is outstanding in its consideration of detail. By the time they published *Sexual Behavior in the Human Female* (1953), Kinsey and his colleagues (Pomeroy, Martin, and

Gebhard) had conducted over 16,000 personal interviews of males and females during a fifteen-year period. They spanned different geographical, urban, and rural parts of the country; different age groups; and members of different religious affiliations, economic levels, and marital statuses. Interviews covered from 300 to 500 items of information and lasted an average of two hours each (Kinsey et al. 1953: 63). Kinsey's ultimate goal was to collect 100,000 interviews. His interviewing techniques stressed interest in respondents, directness in asking questions, adjustment of the language used to suit the social or economic group of the respondent, precision, and thoroughness.

Kinsey was aware of the strengths and weaknesses of his taxonomic approach, and he was quick to point them out. He specified the limits to which generalizations could be made from the types of statistics he used, and he paid particular attention to problems of reliability and validity. He criss-crossed from one field to another to find background data.

Recorded data became the basis for much of the nonstatistical generalization in the books (Kinsey et al. 1953: 83); diaries, calendars of sexual activities, wall inscriptions, erotic art, and fiction were a few of the sources for these data. He also utilized observed data from community studies, clinical studies (from anatomists, gynecologists, obstetricians, psychiatrists, marriage counselors, etc.), and mammalian studies. Previously published anthropological, legal, and statistical studies also provided input for his discussions. The presentation of his results is truly interdisciplinary.

The alarm that readers sounded after the publication of the reports stemmed partially from their disbelief that both men and women had been and were continuing to engage in behavior that was so counter to the values of the time. The late 1940s and the 1950s were probably the most family-oriented period of the twentieth century (Blumstein and Schwartz 1983: 29). Over 95 percent of people in their childbearing years married (Blumstein and Schwartz 1983: 30). Television had replaced movies as the primary carrier of cultural values. At a time when "I Love Lucy," "Father Knows Best," and "I Remember Mama" dominated the air waves, it was difficult for the public to accept the facts about sexual behavior that Kinsey had presented. The outcry was so great that Kinsey's job at the university was threatened, his funding was cut back, and his political inclinations were suspected of being subversive. Obviously Kinsey had hit a delicate nerve in American culture.

Criticisms that he did not consider love and the psychological meaning of the behavior were ill placed, because it was not his intention to delve into these nebulous areas. He concentrated on presenting the frequency and incidence of concrete behaviors as straightforwardly and amorally as possible. Had he been less of a scientist, his results would have been easier to reject. Previous writings on the subject could be dismissed as representing one person's opinion or as limited studies based on the experiences of a few patients or clients. However, it was difficult to attack Kinsey on these grounds. In fact, surveys conducted after 1954 only confirm rather than discredit Kinsey's findings (Brecher 1969: 120).

The majority of the sexual behavior that Kinsey investigated was subject to cultural prohibition in the heyday of the nineteenth-century morality. Most of it concerned nonmarital and nonprocreative sex.

Nonmarital sex seemed to change with the cultural emphases of the times. The incidence of premarital and extramarital sex increased in the generations born after the repressive era in the nineteenth century. By age 18, most females (81%) and males (84%) had experienced premarital petting; of those who had experienced it, most had responded erotically (83% of the females and 100% of the males) (Kinsey et al. 1953: 267). Those born before 1900 were less likely to have engaged in petting by age 35 than those born after 1900. However, the differences between the generations were not as large as one might suppose; 80% of females born before 1900 had experienced petting by age 35; 91% of those born between 1900 and 1909 and nearly 99% of those born between 1910 and 1920 had done so. What differentiated them more markedly was the age they were at their first experiences and their responses to the experiences. Those females born before 1900 were likely to experience petting by age 18; those born after 1900 experienced it earlier, by 15 or 16. Orgasm from petting was more likely for women born after 1900 (32–37%) than for those born before 1900 (15%).

Females were less likely to engage in premarital coitus than in petting. Fifty percent of the women engaged in premarital coitus and 68–98% of the males did, depending on their educational levels. The difference by generation was dramatic for females. Fourteen percent of those born before 1900 involved themselves in premarital coitus, while 36–39% of those born after 1900 did. Kinsey showed that the incidence of premarital sex for females had markedly increased since 1900 and provided evidence to support the idea that women were taking seriously the cultural encouragement to allow themselves to be sexual.

Nevertheless, the degree of devotion to religious principles affected the likelihood of men and women having premarital coitus; 23–30% of the devout females experienced premarital sex, in contrast to 55–63% of the less devout ones. Moral factors (89% F; 21–61% M), fear of pregnancy (44% F; 18–28% M) and fear of discovery (44% F; 14–23% M) were more likely to deter females than males from premarital sex. Fear of venereal disease (14% F; 25–29% M) and lack of opportunity (22% F; 35–52% M) were more likely to dissuade males. Interestingly enough, 69–77% of the women had no regrets for engaging in the practice; those who did express concern were either devout or inexperienced, or else they did not have sex with their fiancés. Most women had premarital coitus with their fiancés and deviated from marital sex only in the direction that the cultural values tolerated, i.e., passion was acceptable in a marital relationship or in one likely to lead to marriage. Overall, the late nineteenth- and early twentieth-century values, which gave women permission to be sexual, had a significant impact on the generations born after 1900. More men and women were engaging in premarital sex and enjoying it, unless they were very devoutly committed to their religions.

Extramarital sex showed a similar rise, probably for similar reasons. Both male and female participants agreed that extramarital sex could have the following benefits: it provides emotional satisfaction, contributes new types of sexual experiences, may improve marital adjustment, and may raise social status among peers (Kinsey et al. 1953: 438). Both males and females were very likely to achieve orgasm in this context (Kinsey et al. 1953: 437). Nevertheless, they recognized that extramarital sex could cause difficulties or even contribute to divorce (Kinsey et al. 1953: 438). By age 25, 4% of the women born before 1900 had had an extramarital relationship, while more than twice as great a proportion of those born after 1900 had (1900–1909, 8%; 1910–1919, 10%; 1920–1929, 12%). By age 40, 22% of those born before 1900 had had an affair, and 30% of those born between 1900 and 1909 had. Overall, 26% of the women and 50% of the men had experienced extramarital relations by age 40.

Even within marriages, sexual practices changed from the nineteenth to the twentieth century. Although all men and women experienced coitus in marriage, they were not equally responsive to the experience. Although nearly all men were orgasmic by the first year of marriage, only 75% of the women were; even after twenty years of marriage, 10% of the wives had never experienced an orgasm in marital coitus (Kinsey et al. 1953: 392). The incidence of orgasm materially increased in the generations of women born after 1900 (Kinsey et al. 1953: 392). The increase was not related to religious background, but more likely stemmed from her previous premarital orgasmic experiences (petting, masturbation, or coitus) and from the cultural exhortation that a woman be sexually responsive within her marriage. Nevertheless, only about three-quarters of a woman's marital copulations led to orgasm, while 100% of a man's did (Kinsey et al. 1953: 393). Nudity during coitus, oral techniques of stimulation, and diversity of positions were added to the sexual repertoire of the younger generations (Kinsey et al. 1953: 393).

The statistics in the Kinsey reports that were probably most shocking to the public were those concerning the incidence of homosexuality. By age 45, approximately 37% of the males and 13% of the females had had homosexual experiences that resulted in orgasm (Kinsey et al. 1953: 487). Furthermore, this incidence had *no* relation to the decade in which the individuals were born (Kinsey et al. 1953: 488). Although females (71%) and males (51%) tended to confine these relationships to one or two partners, a significant number of men had had more than ten partners (22%), in contrast to the low incidence of this practice by females (4%). Although these statistics engendered public horror, they are not surprising in view of the repressive ideas about heterosexual contacts that were current in the nineteenth century. Same-gender friends were thrown into close association in their separate spheres — women in the domestic domain, and men in their educational institutions and workplaces. I have argued that these relationships provided a way to express affection, which was not so easily expressed within the family, except as a "spiritual" love. After sexual love between heterosexual couples was more culturally approved, homosexual relationships continued either as alternatives or additions.

The public horror of homosexuality probably related to anxiety generated by crossing acceptable categories for relationships. By the twentieth century, love was supposed to be confined to heterosexual, maritally-focused relationships. Homosexuality is neither heterosexual nor marital. It threatened the newly established ideal of the companionate marriage and it continued to remind men and women that the choices they had made were not the only alternatives for their lives. The existence of such alternatives made people uncomfortable, because they still had some insecurities about the choices they had made for themselves.

While the incidence of homosexuality created the most public disbelief, that of masturbation did not. Of all of the sexual behaviors investigated, masturbation continued to evoke the most guilt and fear. Most of the men (93%) and women (62%) whom Kinsey and his associates interviewed had engaged in the most severely prohibited sexual behavior of the past: masturbation. Those who masturbated did so for a variety of reasons: as a source of pleasure, as a form of satisfying a physiological need, or as a contribution to psychological well-being (Kinsey et al. 1953: 175). Younger people were much more likely to reach orgasm than those born in the earlier part of the century; orgasmic response was much less likely in devoutly religious respondents, particularly females (Kinsey et al. 1953: 174). The majority of males worried about the practice, while less than half of the females (47%) did. This may have been a product of the view that masturbation was likely to create mental or physical harm and drain a man of his precious energies. It is also possible that men had a more negative view of masturbation, because they had been punished for self-stimulation more frequently than women; erection and ejaculation are more easily detected than signs of female arousal.

It appears that women held true to their nineteenth-century reputation of being more "moral" than men, for they held their behavior in line with cultural values more stringently than the men did. Although 82% of males had experienced orgasm with masturbation by age 15, only 20% of the females had (Kinsey et al. 1953: 173). The data indicate that the fear of masturbation and the guilt created by it persisted through the 1940s.

The picture of sexual behavior that Kinsey painted with his statistics reveals a number of important conclusions about the relationship between cultural values and sociosexual behavior from the nineteenth century through 1950. First, women were more likely to adjust their sexual behavior to the moral standards of the era, while men's behavior was more responsive to such social factors as educational level and socioeconomic status. When it was acceptable for women to be passionate within a love relationship, women gradually increased their participation in premarital sex, extramarital sex, and experimentation with new techniques in marital sex. Second, commitment to religion was a consistently strong cultural force in inhibiting male and female sexual response to any nonmarital, nonprocreative, sexual activity. Even within marriage, religious proscriptions were likely to limit the range of sexual techniques. Third, the main effect of repressive ideology was to inhibit responsiveness and to foster guilt about the prohibited behavior; it did not prevent sexual activity from occurring. Fourth, the effect of repressing a female's sexual response before marriage was to inhibit sexual response in marriage. Orgasm by petting, masturbation, or coitus before marriage appreciably enhanced the woman's ability to have an orgasm in marital coitus. Fifth, males were more likely than females to have continuity in expressing themselves sexually. The major changes in sexual patterns involved the woman's willingness to engage in a wider range of sexual behavior; the types of male outlets remained the same. Culture was a primary force in supporting the female's change in attitude, and it facilitated her physiological response.

In sum, the *types* of sexual behavior engaged in were not appreciably different from one decade to the next. What was different was more extensive participation in them (particularly by women) and increased responsiveness to these activities. Kinsey's reports provided a basis for furthering that process. People who had privately felt that their behavior was perverted or abnormal could breathe a sigh of relief when they realized that their activities fell within a more "normal" range. Secrecy about sexual behavior had bred prejudice and ignorance, which began to wither in the light of recognizing the incidence and frequency of sexual practices. The door was opened even more for enjoying sex. Nevertheless, there remained a disjunction between feelings and behavior, which fostered ambivalence about sex. In any case, the controversies stirred up by the reports stimulated public discussion and aired the issues.

Kinsey's scientific study of sexual behavior segregated it from values and morality. However, he did recognize the impact that cultural and social institutions were likely to make on the incidence and frequency of use of each type of orgasmic outlet. In addition, he presented evidence that linked human to nonhuman sexual behavior and explored the relevance of biological factors in channeling the nature of male and female sexual expression. However, the classification of sexual behavior into different categories presented the public with the potential for continuing a trend begun in the Victorian era — isolating and reifying sexual behavior as a force with an existence of its own. The process of separating out sex as a distinct category in life was to continue for the next few decades.

Scientific and social developments in the 1950s reinforced a process of separating elements of the sexual and reproductive cycles from each other. Masters and Johnson's studies (1966, 1970) are prime examples of how far the investigation of sex as an object of scientific study could go. They took sex into the laboratory for observation and measurement. Even though Kinsey had observed and filmed sexual acts in the course of his research, he published nothing about it (Hunt 1975: 5). The verbal reports he collected were sufficient for the public to regard him and his associates as unwholesome. Dr. William H. Masters initiated an investigation of anatomical and physiological elements of human sexual response at the Department of Obstetrics and Gynecology at Washington University's School of Medicine in 1954 (Masters and Johnson 1966: 3). By using accepted techniques of physiological measurement and the frequent use of color cinematographic recording, he hoped to find out what men and women "do in response to effective sexual stimulation, and why they do it, rather than [rely] on what people say they do or even think their sexual reactions and experiences might be" (Masters and Johnson 1966: 20). By observing, recording, and evaluating patterns of physiological and psychological response to sexual stimulation, he hoped to contribute an understanding of sexual response never previously possible in a medical or behavioral environment (Masters and Johnson 1966: 20). In the initial phase of his research, Masters used prostitutes for subjects. Later on, he used volunteers to continue his studies. Virginia Johnson joined his staff as a researcher in 1957 and became part of the well-known team of Masters and Johnson.

Masters and Johnson were not without their critics. Ministers, moralists, and social scientists raised objections concerning the ethics of intruding into the privacy of the sex act (Salzman 1971: 69). Thomas Szasz raised the thorny question of whether there was a difference between paying a prostitute for her services and paying a sexual surrogate $250 per encounter to help a client cure a sexual dysfunction (Szasz 1980: 60). Since surrogates were paid for sexual services, and since single men who came to the clinic for treatment knew that the clinic would provide them with partners, how was the clinic different from a house of prostitution? Does the label of medical research exempt the behavior from prostitution statutes? It seems that the label must mean exemption from legal consequences, because Masters and Johnson have never been prosecuted for their activities. Instead, the mass media heralded their research in very favorable terms. A feature story in *Time* magazine lauded their investigations for "helping to make it possible for supposedly infertile couples to have children, helping to prolong the enjoyment of a healthy and normal sex life for aging couples at least into their 80s" (in Szasz 1980: 29).

Nevertheless, the research done by Masters and Johnson exploded a number of popular myths about sexual response (Masters and Johnson 1966). First, it emphasizes the similarities rather than the differences between men and women in their sexual responses. Both go through phases of excitement, plateau, orgasm, and resolution. For both, physiological changes are not confined to the genitals, but affect the entire body. Second, it showed that there is no essential physiological difference between a clitoral and a vaginal orgasm. The Freudian claim that clitoral orgasm is an immature sexual response was discredited. Third, it showed that women have the capacity to be more sexually responsive than men; they do not experience a refractory period after orgasm as men do, and they can have multiple orgasms. A woman requires continuous and regular stimulation to reach orgasm, however. Fourth, the relative insensitivity of the inner two-thirds of the vagina means that penis size is not of major importance in effecting adequate vaginal stimulation for a woman. Fifth, Masters and Johnson introduced a therapy format for dealing with sexual dysfunction (Masters and Johnson 1970). It included the following components; (1) the concept that sexual inadequacy is a product of the sexually interacting couple as a "unit," rather than an individual problem; (2) a view that many sexual dysfunctions are learned and can therefore be unlearned; (3) the use of male and female cotherapists to deal with the psychological dimensions of the couple's interaction, by providing support and translation of one's gender behavior in terms which the other can understand; (4) techniques for aiding the man and woman to become more comfortable about the sensations of their bodies and to facilitate the full expression of their physical and psychological feelings in intercourse.

On a cultural level, this research articulated a new conceptualization of sexuality. By providing a physiological baseline of "normal" sexual response (in *Human Sexual Response*, 1966), Masters and Johnson defined new boundaries for labeling abnormality and dysfunction. Their framework represented a 180-degree change from the concepts of the nineteenth century. Rather than being a sign of disease or sinfulness, sexual responsiveness became a "natural" activity. Instead of suppressing and removing sources of sexual desire, physicians and psychotherapists were encouraged to restore their clients' sexual sensitivity. *Human Sexual Inadequacy* (Masters and Johnson 1970) and *The Pleasure Bond* (Masters and Johnson 1976) spelled out the specific ways in which a person could achieve fulfillment. The aim was to clear away the repressive psychological cobwebs that inhibited response and help clients to become fully attuned to the pleasurable sensations that their bodies could produce. The body had become a temple of pleasure. Further, the most heinous activity of the nineteenth century, masturbation, had become one of the keys to sexual salvation.

Redefinition of sexual response by medical and psychological experts encouraged ordinary individuals to think differently about their bodies and their sexual activities. They were aided in feeling good about enjoying themselves. However, in some cases the message was even stronger; you *should* enjoy yourself, and if you don't, there is something wrong with you that requires therapy.

Other researchers were delving into issues that required the analysis of sexuality into still more individual components. John Money at Johns Hopkins University tackled the complex question of how gender identity develops. He dissected the concept of sex into a series of elements (genetic, hormonal, social, cultural, and psychological) and demonstrated that "sex" is not a unitary phenomenon. He suggested "gender" as a more appropriate way of defining categories of sexual differentiation.

Gender role, gender identity, and sexual dimorphism emerged as three major aspects of sexual definition, which usually, but not necessarily, coincided. He extended his investigation of sexual definition into prenatal development and into old age. And, he suggested the possibility of differences in brain organization between men and women. He held out the possibility for a more complete appreciation of the dynamics of sexuality in all of its dimensions (Money and Tucker 1975; Money and Ehrhardt 1977).

Technological changes were hastening a more complete split of sex from procreation. Moore and Price clarified the feedback between the pituitary and the ovarian cycle in 1932 (Peel and Potts 1969: 89). In the late 1930s, Russell Marker developed cheap sources of steroids for use as contraceptives by doing research on plant steroids. By 1940, Sturgis and Albright reported that estrogen could inhibit ovulation (Sturgis and Albright 1940 cited in Peel and Potts 1969: 89). By 1950, steroid hormones cost 1/100th of the price they claimed in the 1940s. After much trial and error in developing oral contraceptives, Searle, Inc., marketed Enovid in the late 1950s and saw its widespread use as a contraceptive in the U.S. by 1959 (Peel and Potts 1969: 90). Unlike the barrier methods of the past, a woman could take "the pill" and engage in "spontaneous" sex without her partner's even knowing whether or not she was using contraception. Although the condom and the diaphragm paved the way for a separation between sex and reproduction, the effectiveness of the pill in preventing conception and the scope it allowed for uninterrupted intercourse culminated in its quick acceptance and popularity with American women in the 1960s.

Scientific analysis of sex carried with it a fragmentation or discrediting of traditional sexual concepts. The ambivalence that these findings generated was expressed in the media.

The star system of the movies was collapsing, and cinema's gods and goddesses with toppling from their pedestals, much as traditional sexual concepts were. There was more recognition of the difference between the roles and the real people who played them. The difference between the person and the personal became more apparent as the decades passed. Audiences wanted more realism in films. What they received were hints of reality. As Haskell put it (1974: 235):

> It was as if the whole period of the fifties was a front, the topsoil that protected the seed of rebellion that was germinating below. The cultural disorientation had begun, but it had yet to be acknowledged . . . The decade, and the stars . . . had an unreal quality. They were all *about* sex, but without sex. The fabulous fifties were a box of Cracker Jacks without a prize; or with the prize distorted into a forty-inch bust, a forty-year-old virgin.

Elvis Presley, Marilyn Monroe, Elizabeth Taylor, and Doris Day played roles that demonstrated the approach/avoidance treatment of sexual expression in the movies. Marilyn Monroe is perhaps the best illustration of the ambivalence and unreality of the time. Her disarming shyness juxtaposed with her voluptuous body projected an image of vulnerability, which at once elicited desire and protectiveness. She was cast in roles that highlighted her efforts to please others rather than fulfill her own physical desires. She thus radiated a sense of spirituality in her behavior, which contrasted with the carnal lust suggested by her body. She was like a little girl trapped in the body of a woman. Her death pointed out the tragedy of a woman who had to deal with being viewed as a sex object; she may have pleased others with her image, but it was a characterization at variance with her identity as a person with a need for love. The split between her role in films and her sense of herself as a real person eventually split her off from life.

The emergence of "rock and roll" gave some outlet for the repressed desires of the young. Although "rock and roll" originally referred to explicitly sexual acts, it was taken over into white, middle-class culture as a label for the upbeat rhythms of the music of the 1950s. Recording stars became the foci for sublimated passion and romanticized sex. Elvis Presley moved his hips and created a sensation.

Both men and women were buying into images of people approaching, yet avoiding sex. Hugh Hefner introduced *Playboy* in the midst of the ambivalence and found a ready readership. The pin-ups of the 1940s became established as a regular part of male fantasies published in "girlie" magazines. Hefner bought the famous nude calendar photo of Marilyn Monroe for $500 and presented her as his first centerfold (Talese 1980: 79).

The sacrosanct unit of the family was also showing signs of change and fragmentation. Although television programs extolled the virtues of family living and promoted a view that home is where the heart is, particularly for women, the image was getting stale. Television acknowledged that conflicts might occur within the family but dismissed them as transitory episodes, which a nurturant mother and a hard-working father could solve if they mutually supported each other and their family members. The distinction between male and female spheres was still clear; males worked outside the home, and women worked within it. Muddying these clear-cut distinctions was the mainstay of comedy. For example, Lucy (in "I Love Lucy") tried a variety of jobs, but found that her efforts were incompetent and laughable. When she worked in a pizza parlor, her dough stuck to the ceiling, and when she tried to package candies at a candy factory, she had to eat chocolates from the conveyer belt because she couldn't wrap them quickly enough. When she finally had a contract in Hollywood to launch her long-desired show-business career, she gave up the opportunity, because Ricky, her husband, reminded her that he was returning to New York with the baby and their friends, the Mertzes, all of whom Lucy would only be able to see occasionally.

Fred and Ethel Mertz and her marriage to Ricky were the anchors of Lucy's leisure-filled existence. The four roles were caricatures of the logical male and the scatter-brained, emotional female. Ricky's willingness to forgive Lucy for her illogical schemes showed his strength and her need to depend on him; it also confirmed the inadvisability of her developing a career of her own. In her comic way, Lucy revealed the frustration of the everyday housewife, to which Betty Friedan gave more serious attention later in *The Feminine Mystique* (1963). Motherhood gave Lucy more purpose in her daily routine. Although motherhood was esteemed, there was still a public aversion to acknowledging the "facts of life" in a direct way. Desi Arnez had to overcome the resistence of the network and the sponsors to incorporate Lucy's pregnancy into the program. It was the first television show in which viewers saw an actual mother-to-be playing a pregnant woman.

Something went wrong with life in the happy kingdom of "Leave It to Beaver" and "Ozzie and Harriet." By the end of the 1950s and the start of the 1960s, the divorce rate was increasing, and the marriage rate was decreasing. The already small nuclear family was fragmenting even further, and "single-parent families" emerged. It is interesting to note that when divorces broke up families in other ethnic groups, they were labeled "broken families"; when the phenomenon hit the white middle class, the illusion of a family still remained, through calling it a "single-parent family." Divorcées entered a marginal social arena in which they had children but were no longer married. There were no rules for how to behave. How does a person "date" when she is older than most singles and has teenage children?

Questions about the nature of sexuality, personal identity, and how to deal with the fragmentation of long-held concepts and social interactions erupted into the "sexual revolution" of the 1960s. However, it might be more accurately called the "sexual evolution" of the 1960s, because the behavior was a product of the gradual changes that preceded it. Without flexible institutions to deal with the stressful situations of individuals, people fell back onto their own resources and did their "own thing," attempting to fashion meaning out of personal chaos. The trend of self-examination that began in the postwar era of the 1940s and 1950s continued into the 1960s. The culture responded to the stress by legitimizing individual efforts to deal with problems. Self-actualization, development of human potential, and growth were concepts that captured the spirit of the times. New social groups gradually emerged, as individuals realized that they were not alone in their confusion; they bonded together to provide mutual support. Problems previously defined as personal became social issues. The private became public and fueled the notion that a brand new set of feelings and behavior had developed from the 1950s to the 1960s. The difference was one of degree, not kind. As old concepts were shattered, new ones took up the pieces of the old and rearranged them in a different and more open way. The public discussion created the illusion that there was more discontinuity from the past than there actually was.

Individuals were obviously questioning the direction they should follow for their lives and were exploring a variety of options. By the late 1960s and early 1970s, fertility dipped. In 1970, 16% of women between 25 and 29 who had ever been married had no children (Blumstein and Schwartz 1983: 31). The marriage rate was low, and divorce was high; this trend continued into the 1970s (Blumstein and Schwartz 1983: 30). In 1960, 28% of the women between 20 and 24 were unmarried (Blumstein and Schwartz 1983: 31). Each of these changes fed into the other. More women were going to college and working before they married and had children; they became aware of the options open to them. An increasing divorce rate siphoned off more women into the labor market. Women's work and its impact on marriage and the family were becoming forces to be reckoned with.

The media picked up on some of the new needs. Following her successful book, *Sex and the Single girl* (1962), Helen Gurley Brown took over the reins of *Cosmopolitan* magazine and transformed it into a vehicle for reconciling women's sexual needs, work, and the family. Single women still wanted men in their lives, and married women wanted to maintain their marriages. Sixty-one percent of the readership was made up of working women, and two-thirds of the readers were married (Faust 1980: 160). The formula was appealing. Women were encouraged to work and to be interested in men and sex. If they did not get married, or even if they were divorced, they had jobs to sustain them before, during, and after they found their men. The magazine presented images of women as sexy, independent, creative, interesting, and self-actualizing (Faust 1980: 161), and its primary message was to "get rid of guilt" about sex, *not* to get rid of sex (Faust 1980: 169).

*Ms.* magazine appeared as another route for integrating the multiple facets of women's lives. Its nonsectarian, feminist message was popular, but it appealed to a more limited audience than the likes of *Cosmopoli-*

*tan* readers. Its first sample issue was designed to stay on the stand for three months, but it sold out in eight days (Steinem 1983: 4). Reader response encouraged the editors to continue their efforts to establish *Ms.* on a monthly basis.

*Ms.* was and still is a significant publication, because its ownership and management are made up of women. Furthermore, it represents a new type of women's magazine, with articles spanning social issues of concern to the modern woman, e.g., health, child care, work, and discrimination. It has gone beyond cosmetics, fashion, and love to present thoughtful analyses about how to integrate women into the public realm.

The women's movement was spawning other literature by women for women, which addressed itself to serious issues of relevance to all women. *Sexual Politics* (1971) by Kate Millett defined the concept of patriarchy as a political institution and presented a theory of power and domination roles in sexual relationships. Robin Morgan collected a series of essays for *Sisterhood Is Powerful* (1970), one of the first anthologies of writings from the women's liberation movement. *Our Bodies, Ourselves* (Boston Women's Health Book Collective 1976) originally appeared in 1971 as an antidote to men's control of women's health. By the time its second edition appeared in 1976, the book had sold over a million copies. As a guide to basic information about women's psychology, physiology, and sexuality, it contextualized activities into women's lives, rather than presenting a mechanized view of sex and reproduction. In addition, it assumed that women have a right to specific, accurate information about their bodies, so that they can make informed decisions about their health. A doctor's authority alone was not sufficient to warrant acceptance of treatment.

While the media were responding to changes in gender roles and concepts by presenting new alternatives to previous orientations, researchers were trying to assess the magnitude of the change that had occurred during the "sexual revolution." Morton Hunt attempted to resurvey the territory Kinsey covered in the 1940s and measure the extent of the change that had taken place since then. In *Sexual Behavior in the 1970s* (1975), Hunt analyzed the results of over 2,000 questionnaires collected in 1972 by the Research Guild from a sample of the American population. Although he said that he could not unequivocally state that the sample was representative of the national population, he believed that the sample was a "reasonably good representation of American adult society" (Hunt 1975: 16). The more than 1,000 items of information included data on individual backgrounds, attitudes toward sex education, and complete sex histories (Hunt 1975: 15). They went beyond the major areas investigated by Kinsey by including information on attitudes as well as on specific behaviors, such an anal intercourse, group sex, sado-masochistic practices, and mate-swapping. The results allow comparison with Kinsey's findings in many important areas.

Of major import was the finding that there was tolerance about a variety of sexual ideas and acts, including those held and engaged in by other people (Hunt 1975: 20). People were giving themselves and others permission to experiment with a wide range of behavior. Depending on the degree of emotional commitment between partners, 60–84% of the males thought premarital sex was acceptable for men, and 44–81% thought it was all right for women; 37–73% of the males thought it was all right for men, and 20–68% thought it was acceptable for women (Hunt 1975: 21). Both men (75%) and women (67%) agreed that a woman does not lose a man's respect if she agrees to have intercourse before marriage.

A variety of contexts and partners for sexual activities were also more acceptable. Many men (50%) and women (50%) refused to agree with a statement that homosexuality was wrong (Hunt 1975: 22). A larger percentage of men (62%) and women (75%) agreed that mate-swapping was wrong. The majority of respondents were in favor of legalizing prostitution and having divorce laws that did not require the presentation of grounds for divorce in court (Hunt 1975: 22).

Specific aspects of sexual interaction were less negatively evaluated than in the past. Both males (80%) and females (100%) agreed that it should not always be the male's prerogative to initiate intercourse (Hunt 1975: 20). More than 75% of both males and females refused to label either cunnilingus or fellatio as wrong, and only 25% were willing to agree that anal intercourse was wrong (Hunt 1975: 23). Women were much less likely than men to condemn masturbation as wrong; 67% of the women, in contrast to 20% of the men, did not condemn the practice (Hunt 1975: 22). Most men and women favored legalization of abortion.

Cultural encouragement for widening the scope of sexual activity to a broad range of nonprocreational behavior came to public fruition in the 1970s. Much of the behavior that fell in line with this view had already been occurring privately throughout the twentieth century.

The behavioral findings that Hunt analyzed demonstrate an accentuation of past trends. Premarital sex was now more common for both males and females. In Kinsey's sample a quarter of the men and two-thirds of the women had not had intercourse by the time they were 25, while only 3% of Hunt's men and one-third of his women had abstained by 25. Of the women in Kinsey's sample who had married by 25, 42–47% had had premarital intercourse, in contrast to 81% in Hunt's sample (Hunt 1975: 34). The gap in the double standard had clearly narrowed, particularly in relation to extramarital sex. Women under 25 were engaging in extramarital sex more frequently than in the past, but men showed only a slight increase. As a result, female participation in extramarital sex in the under-25 age group was almost as great as that of males (Hunt 1975: 37).

Not only were men and women expressing more tolerance in attitudes about sexual behavior but also they were able to behave in more diverse ways. The practice of cunnilingus increased in all age groups, from 40% in Kinsey's survey to 62% in Hunt's; fellatio increased from 40% to 48% (Hunt 1975: 34). Over 90% of the males and 60% of the females had engaged in masturbation (Hunt 1975: 32). More married men masturbated than in the past; 40% in Kinsey's sample engaged in the activity, while 70% in Hunt's did (Hunt 1975: 32). The buttocks and anus joined the arena of other erogenous zones, but they were not as widely accepted as were other erotic foci (Hunt 1975: 35).

Hunt noted that most people regard sexual liberation as the freedom to be selective and to choose those sexual activities that best meet their own emotional needs (Hunt 1975: 31). Although the range of acceptable activities expanded, liberation did not condone behavior that was pathological or that jeopardized marriage or separated sex from affection and love (Hunt 1975: 36). Hunt characterized the basic types of sexual attitudes and behavior that had emerged by the 1970s as belonging to three categories: (1) conservative (obsolescent traditionalism), (2) revolutionary (antiestablishment anarchism), and (3) liberal (emergent progressivism). In his opinion, the liberal style was emerging as the ideal type; it demonstrated a shift to a less repressive, more pleasurable, yet highly organized set of behavior and attitudes, which were integrated with more important values in the society at large (Hunt 1975: 362). In sum, Hunt concluded that "there is no evidence that any radical change or violent discontinuity with the past has occurred" (Hunt 1975: 37).

I agree with Hunt's assessment of developments in the 1970s as continuous with trends of the past. The 1970s and 1980s are decades in which ideology and behavior are still in transition. They are characterized by attempts to define and to expand options for responding to change. A number of different approaches offer ways to adjust and to develop an acceptable solution to the fragmentation of the past. Individual choice and preference highlight these options.

One approach stresses the importance of making the most of anatomy and physiology as a means of adjusting to change. As in the nineteenth century, medical procedures are available to smooth out incongruities between cultural concepts and behavior. These interventions constitute some of the physical repercussions of changing values and increasing technology.

People can now avail themselves of cosmetic surgery to aid them in finding and retaining mates. People are getting older and living longer, yet our culture has remained relatively youth-oriented. At least two factors combine to produce a disproportionately low number of available males relative to females in the later years. First, men generally marry women who are younger than they are. Second, men die earlier than women, so that there are relatively more widows than widowers. Traditionally, men "mature," but women grow old. Cosmetic surgery of the face, breasts, and hips can aid a woman in preserving a youthful appearance, so that she can now retain her attractiveness for a more extended period of time than was formerly the case.

Other procedures go beyond cosmetic changes. Given the current emphasis on being able to achieve adequate sexual response, an impotent man faces a particularly difficult problem when he cannot develop an erection. Rigid and inflatable sexual prostheses are now available for implantation in impotent men. Penil by-pass surgery is another approach to the problem. The surgeon attempts to facilitate the flow of blood to the penis and improve penil circulation. However, the efficacy of the operation is still in doubt (Szasz 1980: 86).

Other operations are available to enhance the sexual response of a woman. James Burt, a gynecologist in Dayton, Ohio, has performed "love surgery" in increase a woman's orgasmic potential (Scully 1980: 65–66). Based on the theory that the design of the vagina is inadequate for maximum orgasm, because the clitoris is not available for direct penile stimulation, Burt attempts to correct the problem surgically: he lengthens the vagina and severs the pubococcygeal muscle (PC muscle) to create a revised vulva with a smaller vaginal opening, which is closer to the clitoris. Despite critics' protests that penile by-pass surgery and "love surgery" are hazardous to patients, such protests are not sufficient to prohibit these operations.

Men and women are also able to consciously and irrevocably terminate their procreative potential by sterilization. This is one of the fastest growing birth control methods in the United States. Tubal ligation (tying the fallopian tubes) or laparoscopic techniques (burning or clipping the tubes) are both means by which a surgeon can sterilize a woman. However, some doctors remove the uterus (hysterectomy) as a means of sterilization, on the grounds that a woman would have no further use for her womb, and it might become cancerous. A male can have a vasectomy (cutting the vas) and thus become sterile.

More sophisticated techniques are now available to aid those couples who want to have children. Sperm banks, in vitro fertilization, and surrogate parents are all options open to infertile couples. Some single women are also using these options. Amniocentesis, sonograms, fetal monitoring, fetal surgery, and caesarian sections facilitate the birth of healthy children. Safe abortions provide an alternative for women who decide to terminate their pregnancies.

Transsexual surgery is the most radical surgical attempt to physically alter a person to conform to culturally acceptable guidelines. In American culture, as in many others, gender identity, gender behavior, and physical appearance are supposed to coincide. A transsexual suffers from a disjunction between his physical appearance as one gender and his identity as another. Since gender roles are initially assigned on the basis of the appearance of the genitals, a transsexual lives in a role that is counter to his gender identity. Therefore, many transsexuals undergo surgical transformations from the physical attributes of one gender to those of the other. Physical males more often shift to females than vice versa.

Male-to-female surgery involves removal of the penis and testes and the creation of an artificial vagina. Female-to-male surgery is more complicated and extended and involves removal of the breasts, uterus, and ovaries. A scrotum may be made from the labia and filled with plastic testicles. Some may have prosthetic devices implanted to make intercourse possible.

The importance of defining the biological dimension of sexuality as a stable framework within which to interpret change comes through in recent research on the brain and in sociobiological theories. Findings such as those presented in *Sex and the Brain* (Durden-Smith and de Simone 1983) indicate that differences in the organization of male and female brains may predispose men and women to different types of behavior. Challenging the current belief that learning accounts for the bulk of gender-typical behavior, the authors suggest that there is a continuity in male and female behavior that is biologically based. Sociobiologists like Donald Symons (*The Evolution of Human Sexuality*, 1979) point out the similarities between human and nonhuman reproductive strategies and suggest that social and psychological patterns of men and women in groups are products of overall reproductive strategies. These points of view have the flavor of a "biology is destiny" position. Nevertheless, they leave room for the role of learning as a behavioral determinant. By strongly stating their case for the importance of biology, they snap us back from our comfortable assumptions that all things are possible with learning and the proper technology.

The mass media (as articulators of cultural concepts) and social groups of the 1970s and 1980s are also attempting to organize the segmented elements of traditional concepts and behavior from the 1950s and 1960s into an integrated network of meaning. Self-help books proliferate, offering advice on everything from how to dress for success and recover from a divorce to how to achieve an orgasm. Many capitalize on physiological information to enhance sexual response. *The Joy of Sex* (Comfort 1972) remains an enlightened and popular guide to the pleasures of sexual enjoyment. *The Love Muscle* (Britton and Dumont 1982), *The G Spot* (Ladas, Whipple, and Perry 1982), and *ESO* (Brauer and Brauer 1983) are guides to the body's pleasure spots. *Becoming Orgasmic: A Sexual Growth Program for Women* (Heiman, LoPiccolo, and LoPiccolo 1976) and *For Yourself: The Fulfillment of Female Sexuality* (Barbach 1976) provide step-by-step treatment for the woman having difficulty in attaining orgasmic response. *Male Sexuality* (1981), by Bernie Zilbergeld, tries to guide men into sexual fulfillment by exploding myths about male sexuality and replacing them with information and exercises to increase pleasure for both sexes.

Others suggest abstention from sex as a way to deal with waves of choice. In *The New Celibacy* (1980), Gabrielle Brown recommends celibacy as a way to develop intimacy and achieve personal growth; it can allow a person to go beyond sex in a relationship and provide a much-needed antidote to the pressures of being "sexy." Celibacy can be a soothing rest from the pursuit of the almighty orgasm.

For those who can afford to go to counselors and sex therapists, a variety of clinics and therapists are available to help clients with treatments for such complaints as orgasmic dysfunction, premature ejaculation, impotence, and lack of sexual desire. Theoretical orientations vary, but many follow the guidelines of Masters and Johnson and Helen Singer Kaplan (1974, 1979).

For those who are single, divorced, gay, lesbian, parents without partners, victims of incest, assault, or rape, or for "problem" families, there are support groups and a growing literature on the special concerns of each group.

Fantasy remains a popular outlet for the frustrations that accompany change. "Harlequin" romance novels, evening television soap operas ("Dallas," "Dynasty," "Falcon Crest," or "Knot's Landing"), pornographic materials, music, videos, and popular men's and women's magazines fill the imagination.

Sex surveys like *The Cosmo Report* (Wolfe 1981), *The Redbook Re-*

*port* (Tavris and Sadd 1975), *Singles: The New Americans* (Simenauer and Carroll 1982), *Love, Sex, and Aging* (Brecher 1984), and the Hite reports on female (1976) and male (1981) sexuality all provide reassurance to those adopting new patterns or continuing previous ones about which they felt guilty; they demonstrate that feelings of uncertainty are shared and that attitudes and behavior are more common than an individual might suppose. They also serve to nip nascent stereotypes in the bud and encourage evaluation of emerging patterns.

Philip Blumstein and Pepper Schwartz provide an overview of the feelings and behavior that couples are expressing in the 1980s. In *American Couples* (1983), they document many of the major changes of male and female roles that are still being processed by American couples. They point to the problems that arise in interpersonal relationships when cultural guidelines for "new" roles are not yet codified. As they put it, "A relationship today can be compared to a smorgasbord, while yesterday's unit was more like Sunday's chicken dinner. Perhaps the older arrangement . . . was not so glorious, but it was structured and orderly . . . Now there are so many decisions that one is liable to make serious errors in judgment. Everything is in flux, and the priorities are not clear" (Blumstein and Schwartz 1983: 46). Their survey allows us to gauge some of the changes that have occurred since Hunt's update of Kinsey's findings.

Their conceptualization of "couples" acknowledges the reality of contemporary forms of relationships. Instead of focusing exclusively on heterosexual, married couples, they include gay and lesbian couples, as well as heterosexual unmarried and cohabiting pairs. This approach changes the emphasis from examining the form of the relationship to concentrating on the dynamics of how two people relate to each other in an intimate relationship, whatever its cultural label. It encourages an appreciation of the common problems that all couples face in reaching basic decisions about their interaction.

Also notable is Blumstein and Schwartz's examination of the relevance of money, work, and sex to both men and women. They do not separate activities into male and female realms, but trace the repercussions of attitudes about income, jobs, and sex for the behavior of both. Sex recedes in importance as a dominating feature of relationships to one of the dimensions of a couple's interaction.

The tone that this book sets is one of balance. The research acknowledges the complexity of relationships by showing how one aspect of a couple's life affects the other. Distribution of money is not merely an economic task but a symbol of trust, commitment, and the guarantee of permanence (Blumstein and Schwartz 1983: 110). Employment may enhance financial assets, but it does not necessarily alter traditional "wifely" roles. Although working men are working and living with working women, they resist participating in housework to an appreciable degree; children and housework remain predominantly female tasks, regardless of whether women work full time outside the home or not (Blumstein and Schwartz 1983: 188). Heterosexual couples may experience sexual difficulties when a work role conflicts with a spouse's self-image or gender expectations. Women want admiration for their job success, but men are more likely to view a woman's work as a helpful adjunct to the household, not an activity that is just as important as a man's work (Blumstein and Schwartz 1983: 326–327).

## Conclusion

Thus far I have documented shifts in sexual attitudes and behavior over time by describing them in their historical context. What remains is for me to assess the meaning of the transformations that I have reviewed. Analysis of these changes as part of a spectrum of cross-cultural variation in sexual experience allows us to put contemporary dilemmas in perspective.

What we have witnessed in our society over the last century-and-a-half is a shift from a restrictive model of sexuality to a more permissive one. In the nineteenth century, the sexual and reproductive cycles overlapped to a large extent, particularly for women. Social and cultural aspects of sexuality conformed quite well to the cross-cultural pattern of restriction. Sex was supposed to be reproductive. This central value entailed a limited definition of sex as heterosexual, genital intercourse and therefore excluded the acceptability of nonmarital, nonprocreative, sexual activity. Celebrations of marriage and birth reinforced the value system. Restrictions on divorce limited the number of sexual and reproductive unions that couples could have.

By the latter part of the twentieth century, the pendulum had swung to the permissive end of the cross-cultural spectrum. At the present time, the sexual and reproductive cycles do not overlap to any significant degree. The central value includes a broad definition of sexuality as both reproductive and nonreproductive intercourse; cultural values do not insist that sex be procreative. Nonprocreative ("recreational") relationships and activities enter the arena of tolerated behavior. Nonmarital unions and divorces are common; there are few social constraints on the number of sexual and reproductive unions that men and women can have.

However, it would be misleading to suppose that Americans were the most restrictive extreme or that they now are the most permissive example of cross-cultural varieties of sexual experience. Even during restrictive times, punishment for deviation from the proscription that sex should occur within marriage and for procreation was not extremely severe. Men's activities with prostitutes were not publicly censured until the late 1800s and early 1900s. Women received the brunt of punishment for deviant activities by their redefinition as "fallen" women; ostracism and prostitution awaited those who dared express sexual desire and/or passion. This is in line with the pattern for the other societies that identify sex with procreation; women's sexual activities are usually limited to assure the assignment of paternity. However, the most restrictive societies usually restrict the nonmarital activities of *both* men and women and punish deviants with death.

Although American attitudes have changed considerably over the years, our permissive orientation is mild compared with that of other societies. Parents still have difficulty communicating with their children about sex and are unlikely to encourage their adolescents to engage in intercourse (as is common in the Maquesas). Far from being perceived as an acceptable expression of sexual feelings, to many people, homosexuality remains a threatening life-style. Definitions of obscenity are still confined to sexually-oriented materials, and the "Moral Majority" has mounted considerable opposition to reproductive and sexual choice. Publicity about sexuality does not mean that we are sexually free in our attitudes or in our behavior.

Despite the seeming revolution in sexual behavior from the nineteenth century to the present, there is continuity in the types of behavior engaged in and in the concepts that are associated with sexuality. Changes in attitude have allowed for more frequent expression of all types of behavior and have transformed the meaning of the basic concepts. Public discussion of matters previously defined as "private" has given the impression that new attitudes and behavior have appeared overnight. Historical data do not uphold this view. We Americans have created some myths about our past to support the contention that a revolution has occurred. According to some accounts, American society has departed from an idyllic, three-generation extended family on the farm, where everyone supported everyone else, to a promiscuous, immoral society in which the family — the cornerstone of our civilization — has been destroyed. Why have we chosen to distort the past and label social change as a revolution? Is American society really on the brink of downfall?

The tone of these questions vascillates from assurances about the nature of change to fear of annihilation. The coherence underlying the seeming conflict between the cultural label of "revolution" and feelings of fear is the process of change itself. Our society is undergoing a rite of passage on a massive scale, which is not yet complete. The phases of rites of passage provide a framework for understanding the form of the feelings and behavior that characterize the history of sexuality in America over the last 150 years.

A rite of passage is a rite that accompanies a change of state. A state is a culturally recognized condition, which can be either stable or recurrent (Turner 1969: 94). The three phases of a rite of passage include separation from one state, a period of liminality, and reaggregation to a different state (Turner 1969: 94). Separation involves symbolic detachment from the fixed social and cultural state of the past. Liminality describes a phase in which the concepts and behavior have few of the attributes of the past or of the coming state; they are betwixt and between traditional conceptual categories and acceptable ways of behaving. Reaggregation consummates the passage. Although we often associate rites of passage with events in an individual's life cycle (initiation, marriage, death), the principles of change operative on an individual level can also apply to major social and cultural transformations.

Symbols play a large role in these changes. Their essence lies in their condensation of multiple meanings, unification of referents that are not of the same logical order, and retention of different poles of significance (physiological, social, and moral) (Turner 1969: 52). Their power derives from their synthesis of apparent conflict. The human body often becomes a focus for symbolic communication, because it is both physical and spiritual. Its biological characteristics include psychological, cultural, and social manifestations. Human bodies express many apparent contradictions: the animal and the human, male and female, life and death, age and youth. They both constrain us and free us. In rites of passage, body symbolism vividly portrays the transformations of the biological nature of humans and of their social life and their cultural life.

The nineteenth century is the traditional state from which the rite of passage progresses. Like the tightness of a corset, the compactness of the ideology of that time left little room for much differentiation in elements of the sexual and reproductive cycles. The major concepts included male, female, body, spirit, domestic life, work, love, sex, marriage, and family. To a large extent, most of these categories overlapped. Males and females joined in marriage to become husbands and wives as well as mothers and fathers. Being female meant exclusive participation in the domestic realm, preferably as a wife and mother; the family was a woman's main charge, and affectionate love bound mother, father, and children together. Participation in the realm of public work was a defining quality of masculinity; the roles of husband and father supplemented this quality. Sex was reified as a concept and was associated with the base qualities of the body. Much of what happened to the body was perceived as involuntary. For example, dysfunctions of the ovaries could drive women insane; eruption of male sexual energy could sap a man of his power. Prostitution was a symbol of the ambivalence of the day. A woman was supposed to lack interest in sex and passion, yet prostitutes were women who displayed these very characteristics. They symbolized the invasion of choice about sexual activity into a world that encourage submission to rules that allowed very little room for choice.

As Americans moved into the twentieth century, they entered a liminal phase of change. Contraception and other technological developments altered the involuntary nature of physiological processes. Contraception meant that coitus did not have to be a procreative activity. This option triggered the first part of the liminal phase, in which separation from traditional ideology occurred through relabelling elements of traditional concepts. As sex separated from procreation, marriage and the family became two distinct phases of the life cycle. Passion was included in the definition of love as it applied to a marital couple, and sex became its vehicle for expression. The body and spirit moved closer together. Roles became more distinct within each phase. The husband/wife bond did not entirely overlap with the father/mother role. Masculinity was still associated with the public realm of work, and femininity was centered at home.

The next part of the liminal phase was more dramatic and involved greater differentiation of elements that had been a part of traditional concepts. Increasing technological specialization was paralleled by greater behavioral separation from traditional patterns. As women entered the primarily male realm of work outside the home, it was more difficult to maintain definitions of females as domestic and males as participants in the work force. Womanhood related to but was not subsumed by being a wife or mother. Manhood expanded to include more nurturant qualities, but questions surrounded attempts to define masculinity. The domestic sphere was no longer the exclusive domain of the nuclear family, presided over by a woman. Households might include a variety of participants in the domestic life: gay and lesbian couples, single heterosexual males and/or females, single parents with children, and widows or widowers. The muddying of the two worlds of men and women had repercussions for the conceptualization of sex. As in household and work arrangements, voluntary choice took precedence over seemingly involuntary patterns of the past.

The sexual dilemmas we face today stem from the apparent lack of structure for our lives. The fragments of the past do not seem to cohere in any meaningful way. However, it is characteristic of liminal periods to be defined as dangerous "dirty" (or polluting), and deadly. This is exactly how the public and the media have chosen to define many of the new options. They have mythologized the past into a stable form, from which the apparent chaos of today's way of living sharply departs. Many of these images are mythical rather than integral parts of the American past. Nevertheless, the contrast persists between a fanciful past and the realities of the present. The label of "revolution" at least provides a framework for conceptualizing the options. Unlike the purpose and determination that characterized the Revolutionary War, the sexual revolution has an involuntary flavor about it, as if it were a typhoon that swept over a terrain of moral restraint and left behind only the battered remains of the structures that had enclosed and protected the inhabitants.

A lack of structure is at once dangerous and powerful. It reminds us of the comfort that predictability provides, as well as the potential range of variations that our lives can have. We are straining to take the next step toward coherence of meaning. We want to reaggregate into a structure, but it is still undefined. Turner labels an unstructured period of liminality as "communitas" (Turner 1969: 96). He argues that the contrast between communitas and structure reaffirms our humanity, because we can feel a unity with each other in this unstructured period; communitas is social and cultural "time out" for us to reflect about the nature of life as well as to prepare for acceptance of our roles to come.

In the 1970s and 1980s, Americans have been moving toward an integration of the fragments of past concepts and behavior. The frustration seems to lie in the amount of choice available to us and the conflict between past structures and future potential. In the past, fantasies transmuted the involuntary into the voluntary. Women initiated and responded to sexual activity. Today, our imagination prefers fantasies that show voluntary options as involuntary. Sexual violence has replaced prostitution as a symbol of dissatisfaction with the current range of choice. Rape, incest, assault, and sado-masochistic pornography replace voluntary choice with images of submission to involuntary forces. Disaster and horror films portray people in the grip of situations beyond their control. Soap operas depict plots against individuals to manipulate their behavior in ways they cannot possibly anticipate. At the same time, they encourage a traditional route of compressing sex, love, marriage, and children into the same package. The grist of the soap opera mill is unhappiness caused by a disjunction between love, sex, marriage, and children. New romantic fiction for women ("sweet savagery") portrays sex and violence in such a way that heroines are often raped, but "never ruined"; their experiences explore a wide range of sexual activities for women but only in contexts over which the women have no control (Faust 1980: 153, 156). They absolve women from the responsibility of choice in sexual relationships and provide vicarious satisfaction for women who have no intention of being permissive in "real" life (Faust 1980: 156). Underlying these diverse cultural forms is the portrayal of predictability.

Attitudes about the body reflect the attempt to develop some predictability about choices. Self-help books promise to give a formula for sexual fulfillment if the participants will arm themselves with knowledge about correct positions, spots, and moves. Counselors, diets, and exercise may hold the key to happiness. However, Szasz warns that people should think carefully about the implications of the new labels and formulas that surround sexual activity. He argues that "one medical epoch's or person's sexual problem may be another epoch's or person's sexual remedy; new medical treatments may be the contemporary substitutes for old-fashioned religious creeds" (Szasz 1980: 164, 165). Finding the "right" sex manual or the "right" sex therapist may not lead to unending sexual or personal fulfillment. Sexologists may conceal moral values and social policies as medical diagnoses and treatments (Szasz 1980: 164).

The emergence from liminality into a new state will come with the recontextualization of our experiences, rather than with desperate attempts to revert to old structures or hang onto whatever seems predictable. We are reaching that point now. Theological, clinical, feminist, academic, and popular writings express the need for balance between sex and the rest of life. In *The End of Sex* (1984), Leonard proposes the renewal of erotic love, which embeds sex in a matrix of creativity, love, and spontaneity. He suggests discarding present usage of the word "sex," because it encourages "dangerous trivialization, fragmentation, and depersonalization of life" (Leonard 1984: 13).

We can draw on a number of sources to reintegrate our lives. Results of the new sex surveys and cross-cultural studies give us ideas about the range of behavior that is possible. Cross-species evidence provides us with general information about the biological constraints on our behavior and the physiological implications of our social and cultural forms. Research on anatomy and physiology provides more information about the workings of our bodies. Sociological and psychological research demonstrate the impact of gender concepts on sexual behavior and feelings. I hope that this book shows how a holistic perspective can weave the biological, social, and cultural dimensions of human sexuality into an integrated framework, which encourages balance among the complex elements of our lives.

# Appendix A
# Research Design and the
# Cross-Cultural Method

Research design is part of the problem-solving process in science. It specifies the sequence of steps that the researcher follows to achieve the objectives of a study. Methodology is an integral component of research design; it is the logical structure that governs the production and organization of information relevant to establishing knowledge about a particular subject (Pelto and Pelto 1978: 2). The scope of methodology includes techniques for data collection and assessment, as well as concepts, hypotheses, and models used to relate data to theoretical propositions. Methodology is a systematic way of defining what constitutes evidence for our beliefs about the world (Johnson 1978: 1–21).

### The Cross-Cultural Method:
### Its Premises and Its Suitability for This Study

The cross-cultural method was used to produce and organize data on social and cultural aspects of the sexual and reproductive cycles. The overall goals of the study guided the choice of this methodology. One major goal was to elucidate the type and extent of variation in human sexuality through systematic description. In order to do this, it was necessary to identify variations of social and cultural elements in different social contexts. This implies the use of a method that enables the investigator to draw upon a large number of cases. The examination of a large and representative number of cases in which the relevant elements appear is the foundation of the cross-cultural method. The fact that this method is sometimes called the hologeistic ("whole earth") method further emphasizes the wide distribution of units on which it relies.

Another goal was to find out whether or not the shared aspects of human sexuality are consistently related to each other and whether they form patterns. A third goal was to provide a basis for explaining the patterns identified. These aims demand a method that will provide a basis for valid generalizations about the relationships between social and cultural elements. The cross-cultural method was developed as a means of making scientifically valid generalizations about the elements of social ("culture-bearing") units.

Because anthropologists can rarely control the relationship between the social and the cultural elements they are investigating or find a situation in which the relevant elements occur in exactly the combination necessary for determining the basis of variation between them, they can make only limited use of the experimental method (Murdock 1966: 97). Cross-culturalists offer the alternative of trying to determine whether posited relationships between social and cultural elements can be statistically substantiated, once the elements have been examined in varying combinations in a wide range of contexts.

The only assumptions necessary for the use of the cross-cultural method are that there are regularities between social and cultural elements and that these can be identified by the examination of a large and representative number of cases. At any one time and place, a social unit will be characterized by a number of social and cultural elements, which may or may not be regularly associated with another; the fact is that they co-occur in the same spatial and temporal dimension. The identification of social units within which these regularities will be found is a definitional problem of sampling. It consists of stating how great a similarity between social and cultural elements of different social groups is sufficient to define the boundaries of a sampling unit. Whether and how these social and cultural elements adjust over time or are integrated is a matter for investigation, not something to be assumed. The regularity and variation that the elements exhibit is something to be explained after they have been identified.

The cross-culturalist wants to know what sorts of statements can be made about the interconnections between these elements and what accounts for the particular configuration of elements that are found. Generalization and explanation of the relation between these elements cannot rely on data from a single case unless its representativeness of other social units is known. In order to determine the conditions under which these same relationships will occur again, a range of units must be studied. The cross-cultural method is a means of identifying a range of social and cultural regularities, despite their social context, and of finding out what elements appear in other groups, under what conditions, and how often (Köbben 1966: 190).

Reliance on a large number of cases and the use of statistical techniques to test hypotheses as well as to sort out regular associations between these elements distinguish the cross-cultural method from other comparative approaches. These techniques of the cross-cultural method also seem to set it apart from one major traditional anthropological approach: the intensive study of a single case or a small number of cases, in which a meticulous study of the elements of a unit is used to provide insight into the interconnection between them.

By definition, cross-culturalists focus less on the context from which the elements under investigation derive than on systematic relationships, which *appear to be* independent of context. This isolation of a social or cultural element from its context is anathema to proponents of the case approach, especially those of a functionalist or historical persuasion. They argue that the uniqueness, pattern, and meaning of the elements in question are lost. In essence, they see the heart of traditional anthropology sacrificed for a few dry bones of data, which take the form of generalizations that may seem trivial, tautological, or boring. How can anyone fathom the richness of a social and cultural milieu when its components are presented as one of a number of cases neatly enumerated in a box as "Table 2"?

A response to these critics lies in reminding them of the aims of each approach. A case study generally focuses on recording and describing the actions and beliefs of members of a specific group, in order to portray their society or culture as accurately as possible. It may emphasize the articulation of elements with one another into a unique pattern, the application of current theories to the unit, or the generation of new hypotheses, which stem from the inclusion of this case study into the body of extant data.

Cross-culturalists ambitiously try to generalize, explain, and construct theories about human societies or cultures. They do this in a variety of ways. One is to identify regularities and variations between social and cultural elements in different social contexts. A second is to test hypotheses about the relationships between these elements. A third is to explain the conditions under which particular configurations of elements are likely to occur.

Although the study of one or a few cases might be adequate to demonstrate a relationship between social and cultural elements in a limited area or in a particular context, it is not sufficient to indicate whether the relationship holds true for higher levels of generalization. Cross-cultural research provides more solid ground for positing generalities, because it indicates the degree to which these same relationships consistently obtain in other social contexts. By pointing out the similarities *and* the differences between social units, the method highlights the unique features of the societies contained in the sample. In addition, a detailed analysis of the cases that are exceptions to the statistical associations between elements can enhance the distinctive characteristics of the units involved. It would be difficult to maintain that human societies are so unique that they have nothing in common. Cross-culturalists want only to sort out which aspects the societies in their samples share and which they do not, in order to try to discover worldwide regularities.

The cross-cultural method can test a hypothesis suggested by a single case and can check the validity of common assumptions derived from the study of a few cases. The results can help anthropologists to rethink their assumptions and the bases for the concepts.

A cross-cultural study complements rather than opposes a single case study. The data base on which cross-culturalists rely is almost exclusively drawn from case studies. Cross-culturalists evaluate the accuracy and completeness of case studies in terms of their own goals. The gaps in information that cross-culturalists find in case studies in the course of their research may become valuable aids to fieldworkers, in pinpointing new areas to investigate. In addition, cross-cultural research may encourage fieldworkers to be more precise in their data collection and analysis. Colson noted that the comparative method has encouraged fieldworkers to collect quantitative material to back up qualitative statements (Colson 1967: 4). As a result, they seem to be "producing more and more meticulous descriptions with a good deal of quantitative material to back up general statements, and at the same time are narrowing their areas of investigation" (Colson 1967: 3). As the quality of the data base becomes more sophisticated, so, too, can be the hypotheses tested cross-culturally. Followers of the case study approach can cooperate with cross-culturalists in adding to the quality of the data and of the generalizations derived from ethnographic studies.

In sum, I used the cross-cultural method because it provided a substantial basis on which I could: (1) indicate the variation in social and cultural aspects of the sexual and reproductive cycles over a wide range of cases; (2) make valid generalizations about social and cultural aspects of the sexual and reproductive cycles; (3) demonstrate the conditions under which specific types of social and cultural aspects of the cycles are associated with one another in varying contexts; and (4) examine the applicability of commonly held concepts relating to sex and reproduction to a variety of social contexts.

## Techniques of the Cross-Cultural Method

The major steps used in implementing the cross-cultural method in this study were: (1) selecting a sample of social units, (2) choosing sources of information that pertain to the sample, (3) developing concepts to include as bases for classification on a code, (4) extracting ("coding") information from the sources, (5) statistically manipulating the data, and (6) analyzing the data in an effort to make generalizations.

### Sampling

Because the testing of hypotheses and the generalizations that are made about particular relationships are based on their occurrence in a large and representative sample, the nature of the sample is an important aspect to consider in evaluating the validity of the generalizations derived from the method. George. P. Murdock, one of the major anthropological proponents of the cross-cultural method in the United States, considers sampling one of the most serious and "vexing" problems of the method (Murdock 1966: 97). He has concentrated a major portion of his efforts on improving the cross-cultural method by refining his sample. He has offered successive proposals for the improvement of sampling techniques in "World Ethnographic Sample" (1957), "Cross-Cultural Sampling" (1966), and "World Sampling Provinces" (1968), but the "Standard Cross-Cultural Sample" (SCCS) represents the "culmination of his efforts (Murdock and White 1969). He describes the SCCS as a "representative sample of the world's known and well-described cultures, 186 in number, each 'pinpointed' to the smallest identifiable sub-groups of the society in question at a specific point in time" (Murdock and White 1969: 329).

*Galton's problem.* One of the major considerations in the construction of the SCCS was to counter Galton's problem. The problem was introduced by Galton in response to Tylor's classic article, "On a Method of Investigating the Development of Institutions" (Tylor 1889), one of the first applications of cross-cultural methodology to anthropological materials. Galton commented that "full information should be given as to the degree in which the customs of the tribes and races which are compared together are independent. It might be, that some of the tribes had derived from a common source, so that they were duplicate copies of the same original" (Tylor 1966: 23). The issue of independence of cases in the sample has plagued cross-cultural researchers ever since that time.

Before Murdock and White constructed the Standard Cross-Cultural Sample, Naroll had offered five solutions for dealing with Galton's problem (Naroll 1961, 1964; Naroll and D'Andrade 1963). Murdock and White incorporated several of Naroll's suggestions and added a sixth solution to Galton's problem, the successive pairs test, which they designed to indicate the scope of areas of historical relatedness (Murdock and White 1969: 348–352). By means of these tests, they tried to eliminate from the sample those societies that exhibited the greatest similarities of social and cultural elements due to spatial contiguity or historical relatedness. This was one way of minimizing historical influences and ensuring independence of cases. Another way by which they tried to counter Galton's problem in the SCCS was to stratify the sample according to world area. Groups of contiguous societies with extremely similar cultures were included together in one "cluster." These clusters, in turn, were grouped into 186 "distinctive world areas" on the basis of similarity in language and other cultural elements. It was from these 186 world areas that the societies included in the SCCS were drawn: one society was chosen from each area. Smaller subsamples of the main sample could be used with equal assurance of their representativeness of the "world's known and well-described cultures" and their freedom from "contamination" from historical influences.

*The sample used for this study.* The sample used for this study is one such subsample from the full SCCS of 186 societies designed by Murdock and White (1969). I chose it in preference to constructing my own or using another sample, because it (1) countered many of the problems previously associated with cross-cultural sampling; (2) was large enough to permit the statistical manipulation of variables; (3) permitted the intercorrelation of results from my study with those previously coded for the same sample; and (4) had an extensive library of original source material available for use in conjunction with it.

I chose the subsample for this study by selecting every third society listed in the SCCS with the exceptions of the Egyptians, who replaced the Riffians; the Lapps, who replaced the Irish; and the Siamese, who replaced the Khmer. In each case, the society following the third one was chosen as an alternative. The Egyptians were substituted because the information on sex and reproduction among the Riffians was sparse. The Lapps were substituted for the Irish, because all of the information for CCCCC (Cross-Cultural Cumulative Coding Center) codes was derived from personal communication with Kane, an anthropologist who was currently conducting research in Ireland. Unfortunately, I was unable to confer with her about my variables when I was coding information for this study. Had I used Arensberg's material, instead of Kane's, I would have been hesitant to intercorrelate my data with that of the CCCCC codes, because of the differences in spatial location and time of investigation of each of the areas involved. The Khmer were replaced by the Siamese, because information on the Khmer for the pinpointed date, 1292, did not contain relevant materials on sex and reproduction. The only information available on these subjects was in descriptions made in the 1800s. Even though it was claimed that the culture had not changed for centuries, I was hesitant to assume that ideas and behavior related to sex and reproduction had remained the same for six centuries.

The 62 societies that make up the sample for this study are listed in the ethnographic bibliography and are arranged according to the world areas that they represent. Each society is identified by its area number, location by geographical region and spatial coordinates, and date to which the information applies. This is followed by a specification of the most useful sources from which the information in the codes is derived.

The 62 societies are distributed as follows:

By geographical region:
    Africa 8 (13%)
    Circum-Mediterranean 12 (19%)
    Eurasia 10 (16%)
    Insular Pacific 10 (16%)
    North America 11 (18%)
    South America 11 (18%)
By subsistence type:
    Advanced agriculture 21 (34%)
    Horticulture 7 (11%)
    Shifting agriculture 4 (6%)
    Domestic animals 4 (6%)
    Exchange 1 (2%)
    Fishing 5 (8%)
    Gathering 4 (6%)
    Hunting 7 (11%)
By descent:
    Bilateral 25 (40%)
    Double 3 (5%)
    Patrilineal 22 (36%)
    Matrilineal 8 (13%)
    Ambilineal 4 (6%)

Compared with the full sample, there is a slight underrepresentation of patrilineal societies (36% in the reduced sample, compared with

41% in the total sample) and a slight overrepresentation of bilateral societies (40% in the reduced sample, as compared with 37% in the total sample). Otherwise, the distribution of the sample societies according to geographical region, subsistence type, and descent rules generally matches that of the total sample of 186. I selected region, subsistence type, and mode of descent for specific mention, because they give some indication of the geographical range and diversity of social types included within the scope of the sample.

*The significance of world area.* The division of the sample into world areas and the grouping of alternate societies into "clusters" facilitated the use of the sample for a purpose which has not received as much attention as Galton's problem: the comparison of traits between culturally similar units within the same world area. Researchers have been so concerned with avoiding similarities stemming from contact between groups in spatially contiguous regions that they have paid less attention to the similarities they find between groups in the same geographical region, even after their sample has been constructed to counter Galton's problem.

The geographical clustering of societies with significant similarities in social and cultural attributes may be an important clue for determining the kinds of conditions that gave rise to the relationships; Chaney and Revilla(1969) suggest that these associations might best be examined in light of historical and ecological circumstances. I therefore crosstabulated all of my variables with world area to find out the degree to which they cluster by region. In this way I hoped to guard against ignoring important bases for explanation of the associations I found. I have noted significant areal contrasts in the text.

*The comparability of units.* Although Galton's comment on Tylor's essay has received more attention, Flower raised another issue about the validity of results obtained from a cross-cultural survey: the comparability of units. He remarked that it seemed to him that the value of the method "depended entirely upon the units of comparison being of equal value" (Tylor 1966: 23). Tylor's response to Flower was that when a community or group of communities follow similar rules, "notwithstanding historical connection and the consequent partial correspondence which may exist between it and other unit systems," they may be taken as a unit (Tylor 1966: 25).

Flower's concern has not disappeared from the issues that crossculturalists must address. It is not unusual to hear someone remark,

"How can you compare a little tribe like the Yahgan with a complex people like the English?" (Naroll 1973: 721).

The crux of the matter lies in remembering the purpose of the sample. In his article on cross-cultural sampling, Murdock said that he wanted his sample to represent "all known cultural types," not all known cultures (Murdock 1966: 99). Therefore, the degree of similarity between the language group and other cultural elements of contiguous groups becomes the main criterion for separating one sampling unit from another. Each sampling unit constitutes one "cultural type" and is comparable with others, in the sense that each group in the unit shares a specific range of cultural elements that are distinctively different from those in another. Just because the properties of these elements vary from one unit to another does not mean that they are not comparable; it only means that they are different, which is as it should be if discovering the range of cultural variation is one aim of the research.

Naroll very nicely sums up the argument presented in this section when he says that the comparability issue is essentially a false one. "There is no special problem of comparability of units among cross-cultural surveys. There is only the general problem in all scientific research of discerning which factors are relevant, which not . . . The question always is: What sort of differences matter for the problem at hand?" (Naroll 1973: 724).

The main focal group to which the data for this study apply is the local community defined for use in the community organization code (Murdock and Wilson 1972: 255). I used the local community in preference to other groups, because it is defined primarily in terms of general criteria, such as social identity, interaction, and residence. Its selection was in line with my desire to use the cross-cultural method to establish types of variation and patterning in social and cultural aspects of the sexual and reproductive cycles. Therefore, it was important to define the focal group within the sampling unit in social and cultural terms and as broadly and parsimoniously as possible, not according to specific characteristics of population, political organization, or religious affiliation.

*The temporal dimension.* Serious flaws can result from failing to include time among the criteria used to select a sample. For example, some researchers obtain their information from precategorized sections of the Human Relations Area Files (HRAF), which are classified according to subject area for each society. Although the information pertains to the same topic, it does not necessarily apply to the same time period. Since societies change over time, the relationships that are found at one time period may not be the same as those present at another. The degree of difference depends upon the amount of time that has elapsed, the nature of social contacts between the sampling unit and other groups, and the types of variables that are under investigation. The danger is that data collected without regard for the time period to which they pertain may create an artificial picture of the social group; they are a patchwork of traits linked by imprecise selection. Consequently, investigation of the conditions that gave rise to the apparent associations between social and cultural elements within a social unit would be futile, because the elements themselves were never associated with each other at the same time; their juncture is an accident of coding, not an end product of the operation of social processes. It therefore seems wise to limit the time period from which information within the sampling units is drawn. But which time period should be chosen?

The main criterion that governed Murdock's choice of dates for the sample societies in the SCCS was the "earliest period for which satisfactory ethnographic data are available or can be reconstructed," unless the descriptive materials were "appreciably richer" for a later period (Murdock and White 1969: 340). This was in line with his effort to sample well-described groups and culture types.

Murdock's emphasis on the adequacy of descriptions is important because it is only on the basis of descriptions that cross-culturalists have data with which to work. It is all very well to design the perfect sample, but it is of little use if there are no data for the units included. Nag sacrificed much of his sampling design in his cross-cultural study of factors affecting fertility for this very reason (Nag 1962: 13).

Murdock's decision to use the earliest time periods possible was made in an effort to counter the effects of acculturation on his sampling units. This consideration is an important one. Had he used the time periods in which the societies were changing, due to contacts with foreign groups, he would have sampled the cultural type to which the society was adjusting, not the indigenous one. This would have resulted in replication of cultural types included in the sampling and would have raised the question of whether they should be considered one case or two for the purposes of statistical analysis. Since Murdock found it impossible to avoid including societies that had been influenced to some degree by the "great colonizing and imperialistic societies of Europe" (Belgians, Dutch, English, French, Germans, Italians, Portuguese, Spanish), the European societies themselves were excluded from the sample; he assumed that their cultures would be reflected in the societies they had colonized or missionized.

This method of choice does not mean that cultures were eliminated because they were affected by their relationships with other social groups; such elimination would have biased the sample against an important type of social process, which modifies elements of culture. It was only when the social change resulted in the duplication of another cultural type that a culture was not chosen.

I have used the same dates that Murdock specified for the sampling units. This was done to facilitate the intercorrelation of my data with the material already coded on other subjects for these units at that time. If material was sparse on sex and reproduction, I preferred to choose another sampling unit and ensure the consistency of dates for all of the coded material, rather than risk the defect of having my data apply to substantially different units.

*Pinpointing.* One of the central conclusions that Murdock made about his sampling procedure was that a group chosen from a sampling unit should be positioned in both time and space. The specification of such a group guards against the interdependence of cases by defining sampling units, yet locates them in time and space by identifying a group within the unit to represent it. Murdock and White devised pinpointing sheets for each of the sample societies to aid in this effort.

A pinpointing sheet specifies the geographical location of the sampling unit, briefly describes the general area in terms of its sociocultural diversity and contact with other groups, indicates why a particular date was chosen for study, notes why a particular locality was chosen as representative of the sampling unit, and includes a bibliography of sources with material relevant to the pinpointed place and date. Appendix B is an example of one of the pinpointing sheets used for this study.

Pinpointing offers a number of advantages and provides a partial solution to many of the difficulties that have plagued cross-cultural researchers. First, it increases the flexibility of the sample for a variety of uses. Comparisons can be made within as well as between sampling units, to determine how a society has changed over time, either in response to its environment or from contact with other social groups. Regional variation may be an important key to understanding the factors that lead to the tenacity of social and cultural elements over time or within a specific area.

Second, identifying a date and a locale within the sampling unit to which the coded data will apply permits the intercorrelation of coded material *as long as researchers use the same sample.* This seems to me to be one of the strongest arguments in favor of using the SCCS. The lengthy process of coding has led many investigators to restrict the scope of their investigations to a few elements instead of considering a range of data, which would increase the sophistication of their analyses. Furthermore, it has not been possible to intercorrelate the findings from the numerous cross-cultural studies that have been made, because the data do not pertain to the same units. If the fund of information gathered by other researchers applied to the same sample, it would be available for everyone's use and thus prevent a duplication of coding efforts. It would then become possible to focus on refining the scope of subsequent studies and yet retain the flexibility to test relationships between a variety of variables.

The fruits of this kind of approach can be seen by the richness of data derived from the use of the SCCS at the Cross-Cultural Cumulative Coding Center (CCCCC), a research unit that functioned at the University of Pittsburgh from 1968 to 1974 under Murdock's direction. Information available for intercorrelation includes coded data on subsistence patterns (Murdock and Morrow 1970), infancy (Barry and Paxson 1971), childhood (Barry et al. 1976), settlement patterns and community organization (Murdock and Wilson 1972), political organization (Tuden and Marshall 1972), technology and the division of labor (Murdock and Provost 1973a), cultural complexity (Murdock and Provost 1973b), and theories of illness (Murdock, Wilson, and Frederick 1978). Other researchers have used the SCCS to develop codes on adolescent initiation ceremonies (Schlegel and Barry 1979), sexual attitudes and practices(Broude and Greene 1976), and the relative status of women (Whyte 1978). Barry and Schlegel (1980) have compiled a collection of codes from the SCCS to accompany the explanation of how the SCCS was chosen. The development of further codes that apply to this sample continues. It was particularly useful for me to have the aforementioned pool of data available for intercorrelation with my variables. It enabled me to test a wider range of hypotheses without spending an extra five years coding the relevant information.

## Data Gathering: Sources

The choice of sources that pertain to the group in the unit sampled is of great importance in any cross-cultural study. It is from these sources that information is extracted to become the data of cross-cultural analysis. Since error may be introduced into the data if the source material is biased, incomplete, poorly described, or inappropriately classified, attempts to ensure accuracy of information in their sources are of particular concern to cross-cultural researchers.

Naroll suggested a means of coping with this problem in *Data Qual-*

*ity Control* (1962). He defined data reliability as general trustworthiness of sources, not consistency of response to tests or other questions (Naroll 1962: 2). As a general means for helping any social scientist cope with the accuracy of oral or written reports, Naroll offered data quality control as an alternative to the largely subjective evaluation of sources by external and internal criticism. His method is especially pertinent to this study, because reports on sexual relationships, like indicators of cultural stress (suicide, drunken brawling, alleged witchcraft), are especially prone to distortion in the sources. As Naroll pointed out, distortion occurs not only because these activities violate Western European mores but also because information about them must be obtained largely by questioning, rather than by direct observation (Naroll 1962: 13).

Naroll's method of data quality control depends upon the assumption that "some records are made under conditions of higher apparent trustworthiness than others" (Naroll 1962: 2). He compared records made under good conditions with reports compiled under poor conditions, to see whether and in what way they might seriously differ. This procedure gave him a basis for detecting the sources of error and for establishing a means of controlling for both random error and bias.

The introduction of random error or bias into correlations results in errors of inference in accepting or rejecting a hypothesis. Random error may be produced by omissions or lack of attention to details in ethnographic reporting. It is called random error, because errors that support or deny the hypothesis are equally likely. Bias, i.e., a systematic tendency to err in one direction, is a much more serious concern for the cross-culturalist. It may result in correlations that either confirm a relationship that does not exist or deny one that does. Naroll concentrated on providing safeguards for different types of bias.

Naroll distinguished three stages of bias: the first can occur in the informant's mind; the second, in the ethnographer's mind; and the third, in the comparativist's mind. First-stage bias arises from erroneous impressions, memories, or stereotypes of a cultural event on the part of an informant (Naroll 1962: 80–81). Naroll suggested controlling this by comparing the report in question with reports known to have been made under better conditions of observation; "better conditions" include those in which the data were collected in the form of case reports or as a consequence of participant observation. Second-stage bias often derives from ethnographers' total reliance on informants for information. They may be embarrassed, fearful, or unwilling to provide accurate statements. The theoretical orientation of ethnographers may also distort the information. Naroll advised the use of a number of controls to contravene these influences. The ethnographers' length of stay in an area, their familiarity with the language, the roles they played in a society, and possibly individual theoretical bents should all be evaluated to control this stage of bias. Third-stage bias can be introduced by the researchers themselves falsifying the data, interpreting vague statements in a manner that upholds their hypotheses, or omitting information that is contrary to their hypotheses. This bias can be controlled by considering the explicitness and generality of the ethnographer's reports and assessing the degree to which the comparativist had to infer information in order to classify it.

All of the above controls for error are implicit in the procedure established for coding materials based on the Standard Cross-Cultural Sample. The pinpointing sheets associated with the sample contain a bibliography of sources that pertain to the pinpointed time and place of the sample society. These are ranked into five categories: (1) principal authority, (2) other dependable primary sources, (3) auxiliary primary sources, (4) useful secondary sources, and (5) other sources. The criteria for the inclusion of a source in one of these categories meet most of the specifications that Naroll outlined for controlling bias in sources. Murdock included the temporal and spatial locations of the ethnographer's fieldwork as criteria for deciding how to classify a source, since this information has an important bearing on justifying the comparability of units for cross-cultural research.

Murdock's categorization of sources on the pinpointing sheets used in the cross-cultural research conducted for this study deals with the issue of informant's and ethnographer's bias. Murdock defined the principal authority as one who had lived in the pinpointed area for a long period of time, knew the language, was a professional ethnologist or scholar, and had written a detailed work, describing many aspects of the life of the people with whom he or she was living. The gradations from principal authority to auxiliary primary source through useful secondary sources alerts the researcher to possible types of bias and deviations from the pinpointed locale and time. The auxiliary ethnographer may have stayed for a shorter period, may not have spoken the language, or may have played a nonscholarly role in the community. Useful secondary sources were compiled from primary ones and were not based on the first-hand observations of the writer. Secondary sources were not used for this study unless there was no information on the topic in the primary sources. This practice is consistent with Naroll's advice to rely on primary sources for correlational study (Naroll 1962: 30). The ranking of sources on the pinpointing sheet provides a convenient guide to the reliability of the sources for the pinpointed date and area; the principal authorities are most likely to provide reliable information, but secondary and other sources are less likely to do so.

Informant's and ethnographer's bias could pose particularly difficult problems in a study of social and cultural aspects of the sexual and reproductive cycles, both because informants might be embarrassed to reveal such information and also because the ethnographer might not approve of or have access to the relevant data. In order to counter these influences, I generally read a minimum of two complete primary sources and compared their accounts. Overall, I read an average of four complete sources for each focal group.

The gender of the ethnographer could be one important reason for distortion of data on sex and reproduction, for women might not reveal details of their sexual relationships to men. Papanek (1974) noted that the problem could be particularly acute in a purdah society, for only a woman fieldworker could hope to reach socially or physically secluded women. Schlegel (1972), on the other hand, found that the gender of the researcher had little to do with the quality of information she gathered about the intimate relationships that occur in the domestic sphere. Even so, I was especially sensitive to the influence that the gender of the ethnographer could have for particular codes. For example, a man might minimize the severity of the ordeal a woman undergoes at first menstruation. Descriptions of "easy" childbirth by men are suspect, since men are quite frequently excluded from births and thus do not have direct information on which to base their descriptions.

Since the reports used for coding were not limited to those compiled by anthropologists, but included some by missionaries, travelers, and administrators, the role of each type of writer and the theoretical orientation of each had to be evaluated. The role of missionary might seem to bias the information most severely, for missionaries tend to disapprove of sexual activities that depart from the restrictive norms of Christianity. Although it is true that there was moral disapproval of these activities in the missionaries' accounts, there also seemed to be a fascination with them, to such an extent that I sometimes derived more details on sexual activities from missionaries than from "scholars." One of the best ethnographies I read was *The Life of a South African Tribe*, a monograph on the Thonga (3), written by the missionary Junod. Part of the serendipity of reading missionaries' accounts was that my knowledge of Latin was useful! When missionaries felt that the material was too delicate to report in English, they often proceeded to report it in Latin for the small community of scholars who might be interested.

Both informant's and ethnographer's bias were usually circumvented by the use of operational definitions for each subject investigated, a careful reading of the source, and a comparison of the statements made in one source with those in another. For example, rather than relying on the judgments of the writers about how mild a menstrual ordeal was, I concerned myself more with descriptions of what actually happened to the women and then made the judgment myself as to whether it was mild or severe, according to the criteria specified in the operational definition of the code. If comparativists rely on the definitions of others for including information in their classifications, they may sacrifice the comparability of their data. Since anthropologists, not to mention amateur ethnographers, do not always use consistent terms of reference, the same terminology may indicate a wide variety of behavior. If the terms rather than the behavior to which they refer are used as a basis for coding, the distributions and correlations may reflect a difference in terminology, rather than a difference in behavior.

The most serious errors in sources used for cross-cultural research in this study were those of omission rather than of commission. Either the writers failed to report items pertinent to the reproductive cycle or else, if they did, their reports did not contain very much detail. As a result, it was difficult to know whether the item was absent or whether the reporter was just not interested in it. This was especially true for information pertaining to abortion, infanticide, and contraception. I also found that the descriptions focused more on kinship relations and marriage than on aspects of the sexual and reproductive cycles. This was evidenced by the relatively higher amount of missing data for such variables as birth celebrations and ordeal at menstruation than for those related to marriage. This bias was handled partly by the elimination of codes for which there was missing data for more than half of the sample and partly by increasing the number of sources I read.

Although it would have been preferable to have had two or more people coding information and then run checks on the reliability of coding, I had neither the financial resources nor student population to accomplish this. I coded all of the material myself over a two-year period.

### Conceptualization and Classification of Information in the Code

In order to put the data into a systematic form for tabulation, a code is set up to provide a basis for organizing the data. The construction of a code for efficiently summarizing and retrieving data from a cross-cultural sample is perhaps one of the most difficult aspects of the cross-cultural process (LeBar 1973). It involves not only the definition of categories into which information will be classified but also a preliminary analysis of the data in terms of the conceptual scheme to which it will ultimately apply. The amount and type of information that will be available for analysis after the coding depend largely on how the code is set up initially. This presents a thorny problem for cross-cultural investigators, for it seems that they have to know in advance the results that they are seeking to find by using the method.

I constructed the categories for this study according to my research goals, the type of statistical techniques I hoped to apply to the variables, and my impression of the range of information that I thought would be available in the sources I was using. I had a better than average impression of the quality and type of information contained in the SCCS sources, because I had read most of them in their entirety over a six-year period at the Cross-Cultural Cumulative Coding Center, in connection with my analysis of settlement patterns and community organization and theories of illness. Appendix C contains the coding manual for the code developed for this study.

*Conceptual focus of the categories.* A conceptual scheme underlies the formation of the categories that make up a code for data collection in cross-cultural research. Concepts are artificial ways of breaking up observations of the world in such a way that they are meaningful to the observer. As such, they reflect the perceptions and world view of the analyst as well as the purposes of the research. They are not "natural" categories awaiting discovery. They are subject to change.

In this study, the major concepts, the "sexual and reproductive cycles" (as introduced and defined in Chapter One), guided the formation of codes to tap the social and cultural dimensions of human sexuality. The codes categorize behavior and beliefs that pertain to human sexuality and that could be linked to each other in a pattern. The purpose of the codes was to provide a framework for collecting information that focused on the sexual and reproductive cycles themselves and not on one particular institutional context within which they were contained. Most of the concepts categorized in the codes were designed to specify the elements of the cycles and to indicate the degree of social and cultural investment in them.

To accomplish my purpose, I tried to devise categories that would retain the complexity of the concepts to which they referred, yet be suitable for assessing their meaning and behavioral concomitants in a diversity of societies. Clear definitions of categories are implied in such a procedure. Operational definitions of concepts enhance the comparability of information and stimulate a re-evaluation of the traditional categories that are applicable to such data. They also strengthen the basis for reliability of findings between different researchers.

For example, "marriage" has different meanings in different societies and is particularly subject to ethnocentric interpretations. Therefore, it was necessary to highlight the core elements of marriage, in order to compare its social and cultural aspects in a variety of social groups. I did not treat marriage as a unitary concept, but broke it down into several components. Although I employed the term "marriage," I defined it in a very specific way, as the main context within which bearing children is not only acceptable but encouraged. I then explored the types of social behavior that such a context might entail: celebrations, rights, problems of maintenance, and dissolution. This approach allowed me to examine the connection between elements of social behavior within the domain of marriage as well as to explore their links with other activities and beliefs associated with sex and reproduction.

I indicated social and cultural aspects of the sexual and reproductive cycles by emphasizing five types of behavior and belief in the codes: (1) positive and negative social rules, (2) positive and negative social actions, (3) spatial and physical differentiation, (4) the social significance of the rules, spatial areas, and actions, and (5) the amount of individual conformity to the rules. All of these types of belief and behavior are ways in which a group of people channels or constrains individual behavior. The more they are applied to sexuality, the more likely I am to conclude that there is social concern with a specific element of the sexual or reproductive cycle.

Positive social rules are usually expressed as preferences, prescriptions, or exhortations, and they state or imply the type of behavior that the individual should exhibit. The codes on choice of spouse, age at marriage, consent to marry, and preferred sex and number of children are of this type. On the other hand, negative social rules generally take the form of threats, taboos, or restrictions; their violation entails punishment, which usually results in individual deprivation. Personal restrictions at menstruation, ordeal at the onset of menstruation, limitations during pregnancy, restrictions after birth, restrictions on occasion for intercourse, extensions of the incest taboo, and restrictions on divorce are coded practices that illustrate such rules. Some codes represent a wide range, from positive to negative rules. The codes on social approval of abortion, social approval of infanticide, restrictions on premarital sex, and restrictions on extramarital sex illustrate this range of variation.

The expenditure of time and material resources devoted to celebrating the enactment of a rule or punishing its violation indicates the strength of social commitment to the rule. Positive group actions can be seen as one way of encouraging conformity to a rule. For example, wedding celebrations, birth celebrations, and celebrations at menstruation may not only emphasize the importance of marriage, birth, and menstruation but also facilitate individual adjustment at each transition. Negative social actions in relation to a rule are more revealing as to the importance of the rule than an explicit statement of its content would be. If a group punishes a person for behaving in a particular way, it is involving itself in the consequences of the individual's behavior and is trying to channel it into more socially acceptable routes. In this way, punishment serves to encourage conformity. The code on "alternatives to barrenness" expresses the social penalties a woman must face if she does not bear children. This type of behavior may be far more important in signifying social concern that women have children than statements about the desirability of having children could ever be. The types of punishments that are meted out to individuals who violate premarital and extramarital rules show how far a society is willing to go in order to prevent deviations from its rules. Other types of punishments are more subtle. For example, harsh restrictions on obtaining a divorce and getting remarried, difficulties in maintaining custody over children, and the infliction of financial loss after a divorce can all be interpreted as punishments (penalties or deprivations) that individuals face if they do not continue to play their expected roles as married people.

Although these codes express the type and strength of social aspects of the sexual and reproductive cycles, they only partially indicate their cultural significance. I therefore included a number of codes that would demonstrate some of the individual and cultural implications that are concerned with phases of the cycle. For example, the codes on the onset of menstruation deal not only with the severity of the ordeal and with the social celebration that attends it but also with the social significance of menstruation. Codes on the regular menstrual cycle include the restrictions that accompany it and a classification of the people who are thought to be harmed if menstrual restrictions are broken. Similar codes are found in connection with pregnancy (purpose of restrictions), restrictions at birth (whom they are thought to protect), abortion (reasons for), infanticide (reasons for), and divorce (grounds for).

The cultural importance of social behavior may also be indicated by spatial and physical indicators, which are not necessarily codified into explicit rules. For example, the spatial segregation of menstruating or parturient women and the segregated living quarters for adolescent boys and adolescent girls mark males off from females at specific points in their life cycles and demonstrate the cultural significance of gender distinctions.

The degree to which individuals respond to these areas of social and cultural concern indicates the strength of social and cultural aspects in shaping individual behavior. Unfortunately, very little information is presented with such precision in ethnographies. There are statements to the effect that "x is frequent" and "y is rare." Consequently, these are the terms incorporated in my classifications to indicate frequency. The analysis of rules and beliefs in relation to the frequency of different types of behavior raises a host of theoretically significant questions that are not only relevant to understanding human sexuality but also pertinent to more general issues about the relationships between society, culture, and the individual. Why do individuals in some societies circumvent the rules, despite the harsh punishments that can be administered to violators? Why does a social group invest one type of behavior with so much meaning?

· These types of indicators of concepts channel interest in comparisons between social and cultural elements of the sexual and reproductive cycles. For instance, it is possible to relate menstrual taboos to those imposed at pregnancy and childbirth, premarital restrictions to extramarital ones, and ceremonies at marriage to those at menstruation and childbirth. Such comparisons facilitate testing hypotheses that are not suggested by conventional ways of clustering material on these subjects in the sources. As Ford noted in his article, "On the Analysis of Behavior for Cross-Cultural Comparisons," "in order to conduct the comparative research necessary to test certain hypotheses, the data must be taken out of its current packaging and re-sorted according to the researcher's purposes" (Ford 1967: 20).

*Number of categories.* Since one of my aims was to determine the range of variation of types of social and cultural aspects of the sexual and reproductive cycles, I hoped to maximize the amount of information I could derive from my codes, as well as to facilitate their use for other types of research problems. I conceptualized the classification of each code variable so that it would be a specific basis for describing the type of variety, as well as an indicator of the range of variation. In order to achieve these objectives, I constructed multiple categories for each variable, in preference to dichotomizing them into presence/absence.

Although the parsimony of a presence/absence scheme was attractive, there was always the danger of losing too much information by noting the occurrence of an element without acknowledging its range of variation. The use of multiple categories allowed me to explore more deeply the complexity of the social and cultural elements I was investigating.

Pretesting the initial categories for each element aided me in deciding upon the final categories for coding material for my full sample of 62 societies. It helped to reveal some of the incompatibilities between the categories I had devised and the information in the sources. The pretest sample of 14 societies represented diverse descent systems, subsistence types, and geographical regions. They were not included as part of the standard sample, but were alternatives to the societies chosen for each of the sampling units.

If a particular category proved to be a cumbersome way of handling the information in the sources, it was modified. In some cases, this meant dividing one category into new, more specific ones, revising its definition, or expanding it so that it could accommodate more information. For example, I added "incompatibility with affines" as a new category under "grounds for divorce," after I found that it was a recurrent exception to the categories I had developed.

In other cases, revision of categories took the form of collapsing or eliminating the ones I had formulated. For example, "danger to father" was eliminated as a reason for pregnancy restrictions, because I found no instances of it. If the information for the whole variable was sparse, I eliminated it.

After I completed the coding of all of the variables in my total sample of 62 societies, I rechecked each coding with the data on which it had been based, to make sure that it was consistent within its context and with the criteria I had developed for classifying it in a particular category. This was possible because I had compiled notes from each source for each coding to show the basis for my judgment. As I coded, I singled out codings that I felt were exceptional to the category in some way by placing asterisks beside them. I then reviewed each one of these, to see if a new category would eliminate its exceptional nature. Although it was always possible to deal with exceptions by using a vague "wastebasket category," such as "other," I preferred to avoid this as much as possible, since one of my aims was to clarify the types of variation in social and cultural aspects of the sexual and reproductive cycles, not to further blur their silhouette.

I could partially attribute the lack of fit between the categories I had devised and the information I found to my own naiveté about the variations in data that I *thought* I would find. On the other hand, I was disappointed to discover that I could ascribe an appreciable measure of it to lack of coverage in the sources. For instance, the information on homosexuality, psychological dimensions of sexuality, and cultural interpretations of contraception was not sufficient to be included in this study. I could not meet the theoretical demands of my study in some cases, because there were no data to satisfy them.

Aside from the amount of data available for inclusion in categories, there was another constraint placed on the number of categories I could set up: the type of statistical techniques I could apply to the information. Although it is conceivable to proliferate an infinite string of categories for the sake of showing cultural variation, to do so would not have been consistent with another aim of my research: to establish whether social and cultural aspects of the sexual and reproductive cycles were related to each other and whether they form patterns. Given the size of my sample, too many categories would spread out the data to an extent that would substantially reduce the possibility of identifying significant correlations between variables. This was one reason why I tried to limit the number of categories I used for each variable. An additional consideration was the conversion of data into a form suitable for operation in the computer. I indicated each category by a numerical rather than a letter symbol, to facilitate the transfer of data from code sheets to computer cards. Since the computer could more easily manipulate data designated by a single rather than a double digit, I decided to limit the number of categories to nine or less for each variable. This arbitrary boundary allowed me to show a considerable range of variation in the elements I coded, yet did not affect their flexibility for statistical analysis.

*Ordering of categories.* The power of the statistical techniques that can be applied to the data depends upon the precision with which categories of different variables can be compared with one another. This means that the arrangement of categories according to a scale of some kind could increase the technical sophistication of the analysis. Cross-culturalists usually do not have data that are exact enough to permit the use of interval or ratio scales; they, like most other social scientists, must be content to use nominal and ordinal scales.

All of the categories for variables in this study are arranged in either nominal or ordinal scales. A nominal scale consists of an unordered set of categories that are exhaustive (contain all cases) and mutually exclusive (no case belongs to more than one). For example, the categories on residence at birth of the first child (temporary matrilocality, permanent matrilocality, ambilocality, neolocality, patrilocality) comprise a nominal scale.

However, I preferred to arrange my categories in ordinal scales if at all possible. These scales consist of categories that are arranged in a series according to the degree to which they are thought to possess a specific characteristic; the position of each category indicates whether it has more or less of the characteristic, but not how much more or less. The order should never be ambiguous, and, as in nominal scales, the categories should be mutually exclusive. Although the categories used in ordinal scales can always be treated as nominal ones, the advantage of ordinal scales is that they can be correlated with other sets of ranked data and add precision to hypothesis-testing.

I specified the characteristic in terms of which I ranked the categories in the identification of each coded element. In some cases, the basis of the ranking was quite obvious. This was so in the codes that expressed gradations like "small," "moderate," or "elaborate." For example, the categories in the code on social celebration at marriage begin with "no celebration" at marriage and proceed to "elaborate celebration."

In other cases, the characteristic on which the scale was based might not be so obvious, because it was designed with a specific concept in mind. For example, the code on consent at marriage is one indicator of the degree of social involvement in a marriage. It begins with a category that shows low social involvement, i.e., individual consent is absolutely necessary. It then progresses to a category that shows the subjugation of individual choice to social prescriptions by the elimination of any form of consultation.

In some cases, the order of the categories was partially nominal, but the identification of the elements may suggest a possible basis for ranking that would be ordinal if the categories were collapsed. I preferred not to collapse nominal categories into ordinal ones when I coded information from the sources, because I wanted to maximize their use as a means of identifying the range of meaning associated with the variable. For example, the code on eating arrangements not only shows variation in whether men and women eat together (one indicator of general sexual differentiation) but also suggests the manner in which the separation was accomplished (spatially, temporally, etc.). The categories retain flexibility for combination in a variety of ways, to test different types of hypotheses.

Where ordinal or potentially ordinal categories were used, they were consistently arranged so that they would relate to social and cultural aspects of the sexual and reproductive cycles. Generally, little social or cultural involvement with the sexual and reproductive cycles was reflected in categories marked by low numbers, while intense social or cultural concern was marked by higher numbers. Since each of the codes did not have the same number of categories, it was not possible to assign an absolute value of social/cultural involvement to each step in the scale. For example, segregation of males and females at meals was assigned a higher number than lack of segregation, because the former requires more social supervision than the latter; as such, it expresses more social concern with the arrangement. The same principle applied in ranking categories for celebration at marriage; a more elaborate celebration entails the expenditure of more time and effort by a group of people than a small one does, and therefore expresses more social involvement.

## Coding

Coding is the data collection phase of the cross-cultural research process. Code sheets facilitate systematic, succinct notations on the information that is relevant to the code. The code sheets designed for this study (an example is shown in Appendix D) contain the name of the society, its world area number, the date on which I coded the information, and the names of the items in the code. I provided space beside the name of each item for entering the symbol for the category that best described the item, as well as for making additional comments about the coding decision. The extra space was systematically used to note the page numbers on which supporting information for the coding decision could be found.

I used a two-page code sheet for each source, because of the large number of items I was coding. For ease in coding, the items were grouped into three main sections. The first, "Sexual Differentiation," provides information on the degree to which men and women are generally distinguished from one another in the basic activities of everyday life. The second section, "The Reproductive Cycle," marks different stages of the reproductive cycle to which social and cultural concern could be attached. The third section, "Sexual Relations," delineates the dimensions of different types of sexual relationships.

The procedure followed in coding was to read the principal authority or authorities first, take notes on the material pertinent to the code, and then enter the symbol for the category that seemed most appropriate for the information on the coding sheet. The page numbers of supporting data were entered beside the symbol for the category decided upon.

I read *complete* sources for each society, rather than confining my attention to sections like "life cycle" or relying on the precategorized sections in HRAF. I followed this rather lengthy procedure in order to cut down on bias resulting from precategorization of information. I did not assume that a writer or classifier for HRAF would put all of the details relevant to my research interest in one place.

When I used HRAF, I used only information in the complete sources that preceded topical divisions. HRAF is a convenient reference library, which contains many complete and hard-to-obtain sources, particularly out-of-date historical materials and sources translated from foreign languages, e.g., Portuguese, Chinese, and Aztec.

In addition to cutting down on classifier's or ethnographer's bias, another advantage that reading complete sources offered was a better understanding of the overall social context within which each of the items was embraced. This not only provided a basis for my formulating new hypotheses, which had not previously occurred to me, but also aided me in explaining significant relationships *and* their exceptions. In his article "Why Exceptions? The Logic of Cross-Cultural Analysis," Köbben (1967) stressed how revealing exceptions to correlations can be in explaining the significance of the most frequent associations. After I found significant relationships, I usually cross-tabulated the categories myself, replacing numerical frequencies for each cell with the names of the societies they represented. I could then refer back to my original notes and try to understand the basis of the exception.

Not only did I read complete sources but I also either read them in the language in which they were originally written or had them translated. Murdock and White (1969: 338) noted that most cross-cultural samples are biased in favor of sources written in English. Since one of their criteria for selecting a society for coding from a sampling area was the fullness of information about it, they tended to select the best-described society, regardless of the language in which the accounts of it were written. Thirty-eight percent of the societies in the SCCS were described in a language other than English, usually in French or German. I read all souces in French, and a colleague of mine, Edith Lauer, read and translated the German material for me. In addition, I used translations that were available in HRAF. By not restricting the use of sources according to the language in which they are written, the scope of material available for a particular society increases. In addition, the possibility that an inadequate source in English will be used in preference to a source of high quality in another language decreases.

After I read a source, I used one pair of coding sheets for coding the information derived from it. A separate pair was used for each source read. This cut down on the amount of information to be processed at one time and provided a basis for comparing the codings among sources. The same process was followed for the other primary and auxiliary primary sources. The category of each source and an assessment of its usefulness for this code was indicated on each code sheet. If the material seemed unclear at that point, or if there was little information relevant to the code, I read the useful secondary sources. Only as a last resort were "other" sources read, as only inferences can generally be made from these sources.

Each code sheet was compared with others to determine the degree of agreement between sources about the code and to provide a basis for a coding on the final sheet. The final sheet reflects my judgment of which category best describes the element in the code. Where the codings for different sources were different, an effort was made to determine whether the error lay in my initial judgment of the material presented by the reporter or whether it was a genuine conflict in information. It was at this point that the ranking of sources proved useful. If there was a discrepancy, the information from the principal authority was generally preferred to that of another source, unless there was some basis for judging that the principal authority's description of a particular characteristic was likely to be erroneous. This could occur in cases where the writer was trying to make a theoretical point but seemed to manipulate data to confirm the point.

If one source was closer to the pinpointing date or locality than another, more weight was given to the former. If there was disagreement between sources, but a weak inference could be made, I indicated this by enclosing the coding in square brackets. If there was some disagreement, but a strong inference could be made, I indicated this by putting parentheses around the coding. If there was *no* information for the code, I indicated this by a dot. If there was some information, but it was insufficient to code, I indicated this by a dash. All of these procedures are consistent with those set up for coding at the Cross-Cultural Cumulative Coding Center. For purposes of computer tabulation of the data, the dot and the dash were treated as missing data. The absence of a characteristic was marked by a special coding category. All of these notations were helpful in rating the amount of comparativist's bias that might influence the coding.

Code symbols from the final code sheets were transferred to a data sheet, which summarized the codings for all of the sample societies. The sample societies were listed down the page by name, world area identification number, and the name of the geographical region wherein they were located. Codings for each item were entered across the page by variable number and name. This summary of all of the codings was used for hand tabulations, as a reference for checking computer cross-tabulations, and for identifying exceptions. Appendix E contains a similar table, which presents the codings for each variable in the code.

*Statistics and Data Analysis*

Data analysis involves the use of statistical and conceptual tools to arrive at conclusions. Statistics as a methodological technique is used to summarize data systematically, to test the degree of association between variables, and to test hypotheses. It provides one type of evidence to support theoretical propositions, which link concepts together in the form of statements or hypotheses. The concepts of theory are the variables in statistics.

In order to facilitate the statistical manipulation of data, the codings on the data sheet were transferred to computer cards. Data for each variable were entered on a separate card for every society in the sample. Dr. Joel Gunn assisted me in setting up a file on social and cultural aspects of the sexual and reproductive cycles. The file was set up in such a way that variables could be intercorrelated with CCCCC variables already on file at the University of Pittsburgh. We later combined the variables in this study with those contained in the CCCCC codes on subsistence economy, division of labor and technology, settlement patterns and community organization, and political organization. The combined file contained a total of 194 items, 86 of which I designed for this study.

Statistics were particularly useful in implementing two goals of this research on human sexuality: (1) finding out the amount of variation in social and cultural aspects of the sexual and reproductive cycles and (2) discovering if and how these aspects were associated with each other in patterns of association.

Initial computer outputs were histograms, frequency distributions, and calculations of the mean, median, and mode for each distribution. These statistics helped to establish the range of variation in social and cultural aspects of the cycles. The results of these distributions are presented throughout the text.

Other statistical manipulations were used to discover the degree of association between variables and the strength of their patterning. The types of statistics used depended upon the types of scales used for data collection and the number of cases available for calculation.

When the data that pertained to two variables were nominal, I used chi square ($X^2$) to determine the degree to which their relationship was due to chance. When the cases in a two-by-two contingency table were fewer than 20 or were between 20 and 40 but with the smallest expected frequency of less than five, I used Fisher's exact test to find out whether or not the association between nominal variables was due to chance.

The association between the variables that had data in the form of ordinal scales could be tested with more powerful statistics than that between variables that had only nominal data. Whereas measures of association for nominal scales assess the degree to which classification in one category can predict classification in another, correlation coefficients for ordinal scales are designed to determine the degree to which the rank of an individual or society on one variable could be used to predict rank on another (Freeman 1968: 79).

I used two statistical measures of association for ordinal scales: the Spearman rho (r) and Goodman and Kruskal's coefficient of association, Gamma (G). In my initial run of the data, I used Spearman's "r" rather than "G," because it was part of the SPSS (Statistical Package for the Social Sciences), which was available for use at the University of Pittsburgh Computing Center. I could therefore test a large number of preliminary hypotheses very quickly. Since ties in rank (cases where several societies occupy the same rank) were inevitable, given the small number of categories I formulated in relation to a relatively large sample, it was important to use a statistic that could take them into account. There is such provision in the SPSS program for the computation of rho. However, Gamma is an easier statistic to use when ties are present, because the formula does not vary in the calculation of tied or untied ranks. When the final descriptions of association were made for this study, I generally used Gamma in lieu of Spearman's rho, because of its greater flexibility when ties are present.

In order to test some hypotheses, it was necessary to measure the degree of association between one variable that was indicated by an ordinal scale with one that was indicated by a nominal one. One way of measuring associations with these types of data was to treat the ordinal scale as if it were a nominal one and to use a statistical technique that applied to nominal scales. This is a less sensitive measure, since it does not make use of the rankings in the ordinal scale. The only statistic available for measuring the association between nominal and ordinal scales is the Wilcoxon coefficient of differentiation, which involves guessing order on one scale from classification on the other (Freeman 1968: 110). I generally used the latter alternative in dealing with associations between nominal and ordinal scales.

The choice of a statistical technique for testing hypotheses based on the association between nominal and ordinal scales is broader than that for measuring association. I chose the Mann-Whitney U test, a variation of the Wilcoxon T test, to evaluate the significance of these hypotheses.

After interrelating social and cultural aspects of the sexual and reproductive cycles with each other, I intercorrelated them with those of other CCCCC codes to test specific hypotheses. Finally, I crosstabulated all variables with their areal classifications, to determine the influence regional clustering might have on the patterning of variables.

As I mentioned earlier, I approached the analysis of cross-tabulations in a very detailed manner. I usually checked the computation of significant associations by hand and identified the societies contained in each cell. This aided in the identification of linked items in the same societies and in the explanation of exceptions to general tendencies. In sum, my procedure linked coded items to the social contexts of which they are a part.

The results of the frequency distributions, contrasts by world area, associations between variables, and specific tests of hypotheses constitute the data upon which conclusions about variations in social and cultural aspects of the sexual and reproductive cycles are based. Data of this sort formed the foundation for descriptions in Chapter Three, Chapter Four, and Chapter Five.

# Appendix B
# An Example of a Pinpointing Sheet

World Area: 147

Sampling Province 160: Southern Plains

Representative of the Province and of Cluster 316: Comanche, Ne3: 177.

Focus: The Comanche as a whole, located from 30° to 38°N and from 98° to 103°W in 1870.

General Area: The Comanche, who speak a Shoshonian language, entered the plains relatively late, coming from the northwest. As early as 1705, however, they were already raiding the Spanish settlements in northeastern New Mexico. They dominated the southern Plains — northwestern Texas, western Oklahoma, southwestern Kansas and southeastern Colorado — from about 1725 to almost 1875. They acquired horses in the seventeenth century and by the eighteenth were raiding the Spaniards in New Mexico and Texas. They were hereditary enemies of the Ute, and in 1838 decimated the pueblo of Pecos and forced its abandonment. By 1870 the range of the buffalo was being seriously curtailed, and the herds completely disappeared about 1878. In 1875 the Comanche capitulated and were assigned a reservation in western Oklahoma. The population of the Comanche was estimated by Mooney to be about 7,000 in 1690. Bent estimated them at 12,000 in 1846. They numbered 4,700 in 1886, 1,380 in 1884, 1,170 in 1910, and 2,200 in 1937.

Selection of Focus: The entire tribe, which was culturally undifferentiated.

Time: The date of 1879 was selected as just prior to the removal to Oklahoma. The last Sun Dance was held in 1878.

Coordinates: Given above, under Focus.

## Bibliography

### 1. Principal Authority

Hoebel, E.A. 1940. The Political Organization and Law-Ways of the Comanche Indians. Memoirs of the American Anthropological Association 54:1–149. HRAF-NO6 #1. (Field work in 1932).
_____ 1939. Comanche and Hekandika Shoshone Relationship System American Anthropologist 41:440–457.
Wallace, E., and E. A. Hoebel. 1952. The Comanches: Lords of the South Plains. Norman, Okla. (Further field work in 1945). HRAF-NO6 #3.

### 2. Other Dependable Primary Sources

Carlson, G. G., and V. H. Jones. 1939. Some Notes on Uses of Plants by the Comanche Indians. Papers of the Michigan Academy of Science, Arts and Letters 5:517:542. HRAF-NO6 #5. (Ethnobotanical field work in 1933).
Gladwin, T. 1948. Comanche Kin Behavior. American Anthropologist 50:73–94. (Field work in 1940). HRAF-NO6 #9.
Linton, R. 1935. The Comanche Sun Dance. American Anthropologist 37:429–428. (Field work in 1933). HRAF-NO6 #6.

### 3. Auxiliary Primary Sources (early)

Lee, N. 1957. Three Years Among the Comanches. Norman, Okla. (Field experience as a captive in 1855–1858, prior to any significant acculturation). HRAF-NO6 #2.
Rister, C. C. 1955. Comanche Bondage, pp. 188–198. Glendale. HRAF-NO6 #10. (Data on culture by a woman captive of 1836–37).

# Appendix C
# Coding Manual

I. Sexual Differentiation. This section deals with the pervasiveness of sexual differentiation in daily life as expressed by the person's physical appearance and the spatial organization of the living arrangements for males and females.

  A. Physical appearance. Each of the following categories specifies a mode of modifying physical appearance; they apply only to the appearance of adults during the daily routine and not to their appearance for temporary occasions such as ceremonial gatherings. If one aspect is not clearly done by one sex or the other, enter both. The categories are ranked according to the severity of physical modification involved.

   1 The amount, style, color, or material of the garment worn.
   2 Paraphernalia, e.g., belts, footwear, headgear and other accessories to the main garment, exclusive of jewelry.
   3 The amount, style, or placement of jewelry.
   4 The style, length, or color of head hair.
   5 The growth of facial hair, e.g., moustaches and beards.
   6 The use of cosmetics, i.e., preparations applied to specific parts of the body to enhance their attractiveness, e.g., facial makeup, body scents, body oils, body paints, tooth blackeners.
   7 The removal of body hair, exclusive of head hair coded under 4, e.g., the removal of facial, axillary, or pubic hair.
   8 The deformation or mutilization of the body, exclusive of the genitals, i.e., a change in the form or the removal of a material part of the body, e.g., tattooing, cicatrization, cranial deformation, ear piercing.
   9 The deformation or mutilation of the genitals, e.g., clitoridectomy, circumcision, sewing the labia together.

  For females (1 on the coding sheet) and for males (2 on the coding sheet), rank the importance of sexual differentiation of up to four of the above modes by placing the numeral for the most important mode first in the coding blank, the second most important, third, etc.

B. Sleeping arrangements. These categories deal with the ways in which mature males and females are differentiated by their spatial arrangement during sleep.

1. Adolescent females. Each of the categories specifies where unmarried but sexually mature females sleep in relation to sexually mature males in the living quarters. The categories are ranked according to the degree of segregation of female from male adolescents.

   1 Girls marry before or very soon after puberty and live in the dwelling of their prospective husband.

   2 Girls sleep in the same dwelling as their parents and sibs. No special section reported for them.

   3 Girls sleep in the same dwelling as their parents but in a particular section or partitioned area for them and/or their female siblings.

   4 Girls sleep in the same dwelling as their parents but in a particular section for their mothers and female children. Males sleep in a separate section.

   5 Girls sleep in the same dwelling as their parents with no partition reported, but the adolescent males sleep in a separate section.

   6 Girls sleep in the same dwelling as their parents with no partition reported, but the adolescent males sleep in a men's house or somewhere other than the natal dwelling.

   7 Girls sleep in the same dwelling as their parents. There is a special section or partitioned area for them. The adolescent males sleep elsewhere.

   8 Girls sleep in the same dwelling as their mother, but adolescent and other mature males sleep elsewhere.

   9 Girls sleep in their own hut or in a separate dwelling for adolescent girls. Adolescent boys sleep in a men's house or some dwelling other than the one in which their parents reside.

2. Married women. Each of the categories specifies where spouses sleep in the living quarters. The categories are ranked according to the degree of spatial separation between the spouses during sleep. The most prominent form of sleeping arrangement should be indicated first in the coding

blank. The number for any important but subsidiary arrangement should be placed after the first numeral.

1 W (wife) sleeps with her H (husband) in their own dwelling. No rooms or partitions between them are specified.

2 W sleeps with her H in a dwelling that contains more than one conjugal family. No partitioned area is reported for them.

3 W sleeps with her H in a partitioned area in a dwelling that contains more than one conjugal family.

4 W sleeps with her H in her dwelling, but he has a dwelling of his own or spends most of his time in the men's house or elsewhere, e.g., with another wife.

5 W sleeps with her H in her own room or section of the dwelling, separate from the section of her H.

6 W sleeps in her dwelling, and her H sleeps in his dwelling or in a men's house except for the times when intercourse is desired.

C. Eating arrangements. This part deals with the way in which the spatial arrangement of the sexes during daily meals differentiate males from females. Each of the categories specifies the placement of adult males in relation to adult females during the main meal of the day, exclusive of arrangements operative during ceremonies or when guests are present. The categories are ranked according to the degree of segregation between males and females during the meal.

1 Men and women eat together. No particular arrangement is specified for the sexes.

2 Men and women eat together. There is a strict positioning of them in the eating area, e.g., positioning according to kinship.

3 Men and women do not eat together in public but certain kin may eat together in private, e.g., husband and wife.

4 Men and women do not eat together and eat in different areas.

5 Men and women do not eat together; the separation is accomplished by their eating at different times.

II. The Reproductive Cycle. This section deals with the amount and type of social emphasis given to specific stages of a woman's reproductive cycle and to the importance of her having children.

A. Menstruation. This part is concerned with the social recognition given to the onset and recurrence of the menstrual flow.

1. The onset of menstruation.

    a. Marking the transition. This deals with the amount of individual ordeal and social celebration involved at the onset of the menses.

    (1) Individual ordeal. The categories are arranged according to the severity of the ordeal.

        1 There is no ordeal reported although there may be a change in physical appearance, living arrangements, or name.

        2 Three is a slight ordeal involved, e.g., a very short or relaxed period of seclusion, a few minor eating taboos, etc.

        3 There is a moderate ordeal involved, e.g., a strict period of seclusion, restraints on movement, numerous eating taboos, etc.

        4 There is a severe ordeal involved, e.g., a painful physical operation such as clitoridectomy, a lengthy seclusion with numerous taboos on movement, eating and social contacts, etc.

    (2) Social celebration. The categories are arranged according to the amount of celebration and the extent of participation in it. If there are differences according to class level, code according to the celebrations for the average individual.

        1 There is no celebration of any kind.

        2 There is a small celebration, e.g., the family group has a party.

        3 There is a moderate celebration, e.g., family, friends, and/or small kin group have a feast, dance, give gifts.

        4 There is an elaborate celebration, e.g., the community, a large kin group, or other large social grouping celebrate or a smaller group has a celebration for an extended period of time.

    b. The social significance. This part deals with how the scope of a woman's position is thought to change with the onset of menstruation. The categories are ranked according to the degree of emphasis placed on her ability to bear children.

1 It is not thought to be especially significant beyond a change in dress, name, etc.

2 Its main significance is that she is an adult who has more social responsibilities.

3 The main significance is that she is now capable of having intercourse, whether or not she actually engages in it.

4 Its main significance is that she is eligible for marriage and can engage in intercourse.

5 Its main significance is that she is eligible for marriage.

6 Its main significance is that she is eligible for marriage and is an adult.

7 Its main significance is that she is eligible for marriage and is capable of bearing children.

8 Its main significance is that she is capable of bearing children.

2. Regular menstruation. This deals with the type of personal restriction and the amount of social danger involved in each recurrence of the menstrual flow.

a. Personal restrictions. The categories are ranked according to the degree to which the woman is socially isolated during her menses.

1 There is no restriction placed on her during this period, and she carries on her activities as usual.

2 There are restrictions placed on her personal activities but not on her social contacts, e.g., cooking taboos, eating taboos, taboos on what she may touch.

3 There are restrictions placed on her personal movements and social contacts, e.g., she must remain in her dwelling or in a certain area of the settlements, she should avoid certain people.

4 There are few restrictions placed on her personal activities and social contacts.

5 There are moderate restrictions placed on her movements and her personal activities, e.g., she is in a partitioned area of the dwelling, she may not cook, she may see only certain people, she cannot engage in her usual economic activities, relaxed seclusion.

6 There are severe restrictions imposed on her movements and personal activities, e.g., she is isolated in

a menstrual hut, she may see few if any people, she may not cook, she may not feed herself.
  b. Social danger. This deals with which person(s) would be most harmed if the woman did not adhere to her menstrual restrictions. The categories are ranked according to how large a group is thought to be endangered by the woman's actions. If more than one category is involved, code the most important danger first, the second most important one, second.
    1 No one is thought to be endangered during this period.
    2 Only the menstruating woman is endangered.
    3 The woman endangers her husband.
    4 The woman endangers men. If both 3 & 4, code as 4.
    5 The woman endangers other women and/or children, e.g., the fertility of other women, newborn children.
    6 The woman endangers anyone with whom she comes in contact.
    7 The woman endangers her social group, e.g., the fertility of the crops, the response of the supernatural to them, harm to an important social functionary.
B. Pregnancy
  1. The personal restrictions. Each category describes a type of restriction that can be applied to a woman during pregnancy. They are ranked according to the degree of segregation from social contacts that is involved. The three most important restrictions should be ranked on the coding sheet with the most important restriction placed first, the second most important, second, etc.
    1 No modification is reported.
    2 She modifies the usual garments she wears and/or the usual care of her body, e.g., she wears more loose-fitting garments, wears amulets to ward off evil spirits, pays special attention to cleanliness, etc.
    3 She modifies the use of her sensory apparatus, e.g., she avoids hearing, seeing, or touching certain things.
    4 She modifies her diet, e.g., she avoids eating certain foods.
    5 She modifies her usual domestic or economic duties, e.g., she does not cook, she has someone else care for the children.

6 She modifies her usual mobility, e.g., she should not leave the settlement, she avoids certain places.

7 Her usual social relations and/or living arrangements are modified, e.g., she may not sleep where she usually does, she cannot be near certain people, she must not behave in the usual manner.

8 She modifies her participation in social groups and activities, e,g., religious events.

2. Purpose of the restrictions. Each category specifies a person(s) whom the restrictions serve to protect from harm. They are ranked according to the extensiveness of the social harm that may result from a woman not modifying her behavior along the expected lines. The code should indicate which person(s) the restrictions are most concerned with protecting.

1 They are to prevent harm to the baby.

2 They are to prevent harm to the mother, e.g., illness, difficult delivery.

3 They are to prevent harm to the baby and the mother, e.g., miscarriage, attacks from the spirits, etc.

4 They are to prevent harm to anyone with whom she comes in contact and/or the social group of which she is a part, e.g., to prevent failure of the crops, to prevent an epidemic.

C. Birth

1. Spatial segregation.

a. Location of the woman when she gives birth. Each category describes where the birth of the first child takes place. The categories are ranked according to the degree of segregation in or from her ordinary dwelling when the woman gives birth.

1 No special place is prepared for the birth of the child; the woman gives birth wherever she happens to be.

2 The woman gives birth in the dwelling where she usually resides, but no special partitions are set up.

3 The woman gives birth in the dwelling where she usually resides but in a partitioned or otherwise demarcated area or room.

4 The woman gives birth in an area near the dwelling where she usually resides, e.g., under the dwelling, in a lean-to near the dwelling.

5 The woman does not give birth in a special dwelling

but in a place outside of the area where most social activity occurs, e.g., on the fringes or outside of the dwelling area.

    6 The woman gives birth in a structure explicitly constructed for the purpose, e.g., a birth hut.

    7 The woman does not give birth in her usual residence but in the dwelling of an affinal relative.

    8 The woman does not give birth in her usual residence but in the dwelling of a consanguineal relative.

  b. Residence of the new parents at the birth of their first child. This indicates where the new mother and her husband are residing when their first child is born.

    1 Temporary matrilocality.

    2 Permanent matrilocality.

    3 Ambilocality.

    4 Neolocality.

    5 Patrilocality.

2. Personal restrictions.

  a. The purpose of the restrictions. Each category indicates why the taboos and restrictions on a woman's personal behavior are imposed after she bears a child. They are ranked according to the degree that the restrictions affect other people.

    1 Restrictions are imposed on her to promote the well-being of her child, e.g., she is cared for so that she can produce milk for the baby.

    2 Restrictions are imposed on her to prevent harm to her and/or to promote her well-being, e.g., other people prepare and bring her food, she does not work, she is indulged.

    3 Restrictions are imposed to prevent harm to her and her baby.

    4 Restrictions are imposed on her to prevent harm to those with whom she comes in contact and/or to prevent harm to her social group.

  b. The duration of the restrictions. Each category specifies a period of time after birth before the woman resumes her usual domestic and economic activities.

    1 0–7 days

    2 8–14 days

    3 15–30 days

    4 31–60 days

5 more than two months.

3. Celebration of birth. This deals with the degree of social concern with the birth of a child as indicated by the amount of celebration after the birth and the extent of social participation in it. The codes apply to the largest social class and exclude such particular occasions as the celebration of multiple births or the birth of an heir to a king. Code for the first born if there is a difference in treatment for different births. If there is a difference for males and females code for the desired sex.

a. Type of celebration.
   1 There is no celebration for the mother or child after birth.
   2 There is no celebration after birth, but people do come to visit, offer congratulations, etc.
   3 There is a minor celebration after the birth, e.g., a small meal, a few drinks, etc.
   4 There is a moderate amount of celebration after the birth, e.g., a feast, dancing.
   5 There is an elaborate celebration after the birth, e.g., elaborate feasting, dancing, many rites performed.

b. When the celebration occurs.
   1 Immediately or a few days after delivery.
   2 After the mother comes out of confinement.
   3 When the baby is named or baptized.
   4 When the baby and mother come out of confinement.
   5 Other

c. The participants. The code indicates the most extensive group which participates in the celebration of the birth. The categories are ranked according to the extensiveness of the group.
   1 No one is involved in a celebration.
   2 The husband's family.
   3 Friends and neighbors.
   4 The wife's kin unit.
   5 Friends of the H and W and "relatives".
   6 The wife's and husband's kin units or relatives of a group more extensive than the family.
   7 The community or large social group to which the H and W belong.

D. Children. This section deals with the ways in which childbearing is socially encouraged or curtailed.

1. Preferred sex and number of children.

    1 They want very few children, regardless of sex.

    2 They prefer to have males rather than females, regardless of number.

    3 They prefer to have females rather than males, regardless of number.

    4 Either sex is acceptable, e.g., the father wants a boy, the mother wants a girl, or they don't care as long as the child is healthy.

    5 They prefer a large number of children, regardless of their sex.

2. Barrenness. This part deals with the amount of social stigma that a woman bears if she is incapable of producing children.

    a.  Explanation of barrenness. The categories are ranked according to the degree to which the woman is blamed for her barrenness.

       1 Barrenness is regarded as the fault of a sterile or impotent H.

       2 Barrenness is regarded as an unfortunate physical condition that has befallen a woman through no fault of her own.

       3 Barrenness is regarded as the fault of others who bear malice towards the woman, e.g., witches.

       4 Barrenness is regarded as the fault of others who break taboos that have ramifications for her fertility.

       5 Barrenness is regarded as the fault of supernatural forces or supernatural beings who are generally malevolent.

       6 Barrenness is regarded as the fault of the woman who is being punished for committing some offense which is not sexual in nature.

       7 Barrenness is regarded as punishment to a woman who has committed some sexual offense, e.g., adultery, incest.

    b.  Penalties for barrenness. The categories are ranked according to the severity of the penalty the woman incurs if she is barren.

       1 No penalties are reported.

       2 Remedies are actively sought to correct the condition, e.g., amulets, potions, ceremonies.

       3 Provision is made for a child by adoption for fosterage.

4 Provision is made for a child by the husband taking an additional wife to bear children or by the wife getting another woman to bear children for her husband.

5 The woman's husband can or does divorce her.

6 The woman is ostracized because she has no children, e.g., jokes are made about her. She is given a subsidiary role in domestic tasks.

7 Other.

3. Control over reproduction.

  a. Contraception. This part deals with the knowledge and use of means to prevent the conception of children. The categories are ranked according to the degree to which the responsibility for contraception devolves upon the woman.

    1 No contraception is known about or used.

    2 Contraception is present, but there is no information on the method.

    3 There is a rudimentary form of contraception, e.g., abstention when the woman is thought most likely to conceive, coitus interruptus.

    4 Contraception is present by implication, e.g., a long post-partum sex taboo or abstention while nursing.

    5 There is a long post-partum sex taboo and rudimentary contraception.

    6 There is a long post-partum sex taboo and the woman practices some intentional form of contraception.

    7 The woman is primarily responsible for contraception, e.g., she has knowledge of rites she can perform to prevent offspring or she swallows a drug.

  b. Abortion. This part deals with the approval of and rationale for action taken to prevent the birth of a child by expelling the fetus before it is viable.

    (1) Social approval. The categories are ranked according to the amount of social disapproval towards abortion.

      1 Abortions occur, but there is no information on frequency.

      2 Abortions are permitted and occur frequently.

      3 Abortions are permitted and occur infrequently.

      4 Abortions are disapproved of but do occur. If they

are infrequent and there is no information on approval, code in this category.

5 Abortions are strongly disapproved of and occur rarely or never.

(2) Rationale for abortions. Each category specifies a reason for which an abortion might be performed. If there is more than one reason, indicate the most frequent reason first on the code sheet, second, etc. up to four important reasons. The categories are ranked according to the degree to which social rather than personal considerations lead to the abortion.

1 No abortions.

2 Concern for the psychological or physical state of the mother, e.g., she does not want more children, she is concerned about her beauty, or she does not want to lose her husband.

3 Revenge, e.g., the woman is angry with her husband.

4 Concern for the child's welfare, e.g., the mother is nursing another which would leave no milk for another, or the couple cannot afford more children.

5 The child was conceived out of wedlock.

6 The child was conceived in an illicit sexual relationship, e.g., adulterous, incestuous, or with a man of the wrong social class or ethnic group.

7 Other.

c. Infanticide. This part deals with the approval of and rationale for killing an infant after he is born.

(1) Social approval. The categories are ranked according to the amount of social disapproval incurred if infanticide occurs.

1 Infanticide occurs, but there is no information on frequency.

2 Infanticide is permitted and occurs frequently.

3 Infanticide is permitted and occurs infrequently.

4 Infanticide is disapproved of but does occur. If it occurs, and there is no information on approval, code here.

(2) Rationale for infanticide. Each category indicates a reason for which an infant might be killed. The categories are ranked according to the degree to which

(2) social rather than personal reasons lead to the infanticide. If there is more than one reason, indicate the most frequent reason first on the code sheet, the next most frequent reason, second, etc., up to four important reasons.

1 No infanticide.

2 The mother's welfare, e.g., she does not want more children, she is afraid of losing her charms, etc.

3 Revenge, e.g., due to argument with husband.

4 Concern for the child's welfare, e.g., the couple cannot support more children or there is no one to suckle the child.

5 The child was born in an unusual position, exhibited some unusual behavior or physical trait at birth, or was deformed, e.g., hair was already present on the child, or the child was born feet first.

6 The child was one of a multiple birth.

7 The child was a female.

8 The child was born of an illicit sexual relationship, i.e., premarital, adulterous, or incestuous.

9 Other.

III. Sexual Relations and their Social Context. This section deals with sexual relations from two perspectives. The first focuses on intercourse and the restrictions that are placed on it. The second focuses on marriage as the most common context within which intercourse and childbearing occur.

A. Intercourse.

1. Restrictions on occasion. Each category specifies an occasion when intercourse is proscribed or strongly preferred not to take place. The categories are ranked according to the degree to which the occasion for intercourse is tied to a social rather than an individual state or activity. If more than one category applies, rank the most important one first on the code sheet, the next most important one, second, etc., up to four restrictions.

1 It cannot occur during menstruation.

2 It cannot occur for some period after childbirth whether because of nursing or a postpartum sex taboo and/or during pregnancy.

3 It cannot occur during menstruation and after childbirth and/or during pregnancy.

4 It cannot occur before, during, or after life cycle events, e.g., after the death of a spouse or at initiation.

5 Other.

6 It cannot occur before, during, and/or after a military expedition.

7 It cannot occur before, during and/or after a major economic activity and/or a manufacturing operation.

8 It cannot occur before, during and/or after a ritual program of some sort, e.g., days of abstinence or power seeking.

9 It cannot occur before, during and/or after non-life cycle ceremonial events, e.g., harvest festivals.

2. Restrictions on partner: the incest taboo.

   a. Extensions of the incest taboo. Each category specifies an extension of the incest taboo beyond the nuclear family. They are ranked according to the degree to which the emphasis is on nonkinship considerations. The coding should indicate the focus of the strongest extension of the incest taboo.

     1 No extension beyond the nuclear family is reported. Note in the comments if the strongest prohibition in the family is Br-Si, Mo-So, or Fa-Dau.

     2 Bilateral extensions by cross or parallel cousins.

     3 Bilateral extension by degree of cousinage from ego.

     4 Other.

     5 Matrilineal extensions, with or without other bilateral extensions.

     6 Patrilineal extensions, with or without other bilateral extensions.

     7 Extensions based on nonkinship considerations, e.g., ritual bonds, household composition, locality, or social class.

   b. Violation of the taboo. The categories are ranked according to the extent of the consequences of violating the incest taboo.

     1 None or mild punishment, e.g., ostracism or a fine.

     2 Moderate punishment, e.g., offenders meet with misfortune such as sickness or bad luck.

     3 Severe punishment, e.g., death, barrenness, or expulsion from the community.

     4 Punishment to others than the offenders, e.g., their family or kin group.

     5 Punishment to the total social group, e.g., an epidemic or crop failure in the community.

     6 Punishment that affects the offenders as well as their

social group, i.e., category '2' or '3' in combination with '5' category.

3. Restrictions according to marital status. This part deals with how strictly a woman must confine her sexual relations to the marital bond.

   a. Premarital sex.

     (1) Restrictions. The categories are ranked according to the degree of prohibition against premarital sex.

       1 It is permitted for both sexes.

       2 It is permitted for both but in limited contexts, e.g., with prostitutes or as part of a ceremony.

       3 It is permitted and not punished unless pregnancy results.

       4 It is permitted for males but not females.

       5 Premarital relations are disapproved but not infrequent in fact.

       6 Insistence on virginity for the woman. There is no information on restrictions on the male.

       7 Premarital relations are strongly disapproved and rare.

     (2) Violation of restrictions. Each category specifies the consequences a woman faces if she violates a premarital sex prohibition.

       1 Neither she nor her partner face punishment.

       2 Her partner is punished, but she is not.

       3 Mild punishment for the women, e.g., temporary ostracism.

       4 Moderate punishment for the woman, e.g., marriage is more difficult or physical punishment.

       5 Severe punishment, e.g., banishment from her social group, or she is killed.

   b. Extramarital sex.

     (1) Restrictions. The categories are ranked according to the strength of the prohibition against extramarital sex.

       1 Permitted for both H and W.

       2 Permitted for both but only in limited contexts, e.g., with particular relatives of the spouse, ceremonial license.

       3 Permitted and not punished unless pregnancy results.

       4 Permitted for the H but not for the W.

     5 Weakly prohibited, e.g., frequent violations or weak punishment.

     6 Strongly prohibited, e.g., occurs rarely or severe punishment.

(2) The punishment. The categories are ranked according to the severity of punishment that a woman receives if she commits adultery.

     1 No punishment or mild punishment, e.g., a warning or a fine.

     2 Generally mild punishment, but she can be killed for it.

     3 Moderate punishment, e.g., a beating or incarceration.

     4 Generally moderate punishment, but she can be killed or divorced for it.

     5 The woman is divorced.

     6 She is generally divorced, but she can be killed for it.

     7 Severe punishment, e.g., permanent physical damage, but she can be killed or divorced for it.

     8 The woman is killed or commits suicide.

(3) Violation: who is punished. The categories are ranked according to the degree to which the woman is punished.

     1 No one is punished.

     2 Only the lover is punished.

     3 Both the woman and her lover are punished, but the lover is punished more severely than the woman.

     4 Both the woman and her lover are punished by almost equally severe punishment.

     5 Both the woman and her lover are punished, but the woman is punished more severely than her lover.

     6 Only the woman is punished.

(4) Violation: who punishes. The categories are ranked according to the degree to which responsibility for punishment of the woman resides with the social group.

     1 No punishment for the women.

     2 The husband punishes his wife and/or her lover, if the wife is not punished.

      3 A representative of the family or kin group of the husband punishes her.

      4 A representative of the family or kin group of the wife punishes her.

      5 The community as a whole or its representative punishes her.

      6 Supernatural consequences fall upon the woman, e.g., mystical retribution or punishment by the ancestral gods.

B. Marriage. This part focuses on the establishment, characteristics, and dissolution of marriage, the most prominent form of legitimate sexual relationship and context for the birth of children.

1. Establishment of marriage.

   a. Age at marriage. Indicate in the first blank of the coding sheet the age of the woman at first marriage and, in the second, the age of the man at marriage.

     1 Under 12 years.

     2 12–15 years (if the source says that boys or girls marry at puberty, code it here).

     3 16–17 years.

     4 18–21 years.

     5 22–25 years.

     6 26 years and older.

   b. Choice of spouse. The categories specify social restrictions which limit an individual's choice of whom he can marry. The categories are ranked according to the degree that nonkinship considerations play an important role. If there is more than one important factor, code the most important one first, the second most important, second, etc.

     1 Bilateral considerations, including not marrying a "relative".

     2 Bilateral considerations, specifically cross and parallel cousins.

     3 Kinship of a matrilineal or matrilateral nature.

     4 Kinship of a patrilineal or patrilateral nature.

     5 The locality where the potential spouse lives.

     6 The tribe to which the potential spouse belongs.

     7 The age or generation of the potential spouse.

     8 The status of the potential spouse.

   c. Agreement to marry. This deals with the extent to which

marriage is a transaction between social groups rather than the couple.

(1) Proposal. Besides the groom, indicate whose proposal is regarded as most necessary in initiating marriage. The categories are ranked according to how extensive a group is involved in initiating marriage.

1 The bride's family or a relative of the bride.

2 The bride's and groom's families.

3 The groom's kin group and the bride's family.

4 The bride's kin group and the groom's family.

5 The kin groups of the bride and groom.

(2) Consent. This indicates how necessary the consent of the prospective spouse is for marriage arrangements to proceed. Code for the bride in the first blank and for the groom in the second.

1 Prospective spouse's consent is necessary, i.e., the marriage cannot take place without it.

2 The prospective spouse is consulted.

3 The prospective spouse is not consulted.

d. The marriage celebration.

(1) Degree of celebration. Each category indicates the degree of social celebration given to the marriage.

1 There is no celebration.

2 There is a small celebration, e.g., a minor acknowledgement or exchange of gifts.

3 There is a moderate celebration, e.g., a feast, dancing, dramatic performances, or extensive gift exchange.

4 There is an elaborate celebration, e.g., it lasts a long period of time, is characterized by lavish dress, has elaborate performances, etc.

(2) Participants. Each category indicates a type of social participant in the wedding. They are ranked according to how extensive the group is.

1 Friends of the couple.

2 The family of the bride or the groom.

3 The kin group of the bride or groom.

4 The families of the bride and groom.

5 The kin groups or "relatives" of the bride and groom.

6 The community.

e. The rights transferred at marriage. This deals with the

rights that are exchanged between a man and woman at marriage. In blank (1), rank in order of importance up to three rights a woman transfers to her husband at marriage; in blank (2), up to three rights a man transfers to a woman at marriage.

1 Rights concerning priority of sexual access.
2 Rights concerning offspring.
3 Rights concerning choice of residence.
4 Rights concerning domestic services.
5 Rights concerning economic labor.
6 Rights concerning choice of residence and economic labor.

   f. Finality. Each category indicates a factor that is important for the firm establishment of a marriage. The categories are ranked according to the degree to which its establishment depends on the groom. The code should reflect the most important obligation that must be met before the marriage is considered final. If there is more than one factor involved, code the most important one first, etc.

1 After children or children of the appropriate sex are born.
2 After cohabitation and the birth of children.
3 After cohabitation.
4 After children are born and after bride price has been paid.
5 After a marriage ceremony.
6 After bride-price has been paid.

2. The dissolution of marriage.
   a. Divorce. This is a legal dissolution of a marriage.
      (1) Grounds. These are the reasons given for dissolving a marriage. For females (blank a.) and for males (blank b.), rank in importance up to three grounds for divorce.

1 There is no divorce.
2 Reproductive problems, e.g., barrenness or impotence.
3 Illicit sexual relationship, e.g., adultery.
4 Physical violence, e.g., beatings.
5 Incompatibility.
6 Desertion or extreme neglect.
7 Incompatibility with affines.

8 Failure in economic or domestic duties, e.g., laziness, poor provider or nonpayment of marriage payments.

9 None or trivial grounds, e.g., another woman or man is more desirable or he or she does not like his or her current spouse.

(2) Restrictions on divorce. The categories are ranked according to the difficulty a woman has in obtaining a divorce.

1 Divorce is allowed for both the H and W.

2 Divorce is more difficult for a man to obtain. There is a prohibition against his obtaining one or a low frequency of men who obtain a divorce.

2 Divorce is difficult and/or has a low frequency for both men and women.

2 Divorce is more difficult for the wife to obtain. There is a prohibition against her obtaining one or a low frequency of wives obtaining a divorce.

(3) Rights over offspring after divorce. The categories are ranked according to the degree to which the husband retains custody over the children after a divorce.

1 No divorce.

2 The wife keeps all of the children.

3 Who has custody of the children depends on the age and/or wishes of the children, e.g., the mother may take the infants.

4 Each spouse has custody of some of the children, e.g., the wife keeps the girls and the husband, the boys.

5 Custody of the children depends on the circumstances of the divorce.

6 The husband has custody of all of the children.

(4) Remarriage after divorce. The categories are ranked according to how difficult it is to remarry after a divorce.

1 Both the H and W may remarry.

2 Both the H and W may remarry, but it is easier for the H.

3 It is difficult for both the H and W to remarry after divorce.

4 No divorce.

(5) Property exchanges after divorce. The categories are ranked in order of the amount of financial loss incurred by the wife when a divorce occurs.

1 There is no divorce.

2 No financial transactions occur after a divorce, or there is an equal division of property.

3 The H or his kin pay compensation.

4 The transactions that occur depend on the circumstances of the divorce.

5 Other.

6 The wife and/or her kin group pay compensation, e.g., return brideprice.

b. Widowhood. This is the dissolution of marriage by the death of the husband.

(1) Remarriage. The categories are ranked in order of the degree of restriction a woman faces to remarry after her husband's death.

1 She may marry anyone she chooses.

2 She may remarry but often chooses not to, e.g., she would suffer financial loss or her children can care for her.

3 She may remarry, but her choice is constrained by the wishes of her family and/or kin group.

4 She may remarry, but first priority is given to marrying a specific relative of her husband's or someone chosen by her husband's kin group, e.g., levirate.

5 She must marry a specific relative of the husband's or someone chosen by her husband's kin group or not remarry.

6 She may not remarry.

(2) Length of time before remarriage.

1 0–6 months.

2 6 months to less than a year.

3 1 year to less than 2 years.

4 More than two years.

5 No remarriage.

# Appendix D
# Code Sheet:
# Social and Cultural Aspects of the
# Sexual and Reproductive Cycles

Society _____        World Area _____

Source _____        Date _____

  I. Sexual Differentiation

    A. Physical Appearance

      1. Females                        _____

      2. Males                           _____

    B. Sleeping Arrangements

      1. Adolescent                   _____

      2. Married                      _____

    C. Eating Arrangements        _____

 II. The Reproductive Cycle

    A. Menstruation

      1. Onset

        a. Marking

          1) Ordeal                _____

          2) Ceremony          _____

        b. Significance            _____

      2. Regular

        a. Restrictions            _____

        b. Danger                _____

    B. Pregnancy

      1. Restrictions              _____

      2. Purpose                 _____

    C. Birth

      1. Segregation             _____

        2. Restrictions
            a. Purpose                    _____
            b. Length                     _____
        3. Celebration
            a. Type                       _____
            b. Participants               _____
    D. Children
        1. Preferred sex                  _____
        2. Barrenness
            a. Explanation                _____
            b. Penalties                  _____
        3. Control of reproduction
            a. Contraception              _____
            b. Abortion
                1) Approval               _____
                2) Rationale              _____
            c. Infanticide
                1) Approval               _____
                2) Rationale              _____
III. Sexual Relations
    A. Intercourse
        1. Occasion                       _____
        2. Incest
            a. Extensions                 _____
            b. Violation                  _____
        3. Marital status
            a. Premarital sex
                1) Restrictions           _____
                2) Violation              _____
            b. Extramarital sex
                1) Restrictions           _____
                2) Punishment             _____
                3) Punished               _____
                4) Punisher               _____
    B. Marriage
        1. Establishment
            a. Age                        _____
            b. Choice                     _____
            c. Agreement
                1) Proposal               _____
                2) Consent                _____

    d. Celebration
      1) Type             _____
      2) Participants     _____
    e. Rights
      1) Woman        _____
      2) Man            _____
    f. Finality             _____
2. Dissolution
    a. Divorce
      1) Grounds
        a) Woman      _____
        b) Man         _____
      2) Restrictions      _____
      3) Offspring        _____
      4) Remarriage      _____
      5) Property        _____
    b. Widowhood
      1) Remarriage      _____
      2) Length         _____

# Appendix E
# Coded Data

| | Female Physical Differentiation | Male Physical Differentiation | Adolescent Sleeping Arrangements | Marital Sleeping Arrangements | Eating Arrangements | Onset of Menstruation: Ordeal | Onset of Menstruation: Celebration | Onset of Menstruation: Significance | Regular Menstruation: Restrictions | Regular Menstruation: Danger |
|---|---|---|---|---|---|---|---|---|---|---|
| 003 Thonga | 841 | 142 | 9 | 4 | 4 | 1 | 1 | – | 5 | 67 |
| 006 Suku | 8 | 295 | 9 | 6 | 4 | 1 | 1 | 5 | 5 | • |
| 009 Hadza | 31 | 248 | 9 | 1 | 4 | 4 | [3] | [1] | 4 | 54 |
| 012 Ganda | 3 | 1 | [9] | 6 | 3 | 2 | (2) | 8 | 4 | 72 |
| 015 Banen | 1 | 19 | 8 | 6 | [3] | • | • | [3] | • | • |
| 018 Fon | 8 | – | 8 | 6 | 4 | 2 | – | • | 5 | • |
| 021 Wolof | 4361 | 419 | 9 | 6 | 4 | (1) | [2] | 5 | 2 | 7 |
| 024 Songhai | 4368 | 542 | 2 | 1 | – | [4] | • | 5 | • | • |
| 027 Massa | 3 | 18 | • | 6 | • | • | • | • | • | • |
| 030 Otoro | 3(1) | 8 | (9) | 6 | – | 1 | 1 | 4 | • | • |
| 033 Kafa | 6431 | 8253 | 4 | 6 | 3 | 1 | 2 | 4 | 5 | – |
| 036 Somali | 3426 | 452 | 6 | 4 | 4 | [–] | 1 | 5 | • | • |
| 039 Kenuzi | 3896 | 5 | 6 | 1* | 4 | [1] | 1 | 6 | 3 | 2 |
| 043 Egyptians | 2364 | 41 | 6 | – | 5 | 2 | 1 | 5 | • | • |
| 045 Babylonians | 42 | 15 | – | – | [1] | • | • | • | • | • |
| 048 Gheg | 316 | 51 | 5 | 2* | 4 | • | • | • | • | • |
| 052 Lapps | 342 | 12 | (2) | 1 | • | – | 1 | • | 5 | 2 |
| 054 Russians | 142 | 12 | [3] | 3 | (1) | • | • | • | • | • |
| 057 Kurd | 3648 | 592 | 1 | (3) | (3) | – | • | • | 4 | – |
| 060 Gond | 814 | 54 | 7 | 5 | • | (1) | 1 | • | 6 | 67 |
| 063 U. Pradesh | 3826 | 512 | 4 | 5 | 4 | 1 | 1 | [3] | 4 | – |
| 066 Khalka | 34 | 427 | (7) | 1 | • | • | • | • | • | • |
| 069 Garo | 1 | 1 | 6 | 3 | (3) | (1) | 1 | 8 | 1 | (1) |
| 072 Lamet | 21 | 21 | 7 | 5 | (1) | [1] | 1 | • | • | • |
| 076 Siamese | 314 | 814 | 6 | 1 | 3 | 2 | 1 | [2] | (2) | – |
| 078 Nicobarese | 14 | 1 | 2 | 2 | 1 | 3 | 4 | 6 | • | • |
| 081 Tanala | 214 | 184 | – | 1 | (2) | (1) | 1 | (1) | 1 | (1) |
| 084 Balinese | 4368 | 24 | 7 | 3 | 5 | 2 | 3 | (2) | 4 | 4 |
| 087 Toradja | 3648 | 93 | 3 | 3 | 3 | 2 | 1 | 3 | 3 | 7 |
| 090 Tiwi | 1 | 7 | 1 | 1 | 1 | 3 | 3 | 3 | 4 | 247 |
| 093 Kimam | 1 | 1 | 2 | 1 | 1 | 2 | 2 | • | 5 | 47 |

| | Female Physical Differentiation | Male Physical Differentiation | Adolescent Sleeping Arrangements | Marital Sleeping Arrangements | Eating Arrangements | Onset of Menstruation: Ordeal | Onset of Menstruation: Celebration | Onset of Menstruation: Significance | Regular Menstruation: Restrictions | Regular Menstruation: Danger |
|---|---|---|---|---|---|---|---|---|---|---|
| 096 Manus | 481 | 34 | 6 | 5 | 3 | 4 | 4 | 2 | – | • |
| 099 Siuai | 2 | 476 | (6) | 1 | (3) | (2) | 1 | 8 | 3 | (1) |
| 102 Mbau Fijians | 81 | 6451 | 6 | 1 | 4 | [4] | [3] | [2] | – | – |
| 105 Marquesans | 63 | 8473 | 6 | 2 | 4 | [2] | 1* | [1] | – | 4 |
| 108 Marshallese | 14 | 81 | 7 | [3] | 2 | 4 | 3 | 4 | 6 | 627 |
| 111 Palauans | 891 | 5 | 8 | 6 | 3 | (1) | 1 | • | – | • |
| 114 Chinese | 1 | 1 | 5 | 3 | 2 | • | • | • | 2 | – |
| 117 Japanese | 214 | 41 | 5 | 3 | 3 | – | 1 | – | 3 | – |
| 120 Yukaghir | 31 | 17 | 3 | 3 | • | 2 | 1 | 3 | 2 | 7 |
| 123 Aleut | 841 | 71 | 2 | [3] | • | 4 | • | • | 5 | 672 |
| 126 Micmac | 31 | – | 5 | 1 | (5) | 2 | • | • | 6 | 47 |
| 129 Kaska | 3481 | 73 | 6 | 1 | 4 | (3) | 6 | 6 | 6 | 72 |
| 132 Bellacoola | • | 5 | [2] | 3 | • | 4 | (1) | 5 | – | 74 |
| 135 Pomo | 134 | 85 | 8 | 6 | 1 | 3 | [3] | 2 | 6 | 27 |
| 138 Klamath | 1(4) | 47 | (2) | 2 | 1 | 3 | 3 | 5 | 6 | 72 |
| 141 Hidatsa | 1 | 26 | [3] | 3 | (1) | – | (1) | 5 | [5] | 7 |
| 144 Huron | 341 | 8624 | [2] | 2 | • | 2 | [1] | [3] | 4 | • |
| 147 Comanche | 1(3)4 | 4728 | 6 | (5) | (1) | [1] | 1 | 7 | 5 | 27 |
| 150 Havasupai | 41 | 213 | – | 1 | 3 | 3 | (2) | 2 | 4 | 7 |
| 153 Aztec | 64 | 128 | 9 | 1 | [–] | • | • | • | • | • |
| 156 Miskito | 641 | 6471 | – | 2 | 5 | – | • | [5] | 5 | 627 |
| 159 Goajiro | 138 | 2 | [2] | 6 | – | 4 | 4 | 6 | • | • |
| 162 Warrau | 63(1) | (1) | 2 | 2 | [1] | [3] | 3 | 5 | [6] | 62 |
| 165 Saramacca | 813 | 1(3) | 6 | 4 | 4 | 1 | (1) | – | 6 | 74 |
| 168 Cayapa | 143 | 14 | 2 | 2 | 5 | [2] | 1 | • | (4) | 1 |
| 171 Inca | 418 | 1834 | 2 | 1 | 2 | 2 | 3 | – | • | • |
| 174 Nambicuara | 7 | 6825 | 5 | 2 | • | 4 | 4 | 5 | 4 | • |
| 177 Tupinamba | 843 | 847 | [2] | 3 | 1 | 4 | [1] | 4 | • | • |
| 180 Aweikoma | 1 | 3 | 2 | 2 | • | • | • | 7 | • | • |
| 183 Abipon | 832 | – | [2] | 1 | • | 4 | • | 7 | • | • |
| 186 Yahgan | 31 | (4) | 3 | 1 | (1) | 3 | (3) | (2) | (2) | • |

| | Pregnancy Restrictions: Type | Pregnancy Restrictions: Purpose | Birth: Location | First Birth: Residence | Birth Restrictions: Purpose | Birth Restrictions: Duration | Birth Celebration: Type | Birth Celebration: Timing | Birth Celebration: Participants | Children: Preferred Gender and Number |
|---|---|---|---|---|---|---|---|---|---|---|
| 003 Thonga | 427 | 1 | 4 | 5 | 1 | 1 | 5 | 4 | 7 | 4 |
| 006 Suku | – | • | • | 5 | • | • | 3 | 4 | [2] | (5) |
| 009 Hadza | 8 | - | 5 | 2 | 3 | 1 | • | • | • | – |
| 012 Ganda | 637 | 1 | 7 | 4 | [3] | 2 | [3] | • | 1 | • |
| 015 Banen | 467 | 3 | 2 | 5 | [1] | 1 | [3] | • | – | 2 |
| 018 Fon | 4 | 2 | 2 | 5 | (2) | 5 | 4 | 1 | (6) | 5 |
| 021 Wolof | • | • | 8 | 1 | • | 1 | 5 | 4 | 5 | 5 |
| 024 Songhai | 3 | 3 | 8 | 1 | 3 | 4 | 5 | 3 | 7 | 5 |
| 027 Massa | • | • | • | 5 | • | • | • | • | • | (3) |
| 030 Otoro | • | • | • | 5 | 1 | • | [3] | – | • | • |
| 033 Kafa | 2 | • | 3 | 5 | – | 3 | 1 | • | 1 | 2 |
| 036 Somali | [–] | • | (2) | 1 | 1 | [–] | 4 | 1 | – | 2 |
| 039 Kenuzi | • | • | (2) | 1 | 3 | 4 | 4 | 1 | 7 | 2 |
| 043 Egyptians | 57 | – | [3] | 1 | 3 | 4 | 4 | 3 | 6 | 2 |
| 045 Babylonians | • | • | • | • | • | • | • | • | • | (2) |
| 048 Gheg | – | (1) | • | 5 | • | • | 2 | 1 | 3 | (2) |
| 052 Lapps | 3 | 1 | – | 5 | 3 | 1 | 3 | 3 | – | 2 |
| 054 Russians | 5 | • | • | 4 | – | – | 4 | 3 | 5 | [2] |
| 057 Kurd | • | • | 3 | 5 | – | 2 | 4 | 3 | 5 | 2 |
| 060 Gond | 3 | • | 3 | 5 | – | [2] | • | • | • | • |
| 063 U. Pradesh | 4673 | • | 3 | • | (1) | 2 | 5 | 1 | 3 | (2) |
| 066 Khalka | • | • | 2 | 5 | 4 | 3 | 3 | 3 | 7 | 4 |
| 069 Garo | 1 | 3 | 3 | 2 | (2) | 1 | 3 | 1 | – | 3 |
| 072 Lamet | (1) | 3 | • | 5 | 3 | 3 | 3 | 1 | • | 5 |
| 076 Siamese | 3875 | 3 | 3 | 1 | 3 | 2 | 3 | 1 | – | 4 |
| 078 Nicobarese | 41 | 1 | 6 | 2 | – | 5 | 1 | • | 1 | • |
| 081 Tanala | 3 | 3 | 6 | 5 | – | 2 | 3 | 1 | 4 | • |
| 084 Balinese | 426 | 3 | (1) | 5 | – | 1 | 4 | 5 | – | 2 |
| 087 Toradja | 4327 | 3 | 3 | 2 | 3 | 1 | 2 | 1 | 5 | 3 |
| 090 Tiwi | 425 | 3 | 5 | 1 | [3] | 2 | 3 | 1 | • | • |
| 093 Kimam | 4 | 3 | 6 | 5 | 1 | 5 | 3 | 5 | 3 | 5 |

| | Pregnancy Restrictions: Type | Pregnancy Restrictions: Purpose | Birth: Location | First Birth: Residence | Birth Restrictions: Purpose | Birth Restrictions: Duration | Birth Celebration: Type | Birth Celebration: Timing | Birth Celebration: Participants | Children: Preferred Gender and Number |
|---|---|---|---|---|---|---|---|---|---|---|
| 096 Manus | 1 | 3 | 8 | 1 | 3 | 3 | 5 | 4 | 7 | • |
| 099 Siuai | 5 | 3 | 8 | 1 | 3 | 4 | 5 | 3 | 7 | 4 |
| 102 Mbau Fijians | 563 | 4 | 2 | 5 | 1 | (3) | 5 | 1 | 6 | 2 |
| 105 Marquesans | 46 | 3 | 6 | 4 | 3 | 2 | - | 1 | - | (5) |
| 108 Marshallese | 652 | 3 | 6 | 2 | 1 | [3] | 5 | 5 | 6 | • |
| 111 Palauans | 748 | 2 | 8 | 1 | - | (1) | 5 | 2 | 6 | 3 |
| 114 Chinese | 345 | 1 | • | - | • | 1 | 5 | 3 | • | 2 |
| 117 Japanese | 423 | (1) | 3 | 5 | 4 | 1 | 3 | 3 | 5 | 2 |
| 120 Yukaghir | 43 | 2 | • | 1 | 4 | 1 | 5 | • | 7 | 2 |
| 123 Aleut | 46 | 1 | 6 | 5 | (2) | [4] | - | 3 | • | 5 |
| 126 Micmac | - | 1 | 5 | 4 | 4 | (1) | - | - | - | 5 |
| 129 Kaska | 34 | 3 | 6 | 2 | 1 | 1 | (4) | • | 3 | • |
| 132 Bellacoola | 43 | 3 | 4 | 5 | 4 | 2 | 4 | 3 | 7 | 5 |
| 135 Pomo | 7463 | 3 | 6 | - | 1 | [1] | 2 | 1 | 6 | • |
| 138 Klamath | • | • | 8 | 1 | 4 | 1 | 2 | - | - | 2 |
| 141 Hidatsa | 437 | 3 | [8] | • | [1] | • | [3] | 3 | - | • |
| 144 Huron | 37 | 4 | 3 | 2 | • | 1 | [3] | • | 3 | 3 |
| 147 Comanche | • | • | 6 | 5 | - | - | (3) | 3 | (3) | 2 |
| 150 Havasupai | 34 | 3 | 2 | 1 | 1 | 1 | 3 | 1 | - | 4 |
| 153 Aztec | 346 | 1 | - | 5 | • | • | 5 | 3 | 5 | • |
| 156 Miskito | 6 | 2 | 6 | 2 | 3 | 2 | [3] | 4 | - | 2 |
| 159 Goajiro | 348 | 3 | 3 | 2 | - | 2 | (5) | (1) | 5 | (5) |
| 162 Warrau | 43 | 1 | 6 | 2 | 4 | 2 | (3) | • | • | 3 |
| 165 Saramacca | 2 | 1 | • | • | - | [2] | 3 | - | • | 4 |
| 168 Cayapa | - | • | (2) | 3 | 2 | [1] | 1 | • | 1 | [5] |
| 171 Inca | 64 | • | • | 5 | - | [1] | 3 | 1 | - | (5) |
| 174 Nambicuara | - | 3 | 2 | 5 | - | 4 | 1 | • | 1 | 1 |
| 177 Tupinamba | 5 | - | • | 2 | - | 1 | 5 | 1 | • | • |
| 180 Aweikoma | • | • | 5 | 3 | - | - | (5) | 1 | 5 | - |
| 183 Abipon | • | • | • | 1 | • | • | - | • | - | [3] |
| 186 Yahgan | 43 | 1 | 2 | 1 | 1 | 2 | 2 | 1 | 3 | 4 |

| | Barrenness: Explanation | Barrenness: Penalties | Contraception: Responsibility | Abortion: Approval | Abortion: Rationale | Infanticide: Approval | Infanticide: Rationale | Intercourse: Restrictions on Occasion | Incest Taboo: Extensions | Incest Taboo: Punishment for Violation |
|---|---|---|---|---|---|---|---|---|---|---|
| 003 Thonga | 4 | 45 | 5 | • | • | 5 | 1 | 7634 | • | • |
| 006 Suku | 21 | 257 | 4 | 4 | 54 | • | • | 35 | 57 | • |
| 009 Hadza | 47 | 1 | • | (5) | 1 | • | • | 73 | 4 | • |
| 012 Ganda | 4 | 652 | 4 | • | • | 3 | 359 | 346 | 6 | 4 |
| 015 Banen | 74 | 24 | 4 | [5] | 9 | • | • | 2 | 6 | 5 |
| 018 Fon | 4 | 24 | 4 | 4 | 56 | 1 | 5 | 24 | 6 | 3 |
| 021 Wolof | 35 | 253 | • | • | • | • | • | 8 | 3 | • |
| 024 Songhai | 5 | 54 | 2 | 1 | 5 | 1 | • | 34 | • | • |
| 027 Massa | 5 | - | • | [4] | • | 3 | 8 | • | • | 4 |
| 030 Otoro | • | - | 7 | 1 | 3 | • | • | 64 | 3 | 4 |
| 033 Kafa | • | [2] | 1 | [5] | 1 | • | • | 3678 | • | 1 |
| 036 Somali | • | 52 | • | 1 | • | 5 | 85 | 36 | 2 | • |
| 039 Kenuzi | 52 | 542 | 1 | 5 | 1 | • | • | 42 | • | • |
| 043 Egyptians | 3 | 25 | 1 | 1 | • | • | • | - | 1 | • |
| 045 Babylonians | • | 534 | • | 1 | 7 | 1 | 9 | 8 | - | 3 |
| 048 Gheg | • | 5 | 4 | • | • | 1 | 5 | - | 6 | • |
| 052 Lapps | [2] | 3 | 1 | • | • | 5 | 1 | 71 | 3 | 1 |
| 054 Russians | • | 57 | 2 | 2 | • | • | • | 8 | • | • |
| 057 Kurd | • | 425 | 1 | - | • | - | - | 3 | 3 | • |
| 060 Gond | 31 | - | • | • | • | 1 | (6) | 743 | 6 | 3 |
| 063 U. Pradesh | 5 | 26 | 5 | 1 | 6 | 5 | 1 | 29 | 7 | 3 |
| 066 Khalka | • | 245 | - | • | • | - | - | 82 | - | • |
| 069 Garo | • | 3 | - | • | • | • | • | 1 | - | • |
| 072 Lamet | 5 | 62 | • | • | • | 1 | 6 | 7 | - | • |
| 076 Siamese | 6 | 3 | 2 | 4 | 5 | 1 | 6 | 92 | 1 | • |
| 078 Nicobarese | • | 253 | - | (2) | • | 1 | 6 | 48 | - | • |
| 081 Tanala | 7(2) | 63 | • | (4) | 5 | 4 | 4 | 2 | 6 | 6 |
| 084 Balinese | 3 | 345 | 7 | 4 | • | (5) | 1 | 1 | 37 | 6 |
| 087 Toradja | 46 | 452 | 7 | 4 | 62 | 4 | 26 | 761 | 37 | 6 |
| 090 Tiwi | • | 3 | • | (2) | 24 | 1 | 6 | 34 | 57 | 3 |
| 093 Kimam | (2) | 3 | • | 4 | 3 | 1 | 5 | 738 | 32 | 1 |

| | Barrenness: Explanation | Barrenness: Penalties | Contraception: Responsibility | Abortion: Approval | Abortion: Rationale | Infanticide: Approval | Infanticide: Rationale | Intercourse: Restrictions on Occasion | Incest Taboo: Extensions | Incest Taboo: Punishment for Violation |
|---|---|---|---|---|---|---|---|---|---|---|
| 096 Manus | 3 | 3 | 7 | • | • | • | • | 2 | 3 | – |
| 099 Siuai | 3 | – | 6 | (5) | 1 | • | • | 2 | 5 | 2 |
| 102 Mbau Fijians | 54 | – | 6 | (2) | 24 | (2) | 724 | 26 | – | – |
| 105 Marquesans | • | 32 | – | 4 | • | 5 | 1 | 768 | 2 | • |
| 108 Marshallese | • | 32 | 5 | (2) | 5 | (3) | 54 | 347 | 5 | 1 |
| 111 Palauans | • | 32 | 4 | 1 | 26 | 1 | • | 24 | 5 | 2 |
| 114 Chinese | • | 53 | • | 2 | 4 | 2 | 74 | 2 | • | • |
| 117 Japanese | • | 32 | 1 | 2 | (2) | 5 | 1 | – | 6 | – |
| 120 Yukaghir | 5 | 52 | – | • | • | 1 | 4 | 3 | 37 | • |
| 123 Aleut | • | 65 | • | 5 | 1 | 5 | 1 | 71 | [5] | 4 |
| 126 Micmac | • | 25 | 4 | 1 | 4 | • | • | 3 | 3 | • |
| 129 Kaska | 2 | 4 | 3 | 5 | 1 | 4 | 8 | 634 | – | 3 |
| 132 Bellacoola | • | 5 | [7] | 1 | 5 | 1 | 284 | 879 | 1 | 1 |
| 135 Pomo | • | 2 | 7 | 1 | 5 | 1 | 2 | 9 | • | • |
| 138 Klamath | 4 | 42 | 4 | • | • | 4 | 85 | 384 | 3 | 4 |
| 141 Hidatsa | • | 32 | • | • | • | • | • | 3 | – | • |
| 144 Huron | • | • | 4 | • | • | • | • | 928 | 53 | • |
| 147 Comanche | • | – | 1 | [2] | • | 1 | 56 | • | 3 | 1 |
| 150 Havasupai | 46 | 42 | 6 | 1 | • | 1 | 6 | 73 | 3 | 1 |
| 153 Aztec | • | 5 | – | 5 | (2) | 5 | 6 | • | 3 | 3 |
| 156 Miskito | • | 526 | 7 | 1 | • | [3] | 857 | 618 | – | • |
| 159 Goajiro | • | • | 7 | (2) | (5) | – | – | 28 | 53 | 1 |
| 162 Warrau | • | [5]6 | [4] | 1 | – | 1 | 5 | 2 | 3 | • |
| 165 Saramacca | 3 | 23 | 4 | 1 | • | – | – | 24 | 57 | 3 |
| 168 Cayapa | • | 53 | [1] | 5 | 1 | 1 | 8 | 4 | 3 | 2 |
| 171 Inca | – | • | (1) | 1 | • | 5 | 1 | 8 | 3 | 3 |
| 174 Nambicuara | 2 | 5 | 5 | [2] | 4 | – | • | 28 | 1 | • |
| 177 Tupinamba | • | 5 | • | 1 | 34 | 1 | 6 | 78 | – | • |
| 180 Aweikoma | • | 2 | • | 1 | 6 | • | • | 24 | 1 | • |
| 183 Abipon | • | • | 4 | (2) | 2 | 2 | 259 | 2 | • | • |
| 186 Yahgan | 2 | 4 | 7 | (2) | 62 | 4 | 573 | 24 | • | • |

| | Premarital Sex: Restrictions | Premarital Sex: Punishment | Extramarital Sex: Restrictions | Extramarital Sex: Punishment | Extramarital Sex: Who is Punished | Extramarital Sex: Who Punishes | Female Age at Marriage | Male Age at Marriage | Choice of Spouse | Marriage: Proposal |
|---|---|---|---|---|---|---|---|---|---|---|
| 003 Thonga | 3 | 2 | 4 | 1 | 2 | 1 | 4 | 4 | 46 | 2 |
| 006 Suku | 7 | 2 | 6 | 4 | 3 | 6 | 4 | • | 275 | 5 |
| 009 Hadza | 3 | 2 | 2 | 3 | 3 | • | 2 | 2 | 25 | 2 |
| 012 Ganda | 3 | 2 | 4 | 7 | 3 | 2 | 2 | 3 | 45 | 5 |
| 015 Banen | 1 | 1 | 2 | 7 | 4 | 6 | – | – | 4 | – |
| 018 Fon | 4 | 4 | 5 | – | – | • | 3 | • | • | 5 |
| 021 Wolof | 7 | 4 | 5 | 4 | 5 | 2 | 3 | 6 | 824 | 2 |
| 024 Songhai | 4 | 3 | 4 | 4 | – | 2 | 2 | 4 | 48 | 2 |
| 027 Massa | 3 | 2 | 6 | 1 | 2 | 1 | • | 6 | 45 | 2 |
| 030 Otoro | 1 | 1 | 5 | 2 | 3 | 5 | 2 | – | 4 | 5 |
| 033 Kafa | 4 | 2 | 4 | 3 | 3 | • | 2 | 4 | 8 | 2 |
| 036 Somali | 6 | 2 | 4 | 5 | 5 | 2 | 4 | 5 | 4 | 3 |
| 039 Kenuzi | 6 | 6 | 6 | 8 | 6 | 2 | 2 | 4 | 26 | 5 |
| 043 Egyptians | 7 | • | 6 | 6 | 4 | 2 | 2 | • | 25 | 5 |
| 045 Babylonians | (4) | • | (4) | 6 | 4 | 2 | – | – | • | 2 |
| 048 Gheg | 6 | 6 | 6 | 6 | 3 | 2 | 2 | 5 | 45 | 2 |
| 052 Lapps | 5 | 3 | 6 | • | • | • | 4 | 6 | 186 | 3 |
| 054 Russians | [7] | 5 | 6 | 7 | 4 | 5 | 5 | 5 | – | 2 |
| 057 Kurd | 6 | 6 | 6 | 8 | 6 | 4 | 1 | 2 | 285 | 5 |
| 060 Gond | 1 | 1 | 5 | 5 | – | 2 | • | • | 42 | 2 |
| 063 U. Pradesh | 4 | 4 | 3 | 7 | 6 | 5 | 2 | 3 | 854 | 2 |
| 066 Khalka | 1 | 1 | 5 | 5 | 5 | 2 | 3 | 4 | 4 | 2 |
| 069 Garo | 3 | 2 | 5 | 1 | 4 | 4 | 4 | 5 | 35 | 2 |
| 072 Lamet | 1 | 1 | • | • | • | • | • | 4 | 48 | 2 |
| 076 Siamese | [5] | – | 5 | – | • | • | 5 | 5 | 857 | 2 |
| 078 Nicobarese | 1 | 1 | 5 | 3 | 4 | 5 | 2 | 3 | 1 | 5 |
| 081 Tanala | 4 | 5 | 5 | 2 | 4 | 2 | 4 | 4 | 427 | 5 |
| 084 Balinese | 1 | 1 | 4 | 5 | – | 2 | 3 | 4 | 458 | – |
| 087 Toradja | 3 | 2 | 5 | – | – | 5 | • | • | 716 | 5 |
| 090 Tiwi | 4 | 2 | 5 | 1 | 3 | 2 | 1 | 6 | 327 | 2 |
| 093 Kimam | 2 | 1 | 2 | 4 | 4 | 2 | – | • | 51 | 5 |

| | Premarital Sex: Restrictions | Premarital Sex: Punishment | Extramarital Sex: Restrictions | Extramarital Sex: Punishment | Extramarital Sex: Who is Punished | Extramarital Sex: Who Punishes | Female Age at Marriage | Male Age at Marriage | Choice of Spouse | Marriage: Proposal |
|---|---|---|---|---|---|---|---|---|---|---|
| 096 Manus | 4 | 6 | 4 | 7 | 4 | 2 | 2 | 4 | 15 | 5 |
| 099 Siuai | 5 | 2 | 5 | 2 | 3 | 4 | • | • | 325 | 2 |
| 102 Mbau Fijians | 4 | 6 | 2 | 3 | 3 | 2 | 3 | 6 | 427 | 2 |
| 105 Marquesans | 1 | 1 | 2 | 4 | 5 | 2 | 4 | • | 12 | 2 |
| 108 Marshallese | 1 | 1 | 2 | 4 | 3 | 2 | 2 | 2 | 328 | 5 |
| 111 Palauans | 1 | 1 | 2 | 5 | 3 | 2 | • | • | 385 | 5 |
| 114 Chinese | 7 | 4 | 6 | 4 | 4 | 2 | - | - | 42 | 2 |
| 117 Japanese | 4 | 4 | 4 | 5 | - | 2 | 5 | 6 | 85 | 2 |
| 120 Yukaghir | 3 | - | - | • | • | • | • | • | 15 | 2 |
| 123 Aleut | (1) | 1 | 2 | 7 | 4 | 2 | • | • | 32 | 5 |
| 126 Micmac | [7] | 3 | [6] | 8 | 4 | 2 | 6 | 6 | 1 | 2 |
| 129 Kaska | 3 | 4 | 4 | 4 | 6 | 2 | 3 | 4 | 36 | 2 |
| 132 Bellacoola | 5 | • | 4 | 4 | 3 | 2 | 2 | 3 | 18 | 5 |
| 135 Pomo | 1 | (1) | - | 7 | - | 2 | • | • | 135 | 2 |
| 138 Klamath | 7 | 4 | 6 | 6 | 3 | 2 | 2 | 3 | 1 | 2 |
| 141 Hidatsa | 5 | 3 | 2 | 5 | 3 | 2 | • | • | 36 | 5 |
| 144 Huron | 1 | (1) | 2 | • | • | • | 2 | • | 13 | 1 |
| 147 Comanche | 1 | 1 | 2 | 7 | 4 | 2 | 3 | 6 | 15 | 2 |
| 150 Havasupai | 5 | - | - | 5 | 4 | 2 | 2 | 5 | 15 | 1 |
| 153 Aztec | 4 | • | 4 | 8 | 4 | 5 | 3 | 4 | 1 | 5 |
| 156 Miskito | - | • | 5 | 4 | 5 | 2 | 2 | 3 | 2 | 1 |
| 159 Goajiro | 3 | 2 | 4 | 4 | 5 | 2 | - | - | 3 | 5 |
| 162 Warrau | 5 | 2 | 5 | 3 | 4 | 5 | 3 | 4 | 5 | 1 |
| 165 Saramacca | 5 | 1 | 1 | 1 | 3 | 2 | 4 | 6 | 365 | 5 |
| 168 Cayapa | 5 | • | 6 | 3 | 4 | 5 | • | • | 1 | 2 |
| 171 Inca | 1 | 1 | 4 | 8 | - | 2 | 3 | 4 | 15 | 2 |
| 174 Nambicuara | 4 | • | 1 | 4 | 4 | 2 | 2 | 3 | 21 | 2 |
| 177 Tupinamba | 1 | 1 | 4 | 6 | 6 | 2 | • | 2 | 4 | - |
| 180 Aweikoma | (1) | 1 | 1 | 4 | 6 | 2 | 4 | 4 | 1 | • |
| 183 Abipon | 7 | • | 6 | - | - | 2 | 4 | 6 | 1 | 1 |
| 186 Yahgan | 7 | 4 | 5 | 4 | 4 | 2 | 3 | 4 | 1 | 1 |

| | Female Consent to Marry | Male Consent to Marry | Marriage Celebration: Type | Marriage Celebration: Participants | Marriage: Female Rights Transferred | Marriage: Male Rights Transferred | Marriage: Final Establishment | Divorce: Female Grounds | Divorce: Male Grounds | Divorce: Restrictions by Gender |
|---|---|---|---|---|---|---|---|---|---|---|
| 003 Thonga | 2 | 2 | 3 | 4 | 624 | • | • | 5 | 582 | 1 |
| 006 Suku | 1 | 1 | 3 | – | 134 | 5 | 4 | 3 | 32 | 1 |
| 009 Hadza | 1 | 1 | 3 | 7 | 143 | 6 | 3 | 84 | – | 2 |
| 012 Ganda | (1) | (1) | 3 | 4 | 541 | 5 | 6 | 94 | 69 | 4 |
| 015 Banen | 1 | – | 4 | 5 | 25 | • | 6 | 9 | – | 2 |
| 018 Fon | 1 | 3 | 4 | 5 | 32 | • | 6 | 578 | 1 | 2 |
| 021 Wolof | 2 | 2 | 4 | 5 | 543 | 5 | 4 | 842 | 325 | 4 |
| 024 Songhai | 3 | – | 4 | 4 | 1 | 5 | 6 | 489 | 239 | 4 |
| 027 Massa | • | • | • | • | 235 | • | 4 | • | 6 | – |
| 030 Otoro | • | • | 2 | 3 | 213 | 5 | 2 | 924 | 653 | 2 |
| 033 Kafa | 3 | 3 | 4 | 7 | 43 | • | • | • | 1 | – |
| 036 Somali | 3 | 2 | 4 | 5 | 264 | 5 | 6 | 852 | 236 | 4 |
| 039 Kenuzi | 3 | 2 | 4 | 7 | 13 | 5 | 1 | 4 | 29 | 4 |
| 043 Egyptians | 3 | 3 | 4 | 7 | 12 | 1 | 1 | – | 271 | 4 |
| 045 Babylonians | 3 | 3 | 2 | 1 | 243 | 5 | 6 | 64 | 238 | 4 |
| 048 Gheg | 3 | 3 | 3 | • | 254 | • | 1 | 4 | 23 | 4 |
| 052 Lapps | 3 | 2 | 3 | 5 | 5 | 5 | • | 1 | 2 | 3 |
| 054 Russians | 1 | 1 | 4 | 7 | 53 | • | 5 | • | 2 | 3 |
| 057 Kurd | 2 | 2 | 4 | 5 | 13 | – | 4 | 5 | 25 | 4 |
| 060 Gond | 1 | 1 | 4 | 7 | 264 | • | 6 | 924 | 3 | 2 |
| 063 U. Pradesh | 3 | 3 | 4 | 7 | 423 | • | 5 | 1 | 1 | 3 |
| 066 Khalka | 1 | – | 4 | 5 | 6 | – | • | 374 | 753 | 4 |
| 069 Garo | 1 | 1 | 3 | 3 | 5 | 6 | 3 | 5 | 5 | 1 |
| 072 Lamet | • | • | – | • | – | – | 1 | • | 8 | – |
| 076 Siamese | 1 | 1 | 2 | 5 | 5 | 5 | 2 | 85 | 85 | 1 |
| 078 Nicobarese | – | – | 2 | 1 | – | 5 | 1 | 26 | 2 | 1 |
| 081 Tanala | 1 | 1 | 4 | 5 | 235 | 5 | 6 | 349 | 873 | 4 |
| 084 Balinese | 1 | 1 | 4 | 3 | 3 | • | 5 | 482 | 385 | – |
| 087 Toradja | 2 | 2 | 3 | 5 | 2 | 6 | 1 | 573 | 52 | 1 |
| 090 Tiwi | 3 | 3 | • | • | 54 | 5 | • | 84 | • | – |
| 093 Kimam | 1 | 1 | • | • | 3 | • | • | • | – | • |

| | Female Consent to Marry | Male Consent to Marry | Marriage Celebration: Type | Marriage Celebration: Participants | Marriage: Female Rights Transferred | Marriage: Male Rights Transferred | Marriage: Final Establishment | Divorce: Female Grounds | Divorce: Male Grounds | Divorce: Restrictions by Gender |
|---|---|---|---|---|---|---|---|---|---|---|
| 096 Manus | 3 | 3 | 4 | 7 | 143 | 5 | 4 | 79 | 82 | 1 |
| 099 Siuai | 2 | 2 | 2 | 5 | 514 | 5 | • | 87 | 873 | (1) |
| 102 Mbau Fijians | 3 | [2] | 2 | 5 | 31 | • | – | • | 3 | – |
| 105 Marquesans | [2] | 1 | 2 | 4 | 12 | • | 1 | 5 | 5 | 1 |
| 108 Marshallese | 2 | 2 | 2 | 2 | – | – | 1 | 563 | 563 | 1 |
| 111 Palauans | 1 | 1 | 2 | 5 | 6 | – | 1 | 547 | 53 | 1 |
| 114 Chinese | 3 | 3 | 4 | 2 | 25 | • | 4 | 1 | 23 | 4 |
| 117 Japanese | 1 | 1 | 4 | 3 | 46 | • | 1 | 5 | 573 | 4 |
| 120 Yukaghir | 3 | 1 | 1 | 2 | • | 6 | 3 | 2 | 2 | (1) |
| 123 Aleut | 2 | 2 | 2 | • | – | – | • | • | 32 | – |
| 126 Micmac | (2) | 1 | 3 | 5 | • | 6 | 1 | 52 | 52 | • |
| 129 Kaska | 1 | 1 | 3 | 5 | 5 | 2 | 5 | 943 | 93 | • |
| 132 Bellacoola | 2 | 1 | 4 | 7 | 61 | 5 | 5 | 4 | 283 | 3 |
| 135 Pomo | 2 | 2 | 3 | 5 | – | – | • | – | – | • |
| 138 Klamath | 2 | 2 | 3 | 5 | 3 | • | 6 | 352 | 35 | 1 |
| 141 Hidatsa | 2 | 2 | 2 | 4 | 5 | 6 | 1 | 34 | 358 | 1 |
| 144 Huron | 2 | 2 | 2 | 5 | • | 6 | 1 | • | 5 | 1 |
| 147 Comanche | 3 | 2 | 1 | • | 41 | 5 | 3 | 7 | 85 | – |
| 150 Havasupai | 2 | 2 | 2 | 2 | 43 | 5 | 1 | 5 | 53 | 3 |
| 153 Aztec | 2 | 2 | 4 | 7 | 14 | 5 | • | 846 | 286 | 3 |
| 156 Miskito | 2 | 1 | • | • | • | 6 | 1 | 845 | 25 | – |
| 159 Goajiro | 3 | 2 | 3 | 4 | 541 | 6 | • | 84 | 836 | • |
| 162 Warrau | 2 | 1 | 3 | 7 | • | 6 | • | – | – | • |
| 165 Saramacca | 2 | 2 | 2 | 4 | 415 | 5 | 6 | 258 | 529 | 2 |
| 168 Cayapa | 1 | 1 | 4 | 5 | • | 5 | • | 1 | 2 | 3 |
| 171 Inca | 2 | 2 | 3 | 4 | 3 | • | • | 1 | 1 | 3 |
| 174 Nambicuara | 2 | [2] | 2 | • | – | • | • | • | 92 | • |
| 177 Tupinamba | – | – | 1 | • | 5 | 2 | – | 46 | 592 | 4 |
| 180 Aweikoma | 1 | 1 | 1 | • | 4 | 6 | 1 | • | 3 | 1 |
| 183 Abipon | 2 | 1 | 2 | 4 | 4 | 3 | 1 | • | 9 | – |
| 186 Yahgan | 1 | 1 | 4 | 7 | 61 | 5 | 1 | 438 | 83 | 1 |

| | Divorce: Child Custody | Divorce and Remarriage | Divorce: Property Settlement | Widow Remarriage: Restrictions | Widow Remarriage: Timing |
|---|---|---|---|---|---|
| 003 Thonga | 5 | • | 4 | 4 | 3 |
| 006 Suku | 3 | (1) | 6 | 4 | • |
| 009 Hadza | 5 | 1 | 6 | 5 | 1 |
| 012 Ganda | 6 | – | 6 | (6) | • |
| 015 Banen | 6 | 1 | 6 | 4 | 3 |
| 018 Fon | – | 1 | – | (5) | • |
| 021 Wolof | 3 | 1 | 4 | 1 | 1 |
| 024 Songhai | 6 | 2 | 4 | 1 | 1 |
| 027 Massa | – | – | 6 | 4 | • |
| 030 Otoro | 2 | 1 | 6 | 5 | 3 |
| 033 Kafa | 3 | • | 3 | 5 | – |
| 036 Somali | 6 | 2 | 4 | 5 | 1 |
| 039 Kenuzi | 3 | 1 | 3 | 2 | 4 |
| 043 Egyptians | 3 | 3 | 3 | 2 | • |
| 045 Babylonians | • | 2 | 3 | – | • |
| 048 Gheg | • | • | • | – | • |
| 052 Lapps | 1 | 4 | 1 | 1 | • |
| 054 Russians | • | 1 | 4 | 2 | • |
| 057 Kurd | 3 | • | 4 | 2 | • |
| 060 Gond | 6 | 1 | – | 4 | • |
| 063 U. Pradesh | 1 | 4 | 1 | 6 | 5 |
| 066 Khalka | 4 | 2 | 4 | 2 | • |
| 069 Garo | • | 1 | 4 | (5) | • |
| 072 Lamet | 4 | • | • | 4 | • |
| 076 Siamese | 3 | 1 | 2 | (1) | • |
| 078 Nicobarese | – | 1 | • | 1 | 4 |
| 081 Tanala | 6 | 2 | 3 | 1 | 3 |
| 084 Balinese | 5 | 1 | 6 | 1 | 1 |
| 087 Toradja | 3 | 1 | 4 | 1 | 1 |
| 090 Tiwi | • | 1 | • | 4 | 1 |
| 093 Kimam | • | • | • | (1) | • |

| | Divorce: Child Custody | Divorce and Remarriage | Divorce: Property Settlement | Widow Remarriage: Restrictions | Widow-Remarriage: Timing |
|---|---|---|---|---|---|
| 096 Manus | 6 | 1 | • | 1 | 3 |
| 099 Siuai | 6 | • | 6 | 1 | 2 |
| 102 Mbau Fijians | 5 | • | – | 6 | 6 |
| 105 Marquesans | 3 | 1 | • | 4 | • |
| 108 Marshallese | [2] | 1 | • | 1 | 1 |
| 111 Palauans | 5 | 1 | 3 | – | • |
| 114 Chinese | • | – | 4 | 5 | 4 |
| 117 Japanese | • | (1) | • | 2 | – |
| 120 Yukaghir | • | • | • | • | • |
| 123 Aleut | 2 | (1) | 4 | [4] | • |
| 126 Micmac | • | • | 2 | 2 | 3 |
| 129 Kaska | 3 | • | [4] | 4 | 4 |
| 132 Bellacoola | 3 | • | 4 | 5 | 2 |
| 135 Pomo | 4 | 1 | 2 | 4 | 3 |
| 138 Klamath | 5 | – | 4 | 5 | 3 |
| 141 Hidatsa | 2 | 1 | • | 5 | – |
| 144 Huron | 4 | 1 | 2 | 4 | 3 |
| 147 Comanche | 6 | – | – | 4 | • |
| 150 Havasupai | 2 | 1 | • | 4 | 2 |
| 153 Aztec | 4 | (1) | [2] | 4 | • |
| 156 Miskito | 2 | • | 6 | 4 | 3 |
| 159 Goajiro | 5 | • | 4 | 5 | • |
| 162 Warrau | 2 | – | 2 | 4 | • |
| 165 Saramacca | 2 | 2 | 4 | 4 | 2 |
| 168 Cayapa | 1 | 4 | 1 | 1 | • |
| 171 Inca | 1 | 4 | 1 | 5 | • |
| 174 Nambicuara | • | • | • | 4 | • |
| 177 Tupinamba | • | 2 | • | 5 | 2 |
| 180 Aweikoma | – | 1 | 2 | • | • |
| 183 Abipon | • | 1 | • | 1 | – |
| 186 Yahgan | 4 | 1 | 2 | 4 | 1 |

# Ethnographic Bibliography

Ethnographic sources for the societies listed below can be located from the text by referring to the identification number of the society (explained below), which is contained in parentheses beside the mention of the society in the text. The identification number corresponds to the numbering of the societies in the ethnographic bibliography.

The sources that were used for coding information on the sixty-two sample societies used in this study are listed below. Each list of sources is preceded by relevant information about the sample society. The number preceding the name of the society is the Standard Cross-Cultural Sample (Murdock and White 1969) identification number for the world area that the society represents. The following information is listed with the name of the society: the geographical region in which it is located (A); the community to which most of the information pertains (C); the geographical coordinates of the society (L); and the date to which most of the coded information pertains (D). Below the name of each society are listed the sources most useful for retrieving information on sociocultural aspects of the sexual and reproductive cycles.

3. Thonga. A: A. C: village of the Ronga subtribe. L: 25°50′S, 32°20′E. D: 1895.
   Junod, H. A.
      1927   The Life of a South African Tribe. 2d edit. 2 vols. London.
6. Suku. A: A. C: "lineage center" in Feshi Territory. L: 6°S, 18°E. D: 1920.
   Holemans, K.
      1959   Etudes sur l'alimentation en milieu coutumier du Kwango: II-
             L'Enquete familiale directe. Annales de al Societe Belge de Medecine Tropi-
             cale 39:361–374.
   Kopytoff, I.
      1964   Family and Lineage among the Suku of the Congo. In The Family
             Estate in Africa. R. F. Gray and P. H. Gulliver, eds. pp. 83–116. Boston.
      1965   The Suku of Southwestern Congo. In Peoples of Africa. J. L. Gibbs, Jr.,
             ed. pp. 441–477. New York.

495

Torday, E., and T. A. Joyce
    1906    Notes on the Ethnography of the Bayaka. Journal of the Royal Anthro-
        pological Institute 36:39–58.
Van de Ginste, F.
    1947    Le mariage chez les Basuka. Bulletin des Jurisdictions Indigenes et du
        Droit Coutumier Congolais, nos. 1–2.
9. Hadza. A: A. C: "camp." L: 3°20′ to 4°10′S, 34°40′ to 35°25′E. D: 1930.
Bagshawe, F. J.
    1925    The People of the Happy Valley. Journal of the (Royal) African Society
        24:117–130.
Bleek, D. F.
    1931    The Hadzapi or Watindiga of Tanganyika Territory. Africa 4:273–286.
Huntingford, G. W. B.
    1953    The Southern Nilo-Hamites. London.
Kohl-Larsen, L.
    1958    Wildbeuter in Ostafrika: Die Tindiga. Berlin.
Woodburn, J.
    1964    The Social Organization of the Hadza of North Tanzania. Ph.D. disser-
        tation, University of Cambridge.
12. Ganda. A: A. C: neighborhood in the Kyaddondo district. L: 0°20′N, 32°30′E. D:
    1875.
Kagwa, A.
    1934    The Customs of the Baganda, E. B. Kalibala, trans. M. Mandelbaum,
        ed. New York.
Mair, L. P.
    1940    Native Marriage in Baganda. London.
Murdock, G. P.
    1934    The Ganda of Uganda. *In* Our Primitive Contemporaries. pp. 508–550.
        New York.
Roscoe, J.
    1911    The Baganda. London.
Southwold, M.
    1965    The Ganda. *In* Peoples of Africa. J. L. Gibbs, Jr., ed. pp. 81–118. New
        York.
15. Banen. A: A. C: clan territory of the Ndiki subtribe. L: 4°35′ to 4°45′N, 10°35′ to
    11°E. D: 1935.
Dugast, I.
    1955    Monographie de la tribu des Ndiki. Travaux et Memoires de l'Institut
        d'Ethnologie 58:*1*, 1–824. Paris.
    1959    Monographie de la tribu des Ndiki. Travaux et Memoires de l'Institut
        d'Ethnologie 58:*2*, 1–635. Paris.
McCulloch, M., M. Littlewood, and I. Dugast
    1954    Peoples of the Central Cameroons. London.
18. Fon. A: A. C: city and environs of Abomey in 1890. L: 7°12′N, 1°56′E. D: 1890.
Burton, R.
    1864    A Mission to Gelele, King of Dahome. 2 vols. London.
Herskovits, M. J.
    1938    Dahomey. 2 vols. New York.

21. Wolof. A: C. C: village of Upper and Lower Salum. L: 13°45′N, 15°20′E. D: 1950.
Ames, D. W.
 1953 Plural Marriage among the Wolof in the Gambia. Ph.D. dissertation, Northwestern University.
 1959 Wolof Co-operative Work Groups. *In* Continuity and Change in African Cultures. W. R. Bascom and M. J. Herskovits, eds. pp. 224–237. Chicago.
Basset, R.
 1888–89 Folk-lore Wolof. Melusine 4:57–59, 84–91, 132–133, 234–235. Paris.
Berenger-Feraud, L. J. B.
 1879 Les Ouolofs. *In* Les Peuples de la Senegambie. pp. 1–62. Paris.
Campistron, M.
 1939 Coutume Ouolof du Cayor. Publications du Comite d'Etudes Historiques et Scientifiques de l'Afrique Occidentale Francaise, ser. A, 8:111–146.
Falade, S.
 1963 Women of Dakar and the Surrounding Urban Area. *In* Women of Africa. D. Paulme, ed. pp. 217–229. London.
Fayet, J. J. C.
 1939 Coutume des Ouolof Musulmans. Publications du Comite d'Etudes Historiques et Scientifiques de l'Afrique Occidentale Francaise, ser. A, 8:147–193.
Gamble, D. P.
 1957 The Wolof of Senegambia. London.
Gorer, G.
 1935 Africa Dances. London.
Leca, N.
 1935 Les pecheurs de Guet N'Dar. Publications du Comite d'Etudes Historiques et Scientifiques de l'Afrique Occidental Francaise, ser. A, 2:1–82.
24. Songhai. A: C. C: village in the Bamba division. L: 16° to 17°15′N, 0°10′ to 3°10′W. D: 1940.
Barth, H.
 1857 Travels and Discoveries in North and Central Africa. 5 vols. London.
Jacquemond, M. S.
 1959 Les pecheurs de boucle du Niger. Paris.
Miner, H.
 1953 The Primitive City of Timbuctoo. Princeton.
Proust, A.
 1954 Notes sur les songhay. Bulletin de l'Institut Francais d'Afrique Noire, ser. 3, 16:167–213.
Rouch, J.
 1954 Les Songhay. Paris.
27. Massa. A: A. C: Neighborhood in Cameroon. L: 10° to 11°N, 15° to 16°E. D: 1910.
Garine, I. de
 1964 Les Massa du Cameroun. Paris.
Lambezat, B.
 1961 Les populations paiennes du Nord-Cameroun et de l'Adamaoua. Paris.
30. Otoro. A: A. C: "hill community". L: 11°20′N, 30°40′E. D: 1930.
Nadel, S. F.
 1947 The Nuba. London.

33. Kafa. A: C. C: neighborhood. L: 6°50′ to 7°45′N, 35°30′ to 37°30′E. D: 1905.
   Beiber, J. F.
      1920–23   Kaffa. 2 vols. Munster.
   Huntingford, G. W. B.
      1955   The Kingdoms of Kafa and Janjero. London.
36. Somali. A: C. C: "encampment" of the Dolbahanta subtribe. L: 7° to 11°N, 45°30′ to 49°E. D: 1900.
   Burton, R. F.
      1957   First Footsteps in East Africa. London.
   Drake-Brockman, R. E.
      1912   British Somaliland. London.
   Lewis, I. M.
      1955   Peoples of the Horn of Africa. London.
      1961   A Pastoral Democracy. London.
      1962   Marriage and the Family in Northern Somaliland. East African Institute for Social and Economic Research. Kampala.
      1965   The Northern Pastoral Somali of the Horn. *In* Peoples of Africa, James L. Gibbs, Jr., ed. pp. 319–360. New York.
   Paulitschke, P.
      1888   Beitrage zur Ethnographie and Anthropologie der Somal, Galla und Harari, pp. 13–40, 98–99. Leipzig.
   Puccioni, N.
      1936   Athropologia e etnografia delle genti della Somalia 3:1–140. Bologna.
39. Kenuzi Nubians. A: C. C: village in Dahmit. L: 22° to 24°N, 38°45′E. D: 1900.
   Callender, C., and R. El Guindi
      1971   Life Crisis Rituals among the Kenuz. Case Western Reserve University Studies in Anthropology 3.
   Herzog, R.
      1957   Die Nubier. Berlin.
43. Egyptians. A: C. C: town and environs of Silwa. L: 24°45′N, 33°E. D: 1950.
   Ammar, H.
      1954   Growing up in an Egyptian Village. London.
45. Babylonians. A: C. C: city and environs of Babylon. L: 32°35′N, 44°45′E. D: 1750 B.C.
   Delaporte, L. J.
      1925   Mesopotamia. New York.
   Driver, G. F., and J. C. Miles
      1952–55   The Babylonian Laws. 2 vols. Oxford.
   Gadd, G. J.
      1965   Hammurabi and the End of His Dynasty. Cambridge Ancient History, rev. ed., fascicle 35. Cambridge.
   Saggs, H. W. F.
      1962   The Greatness that Was Babylon: A Sketch of Ancient Civilization of the Tigris-Euphrates Valley. London.
      1965   Everyday Life in Babylonia and Assyria. New York.
   Thompson, R. C.
      1923   The Golden Age of Hammurabi. Cambridge Ancient History 1:494–551. New York.

48. Gheg Albanians. A: C. C: village. L: 41°20' to 42°40'N, 19°30' to 20°50'E. D: 1910.
Coon, C. S.
1950    The Mountain of Giants: A Racial and Cultural Study of the North Albanian Mountain Ghegs. Papers of the Peabody Museum of Archaeology and Ethnology, Harvard Univeristy 23:3, 1–105.
Durham, M. E.
1909    High Albania. London.
1928    Some Tribal Origins, Laws and Customs of the Balkans. London.
Hasluck, M.
1954    The Unwritten Law in Albania. Cambridge.
Lane, R. W.
1923    Peaks of Shala. New York.
52. Lapps. A: C. C: band in Konkama district. L: 68°20' to 69°5'N, 20°5' to 23°E. D: 1950.
Bernatzik, H. A.
1938    Overland with the Nomad Lapps. V. Ogilvie, trans. New York.
Karsten, R.
1955    The Religion of the Samek. Leiden.
Pehrson, R. N.
1957    The Bilateral Network of Social Relations in Konkama Lapp District. Indiana University Publications, Slavic and East European Series 5:1–128.
Turi, J.
1931    Turi's Book of Lapland, E. G. Nash, trans. New York.
Whitaker, I.
1955    Social Relations in a Nomadic Lappish Community. Oslo of Norsk Folkmuseum 2:1–178.
54. Russians. A: C. C: peasant village of Viriatino. L: 52°40'N, 41°20"E. D: 1955.
Belov, F.
1955    The History of a Collective Farm. New York.
Benet, S., ed.
1970    The Village of Viriatino. New York.
Dunn, S. P.
1971    Structure and Functions of the Soviet Rural Family. *In* The Soviet Rural Community. J. R. Millar, ed. pp. 325–345. Urbana.
Dunn, S. P., and E. Dunn
1967    The Peasants of Central Russia. New York.
57. Kurd. A: C. C: the town and environs of Rowanduz. L: 36°30'N, 44°30'E. D: 1951.
Barth, F.
1953    Principles of Social Organization in Southern Kurdistan. Universitets Etnografiske Museum Bulletin 7:1–146.
1954    Father's Brother's Daughter Marriage in Kurdistan. Southwestern Journal of Anthropology 10:164–171.
Hansen, H. H.
1961    The Kurdish Woman's Life. Copenhagen Ethnographic Museum Record 7:1–213.
Leach, E. R.
1940    Social and Economic Organization of the Rowanduz Kurds. London School of Economics, Monographs on Social Anthropology 3:1–74.

Masters, W. M.

    1953  Rowanduz: A Kurdish Administrative and Mercantile Center. Ph.D. dissertation, University of Michigan.

60. Gond. A: E. C: Hill Maria village. L: 19°15′ to 20°N, 80°30′ to 81°20′E. D: 1930.

Grigson, W. V.

    1938  The Maria Gonds of Bastar. London.

63. Uttar Pradesh. A: E. C: village and environs of Senapur. L: 25°55′N, 83°E. D: 1945.

Cohn, B. S.

    n.d.  Chamar Family in a North Indian village. Ms.

Luschinsky, M. S.

    1963  The Life of Women in a Village of North India: A Study of Role and Status. Ph.D. dissertation, Cornell University.

Opler, M. E. and R. D. Singh

    1952  Economic, Political and Social Change in a Village of North Central India. Human Organization 11:5–12.

Rowe, W. L.

    1960  The Marriage Network and Structural Change in a North Indian Community. Southwestern Journal of Anthropology 16:299–311.

66. Khalka Mongols. A: E. C: camp in Narobanchin territory. L: 47° to 47°20′N, 95°10′ to 97° E. D: 1920.

Ballis, W. B., ed.

    1956  Mongolian People's Republic. 3 vols. New Haven.

Maiskii, I.

    1921  Sovremennaia Mougoiia Irkutsk.

Vreeland, H. H.

    1954  Mongol Community and Kinship Structure. New Haven.

69. Garo. A: E. C: village and environs of Rengsanggri. L: 26°N, 91°E. D: 1955

Burling, R.

    1963  Rengsanggri: Family and Kinship in a Garo Village. Philadelphia.

72. Lamet. A: E. C: village of Mokola Panghay. L: 20°N, 100°40′E. D: 1940.

Izikowitz, K. G.

    1941  Fastening the Soul: Some Religious Traits among the Lamet. Goteborgs Hogskolas Arsskrift 47:*14*, 1–32.

    1943  The Community House of the Lamet. Ethnos 1943:1–2.

    1951  Lamet: Hill Peasants in French Indo-China. Etnologiska Studier 17:1–375. Goteborg.

Needham, R.

    1960  Alliance and Classification among the Lamet. Sociologus N.F. 10:97–119.

76. Siamese. A: E. C: "natural community" of Bang Chan. L: 14°N, 100°52′E. D: 1955.

Hanks, J. R.

    1963  Maternity and Its Rituals in Bang Chan. Ms.

Hanks, L. M., Jr., and J. R. Hanks

    1961  Thailand: Equality between the Sexes. *In* Women in the New Asia. B. J. Ward, ed. pp. 424–451.

Sharp, R. L., H. M. Hauck, K. Janlekha, and R. B. Textor

    1954  Siamese Village. Bangkok.

78. Nicobarese. A: E. C: village in Car Nicobar. L: 7°N, 93°45'E. D: 1870.
Hockett, Mrs. C. F.
  1932   The Nicobarese. Ms.
Man, E. H.
  1885   A Brief Account of the Nicobar Islands. Journal of the Royal Anthropological Institute 15:428–451.
  1888   The Nicobar Islanders. Journal of the Royal Anthropological Institute 18:354–394.
  1932   The Nicobar Islands and Their People. Guilford.
Whitehead, G.
  1924   In the Nicobar Islands. London.
81. Tanala. A: E. C: village of the Menabe subtribe. L: 20°S, 48°E. D: 1925.
Linton, R.
  1933   The Tanala: A Hill Tribe of Madagascar. Publications of the Field Museum of Natural History, Anthropological Series 22: 1–334.
  1939   The Tanala of Madagascar. *In* The Individual and His Society. A. Kardiner, ed. pp. 251–290. New York.
84. Balinese. A: I. C: village of Tihingan. L: 8°30'S, 115°20'E. D: 1958.
Belo, J.
  1936   A Study of the Balinese Family. American Anthropologist 38:12–31.
Covarrubias, M.
  1937   The Island of Bali. New York.
Franken, H. J., R. Goris, C. J. Grade, V. E. Korn, and J. L. Swellengrebel
  1960   Bali: Studies in Life, Thought and Ritual. The Hague.
Geertz, C.
  1959   Form and Variation of Balinese Village Structure. American Anthropologist 61:991–1012.
  1967   Tihingan. *In* Villages in Indonesia. Koentjaraningrat, ed. pp. 210–243. Ithaca.
Geertz, C. and H. Geertz
  1959   The Balinese Kinship system. Unpublished Ms.
87. Toradja. A: I. C: village of the Bare'e subgroup. L: 2°S, 121°E. D: 1910.
Adriani, N., and A. C. Kruijt.
  1912   De Bare'e-sprekende Toradja's van Midden-Celebes. 3 vols. Batavia.
Downs, R. E.
  1956   The Religion of the Bare'e-speaking Toradja of Central Celebes. Gravenhage.
90. Tiwi. A: I. C: band. L: 11° to 11°45'S, 130° to 132°E. D: 1929.
Basedow, H.
  1913   Notes on the Natives of Bathurst Island. Journal of the Royal Anthropological Institute 48:291–323.
Goodale, J. C.
  1959   The Tiwi Women of Melville Island, North Australia. Ph.D. dissertation, University of Pennsylvania.
  1971   Tiwi Wives: A Study of the Women of Melville Island. Seattle.
Harney, W. E., and A. P. Elkin
  1943   Melville and Bathurst Islanders. Oceania 8:228-234.
Hart, C. W. M.
  1930   The Tiwi of Melville and Bathurst Islands. Oceania 1:167–180.

Hart, C. W. M., and A. R. Pilling

    1960   The Tiwi of North Australia. New York.

Mountford, C. P.

    1958   The Tiwi: Their Arts, Myth and Ceremony. London.

Pilling, A. R.

    1957   Law and Feud in an Aboriginal Society of North Australia. Ph.D. dissertation, University of California at Berkeley.

93. Kimam. A: I. C: village of Bamol. L: 7°30′S, 138°30′E. D: 1960.

Serpenti, L. M.

    1965   Cultivators in the Swamps. Assen.

96. Manus. A: I. C: village of Peri. L: 2°10′S, 147°10′E. D: 1929.

Fortune, R. F.

    1935   Manus Religion. Memoirs of the American Philosophical Society 3:1–372.

Mead, M.

    1930a.   Growing Up in New Guinea. New York.

    1930b.   Melanesian Middlemen. Natural History 30:115–130.

    1934   Kinship in the Admiralty Islands. Anthropological Papers of the American Museum of Natural History 34:180–358.

    1937   The Manus of the Admiralty Islands. *In* Cooperation and Competition among Primitive Peoples. M. Mead, ed. pp. 210–239.

99. Siuai. A: I. C: village of the northeastern group. L: 7°S, 155°20′E. D: 1939.

Oliver, D. L.

    1949   Studies in the Anthropology of Bougainville. Papers of the Peabody Museum of American Archaeology and Ethnology, Harvard University 29:*1*, 1–26; *2*, 1–38; *3*, 1–28; *4*, 1–97.

    1955   A Solomon Island Society. Cambridge.

102. Fijians. A: I. C: island of Mbau. L: 18°S, 178°35′E. D: 1840.

Deane, W.

    1921   Fijian Society. London

Roth, G. K.

    1953   Fijian Way of Life. Melbourne

Thomson, B.

    1908   The Fijians: A Study of the Decay of Custom. London.

Toganivalu, D.

    1911   The Customs of Bau before the Advent of Christianity. Transactions of the Fijian Society.

Waterhouse, J.

    1866   The King and People of Fiji. London.

Williams, T.

    1884   Fiji and the Fijians. London.

105. Marquesans. A: I. C: "tribe" of southwestern Nuku Hiva. L: 8°55′S, 140°10′W. D: 1800.

Dodge, E. D., ed.

    1940   An Account of the Marquesas Islands in 1825. Journal of the Polynesian Society 49:382–392.

Handy, E. S. C.

    1923   The Native Culture in the Marquesas. Bernice P. Bishop Museum Bulletin 9:1–358.

LaBarre, R.
  1934   Marquesan Culture. Ms.
Linton, R.
  1939   Marquesan Culture. *In* The Individual and His Society. A. Kardiner,
         ed. pp. 138–196. New York.
Lisiansky, R.
  1814   A Voyage Round the World in the Years 1803–06. London.
Maranda, P.
  1964   Marquesan Social Structure. Ethnohistory 11: 301–379.
Porter, D.
  1823   A Voyage in the South Seas in the Years 1812–14. London.
Sheahan, G. M., ed.
  1952   Marquesan Source Materials. Ms.
Stewart, C. S.
  1831   A Visit to the South Seas. New York.
Suggs, R. C.
  1963   Marquesan Sexual Behavior. Ms.
  1966   Marquesan Sexual Behavior. New York.
Tautain
  1895   Etude sur le mariage chez les Polynesiens des Iles Marquises. L'Anthro-
         pologie 6:640–661.
  1896   Notes sur l'ethnographie des Iles Marquises. L'Anthropologie 7:542–52.
108. Marshallese. A: I. C: village of Jaluit atoll. L: 6°N, 169°15′E. D: 1900.
Erdland, P. A.
  1914   Die Marshall-Insulaner. Anthropos Bibliothek Ethnological Mono-
         graphs 2:1–376. Munster i. W.
Finsch, O.
  1881   Bilder aus dem Stillen Ocean: 1 Kriegsfuhrung auf dem Marshall-
         Inseln. Die Gartenlaube 29:700–702.
  1893   Ethnologische Erfahrungen und Belegstucke aus der Sudsee. Annalen
         des. K. K. Naturhistorischen Hofmuseums 8:2, 119–182.
Knapp, C.
  1888   Religiose Anschauungen der Marschallinsulaner. Mitteilungen von Fors-
         chungsreisenden und Gelehrten aus den Deutschen Schutzgebiiten 1:63–81.
         Berlin.
Kramer, A., and H. Nevermann
  1938   Ralik-Ratak. Ergebnisse aus der Sudsee-Expedition 1908–10. G. Thile-
         nius, ed. 2:xi, 1–438. Hamburg.
Mason, L. E.
  1947   The Economic Organization of the Marshall Islands. Ms.
  1954   Relocation of the Bikini Marshallese. Ph.D. dissertation, Yale Univer-
         sity.
Senfft, A.
  1903   Die Marshall-Insulaner. Rechtsverhaltnisse von eingeborenen Volkern
         in Afrika und Ozeanien. S. R. Steinmetz, ed. pp. 425–455. Berlin.
Wedgewood, C.
  1942   Notes on the Marshall Islands. Oceania 13:1–23.
111. Palauans. A: I. C: village on Koror island. L: 7°N, 134°30′E. D: 1873.
Barnett, H. G.
  1949   Palauan society. Eugene.

1960   Being a Palauan. New York.

Force, R. W. and M. Force
1971   Just One House: A Description and Analysis of Kinship in the Palau Islands. Ms.

Kramer, A.
1929   Palau. Ergebnisse aus der Sudsee-Expedition 1908–1910. G. Thilenius, ed. 2, B, III. Hamburg.

Kubary, J. S.
1873   Die Palau-Inseln in der Sudsee. Journal des Museum Godeffroy 1:181–238. Hamburg.
1888   Die Religion der Palauer. Allerlei aus Volks- und Menschenkunde, A. Bastian, ed. 1:1–99. Berlin.
1900   Die Verbrechen und das Strafverfahre auf den Palau-Inseln. Die mikronesischen Kolonien aus ethnologischen Gesichtsprunkten, A. Bastian, ed. 2:1–36. Berlin.

114. Chinese. A: E. C: village of Kaihsienkung in northern Chekiang. L: 31°N, 120°5′E. D: 1936.

Fei, H.
1946   Peasant Life in China. New York.

117. Japanese. A: E. C: the *buraku* of Niiike. L: 34°30′N, 133°40′E. D: 1950.

Beardsley, R. K., J. W. Hall, and R. E. Ward.
1959   Village Japan. Chicago.

Befu, H.
1962   Corporate Emphasis and Patterns of Descent in the Japanese Family. *In* Japanese Culture. Robert J. Smith and R. K. Beardsley, eds. Viking Fund Publications in Anthropology 34:34–41. New York.

Cornell, J. B., and R. J. Smith
1956   Two Japanese Villages. Ann Arbor.

DeVos, G.
1965   Social Values and Personal Attitudes in Primary Human Relations in Niiike. University of Michigan Center for Japanese Studies Occasional Papers.

DeVos, G., and H. Wagatsuma
1961   Value Attitudes toward Role Behavior of Women in Two Japanese Villages. American Anthropologist 63:1204–1230.

Norbeck, E.
1954   Takashima: A Japanese Fishing Community. Salt Lake City.

120. Yukaghir. A: E.C: local group of the upper Kolyma River. L: 63° to 70°N, 150° to 157°E. D: 1900.

Jochelson, W.
1926   The Yukaghir and Yukaghirized Tungus. Memoirs of the American Museum of Natural History 12:1–469.

123. Aleut. A: N. C: village of the Unalaska division. L: 53° to 57°30′N, 158° to 170°W. D: 1778.

Cook, J.
1785   A Voyage to the Pacific Ocean. London.

Langsdorff, G. H. von
1817   Voyages and Travels. London.

Lantis, M., ed.

    1970  Ethnohistory in Southwestern Alaska and the Southern Yukon. Lexington, Kentucky.

Sarytschew, G.

    1806  Account of a Voyage of Discovery to the North-east of Siberia, the Frozen Ocean, and the North-east Sea, 2 vols. London.

Sauer, M.

    1802  An Account of a Geographical and Astronomical Expedition to the Northern Parts of Russia. London.

Veniaminov, I. E. P.

    1840  Sapiski ob ostrovakh unalashkinskago otdela. St. Petersburg.

126. Micmac. A: N. C: band on the mainland. L: 43°30' to 50°N, 60° to 66°W. D: 1650.

Denys, N.

    1908  The Description and Natural History of the Coasts of North America. W. F. Ganong, ed. Publications of the Champlain Society 2:1–625.

LeClercq, C.

    1910  New Relation of Gaspesia. W. F. Ganong, ed. Publications of the Champlain Society 5:1–452.

Maillard, A. S.

    1758  An Account of the Customs and Manners of the Micmakis and Maricheets. London.

Parsons, E. C.

    1928  Micmac Notes. Journal of American Folk-Lore 39:460–485.

Wallis, W. D., and R. S. Wallis

    1955  The Micmac Indians of Eastern Canada. Minneapolis.

129. Kaska. A: N. C: band on the upper Liard River. L: 60°N, 131°W. D: 1900.

Honigmann, J. J.

    1947  Witch-Fear in Post-contact Kaska Society. American Anthropologist 49:222–243.

    1954  The Kaska Indians: An Ethnographic Reconstruction. Yale University Publications in Anthropology 51:1–163.

Teit, J. A.

    1956  Field Notes on the Tahltan and Kaska Indians, 1912–1915. Anthropologica 3:39–171.

132. Bellacoola. A: N. C: village. L: 52°20'N, 126° to 127°W. D: 1880.

Boas, F.

    1891  The Bilqula. Reports of the British Association for the Advancement of Science 61:408–424.

McIlwraith, T. F.

    1948  The Bella Coola Indians. 2 vols. Toronto.

135. Eastern Pomo. A: N. C: village of Cigom. L: 39°N, 123°W. D: 1850.

Gifford, E. W.

    1926  Clear Lake Pomo Society. University of California Publications in American Archaeology and Ethnology 18:287–390.

Gifford, E. W., and A. L. Kroeber.

    1937  Culture Element Distributions: IV, Pomo. University of California Publications in American Archaeology and Ethnology 37:117–254.

Kroeber, A. L.

    1953  Handbook of the Indians of California. Berkeley.

Loeb, E. M.
  1926 Pomo Folkways. University of California Publications in American Archaeology and Ethnology 19:149–404.
138. Klamath. A: N. C: village. L: 42° t 43°15'N, 121°20' to 122°20'W. D: 1860.
  Gatschet, A. S.
    1890 The Klamath Indians of Southwestern Oregon. United States Geographical and Geological Survey of the Rocky Mountain Region, Contributions to North American Ethnology 2. 2 vols. Washington, D.C.
  Pearsall, M.
    1950 Klamath Childhood and Education. Anthropological Records 9:339–353.
  Spier, L.
    1930 Klamath Ethnography. University of California Publications in American Archaeology and Ethnology 30:1–328.
  Stern, T.
    1965 The Klamath Tribe. Seattle.
  Voegelin, E. W.
    1942 Culture Element Distributions: 20, Northeast California. Anthropological Records 7:47–251.
141. Hidatsa. A: N. C: Hidatsa proper village. L: 47°N, 101°W. D: 1836.
  Bowers, A. W.
    1965 Hidatsa Social and Ceremonial Organization. Bulletins of the Bureau of American Ethnology 194:1–528.
  Curtis, E. S.
    1909 The North American Indian 4:129–172, 180–196. Cambridge.
  Lowie, R. H.
    1917 Social Life of the Hidatsa. Anthropological Papers of the American Museum of Natural History 11:221–293, 323–358.
  Wied-Neuwied, M. zu
    1906 Travels in the Interior of North America. *In* Early Western Travels. R. G. Thwaites, ed. 22:357–366; 23:252–385.
  Wilson, G. L.
    1917 Agriculture of the Hidatsa Indians. University of Minnesota Studies in the Social Sciences 4:1–129.
    1924 The Horse and Dog in Hidatsa Culture. Anthropological Publications of the American Museum of Natural History 15:127-311.
    1934 The Hidatsa Earth Lodge. Anthropological Publications of the American Museum of Natural History 33:341–420.
144. Huron. A: N. C: village of the Attingnawantan and Attigneenongnahac tribes. L: 44° to 45°N, 78° to 80°W. D: 1634.
  Kinietz, W. V.
    1940 The Indians of the Great Western Lakes 1615–1760. Occasional Contributions from the Museum of Anthropology of the University of Michigan 10:1–427.
  Tooker, E.
    1964 An Ethnography of the Huron Indians 1615–1649. Bulletins of the Bureau of American Ethnology 190:1–183.
  Trigger, B. G.
    1969 The Huron. New York.

147. Comanche. A: N. C: band. L: 30° to 38°N, 98° to 103°W. D: 1870.
  Gladwin, T.
    1948   Comanche Kin Behavior. American Anthropologist 50:73–94.
  Hoebel, E. A.
    1940   The Political Organization and Law-Ways of the Comanche Indians. Memoirs of the American Anthropological Association 54:1–149.
  Lee, N.
    1957   Three Years among the Comanches. Norman, Okla.
  Wallace, E., and E. A. Hoebel
    1952   The Comanches: Lords of the South Plains. Norman, Okla.
150. Havasupai. A: N. C: Havasupai tribe. L: 35°20′ to 36°20′N, 111°20′ to 113°W. D: 1918.
  Cushing, F. H.
    1882   The Nation of the Willows. Atlantic Monthly 50:374, 541–559.
  Hassler, E.
    n.d.   Havasupai. Ms.
  The Havasupai and the Hualapi
    1940   Arizona State Teachers College Bulletin 21:1–18.
  Iliff, F. G.
    1954   People of the Blue Water, pp. 102–205. New York.
  Smithson, C. L.
    1959   The Havasupai Woman. Department of Anthropology, University of Utah, Anthropological Papers 38:1–170.
  Spier, L.
    1928   The Havasupai Ethnography. Anthropological Papers of the American Museum of Natural History 24:81–408.
153. Aztec. A: N. C: city and environs of Tenochtitlan. L: 19°N, 99°10′W. d: 1520.
  Carrasco, P.
    1962   The Social Organization of Ancient Mexico.
  Diaz del Castillo, B.
    1956   The Discovery and Conquest of Mexico 1517–1521. G. Garcia, ed. New York.
  Murdock, G. P.
    1934   Our Primitive Contemporaries, pp. 359–402. New York.
  Sahagun, B. de
    1950–57   Florentine Codex: General History of the Things of New Spain. A. J. O. Anderson and C. F. Dibble, trans. Monographs of the School of American Research 14: parts 2,3,4,8,9,13, and 14. Santa Fe.
  Soustelle, J.
    1961   Daily Life of the Aztecs. New York.
  Vaillant, G. C.
    1941   Aztecs of Mexico. New York.
156. Miskito. A: S. C: village near Cape Gracias a Dios. L: 15°N, 91°W. D: 1921.
  Conzemius, E.
    1932   Ethnographic Survey of the Miskito and Sumu Indians. Bulletins of the Bureau of American Ethnology 106:1–191.
  Helms, M. W.
    1969   The Cultural Ecology of a Colonial Tribe. Ethnology 8:76–84.

Kirchhoff, P.
n.d.    The Caribbean Lowland Tribes. The Mosquito, Sumo, Paya, and Jica-
que. Handbook of South American Indians. 4, pp. 219–229.
Pijoan, M.
1946    The Health and Customs of the Miskito Indians of Northern Nicaragua.
Mexico: Instituto Indigenista Interamericano.
159. Goajiro. A: S. C: local group. L: 11°30′ to 12°20′N, 71°30′W. D: 1947.
Armstrong, J. M., and A. Metraux
1948    The Goajiro. Bulletins of the Bureau of American Ethnology 143:iv,
360–383.
Bolinder, G.
1957    Indians on Horseback, pp. 47–164. London.
Gutierrez de Pineda, V.
1948    Organizacion social en la Guajira. Revista del Instituto Etnologico Nacional 3:ii, 1–255. Bogota.
Pineda Giraldo, R.
1950    Aspectos de la magia en la Guajira. Revista del Instituto Etnologico
Nacional 3:i, 1–164, Bogota.
Santa Cruz, A.
1941    Aspects of the Avunculate in Guajiro Culture. Primitive Man 14:1–13.
1960    Acquiring Status in Goajiro Society. Anthropological Quarterly
33:115–127.
Simons, F. A. A.
1885    An Exploration of the Goajira Peninsula. Proceedings of the Royal Geographical Society n.s. 7:781–796, 840.
162. Warrau. A: S. C: "rancheria" L: 8°30′ to 9°50′N to 60°40′ to 62°30′W. D: 1935.
Hill, G. W., et al.
1956    Los Guarao del delta Amacuro. Caracas.
Kirchhoff, P.
1948    The Warrau. Bulletins of the Bureau of American Ethnology 143:iii,
869–881.
Plassard, L.
1868    Les Guaraunos et le delta de l'Orenoque. Bulletin de la Societe de Geog-
raphie 15:568–592. Paris.
Roth, W. E.
1915    An Enquiry into the animism and Folklore of the Guiana Indians. Annual Reports of the Bureau of American Ethnology 30:103–386.
Suarez, M. M.
1968    Los Warao: Indigenas del Delta del Orinoco. Caracas.
Turrado Moreno, A.
1945    Etnografia de los Indios Guaraunos. Caracas.
Wilbert, J.
1958    Die soziale und politische Organisation der Warrau. Kolner Zeitschrift
fur soziologie und Sozialpsychologie n.s. 10:272–291.
165. Saramacca. A: S. C: village L: 3° to 4°N, 55°30′ to 56°W. D: 1932.
Herskovits, M. J., and F. S. Herskovits
1934    Rebel Destiny: Among the Bush Negroes of Dutch Guiana.
Hurault, Jean
1959    Etude demographique comparee des Indiens Oayana et des noirs refugies Boni de Haut-Maroni. Population 14:509–534.

1961    Les noirs refugies Boni de la Guyane Grancaise. Institut Francais d'Afrique Noire 13.

Kahn, M. C.
1931    Djuka: The Bush Negroes of Dutch Guiana. New York.

Price, Richard
1971    Saramaka Social Structure: Analysis of a "Bush Negro" Society. Ph.D. dissertation, Yale University.

168. Cayapa. A: S. C: district of Punta Venado. L: 1°N, 79°W. D: 1908.
Altschuler, M.
1965    The Cayapa: A Study in Legal Behavior. Ph.D. dissertation, University of Minnesota.
1972    Cayapa Personality and Sexual Motivation. *In* Human Sexual Behavior. D. S. Marshall and R. C. Suggs, eds. pp. 38–58. Englewood Cliffs, N.J.

Barrett, S. A.
1925    The Cayapa Indians of Ecuador. Indian Notes and Monographs 40:1–476.

Heimann, M.
1932    Die Cayapa-Indianer. Zeitschrift fur Ethnologie 63:281–287.

Murra, J.
1948    The Cayapa and Colorado. Bulletins of the Bureau of American Ethnology 143:iv, 277–291.

171. Inca. A: S. C: *ayllu* in the vicinity of Cuzco. L: 13°30′S, 72°W. D: 1530.
Cobo, B.
1890–95    Historia del Neuvo Mundo. 4 vols. Seville.

Mason, J. A.
1957    The Ancient Civilizations of Peru. London.

Metraux, A.
1970    The History of the Incas. G. Ordish, trans. New York.

Murdock, G. P.
1934    Our Primitive Contemporaries, pp. 403–450. New York.

Polo de Ondegardo, J.
1916    Los errores y supersticiones de los indios. H. H. Urteaga and C. A. Romero, eds. Col. Lib. Doc. Ref. Hist., Peru, ser. 1, 3:1–43.
1916    Relacion de los fundamentos acerca del notable dano que resulta de no guardar a los indios sus fueros. H. H. Urteaga and C. A. Romero, eds. Col. Lib Doc. Ref. Hist., Peru, ser. 1, 3:45–188.
1917    Del linage de los ingas y como conquestaron. H. H. Urteaga, ed. Col. Lib. Doc. Ref. Hist. Peru, ser: 1, 4:45–138.

Rowe, J. H.
1946    Inca Culture at the Time of the Spanish Conquest. Bulletins of the Bureau of American Ethnology 143:ii, 183–330.

174. Nambicuara. A: S. C: "group" of Cocozu Nambicuara. L: 12°30′ to 13°30′S, 50°30′ to 59°W. D: 1940.
Lévi-Strauss, C.
1943    The Social Use of Kinshp Terms among Brazilian Indians. American Anthropologist 45:398–409.
1948a    The Nambicuara. Bulletins of the Bureau of American Ethnology 143:iii, 361–369.
1948b    La vie familiale et sociale des Indiens Nambikwara. Journal de la Societe des Americanistes de Paris 37:1–131.

1955 Tristes Tropiques. Paris.

Oberg, K.
1953 Indian Tribes of Northern Mato Grosso, Brazil. Publications of the Institute of Social Anthropology, Smithsonian Institution 15:82–105.

Roquette-Pinto, E.
1935 Rondonia. 3d ed. Brasiliana 39:1–401.

177. Tupinamba. A: S. C: village in the vicinity of Rio de Janeiro. L: 22°35′ to 23°S, 42° to 44°30′W. D: 1550.

Anchieta, J. de
1846 Informacao dos casamentos dos indios do Brasil. Revista Trimensal de Historia e Geographia 8:254–262.

Cardim, F.
1906 A Treatise on Brasil. Haykuytus Posthumus or Purchas His Pilgrimes 16:417–517. Glascow.

Léry, J. de
1880 Histoire d'un voyage faict en la terre du Breseil. P. Gaffarel, ed. Paris.
1906 Extracts out of the Historie of John Lerius. S. Purchas, ed. Hakluytus Posthumus or Purchas His Pilgrimes 16:518–579. Glascow.

Métraux, A.
1948 The Tupinamba. Bulletins of the Bureau of American Ethnology 143:iii, 95–133.

Staden, H.
1928 The True Story of His Captivity. M. Letts, ed. London.

Thevet, A.
1878 Les singularitez de la France antarctique. P. Gaffarel, ed. Paris.

180. Aweikoma. A: S. C: band. L: 28°S, 50°W. D: 1913.

Henry, J.
1941 Jungle People. New York.

Métraux, A.
1947 Social Organization of the Kaingang and Aweikoma. American Anthropologist 49:148–151.

Paula, J. M. de
1924 Memoria sobre os Botocudos do Parana e Santa Catharina. Proceedings of the International Congress of Americanists 20:i, 117–138.

183. Abipon. A: S. C: band. L: 27° to 29°S, 59° to 60°W. D: 1750.

Dobrizhoffer, M.
1822 An Account of the Abipones, 3 vols. London.

186. Yahgan. A: S. C: "local group" L: 54°30′ to 56°30′S, 67° to 76°W. D: 1865.

Gusinde, M.
1937 Die Feuerland-Indianer 2: Yamana. Modling bei Wien.

# Selected Bibliography

All references cited in the text and appendixes are included below, with the exception of ethnographic works that served as sources for the 62 sample societies on which the cross-cultural research for this study was based. These sources are included in the Ethnographic Bibliography.

Aberle, David
    1973   Matrilineal Descent in Cross-Cultural Perspective. *In* Matrilineal Kinship, David M. Schneider and Kathleen Gough, eds. pp. 655–727. Berkeley: University of California Press.
Ardrey, Robert
    1961   African Genesis. London: Collins.
Athanasiou, Robert, Philip Shaver, and Carol Tavris
    1970   Sex. Psychology Today 4:37–52.
Ayres, Barbara
    1967   Pregnancy Magic: A Study of Food Taboos and Sex Avoidances. *In* Cross-Cultural Approaches: Readings in Comparative Research, Clellan S. Ford, ed. pp. 111–125. New Haven: HRAF Press.
Barash, David P.
    1977   Sociobiology and Behavior. New York: Elsevier North-Holland.
Barbach, Lonnie G.
    1976   For Yourself: The Fulfillment of Female Sexuality. Garden City, N.Y.: Anchor Press/Doubleday.
Barfield, Ashton
    1976   Biological Influences on Sex Differences in Behavior. *In* Sex Differences: Social and Biological Perspectives, Michael S. Teitelbaum, ed. pp. 62–121 Garden City, N.Y.: Anchor Press/Doubleday.
Barker-Benfield, G. J.
    1978   The Spermatic Economy: A Nineteenth-Century View of Sexuality. *In* The American Family in Social-Historical Perspective, Michael Gordon, ed. pp. 374–402. 2d ed. New York: St. Martin's Press.
Barnes, John A.
    1971   Three Styles in the Study of Kinship. Berkeley: University of California Press.
Barry, Herbert A., III, Margaret K. Bacon, and Irvin L. Child
    1957   A Cross-Cultural Survey of Some Sex Differences in Socialization. Journal of Abnormal and Social Psychology 55: 327–332.
Barry, Herbert A., III, Irvin L Child, and Margaret K. Bacon

1959 The Relation of Child Training to Subsistence Economy. American Anthropologist 61:51–63.

Barry, Herbert A., III, Lili Josephson, Edith Lauer, and Catherine Marshall
1976 Traits Inculcated in Childhood: Cross-Cultural Codes 5. Ethnology 15: 83–114.
1977 Agents and Techniques for Child-Training; Cross-Cultural Codes 6. Ethnology 16: 191–230.

Barry, Herbert A., III, and Leonora M. Paxson
1971 Infancy and Early Childhood: Cross-Cultural Codes 2. Ethnology 10: 466–508.

Barry, Herbert A., III, and Alice Schlegel
1980 Cross-Cultural Samples and Codes. Pittsburgh: University of Pittsburgh Press.

Bart, Pauline B.
1972 Depression in Middle-Aged Women. *In* Woman in Sexist Society, Vivian Gornick and Barbara K. Moran, eds. pp. 163–186. New York: New American Library.

Beach, Frank A.
1974 Human Sexuality and Evolution. *In* Reproductive Behavior, William Montagna and William A. Sadler, eds. pp. 333–365. New York: Plenum Press.

Beigel, Hugo G.
1953 The Meaning of Coital Postures. Indiana Journal of Sex 4: 136–143.

Benedeck, Therese, and Boris B. Rubenstein
1942 The Sexual Cycle in Women: The Relation between Ovarian Function and Psychodynamic Processes. Psychosomatic Medical Monographs III (1 and 2). Washington, D.C.: National Research Council.

Bennett, Kenneth A.
1979 Fundamentals of Biological Anthropology. Dubuque, Iowa: William C. Brown.

Benson, Herbert, with Miriam Z. Klipper
1976 The Relaxation Response. New York: William Morrow.

Bettelheim, Bruno
1968 Symbolic Wounds: Puberty Rites and the Envious Male. New York: Macmillan/Collier Books.

Blumstein, Philip, and Pepper Schwartz
1983 American Couples: Money, Work, Sex. New York: William Morrow.

Bohannan, Paul, and John Middleton, eds.
1968 Marriage, Family, and Residence. Garden City, N.Y.: Natural History Press.

Boston Women's Health Book Collective
1976 Our Bodies, Ourselves: A Book by and for Women. 2d ed. New York: Simon and Schuster (first published in 1971).

Bowlby, John
1969 Attachment and Loss I: Attachment. New York: Basic Books.

Brain, Robert
1979 The Decorated Body. New York: Harper and Row.

Brauer, Alan P., and Donna Brauer
1983 ESO: How You and Your Lover Can Give Each Other Hours of Extended Sexual Orgasm. New York: Warner Books.

Brecher, Edward M.
1969 The Sex Researchers. Boston: Little, Brown.

1984   Love, Sex, and Aging: A Consumers Union Report. Boston: Little Brown.
Britton, Bryce, and Belinda Dumont
1982   The Love Muscle: Every Woman's Guide to Intensifying Sexual Pleasure. New York: New American Library.
Bronowski, Jacob
1973   The Ascent of Man. Boston: Little, Brown.
Broude, Gwen J.
1980   Extramarital Sex Norms in Cross-Cultural Perspective. Behavior Science Research 15: 181–218.
Broude, Gwen J., and Sarah J. Greene
1976   Cross-Cultural Codes on Twenty Sexual Attitudes and Practices. Ethnology 15: 409–429.
Brown, Gabrielle
1980   The New Celibacy: Why More Men and Women Are Abstaining from Sex — and Enjoying It. New York: McGraw-Hill.
Brown, Helen Gurley
1962   Sex and the Single Girl. New York: Random House.
Brown, Judith K.
1963   A Cross-Cultural Study of Female Initiation Rites. American Anthropologist 65: 837–853.
1970   A Note on the Division of Labor by Sex. American Anthropologist 72: 1073–1078.
Brownmiller, Susan
1984   Femininity. New York: Linden Press/Simon and Schuster.
Buchler, Ira R., and Henry A. Selby
1968   Kinship and Social Organization: An Introduction to Theory and Method. New York: Macmillan.
Campbell, Bernard G.
1967   Human Evolution: An Introduction to Man's Adaptations. Chicago: Aldine.
Campbell, J. K.
1974   Honour, Family, and Patronage. New York/Oxford: Oxford University Press.
Carpenter, Edward
1911   Love's Coming of Age. New York: Mitchell Kennerley.
Carroll, Vern, ed.
1970   Adoption in Eastern Oceania. Association for Social Anthropology in Oceania Monographs 1. Honolulu: University of Hawaii Press.
Castaneda, Carlos
1971   A Separate Reality: Further Conversations with Don Juan. New York: Simon and Schuster.
Chaney, Richard P., and Rogelio R. Revilla
1969   Sampling Methods and Interpretation of Correlation: A Comparative Analysis of Seven Cross-Cultural Samples. American Anthropologist 71: 597–633.
Clignet, Remi
1970   Many Wives, Many Powers. Evanston, Ill.: Northwestern University Press.
Cohen, Yehudi A.
1964   The Transition from Childhood to Adolescence: Cross-Cultural Studies of Initiation Ceremonies, Legal Systems, and Incest Taboos. Chicago: Aldine.
Colson, Elizabeth
1967   The Intensive Study of Small Sample Communities. In The Craft of Social Anthropology, A. L. Epstein, ed. pp. 3–15. London/New York: Tavistock.

Comfort, Alex, ed.
    1972    The Joy of Sex: A Cordon Bleu Guide to Lovemaking. New York: Simon and
        Schuster.
    1974    More Joy of Sex. New York: Simon and Schuster.
Cott, Nancy F.
    1972    Root of Bitterness: Documents of the Social History of American Women.
        New York: E. P. Dutton.
Dalton, Katharina
    1964    The Premenstrual Syndrome. Springfield, Ill.: C. C. Thomas.
Daly, Martin, and Margo Wilson
    1978    Sex, Evolution, and Behavior: Adaptations for Reproduction. North Scituate,
        Mass.: Duxbury Press.
Dan, Alice J., Effie A. Graham, and Carol P. Beecher, eds.
    1980    The Menstrual Cycle, 1: A Synthesis of Interdisciplinary Research. New York:
        Springer.
Darwin, Charles
    1859    On the Origin of Species by Means of Natural Selection, or The Preservation
        of Favoured Races in the Struggle for Life. London: Watts.
Davis, Katherine B.
    1922    A Study of the Sex Life of the Normal Married Woman, Part I: The Use of
        Contraceptives. Journal of Social Hygiene 8: 173–189.
Degler, Carl N.
    1978    What Ought to Be and What Was: Women's Sexuality in the Nineteenth
        Century. In The American Family in Social-Historical Perspective, Michael Gor-
        don, ed. pp. 403–425. 2d ed. New York: St. Martin's Press.
Devereux, George
    1937    Homosexuality among the Mohave Indians. Human Biology 9: 498–597.
    1955    A Study of Abortion in Primitive Societies: A Typological, Distributional, and
        Dynamic Analysis of the Prevention of Birth in 400 Pre-Industrial Societies. New
        York: Julian Press.
Divale, William T.
    1975    An Explanation for Matrilocal Residence. In Being Female: Reproduction,
        Power, and Change, Dana Raphael, ed. pp. 99–108. The Hague/Paris: Mouton.
Doty, Richard L.
    1981    Olfactory Communication in Humans. Chemical Senses 6 (4): 351–376.
Douglas, Mary
    1966    Purity and Danger: An Analysis of Concepts of Pollution and Taboo. New
        York: Praeger.
Durden-Smith, Jo, and Diane de Simone
    1983    Sex and the Brain. New York: Arbor House.
Ember, Carol R., and Melvin Ember
    1983    The Evolution of Human Female Sexuality: A Cross-Species Perspective. Pa-
        per presented at the 12th annual meeting of the Society for Cross-Cultural Re-
        search, Washington, D.C., February 19th.
Ember, Melvin, and Carol R. Ember
    1971    The Conditions Favoring Matrilocal vs. Patrilocal Residence. American An-
        thropologist 73: 571–594.
    1979    Male-Female Bonding: A Cross-Species Study of Mammals and Birds. Behav-
        ior Science Research 14 (1): 37–56.
Epstein, Barbara

1983    Family, Sexual Morality, and Popular Movements in Turn-of-the-Century America. *In* Powers of Desire: The Politics of Sexuality, Ann Snitow, Christine Stansell, and Sharon Thompson, eds. pp. 117–130. New York: Monthly Review Press.

Faust, Beatrice
1980    Women, Sex, and Pornography: A Controversial and Unique Study. New York: Macmillan.

Feagin, Joe R.
1978    Racial and Ethnic Relations. Englewood Cliffs, N.J.: Prentice-Hall.

Festinger, Leon, Henry W. Riecken, and Stanley Schachter
1964    When Prophecy Fails. New York: Harper and Row.

Fisher, Lawrence E.
1980    Relationships and Sexuality in Contexts and Culture: The Anthropology of Eros. *In* Handbook of Human Sexuality, Benjamin B. Wolman and John Money, eds. pp. 164–189. Englewood Cliffs, N.J.: Prentice-Hall.

Fisher, Seymour
1973    The Female Orgasm: Psychology, Physiology, Fantasy. New York: Basic Books.

Ford, Clellan S.
1964    A Comparative Study of Human Reproduction. Yale University Publications in Anthropology 32. New Haven: HRAF Press.
1967    On the Analysis of Behavior for Cross-Cultural Comparisons. *In* Cross-Cultural Approaches: Readings in Comparative Research, Clellan S. Ford, ed. pp. 3–21. New Haven: HRAF Press.

Ford, Clellan S. and Frank A. Beach
1972    Patterns of Sexual Behavior. New York: Harper Colophon Books (first published by Harper and Row in 1951).

Fortes, Meyer
1969    Kinship and the Social Order: The Legacy of Lewis Henry Morgan. Chicago: Aldine.

Fox, Robin
1974    Kinship and Marriage: An Anthropological Perspective. Baltimore: Penguin Books.
1980    The Red Lamp of Incest. New York: E. P. Dutton.

Frank, Robert L.
1931    The Hormonal Causes of Premenstrual Tension. Archives of Neurology and Psychiatry 26: 1053–1057.

Freeman, Linton C.
1968    Elementary Applied Statistics: For Students in Behavioral Science. New York: Wiley.

Freud, Sigmund
1950    Totem and Taboo, authorized translation by James Strachey. New York: W. W. Norton (first published in Imago, 1–2, 1912–13).

Friedan, Betty
1963    The Feminine Mystique. New York: Norton.

Friedl, Ernestine
1975 Women and Men: An Anthropologist's View. New York: Holt, Rinehart, and Winston.

Frisch, Rose E., and Janet W. McArthur

1974   Menstrual Cycles: Fatness as a Determinant of Minimum Weight for Height Necessary for Their Maintenance or Onset. Science 185: 949–951.

Frisch, Rose E., and Roger Revelle
1970   Height and Weight at Menarche and a Hypothesis of Critical Body Weights and Adolescent Events. Science 169: 397–399.

Gebhard, Paul H.
1966   Factors in Marital Orgasm. Journal of Social Issues 22 (2): 88–95.
1981   Review of *Human Sexuality: A Comparative and Developmental Perspective*, edited by Herant A. Katchadourian. American Ethnologist 8 (1): 205–206.

Gerard, Alice
1970   Please Breast-Feed Your Baby. New York: New American Library.

Golanty, Eric
1975   Human Reproduction. New York: Holt, Rinehart, and Winston.

Goldstein, Bernard
1976   Human Sexuality. New York: McGraw-Hill.

Gombrich, Ernst H. J.
1960   Art and Illusion: A Study in the Psychology of Pictorial Representation. New York: Pantheon Books.

Goodenough, Ward H.
1970   Description and Comparison in Cultural Anthropology. Chicago: Aldine.

Goodlin, Robert C., et al.
1971   Orgasm during Late Pregnancy — Possible Deleterious Effects. Obstetrical Gynecology 38: 916.

Goody, Jack
1969   Comparative Studies in Kinship. Stanford, Calif.: Stanford University Press.
1976   Production and Reproduction. New York: Cambridge University Press.

Gordon, Michael, ed.
1978   The American Family in Social-Historical Perspective. 2d ed. New York: St. Martin's Press.

Gordon, Richard E., Katherine K. Gordon, and Max Gunther
1961 The Split Level Trap. New York: B. Geis Associates, distributed by Random House.

Gough, E. Kathleen
1968 The Nayars and the Definition of Marriage. *In* Marriage, Family, and Residence, Paul Bohannan and John Middleton, eds. pp. 49–71. Garden City, N.Y.: Natural History Press.

Gregersen, Edgar
1983   Sexual Practices: The Story of Human Sexuality. New York: Franklin Watts.

Guyton, Arthur C.
1966   Textbook of Medical Physiology. 3d ed. Philadelphia: Saunders.

Hall, Edward T.
1959   The Silent Language. Greenwich, Conn.: Fawcett.

Hareven, Tamara K.
1982 American Families in Transition: Historical Perspectives on Change. *In* Normal Family Processes, Froma Walsh, ed. pp. 446–465. New York: Guilford Press.

Harlow, Harry F.
1973   Learning to Love. New York: Ballantine Books.

Harlow, Harry F., and Margaret Harlow
1962   Social Deprivation in Monkeys. Scientific American 207 (5): 136–146.

Harlow, Margaret, and Harry F. Harlow

1966   Affection in Primates. Discovery 27: 11–17.

Harragan, Betty L.
1977   Games Mother Never Taught You. New York: Rawson Associates.

Harrell, Barbara B.
1981   Lactation and Menstruation in Cultural Perspective. American Anthropologist 83 (4): 796–823.

Haskell, Molly
1974   From Reverence to Rape: A Treatment of Women in the Movies. Baltimore: Penguin Books.

Heiman, Julia, Leslie LoPiccolo, and Joseph LoPiccolo
1976   Becoming Orgasmic: A Sexual Growth Program for Women. Englewood Cliffs, N.J.: Prentice-Hall.

Henley, Nancy M.
1977   Body Politics: Power, Sex, and Nonverbal Communication. Englewood Cliffs, N.J.: Prentice-Hall.

Hinsie, Leland E., and Robert J. Campbell
1970   Psychiatric Dictionary. 4th ed. London: Oxford University Press.

Hite, Shere
1976   The Hite Report: A Nationwide Study of Female Sexuality. New York: Macmillan
1981   The Hite Report on Male Sexuality. New York: Alfred A. Knopf.

Holloway, Ralph
1966   Cranial Capacity, Neural Reorganization, and Hominid Evolution: A Search for More Suitable Parameters. American Anthropologist 68 (1): 103–121.

Holy Bible
1952   Revised Standard Version. New York: Harper.

Hrdy, Sarah B.
1981   The Woman That Never Evolved. Cambridge, Mass.: Harvard University Press.

Hunt, Morton
1975   Sexual Behavior in the 1970s. New York: Dell.

Johnson, Allen W.
1978   Quantification in Cultural Anthropology: An Introduction to Research Design. Stanford, Calif.: Stanford University Press.

Jolly, Alison
1972   The Evolution of Primate Behavior. New York: Macmillan.

Jolly, Clifford J.
1970   The Seed-Eaters: A New Model of Hominid Differentiation Based on a Baboon Analogy. Man 5: 5–25.

Kapferer, Bruce
1979   Mind, Self, and Other in Demonic Illness: The Negation and Reconstruction of Self. American Ethnologist 6 (1): 110–133.

Kaplan, Helen S.
1974   The New Sex Therapy, 1. New York: Brunner/Mazel.
1979   Disorders of Sexual Desire; The New Sex Therapy, 2. New York: Brunner/Mazel.

Katchadourian, Herant A., and Donald T. Lunde
1975   Fundamentals of Human Sexuality. 2d ed. New York: Holt, Rinehart, and Winston.

Kennedy, David M.

1970 Birth Control in America: The Career of Margaret Sanger. New Haven, Conn.: Yale University Press.

Key, Ellen
1911 Love and Marriage. New York: G. P. Putnam's Sons.

Kinsey, Alfred C., Wardell B. Pomeroy, and Clyde E. Martin
1948 Sexual Behavior in the Human Male. Philadelphia: Saunders.

Kinsey, Alfred C., Wardell B. Pomeroy, Clyde E. Martin, and Paul H. Gebhard
1953 Sexual Behavior in the Human Female. Philadelphia: Saunders.

Kobben, Andre J.
1966 New Ways of Presenting an Old Idea: The Statistical Method in Social Anthropology. *In* Readings in Cross-Cultural Methodology, Frank W. Moore, ed. pp. 166–192. New Haven, Conn.: HRAF Press.
1967 Why Exceptions? The Logic of Cross-Cultural Analysis. Current Anthropology 8: 3–19.

Komnenich, Pauline, Sister Nathalie Elder, Maryellen McSweeney, and Janice Noack
1981 The Menstrual Cycle, 2: Research and Implications for Women's Health. New York: Springer.

Konner, Melvin
1982 The Tangled Wing: Biological Constraints on the Human Spirit. New York: Holt, Rinehart, and Winston.

Koran
1930 Translated from the original Arabic by George Sale. New York: A. L. Burt.

Kosnik, Anthony, et al.
1977 Human Sexuality; New Directions in American Catholic Thought. New York: Paulist Press.

Krafft-Ebing, Richard von
1886 Psychopathia Sexualis. 1st ed. Stuttgart: F. Enke.
1906 Psychopathia Sexualis, English translation by F. J. Rebman. 12th ed. New York: Rebman.

Kuhn, Thomas S.
1962 The Structure of Scientific Revolutions. Chicago: University of Chicago Press.

Ladas, Alice K., Beverly Whipple, and John D. Perry
1982 The G Spot and Other Discoveries about Human Sexuality. New York: Holt, Rinehart, and Winston.

Leach, Edmund R.
1955 Polyandry, Inheritance, and the Definition of Marriage. Man 55: 182–186.

LeBar, Frank M.
1973 Coding Ethnographic materials. *In* A Handbook of Method in Cultural Anthropology, Raoul Naroll and Ronald Cohen, eds. pp. 707–720. New York: Columbia University Press.

Leo, John
1984 The Revolution Is Over. Time, April 9, pp. 74–78, 83.

Leonard, George
1984 The End of Sex: Erotic Love after the Sexual Revolution. Toronto/New York: Bantam Books, published by arrangement with J. P. Tarcher.

Lessing, Doris
1973 The Summer before the Dark. New York: Knopf.

Lévi-Strauss, Claude
1956 The Family. *In* Man, Culture, and Society, Harry L. Shapiro, ed. pp. 261–285. New York: Oxford University Press.

1963   Structural Anthropology, translated from the French by Claire Jacobson and Brooke G. Schoepf. New York: Basic Books.

1969   The Elementary Structures of Kinship, translated from the French by James H. Bell and John R. von Sturmer, Rodney Needham, ed. Boston: Beacon Press.

Lindenbaum, Shirley

1972   Sorcerers, Ghosts, and Polluting Women: An Analysis of Religious Belief and Population Control. Ethnology 11: 241–253.

Lovejoy, C. Owen

1981   The Origin of Man. Science 211 (January 23): 341–350.

MacKinnon, P. C. B. and I. L. MacKinnon

1956   Hazards of the Menstrual Cycle. British Medical Journal 1: 55.

Mair, Lucy

1971   Marriage. Baltimore: Penguin Books.

Malinowski, Bronislaw

1929   The Sexual Life of Savages in North-Western Melanesia: An Ethnographic Account of Courtship, Marriage, and Family Life among the Natives of the Tro-briand Islands, British New Guinea. London: Routledge and Sons.

1965   Sex and Repression in Savage Society. Cleveland, Ohio, and New York: World Publishing Co.

Malloy, John T.

1978   The Woman's Dress for Success Book. New York: Warner Books.

Martin, M. Kay, and Barbara Voorhies

1975   Female of the Species. New York and London: Columbia University Press.

Marx, Jean L.

1979   Dysmenorrhea: Basic Research Leads to a Rational Therapy. Science 205: 175–176.

Masters, William H., and Virginia E. Johnson

1966   Human Sexual Response. Boston: Little, Brown.

1970   Human Sexual Inadequacy. Boston: Little, Brown.

1976   The Pleasure Bond: A New Look at Sexuality and Commitment. New York: Bantam Books

McClintock, Martha K.

1971   Menstrual Synchrony and Suppression. Nature 229: 244–245.

McQueen, M.

1981   Black Woman, White Man. The Washington Post, January 25, p. C1.

Mead, Margaret

1930   Growing Up in New Guinea: A Comparative Study of Primitive Education. New York: W. Morrow.

1949   Male and Female: A Study of the Sexes in a Changing World. New York: W. Morrow.

1968   Sex and Temperament in Three Primitive Societies. New York: Dell.

Michelmore, Susan

1964   Sexual Reproduction. Garden City, N.Y.: Natural History Press.

Millett, Kate

1971   Sexual Politics. New York: Avon Books.

Money, John

1980   Love and Love Sickness: The Science of Sex, Gender Difference, and Pair Bonding. Baltimore and London: Johns Hopkins University Press.

Money, John, ed.

1965   Sex Research: New Developments. New York: Holt, Rinehart, and Winston.

Money, John, and Anke A. Ehrhardt
    1977   Man and Woman, Boy and Girl: The Differentiation and Dimorphism of
        Gender Identity from Conception to Maturity. Baltimore and London: Johns
        Hopkins University Press.
Money, John, and Patricia Tucker
    1975   Sexual Signatures: On Being a Man or a Woman. Boston/Toronto: Little,
        Brown.
Montagu, Ashley
    1957   The Reproductive Development of the Female, with Especial Reference to
        the Period of Adolescent Sterility: A Study in the Comparative Physiology of
        Infecundity of the Adolescent Organism. New York: Julian Press.
Morgan, Edmund S.
    1978   The Puritans and Sex. *In* The American Family in Social-Historical Perspec-
        tive, Michael Gordon, ed. pp. 363–373. 2d ed. New York: St. Martin's Press.
Morgan, Robin, ed.
    1970   Sisterhood Is Powerful: An Anthology of Writings from the Women's Libera-
        tion Movement. New York: Random House.
Morris, Desmond
    1967   The Naked Ape. London: Constable.
Morris, Jan
    1975   Conundrum. New York: New American Library.
Mosher, Clelia Duel
    1980   The Mosher Survey: Sexual Attitudes of 45 Victorian Women. Edited by
        James MaHood and Kristine Wenburg. New York: Arno Press.
Munroe, Robert L., and Ruth H. Munroe
    1975   Cross-Cultural Human Development. Monterey, Calif.: Brooks/Cole.
Murdock, George P.
    1957   World Ethnographic Sample. American Anthropologist 59: 664–687.
    1963   Outline of World Cultures. 3d ed. New Haven, Conn.: HRAF Press.
    1965   Social Structure. New York: Free Press (first published by Macmillan in
        1949).
    1966   Cross-Cultural Sampling. Ethnology 5: 97–114.
    1968   World Sampling Provinces. Ethnology 7: 305–326.
Murdock, George P., et al.
    1964   Outline of Cultural Materials. 4th ed. New Haven, Conn.: HRAF Press.
Murdock, George P., and Diana O. Morrow
    1970   Subsistence Economy and Supportive Practices: Cross-Cultural Codes 1. Eth-
        nology 9: 302–330.
Murdock, George P., and Caterina Provost
    1973a  Factors in the Division of Labor by Sex: A Cross-Cultural Analysis. Ethnol-
        ogy 12: 203–225.
    1973b  Measurement of Cultural Complexity. Ethnology 12: 379–392.
Murdock, George P., and Douglas R. White
    1969   Standard Cross-Cultural Sample. Ethnology 8: 329–369.
Murdock, George P., and Suzanne F. Wilson
    1972   Settlement Patterns and Community Organization: Cross-Cultural Codes 3.
        Ethnology 11: 254–295.
Murdock, George P., Suzanne F. Wilson, and Violetta Frederick
    1978   World Distribution of Theories of Illness. Ethnology 17: 449–470.
My Secret Life

1966    New York: Grove Press (first publicly imprinted edition).
Nag, Moni
    1962    Factors Affecting Human Fertility in Nonindustrial Societies: A Cross-Cultural Study. Yale University Publications in Anthropology 66. New Haven, Conn.: HRAF Press.
Napheys, George H.
    1869    The Physical Life of Woman: Advice to the Maiden, Wife, and Mother. Philadelphia: G. Maclean.
Napier, Prue
    1973    Monkeys and Apes. Toronto/New York: Bantam Books.
Naroll, Raoul
    1961    Two Solutions to Galton's Problem. Philosophy of Science 28: 15–39.
    1962    Data Quality Control — A New Research Technique: Prolegomena to a Cross-Cultural Study of Culture Stress. New York: Free Press of Glencoe.
    1964    A Fifth Solution to Galton's Problem. American Anthropologist 66: 863–867.
    1973    The Culture-Bearing Unit in Cross-Cultural Surveys. *In* A Handbook of Method in Cultural Anthropology, Raoul Naroll and Ronald Cohen, eds. pp. 721–765. New York and London: Columbia University Press.
Naroll, Raoul, and Roy G. D'Andrade
    1963    Two Further Solutions to Galton's Problem. American Anthropologist 63: 1053–1067.
Needham, Rodney, ed.
    1971    Rethinking Kinship and Marriage. A.S.A. Monographs 11. London/New York: Tavistock Publications.
Nelson, Harry, and Robert Jurmain
    1982    Introduction to Physical Anthropology. St. Paul, Minn.: West.
Neugarten, Bernice L., and Ruth J. Kraines
    1965    Menopausal Symptoms in Women of Various Ages. Psychosomatic Medicine 273 (3):266.
Newman, Gustave, and Claude R. Nichols
    1960    Sexual Activities and Attitudes in Older Persons. Journal of the American Medical Association 173: 33–35.
Newman, Herbert F.
    1970    Vibratory Sensitivity of the Penis. Fertility and Sterility 21(11): 791–793.
Newton, Niles
    1975    Birth Rituals in Cross-Cultural Perspective: Some Practical Applications. *In* Being Female: Reproduction, Power, and Change, Dana Raphael, ed. pp. 37–48. The Hague/Paris: Mouton (distributed in the U.S. by Aldine).
Offir, Carole W.
    1982    Human Sexuality. New York: Harcourt Brace Jovanovich.
Ortner, Sherry B.
    1974    Is Female to Male as Nature Is to Culture? *In* Woman, Culture, and Society, Michelle Z. Rosaldo and Louise Lamphere, eds. pp. 67–87. Stanford, Calif.: Stanford University Press.
Ortner, Sherry B., and Harriet Whitehead
    1981    Sexual Meanings: The Cultural Construction of Gender and Sexuality. Cambridge: Cambridge University Press.
Otterbein, Keith
    1968    Internal War: A Cross-Cultural Study. American Anthropologist 70: 277–289.
Otterbein, Keith, and Charlotte Otterbein

1965    An Eye for an Eye: A Cross-Cultural Study of Feuding. American Anthropologist 67: 1470–1482.

Papanek, Hanna
1974    The Woman Field Worker in a Purdah Society. *In* Many Answers: A Reader in Cultural Anthropology, Norman Alger, ed. pp. 328–335. St. Paul, Minn.: West.

Parsons, Talcott
1964    The Social System. New York: Free Press of Glencoe.

Pearsall, Ronald
1969    The Worm in the Bud: The World of Victorian Sexuality. Toronto: Macmillan.

Peel, John, and Malcolm Potts
1969    Textbook of Contraceptive Practice. London: Cambridge University Press.

Peiss, Kathy
1983    "Charity Girls" and City Pleasures: Historical Notes on Working-Class Sexuality, 1880–1920. *In* Powers of Desire: The Politics of Sexuality, Ann Snitow, Christine Stansell, and Sharon Thompson, eds. pp. 74–87. New York: Monthly Review Press.

Pelto, Pertti J., and Gretel H. Pelto
1978    Anthropological Research: The Structure of Inquiry. 2d ed. Cambridge: Cambridge University Press.

Pilbeam, David
1978    Rearranging Our Family Tree. Human Nature 1: 38–45.

Pliny the Elder
1938–63    Natural History. English translation by H. Rackham. 10 vols. Cambridge, Mass.: Harvard University Press.

Price-Williams, Douglass R.
1975    Explorations in Cross-Cultural Psychology. San Francisco: Chandler and Sharp.

Raphael, Dana
1966    The Lactation-Suckling Process within a Matrix of Supportive Behavior. Ph.D. dissertation, Columbia University.
1976    The Tender Gift: Breastfeeding. New York: Schocken Books.

Raphael, Dana, ed.
1975    Being Female: Reproduction, Power, and Change. The Hague/Paris: Mouton (distributed in the U.S. by Aldine).

Robinson, Paul
1976    The Modernization of Sex: Havelock Ellis, Alfred Kinsey, William Masters and Virginia Johnson. New York: Harper Colophon Books.

Robson, John R. K.
1975    Nutrition and Pregnancy. *In* Being Female: Reproduction, Power, and Change, Dana Raphael, ed. pp. 49–53. The Hague/Paris: Moutin (distributed in the U.S. by Aldine).

Rosaldo, Michelle Z., and Louise Lamphere
1974    Woman, Culture, and Society. Stanford, Calif.: Stanford University Press.

Rosenblatt, Paul C., et al.
1973    A Cross-Cultural Study of Responses to Childlessness. Behavior Science Notes 8: 221–231.

Rosenblatt, Paul C., and Michael R. Cunningham
n.d.    Sex Differences in Cross-Cultural Perspective. Ms.

Rosenblatt, Paul C., and William J. Hillabrant

1972   Divorce for Childlessness and the Regulation of Adultery. Journal of Sex Research 8: 117–127.

Rowell, Thelma
1974   Social Behaviour of Monkeys. Baltimore: Penguin Books.

Rugoff, Milton
1971   Prudery and Passion. New York: G. P. Putnam's Sons.

Salzman, Leon
1971   Sex Research. *In* The New Sexual Revolution, Lester A. Kirkendall and Robert N. Whitehurt, eds. pp. 63–76. New York: Donald W. Brown.

Sanday, Peggy R.
1973   Toward a Theory of the Status of Women. American Anthropologist 75: 1682–1700.

1974   Female Status in the Public Domain. *In* Woman, Culture, and Society, Michelle Z. Rosaldo and Louis Lamphere, eds. pp. 189–206. Stanford, Calif.: Stanford University Press.

1982   Female Power and Male Dominance: On the Origins of Sexual Inequality. Cambridge: Cambridge University Press.

Sanger, Margaret
1922   The Pivot of Civilization. New York: Brentano's.

Sarvis, Betty, and Hyman Rodman
1974   The Abortion Controversy. 2d ed. New York and London: Columbia University Press.

Saucier, Jean-Francois
1972   Correlates of the Long Postpartum Sex Taboo: A Cross-Cultural Study. Current Anthropology 13: 238–258.

Schaefer, Leah C.
1973   Women and Sex. New York: Pantheon Books.

Schlegel, Alice
1972   Male Dominance and Female Autonomy: Domestic Authority in Matrilineal Societies. New Haven, Conn.: HRAF Press.

Schlegel, Alice, ed.
1977   Sexual Stratification: A Cross-Cultural View. New York: Columbia University Press.

Schlegel, Alice, and Herbert Barry, III
1979   Adolescent Initiation Ceremonies: A Cross-Cultural Code. Ethnology 18(2): 199–210.

1980   The Evolutionary Significance of Adolescent Initiation Ceremonies. American Ethnologist 7(4): 696–715.

Schneider, David M.
1974   The Distinctive Features of Matrilineal Descent Groups. *In* Matrilineal Kinship, David M. Schneider and Kathleen Gough, eds. pp. 1–29. Berkeley: University of California Press.

Schneider, David M., and Kathleen Gough, editors
1974   Matrilineal Kinship. Berkeley: University of California Press.

Schneider, Jane
1971   Of Vigilance and Virgins: Honor, Shame, and Access to Resources in Mediterranean Societies. Ethnology 10: 1–24.

Scully, Diana
1980   Men Who Control Women's Health: The Miseducation of Obstetrician-Gynecologists. Boston: Houghton Mifflin.

Service, Elman R.
   1978   The Arunta of Australia. *In his* Profiles in Ethnology, pp. 13–34. 3d ed. New York: Harper and Row.
Sheehy, Gail
   1976   Passages: Predictable Crises of Adult Life. New York: Dutton.
Sherfey, Mary Jane
   1973   The Nature and Evolution of Human Sexuality. New York: Vintage Books.
Simenauer, Jacqueline, and David Carroll
   1982   Singles: The New Americans. New York: Simon and Schuster.
Slater, Mariam K.
   1959   Ecological Factors in the Origin of Incest. American Anthropologist 61: 1042–1059.
Smith, Daniel S.
   1978   The Dating of the American Sexual Revolution: Evidence and Interpretation. *In* The American Family in Social-Historical Perspective, Michael Gordon, ed. pp. 426–438. 2d ed. New York: St. Martin's Press.
Smith-Rosenberg, Carroll
   1978   The Female World of Love and Ritual: Relations between Women in Nineteenth-Century America. *In* The American Family in Social-Historical Perspective, Michael Gordon, ed. pp. 334–358. 2d ed. New York: St. Martin's Press.
Snitow, Ann, Christine Stansell, and Sharon Thompson, eds.
   1983   Powers of Desire: The Politics of Sexuality. New York: Monthly Review Press.
Sochen, June
   1974   Herstory: A Woman's View of American History. New York: Alfred.
Spencer, Baldwin, and F. J. Gillen
   1899   The Native Tribes of Central Australia. New York: Macmillan.
Steinem, Gloria
   1983   Outrageous Acts and Everyday Rebellions. New York: Holt, Rinehart, and Winston.
Stephens, William N.
   n.d.   A Cross-Cultural Study of Modesty and Obscenity. Ms.
   1961   A Cross-Cultural Study of Menstrual Taboos. Genetic Psychology Monographs 64: 384–416.
   1962   The Oedipus Complex: Cross-Cultural Evidence. New York: Free Press of Glencoe.
   1963   The Family in Cross-Cultural Perspective. New York: Holt, Rinehart, and Winston.
Symons, Donald
   1979   The Evolution of Human Sexuality. New York/Oxford: Oxford University Press.
Szasz, Thomas
   1980   Sex by Prescription. Garden City, N.Y.: Anchor Press/Doubleday.
Talese, Gay
   1980   Thy Neighbor's Wife. Garden City, N.Y.: Doubleday.
Tannahill, Reay
   1980   Sex and History. New York: Stein and Day.
Tanner, James M.
   1962   Growth in Adolescence: With a General Consideration of the Effects of Heredity and Environmental Factors upon Growth and Maturation from Birth to Maturity. 2d ed. Oxford: Blackwell Scientific Publications.

Tanner, Nancy M.
    1981   On Becoming Human. New York: Cambridge University Press.
Tavris, Carol, and Susan Sadd
    1975   The Redbook Report on Female Sexuality: 100,000 Married Women Disclose
           the Good News about Sex.
Teitelbaum, Michael S., ed.
    1976   Sex Differences: Social and Biological Perspectives. New York: Anchor Books.
Time-Life Books
    1969–70   This Fabulous Century. 8 vols. New York: Time-Life Books.
Trimberger, Ellen K.
    1983   Feminism, Men, and Modern Love: Greenwich Village, 1900–1925. *In*
           Powers of Desire: The Politics of Sexuality, Ann Snitow, Christine Stansell, and
           Sharon Thompson, eds. pp. 131–152. New York: Monthly Review Press.
Trivers, Robert L.
    1972   Parental Investment and Sexual Selection. *In* Sexual Selection and the De-
           scent of Man 1871–1971, Bernard Campbell, ed. pp. 136–179. Chicago: Aldine.
Tuden, Arthur, and Catherine Marshall
    1972   Political Organization: Cross-Cultural Codes 4. Ethnology 11: 436–464.
Turner, Victor W.
    1966   Color Classification in Ndembu Ritual. *In* Anthropological Approaches to the
           Study of Religion, Michael Banton, ed. pp. 47–84. A.S.A. Monograph No. 3.
           London: Tavistock.
    1967   The Forest of Symbols: Aspects of Ndembu Ritual. Ithaca, N.Y.: Cornell
           University Press.
    1969   The Ritual Process: Structure and Anti-Structure. Chicago: Aldine.
Tylor, Edward B.
    1889   On a Method of Investigating the Development of Institutions; Applied to
           Laws of Marriage and Descent. Journal of the Royal Anthropological Institute 18:
           245–269.
    1966   On a Method of Investigating the Development of Institutions; Applied to
           Laws of Marriage and Descent. *In* Readings in Cross-Cultural Methodology,
           Frank W. Moore, ed. pp. 1–25. New Haven, Conn.: HRAF Press.
Udry, J. Richard, and Naomi M. Morris
    1968   Distribution of Coitus in the Menstrual cycle. Nature 220: 593–597.
Unwin, Joseph D.
    1934   Sex and Culture. London: Oxford University Press.
Vandenberg, J.
    1972   Implications of Hurried Puberty. San Francisco Chronicle. August 13.
van Gennep, Arnold
    1960   The Rites of Passage. Translated by Monika B. Vizedom and Gabrielle L.
           Caffee. Chicago: University of Chicago Press.
van Lawick-Goodall, Jane
    1971   In the Shadow of Man. Boston: Houghton Mifflin.
van de Velde, Theodoor
    1926   Ideal Marriage, Its Physiology and Technique. English, authorized transla-
           tion by Stella Brown (1930). New York: Random House.
Wagner, Nathaniel N., and Don A. Solberg
    1974   Pregnancy and Sexuality. Medical Aspects of Human Sexuality 8(3): 44–79.
Walker, Alexander

1966    The Celluloid Sacrifice: Aspects of Sex in the Movies. New York: Hawthorn Books.

Wallace, Anthony F. C.
1970    Culture and Personality. 2d ed. New York: Random House.

Washburn, Sherwood L., and Ruth Moore
1980    Ape into Human: A Study of Human Evolution. 2d ed. Boston: Little, Brown.

Weideger, Paula
1977    Menstruation and Menopause: The Physiology and Psychology, the Myth and the Reality. New York: Dell.

Weiss, Alfred D.
1960    Sensory Functions. *In* Handbook of Aging and the Individual: Psychological and Biological Aspects, James E. Birren, ed. pp. 503–542. Chicago and London: University of Chicago Press.

Welter, Barbara
1978    The Cult of True Womanhood: 1820–1860. *In* The American Family in Social-Historical Perspective, Michael Gordon, ed. pp. 313–333. 2d ed. New York: St. Martin's Press.

Westermarck, Edward
1925    The History of Human Marriage. 3 vols. 5th ed. London: Macmillan.

White, Douglas R., Michael L. Burton, Lilyan A. Brudner, and Joel D. Gunn.
1975    Implicational Structures in the Sexual Division of Labor. Social Science Working Papers #83. School of Social Science. University of California at Irvine.

White, Edmund, and Dale M. Brown
1973    The First Men. New York: Time-Life Books.

Whiting, John W. M.
1964    The Effects of Climate on Certain Cultural Practices. *In* Explorations in Cultural Anthropology: Essays in Honor of George Peter Murdock, Ward H. Goodenough, ed. pp. 511–544. New York: McGraw-Hill.
1965    Menarcheal Age and Infant Stress in Humans. *In* Sex and Behavior, Frank A. Beach, ed. New York: Wiley.

Whiting, John W. M., and Irvin Child
1953    Child Training and Personality: A Cross-Cultural Study. New Haven: Yale University Press.

Whiting, John W. M., Richard Kluckhohn, and Albert Anthony
1958    The Function of Male Initiation Ceremonies at Puberty. *In* Readings in Social Psychology, Eleanor E. Maccoby, Theodore M. Newcomb, and Eugene L. Hartley, eds. pp. 359–370. New York: Henry Holt.

Whyte, Martin K.
1978    Cross-Cultural Codes Dealing with the Relative Status of Women. Ethnology 17: 211–237.

Williams, George C.
1975    Sex and Evolution. Princeton, N.J.: Princeton University Press.

Wilson, Monica
1963    Good Company: A Study of Nyakyusa Age-Villages. Boston: Beacon Press.

Wilson, Suzanne Frayser
1975    Matri-Patrilocality and the Birth of the First Child. *In* Being Female: Reproduction, Power, and Change, Dana Raphael, ed., pp. 73–86. The Hague/Paris: Mouton (distributed in the U.S. by Aldine).
1976    Sociocultural Aspects of the Sexual and Reproductive Cycles: A Cross-

Cultural Study. Ph.D. dissertation, Cornell University. Ann Arbor, Mich.: University Microfilms, no. 77-11, 028.

Wolf, Arthur P.
1966   Childhood Association, Sexual Attraction, and the Incest Taboo: A Chinese Case. American Anthropologist 68: 883–898.

Wolfe, Linda
1981   The Cosmo Report. New York: Arbor House.

Wolman, Benjamin B., and John Money
1980   Handbook of Human Sexuality. Englewood Cliffs, N.J.: Prentice-Hall.

Worden, R.
1974   Arabs Kill Wives Who "Dishonor." April 4, p. 14-A. Baltimore: The News American.

Yorburg, Betty
1974   Sexual Identity: Sex Roles and Social Change. New York/London: John Wiley.

Young, Frank W.
1965   Initiation Ceremonies: A Cross-Cultural Study of Status Dramatization. Indianapolis/New York: Bobbs-Merrill.

Young, Frank W., and Albert S. Bacdayan
1965   Menstrual Taboos and Social Rigidity. Ethnology 4: 225–240.

Zilbergeld, Bernie
1981   Male Sexuality: A Guide to Sexual Fulfillment. 4th printing. New York: Bantam Books, published by arrangement with Little, Brown.

# Index

Compiled by Thomas J. Whitby, Ph.B., M.A.

All references are page numbers except where App. E appears following the name of a society, e.g., Abipon: App. E (183). This refers to Appendix E; the number in parenthesis is the SCCS identification number of the society.

540 *Varieties of Sexual Experience*

Palauans: App. E (111)
  tattooing by women, 172
  views on sex and food, 2
Paradigms, 12
Parent/child dependency, 356
  at maturity, 71
  during infancy, 71
Parental care, 31
Parsons, Talcott, 144
*Passages* (Sheehy), 239
Patrilineage
  contrasted with matrilineage, 109
Patrilineal kinship systems
  and patrilocality, 347
  importance of father/son bond,
    342
  significance of paternity in, 343
  status of motherhood in, 340–341
Patrilocality, 351
  and lineal kinship systems, 347
  defined, 346
Patterns of behavior, 8, 323
*Patterns of Sexual Behavior* (Ford
    and Beach), 186
Paul, Saint
  views on sex, 366
Peiss, Kathy, 379
Pelvis
  location of genitals in, 58
  size of, relative to brain size, 62
  structure of, in bipeds, 58
Penis, 25, 27–28
  erection slower in older men,
    235
  position in upright posture, 58
  size in human males, 60
Perfectionists, 369
Physical appearance
  coding of, App. C, 455–456
  role in sexual differentiation,
    170–174
  unattractive traits in men and
    women, 187
  *See also* Body decoration, Body
    mutilation, Grooming, Jewelry
*The Physical Life of Woman*
    (Napheys), 368–369, 383
Pilbeam, David, 47

Pituitary
  as source of hormones, 124
  *See also* Hypothalamus
Placenta, 302–304, 311
*The Pleasure Bond* (Masters and
    Johnson), 404
Polyandry
  among the Marquesans, 256
Polygamy, 252–257
Polygyny, 252–257, 268, 351, 357
  affected by age differences at
    marriage, 252
  full and limited, distinguished,
    253
  sexual status of women under,
    199
Pomo: App. E (135)
  contraceptive practice of, 294
  postpartum celebrations, 319
  pregnancy restrictions on, 306
  restrictions on, during
    menstruation, 223–224
Ponape
  foreplay among, 189
Pornography
  in America, 369
Postmarital residence patterns
  in relation to the conflict
    management, 279–280
  influence on reproductive
    relationships, 278
Postnatal care. *See* Infant care
Postpartum sex taboo, 294–295
Predation, 54
Pregnancy, 302–307
  coding of, App. C, 460–461
  physiological explanation of,
    302–305
  rationales for restrictions on, 307
  restrictions on women during,
    305
  sexual activity during, 40–41, 307
  *See also* Childbirth, Labor
    (obstetrics)
Prehominids. *See* Hominids
Premarital sex, 202–206, 214–218,
    390, 398
  coding of, App. C, 469
  double standard in some societies,
    203

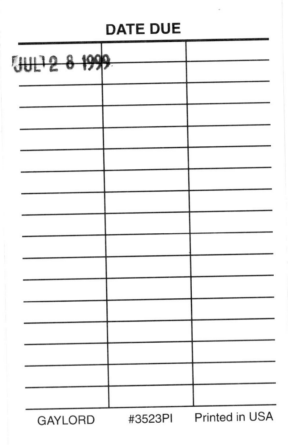

## DATE DUE

| JUL 2 8 1999 | | |
|---|---|---|
| | | |
| | | |
| | | |
| | | |
| | | |
| | | |
| | | |
| | | |
| | | |
| | | |
| | | |
| | | |
| | | |
| | | |
| | | |
| | | |
| | | |

GAYLORD      #3523PI      Printed in USA